Die Erfindung der Neuen Wilden

The Invention of the Neue Wilde

Diese Publikation wurde gefördert von der
Peter und Irene Ludwig Stiftung /
This catalogue was sponsored by the
Peter and Irene Ludwig Foundation

Die Erfindung der Neuen Wilden. Malerei und Subkultur um 1980

The Invention of the Neue Wilde: Painting and Subculture around 1980

Herausgegeben von / Edited by
Benjamin Dodenhoff, Ramona Heinlein
Ludwig Forum für Internationale Kunst Aachen

Verlag der Buchhandlung Walther König, Köln

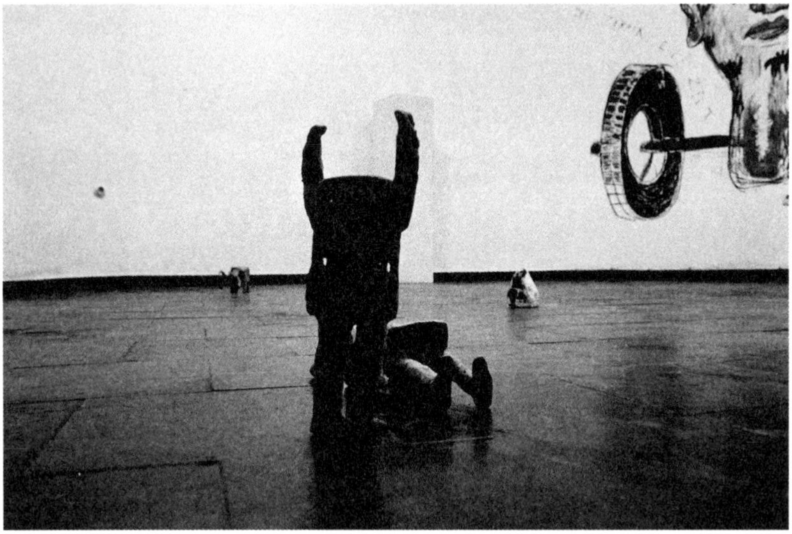

Grußworte / Forewords

Essays

Drucksachen / Printed Matter

Interviews

Drucksachen / Printed Matter

Reprints

In German cultural history, to be wild is an age-old topos, particularly in literature but also in the visual arts. The idea of the "wild man," or person, who represents an alternative to civilization, ostracized or willfully outside of society, requires a critical view of the conditions of the "civilized" as well as an appreciation for (or even discomfort with) the sublimity of the other, of the "wild one."

The conclusion of the research project *Plattform Aachen*,[1] an investigation that ran from 2013 to 2017 into international art movements related to Aachen by the Ludwig Forum für Internationale Kunst, serves as evidence of the high level of research being carried out in art museums. This research exposes issues that are inherently topical, without regard to the curatorial mainstream. While the projects *Plattform Aachen* and *The Invention of the Neue Wilde* hopefully only mark a provisional point and represent a transitional period, there is an opportunity for others to take up the now quite extensive holdings on the history of the institution and Aachen art initiatives that likewise made international history. Alongside the concurrent sister project *Video Archive*,[2] in recent years artistic activities of international import that began here since the 1960s have been curatorially and academically reappraised. The information and documents obtained in doing so are ready for use in further projects. What began at the Ludwig Forum in 2011 with the research and exhibition project *Nie wieder störungsfrei!* (Never Trouble-Free Again!),[3] now finds its historically consistent continuation in *The Invention of the Neue Wilde*. With this, numerous studies of recent German art history were carried out, presenting in depth the phase from the mid-1960s to the mid-1980s from the

1 See the website created in connection with this: www.zeitsprungaachen.de. With funding from the state of North Rhine-Westphalia, the Youth and Cultural Foundation of the Sparkasse Aachen, the Friends of the Ludwig Forum, Deutsche Bahn, and the Peter and Irene Ludwig Foundation, a comprehensive archive of art locations and art events since the 1960s has been developed since 2013 under the title *Plattform Aachen*.

2 The research project *Video Archive*, funded by the Volkswagen Foundation, ran from 2012 to 2017. In the course of this project, the avant-garde video art inventory of the Ludwig Forum was digitized and processed by art historians. Since 2015, there has been a video viewing area in the library of the Ludwig Forum that makes the inventory accessible. In fall 2018, the accompanying scholarly website went live.

3 *Nie wieder störungsfrei! Aachen Avantgarde seit 1964*, ed. Brigitte Franzen, Annette Lagler, and Myriam Kroll, exh. cat. Ludwig Forum für Internationale Kunst Aachen, Bielefeld 2011.

Wild zu sein ist in der deutschen Kulturgeschichte, insbesondere in der Literatur, aber auch in der bildenden Kunst, ein jahrhundertealter Topos. Die Idee vom „wilden Mann“, vulgo Mensch, der eine Gegenwelt zur Zivilisation darstellt, ausgegrenzt oder selbstständig absentiert, fordert den kritischen Blick auf die Zustände des „Zivilisierten“ ebenso wie die Bewunderung (oder auch das Unbehagen an) gewissermaßen der Erhabenheit des anderen, eben des „Wilden“.

Dass nun ausgehend vom 2013 bis 2017 betriebenen Forschungsprojekt *Plattform Aachen*[1] die vom Ludwig Forum für Internationale Kunst realisierte Untersuchung internationaler Kunstströmungen mit Bezug zu Aachen zu einem Abschluss kommt, ist ein Beweis dafür, wie hoch Forschung an Kunstmuseen einzuschätzen ist. Sie fördert Themen zutage, denen eine Aktualität innewohnt, unabhängig vom kuratorischen Mainstream. Da die Projekte *Plattform Aachen* und *Die Erfindung der Neuen Wilden* hoffentlich einen lediglich vorläufigen Punkt markieren und einen Übergang definieren, ergeben sich Freiräume für andere, sich der mittlerweile sehr umfangreichen Bestände zur Geschichte der Institution und zu den Aachener Kunstinitiativen anzunehmen, die von hier aus auch international Geschichte geschrieben haben. Gemeinsam mit dem zeitgleich laufenden Schwesterprojekt *Videoarchiv*[2] sind in den letzten Jahren wichtige Ereignisse international bedeutender Kunstaktivitäten seit den 1960er-Jahren kuratorisch und wissenschaftlich aufgearbeitet worden, die hier ihren Ausgang nahmen. Die so gewonnenen Informationen und Dokumente stehen für weitere Projekte bereit. Was 2011 am Ludwig Forum mit dem Forschungs- und Ausstellungsprojekt *Nie wieder störungsfrei!*[3] begann, findet in *Die Erfindung der Neuen Wilden* nun seine historisch folgerichtige Fortsetzung. Damit wurden zahlreiche Untersuchungen der jüngsten deutschen Kunstgeschichte geleistet, die die Phase von Mitte der 1960er- bis Mitte der 1980er-Jahre aus der Perspektive Westdeutschlands tiefgreifend herausgearbeitet haben. In dieser Zeit

1 Vgl. die in diesem Zusammenhang entstandene Website www.zeitsprungaachen.de. Gefördert vom Land Nordrhein-Westfalen, der Jugend- und Kulturstiftung der Sparkasse Aachen, den Freunden des Ludwig Forum, der Deutschen Bahn und der Peter und Irene Ludwig Stiftung, fand unter dem Titel *Plattform Aachen* ab 2013 der Aufbau eines umfassenden Archivs zu Kunstorten und Kunstereignissen seit den 1960er-Jahren statt.

2 Das Forschungsprojekt *Videoarchiv*, gefördert von der Volkswagen-Stiftung, lief von 2012 bis 2017. Im Zuge dieses Projekts wurden die Bestände der Avantgarde-Videokunst des Ludwig Forum digitalisiert und kunstwissenschaftlich bearbeitet. In der Bibliothek des Ludwig Forum befindet sich seit 2015 ein Video-Sichtplatz, der die Bestände zugänglich macht. Im Herbst 2018 ging die zugehörige wissenschaftliche Website online.

3 *Nie wieder störungsfrei! Aachen Avantgarde seit 1964*, Ausstellungsprojekt und Katalog (hg. v. Brigitte Franzen, Annette Lagler und Myriam Kroll, Bielefeld 2011).

West German perspective. During this time, the Neue Galerie – Sammlung Ludwig, later the Ludwig Forum für Internationale Kunst, launched not only the development of a "new type of museum" from Aachen but also a new model for collectors.

We would like to warmly congratulate the curators of the exhibition, Benjamin Dodenhoff and Ramona Heinlein, the research project assistants from the very beginning, Lene ter Haar and Nicodemus Schulz, as well as Julia Küchle, Stefanie Raupach, and Marlen Lienkamp, who joined later, for their ambitious and focused work on the projects *Plattform Aachen* and *The Invention of the Neue Wilde*. We would also like to thank our co-sponsors, above all the Friends of the Ludwig Forum, the Youth and Cultural Foundation of the Sparkasse Aachen, Deutsche Bahn, and the state of North Rhine-Westphalia. It is wonderful that over the years the Ludwig Forum has been able to count on such lasting support that encourages penetrating and explorative curiosity rather than easy acclaim.

The thrill of looking into the art world from Aachen, whether toward Berlin and Hamburg or further afield, can be incredibly fruitful, successfully demonstrated by both this project and previous research on artists such as Valdis Āboliņš.

Brigitte Franzen
Chairwoman of the Peter and Irene Ludwig Foundation

lief mit der Neuen Galerie – Sammlung Ludwig, dem späteren Ludwig Forum für Internationale Kunst, von Aachen aus nicht nur die Entwicklung eines „neuen Typs Museum“, sondern auch die eines neuen Sammlermodells „vom Stapel“.

Den Kurator*innen der Ausstellung, Benjamin Dodenhoff und Ramona Heinlein, sowie den Mitarbeiter*innen des Forschungsprojektes der ersten Stunde Lene ter Haar und Nikodemus Schulz sowie später Julia Küchle, Stefanie Raupach und Marlen Lienkamp gratulieren wir herzlich zur ambitionierten und konzentrierten Arbeit an den Projekten *Plattform Aachen* und *Die Erfindung der Neuen Wilden*. Und wir danken unseren Ko-Förderern, allen voran den Freunden des Ludwig Forum, der Jugend- und Kulturstiftung der Sparkasse Aachen, der Deutschen Bahn und dem Land Nordrhein-Westfalen. Es ist wunderbar, dass sich das Ludwig Forum auf eine so nachhaltige Förderung, die nicht den schnellen Applaus, sondern eher die durchdringende forschende Neugier unterstützt, über all die Jahre verlassen konnte.

Der Spannungsbogen, von Aachen aus in die Kunstwelt zu schauen, ob nach Berlin und Hamburg oder weit darüber hinaus, kann sehr fruchtbar sein, wie unter anderem dieses Projekt, aber auch die vorangegangenen Untersuchungen zum Beispiel zu Valdis Āboliņš erfolgreich bewiesen haben.

Brigitte Franzen
Vorständin der Peter und Irene Ludwig Stiftung

It is not often that the history of a museum and the activities of its directors or curators are directly connected to the authorship of an art-historical term. The Neue Galerie – Sammlung Ludwig, now the Ludwig Forum für Internationale Kunst Aachen, and its founding director Wolfgang Becker accomplished this in the 1980s with the concept of the "Neue Wilde." This publication marks the conclusion of the academic research project *The Invention of the Neue Wilde,* which began in 2017, and the exhibition of the same name that examine this artistic development and, above all, the various (sub-)cultural spheres of influence on the Neue Wilde and their art from a distance of around four decades, promising a certain degree of neutrality.

The exhibition and publication are an excellent example of how an institution's own collection can be used as a basis for interrogating certain issues from its history. This seems particularly important at a time when even cultural institutions are obliged to critically address their history and to become aware of their role as agents in the "art operating system" (*Betriebssystem Kunst,* Thomas Wulffen). The exhibition and publication, however, are not merely self-reflections, but instead explore the art of the Neue Wilde in a larger context, revealing how closely intertwined visual art, punk and new wave music, and the subculture at the time were at the hot spots of the movement. The works from the collection of Peter and Irene Ludwig thus serve as a prism through which the history of the Neue Wilde can be newly considered: the exhibition and publication investigate the origins of the art movement, before gallerists, collectors like the Ludwigs, and curators like Becker discovered and supported their art.

As a consequence of the exhibition, many of the Neue Wilde artists, with whom our curators communicated closely, returned to the "birthplace" of the term and—in addition to numerous loans from their early work—contributed valuable information to this publication. Our heartfelt thanks go to all of them. Without the substantial support of the Peter and Irene Ludwig Foundation and the Ministry of Culture and Science of North Rhine-Westphalia, the project would not have been realized, and for this I would also like to express my sincerest gratitude. I would also like to thank the Friends of the Ludwig Forum for their support. Benjamin Dodenhoff and Ramona Heinlein developed the concept for the research project, exhibition, and final publication, and brought them all to a very successful

Es kommt nicht oft vor, dass die Geschichte eines Museums und die Aktivitäten seiner Direktor*innen oder Kurator*innen direkt mit der Urheberschaft eines kunsthistorischen Terminus verbunden sind. Der Neuen Galerie – Sammlung Ludwig, dem heutigen Ludwig Forum für Internationale Kunst Aachen, und ihrem Gründungsdirektor Wolfgang Becker ist dies in den 1980er-Jahren mit dem Begriff der „Neuen Wilden" gelungen. Das 2017 initiierte wissenschaftliche Forschungsprojekt *Die Erfindung der Neuen Wilden* und die gleichnamige Ausstellung, deren Abschluss die vorliegende Publikation bildet, untersuchen aus der eine gewisse Neutralität versprechenden Distanz von rund vier Jahrzehnten diese künstlerische Entwicklung und vor allem die verschiedenen (sub-)kulturellen Einflusssphären auf die Neuen Wilden und ihre Kunst.

Ausstellung und Publikation sind ein sehr gelungenes Beispiel dafür, wie sich Fragestellungen aus der Geschichte der eigenen Sammlung heraus entwickeln lassen. Dies erscheint besonders wichtig in einer Zeit, in der gerade auch Kulturinstitutionen angehalten sind, sich kritisch mit ihrer eigenen Geschichte auseinanderzusetzen und sich ihrer Rolle als Akteure im „Betriebssystem Kunst" (Thomas Wulffen) bewusst zu werden. Ausstellung und Publikation bleiben aber nicht bei einer reinen Selbstreflexion stehen, sondern beleuchten die Kunst der Neuen Wilden in einem größeren Kontext, zeigen auf, wie eng verflochten bildende Kunst, Punk- und New Wave-Musik sowie die Subkultur zu der Zeit an den Brennpunkten der Bewegung waren. Die Werke aus der Sammlung von Peter und Irene Ludwig dienen folglich als ein Prisma, durch das die Geschichte der Neuen Wilden neu betrachtet werden kann: Ausstellung und Publikation untersuchen, woher die Kunstbewegung eigentlich kam, bevor Galerist*innen, Sammler*innen wie die Ludwigs und Kurator*innen wie Becker ihre Kunst entdeckten und förderten.

Viele der Künstler*innen der Neuen Wilden, mit denen unsere Kurator*innen im engen Austausch waren, sind aufgrund der Ausstellung an den „Geburtsort" des Begriffs zurückgekehrt und haben neben zahlreichen Leihgaben aus ihrem Frühwerk auch wertvolle Informationen zur vorliegenden Publikation beigesteuert. Hierfür sei ihnen sehr herzlich gedankt. Ohne die substanzielle Förderung der Peter und Irene Ludwig Stiftung sowie des Ministeriums für Kultur und Wissenschaft des Landes Nordrhein-Westfalen wäre das Projekt nicht zu realisieren gewesen, wofür ich ebenfalls meinen herzlichsten Dank zum Ausdruck bringen möchte. Auch danke ich dem Verein der Freunde des Ludwig Forum für die gewährte Unterstützung. Benjamin Dodenhoff

conclusion, ultimately demonstrating the great importance of research in museums, which themselves are a tremendous source for the creation and public dissemination of cultural education. So finally, many thanks to both of you.

Andreas Beitin
Director of the Ludwig Forum für Internationale Kunst Aachen

und Ramona Heinlein haben das Forschungsprojekt, die Ausstellung sowie die abschließende Publikation konzeptuell entwickelt und zu einem sehr erfolgreichen Abschluss geführt, der nicht zuletzt auch verdeutlicht, wie wichtig Forschung in Museen ist, denn dadurch wird ein maßgeblicher Teil an kultureller Bildung geleistet und der Öffentlichkeit zur Verfügung gestellt. Ihnen beiden gilt abschließend ein großer Dank.

Andreas Beitin
Direktor des Ludwig Forum für Internationale Kunst Aachen

Benjamin Dodenhoff
Einführung
Die Erfindung der Neuen Wilden. Der Malereiboom um 1980 im Spiegel der Sammlung Ludwig

Benjamin Dodenhoff
Introduction
The Invention of the Neue Wilde: The Painting Boom around 1980 as Reflected in the Ludwig Collection

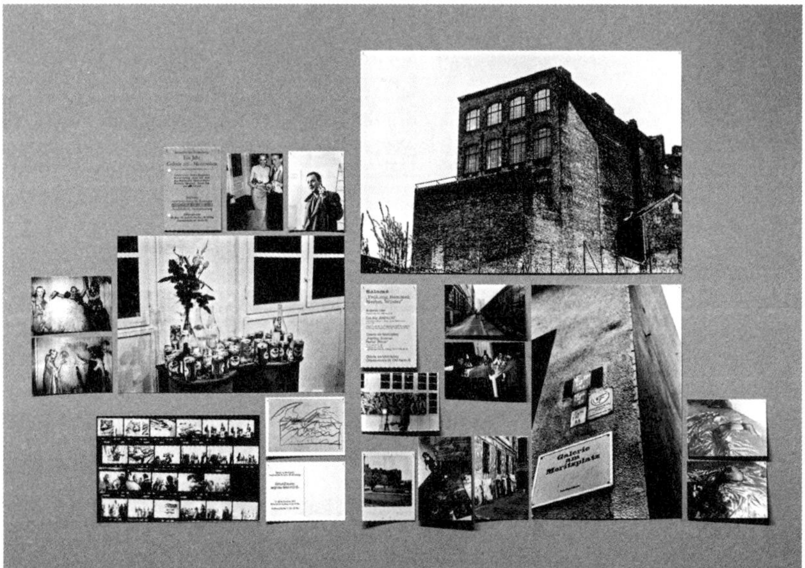

Die Erfindung der Neuen Wilden. Malerei und Subkultur um 1980 / The Invention of the Neue Wilde: Painting and Subculture around 1980, Ludwig Forum für Internationale Kunst Aachen, 2018/19

Kein anderer kunsthistorischer Begriff hat die deutsche Kunstszene zu Beginn der 1980er-Jahre so sehr geprägt wie jener der „Neuen Wilden“. Die Wortschöpfung taucht exakt zum richtigen Zeitpunkt auf, um ein begrifflich noch nicht konturiertes Phänomen festzuschreiben, das in den nachfolgenden Jahren omnipräsent werden sollte. Ab 1980 stürmten junge Künstler*innen die Ausstellungshäuser mit großformatigen Leinwandarbeiten, die durch figurative Darstellungen in ungestümem Farbgestus auffielen. Die üppige Motivwelt, changierend zwischen unmittelbarem Witz und lustvoller Provokation, stand in scharfem Kontrast zur Semantik von Konzeptkunst und Minimal Art, die im Kunstdiskurs der vorangegangenen Jahre als dominierend wahrgenommen wurden. Die neue Welle figurativer Malerei hatte viele Zentren und Protagonist*innen: etwa die Galerie am Moritzplatz, ein 1977 in Eigenregie gegründeter Off-Space in Westberlin, zu dessen Umfeld Künstler*innen wie Rainer Fetting, Helmut Middendorf, Salomé, Anne Jud und Bernd Zimmer gehörten, oder die Kölner Ateliergemeinschaft Mülheimer Freiheit, der Künstler wie Hans Peter Adamski, Peter Bömmels, Walter Dahn und Jiří Georg Dokoupil angehörten. Weitere Impulse kamen von den zeitweise in Hamburg arbeitenden Martin Kippenberger, Werner Büttner und Albert Oehlen sowie dessen in Düsseldorf lebendem Bruder Markus Oehlen, die häufig verkürzt schlicht als „die Hamburger“ bezeichnet wurden. Dies sind nur einige der bekanntesten Namen aus einer Liste von Künstler*innen, die sich beliebig erweitern ließe, denn der Begriff „Neue Wilde“ war eine eher vage, immer auch umstrittene Umschreibung für eine Reihe von Künstler*innen, die in der Öffentlichkeit als eine Art Bewegung wahrgenommen wurden, ohne dass sie selbst sich als zusammenhängende Gruppe verstanden hätten. Diese Bezeichnung, unter der diese Künstler*innen häufig kunsthistorisch zusammengefasst werden, wurde im Zuge einer Ausstellung geboren, die 1980 in der Neuen Galerie – Sammlung Ludwig in Aachen stattfand, dem späteren Ludwig Forum für Internationale Kunst. Die Begriffsbildung an diesem Ort gab den initialen Impuls für die Kurator*innen des Ludwig Forum, eben hier in einem Forschungs- und Ausstellungsprojekt den Ursprüngen des kunsthistorischen Mythos der Neuen Wilden nachzugehen.
Im Kern als eine Präsentation der hauseigenen Bestände der Sammlung Ludwig konzipiert, ging es dabei nicht um eine Best-of-Schau von Gemälden. Wir wollten stattdessen am Fallbeispiel des „Booms“ der Neue Wilden im Spiegel der Sammlung Ludwig zeigen, wie das Wechselverhältnis zwischen Künstler*innen, Händler*innen, Sammler*innen und Betrachter*innen zeitgenössischer Kunst sowie den mit ihr befassten

No other art-historical term had a greater influence on the German art scene at the beginning of the 1980s than that of "Neue Wilde." The coinage surfaced at exactly the right time to define a phenomenon still lacking conceptual contours but that would become ubiquitous in the years that followed. From 1980 onward, young artists stormed the exhibition venues with large-format canvases distinguished by figurative depictions gesturally rendered in boisterous colors. Its lavish world of motifs, alternating between direct gag and joyful provocation, stands in sharp contrast to the semantics of Conceptual and Minimal Art, which had been perceived as dominating the art discourse of the preceding years. The new wave of figurative painting had a number of hubs and protagonists, such as Galerie am Moritzplatz, an independent, self-organized gallery in West Berlin, founded in 1977, with which artists such as Rainer Fetting, Helmut Middendorf, Salomé, Anne Jud, and Bernd Zimmer were associated, or the Cologne studio community Mülheimer Freiheit that included the artists Hans Peter Adamski, Peter Bömmels, Walter Dahn, and Jiří Georg Dokoupil. Further stimuli came from Martin Kippenberger, Werner Büttner, and Albert Oehlen, who all temporarily worked in Hamburg, and the latter's Düsseldorf-based brother Markus Oehlen. They were often called "die Hamburger." These are just a few of the best-known names from a list of artists that could be arbitrarily extended, since the term "Neue Wilde" was a rather vague and invariably contested description of numerous artists publicly perceived as a sort of movement, even though they did not regard themselves as a coherent group. The term under which these artists are frequently subsumed from an art-historical perspective was born in the wake of a show held in 1980 at the Neue Galerie – Sammlung Ludwig in Aachen, later the Ludwig Forum für Internationale Kunst. The creation of the concept at its predecessor institution provided the initial impulse for the curators of the Ludwig Forum to explore the origins of the art-historical myth of the Neue Wilde in an on-site research and exhibition project. Basically conceived as a presentation of the holdings of the Ludwig Collection, our aim was not to stage a "best of" painting show. Instead, we wanted to use the example of the "boom" of the Neue Wilde as reflected in the Ludwig Collection to show how the interrelations between artists, traders, collectors, and viewers of contemporary art, as well as the art historians dealing with it, create a dynamic field of tension that

Kunsthistoriker*innen ein dynamisches Spannungsfeld erzeugt, das längst nicht mehr monokausal beschrieben werden kann. Das Projekt hatte zum Ziel, die Akteur*innen der verschiedenen Ebenen der Kunstproduktion und -rezeption in den Fokus zu nehmen, eine Perspektive, die als ergänzendes Korrektiv neben die traditionelle Betrachtung des Kunstwerks als ästhetischem Objekt und des Künstlers als genialischem Urheber treten soll. Dabei ging es vor allem auch darum, die Malerei historisch zu verorten, ihre enge Verzahnung mit vielfältigen Phänomenen des Zeitgeists aufzuzeigen und ihre Nähe zu den subkulturellen Szenen ihrer Entstehungszeit als einen der Hauptaspekte ihrer Faszination darzustellen. Neben die großformatigen Leinwandarbeiten der Sammlung Ludwig treten in der Ausstellung daher rund dreihundert Fotos, Plakate, Dokumente, Schallplatten und Filme aus der experimentellen Frühzeit jener Künstler*innen, die wenig später als „Neue Wilde“ bekannt wurden.

Aachen 1980 – Sammlung Ludwig und die Nouveaux Fauves

Seit 1970 gestaltete Museumsdirektor Wolfgang Becker für die Neue Galerie – Sammlung Ludwig in Aachen ein vielfältiges Ausstellungsprogramm, das ausgehend von den Sammlungsaktivitäten Peter und Irene Ludwigs den aktuellsten künstlerischen Strömungen nachspürte. 1967, drei Jahre vor der Gründung der Neuen Galerie, präsentierten sie im Aachener Suermondt-Museum erstmals eine größere Auswahl der von ihnen zusammengetragenen Werke vor allem der amerikanischen Pop-Art, die sie in den folgenden Jahren immer weiter als Sammlungsschwerpunkt ausbauten. Peter Ludwig war geschäftlich häufig in New York, wo er ganze Konvolute früher Werke von Künstler*innen wie Jasper Johns, Andy Warhol und Roy Lichtenstein erwarb. Hinzu kamen Werke des Hyperrealismus, der Minimal Art, des Abstrakten Expressionismus und verschiedene Einzelpositionen aktueller Kunst. Doch wuchs die Sammlung des Ehepaars Ludwig in verschiedene Richtungen weiter. 1975 erwarben sie ihre ersten beiden Arbeiten von A. R. Penck in der Galerie Michael Werner und fünf Gemälde von Georg Baselitz bei Werner und Rudolf Zwirner. Diese Ankäufe markieren das zunehmende Interesse der Ludwigs an der zeitgenössischen deutschen Kunst. So gelangten über Werner und Zwirner in den kommenden Jahren auch Werke unter anderem von Anselm Kiefer, Markus Lüpertz oder Jörg Immendorff in die Sammlung.[1]

Die Schau *Les Nouveaux Fauves – Die Neuen Wilden* war als Präsentation der Neuankäufe des Ehepaars Ludwig konzipiert. Als

can by no means be described in a singular fashion. The project's intention was to focus on the actors at various levels of art production and reception, a perspective meant to serve as a complementary corrective to the traditional view of the artwork as an aesthetic object and of the artist as a genius creator. At issue was, above all, to situate this painting historically, to highlight its close interconnection with diverse phenomena of the zeitgeist, and to portray the proximity to the subcultural scenes of its time as one of the main sources for its fascination. Along with the large-format canvases of the Ludwig Collection, the show therefore features around three hundred photographs, posters, documents, records, and films from the experimental early phase of those artists who later became known as the Neue Wilde.

Aachen 1980: The Ludwig Collection and the Nouveaux Fauves

Since 1970, the museum's director Wolfgang Becker had been organizing a diverse exhibition program for the Neue Galerie – Sammlung Ludwig in Aachen that traced the most current artistic movements based on the collecting activities of Peter and Irene Ludwig. In 1967, three years before the founding of the Neue Galerie, they presented a larger selection of their collected works for the first time at the Suermondt-Museum in Aachen, mostly American Pop Art that would become a growing focus of their collection in the following years. Peter Ludwig was often in New York for business, and he would acquire entire groups of early works by artists such as Jasper Johns, Andy Warhol, and Roy Lichtenstein, but also works of Hyperrealism, Minimal Art, Abstract Expressionism, and various individual artistic positions of contemporary art. Yet the Ludwigs' collection continued to expand in different directions. In 1975, they purchased their first two works by A. R. Penck from Galerie Michael Werner and a total of five paintings by Georg Baselitz from Werner and Rudolf Zwirner. These acquisitions marked their increasing interest in contemporary German art. In the following years, more works by German artists were added to the collection by way of Werner and Zwirner, including pieces by Anselm Kiefer, Markus Lüpertz, and Jörg Immendorff.[1]

The exhibition *Les Nouveaux Fauves – Die Neuen Wilden* was conceived as a presentation of the Ludwigs' new acquisitions.

thematischen Faden verknüpfte Wolfgang Becker künstlerische Positionen, die auf unterschiedliche Weise Bezüge zu den historischen Fauves der französischen Kunst zu Beginn des 20. Jahrhunderts aufwiesen. Hierzu gehörten US-amerikanische Künstler*innen der damals neuen Pattern and Decoration-Bewegung genauso wie die französische Künstlergruppe Supports/Surfaces, die bereits seit Mitte der 1960er-Jahre aktiv war. Als deutscher Beitrag wurden Arbeiten von Baselitz, Immendorff, Lüpertz und Penck gezeigt. Keiner von ihnen war Teil jener Künstler*innen, die später als „Neue Wilde" bezeichnet wurden. Trotzdem verfing der griffige Terminus sofort. Während die Fachpresse und die Kunstwissenschaft ihn eher zurückhaltend aufnahmen, wurde er in den Massenmedien ab 1980 schnell als feststehender Begriff für die deutschen Maler*innen gebräuchlich, die eine Generation jünger waren als die in der Ausstellung gezeigten. Möglich war die Umwidmung des Begriffs durch die Herleitung, die Wolfgang Becker in der Einleitung zur Ausstellung formulierte. Als verbindende Charakteristika der Kunst der Neuen Wilden nennt er hier „Farbigkeit – Hitze – gestalteter Ausdruck – Spontaneität – Lockerheit – Unruhe – Emotion – Erlebnis – Geschichte – Orient – Gesamtkunstwerk – Synthese – Kommunikation – Praxis"[2] und grenzt sie im Folgenden ab von einer Kunst, die als „farblos, kalt, ausdruckslos, kalkulierend, besessen, ruhig, emotionslos, geschichtslos, akademisch, analytisch, kommunikationsarm und praxisfremd"[3] beschrieben wird. Becker formuliert hier die damals virulente Dichotomie zwischen der wieder stärker wahrgenommenen „expressiven" Malerei auf der einen Seite und der „bildnerische[n] Askese und Kopflastigkeit der minimal und conceptual art"[4] auf der anderen. Das entspricht einer Erzählung, die für den Diskurs zur neuen figurativen Malerei um 1980 prägend war und nicht zuletzt vom Kunstkritiker Wolfgang Max Faust in diversen einflussreichen Texten umfassend ausgearbeitet wurde.[5] Beckers

1 Unter den erworbenen Arbeiten befanden sich Schlüsselwerke wie *Café Deutschland I* (1977/78) von Jörg Immendorff, *Die Große Nacht im Eimer* (1962/63) von Georg Baselitz oder *Der Übergang* (1963) von A. R. Penck. Während von den meisten Malern vor allem frisch entstandene Arbeiten in die Sammlung gelangten, ist den Sammlungskomplexen von Penck und Baselitz die Bestrebung anzumerken, auch Beispiele älterer Werkphasen der Künstler nachzukaufen, sodass sich ein Querschnitt des Gesamtœuvres ergibt. Dies gelang unter anderem durch den Ankauf großer Konvolute von Papierarbeiten.

2 Wolfgang Becker, „Les Nouveaux Fauves / Die Neuen Wilden: Vorschlag zu einer Untersuchung", in: *Les Nouveaux Fauves – Die Neuen Wilden*, Ausst.-Kat. Neue Galerie – Sammlung Ludwig, Aachen 1980, Wiederabdruck im vorliegenden Band S. 374–381, Zitat S. 375.

3 Ebd.

4 Ebd., S. 379.

As a thematic thread, Wolfgang Becker connected artistic positions that in different ways revealed references to the Fauves of early twentieth-century French art. They included American artists of the then new Pattern and Decoration movement as well as the French artists group Supports/Surfaces, who had been active since the mid-1960s. The German contributions included works by Baselitz, Immendorff, Lüpertz, and Penck. None of the pieces belonged to the artists that were later called the Neue Wilde. Nevertheless, the catchy term immediately gained traction. While the specialist press and art theorists used it rather cautiously, beginning in 1980 it quickly became widespread in the mass media as an established term for German painters a generation younger than those featured in the exhibition. The rededication of the term became possible given how Wolfgang Becker formulated its derivation in the introduction to the show. As common characteristics of the art of the Neue Wilde he mentioned "colorfulness—heat—expression—spontaneity—casualness—unrest—emotion—experience—history—orient—Gesamtkunstwerk—synthesis—communication—praxis,"[2] distinguishing it from an art he described as "colorless, cold, expressionless, calculating, obsessive, calm, emotionless, ahistorical, academic, analytical, uncommunicative, and out of touch with praxis."[3] Becker formulated what was then a virulent dichotomy: between the revitalized "expressive" painting on one side, and the "pictorial asceticism and intellectualism of Minimal and Conceptual Art" on the other.[4] He was therefore in line with a narrative that shaped the discourse on the new figurative painting around 1980, and that was extensively elaborated not least by the art critic Wolfgang Max Faust in various influential texts.[5] Becker's characterization of the Neue

1 Among the paintings acquired were key works such as Jörg Immendorff's *Café Deutschland I* (1977–78), Georg Baselitz's *Die Große Nacht im Eimer* (1962–63), or A. R. Penck's *Der Übergang* (1963). While most painters are represented in the collection by newly created works, one can see an effort made with respect to the collections of works by Penck and Baselitz to subsequently acquire examples from older work periods, resulting in a cross section of their entire oeuvre. This was achieved, for example, by purchasing large numbers of works on paper.

2 Wolfgang Becker, "Les Nouveaux Fauves / Die Neuen Wilden: Vorschlag zu einer Untersuchung," in *Les Nouveaux Fauves – Die Neuen Wilden,* exh. cat. Neue Galerie – Sammlung Ludwig, Aachen 1980, n.p.; reprinted in translation in the present volume as "Les Nouveaux Fauves / Die Neuen Wilden: Proposal for a Study," pp. 374–381, here p. 374.

3 Ibid.

4 Ibid., p. 378.

Charakterisierung der Neuen Wilden ließ sich so gut zur Beschreibung der jüngsten deutschen Maler*innen-Generation heranziehen, dass es schlicht keine Rolle spielte, dass deren Bilder in seiner Ausstellung 1980 gar nicht zu sehen waren. Die Taufe der Neuen Wilden fand gewissermaßen in Abwesenheit der Täuflinge statt.

Malerei und Subkultur um 1980

Als verbindendes Element, das es ermöglichte, die Künstler*innen aus Berlin, Hamburg und Köln unter dem Gruppensignet „Neue Wilde" zusammenzufassen, ließe sich – neben der offensichtlichen Zugehörigkeit zur selben Generation – schnell die Praxis der figurativen Malerei ausmachen. Übersehen wird dabei allerdings, dass die Haltungen der einzelnen Künstler*innen zur Malerei ebenso divers waren wie die Themen und Motive ihrer Bilder. Beispielhaft lässt sich das an drei Protagonisten nachvollziehen: Salomé, Peter Bömmels und Martin Kippenberger. Salomés frühe Bilder stehen in engem Austausch mit seiner Aktivität als Performancekünstler, die Leinwand nutzt er als Aktionsfeld.[6] Die gemalten Figuren, häufig Selbstporträts, sind immer lebensgroß. Eine Verkleinerung der Figur bedeutete schon eine Ebene der Abstraktion, die dem Verlangen nach einem möglichst unmittelbaren Ausdruck des Körpers auf der Leinwand zuwider gelaufen wäre. Salomés Malerei zielt auf eine Konfrontation des Publikums mit der – nicht selten stark sexuell konnotierten – physischen Präsenz des Malers in seinem Werk. Nicht zuletzt durch die Dynamik des Farbauftrags ist diese Malerei als performativ aufzufassen, die sowohl an Aspekte des klassischen Expressionismus vom Beginn des 20. Jahrhunderts als auch an das Action-Painting der 1950er-Jahre anknüpft. Die Konzentration auf die Figur und die starkfarbige Malweise von Ersterem überblendet er mit der Wucht, Spontaneität und körperlichen Unmittelbarkeit des Zweiteren. Die Bezeichnung Neo-Expressionismus charakterisiert seine Malerei also im doppelten Sinne. Zugleich eignet sich Salomé den virilen expressionistischen Gestus in einem Akt der Emanzipation an, indem er ihn im Sinne seines dezidiert schwulen Bildprogramms umdeutet.

5 Vgl. etwa Wolfgang Max Faust, „‚Du hast keine Chance. Nutze sie!' With It and Against It: Tendencies in Recent German Art", in: *Artforum*, September 1981, S. 33–39, Wiederabdruck im vorliegenden Band S. 390–405.

6 Zum Zusammenhang zwischen Salomés performativen Selbstinszenierungen und seiner Malerei vgl. Katrin Köppert, „Queere ‚Indianer' und exotische Terrortunten. Die ‚Kunst' des Ethnic Drag bei Castelli und Salomé", im vorliegenden Band S. 62–85.

Wilde applied so well in describing the youngest generation of German painters that it simply no longer mattered that their pictures were not displayed at his show in 1980. The Neue Wilde was baptized, so to speak, without the candidates being present.

Painting and Subculture around 1980

As a connecting element that allows the artists from Berlin, Hamburg, and Cologne to be grouped together under the common label of "Neue Wilde," the practice of figurative painting quickly comes to mind—in addition, of course, to their belonging to the same generation. What this neglects, however, is that the attitudes of the individual artists toward painting were just as diverse as the themes and motifs of their pictures. This can be exemplified by three protagonists: Salomé, Peter Bömmels, and Martin Kippenberger.

Salomé's early paintings are closely linked to his activities as a performance artist. He uses the canvas as a field of action.[6] The painted figures, often self-portraits, are always life-size. Reducing the size of the figure would have already implied a level of abstraction running counter to the desire to express the body on the canvas as directly as possible. Salomé's painting aims at confronting the viewer with the—often sexually explicit—physical presence of the painter. Not least due to the dynamic application of color, one can grasp this type of painting as performative, latching on to aspects of classic, early twentieth-century Expressionism as well as of 1950s Action Painting. He combines the focus on the figure and the gaudily colored painting style of the former with the power, spontaneity, and corporeal directness of the latter. Thus the term "Neo-Expressionism" characterizes his painting in a double sense. At the same time, however, Salomé appropriates the virile Expressionist gesture in an act of emancipation to reinterpret it for the purpose of his decidedly queer imagery.

At the center of Peter Bömmels's work is the idea of dilettantism. He is an autodidact, both as a music journalist and

5 See, for example, Wolfgang Max Faust, "'Du hast keine Chance. Nutze sie!' With It and Against It: Tendencies in Recent German Art," *Artforum* 20, no. 1, September 1981, pp. 33–39; reprinted in the present volume, pp. 390–405.

6 On the connections between Salomé's performative self-staging and painting, see Katrin Köppert, "Queer 'Indians' and Exotic Terrorist Drags: The 'Art' of Ethnic Drag in Castelli and Salomé," in the present volume, pp. 62–85.

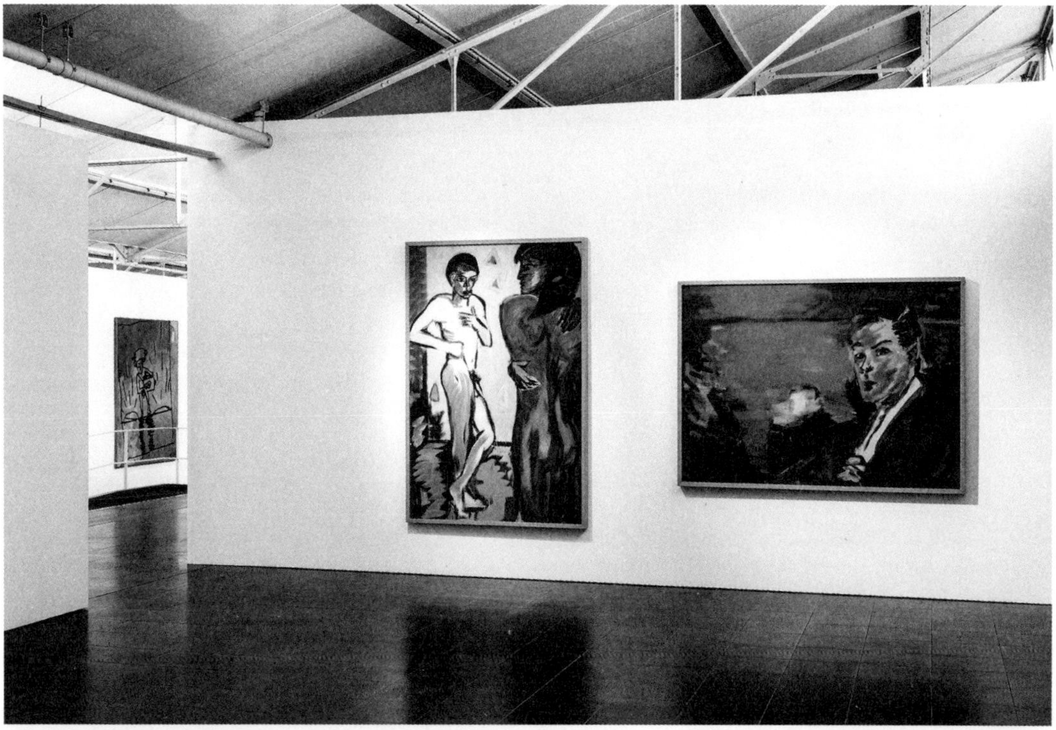

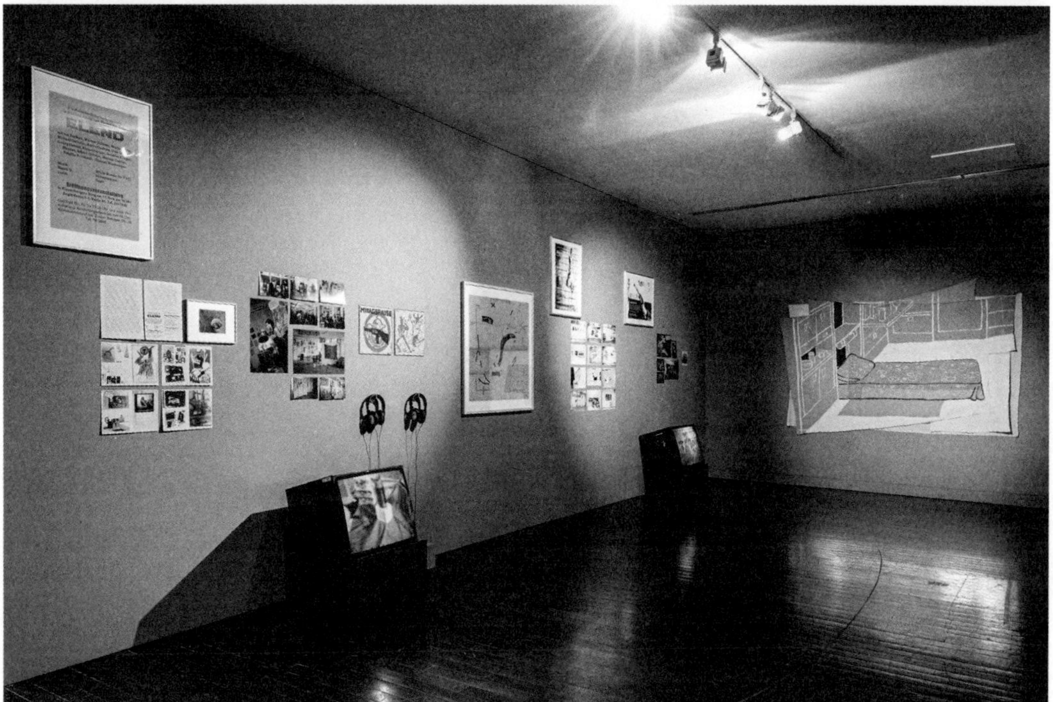

Die Erfindung der Neuen Wilden. Malerei und Subkultur um 1980 / The Invention of the Neue Wilde: Painting and Subculture around 1980, Ludwig Forum für Internationale Kunst Aachen, 2018/19

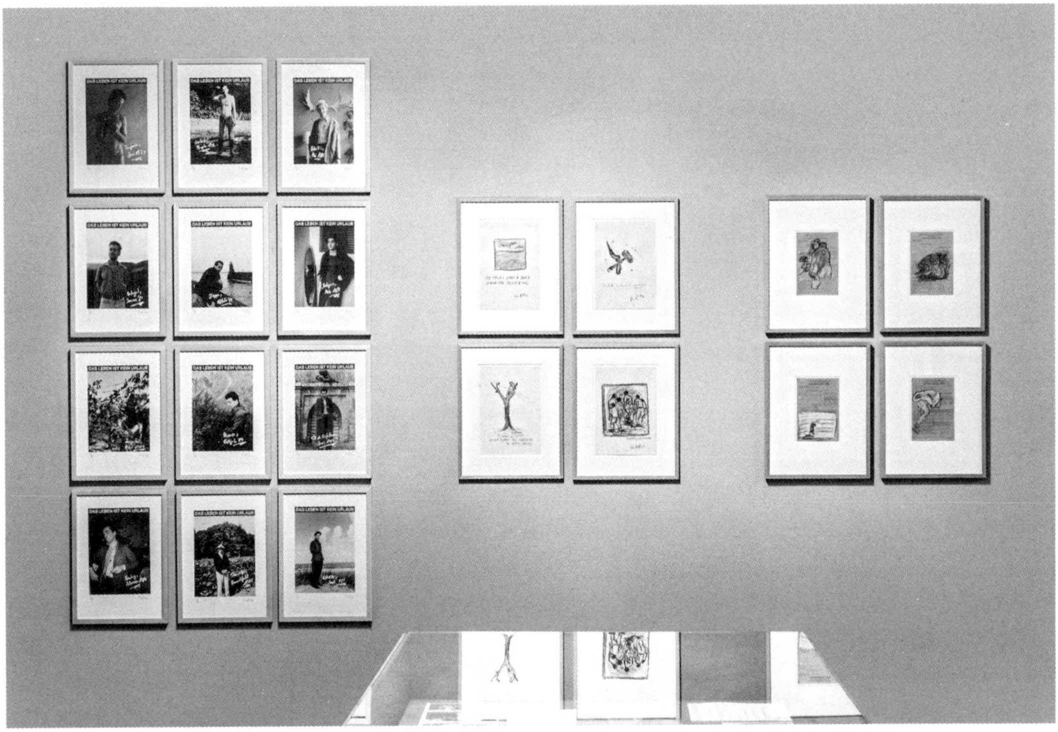

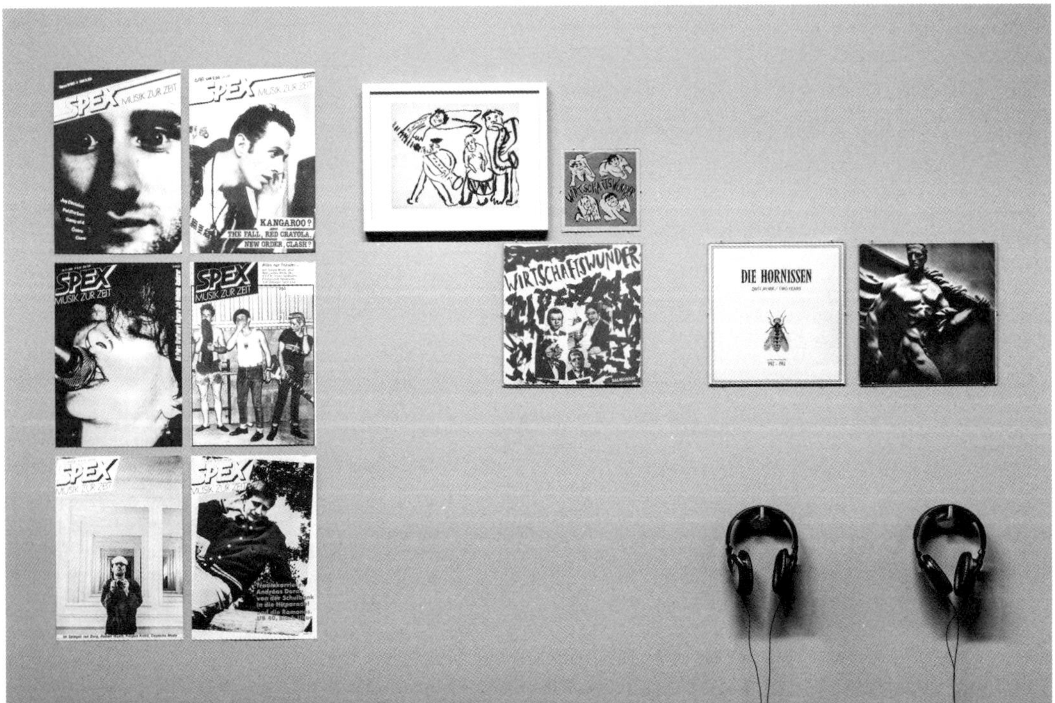

Die Erfindung der Neuen Wilden. Malerei und Subkultur um 1980 / The Invention of the Neue Wilde: Painting and Subculture around 1980, Ludwig Forum für Internationale Kunst Aachen, 2018/19

Im Zentrum des Schaffens von Peter Bömmels steht die Idee des Dilettantismus. Als Musikjournalist wie auch als bildender Künstler ist er Autodidakt. Beflügelt durch die gruppendynamischen Prozesse mit seinen Malerkollegen der Mülheimer Freiheit, geht es in seinen frühen Arbeiten um die Möglichkeit, überhaupt etwas zu erfinden und zu schaffen, das keiner Tradition und keinem festgelegten Bildprogramm verpflichtet wäre. Gemäß seiner Affinität zur geschriebenen Sprache und der Lust am Fabulieren entstanden ins Bild gesetzte Sprachspiele und versponnene Geschichten. Expressivität im Sinne einer impulsiven Selbstäußerung ist nicht der Antrieb hinter Bömmels' Bildern. Vielmehr geht es um sprachlichen und formalen Witz sowie eine oftmals surreal anmutende Metaphorik, die eher gelesen als erfahren werden soll.

Kippenberger schließlich produziert während seiner Berliner Zeit kaum Gemälde. Um 1980 entstehen vor allem Fotografien, Plakate, Postkarten und andere Drucksachen, die in unablässiger Frequenz publiziert werden. Eine der wenigen malerischen Arbeiten dieser Zeit ist die Serie *Lieber Maler, male mir* (1981), für die Kippenberger lediglich die fotografischen Vorlagen schuf, um einen professionellen Plakatmaler mit der malerischen Umsetzung zu beauftragen. Hier zeigt sich die ironisch distanzierte Haltung Kippenbergers gegenüber der Figur des Malers generell. Als Bildmotive konnten fotografische Schnappschüsse oder Ausschnitte aus Zeitschriften und anderen Druckerzeugnissen dienen. Erst in der collageartigen Zusammenstellung verschiedener Bildquellen, und versehen mit oftmals abstrusen, gerne auch frivolen Bildtiteln, entwickeln die Gemälde ihren anarchischen Witz. Die Ironie, mit der Kippenberger die tradierte Erwartungshaltung gegenüber dem klassischen Tafelbild bricht, etwa durch die Verwendung kalauernder Bildinhalte, ermöglicht ihm überhaupt erst, Malerei als Medium in Betracht zu ziehen. Kippenbergers Malerei ist eine Metamalerei, die sich ihres Unvermögens, eine authentische Selbstäußerung zu artikulieren, jederzeit bewusst ist und den Maler als lächerliche Figur vorführt.[7]

Bei aller Diversität in den skizzierten Einzelpositionen gibt es allerdings auch große Gemeinsamkeiten. Dazu zählt zum einen die grundlegende Unbekümmertheit, mit der die Künstler*innen sich die Malerei zu eigen machten. Sowohl die Selbstverständlichkeit und Konsequenz, mit denen Salomé die Leinwand als Ausdrucksmedium

7 Zur Figur des Künstlers im Werk der Hamburger vgl. Ramona Heinlein, „Wir behaupten die Welt. Künstlerische Selbstinszenierung an den Rändern der Malerei", im vorliegenden Band S. 40–61.

a visual artist. Inspired by the group dynamics that he developed with his painter colleagues of the Mülheimer Freiheit, his early works deal with the possibility of inventing and creating something that would not be bound to any tradition or defined pictorial program. In accordance with his affinity for written language and his delight in storytelling, he created visual language games and told tales. But it is not expressivity in the sense of impulsive self-expression that is the driving force behind Bömmels's paintings. It is instead linguistic and formal wit and an oftentimes surreal imagery that should be read rather than experienced.

For his part, Martin Kippenberger ultimately realized very few paintings during his time in Berlin. Around 1980, he was mainly producing photographs, posters, postcards, and other printed materials that he churned out at an unrelenting pace. One of the few painterly works from this period is the series *Lieber Maler, male mir* (Dear Painter, Paint for Me, 1981), for which Kippenberger only created the photographic templates, which he then commissioned a professional billboard painter to paint. It is here where Kippenberger's ironically distanced attitude toward the figure of the painter is revealed. Snapshots or clippings from magazines and other printed matter generally served as picture motifs. Only through the collage-like assembly of the various image sources and the oftentimes fanciful and also frivolous titles assigned to them do the paintings unfold their anarchic wit. It is the irony with which Kippenberger frustrates what one traditionally expects from the panel painting, such as through his use of puns as pictorial content, that even allows him to consider painting as a viable medium. Kippenberger's painting is meta-painting that is invariably conscious of its inability to articulate authentic self-expression, and which reveals the painter as a ridiculous figure.[7]

Despite all the diversity in the individual artistic positions outlined above, there were also great similarities. For one, the elemental recklessness with which the artists made painting their own: the naturalness and consistency with which Salomé uses the canvas as a means of expressing his corporeality, Bömmels' poetic dilettantism, and Kippenberger's ironic meta-painting all spring from an impulsive desire to articulate oneself artistically.

7 On the figure of the artist in the work of the Hamburg artists, see Ramona Heinlein, "We Assert the World: Artistic Self-Staging at the Fringes of Painting," in the present volume, pp. 40–61.

seiner Körperlichkeit nutzt, als auch der poetische Dilettantismus Bömmels' und die ironische Metamalerei Kippenbergers entspringen einer impulsiven Lust, sich künstlerisch zu artikulieren. Die Neuen Wilden bilden damit einen Gegenentwurf zur konzeptuellen Reflexion des Mediums Malerei, wie sie etwa Gerhard Richter seit den 1960er-Jahren betrieb. Zum anderen lässt sich als weitere große Konstante und Gemeinsamkeit in den Aktivitäten der Künstler*innen die Nähe zu den verschiedensten Subkulturen ihrer Zeit konstatieren. Anregungen für die Spielarten ihrer ästhetischen Grundhaltung und die konkreten Themen und Motive ihrer Malerei fanden sie abseits der Akademien und des hegemonialen Kunstdiskurses: in der sexuellen Freizügigkeit der Schwulenszene, im DIY-Geist der Punk- und New-Wave-Bewegung und im Nachtleben der Kneipen und Undergroundläden der Großstädte. Die hier gewonnenen Eindrücke wurden mannigfaltig künstlerisch verarbeitet. Gerade in ihren Frühwerken experimentierten fast alle Künstler*innen auch mit Medien jenseits der Malerei. Salomé machte Performances, Helmut Middendorf drehte Super-8-Filme, Walter Dahn fotografierte, Martin Kippenberger organisierte Konzerte, Ausstellungen und Aktionen für den Underground-Club S.O.36, es entstanden Plakate, Bücher, Objekte und Installationen. In der ersten Ausstellung[8] der Kölner Künstler etwa hing keine einzige Leinwand (Abb. S. 336–341). Ihre breiten Pinselstriche zogen sich stattdessen über Wände, Böden und Decken, darüber hinaus gab es Collagen, Papierrisse und Objekte zu sehen. Und immer wieder erschienen Schallplatten, auf denen die Künstler*innen entweder selbst zu hören oder an denen sie auf unterschiedlichste Weise beteiligt waren.[9] Will man die Wucht nachvollziehen, mit der die Neuen Wilden die Bühne der Kunstwelt eroberten, muss man sich dieser explosiven Mischung aus subkulturellen Themen und medialer Experimentierfreude gewahr werden. Sie war die Quelle, aus der die Malerei ihre überbordende Energie zog. Es gehört allerdings auch zur Geschichte der Neuen Wilden, dass der multimediale Aspekt ihrer Kunst bei vielen Künstler*innen in den Hintergrund trat, sobald die kommerziellen Galerien und die institutionellen Ausstellungshäuser sie entdeckten und sich fast ausschließlich auf ihre Malerei fokussierten.

8 *Auch wenn das Perlhuhn leise weint*, Hahnentorburg Köln, 1980.

9 Zu den Musikprojekten vgl. Christian Höller, „While the Guinea Fowl Gently Weeps. Über Maler-Musik und Künstler-Bands, 1979–1984“, im vorliegenden Band S. 86–109.

The Neue Wilde thus represented a counter-model to the conceptual reflection on the medium of painting as practiced since the 1960s by someone such as Gerhard Richter. Also, the artists had in common a steady closeness to the diverse subcultures of their time. The inspiration for their varied aesthetic approaches and their paintings' concrete subjects and motifs did not come from the academies and hegemonic art discourse, but by the sexual openness of the gay scene, the DIY spirit of the punk and new wave movements, and the nightlife in the bars and underground spots in the big cities. The impressions they received in these milieus were explored artistically, and in countless ways. Especially in their early works, almost all of the artists experimented with media outside painting: Salomé realized performances; Helmut Middendorf shot Super-8 films; Walter Dahn took photographs; Martin Kippenberger organized concerts, exhibitions, and actions for the underground club S.O.36; and posters, books, objects, and installations were produced. At the first exhibition by the Cologne-based artists,[8] for example, not a single canvas was on display (figs. pp. 336–341). Instead, their broad brushstrokes covered the walls, floors, and ceilings, and one could find collages, paper cutouts, and objects. Records were also frequently released, either with music by the artists themselves or with which they were involved in other ways.[9] To understand the force with which the Neue Wilde conquered the art world, one must first become aware of the explosive mix of subcultural themes and the pleasure taken in media experimentation. It was the source from which their painting drew its exuberant energy. However, another facet of the history of the Neue Wilde is the fact that the multimedia nature of many of the artists' work receded to the background once they were discovered by commercial galleries and institutional exhibition venues that focused almost exclusively on painting.

Germany / New York 1982: Media, Market, and Museum Breakthrough

In many respects, 1982 marked the peak of the Neue Wilde phenomenon. Galleries, museums, and art associations throughout

8 *Auch wenn das Perlhuhn leise weint*, Hahnentorburg, Cologne, 1980.

9 On the music projects, see Christian Höller, "While the Guinea Fowl Gently Weeps: On Painters' Music and Artists' Bands, 1979–1984," in the present volume, pp. 86–109.

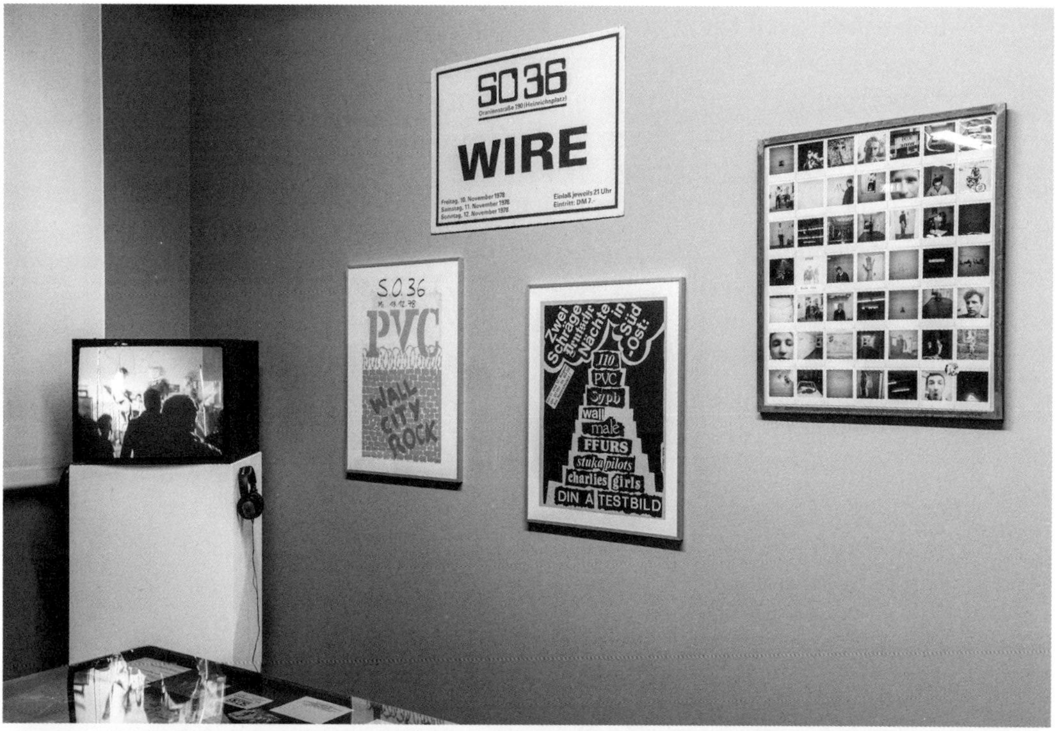

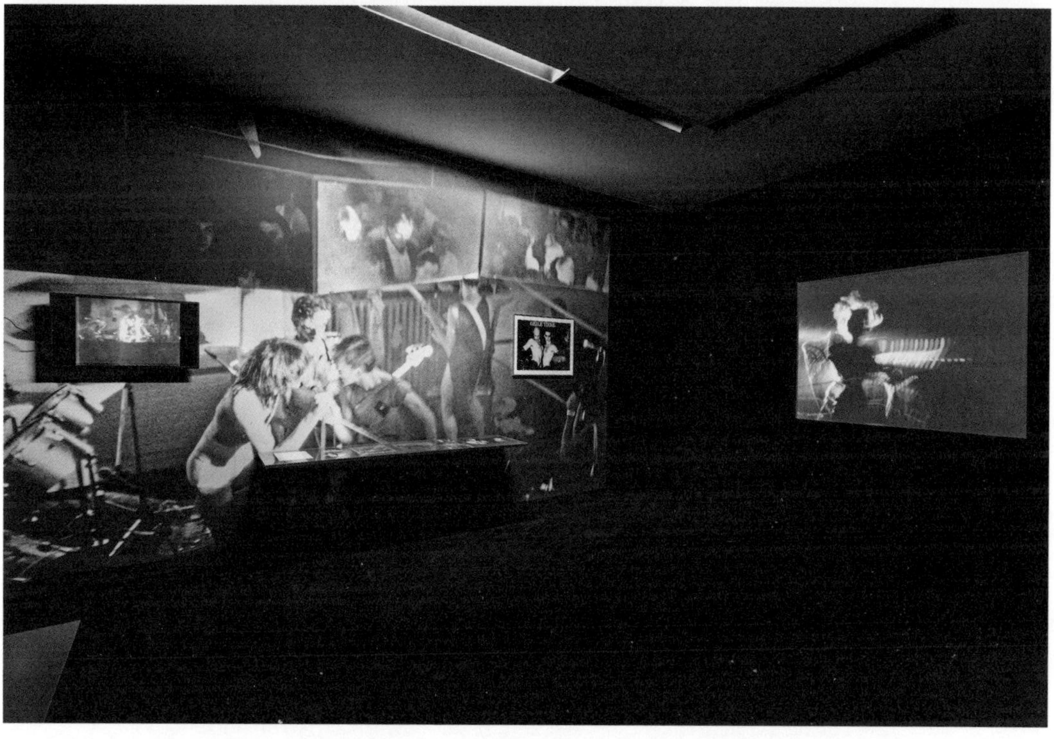

Die Erfindung der Neuen Wilden. Malerei und Subkultur um 1980 / The Invention of the Neue Wilde: Painting and Subculture around 1980, Ludwig Forum für Internationale Kunst Aachen, 2018/19

Europe presented their work. In February, the Museum Folkwang in Essen showed *10 junge Künstler aus Deutschland* (10 Young Artists from Germany), with artists from the scenes in Berlin and Cologne. Almost all of the same, in fact male, painters, along with Hamburg-based Albert Oehlen, were presented as *12 Künstler aus Deutschland* (12 Artists from Germany) from March at the Kunsthalle Basel and from May at the Museum Boymans-van Beuningen in Rotterdam. A year earlier, the Berlin scene had launched their touring exhibition *Im Westen nichts Neues* (All Quiet on the Western Front) at the Kunstmuseum Luzern, with stops in early 1982 at the Centre d'Art Contemporain in Geneva and the Neue Galerie – Sammlung Ludwig in Aachen. This was followed by *Känsla och Hårdhet / Gefühl und Härte* (Feeling and Hardness) in Stockholm and Munich, and *Tendenzen 82* in Ulm. The list could go on. Representatives of the Neue Wilde also made it to major survey exhibitions that year, with many of them featured in the mammoth show *Zeitgeist* at the Martin-Gropius-Bau in Berlin, while Salomé, Dahn, and Dokoupil also exhibited at Documenta 7 in Kassel.

In January, the artists of the Mülheimer Freiheit had already appeared live on *Bio's Bahnhof,* a television show dedicated to music on the German network ARD. The approximately ten-minute-long interview, immediately following the appearance of the band The Wirtschaftswunder,[10] says quite a lot about the reputation that the Neue Wilde already enjoyed in the eyes of the public. Walter Dahn, in particular, delighted in playing the role of the "wild painter" in the conversation with the show's host, Alfred Biolek. Wearing a sleeveless denim jacket and sunglasses and with a smoking cigar in his hand, he describes himself as an "honest painter-pig"[11] tormenting himself daily for the sake of art and having just come from the studio with his fingers still smeared with paint. When he explains to an astonished Biolek that he completes some of his paintings in just five minutes,

10 Jiří Georg Dokoupil, whose brother Tom Dokoupil played guitar with The Wirtschaftswunder, and Walter Dahn had painted a huge canvas depicting comic-like figures that was raised behind the band at the beginning of their performance. As an additional artistic contribution to the show, the artists arranged a distorting effect with the broadcast direction that reminded one of an image interference during the band's performance.

11 The magazine *Konkret* adopted Dahn's self-description four months later for their report on the Neue Wilde; see "Ehrliche Malschweine – Die Kunst der 'Neuen Wilden,'" *Konkret,* no. 5, May 1982, pp. 104–12.

Deutschland / New York 1982 – Medien, Markt und musealer Durchbruch

Das Jahr 1982 markierte in vielerlei Hinsicht den Höhepunkt des Phänomens der Neuen Wilden. Galerien, Museen und Kunstvereine in ganz Europa präsentierten ihre Bilder. Im Februar zeigte das Museum Folkwang in Essen *10 junge Künstler aus Deutschland,* die sich aus der Berliner und Kölner Szene rekrutierten. Fast die gleichen, übrigens ausschließlich männlichen Maler, ergänzt durch den Hamburger Albert Oehlen, werden als *12 Künstler aus Deutschland* ab März in der Kunsthalle Basel und ab Mai im Museum Boijmans van Beuningen in Rotterdam präsentiert. Schon im Vorjahr war die Berliner Szene mit der Ausstellungstour *Im Westen nichts Neues* im Kunstmuseum Luzern gestartet, die Anfang 1982 weiter ins Centre d'Art Contemporain nach Genf und in die Neue Galerie – Sammlung Ludwig nach Aachen wanderte. Es folgten *Gefühl und Härte* in Stockholm und München und *Tendenzen 82* in Ulm. Die Liste ließe sich weiter fortführen. Auch in die großen Überblicksschauen des Jahres schafften es Vertreter der Neuen Wilden, viele von ihnen in die Mammutausstellung *Zeitgeist* im Berliner Martin-Gropius-Bau, Salomé, Dahn und Dokoupil zudem auf die documenta 7 in Kassel.

Bereits im Januar waren die Künstler der Mülheimer Freiheit live in der ARD-Sendung *Bio's Bahnhof* aufgetreten. Das zirka zehnminütige Interview, das unmittelbar auf einen Auftritt der Gruppe The Wirtschaftswunder folgte,[10] verrät ungemein viel über den Ruf, der den Neuen Wilden in der Wahrnehmung der breiten Öffentlichkeit vorauseilte. Besonders Walter Dahn genießt es im Gespräch mit Moderator Alfred Biolek sichtlich, der Rolle des „wilden Malers" gerecht zu werden. Mit ärmelloser Jeansjacke, Sonnenbrille und qualmender Zigarre in der Hand bezeichnet er sich als „ehrliches Malschwein"[11], das sich jeden Tag für die Kunst quäle, eben erst aus dem Atelier komme und noch Farbe an den Fingern habe. Als er dem staunenden Biolek erklärt, dass einige seiner Bilder innerhalb von fünf Minuten fertig seien,

10 Jiří Georg Dokoupil, dessen Bruder Tom Dokoupil bei The Wirtschaftswunder Gitarre spielte, hatte zusammen mit Walter Dahn eine riesige Leinwand mit Comic-haften Figuren bemalt, die zum Anfang des Auftritts hinter der Band hochgefahren wurde. Als zusätzlichen künstlerischen Beitrag zur Sendung hatten die Künstler im Vorfeld einen verfremdenden Effekt mit der Bildregie abgesprochen, der an eine Bildstörung während der Darbietung der Band denken ließ.

11 Die Selbstbeschreibung Dahns übernahm die Zeitschrift *Konkret* vier Monate später für ihre Reportage über die Neuen Wilden, vgl. „Ehrliche Malschweine – Die Kunst der ‚Neuen Wilden'", in: *Konkret,* Nr. 5, Mai 1982, S. 104–112.

a smirking Bömmels conspiratorially murmurs to Dokoupil sitting next to him, "That's not true at all." The image of the "dropouts and punks of the palette," as Biolek addresses the artists, was enticing for the mass media, including the yellow press, with all the clichés used to latch on to the romantic image of the artist as a rebellious outsider. In May 1982, the youth magazine *Twen* interviewed the Hamburg painters.[12] *Der Spiegel* granted the "Sturmflut der Bilder" (Storm Surge of Pictures)—as the title went—a total of ten richly illustrated pages and did not fail to mention the musical experiments of the artists from Berlin, Hamburg, and Cologne, perhaps to subtly place them in the context of the Rolling Stones, to whom the cover story was dedicated.[13] In October of the preceding year, *Stern* and *Art. Das Kunstmagazin* had already jumped onto the bandwagon with long reports on the Neue Wilde, the latter under the headline "Triumph der Wilden" (Triumph of the Wild Ones) with numerous photos of "wild" artists in their studios.[14]

Major collectors such as Peter and Irene Ludwig could no longer ignore the success of the Neue Wilde. Their paintings surfaced in the art world at a time when the Ludwigs had just started casting a glance at the painting of German contemporaries such as Penck, Lüpertz, and Baselitz. Their interest in the most recent generation of German painters may have been triggered by the acquisition of the painting *Tiere* (1981), a colossal collective work by Salomé and Luciano Castelli nearly ten meters wide (fig. p. 178). This was followed by a work by Helmut Middendorf (*Reise ans Ende der Nacht,* 1981; fig. p. 206) that the Ludwigs purchased directly from the Aachen show *Im Westen nichts Neues,* and two works by Rainer Fetting (*Rafael-Sunset,* 1981, and *Zwei Figuren,* 1981; both figs. p. 25 top). When the Stuttgart gallerist Max Hetzler opened his first branch in Cologne in 1983, the Ludwigs bought their first two works by Werner Büttner (*Lob des Bettes III,* 1983, and *Spuren des Picknicks der KPD/ML-Ortsgruppe Krefeld,* 1981; fig. p. 278) from the opening exhibition. Later, a fifteen-part work by Kippenberger (*Nieder mit dem Idealismus!,*

12 "Wild und heftig? Hart und wahr! Neue deutsche Maler," *Twen,* no. 5, May 1982, pp. 18–31.

13 "Sturmflut der Bilder – Junge Malerei in Deutschland auf der Erfolgswelle und im Meinungsstreit," *Der Spiegel,* no. 22, May 1982, pp. 172–82.

14 "Die neue Malwut," *Stern,* no. 41, October 1981, pp. 39–60; "Malerei '81: Triumph der Wilden," *Art. Das Kunstmagazin,* no. 10, October 1981, pp. 22–43.

raunt ein feixender Bömmels dem neben ihm sitzenden Dokoupil verschwörerisch „Das stimmt gar nicht…" zu. Das Image der „Drop-Outs und Punks der Palette", wie Alfred Biolek die Künstler anspricht, war in all der Klischeehaftigkeit, mit der es an das romantische Künstlerbild des rebellischen Außenseiters anknüpfte, für die Massenmedien bis hin zum Boulevard verlockend. Im Mai 1982 ließ das Jugendmagazin *Twen* die Hamburger Maler zum Interview auflaufen.[12] Der *Spiegel* räumte der „Sturmflut der Bilder" – so der Titel – ganze zehn reich bebilderte Seiten ein und versäumte es nicht, auch auf die musikalischen Experimente der Künstler*innen aus Berlin, Hamburg und Köln zu verweisen, vielleicht auch, um sie damit subtil in einen Zusammenhang mit den Rolling Stones zu bringen, denen die Coverstory der Ausgabe gewidmet war.[13] Im Oktober des Vorjahres waren bereits die Illustrierte *Stern* und das Kunstmagazin *Art* mit großen Reportagen auf den Hype um die Neuen Wilden aufgesprungen, Letzteres unter Verwendung der Überschrift „Triumph der Wilden" mit zahlreichen Fotos „wilder" Künstler in ihren Ateliers.[14]

Auch Großsammler*innen wie Peter und Irene Ludwig konnten den enormen Erfolg der Neuen Wilden nicht ignorieren. Ihre Bilder tauchten ja ohnehin zu einem Zeitpunkt in der Kunstwelt auf, als das Ehepaar Ludwig gerade damit begonnen hatte, einen Blick auf die Malerei deutscher Zeitgenossen wie Penck, Lüpertz oder Baselitz zu werfen. Als Initialzündung für das Interesse an der allerjüngsten Generation deutscher Maler*innen mag der Erwerb des Gemäldes *Tiere* (1981) gewirkt haben, eine kolossale Gemeinschaftsarbeit von Salomé und Luciano Castelli von fast zehn Meter Breite (Abb. S. 178). Es folgten eine Arbeit von Helmut Middendorf, die die Ludwigs direkt aus der Aachener Ausstellung *Im Westen nichts Neues* heraus erwarben (*Reise ans Ende der Nacht*, 1981, Abb. S. 206), und zwei Arbeiten von Rainer Fetting (*Rafael-Sunset*, 1981, und *Zwei Figuren*, 1981, beide Abb. S. 25 oben). Als der Stuttgarter Galerist Max Hetzler 1983 seine erste Dependance in Köln eröffnete, erwarben die Ludwigs aus der Eröffnungsausstellung ihre ersten beiden Arbeiten von Werner Büttner (*Lob des Bettes III*, 1983, und *Spuren des Picknicks der KPD/ML-Ortsgruppe Krefeld*, 1981, Abb. S. 278). Ebenfalls über Hetzler kamen später eine 15-teilige Arbeit Kippenbergers (*Nieder mit dem Idealismus!*,

12 „Wild und heftig? Hart und wahr! Neue deutsche Maler", in: *Twen*, Nr. 5, Mai 1982, S. 18–31.

13 „Sturmflut der Bilder – Junge Malerei in Deutschland auf der Erfolgswelle und im Meinungsstreit", in: *Der Spiegel*, Nr. 22, Mai 1982, S. 172–182.

14 „Die neue Malwut", in: *Stern*, Nr. 41, Oktober 1981, S. 39–60; „Malerei '81: Triumph der Wilden", in: *Art. Das Kunstmagazin*, Nr. 10, Oktober 1981, S. 22–43.

1982–83; fig. p. 283), works by Albert Oehlen (*Ohne Titel [Seerosen]*, 1982; fig. p. 276 and *Ohne Titel [Tür]*, 1982) and Markus Oehlen (*Ohne Titel [28/87]*, 1987) were also acquired for the collection via Hetzler, plus a portfolio of graphics by all four artists edited by Max Hetzler (*laque des hommes*, 1983, figs. pp. 284–285). Not least due to their collaboration with Hetzler, the four were publicly regarded as a kind of group: the "Hetzler Boys." At the Galerie Paul Maenz in Cologne, the Ludwigs acquired works by the Mülheimer Freiheit—by Bömmels (*Deutsches Leben*, 1984; fig. p. 348), Dahn (*Ohne Titel*, 1984, *Zweites Asthma*, 1982, and *ohne Titel [der Fotograf]*, 1986; fig. p. 346), and Dokoupil (*Mann mit Schnurrbart*, 1984, and *Gott, zeig mir deine Eier*, 1982; fig. p. 350). Maenz substantially altered his program that had formerly specialized in Minimal and Conceptual Art to accommodate the young painters. The wave of success of the Neue Wilde spread all the way to New York—boosted by the excellent international network that the professional art trade maintained.[15] At the beginning of the 1980s, German painting descended upon the New York gallery scene with such great force that the American press already wrote about the "end of the American era" on the art market.[16] Strangely enough, it was also a New York gallery in which Peter Ludwig bought the two works by Rainer Fetting, when he had his first solo show at Mary Boone in late 1981. In a certain sense, the paintings returned to Germany as re-imports. In the end, one can find at least one work by almost all of the better-known names of the Neue Wilde in the Ludwig Collection. However, the interest of the Ludwigs in the painting of young German artists did not result in a systematic collecting focus that could be compared, for example, with the groups of works by Penck or Baselitz. It is also striking that no female artists can be found among the works. In this respect, the inventory of the Ludwig Collection is unfortunately all too symptomatic of the art

15 On the international success of German painting around 1980, see Catherine Dossin, "The Return to Painting and the European Comeback of the 1980s: Beyond Marketing and Zeitgeist," in the present volume, pp. 110–131.

16 See Carter Ratcliff, "The End of the American Era," *Saturday Review*, September 1981, p. 42. Notably, the American—as opposed to the German—public rarely distinguished between the Neue Wilde artists and the painters of the preceding generation such as Penck or Baselitz. See, for example, Robert Hughes, "Upending the New German Chic—Neoexpressionism Enters the Flophouse of Late Modernity," *Time*, January 1982, pp. 66–67. Ratcliff broadens the scope even more, combining the young German painters with the Italian painters of the Transavanguardia to establish a wave of Neo-Expressionist European paintings.

1982/83, Abb. S. 283) und Werke von Albert Oehlen (*Ohne Titel (Seerosen)*, 1982, Abb. S. 276, und *Ohne Titel (Tür)*, 1982) sowie Markus Oehlen (*Ohne Titel (28/87)*, 1987) in die Sammlung. Hinzu kam eine Grafikmappe mit Arbeiten aller vier Künstler, die Max Hetzler herausgegeben hatte (*laque des hommes*, 1983, Abb. S. 284–285). Nicht zuletzt durch ihre Zusammenarbeit mit Hetzler wurden die vier in der Öffentlichkeit als eine Art Gruppe, als „Hetzler-Boys" wahrgenommen. In der Kölner Galerie Paul Maenz erwarben die Ludwigs Werke der Mülheimer Freiheit – von Bömmels (*Deutsches Leben*, 1984, Abb. S. 348), Dahn (*Ohne Titel*, 1984, *Zweites Asthma*, 1982, und *Ohne Titel (Der Fotograf)*, 1986, Abb. S. 346) und Dokoupil (*Mann mit Schnurrbart*, 1984, und *Gott, zeig mir deine Eier*, 1982, Abb. S. 350). Maenz hatte sein vormals auf Minimal Art und Konzeptkunst spezialisiertes Programm zugunsten der jungen Maler weitgehend umgestellt. Die Erfolgswelle der Neuen Wilden reichte bis nach New York – begünstigt auch durch das hervorragende internationale Netzwerk, über das der professionelle Kunsthandel verfügte.[15] Anfang der 1980er-Jahre brach die deutsche Malerei so kraftvoll über die New Yorker Galerieszene herein, dass in der US-amerikanischen Presse bereits vom „Ende der amerikanischen Ära"[16] auf dem Kunstmarkt die Rede war. Skurrilerweise war es auch eine New Yorker Galerie, in der Peter Ludwig die beiden Arbeiten von Rainer Fetting erwarb, als dieser Ende 1981 seine erste Einzelausstellung bei Mary Boone hatte. So kamen die Gemälde gewissermaßen als Reimport zurück nach Deutschland. Letztlich findet sich von fast jedem der bekannteren Namen der Neuen Wilden mindestens eine Arbeit in der Sammlung Ludwig. Trotzdem bildete sich aus dem Interesse der Ludwigs für die Malerei der jungen Künstler kein systematisch verfolgter Sammlungsschwerpunkt heraus, der etwa mit den Konvoluten von A. R. Penck oder Georg Baselitz vergleichbar wäre. Auffällig ist auch, dass sich unter den Arbeiten keine einzige weibliche Position befindet. Hierin entpuppt sich der Bestand der Sammlung Ludwig leider als allzu

15 Zum internationalen Erfolg der deutschen Malerei um 1980 vgl. Catherine Dossin, „Die Rückkehr zur Malerei und das europäische Comeback der 1980er-Jahre: Jenseits von Marketing und Zeitgeist", im vorliegenden Band S. 110–131.

16 Vgl. Carter Ratcliff, „The End of the American Era", in: *Saturday Review*, September 1981, S. 42. Auffällig ist, dass die amerikanische Öffentlichkeit im Gegensatz zur deutschen selten zwischen den Künstler*innen der Neuen Wilden und den Maler*innen der vorangegangenen Generation wie Penck oder Baselitz unterschied. Vgl. z. B. Robert Hughes, „Upending the New German Chic – Neoexpressionism Enters the Flophouse of Late Modernity", in: *Time*, Januar 1982, S. 66–67. Ratcliff spannt den Rahmen sogar noch weiter und fasst die junge deutsche Malerei mit der italienischen Kunst der Transavanguardia zu einer Welle neo-expressionistischer europäischer Malerei zusammen.

market circa 1980: the renowned galleries from which not only the Ludwigs regularly purchased did not work with any of the female artists from the Neue Wilde milieu. The female painters were quite obviously unable to benefit from the success of their male colleagues as far as their representation by large, commercial galleries was concerned. This is surprising, especially in light of the fact that female artists participated in the self-organized exhibitions at Moritzplatz, for example, or the three shows organized by Martin Kippenberger: *Elend* [Misery], *Aktion Pisskrücke* [Action Piss Crutch], and *Finger für Deutschland* [Finger for Germany]. The absence of women in the Ludwig Collection has remained visible in the painting section of our exhibition as a gaping hole so as to open up debate about this aspect of collecting. And it was thus all the more important in our cross-media section to feature outstanding works by female artists, including Hilka Nordhausen (fig. p. 326), Anne Jud (fig. p. 210), Brigitta Rohrbach (figs. pp. 236, 237), and Bettina Semmer, to show that the inventiveness of the Neue Wilde cannot be told as a purely male story. Both the exhibition and the present publication seek to not only tell the story of the Neue Wilde through their painting but to radically broaden the perspective. The time seemed to be right to re-examine the art-historical construct of the Neue Wilde. With the research work of the project *The Invention of the Neue Wilde* as well as the contributions to this publication, we hope to point to undiscovered paths beyond the conventional narrative.

symptomatisch für den Kunstmarkt um 1980: Die namhaften Galerien, in denen nicht nur die Ludwigs regelmäßig kauften, arbeiteten mit keiner der Künstlerinnen aus dem Umfeld der Neuen Wilden zusammen. Von dem Erfolg ihrer männlichen Kollegen konnten die Malerinnen offensichtlich nicht profitieren, wenn es um eine Platzierung in den großen kommerziellen Galerien ging. Das erstaunt vor allem angesichts der Tatsache, dass in den selbstorganisierten Ausstellungen etwa am Moritzplatz oder der von Martin Kippenberger initiierten Ausstellungstrias *Elend, Aktion Pisskrücke* und *Finger für Deutschland* durchaus Künstlerinnen vertreten waren. Die Leerstelle an weiblichen Positionen in der Sammlung Ludwig ist im Malereiteil unserer Ausstellung als klaffende Lücke weiterhin sichtbar geblieben, um diesen Aspekt der Sammeltätigkeit offen zur Diskussion zu stellen. Umso wichtiger war es uns, im medienübergreifenden Teil der Ausstellung mit herausragenden Arbeiten von Künstlerinnen wie Hilka Nordhausen (Abb. S. 326), Anne Jud (Abb. S. 210), Brigitta Rohrbach (Abb. S. 236, 237) und Bettina Semmer zu zeigen, dass die Erfindung der Neuen Wilden nicht als eine rein männliche Geschichte erzählt werden kann. Sowohl die Ausstellung als auch die vorliegende Publikation sind zudem der Versuch, die Geschichte der Neuen Wilden nicht allein aus ihrer Malerei heraus zu erzählen, sondern die Perspektive auf ihre Kunst drastisch zu erweitern. Es schien an der Zeit, das kunsthistorische Konstrukt der Neuen Wilden neu zu hinterfragen. Mit der Forschungsarbeit des Projekts *Die Erfindung der Neuen Wilden* sowie den Beiträgen in der vorliegenden Publikation hoffen wir, unentdeckte Wege abseits des gängigen Narrativs aufzeigen zu können.

Ramona Heinlein
Wir behaupten die Welt Künstlerische Selbstinszenierung an den Rändern der Malerei

Ramona Heinlein
We Assert the World Artistic Self-Staging at the Fringes of Painting

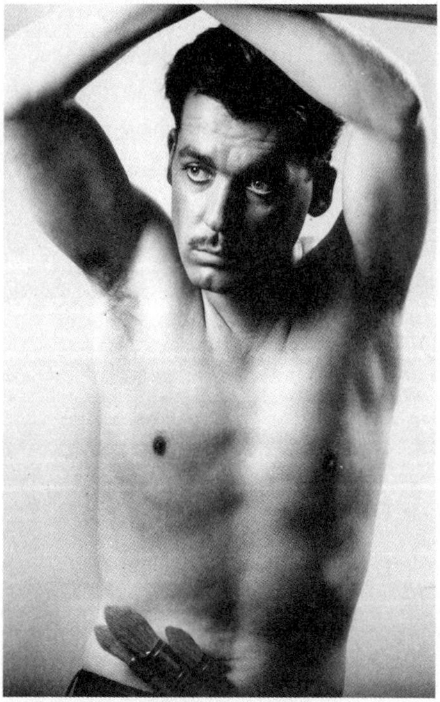

Einladung / Invitation, Werner Büttner, *La Luta Continua*, Galerie Max Hetzler, Köln / Cologne, 1984

„Wir bedauern, daß wir durch unpräzise Ausdrucksweise den Eindruck von Angeberei vermitteln. [...] Es ist Scheiße, daß wir unsere Wohnung nicht oft genug aufräumen. [...] Es tut uns leid, daß sich nicht mehr Leute unsere Bilder leisten können. Wir bereuen zutiefst unsere Manieriertheit, die uns Wörter bilden ließ wie fiffen, faufen und ferfaufen. Wir bereuen zutiefst unsere Esoterik, die uns Sätze sagen ließ wie: ‚Eini Bieri, bitti!' Es tut uns leid, daß wir in unserer Arbeit bisher nicht klar genug geworden sind und für viele Mißverständnisse gesorgt haben."[1]

Dass es sich bei der Entschuldigung von Werner Büttner, Martin Kippenberger und Albert Oehlen nicht um ein aufrichtiges Bekenntnis, sondern um eine zwielichtige Behauptung handelt, liegt nahe. So scheint die Äußerung doch nicht aus Scham, sondern viel eher zur Exponierung der offenbar fragwürdigen Lebensführung geäußert worden zu sein. Schließlich findet sie sich in direkter Nachbarschaft zu diversen Geschichten, die unverfroren von dem gemeinsamen Bordellbesuch oder dem aus dem Ruder gelaufenen Trinkgelage der Künstler berichten: „Nachdem er im Krankenhaus seinen Namen mit Werner Büttner angegeben hatte, wurde ihm die Bierflasche entfernt, in der seine Zunge festgepfropft war. In die Kneipe ist Werner Büttner nie wieder gegangen. Albert Oehlen auch nicht"[2], heißt es in einem lehrstückartigen Abschnitt, in dem sich die beiden Künstler bewusst als Negativbeispiel präsentieren.

Durch die überzogene Darstellung und die ironische Brechung der Entschuldigung veralbern die Künstler allerdings nicht nur sich selbst, sondern auch jede Kritik an ihrem „untugendhaften" Verhalten. Wer den betont banalen Wortschöpfungen der Künstler ernsthaft mit Bedeutungssuche oder Kritik begegnet, wird der Lächerlichkeit preisgegeben. Hinter der vermeintlich demütigen Entschuldigung verbirgt sich nicht nur eine spielerische Herabwürdigung der eigenen Person, sondern zugleich eine Überlegenheitsgeste, die den Tadel für die eigenen Zwecke vereinnahmt – auf den ersten Blick ein Taschenspielertrick, sicherlich, und doch: Die Entschuldigung und die

1 Werner Büttner, Martin Kippenberger und Albert Oehlen, *Wahrheit ist Arbeit*, Essen 1984, S. 39f.

2 Ebd., S. 71. Erstmalig veröffentlicht wurde dieser Text in dem Ausstellungskatalog Werner Büttner und Albert Oehlen, *Jenseits konstanter Bemühungen um braven Erfolg*, Produzentengalerie Hamburg 1983. Ähnlich betont intime Geschichten über das Leben der Künstler finden sich in Briefform in dem Ausstellungskatalog *Büttner/Oehlen. Rechts blinken, links abbiegen*, nGbK, Berlin 1982.

> We regret that, with our imprecise style, we give the impression of showing off.... It sucks that we don't clean up our apartment often enough.... We're sorry that there aren't more people who can afford our paintings. We deeply regret our mannerisms that made us coin words like *fiffen, faufen, and ferfaufen.* We deeply regret our esotericism that made us utter sentences like "Eini Bieri, bitti!" We're sorry that we have not yet become clear enough in our work and have caused so many misunderstandings.[1]

It is pretty obvious that the apology offered by Werner Büttner, Martin Kippenberger, and Albert Oehlen is not a sincere confession but rather a dubious assertion, expressing less a sense of shame than exposing an apparently questionable lifestyle, or so it seems. After all, the statement appears among various stories providing brazen accounts of the artists' visits together to brothels or drinking sprees that got out of control: "After giving his name as Werner Büttner in the hospital, they removed the beer bottle in which his tongue had gotten stuck. Werner Büttner never went back to that bar. Neither did Albert Oehlen."[2] This is a passage in a section resembling a learning play in which the two artists deliberately present themselves as negative examples.

However, through the exaggerated description and the ironic breaks in the apology, the artists ridicule not only themselves but also any criticism of their "non-virtuous" behavior. Anyone earnestly searching for meaning in or criticizing their expressly banal neologisms is exposed to ridicule. Lurking behind the allegedly humble excuse is not only a playful denigration of one's own person but also a gesture of superiority that appropriates the reprimand for its own purposes—a sleight of hand at first glance, certainly, and yet: the apology and the attendant stories should be taken seriously as belonging to a strategy of conceiving and staging oneself that is characterized by precisely this Janus-faced

1 Werner Büttner, Martin Kippenberger, and Albert Oehlen, *Wahrheit ist Arbeit,* Essen 1984, pp. 39–40.

2 Ibid., p. 71. The text was first published in the exhibition catalogue Werner Büttner and Albert Oehlen, *Jenseits konstanter Bemühungen um braven Erfolg,* Produzentengalerie Hamburg, 1983. Similar, expressly intimate stories about the life of the artists can be found in the form of a correspondence in Büttner and Oehlen's exhibition catalogue *Büttner / Oehlen. Rechts blinken – links abbiegen,* nGbK, Berlin 1982.

Geschichten, die sie begleiten, sind durchaus ernst zu nehmen. Und zwar als Teil einer Strategie des Sich-Entwerfens und -Inszenierens, die durch ebenjenes januskopfige Changieren zwischen Selbsterniedrigung und Selbstermächtigung gekennzeichnet ist. Die damit einhergehende Markierung und Verunsicherung der Grenze zwischen Werk und Leben der Künstler zeigt sich vor allem auch in den vermeintlichen Nebenprodukten, zum Beispiel in den Texten, Büchern, Einladungskarten und Postern. Dabei dringen die künstlerischen Praktiken über die klassische Werkform der Malerei hinaus gerade in jene Randgebiete vor, in denen unklar wird, was noch als „Werk“ zu fassen wäre oder schon in den Bereich „Leben“ fiele.[3]

Die Entschuldigung der Künstler wird in der Publikation *Wahrheit ist Arbeit* ausgesprochen, die 1984 begleitend zur gleichnamigen Ausstellung des Museum Folkwang Essen erschienen ist.[4] Bei dieser Bild-Text-Montage handelt es sich nicht um einen klassischen informativen Begleitkatalog, sondern um ein eigenständiges Künstlerbuch, das als zentrale Quelle zur Auseinandersetzung mit der Praxis der bisweilen eng zusammenarbeitenden Künstler bis Mitte der 1980er-Jahre zu betrachten ist. Diverse, teilweise bereits separat geschriebene und publizierte Texte der Künstler, die von statementhaften Äußerungen bis hin zu legendenhaften Geschichten über das eigene Leben reichen, sind hier zu einem Fließtext zusammengefügt und mit Fußnoten „belegt“. Zur Beweisführung werden Texte von Karl Popper über Erving Goffman bis hin zu Rainald Goetz, Nicola Reidenbach oder Diedrich Diederichsen angeführt. Die Affinität zu alltäglichen Anekdoten bei scheinbar wissenschaftlicher Methodik ist allerdings keineswegs im Sinne demokratischer Zugänglichkeit misszuverstehen. Die verklausulierte, zu Recht als „chaotische[s] Bedeutungstheate[r]“[5] bezeichnete Publikation soll nicht klar verständlich sein. Die von den Künstlern vermeintlich bedauerten „Mißverständnisse“ zwischen ihnen und dem Publikum scheinen gewollt. So sind Text und Abbildungen durchzogen von einem diffizilen und dabei keineswegs auserklärten Verweissystem, das von

3 Isabelle Graw verweist in Bezug auf die Selbstinszenierung Kippenbergers auf die Hybridität von dessen Werk, besteht aber auf einer „Sonderstellung“ der Malerei. Vgl. Isabelle Graw, „‚Hallo hier bin ich, das muss reichen‘. Die Persona im Produkt bei Martin Kippenberger“, in: dies., *Die Liebe zur Malerei. Genealogie einer Sonderstellung*, Zürich 2017, S. 159.

4 Vgl. dazu auch Zdenek Felix, „Wahrheit ist Arbeit“, in: Andreas Beitin und Peter Weibel (Hg.), *Werner Büttner. Gemeine Wahrheiten*, Ausst.-Kat. ZKM | Zentrum für Kunst und Medien Karlsruhe, Ostfildern 2013, S. 390–396.

5 Diedrich Diederichsen, „‚Virtueller Maoismus‘. Das Wissen von 1984“, in: Helmut Draxler (Hg.), *Malen ist Wahlen*, Ausst.-Kat. Kunstverein München, Stuttgart 1992, S. 38.

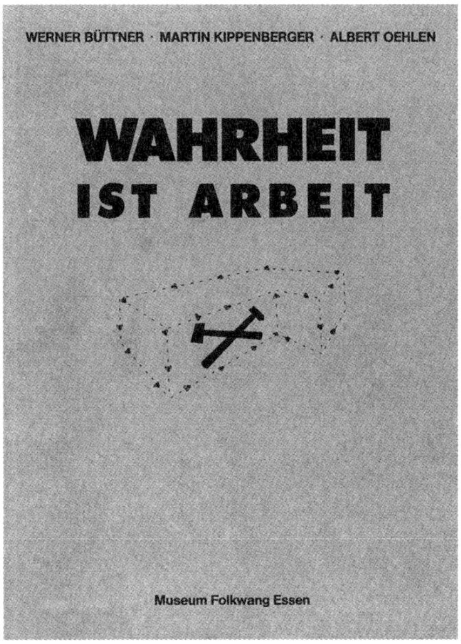

Werner Büttner, Martin Kippenberger, Albert Oehlen, *Wahrheit ist Arbeit*, 1984
Künstlerbuch / artist's book

vacillation between self-abasement and self-empowerment. The marking and simultaneous blurring of the borders between the work and life of the artists is displayed above all in the reputed side products, the texts, books, invitation cards, and posters, for example, in which the artistic practices extend beyond the classic work form of painting to fringe areas where it becomes unclear what is to be understood as a "work" and what already belongs to the area of "life."[3]

The artists' apology was made in the book *Wahrheit ist Arbeit* (Truth is Work) published in 1984 in conjunction with the eponymous exhibition at Museum Folkwang Essen.[4] This image-text montage is not an informative exhibition catalogue in the classical sense, but an autonomous artists' book that must be regarded as a central source when engaging with the praxis of

3 Referring to Kippenberger's self-staging, Isabelle Graw points out the hybridity of his work but insists on the "special status" of painting. See Isabelle Graw, "Hi, Here I Am, That Must be Enough—The Persona and the Product in Martin Kippenberger's Work," in *The Love of Painting: Genealogy of a Success Medium,* Berlin 2018, p. 162.

4 See Zdenek Felix, "Wahrheit ist Arbeit," in *Werner Büttner. Gemeine Wahrheiten,* ed. Andreas Beitin and Peter Weibel, exh. cat. ZKM | Center for Art and Media Karlsruhe, Ostfildern 2013, pp. 390–96.

Mao Zedong, dem Jazz-Musiker Eric Dolphy, dem romantischen Lyriker Joseph von Eichendorff über Bertolt Brecht und den Filmregisseur Brian De Palma bis hin zum Verhaltensforscher Konrad Lorenz und dem Stasi-Chef Erich Mielke reicht.

Bei den Werken, die in diesen Referenzrahmen eingebettet sind, handelt es sich – parallel zu dessen Eklektizismus – nicht nur um Gemälde. Anstatt nur für sich stehender Malereitableaus sind auch Schallplatten, Zeichnungen, Büchercover und Einladungskarten abgedruckt, die Zeugnis ablegen von der verschiedene Medien und Künste umspannenden Praxis der Beteiligten. So wurde veranstaltet, performt, musiziert, geschrieben und auch verlegt. Dabei situieren sich die Künstler dezidiert in einem Kreis aus Kulturschaffenden einer durchaus genreübergreifenden Szene.[6] Schließlich sind auch Werke und Fotografien von Musikern und Künstler*innen aus dem Umfeld von Büttner, Oehlen und Kippenberger abgedruckt, etwa von Andreas Dorau, Sven-Åke Johansson, Rosemarie Trockel, Hubert Kiecol, Markus Oehlen oder Meuser. In *Wahrheit ist Arbeit* zeigt sich so das netzwerkartige Bild einer „künstlerisch-kommunikativen Praxis"[7], die sich nicht nur in objekthaften Werkformen, sondern auch in schwer greifbaren Praxisformen, im Sozialen und Kollaborativen, im Behaupten und Posieren äußert.

Zahlreiche mitunter alberne und deshalb nicht minder ikonische Fotos auf Plakaten, Buchcovern und Einladungskarten, aber auch Berichte und Schnappschüsse vom öffentlichen Auftreten bis hin zum buchstäblichen Performen als Musiker auf der Bühne bezeugen, dass nicht nur das *Schreiben* am eigenen Mythos Bestandteil der künstlerischen Praxis ist. Bereits 1974 gibt Kippenberger einen Briefmarkenbogen mit seinem Konterfei heraus. Zu seiner Ausstellung *La Luta Continua* in der Galerie Max Hetzler lädt Büttner 1984 mit einer Oben-ohne-Aufnahme ein, die geschminkten Augen exaltiert nach

6 Kippenberger veranstaltete Ende der 1970er-Jahre in seinem Berliner Projektraum Kippenbergers Büro Ausstellungen, war für kurze Zeit Teilhaber des Clubs S.O.36, schrieb kleine Texte und Gedichte und produzierte Poster, Flyer und Künstlerbücher. Auch Büttners und Oehlens Schaffen weist eine starke Affinität zu Drucksachen, zum Schreiben und Publizieren auf. Anfänglich verfassten sie zum Beispiel Rezensionen für die Musikzeitschrift *Sounds,* 1985 gründeten sie den Meterverlag. Zudem war die Kombination von Zeichnung und Text ein beliebtes Format der Künstler. Vgl. dazu die Zeitschrift *Dum Dum Nr. 3,* in: Büttner/Oehlen 1983 (wie Anm. 2). Zu den Musikprojekten vgl. Christian Höllers Beitrag „While the Guinea Fowl Gently Weeps. Über Maler-Musik und Künstler-Bands, 1979–1984" in der vorliegenden Publikation, S. 86–109.

7 Diedrich Diederichsen, „Der Selbstdarsteller. Martin Kippenberger zwischen 1977 und 1983", in: Eva Meyer-Hermann und Susanne Neuburger (Hg.), *Nach Kippenberger,* Ausst.-Kat. Museum Moderner Kunst Stiftung Ludwig Wien, Wien 2003, S. 46.

these artists who until the mid-1980s oftentimes worked in close collaboration. Diverse texts, including some previously written and published, that range from statement-like pronouncements to legendary stories about their own lives are assembled into a continuous text and "proven" with footnotes. Texts from Karl Popper and Erving Goffman to Rainald Goetz, Nicola Reidenbach, and Diedrich Diederichsen are employed as documentary evidence. But the affinity for prosaic anecdotes with an ostensibly scientific method should by no means be misunderstood in terms of democratic accessibility. The cryptic publication aptly described as a "chaotic theater of meaning"[5] is not meant to be readily comprehensible. The "misunderstandings" between the artists and the audience that they supposedly regret appear intentional. The text and the illustrations are thus permeated by a reference system that is in no way meaningfully explained. It includes, among others, Mao Zedong, the jazz musician Eric Dolphy, the Romantic poet Joseph von Eichendorff, Bertolt Brecht, the film director Brian De Palma, the behavioral scientist Konrad Lorenz, and the Stasi chief Erich Mielke.

The works embedded in this frame of reference are—paralleling its eclecticism—not only standalone paintings but also records, drawings, book covers, and invitation cards bearing witness to the praxis of the participants that spans different media and art forms. The artists organized events, performed, played music, wrote, and published, firmly positioning themselves in a circle of cultural producers of a scene that indeed worked across genres.[6] Finally, also featured are works and photographs by musicians and artists associated with Büttner, Oehlen, and Kippenberger, including Andreas Dorau, Sven-Åke Johansson, Rosemarie Trockel, Hubert Kiecol, Markus Oehlen, and Meuser.

5 Diedrich Diederichsen, "'Virtueller Maoismus'. Das Wissen von 1984," in *Malen ist Wahlen*, ed. Helmut Draxler, exh. cat. Kunstverein München, Stuttgart 1992, p. 38.

6 In the late 1970s, Kippenberger organized exhibitions in his project space Kippenbergers Büro in Berlin, he was co-proprietor of the club S.O.36, wrote small texts and poems, and produced posters, flyers, and artist's books. Büttner and Oehlen also revealed a strong affinity for printed materials, writing, and publishing in their work. They first wrote reviews for the music magazine *Sounds*, and in 1985 founded the publishing company Meterverlag. In addition, the combination of drawing and text was a favorite format of theirs. See the magazine *Dum Dum Nr. 3*, in Büttner and Oehlen 1983 (see note 2). On the music projects, see Christian Höller's text "While the Guinea Fowl Gently Weeps: On Painters' Music and Artists' Bands, 1979–1984" in this publication, pp. 86–109.

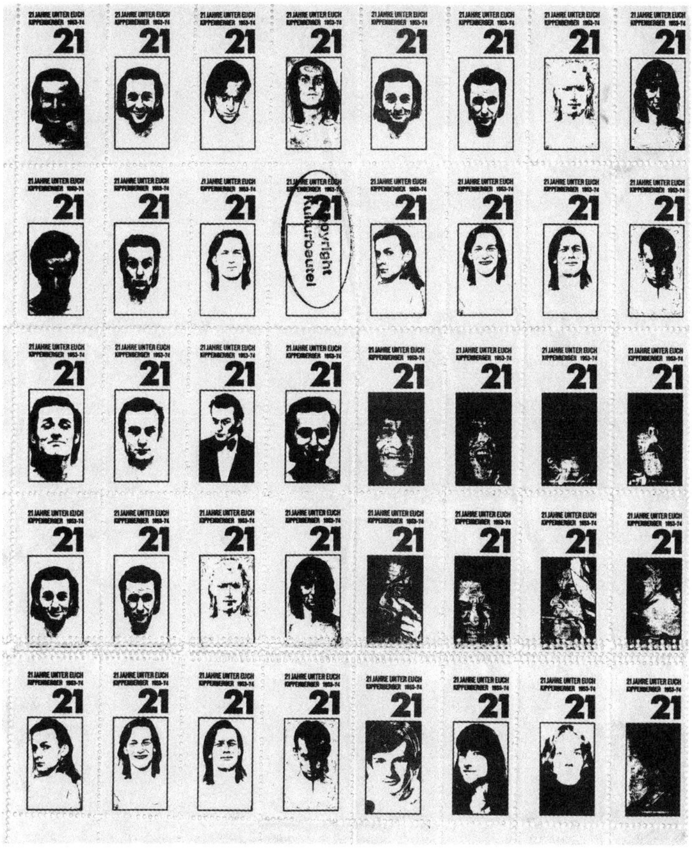

Martin Kippenberger, *21 Jahre unter Euch – Kippenberger 1953–1974*, 1974
Briefmarkenbogen, Offset auf Papier / sheet of stamps, offset on paper, 30 × 21,5 cm

oben gerichtet, aus der Hose ragen die Pinsel. Der 1984 erschienenen LP *Rache der Erinnerung* ist ein Poster mit einer männerbündlerischen Sauna-Aufnahme der Beteiligten beigelegt. Neben Büttner, Markus und Albert Oehlen sowie Kippenberger sind der offensiv breitbeinig sitzende Jörg Immendorff und der betont nachlässig dazucollagierte A. R. Penck zu sehen. Ein ähnliches die Künstler als Band oder Gang inszenierendes Foto zeigt auch das Cover der Publikation *Wer diesen Katalog nicht gut findet muß sofort zum Arzt* von 1983. Draufgängerisch posieren die Künstler auf einer Motorhaube.

Dass es für das Sich-Abarbeiten an der Künstlerfigur zahlreiche kunsthistorische Vorbilder gibt, ist unumstritten.[8] Als fruchtbarer

8 Sigmar Polke, bekannt für seine betont unseriöse, clowneske Selbstinszenierung, wird häufig als maßgeblicher Einfluss der Künstler hervorgehoben. Vgl. zum Beispiel Graw 2017 (wie Anm. 3), S. 167f.

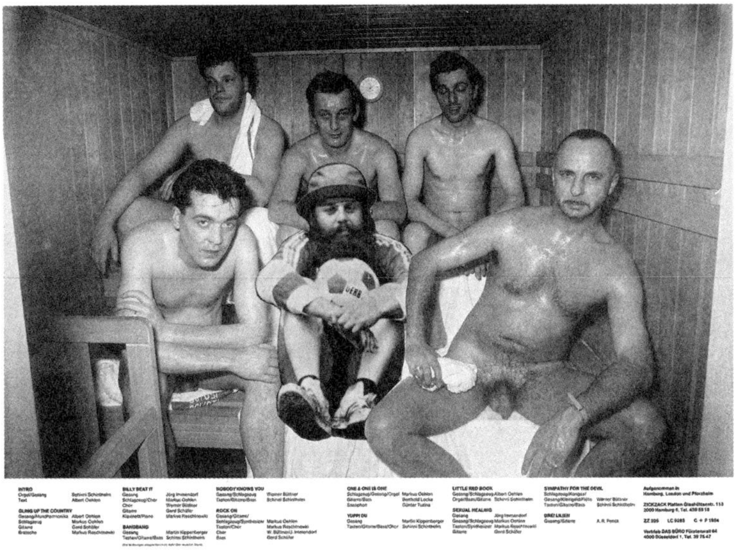

Werner Büttner, Jörg Immendorff, Martin Kippenberger, Albert Oehlen, Markus Oehlen, A. R. Penck, *Rache der Erinnerung*, 1984
Inlay der / of the LP, ZickZack Platten

Wahrheit ist Arbeit thus draws the web-like portrayal of a "mode of artistic communication"[7] manifesting itself not only in works as objects but also in intangible forms of praxis, in the social and the collaborative, in asserting and posing.

Numerous occasionally silly but no less iconic photos on posters, book covers, and invitation cards, as well as accounts and snapshots of public appearances, all the way to actual stage performances as musicians, provide evidence that not only *writing* about one's own myth is an element of their artistic praxis. As early as 1974, Kippenberger published a sheet of stamps with his countenance on them. In 1984, Büttner invited the audience to his show *La Luta Continua* at Galerie Max Hetzler with a photo depicting him topless, his painted eyes gazing exactedly upward, brushes sticking out of his pants. The LP *Rache der Erinnerung* (The Revenge of Memory) from 1984 includes a poster supplement with a picture of the male-bonding participants in a sauna—alongside Büttner, Markus and Albert Oehlen, and Kippenberger, it features Jörg Immendorff seated with his legs aggressively spread and A. R. Penck added in a deliberately careless collage.

7 Diedrich Diederichsen, "'Selbstdarsteller': Martin Kippenberger between 1977 and 1983," in *Nach Kippenberger*, ed. Eva Meyer-Hermann and Susanne Neuburger, exh. cat. Museum Moderner Kunst Stiftung Ludwig Wien, Vienna 2003, p. 45.

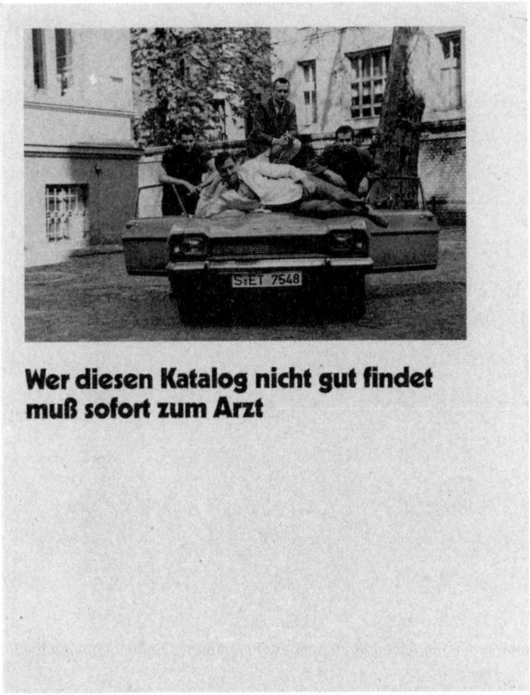

Werner Büttner, Martin Kippenberger, Albert Oehlen, Markus Oehlen, *Wer diesen Katalog nicht gut findet muß sofort zum Arzt*, Galerie Max Hetzler, Stuttgart 1983

Anknüpfungspunkt für die Lust der Künstler an der Darstellung des eigenen Lebensentwurfs und -umfelds mögen auch die um 1980 aufkommende Pop-Begeisterung in den Großstädten Deutschlands und die damit eng verbundene Neupositionierung der Linken gelten, in deren Umfeld sich diese bewegten:

> „Wir brauchen keine Kulturverteidigung. Lieber geil angreifen, kühn totalitär roh kämpferisch und lustig, so muß geschrieben werden, so wie der heftig denkende Mensch lebt. [...] Wir brauchen noch mehr Reize, noch viel mehr Werbung Tempo Autos Modehedonismen Pop und nochmal Pop."[9]

Angesichts bundesrepublikanischer Kleinbürgerlichkeit und postmoderner Entfremdungserfahrung, die die avantgardistische Fortschrittsutopie als unzulänglich erscheinen ließ, taumelte die von Rainald Goetz

9 Rainald Goetz, „Subito", in: ders., *Hirn*, Frankfurt am Main 1986, S. 20f.

A similar photo can be found on the cover of the publication *Wer diesen Katalog nicht gut findet muß sofort zum Arzt* (Whoever Doesn't Like This Catalogue Must Go See a Doctor at Once) from 1983 depicting the artists as a band or gang posing like daredevils on the hood of a car.

It is indisputable that there are numerous art-historical models for working with the artist figure.[8] A productive point of departure for the pleasure the artists took in representing their own concept and environment for living may also have been the enthusiasm for pop commencing around 1980 in Germany's big cities, along with the attendant repositioning of the Left, among whom they moved:

> We do not need a defense of culture. We prefer to attack, boldly totalitarian brutishly combative and funny, that is how we must write, just like the intensely thinking human lives.... We need even more stimuli, much more advertising speed cars fashion-hedonism pop and more pop.[9]

In light of the petit-bourgeois mentality and postmodern experience of alienation in the Federal Republic that made the avant-gardist utopia of progress appear inadequate, the scene described by Rainald Goetz lurched toward a spirit of setting off. They attempted the delicate balancing act of declaring as opponents not only conservatives but also the 1970s leftists who, with the collapse of the radical K-Gruppen and the rise of the seemingly escapist environmental movement, they simply could not join. The desired reorientation was sought less in university debates or at moralistic communal-living tables than in the sometimes hedonistic "designing of oneself"[10] in clubs and bars. Though they still saw themselves as leftists, left-wing radicalism was no longer to be established by means of a revolutionary praxis but rather a radical habitus. One's own *stance* gained new

8 Sigmar Polke, known for his expressly unserious, clownesque self-staging, is often mentioned as having had a crucial influence on the artists. See, for example, Graw 2018 (see note 3), pp. 169–70.

9 Rainald Goetz, "Subito," in *Hirn*, Frankfurt am Main 1986, pp. 20–21.

10 Nadja Geer, "'If you have to ask, you can't afford it'. Pop als distinktiver Selbstentwurf der 1980er Jahre," in *Popgeschichte*, vol. 2: *Zeithistorische Fallstudien 1958–1988*, ed. Bodo Mrozek, Alexa Geisthövel, and Jürgen Danyel, Bielefeld 2014, p. 352.

beschriebene Szene in Aufbruchstimmung. Dabei wurde der Spagat versucht, sich nicht nur die Konservativen, sondern auch die Linke der 1970er-Jahre, die mit dem Zusammenbruch der radikalen K-Gruppen und der als Flucht wahrgenommenen Ökobewegung nicht länger als anschlussfähig galt, zum Gegner zu erklären. Die ersehnte Neuorientierung wurde weniger in den Debatten innerhalb der Universitäten oder an moralisierenden WG-Tischen, sondern in der bisweilen hedonistischen „Ausgestaltung des eigenen Selbst“[10] in Clubs und Kneipen gesucht. Zwar verstand man sich nach wie vor als links, jedoch sollte Linksradikalismus nicht mehr mittels revolutionärer Praxis, sondern über einen radikalen Habitus etabliert werden. So nimmt die eigene *Haltung* eine neue Relevanz ein, die sich – allerdings möglichst weit entfernt vom Moralismus der ernsthaften, vermeintlich ungebrochen authentischen Haltung von Hippie- und Sozialreformertum – in Drastik, Ironie und Distanz übte. Dabei erschienen gerade die Mythen und Posen der Popmusik in ihrer Künstlichkeit selbst attraktiv, die nun nicht länger als das kommerzielle und korrumpierte Andere der tiefgründigen Kunst ausgeschlossen werden sollten.[11] Die erfahrene Unmöglichkeit von Authentizität galt es nicht zu verdrängen, sondern freudig zu exponieren: „Wir behaupten die Welt“[12] lautete die Antwort der „fröhlich politisch Verzweifelten“[13].

Neben der Vermischung bildungsbürgerlicher und popkultureller Referenzen und einem bisweilen durchaus „kühnen“, „rohen“, „kämpferischen“ Ton ist eine dezidiert anti-authentische Haltung auch in *Wahrheit ist Arbeit* zentral. Schließlich fügt sich die Publikation gerade nicht zu einem ganzheitlichen Bild der Künstleridentität zusammen. Zwar regen die Text-Bild-Kombinationen die Bedeutungssuche an und suggerieren mit den privaten Anekdoten – sogar Fotografien der mutmaßlich eigenen Mütter sind abgebildet – Intimität, doch diese wird bewusst nicht eingelöst. Was hier geäußert wird, sind keine

10 Nadja Geer, „‚If you have to ask, you can’t afford it‘. Pop als distinktiver Selbstentwurf der 1980er Jahre“, in: Bodo Mrozek, Alexa Geisthövel und Jürgen Danyel (Hg.), *Popgeschichte*, Bd. 2: *Zeithistorische Fallstudien 1958–1988*, Bielefeld 2014, S. 352.

11 Vgl. Diedrich Diederichsen, „Peinlich. Über das Peinliche des Unpeinlichen in der Kunst“, in: *Spex*, 4, April 1985, S. 19, Wiederabdruck im vorliegenden Band S. 422–427, sowie ders., „Im Kino onanierend“, in: Götz Adriani (Hg.), *Obsessive Malerei. Ein Rückblick auf die Neuen Wilden*, Ausst.-Kat. Museum für Neue Kunst, ZKM Karlsruhe, Ostfildern-Ruit 2003, S. 171f. Auch Graw verweist auf das „Haltungscredo“ der 1980er-Jahre, vgl. dies. 2017 (wie Anm. 3), S. 166f. Zu einer Analyse von linker Subkultur, Pop und Pose im Deutschland der 1980er-Jahre, vgl. Geer 2014 (wie Anm. 10), S. 337–357.

12 Max Dax, „Eines von mehreren möglichen Vorworten“, in: ders. und Anne Waak (Hg.), *Spex. Das Buch. 33 1/3 Jahre Pop*, Berlin 2013, S. 5.

13 Diederichsen 2003 (wie Anm. 11), S. 172.

relevance, expressing itself in hyperbole, irony, and detachedness, albeit at the greatest possible remove from the earnest and seemingly authentic moralistic stance of hippies and social reformers. In this context, the artificiality of the myths and poses of pop music appeared attractive and no longer had to be rejected as the commercial and corrupted other of profound art.[11] The experienced impossibility of authenticity was not to be suppressed anymore, but joyfully displayed: "We assert the world"[12] was the answer given by the "joyful politically desperate."[13]

Alongside the mixture of references drawn from an educated middle-class milieu and from pop culture, and the occasionally "bold," "brutish," and "combative" tone, playing a central role in *Wahrheit ist Arbeit* is a decidedly anti-authentic stance. After all, a unified picture of an artistic identity is exactly that which the publication does not stitch together. Although the text-image combinations prompt one to search for meaning and suggest intimacy through private anecdotes—even photographs presumaly of the artists' mothers are included—this promise is left deliberately unfulfilled. There are no emotional outpourings from the "inside" of the artist's soul. Instead, Rainald Goetz ponders in great detail about rectal ailments in a "guest" text added as a footnote.[14] Elsewhere, black-and-white photographs of the—traditionally creative—artists' hands are accompanied by a list of diverse actions ranging from the mundane to the absurd ("We wiped our asses and took the caper that got on our nerves out from under the door."[15]). And a stereotypically dressed painter vomits on a canvas on the floor in the style of Pollock when he sees his chubby model.[16] The myth of the creative process and the painting as bearing

11 See Diedrich Diederichsen, "Peinlich. Über das Peinliche des Unpeinlichen in der Kunst," *Spex*, no. 4, April 1985, p. 19, reprinted in translation in the present volume, pp. 422–427, as well as Diederichsen, "Im Kino onanierend," in *Obsessive Malerei. Ein Rückblick auf die Neuen Wilden*, ed. Götz Adriani, exh. cat. ZKM Karlsruhe, Ostfildern-Ruit 2003, pp. 171–72. Graw also refers to the "credo of stance" in the 1980s; see Graw 2018 (see note 3), pp. 168–69. For an analysis of left-wing subculture, pop, and pose in 1980s Germany, see Geer 2014 (see note 10), pp. 337–57.

12 Max Dax, "Eines von mehreren möglichen Vorworten," in *Spex. Das Buch. 33 1/3 Jahre Pop*, ed. Max Dax and Anne Waak, Berlin 2013, p. 5.

13 Diederichsen 2003 (see note 11), p. 172.

14 Rainald Goetz, "Warum die Hose runter muß," in Büttner et al. 1984 (see note 1), pp. 92–95.

15 Büttner et al. 1984 (see note 1), pp. 74–75.

16 Ibid., p. 26. Kippenberger's painting *Im Atelier (aus der vierteiligen Folge: Leicht verständliche Mysterien)*, 1983. See Stefan Hartmann, *Martin Kippenberger und die Kunst der Persiflage*, Munich 2013, pp. 20–21.

empfindsamen Ergüsse aus dem „Inneren" der Künstlerseele. Stattdessen sinniert Rainald Goetz in einem als Fußnote beigefügten „Gast"-Text in aller Ausführlichkeit über Rektalerkrankungen.[14] Schwarz-Weiß-Fotografien der – traditionell schöpferischen – Künstlerhände sind an anderer Stelle begleitet von einer Aufzählung allerlei alltäglicher bis absurder Handlungen. („Wir haben uns den Arsch abgewischt und die Kaper, die uns auf die Nerven ging, unter der Tür hervorgeholt."[15]) Und ein klischeehaft gekleideter Maler übergibt sich beim Anblick seines dicklichen Modells auf die in Pollock'scher Manier am Boden liegende Leinwand.[16] Es ist der Mythos des Schaffensprozesses sowie des Gemäldes als unmittelbarem Zeugnis der einzigartigen Subjektivität des Künstlers, der durch unsentimentale Herabwürdigung diskreditiert wird. Auf das Pathos ernster Tiefgründigkeit und unmittelbaren Ausdrucks wird mit konfrontativ schlechtem Benehmen, mit Abjektem und politisch Unkorrektem reagiert – gerne im Gewand eines gewitzten (und deshalb nicht minder haarsträubend sexistischen) Machismo.[17] Der eigene Fehltritt wird dabei nicht kaschiert, sondern offensiv ausgestellt: „Ich bin ein Arschloch. Aber ihr seid auch Arschlöcher."[18]

Bei den (auto-)biografisch anmutenden Geschichten und Äußerungen in *Wahrheit ist Arbeit* handelt es sich freilich um hochgradig stilisierte Darbietungen einer betont exzessiven Lebensführung, deren Autoren, so unterstreicht die maßlose Übertreibung, nicht nur um deren Konstruiertheit wissen, sondern ihren Fiktionscharakter durch den bisweilen legendenhaften Ton gezielt forcieren. Die Grenze zwischen Protagonisten und Autoren verschwimmt, die Gemachtheit der Figuren- und Selbstentwürfe wird betont. Gleichzeitig binden die Abbildungen die Geschichten an real existierende beziehungsweise überprüfbare Begebenheiten, künstlerische Produkte und freundschaftliche Beziehungen. So rückt gerade die Unbeantwortbarkeit der Frage „Ist das etwa wahr?", die mit jedem Mythos einhergeht, in den

14 Rainald Goetz, „Warum die Hose runter muß", in: Büttner/Kippenberger/Oehlen 1984 (wie Anm. 1), S. 92–95.

15 Büttner/Kippenberger/Oehlen 1984 (wie Anm. 1), S. 74f.

16 Ebd., S. 26. Hierbei handelt es sich um Kippenbergers Gemälde *Im Atelier (aus der vierteiligen Folge: Leicht verständliche Mysterien)*, 1983. Vgl. Stefan Hartmann, *Martin Kippenberger und die Kunst der Persiflage*, München 2013, S. 20f.

17 Zum Männerbündlerischen vgl. „Rochelle Feinstein und Kerstin Stakemeier im Gespräch. Die Gang- und Post-Gang-Malerei von Albert Oehlen", in: Achim Hochdörfer (Hg.), *Albert Oehlen. Malerei*, Ausst.-Kat. Museum Moderner Kunst Stiftung Ludwig Wien, Köln 2013, S. 67.

18 Werner Büttner, „Von der Methode", in: ders., *Schrecken der Demokratie*, Köln 1983, S. 5.

direct witness to the unique subjectivity of the artist is discredited through unsentimental degradation. The response to the pathos of earnest profundity and direct expression is confrontational bad behavior, the abject, and political incorrectness—preferably in the guise of a shrewd (but therefore no less appalling) machismo.[17] One's own misconduct is not concealed but aggressively exposed: "I am an asshole. But you are assholes too."[18]

The apparently (auto-)biographical stories and statements in *Wahrheit ist Arbeit* are, in fact, highly stylized skits of a decidedly excessive lifestyle, whose authors—as underscored by the exorbitant exaggerations—are not only aware of their constructedness but also deliberately promote the fictional character by striking an at times legendary tone. The border between protagonists and authors is blurred, while the fabricated nature of the constructed characters and self-representations is stressed. At the same time, the illustrations tie the stories to actually existing or verifiable occurrences, artistic products, and friendships, thus bringing to the fore the unanswerability of the question "Is that really true?" that goes hand in hand with any myth. What the artists revolve around and make use of in their variegated and, above all, cross-media self-portrayals is the special ambiguity of the figure of the artist, something also characteristic of pop stars. Unlike the classic theater actor who after the play leaves behind the domain of the stage—clearly separated from the empirical audience area—and with it his or her role, here the identity and performativity of the artist remain inextricably linked. What is "real" and what is merely performed or staged must remain structurally unclear.[19] Their own "flawed" life, which Büttner, Oehlen, and Kippenberger consciously expose to judgment, as in their extensive apology, is therefore both fictive and real—an uncertainty extending beyond the edges of the artists' book to the interview situation. It is not for nothing that in a conversation

17 On male bonding, see "Rochelle Feinstein und Kerstin Stakemeier im Gespräch. Die Gang- und Post-Gang-Malerei von Albert Oehlen," in *Albert Oehlen. Malerei*, ed. Achim Hochdörfer, exh. cat. Museum Moderner Kunst Stiftung Ludwig Wien, Cologne 2013, p. 67.

18 Werner Büttner, "Von der Methode," in *Schrecken der Demokratie*, Cologne 1983, p. 5.

19 Graw uses the term "persona" for this. See Graw 2018 (see note 3), pp. 159–60. On the paradoxical simultaneity of role and identity, mainly with regard to the pop star and his "pose," see Diedrich Diederichsen, *Über Popmusik*, Cologne 2014, pp. 133–41.

Mittelpunkt. Was die Künstler bei ihren mannigfaltigen und vor allem medienübergreifenden Selbstdarstellungen also umkreisen und sich zunutze machen, ist die besondere Doppelbödigkeit der Künstlerfigur, die auch den Popstar auszeichnet. Anders als beim/bei der klassischen Theaterschauspieler*in, die nach Ende des Stücks die fiktive, klar vom empirischen Zuschauerraum getrennte Bühnensphäre und damit auch seine/ihre Rolle zurücklässt, bleiben hier Identität und Performativität des/der Künstler*in untrennbar miteinander verbunden. Was nun „echt" und was nur gespielt beziehungsweise inszeniert ist, muss strukturell im Unklaren bleiben.[19] Das eigene „fehlerhafte" Leben, das Büttner, Oehlen und Kippenberger auch in ihrer ausführlichen Entschuldigung ganz bewusst zur Beurteilung stellen, ist also ein fiktives und doch ein wirkliches zugleich – eine Verunsicherung, die über die Ränder der Künstlerbücher hinaus bis in die Interviewsituation reicht. Nicht umsonst äußert Walter Grasskamp 1984 in einem Gespräch mit Büttner sein Misstrauen, was die „Wahrheit" von dessen Biografie angeht.[20]

Bei aller ironischen Distanzierung gegenüber einer ernsthaften Huldigung der Künstlerfigur bleibt das Bild des nonkonformen Enfant terrible genauso wie die Verschränkung von Kunst und einem rebellischen, unbürgerlichen Lebensstil letztlich natürlich dem gängigen Klischee vom avantgardistischen Bohemien verpflichtet.[21] Überhaupt bringt die herausgestellte Entmystifizierung und Entmachtung der Künstler deren Re-Mystifizierung und Re-Autorisierung mit sich. So geht das strategisch inszenierte Selbst nicht in der Rolle auf. Denn in dem Zuge, in dem die direkte Verbindung zwischen den Künstlern und ihrem Werk veralbert und der Zugriff auf deren authentisches, ja wahres Wesen verunmöglicht wird, wird diese dennoch genährt und forciert. Das bewusste Aussetzen der Unterscheidbarkeit von Rolle und Identität, Performance und Wahrheit kann somit nicht nur als Strategie des Sich-Verbergens, sondern eben auch als eine des Sich-Zeigens verstanden werden. Zwar kommuniziert die Selbstdarstellung, die das

19 Graw führt hierfür den Begriff der „Persona" ein. Vgl. Graw 2017 (wie Anm. 3), S. 156. Zur paradoxen Gleichzeitigkeit von Rolle und Identität, in erster Linie bezogen auf den Popstar und dessen „Pose", vgl. Diedrich Diederichsen, *Über Popmusik*, Köln 2014, S. 133–141.

20 Vgl. „Walter Grasskamp im Gespräch mit Werner Büttner", in: Christos M. Joachimides (Hg.), *Ursprung und Vision*, Ausst.-Kat. Palacio de Velázquez, Madrid, Berlin 1984, S. 14.

21 Vgl. „Hal Foster im Gespräch mit Achim Hochdörfer. Oehlen als Schönberg – ein wilder Gedanke!", in: Hochdörfer 2013 (wie Anm. 17), S. 141.

22 Vgl. ebd.

with Büttner in 1984, Walter Grasskamp voiced the suspicion regarding the "truth" of his biography.[20]

Despite all the ironic distance from a serious homage to the figure of the artist, the image of the nonconformist enfant terrible, just like the interweaving of art and a rebellious, anti-bourgeois lifestyle, are ultimately bound to the common cliché of the avant-garde bohemian.[21] The exposed demystification and disempowerment of the artists, in general, entail their re-mystification and re-authorization. The strategically staged self does not only play a role. For in ridiculing the direct connection between the artists and their work and in denying access to their authentic, true personalities, these personalities are nurtured and advanced all the same. The deliberate suspension of the distinction between role and identity, performance and truth, can therefore be read as a strategy not only of self-concealment but equally of self-exposure. The type of self-promotion replacing expressivity with eccentricity also communicates the awareness of the impossibility of authenticity.[22] But that does not mean that it is completely supplanted by the performativity of the role. Instead, authenticity is preserved as a potentiality—a game that can indeed be used to position oneself in an identity-forming manner.

Finally, *Wahrheit ist Arbeit* must also be viewed against the backdrop of the painting euphoria in the 1980s and the appropriation of various painterly practices by the—criticized or welcomed—rehabilitation of "expressive" painting and untamed "subjective articulation." The fact that the artists incorporate their paintings in a cross-media, decidedly unserious, anti-authentic praxis that rejects any insinuation of a naïve romanticism of immediacy can presumably also be understood as an attempt at self-localization and demarcation (that by the same token cannot, of course, be voiced too seriously).[23] The attempt to keep control of the reception and classification of one's work is also in line with

20 See "Walter Grasskamp im Gespräch mit Werner Büttner," in *Ursprung und Vision*, ed. Christos M. Joachimides, exh. cat. Palacio Velázquez, Madrid, Berlin 1984, p. 14.

21 See "Hal Foster im Gespräch mit Achim Hochdörfer. Oehlen als Schönberg – ein wilder Gedanke!," in Hochdörfer 2013 (see note 17), p. 141.

22 Ibid.

23 Dissociations from proponents of "neo-expressive" painting can be found in the catalogue of Werner Büttner, Georg Herold, and Albert Oehlen, *Facharbeiterficken. Gemeinsame Arbeiten 79/80/81*, Hamburg 1982. On the debates relating to the return of expressivity in 1980s painting, see Achim Hochdörfer, "How the World Came In," in *Painting 2.0: Expression in the Information Age*, ed. Manuela Ammer et al., exh. cat. Museum Brandhorst, Munich 2016, pp. 20–21.

Expressive durch das Exzentrische ersetzt, das Bewusstsein über die Unmöglichkeit von Authentizität mit.[22] Das bedeutet allerdings nicht, dass diese durch die Performativität der Rolle vollständig ersetzt wird. Vielmehr bleibt Authentizität als Potenzialität erhalten – ein Spiel, das durchaus zur identitätsstiftenden Selbstpositionierung genutzt wird.

Schließlich ist *Wahrheit ist Arbeit* auch vor dem Hintergrund der Malereieuphorie der 1980er-Jahre und der Vereinnahmung sämtlicher malerischer Praktiken durch eine – kritisierte oder begrüßte – Rehabilitation von „expressiver" Malerei und ungebändigtem „Ausdruck" zu betrachten. Dass die Künstler ihre Gemälde demgegenüber in eine medienübergreifende, betont unernste, anti-authentische Praxis einbetten, die jeden Anschein von naiver Unmittelbarkeitsromantik zurückweist, kann mutmaßlich auch als Versuch einer Selbstverortung und Abgrenzung verstanden werden (die gleichzeitig natürlich nicht allzu ernsthaft geäußert werden kann).[23] Der Versuch, die Kontrolle über die Rezeption und Einordnung des eigenen Werks zu behalten, schließt auch an die überzogen totalitäre Forderung nach eigenen Kritiker*innen an, die Büttner 1984 in einem Interview äußert: „Für uns hängt das mit Rechthaberei zusammen: jemand, der Bilder malt und davon überzeugt ist, daß er recht hat, die so zu malen, der muß zwangsweise fordern, daß er eigene Kritiker kriegt."[24]

Der Wille zur Distinktion zeigt sich in *Wahrheit ist Arbeit* zudem in dem gewollt unauflösbaren Geflecht origineller Referenzen, das nicht nur als Verweigerung eines einheitlichen nachvollziehbaren Sinns, sondern auch als Inszenierung des eigenen Spezialwissens sichtbar wird. Trotz brachialer Sprache und betont niveauloser Plots kommt *Wahrheit ist Arbeit* mithin überraschend snobistisch daher und beschert den Künstlern jenen Vorwurf der Angeberei, für den sie sich im gleichen Atemzug fadenscheinig „entschuldigen".[25]

Der vermeintliche Taschenspielertrick der Entschuldigung ist also als Versuch einer Dekonstruktion authentischer Subjektivität und

23 Abgrenzungen von Vertreter*innen der „neo-expressiven" Malerei finden sich zum Beispiel in dem Katalog von Werner Büttner, Georg Herold und Albert Oehlen, *Facharbeiterficken. Gemeinsame Arbeiten 79/80/81*, Hamburg 1982. Zu den Debatten um die Rückkehr des Expressiven in der Malerei der 1980er-Jahre vgl. Achim Hochdörfer, „How the World Came in: Medien der Expression in der Malerei seit den 1960er-Jahren", in: Manuela Ammer, Achim Hochdörfer und David Joselit (Hg.), *Painting 2.0. Malerei im Informationszeitalter*, Ausst.-Kat. Museum Brandhorst, München 2016, S. 20f.

24 „Büttner im Gespräch mit Grasskamp und A. Oehlen", in: Joachimides 1984 (wie Anm. 20), S. 150.

25 Zur „Sophistication" als Strategie eines „distinktiven Selbstentwurfs" der Pop-Intellektuellen der 1980er-Jahre vgl. weiterführend Nadja Geer, *Sophistication. Zwischen Denkstil und Pose*, Göttingen 2012.

the overblown totalitarian demand for critics of one's own that Büttner made in an interview in 1984: "For us, that has to do with the insistence on being right: someone who paints pictures and is convinced that he is right in painting them that way must compulsorily demand critics of his own."[24]

The will to distinction is also present in *Wahrheit ist Arbeit* through the intentionally irresolvable tangle of original references that appears not only as the refusal of a unified, comprehensible meaning, but also as the mise-en-scène of one's own specialist knowledge. Despite its brute language and decidedly lowbrow plots, *Wahrheit ist Arbeit* occasionally makes a surprisingly snobby impression and earns the artists the accusation of showing off, for which, in the same breath, they make a spurious "apology."[25] The alleged apology as a sleight of hand is therefore to be understood both as a bid to deconstruct authentic subjectivity and as a strategy of self-representation. The alliance between artistic praxis and a bohemian lifestyle forged in *Wahrheit ist Arbeit* with its targeted destabilization of the border between work and person can thus be taken seriously as an arena in which the remaining free spaces for subjectivity are negotiated.[26] The emerging paradoxes, inconsistencies, and contradictions are caused precisely by the struggles for the seemingly unbridgeable dualism of authenticity and role, truth and performance. These transgressions lead from the fringe areas right to the heart of the conflict related to art, and, even more so, painting. The hardened fronts between allegedly reactionary expressionism and critical conceptuality turn painting—which advanced critics long automatically identified with the former—into a disputatious endeavor that these artists do not want to give up,[27] be it, for instance, on account of disillusionment, or the "fear of doing something wrong."[28]

24 "Büttner im Gespräch mit Grasskamp und A. Oehlen," in Joachimides 1984 (see note 20), p. 150.

25 For more details on "sophistication" as a strategy of a distinctive self-design of the 1980s pop intellectual, see Nadja Geer, *Sophistication. Zwischen Denkstil und Pose*, Göttingen 2012.

26 Hochdörfer speaks of "showing solidarity with the subject in crisis." See Hochdörfer and Foster 2013 (see note 21), p. 141.

27 See, for example, Douglas Crimp, "The End of Painting," *October* 16 (1981), p. 73. On calling into question the mentioned fronts, see Isabelle Graw, "Conceptual Expression: On Conceptual Gestures in Allegedly Expressive Painting, Traces of Expression in Proto-Conceptual Works, and the Significance of Artistic Procedures," in *Art After Conceptual Art*, ed. Sabeth Buchmann and Alexander Alberro, Cambridge, MA and London 2006, pp. 119–34.

28 Büttner et al. 1984 (see note 1), p. 29.

als Strategie eines Selbstentwurfs zugleich zu verstehen. Die Allianz aus künstlerischer Praxis und bohemehaftem Lebensstil in *Wahrheit ist Arbeit* kann mit ihrer gezielten Destabilisierung der Grenze zwischen Werk und Person dementsprechend als Arena der Aushandlung der verbleibenden Freiräume für Subjektivität ernst genommen werden.[26] Die darin aufscheinenden Paradoxien, Ungereimtheiten und Widersprüche sind ebenjenen Kämpfen um den scheinbar unüberbrückbaren Dualismus von Authentizität und Rolle, Wahrheit und Performance geschuldet. Diese Grenzüberschreitungen führen von den Randgebieten direkt in das Zentrum des Konflikts um die Kunst, oder noch mehr um die Malerei. Die verhärteten Fronten zwischen vermeintlich reaktionärem Expressionismus und kritischer Konzeptualität machen die Malerei – von der avancierten Kritik lange Zeit automatisch mit Ersterem identifiziert – zu einem streitbaren Unterfangen, das von den Künstlern allerdings nicht – etwa aus Desillusionierung oder aus „Angst, etwas falsch zu machen“[27] – aufgegeben werden will.[28]

> „Die Suche nach der Wahrheit ist eine der vornehmsten Aufgaben des Menschen, umso mehr, als es gar keine Wahrheit gibt, wie Karl. R. Popper ganz richtig behauptet, sondern es gibt nur stetige Wahrscheinlichkeitsstufen, deren obere und untere, unerreichbare Grenzen, Wahrheit und Falschheit sind. [...] Die Kunst, die als gute Kunst – Kunst ist immer gut, sonst ist sie keine Kunst – ihrer Zeit immer voraus ist, wußte alles schon immer. Die Angst, die Wahrheit zu verpassen, führte zur Ausschaltung des Ungesicherten, zur unkritisierbaren Aussage: Hier, ich bin ein Kunstwerk oder das Kunstwerk wurde auf die Phantasie des Künstlers zurückgeführt und damit konkret gemacht. Daß sich die Phantasie des Künstlers im Bild konkretisierte, daran nahm niemand Anstoß [...]. Die Suche nach der Wahrheit war ersatzlos vom Stundenplan gestrichen, und damit die Wahrheit, behaupten wir, und wer nichts behauptet, hat auch keinen Anspruch auf die Wahrheit. [...]

26 Hochdörfer spricht von einer „Solidarisierung mit dem kriselnden Subjekt“. Vgl. Hochdörfer/Foster 2013 (wie Anm. 21), S. 141.

27 Büttner/Kippenberger/Oehlen 1984 (wie Anm. 1), S. 29.

28 Vgl. zum Beispiel Douglas Crimp, „The End of Painting“, in: *October*, Nr. 16, 1981, S. 73. Zur Infragestellung der genannten Frontstellung vgl. Isabelle Graw, „Konzeptuelle Expression: Über konzeptuelle Gesten in vermeintlich expressiver Malerei, Spuren von Ausdruck in protokonzeptuellen Arbeiten und den Stellenwert künstlerischer Verfahren“, in: Sabeth Buchmann und Alexander Alberro (Hg.), *Art After Conceptual Art*, Wien 2006, S. 135–150.

> The search for truth is one of man's noblest tasks, even more so as there is no truth, as Karl. R. Popper quite correctly states, but only continuous stages of probability whose upper and lower, unreachable limits are truth and falsehood.... The art, which as good art—art is always good, otherwise it isn't art—is always ahead of its time, always already knew everything. The fear of missing the truth has led to the elimination of what is uncertain, to the statement that cannot be criticized: here, I am an artwork; or the artwork was traced back to the imagination of the artist and thus made concrete. Nobody took offense at the imagination of the artist becoming concrete in the picture.... The search for truth was completely deleted from the timetable, and with it truth, we assert, and whoever asserts nothing cannot lay claim to the truth.... The truth can only be used briefly, but one can prolong it by letting it get into a picture.[29]

This is not just the witty gesture of a leftist citing Popper, of all people, and with him the antagonist of the "false prophets"[30] Hegel and Marx, because what also reveals itself here is a serious questioning of the still existing possibilities of art as the traditional guarantor of lost truth. The process of searching for *the* truth, which is of course inaccessible, can only be expressed in the form of making potentially "false" assertions—reckoning with mistakes and failure, then, to oppose a pluralism that completely dissolves the dichotomy of truth and falsehood. That precisely art, or painting, is supposed to be the place of falsifiable statements is indeed an intentionally paradoxical statement. And yet it can be understood as a plea to neither forfeit art's work on "truth" in favor of the mystical aura of imagination, nor restrict art to working on its own concept.[31] The will to express is replaced by the will to assert that, despite all dubiousness, is indeed at the same time once again a confession.

29 Ibid., pp. 28–29.

30 Karl R. Popper, *The Open Society and Its Enemies*, vol. 2: *The High Tide of Prophecy: Hegel, Marx, and the Aftermath*, London and New York 1952.

31 See also Diederichsen 1992 (see note 5), p. 36.

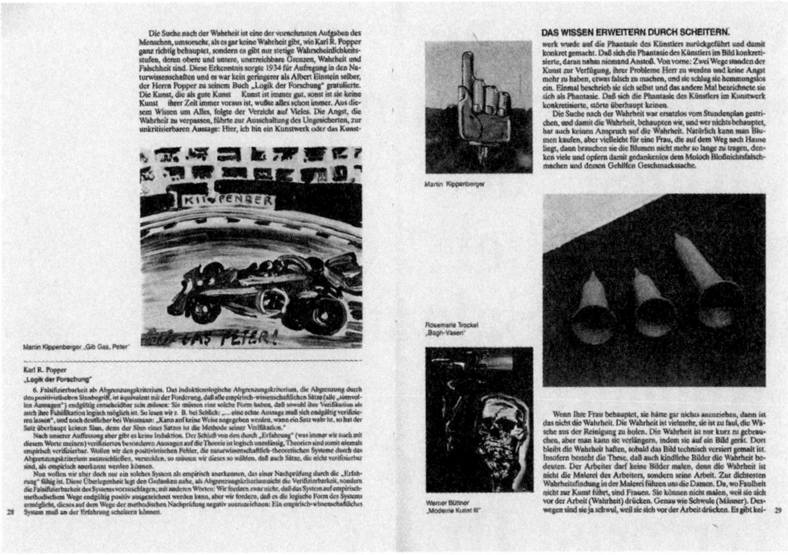

Die Suche nach der Wahrheit ist eine der vornehmsten Aufgaben des Menschen, umsomehr, als es gar keine Wahrheit gibt, wie Karl R. Popper ganz richtig behauptet, sondern es gibt nur stetige Wahrscheinlichkeitsstufen, deren obere und untere, unerreichbare Grenzen, Wahrheit und Falschheit sind. Diese Erkenntnis sorgte 1934 für Aufregung in den Naturwissenschaften und es war kein geringerer als Albert Einstein selber, der Herrn Popper zu seinem Buch „Logik der Forschung" gratulierte. Die Kunst, die als gute Kunst   Kunst ist immer gut, sonst ist sie keine Kunst   ihrer Zeit immer voraus ist, wußte alles schon immer. Aus diesem Wissen um Alles, folgte der Verzicht auf Vieles. Die Angst, die Wahrheit zu verpassen, führte zur Ausschaltung des Ungesicherten, zur unkritisierbaren Aussage: Hier, ich bin ein Kunstwerk oder das Kunst-

Martin Kippenberger „Gib Gas, Peter"

Karl R. Popper
„Logik der Forschung"

6. Falsifizierbarkeit als Abgrenzungskriterium. Das induktionslogische Abgrenzungskriterium, die Abgrenzung durch den positivistischen Sinnbegriff, ist äquivalent mit der Forderung, daß alle empirisch-wissenschaftlichen Sätze (alle „sinnvollen Aussagen") endgültig entscheidbar sein müssen: Sie müssen eine solche Form haben, daß sowohl ihre Verifikation als auch ihre Falsifikation logisch möglich ist. So lesen wir z. B. bei Schlick: „... eine echte Aussage muß sich endgültig verifizieren lassen", und noch deutlicher bei Waismann: „Kann auf keine Weise angegeben werden, wann ein Satz wahr ist, so hat der Satz überhaupt keinen Sinn, denn der Sinn eines Satzes ist die Methode seiner Verifikation."

Nach unserer Auffassung aber gibt es keine Induktion. Der Schluß von den durch „Erfahrung" (was immer wir auch mit diesem Worte meinen) verifizierten besonderen Aussagen auf die Theorie ist logisch unzulässig. Theorien sind somit niemals empirisch verifizierbar. Wollen wir den positivistischen Fehler, die naturwissenschaftlich-theoretischen Systeme durch das Abgrenzungskriterium auszuschließen, vermeiden, so müssen wir dieses so wählen, daß auch Sätze, die nicht verifizierbar sind, als empirisch anerkannt werden können.

Nun wollen wir aber doch nur ein solches System als empirisch anerkennen, das einer Nachprüfung durch die „Erfahrung" fähig ist. Diese Überlegenheit legt den Gedanken nahe, als Abgrenzungskriterium nicht die Verifizierbarkeit, sondern die Falsifizierbarkeit des Systems vorzuschlagen; mit anderen Worten: Wir fordern zwar nicht, daß das System auf empirisch-methodischem Wege endgültig positiv ausgezeichnet werden kann, aber wir fordern, daß es die logische Form des Systems ermöglicht, dieses auf dem Wege der methodischen Nachprüfung negativ auszuzeichnen: Ein empirisch-wissenschaftliches
28 System muß an der Erfahrung scheitern können.

Martin Kippenberger

DAS WISSEN ERWEITERN DURCH SCHEITERN.

werk wurde auf die Phantasie des Künstlers zurückgeführt und damit konkret gemacht. Daß sich die Phantasie des Künstlers im Bild konkretisierte, daran nahm niemand Anstoß. Von vorne: Zwei Wege standen der Kunst zur Verfügung, ihrer Probleme Herr zu werden und keine Angst mehr zu haben, etwas falsch zu machen, und sie schlug sie hemmungslos ein. Einmal beschrieb sie sich selbst und das andere Mal bezeichnete sie sich als Phantasie. Daß sich die Phantasie des Künstlers im Kunstwerk konkretisierte, störte überhaupt keinen.

Die Suche nach der Wahrheit war ersatzlos vom Stundenplan gestrichen, und damit die Wahrheit, behaupten wir, und wer nichts behauptet, hat auch keinen Anspruch auf die Wahrheit. Natürlich kann man Blumen kaufen, aber vielleicht für eine Frau, die auf dem Weg nach Hause liegt, dann brauchen sie die Blumen nicht mehr so lange zu tragen, denken viele und opfern damit gedankenlos dem Moloch Bloßnichtsfalschmachen und dessen Gehilfen Geschmackssache.

Rosemarie Trockel
„Bagh-Vasen"

Werner Büttner
„Moderne Kunst III"

Wenn Ihre Frau behauptet, sie hätte gar nichts anzuziehen, dann ist das nicht die Wahrheit. Die Wahrheit ist vielmehr, sie ist zu faul, die Wäsche aus der Reinigung zu holen. Die Wahrheit ist nur kurz zu gebrauchen, aber man kann sie verlängern, indem sie auf ein Bild gerät. Dort bleibt die Wahrheit haften, sobald das Bild technisch versiert gemalt ist. Insofern besteht die These, daß auch kindliche Bilder die Wahrheit bedeuten. Der Arbeiter darf keine Bilder malen, denn die Wahrheit ist nicht die Malerei des Arbeiters, sondern seine Arbeit. Zur dichtesten Wahrheitsfindung in der Malerei führen uns die Damen. Da, wo Faulheit nicht zur Kunst führt, sind Frauen. Sie können nicht malen, weil sie sich vor der Arbeit (Wahrheit) drücken. Genau wie Schwule (Männer). Deswegen sind sie ja schwul, weil sie sich vor der Arbeit drücken. Es gibt kei- 29

Werner Büttner, Martin Kippenberger, Albert Oehlen, *Wahrheit ist Arbeit*, 1984

> Die Wahrheit ist nur kurz zu gebrauchen, aber man kann sie verlängern, indem sie auf ein Bild gerät."[29]

Es ist nicht nur eine gewitzte Geste, als Linker Popper und damit ausgerechnet den Antagonisten der „falschen Propheten"[30] Hegel und Marx zu zitieren. Denn zugleich zeigt sich hier eine ernsthafte Befragung der noch vorhandenen Möglichkeiten der Kunst als traditioneller Bürgin der verlorenen Wahrheit. Der Prozess der Suche nach *der* Wahrheit, die als solche freilich nie zu erreichen ist, kann sich nur als Aufstellen potenziell „falscher" Behauptungen äußern – als eine Inkaufnahme von Irren und Scheitern also, die sich gegen einen Pluralismus wendet, der die Dichotomie von Wahrem und Falschem gänzlich auflöst. Dass gerade die Kunst, oder die Malerei, der Ort falsifizierbarer Aussagen sein soll, ist natürlich eine gewollt paradoxe Aussage. Und lässt sich doch gleichzeitig als Plädoyer verstehen, die Arbeit an der „Wahrheit" in der Kunst weder zugunsten der mystischen Aura der Fantasie preiszugeben, noch sie auf die Arbeit an ihrem eigenen Begriff zu beschränken.[31] An die Stelle des Willens zum Ausdruck tritt der Wille zur Behauptung, der bei aller Zwielichtigkeit dann eben doch zugleich ein Bekenntnis ist.

29 Büttner/Kippenberger/Oehlen 1984 (wie Anm. 1), S. 28f.

30 Karl R. Popper, *Die offene Gesellschaft und ihre Feinde*, Bd. 2: *Falsche Propheten: Hegel, Marx und die Folgen*, Bern 1958.

31 Vgl. auch Diederichsen 1992 (wie Anm. 5), S. 36.

Katrin Köppert

Queere „Indianer“ und exotische Terrortunten Die „Kunst“ des Ethnic Drag bei Castelli und Salomé

Katrin Köppert

Queer “Indians” and Exotic Terrorist Drags The “Art” of Ethnic Drag in Castelli and Salomé

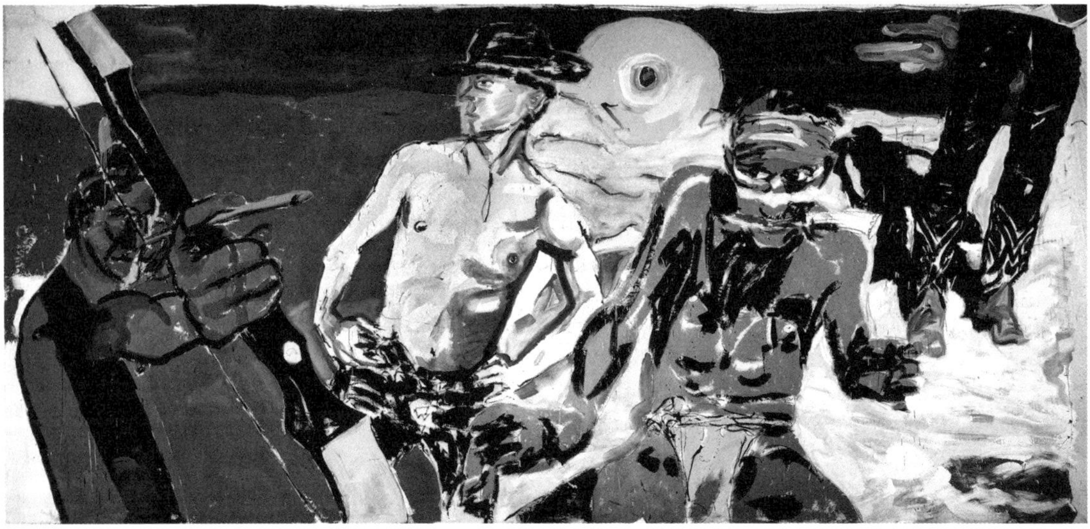

Luciano Castelli, Rainer Fetting, *Room Full of Mirrors*, 1982
Öl auf Leinwand / oil on canvas, 500 × 1000 cm

Neue Wilde. Zwei Worte – und ich bin draußen. Aus der Perspektive einer queeren und postkolonialen Kunst- und Medienwissenschaft verbirgt sich in diesen zwei Worten zur Beschreibung[1] der Malerei der Berliner Neuen Wilden[2] um Elvira Bach, Luciano Castelli, Rainer Fetting, Helmut Middendorf, Salomé und Bernd Zimmer Anfang der 1980er-Jahre ein weißer, westlicher und heteronormativer Signifikatenüberschuss der Extraklasse.

Im chronopolitischen Modus der Neuheitsverkündigung artikuliert sich das ganze auf Fortschritt geeichte Paradigma der westlichen Moderne. Da dieses im 19. Jahrhundert eng an die Konsolidierung eines Familienkonzepts geknüpft wurde, in dessen Zentrum die Liebe und deren Früchte (Kinder) standen, schlich sich in jedes Modernitätsversprechen das Bekenntnis zur heterosexuellen Reproduktion.[3] „Neu“ zu sagen meint – wenngleich etwas zusammengekürzt – die Marginalisierung nicht-reproduktiver, queerer Lebensweisen, was – wie noch zu sehen sein wird – insbesondere für die Berliner Neuen Wilden und deren Ästhetik geradezu paradox erscheint. Daher also ein erstes Zaudern. Das zweite stellt sich ein, wenn das „Wilde“ das Neue sein soll beziehungsweise das Wörtchen „neu“ die Affirmation eines Begriffs des Wilden darstellt, der innerhalb der Kunstgeschichte mehr als problematische Implikationen birgt. Sicherlich lässt sich das Wilde als das Ungestüme verstehen, das sich der unterkühlten Durchdachtheit der aneinanderschmiegenden Farbgeometrien des Minimalismus der frühen Nachkriegszeit entgegenstemmt.[4] Nur erlebt mit dem chaotischen Wimmeln der Farbaufträge, dem Stöbern im „Großwildjäger-Repertoire des Kolonialismus“[5] mit Tiger- und Zebrafellen und der

1 Der Begriff „Neue Wilde“ geht auf die von Wolfgang Becker kuratierte Ausstellung *Les Nouveaux Fauves – Die Neuen Wilden* aus dem Jahr 1980 zurück. Becker bezieht sich mit dem Begriff auf die französischen Fauves des frühen 20. Jahrhunderts, die er in der Ausstellung mit deutschen und nordamerikanischen Malereipositionen der 1970er-Jahre kombinierte. Neben Georg Baselitz, Jörg Immendorff, Markus Lüpertz und A. R. Penck zeigte er Neil Jenney, Miriam Schapiro und Robert Zakanitch. Obwohl Becker keine Werke der Berliner Künstler*innengruppe ausstellte, wurde der Begriff in der medialen Diskussion sehr schnell für deren Schaffen verwendet und steht heute vornehmlich für deren Malerei. Wolfgang Becker (Hg.), *Les Nouveaux Fauves – Die Neuen Wilden*, Ausst.-Kat. Neue Galerie – Sammlung Ludwig Aachen, Aachen 1980.

2 Die Künstler*innenbewegung Neue Wilde entstand in mehreren bundesdeutschen Städten. Neben Berlin waren Köln, Düsseldorf und Hamburg maßgeblich.

3 Zur queer-theoretischen Auseinandersetzung mit „straight time“, also der Heteronormalisierung von Zeit insbesondere durch die Moderne, sowie mit Formen queerer Unterbrechungen vgl. Elizabeth Freeman, *Time Binds. Queer Temporalities, Queer Histories*, Durham und London 2010; Elizabeth Grosz, *The Nick of Time: Politics, Evolution, and the Untimely*, Durham 2004; Judith Halberstam, *In a Queer Time and Place: Transgender Bodies, Subcultural Lives*, New York und London 2005.

Neue Wilde. Two words—and I'm gone. From the perspective of queer and postcolonial art and media studies, these two words used to describe[1] the painting of the Berlin Neue Wilde[2] that included Elvira Bach, Luciano Castelli, Rainer Fetting, Helmut Middendorf, Salomé, and Bernd Zimmer in the early 1980s bear an excess of white, Western, and heteronormative signifiers extraordinaire.

In the chronopolitical mode of proclaiming novelty is articulated the entire progress-calibrated paradigm of Western modernity. As in the nineteenth century, this was closely tied to the consolidation of a family concept, at the center of which stood love and its fruits (children)—the commitment to heterosexual reproduction crept into every promise of modernity.[3] To say "new" implies—although somewhat abbreviated—the marginalization of nonreproductive, queer lifestyles, something that appears downright paradoxical with regard to the Berlin Neue Wilde, as we shall see. Thus my initial hesitation. The second one sets in when the "wild" is supposed to be the new, or when the little word "new" marks the affirmation of a concept of the wild that in art history has more than troubling implications. The wild can certainly be understood as boisterousness making a stand against the highly reserved sophistication of the nestling color geometries of early postwar Minimalism.[4] Except that the chaotic bristling of the color applications as well as the foraging in the "big-game hunter repertoire of colonialism"[5] with tiger and zebra hides and the "Indian folklore" of artistic primitivism of the first half of the twentieth century experiences a renaissance that at

1 The term "Neue Wilde" harks back to the 1980 exhibition *Les Nouveaux Fauves – Die Neuen Wilden* curated by Wolfgang Becker. It makes reference to the French Fauves of the early twentieth century that Becker juxtaposed with German and North American painting positions of the 1970s. Alongside Georg Baselitz, Jörg Immendorff, Markus Lüpertz, and A. R. Penck, he showed Neil Jenney, Miriam Schapiro, and Robert Zakanitch. Although Becker did not present works by the Berlin-based artist group, the term was quickly used by the media for their art and today denotes primarily their painting. *Les Nouveaux Fauves – Die Neuen Wilden*, ed. Wolfgang Becker, exh. cat. Neue Galerie – Sammlung Ludwig Aachen, Aachen 1980.

2 The artist movement Neue Wilde emerged in several West German cities. Berlin was leading, along with Cologne, Düsseldorf, and Hamburg.

3 On the queer-theoretical debate on "straight time," i.e., the heteronormalization of time in particular through modernity as well as forms of queer disruptions, see Elizabeth Freeman, *Time Binds: Queer Temporalities, Queer Histories*, Durham and London 2010; Elizabeth Grosz, *The Nick of Time: Politics, Evolution, and the Untimely*, Durham 2004; Judith Halberstam, *In a Queer Time and Place: Transgender Bodies, Subcultural Lives*, New York and London 2005.

„Indianerfolklore“ der künstlerische Primitivismus der ersten Hälfte des 20. Jahrhunderts eine Renaissance, die mich erst einmal auf Abstand zu den Werken, aber auch zu der diesen Aspekt zumeist ignorierenden Rezeption der Neuen Wilden bringt.

Gleichzeitig geht von den Fotografien, Performances und Gemälden etwas aus, das einer genaueren Überprüfung lohnt. Aufgrund bestimmter motivischer Setzungen, transmedialer Verfahren und stilistischer Eigenheiten aus dem Spektrum queerer Medienpraktiken sprechen die Arbeiten auf eine intime und vertraute Weise zu mir. Auch aus dem Zusammenhang der postkolonialen Zirkulation von Zeichen heraus erscheinen sie mir nicht als eine bruchlose Wiederauflage primitivistischer Signaturen des frühen 20. Jahrhunderts. Doch was dann? Handelt es sich hier um die Dekonstruktion von Primitivismus? Was ist die Funktion, sich zu diesem (kunst-)historischen Zeitpunkt als „Indianer“ oder „Geisha“ selbst ins Bild zu bringen? Macht es einen Unterschied, dies in der Malerei zu betreiben oder in den zwischen Kunst- und Privatraum, Galerie und Subkultur changierenden performativen und fotografischen Selbstinszenierungen? Welche Medialität hat die „Kunst“ des Ethnic Drag[6], das heißt die Aneignung indigener Kulturen, die – wie es von der Queeren Theorie für Geschlecht formuliert wurde[7] – Ethnie „als Produktion von identitätskonstruierenden Wiederholungsakten ohne Original sieht“[8]? Handelt es sich überhaupt um Kunst, oder müssen wir die Fotografien und Performances – wie so oft unterstellt – als Vorarbeiten für die Malerei betrachten? Haben sie nicht einen eigenen künstlerischen Stellenwert, wenngleich dieser von den privaten Archiven der fotografischen Selbstaufzeichnung im

4 So beschreiben es unter anderem Ernst Busche, Christos M. Joachimides und Götz Adriani. Ernst Busche, „Notizen zur Malerei von Rainer Fetting, Helmut Middendorf, Salomé und Bernd Zimmer“, in: Haus am Waldsee (Hg.), *Heftige Malerei. Rainer Fetting, Helmut Middendorf, Salomé, Bernd Zimmer*, Ausst.-Kat. Haus am Waldsee Berlin, Berlin 1980; Christos M. Joachimides (Hg.), *Die wiedergefundene Metropole. Neue Malerei in Berlin*, Ausst.-Kat. Palais des Beaux-Arts Brüssel, Berlin 1984; Götz Adriani, „Vorwort“, in: ders. (Hg.), *Obsessive Malerei. Ein Rückblick auf die Neuen Wilden*, Ausst.-Kat. Museum für Neue Kunst, ZKM Karlsruhe, Ostfildern 2003, S. 7.

5 Gabriele Dietze, *Weiße Frauen in Bewegung. Genealogien und Konkurrenzen von Race- und Genderpolitiken*, Bielefeld 2013, S. 23.

6 Katrin Sieg, *Ethnic Drag. Performing Race, Nation, Sexuality in West Germany*, Ann Arbor 2002.

7 Judith Butler, *Das Unbehagen der Geschlechter*, Frankfurt am Main 1991 [1990]; Judith Butler, *Körper von Gewicht. Die diskursiven Grenzen des Geschlechts*, Frankfurt am Main 1997 [1993].

8 Ulrike Bergermann, „Federn lassen. Aktuelles zur Appropriation“, in: *Gender Blog, Zeitschrift für Medienwissenschaft (ZfM)*, www.zfmedienwissenschaft.de/online/blog/federn-lassen-aktuelles-zur-appropriation, 2017 (zuletzt abgerufen am 26.09.2018).

first prompts me to distance myself from the works as well as the reception of the Neue Wilde, which mostly ignores this aspect.

At the same time, something emanates from the photographs, performances, and paintings that is worth closer examination. Due to certain motivic postulates, transmedial procedures, and stylistic idiosyncrasies from the spectrum of queer media practices, the works speak to me in an intimate and familiar manner. Even from the perspective of the postcolonial circulation of signs, they do not seem to be a seamless revival of primitivistic signifiers of the early twentieth century. But what are they? Deconstructions of primitivism? What is the function of depicting oneself at this (art-)historical point in time as an "Indian" or "geisha"? Is there a difference between doing so in painting and in the performative and photographic self-staging taking place in art and private spaces, in galleries and the subculture? What kind of mediality is inherent in the "art" of ethnic drag,[6] meaning the appropriation of indigenous cultures that—as has been formulated by queer theory with respect to gender[7]—grasps ethnicity as the "production of identity-forging repetitive acts without an original"?[8] Is it even art? Or must we consider the photographs and performances—as often assumed—as preparatory works for painting? Do they not possess an artistic significance of their own, even though they are inspired and guided by the private archives of photographic self-recording in the context of homosexual self-assurance, or by the images of gay heroes circulating in popular cultures? Do they not gain a status within art precisely because of this transgression

4 That is how Ernst Busche, Christos M. Joachimides, and Götz Adriani describe it. Ernst Busche, "Notizen zur Malerei von Rainer Fetting, Helmut Middendorf, Salomé und Bernd Zimmer," in *Heftige Malerei. Rainer Fetting, Helmut Middendorf, Salomé, Bernd Zimmer,* ed. Thomas Kempas, exh. cat. Haus am Waldsee, Berlin 1980; *Die wiedergefundene Metropole. Neue Malerei in Berlin,* ed. Christos M. Joachimides, exh. cat. Palais des Beaux-Arts, Brussels, Berlin 1984; Götz Adriani, "Vorwort," in *Obsessive Malerei. Ein Rückblick auf die Neuen Wilden,* ed. Götz Adriani, exh. cat. Museum für Neue Kunst, ZKM Karlsruhe, Ostfildern 2003, p. 7.

5 Gabriele Dietze, *Weiße Frauen in Bewegung. Genealogien und Konkurrenzen von Race- und Genderpolitiken,* Bielefeld 2013, p. 23.

6 Katrin Sieg, *Ethnic Drag: Performing Race, Nation, Sexuality in West Germany,* Ann Arbor 2002.

7 Judith Butler, *Gender Trouble: Feminism and the Subversion of Identity,* New York 1990; Judith Butler, *Bodies That Matter: On The Discursive Limits of "Sex,"* New York 1993.

8 Ulrike Bergermann, "Federn lassen. Aktuelles zur Appropriation," *Gender Blog, Zeitschrift für Medienwissenschaft,* June 27, 2017 (update), www.zfmedienwissenschaft.de/online/blog/federn-lassen-aktuelles-zur-appropriation.

Kontext homosexueller Selbstvergewisserung inspiriert und angeleitet ist, oder von den innerhalb populärer Kulturen zirkulierenden Bildern schwuler Heroen? Erlangen sie nicht gar aufgrund dieser Grenzüberschreitung beziehungsweise gegenseitigen Durchdringung einen Status innerhalb der Kunst, der ihren primitivistischen Gehalt umlenkt?

Queere „Indianer“: Luciano Castelli

Aus leicht erhöhter Position schauen wir auf ein Zwischenwesen: Paillettenkleid und Glitzerstaub stehen dem Schlangenmuster der Stiefel und den Federn in den Haaren gegenüber (Abb. S. 160). Handelt es sich um eine Frau oder einen Mann, einen „Indianer“ oder eine das Bein hochwerfende Frau in Flapper-Ästhetik? Stellen die Federn einen Bezug zur Natur und ihren animalischen Lebewesen her und die glitzernden, seit den 1950er-Jahren industriell gefertigten Kunststoff-Pailletten eine Verbindung zur Camp-Attitude, einer Haltung, die sich gegen Natur wendet und alles Artifizielle in einem Modus der Übertreibung affirmiert?[9] Ist die Figur mit den grotesk aussehenden abgespreizten und verdrehten Beinen eine Diva oder eine Kreatur[10]? Und nicht zuletzt: Haben wir es hier mit einem beiläufigen Schnappschuss zu tun oder einer hochgradig inszenierten Selbstdarstellung, einer absichtsvoll künstlerischen Fotografie?

Es sind viele Gegensätze, die sich in diesem von Luciano Castelli 1973 aufgenommenen Selbstporträt feststellen ließen, und dennoch bilden sie eine Koexistenz, aus der heraus sich nur schwerlich ein hierarchisches Verhältnis ableiten lässt. Es scheint, als würde zitiert, aber nicht appropriiert; als würde angeeignet, aber für nichts Eigenes, nichts Eigentliches. Das Zitierte amalgamiert zu etwas anderem, das abseits der Zeichenkette des Indianerbildes steht oder eines Bildes der Neuen Frau, die sich in den Roaring Twenties mittels Federschmuck und weiterer Race-Signaturen aus dem Korsett der viktorianischen

9 Vor allem Susan Sontag hatte in „Notes on ‚Camp‘“ einen Begriff von Camp etabliert, der in einem offenen Widerspruch zur Natur steht. Da sich Sontag dabei explizit auf acht Mottos bezieht, die von Oscar Wilde stammen, verstärkt sie die historisch gewachsene Verknüpfung zwischen Künstlichkeit und Homosexualität. Susan Sontag, „Notes on ‚Camp‘“, in: dies., *Against Interpretation and Other Essays*, New York 1966, S. 275–292.

10 Juliane Rebentisch – in kritischer Auseinandersetzung mit Sontags Begriffsbestimmung camper Ästhetik – verweist im Zusammenhang ihrer Betrachtung der Ästhetik von Jack Smith darauf, dass insbesondere die kreatürliche Dimension der Diva auf die Natur in der Geschichte hindeutet. Damit wendet sie sich gegen das nahezu naturalisierte Verhältnis der Homosexualität zur Artifizialität. Juliane Rebentisch, „Über eine materialistische Seite von Camp. Naturgeschichte bei Jack Smith“, in: *Zeitschrift für Medienwissenschaft (ZfM)*, 8, 1, 2013, S. 166.

or interpenetration that diverts their primitivistic content in other directions?

Queer "Indians": Luciano Castelli

From a slightly elevated position, we gaze at an in-between being: sequin dress and glitter contrast the snakeskin pattern of the boots and the feathers in the hair (p. 160). Is it a woman or a man, an "Indian" or a woman dressed as a flapper raising her leg? Do the feathers establish a relation to nature and its animalistic beings, and do the glittering artificial sequins manufactured industrially since the 1950s reference a camp attitude, a stance directed against nature, affirming everything that is artificial in an exaggerated fashion?[9] Is the figure with the grotesquely splayed out and twisted legs a diva or a creature?[10] And not least: Is this a snapshot taken in passing or a highly contrived self-image, a deliberately artful photograph?

There are so many contradictions that can be detected in the self-portrayal of Luciano Castelli from 1973, and yet they cohere in such a way that it is quite difficult to derive a hierarchical relationship. It seems as if things were being cited but not taken possession of; as if they were being appropriated but not for one's own cause or for anything essential. That which is cited amalgamates to something going beyond the chain of signifiers of the image of the Indian or the new woman of the Roaring Twenties who liberated herself from the corset of the Victorian or Wilhelmine era with feather headdresses and other racial signifiers, thus self-ethnicizing.[11] At issue here is not emancipation at the cost of others, however, because whom—as the picture asks—would the headdress assist in becoming a self of equal status? Does something essential crystallize here that as a political subject

9 Especially Susan Sontag established a concept of camp in "Notes on 'Camp'" that clearly contradicts nature. Because Sontag explicitly references eight mottos by Oscar Wilde, she strengthens the historical ties between artificiality and homosexuality. Susan Sontag, "Notes on 'Camp,'" in *Against Interpretation and Other Essays*, New York 1966, pp. 275–92.

10 In a critical assessment of Sontag's definition of camp aesthetic, Juliane Rebentisch points out in her discussion of Jack Smith's aesthetic that it is above all the animal dimension of the diva that indicates nature in history. She thus opposes the almost naturalized relationship between homosexuality and artificiality. Juliane Rebentisch, "Über eine materialistische Seite von Camp. Naturgeschichte bei Jack Smith," *Zeitschrift für Medienwissenschaft* 8, no. 1 (2013), p. 166.

11 Dietze 2013 (see note 5), pp. 175–76.

beziehungsweise wilhelminischen Epoche befreite und hierfür selbstethnisierte.[11] Hier geht es nicht um die Emanzipation auf Kosten eines anderen. Denn – so fragt das Bild – wem würde denn durch den Federschmuck zu einem gleichgestellten Selbst verholfen? Lässt sich hier etwas Wesenhaftes herausschälen, das als politisches Subjekt das Recht auf Gleichheit beansprucht? Oder handelt es sich nicht vielleicht um die Verweigerung eines solchen Subjektbegriffs? Befinden wir uns nicht vielmehr in einem Übergangsraum, einem Zwischenraum, aus dem heraus nicht zuletzt ein Kunstbegriff generiert wird, der, anders als die Rezeption es will, gar nichts mehr mit dem Modernebegriff und all seinen Implikationen wie Künstlersubjekt, Originalität, Anti-Traditionalität zu tun hat?

Kea Wienand konstatiert in Bezug auf Rainer Fettings nahezu zehn Jahre später entstandene „Indianerbilder“[12], dass sie das Zitathafte ausstellen und in diesem Zusammenhang die Konstruktionsweisen rassistischer und heterosexistischer Stereotypen verhandeln würden.[13] Anders als die „Indianerromantik“, die das Nachkriegsdeutschland erfasst hatte, seien sie nicht im Sinne eines Begehrens entstanden, sich von der nationalsozialistischen Schuld zu befreien. Als eine solche Wiedergutmachungsfantasie hatte Katrin Sieg das „Indianerbild“ nach 1945 bewertet.[14] Es diente der Verlagerung des nationalsozialistischen Genozids in die USA und konnte außerdem als Lieferant von Naturnähe deutsche Tugenden wieder in die Mitte der Aufmerksamkeit stellen.[15] Fettings Gemälde seien jedoch – anders als zum Beispiel Beuys' Kojoten-Performance – nicht mythisch aufgeladen, sondern spielerisch und überdreht. Als Übertreibung suggerieren sie nicht Authentizität,

11 Dietze 2013 (wie Anm. 5), S. 175ff.

12 Hier sei angemerkt, dass diese Bilder auf den mit Luciano Castelli 1982 gedrehten Super-8-Film *Room Full of Mirrors* zurückgehen. In Rückgriff auf Matthias Liebel beschreibt Kea Wienand den Film folgendermaßen: „[D]ie beiden Künstler [filmten sich] selbst in der Rolle jeweils eines ‚Indianers‘. Castelli hatte dafür seinen gesamten Körper rot, Fetting seinen – wie in seiner später gemalten Selbstdarstellung – blau eingefärbt. Auch die im ‚Selbstporträt eines Indianer‘ [sic!] erkennbaren gelben Striche im Gesicht der Figur entsprechen seiner filmischen Verkleidung. Die Handlung des Films entwickelt sich nicht als kontinuierliche Abfolge, sondern einzelne Szenen wurden ähnlich einer Collage aneinandergereiht. Dabei wird ein Plot erkennbar, der klassische ‚Indianerfilme‘ nachstellt.“ Kea Wienand, *Nach dem Primitivismus? Künstlerische Verhandlungen kultureller Differenz in der Bundesrepublik Deutschland, 1960–1990. Eine postkoloniale Relektüre*, Bielefeld 2015, S. 238.

13 Ebd., S. 238–250.

14 Sieg 2002 (wie Anm. 6).

15 Hartmut Lutz, *„Indianer“ und „Native Americans“. Zur sozial- und literaturhistorischen Vermittlung eines Stereotyps*, Hildesheim 1985; Hartmut Lutz, „German Indianthusiasm. A Socially Constructed German National(ist) Myth“, in: Colin G. Calloway u. a. (Hg.), *Germans and Indians. Fantasies, Encounters, Projections*, Lincoln 2002, S. 167–184.

claims the right to equality? Or is it instead the rejection of such a concept of the subject? Aren't we in fact in a transitional, intermediate space from which, not least, a concept of art is generated that, unlike what its reception seeks, no longer has anything to do with the concept of modernity and all its implications, such as the artist as subject, originality, and anti-traditionalism?

With regard to Rainer Fetting's "Indian paintings"[12] made almost ten years later, Kea Wienand points out that they openly allude to and, in this context, negotiate the manner in which racist and heterosexist stereotypes are constructed.[13] Unlike the "Indian romanticism" that had gripped postwar Germany, they were not made based on the desire to free oneself from National Socialist guilt. Katrin Sieg describes the "image of the Indian" after 1945 as such a reparation fantasy,[14] serving to shift the National Socialist genocide to the United States and, by providing a closeness to nature, once again place the focus on German virtues.[15] However, Fetting's paintings—unlike Joseph Beuys's coyote performance, for example—are not mythically charged but playful and overwrought. As exaggerations they do not suggest authenticity but expose stereotypical projections,[16] one of which was that of the virile masculinity of the "Indians" in the nineteenth century.[17] By crossing his figures of "Indians" with the history of representing homosexual masculinity, and by integrating postures into the

12 It must be noted that these pictures go back to the Super-8 film *Room Full of Mirrors* shot with Luciano Castelli in 1982. Making recourse to Matthias Liebel, Kea Wienand describes the film as follows: "[T]he two artists [filmed] themselves each in the role of an 'Indian.' Castelli painted his entire body red, Fetting his—like in a portrait he painted later—blue. The yellow lines in the face of the figure discernible in 'Selbstporträt eines Indianer' [*sic*] also correspond with his costume in the film. The plot does not evolve as a continuous sequence, individual scenes were instead stringed together like a collage, in which the plot becomes recognizable as an imitation of classical 'Indian movies.'" Kea Wienand, *Nach dem Primitivismus? Künstlerische Verhandlungen kultureller Differenz in der Bundesrepublik Deutschland, 1960–1990. Eine postkoloniale Relektüre,* Bielefeld 2015, p. 238.

13 Ibid., pp. 238–50.

14 Sieg 2002 (see note 6).

15 Hartmut Lutz, *"Indianer" und "Native Americans". Zur sozial- und literaturhistorischen Vermittlung eines Stereotyps*, Hildesheim 1985; Hartmut Lutz, "German Indianthusiasm: A Socially Constructed German National(ist) Myth," in *Germans and Indians: Fantasies, Encounters, Projections,* ed. Colin G. Calloway et al., Lincoln, NE 2002, pp. 167–84.

16 Wienand 2015 (see note 12), p. 250.

17 Julie Schimmel, "Inventing the Indian," in *The West as America: Rethinking Images of the Frontier, 1820–1920,* ed. Nancy K. Anderson et al., exh. cat. National Museum of American Art, Washington, DC 1991, pp. 149–89.

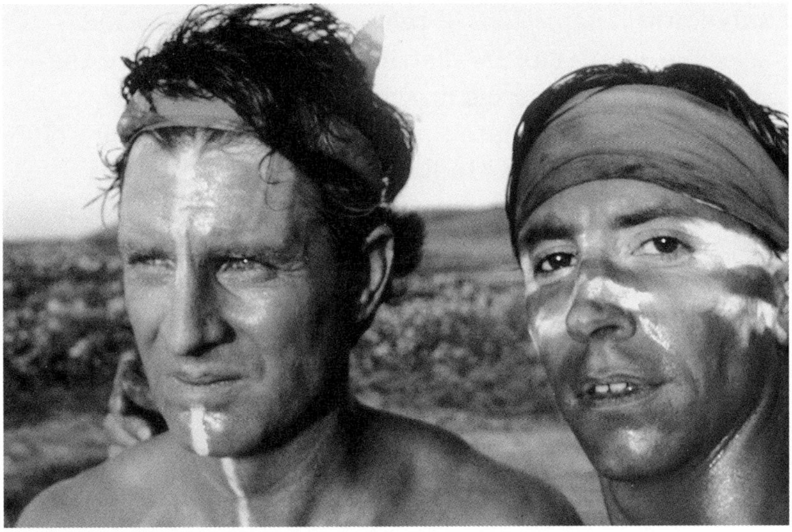

Luciano Castelli, Rainer Fetting, *Room Full of Mirrors*, 1982
Filmstill / still, Super 8, 33:50 Min.

sondern lassen die stereotypen Projektionen aufscheinen.[16] Eine solche Projektion stellte im 19. Jahrhundert die virile Männlichkeit von „Indianern“ dar.[17] Indem Fetting seine „Indianer“-Figuren mit der Darstellungsgeschichte schwuler Männlichkeit kreuzt und Körperhaltungen in das Sujet subkultureller Darstellungen der sogenannten Homo-Presse und populärkultureller Bildwelten der Jugendkultur einpflegt, widersetzt er sich der Vorstellung des „Indianers“ als Prototyp heroischer maskuliner Männlichkeit. Er gliedert seine Aneignung nicht in die geschlechternormative Aneignungsgeschichte des Bildes des „Indianers“ ein, sondern produziert eine Irritation, die Spekulationen darüber anstößt, ob hier die Homosexualität des Künstlers ins Bild gebracht würde oder die Homoerotik der indigenen Kulturen Nordamerikas. Insofern Letztere im Kontext der westlichen Kulturgeschichte der Imagination weißer Überlegenheit diente,[18] ist wichtig zu betonen, dass die Sichtbarmachung des Ersteren für eine Verschiebung in der hegemonialen Visualisierung des „Indianers“ sorgt. Homosexualität, die hier auf Bilder und Medienpraktiken des gelebten schwulen Alltags

16 Wienand 2015 (wie Anm. 12), S. 250.

17 Julie Schimmel, „Inventing the Indian“, in: Nancy K. Anderson u. a. (Hg.), *The West as America*, Ausst.-Kat. National Museum of American Art, Washington, D.C. 1991, S. 149–189.

18 Lutz 1985 (wie Anm. 15); Sieg 2002 (wie Anm. 6); Susanne Zantop, „Close Encounters: Deutsche und Indianer“, in: Calloway u. a. 2002 (wie Anm. 15), S. 3–14.

subject of sub-cultural depictions of the so-called gay press and the pop imagery of youth culture, Fetting defies the notion of the "Indian" as a prototype of heroic masculine virility. He does not inscribe his appropriation into the gender-normative history of appropriating the image of the "Indian," but instead produces a confusion that gives rise to speculations about whether what is depicted is the homosexuality of the artist or the homoeroticism of North America's indigenous cultures. Insofar as the latter served the imagination of white superiority in the context of Western cultural history,[18] it is important to stress that the visualization of the former prompts a shift in the hegemonic visualization of the "Indian." Homosexuality, which in this case draws from images and media practices of lived gay everyday life, in other words, producing, dealing with, and trading amateur photographs and semiofficial mail-order booklets, or the repurposing of hetero-sexual press organs such as the physique magazines of the 1950s or *Playgirl* from 1973 onward, forms the concrete horizon of experience in Fetting's paintings, thus transforming the stereotyping of the "Indian" detached from everyday knowledge.

The case is a bit different in Castelli's self-portrait (p. 160). Castelli does not fall back on the experiential horizon of gay identity or homosexual practices. Catering to the aesthetic of drag queens and terrorist drags,[19] he stages himself not as a gay man but as a self-proclaimed hetero trans. The intention of the queers at the time was not to perfectly imitate femininity but to stage themselves as an inherently ambiguous sex so as to undermine gender norms.[20] For example, beards were not shaven despite the drag, or fake breasts were exposed—such as here in a photograph of the artist Salomé.

Looking at Castelli's flat breast in drag reveals that ambiguity was to be created—regardless of sexuality. So one could say that the cited "Indian image" loses even more of its truthfulness due to the incongruence of image and reality with respect to sexuality. Queerness that has the effect of exposing the gender

18 Lutz 1985 (see note 15); Sieg 2002 (see note 6); Susanne Zantop, "Close Encounters: Deutsche und Indianer," in Calloway et al. 2002 (see note 15), pp. 3–14.

19 José Esteban Muñoz, "'The White to Be Angry': Vaginal Davis's Terrorist Drag," in "Queer Transexions of Race, Nation, and Gender," special issue, *Social Text* 52/53 (Fall/Winter 1997), pp. 80–103.

20 Volker Woltersdorff, "'All those beautiful boyz ... and criminal queers' – Vom Erbe der Terrortunten," in *Rosa Radikale: Die Schwulenbewegung der 1970er Jahre*, ed. Andreas Pretzel and Volker Weiß, Hamburg 2012, p. 224.

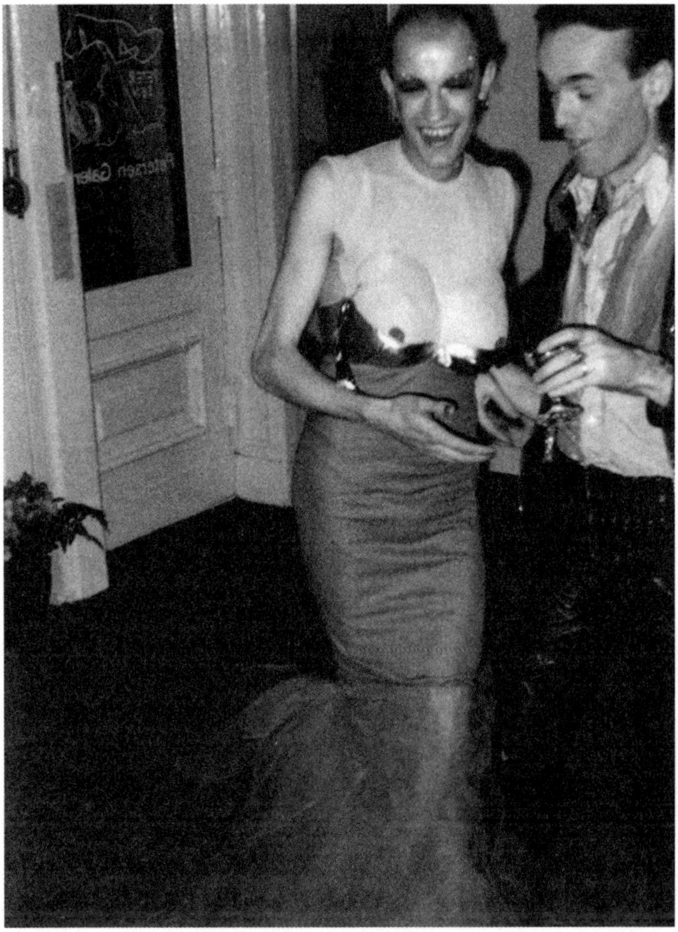

Salomé und / and Jürgen Klauke, Galerie Petersen, Berlin, 1977

zurückgreift, also das Selbermachen, Handeln oder Tauschen von Amateurfotografien und halboffiziellen Mail-Order-Heften beziehungsweise das Umnutzen von heterosexuellen Presseorganen wie Physique-Magazinen aus den 1950er-Jahren oder *Playgirl* ab 1973, stellt den konkreten Erfahrungshorizont der Bilder Fettings dar und transformiert daher die vom Alltagswissen entbundenen Stereotypisierungen des „Indianers“.

Bei Castellis Selbstporträt (Abb. S. 160) verhält es sich ein bisschen anders. Castelli greift nicht auf einen Erfahrungshorizont schwuler Identität oder homosexueller Praktiken zurück. Die Ästhetik der Fummeltrinen und Terrortunten bedienend, inszeniert sich Castelli nicht als schwuler Mann, sondern als selbsternannte Hetero-Transe. Das Ansinnen der Tunten dieser Zeit war es, Weiblichkeit nicht perfekt

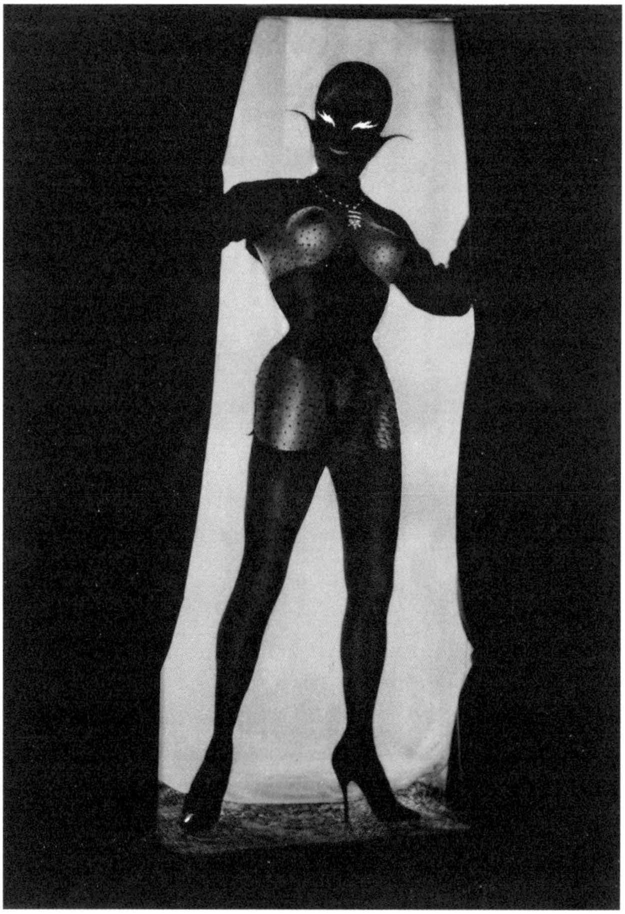

Pierre Molinier, *Le Chaman, planche 1 du Chaman*, 1967/68
Vintage-Silbergelatinedruck / vintage gelatin silver print,
20 × 13 cm

stereotype of the "Indian" as a construction is intensified to such a degree that there is no longer a representational relationship between image and reality. The image is not the depiction of an original reality outside the picture. It only shows us the character of constructedness.

In a certain respect, Castelli stands in the tradition of Pierre Molinier and Jürgen Klauke, male heterosexual artists who offered themselves in drag as erotic objects to the gaze of the audience. One could say that travesty allows the male artist to present himself as an object of an erotic voyeurism that has rarely been realized in the history of Western European art. What distinguishes the presentation—and this brings us to the role of

zu imitieren, sondern als in sich uneindeutiges Geschlecht zu inszenieren, um Geschlechternormen zu unterlaufen.[19] So wurden Bärte trotz des Fummels, den man trug, nicht rasiert oder Brustimitate – wie in einer Fotografie, die den Künstler Salomé zeigt (Abb. S. 73) – ausgestellt.

Der Blick auf die flache Brust Castellis in Drag verrät, dass Uneindeutigkeiten geschaffen werden sollten – und das unabhängig von der Sexualität. Somit ließe sich behaupten, dass das zitierte „Indianerbild“ aufgrund der zwischen Bild und Realität nicht abgeglichenen Sexualität zusätzlich an Wahrheitsgehalt verliert. Queerness, die bewirkt, Geschlechterstereotype des „Indianers“ als Konstruktionen herauszustellen, potenziert sich insofern, als zwischen Bild und Realität kein Abbildungsverhältnis mehr herrscht. Das Bild ist nicht die Abbildung einer originären Realität außerhalb des Bildes. Es zeigt uns lediglich den Konstruktionscharakter auf.

Nun steht Luciano Castelli gewissermaßen in der Tradition von Pierre Molinier und Jürgen Klauke, männlicher heterosexueller Künstler also, die sich in Drag als erotische Objekte dem Auge des Publikums anboten. Travestie – so könnte gesagt werden – erlaubt die Selbstdarstellung des männlichen Künstlers als Objekt einer in der westeuropäischen Kunstgeschichte sehr selten umgesetzten erotischen Schaulust. Was die Darstellung unterscheidet – und hiermit komme ich auf die Rolle der Fotografie zu sprechen – ist die Frage nach dem Stellenwert der Fotografie im System der Künste.

Moliniers Gestaltungsvermögen zum Beispiel entspricht der subjektiven Fotografie der 1950er- und 60er-Jahre. Die subjektive Fotografie und die damit im Zusammenhang stehende subjektive Kreativität und Rezeption war die durchgängige Signatur einer ganzen Epoche.[20] Subjektivität artikulierte sich jedoch nicht nur durch Selbstdarstellung oder eine autoporträtistische Markierung schöpferischer Kreativität, sondern auch durch das technisch informierte Gestaltungsvermögen und die von Bedeutung befreite, also wieder abstrakte und surreale Form. Molinier fotografiert surrealistisch und entwirft einen der anatomischen „Korrektheit“ widersprechenden imaginären Körper. Er zerstückelt die Bilder seines Körpers in weiblichem Drag und montiert die Fragmente zu einer Collage, die die Zeichenhaftigkeit und somit Austauschbarkeit des weiblichen Körpers im fetischisierenden Blick zur Darstellung bringt.

19 Volker Woltersdorff, „‚All those beautiful boyz ... and criminal queers‘ – Vom Erbe der Terrortunten“, in: Andreas Pretzel und Volker Weiß (Hg.), *Rosa Radikale: Die Schwulenbewegung der 1970er Jahre,* Hamburg 2012, S. 224.

20 Wolfgang Kemp, *Theorie der Fotografie III. 1945–1980,* München 1983, S. 19.

photography—is the question pertaining to the status of photography within the system of the arts.

Molinier's creative skills, for example, correspond with the subjective photography of the 1950s and 1960s. Subjective photography and the attendant subjective creativity and reception were the hallmarks of an entire era.[21] However, subjectivity articulates itself not only through self-presentation or the marking of creativity through self-portraiture but also through technically informed creative skills and form freed from meaning—which thus becomes abstract and surreal again. Molinier shoots photos in a surrealistic style and projects an imaginary body that contradicts anatomical "correctness." He fragments the images of his body in female drag and assembles them into a collage that visualizes the semiotic character and thus the exchangeability of the female body under a fetishizing gaze.

Castelli's photography lacks not only surrealistic fragmentation but also expressive assertiveness aiming for technical perfection. One rather gets the impression as if it were a fleeting gaze, as if he had been stopped on his way to the toilet at a dance performance, quickly positioned against the wall, and photographed. The gaping mouth and wide-open eyes also give the impression that he is about to strike a pose. Photography appears here as a snapshot—or rather in the aesthetic of the snapshot. In this respect, it loses its claim to the artistic conceptuality and media-technological sophistication it had gained through subjective photography. At the same time, however, we learn that the self-portrait was made with a self-timer. Thus the technical effort to create this picture must have been greater than its aesthetic suggests. In a certain respect, a reflective relationship to the pose had to be established. Even if the shutter was released sooner than Castelli had planned, he must have thought about which picture section he wanted to show and which pose he wanted to strike. So photography is conducted here in the intermediate space between snapshot and art photography. In my view, this finds itself in an interesting interrelationship to the painting of the Neue Wilde.

Since its beginnings, photography has been determined by defining itself as either art, non-art, or anti-art. It has often been overlooked that, in this respect, photography contributed

21 Wolfgang Kemp, *Theorie der Fotografie,* vol. 3: *1945–1980,* Munich 1983, p. 19.

Nicht nur fehlt Castellis Fotografie die surrealistische Fragmentierung, sondern auch die auf technische Perfektion zielende Durchsetzung seines Ausdrucks. Eher erhält man den Eindruck, es handele sich um einen flüchtigen Blick, als wäre er bei einer Tanzveranstaltung auf dem Weg zur Toilette aufgehalten, schnell vor die Wand gestellt und abfotografiert worden. So auch wirken der offene Mund und die aufgerissenen Augen, als wäre er noch dabei, eine Pose einzunehmen. Fotografie erscheint hier als Schnappschuss – oder vielmehr in der Ästhetik des Schnappschusses. Insofern verliert sie ihren durch die subjektive Fotografie erlangten Anspruch auf das künstlerisch Konzeptionelle und medientechnisch Aufwendige. Gleichzeitig erfahren wir, dass es sich um ein mit Selbstauslöser hergestelltes Selbstporträt handelt. Der technische Aufwand, dieses Bild herzustellen, muss also größer gewesen sein, als die Ästhetik vermuten lässt. Zur Pose muss in gewisser Hinsicht ein reflektierendes Verhältnis erzeugt worden sein. Wenngleich der Selbstauslöser schneller ausgelöst haben mag, als Castelli dies plante, muss er dennoch darüber nachgedacht haben, welchen Bildausschnitt er zeigen, welche Körperhaltung er einnehmen möchte. Fotografie findet also im Zwischenraum von Schnappschuss- und Kunstfotografie statt. Mit der Malerei der Neuen Wilden steht dies meiner Meinung nach in einem interessanten Wechselverhältnis.

Die Fotografie ist seit ihren Anfängen davon bestimmt, sich als Kunst, Nicht-Kunst oder Anti-Kunst zu definieren. Dabei wurde oft übersehen, dass die Fotografie nicht unwesentlich der bildenden Kunst zu ihrer Bestimmung verholfen hat. So schreibt Peter Geimer, dass durch das Erscheinen der Fotografie die Malerei zu sich selbst, das heißt zu ihrer abstrakten Formgebung gekommen sei.[21] Da sich die Kapazität der Fotografie auf die Abbildung der Realität beschränken würde,[22] könne sich die Malerei von ihrem „zwanghaften Realismus“[23] befreien und zu ihrer „ästhetischen Autonomie“[24] zurückfinden.

Das erscheint bei den Berliner Neuen Wilden in vielerlei Hinsicht nicht stimmig. Aufgrund von Inszenierung, Übertreibung und Theatralität ist bei der Fotografie der Berliner Neuen Wilden kein authentisches, referenzielles Verhältnis zwischen Bild und Realität gegeben. Fotografie hält sich im Zwischenraum von Abbildung und Bildgebung auf. Gleichzeitig stellt der von den Neuen Wilden praktizierte

21 Peter Geimer, *Theorien der Fotografie zur Einführung*, Hamburg 2009, S. 173.

22 Wolfgang Kemp, *Theorie der Fotografie II. 1912–1945*, München 1979, S. 13.

23 André Bazin, „Ontologie des photographischen Bildes“, in: Robert Fischer (Hg.), *Was ist Film?*, Berlin 2004, S. 40.

24 Ebd., S. 40.

substantially to the visual arts finding their purpose and calling. Peter Geimer, for instance, states that through the emergence of photography painting found itself, meaning its abstract forming (*Formgebung*).[22] Since the capacity of photography, in his view, is limited to the depiction of reality,[23] painting can free itself from the "obsession with realism"[24] and find its way back to its "aesthetic autonomy."[25]

In many regards, this appears inconsistent in the case of the Berlin Neue Wilde. Due to its staging, exaggeration, and theatricality, there is no authentic, referential relationship between image and reality in their photography. It is situated in the intermediate space between depiction and imaging. At the same time, the recourse to figurative painting made by the Neue Wilde is not a commitment to realism. The expressive, provisional, and fleeting brushstroke denies figurativeness its "reality content." In this sense, I do not understand their painting as a distancing from a form of photography that merely vouches for reality, nor do I regard photography as a preliminary medium for the artistic program of painting. Instead, I contend that with the Berlin Neue Wilde artistic expression can be traced as media-indifferent. It doesn't matter which medium produces the image, only that the image is produced. Thus, the Berlin Neue Wilde can be classified differently in art-historical terms than has previously been the case. It has often been claimed that they dissociated themselves from the dominance of Conceptual and Minimal Art of the early postwar years by taking up the paintbrush. Diedrich Diederichsen, on the other hand, claims that if there was something that they opposed, it was the media art predominant in the 1970s.[26] I find both to be little plausible. Aren't they instead an example of "work on visual culture" that, rather than committing to the "self-reflective engagement with their medial conditions,"[27] addresses the issue of representation as a transmedial construction of images? Here is another related example.

22 Peter Geimer, *Theorien der Fotografie zur Einführung*, Hamburg 2009, p. 173.

23 Wolfgang Kemp, *Theorie der Fotografie*, vol. 2: *1912–1945*, Munich 1979, p. 13.

24 André Bazin, "The Ontology of the Photographic Image," *Film Quarterly* 13, no. 4 (Summer 1960), p. 7.

25 Ibid., p. 9.

26 Diedrich Diederichsen, "Im Kino onanierend," in Adriani, ed., 2003 (see note 4), pp. 170–80.

27 Juliane Rebentisch, *Theorien der Gegenwartskunst zur Einführung*, Hamburg 2017, pp. 150–51.

Rückgriff auf die figurative Malerei kein Bekenntnis zum Realismus dar. Der expressive, provisorische und flüchtige Pinselstrich verweigert dem Figürlichen seinen Realitätsgehalt. Insofern verstehe ich diese Malerei nicht als eine Absetzbewegung von der nur Realität verbürgenden Fotografie. Die Fotografie betrachte ich aber auch nicht als ein das künstlerische Programm der Malerei vorbereitendes Medium. Stattdessen möchte ich behaupten, dass sich bei den Berliner Neuen Wilden der künstlerische Ausdruck als medienindifferent nachzeichnen lässt. Es spielt keine Rolle, welches Medium das Bild hervorbringt, es spielt nur eine Rolle, dass Bilder entstehen. In diesem Sinne ließen sich die Berliner Neuen Wilden kunsthistorisch noch einmal anders einordnen, als bisher in der Rezeption geschehen. Oft wurde behauptet, sie hätten sich, indem sie zum Pinsel griffen, gegen die Dominanz von Konzeptkunst und Minimal Art der frühen Nachkriegszeit abgegrenzt. Diedrich Diederichsen hingegen meint, dass sie sich wenn, dann eher gegen die in den 1970er-Jahren dominante Medienkunst gewandt hätten.[25] Beides erscheint mir wenig plausibel. Sind sie nicht vielmehr Beispiel einer „Arbeit an der visuellen Kultur“, die, statt sich der „selbstreflexiven Auseinandersetzung mit ihren medialen Bedingungen“[26] zu widmen, die Frage der Repräsentation als eine der transmedialen Konstruktion von Bildern angeht? Dazu noch ein anderes Beispiel.

Exotische Terrortunten: Salomé als Geisha

In der 1981 auf dem 3. Internationalen Symposium für Performance-Art in Lyon präsentierten und als Video vorliegenden Performance *The Bitch and Her Dog* sind die Künstler Luciano Castelli und Salomé in einer jeweils anderen und dennoch das primitivistische Vokabular des Animalischen und Exotischen einlösenden Verkleidung zu sehen. Castelli als Inkarnation eines gefleckten Hundes wird von Salomé als Geisha an der Leine durch den öffentlichen Raum geführt. Die Performance erinnert an die legendäre Aktion *Aus der Mappe der Hundigkeit* von Valie Export und Peter Weibel. War es da die weiße Frau, die ihren Mann wie einen Hund an der Leine ausführte, um die Beziehung der Geschlechter als Herrschaftsspiel zu thematisieren, sind es hier Geisha und Dalmatiner, die auf ihre jeweils spezifische Domestizierungsgeschichte durch den Westen hinweisen. War der Dalmatiner während

25 Diedrich Diederichsen, „Im Kino onanierend“, in: Adriani 2003 (wie Anm. 4), S. 170–180.

26 Juliane Rebentisch, *Theorien der Gegenwartskunst zur Einführung*, Hamburg 2017, S. 150f.

Exotic Terrorist Drags: Salomé as Geisha

In the performance *The Bitch and Her Dog* presented in 1981 at the 3rd International Symposium of Performance Art in Lyon and available as a video, the artists Luciano Castelli and Salomé appear in different costumes that each in their own way adhere to the primitivistic vocabulary of the feral and exotic. Castelli as the incarnation of a spotted dog is led on a leash through public space by Salomé as a geisha. The performance is reminiscent of the legendary action *Aus der Mappe der Hundigkeit* (From the Underdog File) by Valie Export and Peter Weibel. While in that case it was a white woman walking her man like a dog on a leash to address gender relations as a game of domination, here it is a geisha and a Dalmatian that both refer to their specific histories of domestication by the West. While the Dalmatian was very popular as a carriage dog during the Victorian age, the geisha was an object of sexual desire up until the first half of the twentieth century. Without going into the geisha's (colonial) history (of appropriation) in more detail, what is striking is the encounter of two narratives, especially when calling to mind that the geisha in the performance is embodied by the gay artist Salomé.

His artist's name can be read as a reference to perhaps the most significant drama of Anglo-French decadence. It was written by Oscar Wilde, who was in prison when the play premiered in 1896, accused of same-sex intercourse. The figure of Salome allowed Wilde to reflect upon sexuality and gender beyond the limits of the bi-gender system and heteronormativity.[28] Moreover, Salome was increasingly viewed due to a cultural and historical mix-up as a transvestite.[29]

Salomé—as I would like to suggest—refers back through his very name to the drama's queer reception history. By performing as a geisha, he simultaneously integrates a far more complex constellation. It is not only that Salome's dance for Herod parallels the function of the geisha as the mysterious female entertainer of a male audience, but one can also discern a direct historical intertwining of the figures that is interesting in postcolonial terms

28 Renate Lorenz, *Queer Art: A Freak Theory*, Bielefeld 2012, p. 97.

29 The mix-up was caused by an alleged photographic depiction of Oscar Wilde that actually showed the singer Alice Guszalewicz dressed as Salome. Despite the successful correction that was made, the narrative of Salome as a transvestite prevailed. Ibid, pp. 96–97.

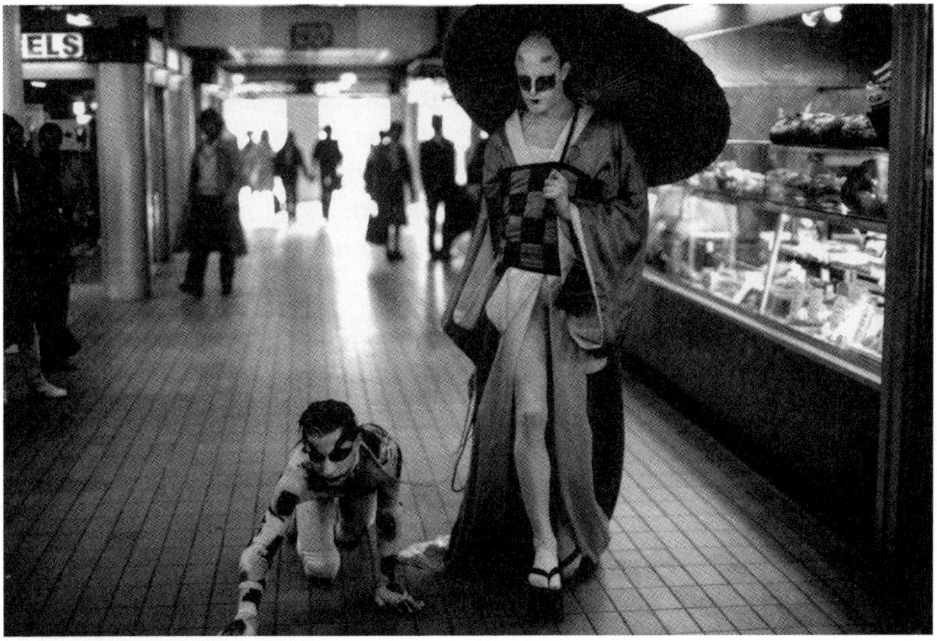

Salomé, Luciano Castelli, *The Bitch and Her Dog*, 1981
Filmstill / still, Video, 11:24 Min.

der viktorianischen Zeit als Kutschenbegleithund sehr populär, ist es die Geisha als Objekt der sexuellen Begierde bis in die erste Hälfte des 20. Jahrhunderts gewesen. Ohne auf die (koloniale Aneignungs-) Geschichte der Geisha genauer einzugehen, fällt das Aufeinandertreffen zweier Erzählungen auf, wenn wir uns vergegenwärtigen, dass die Geisha in der Performance durch den schwulen Künstler Salomé verkörpert wird.

Dessen Künstlername lässt sich als Referenz auf das wohl wichtigste Drama der anglo-französischen Décadence lesen. Geschrieben wurde es von Oscar Wilde, der zur Zeit der Erstaufführung 1896 im Gefängnis saß, weil ihm gleichgeschlechtlicher Sexualverkehr vorgeworfen wurde. Die Figur der Salome diente Wilde als Möglichkeit, über Sexualität und Geschlecht außerhalb von Zweigeschlechtlichkeit und Heteronormativität nachzudenken.[27] Hinzu kommt, dass Salome aufgrund einer Verwechslung kulturgeschichtlich zunehmend als Transvestitin betrachtet wurde.[28]

27 Renate Lorenz, *Queer Art. A Freak Theory*, Bielefeld 2012, S. 97.

28 Bei der Verwechslung ging es um eine vermeintliche fotografische Darstellung von Oscar Wilde, die eigentlich die Sängerin Alice Guszalewicz zeigte, verkleidet als Salome. Trotz erfolgreicher Richtigstellung setzte sich das Narrativ von Salome als Transvestitin durch. Lorenz 2012 (wie Anm. 27), S. 96f.

and relevant to the question of how Salomé's performance can be understood.

Loïe Fuller, an American dancer and filmmaker, became legendary in the early twentieth century for her dance of Salome, and made a name for herself with the lighting design of the veil. It was she who invited the actress Sadayakko, famous for her performance of Salome in Japan, to dance with her in Paris. As Jeanne Scheper formulates it, Fuller employed orientalism to underpin her connection to a modern future.[30] In Japan, Sadayakko actually represented a staging of Salome that followed Japanese traditions and took up attributes of the geisha. This changed when the younger Matsui Sumako was cast as Salome around 1914. According to Maho Hidaka, her performance, which was characterized by airy garments and more nudity, established a new, more liberated form of female eroticism in Japan.[31] Because this unveiling oriented toward Western codes made the play *Salome* popular in Japan at a time when theater was becoming hetero-normalized,[32] the question arises as to what it means when the artist Salomé stages himself as a geisha. At first, one could maintain that he, like Fuller, uses features of anachronistic femininity—meaning the veiled and premodern corporeality with heavy and opaque fabrics alluding to the performance of Sadayakko—as instruments to confirm himself as avant-garde. But that conceals the queer and temporally anticipating implication that the performance of Sadayakko already possessed. As a female performer of Salome, Sadayakko had chosen an aesthetic that went back to the history of representing the geisha on stage, traditionally played by a male imitating a woman. As a woman, she performed the performance of a man performing a woman. Salomé, in turn, who now, as a man, in a certain respect performs a woman imitating a man performing a woman, exaggerates this play to such a degree that no original is discernible anymore. All we have is a copy of a copy.

This aspect is repeated on another level when taking into account the indifference to the choice of media. The unique features of the aesthetic media no longer seem to matter, thus video,

30 Jeanne Scheper, *Moving Performances: Divas, Iconicity, and Remembering the Modern Stage*, New Brunswick, NJ 2016, pp. 67–72.

31 Maho Hidaka, "The Sexual Transfiguration of the Japanese Salomé, 1909–2009," in *Wilde's Other Worlds*, ed. Michael F. Davis and Petra Dierkes-Thrun, New York and London 2018.

32 Scheper 2016 (see note 30), pp. 70–72.

Salomé – so möchte ich hiermit nahelegen – rekurriert allein schon mittels seiner Namensgebung auf die queere Rezeptionsgeschichte des Dramas. Gleichzeitig flicht er mit der Performance als Geisha eine ungleich komplexere Konstellation ein. Nicht nur, dass Salomes Tanz für Herodes die Funktion der Geisha als mysteriöser weiblicher Unterhalterin eines männlichen Publikums parallelisiert, lässt sich eine direkte historische Verflechtung der Figuren feststellen, die in postkolonialer Hinsicht interessant und für die Frage relevant ist, wie Salomés Performance verstanden werden kann.

Loïe Fuller, eine US-amerikanische Tänzerin und Filmemacherin, war Anfang des 20. Jahrhunderts für den Tanz der Salome legendär und machte sich aufgrund der lichttechnischen Inszenierung des Schleiers einen Namen. Sie war es, die die für die Aufführung der Salome in Japan sehr bekannte Schauspielerin Sadayakko nach Paris einlud, um mit ihr zu tanzen. Fuller – so formuliert es Jeanne Scheper – nutzte Orientalismus, um ihren Bezug zum Futuristischen zu untermauern.[29] Tatsächlich stand Sadayakko in Japan für die eher an japanische Traditionen angelehnte und Attribute der Geisha aufgreifende Darstellung der Salome. Mit der Besetzung der jüngeren Matsui Sumako als Salome um 1914 änderte sich dies. Ihre sich durch luftige Gewänder und mehr Nacktheit auszeichnende Performance begründete laut Maho Hidaka in Japan eine neue, freiheitlichere Form weiblicher Erotik.[30] Insofern diese sich an westlichen Codes orientierende Enthüllung das Stück *Salome* in Japan zu einer Zeit populär werden ließ, als sich das Theater hetero-normalisierte,[31] steht die Frage nach der Bedeutung der Inszenierung des Künstlers Salomé als Geisha im Raum. Auf den ersten Blick ließe sich behaupten, er würde wie Fuller Merkmale anachronistischer Weiblichkeit – also die sich mit schweren und blickdichten Stoffen an die Performance von Sadayakko anlehnende, verhüllte und vormoderne Körperlichkeit – für die Selbstvergewisserung der eigenen Zugehörigkeit zur Avantgarde instrumentalisieren. Das verdeckt aber die queere und der Zeitlichkeit vorgreifende Implikation, die schon dem Spiel Sadayakkos eigen war. Diese hatte als weibliche Darstellerin der Salome eine Ästhetik gewählt, die auf die Darstellungsgeschichte der Geisha auf der Bühne zurückging, in der traditionell

29 Jeanne Scheper, *Moving Performances: Divas, Iconicity, and Remembering the Modern Stage,* New Brunswick u. a. 2016, S. 67ff.

30 Maho Hidaka, „The Sexual Transfiguration of the Japanese Salomé, 1909–2009“, in: Michael F. Davis und Petra Dierkes-Thrun (Hg.), *Wilde's Other Worlds,* New York und London 2018.

31 Scheper 2016 (wie Anm. 29), S. 70ff.

performance, photography, and painting become interchangeable. Motifs circulate across media; they are subjected to the technical reproducibility of photography and the hardly distinguishable painting cycles of Salomé. Much of it is original, but nothing is originary anymore. That is not a flaw—as one could read into the derogatory name “Neue Wilde”—but a quality of the Berlin Neue Wilde. To measure the artists of the Neue Wilde using concepts of modernism appears misleading, even though they extensively cite modernism. But this is done in a critical and, above all, queer fashion. Therefore, the significance of the Neue Wilde must be reassessed not only in the system of art but also in view of the history of a queer theory that since the early 1990s has been inspired by both everyday life and aesthetics.

ein männlicher Darsteller die Frau mimte. Sadayakko performte nun als Frau die Performance eines Mannes als Frau. Salomé wiederum, der nun gewissermaßen als Mann die Frau performt, die den eine Frau performenden Mann nachahmt, überdreht dieses Spiel dermaßen, dass kein Original mehr erkennbar ist. Es gibt nur noch die Kopie von der Kopie.

Dieser Aspekt wiederholt sich auf einer anderen Ebene, bedenkt man die Indifferenz gegenüber der Medienwahl. Die Eigenheiten der ästhetischen Medien scheinen keine Rolle mehr zu spielen, weswegen Video, Performance, Fotografie und Malerei austauschbar werden. Motive zirkulieren über die Medien hinweg, werden der technischen Reproduzierbarkeit der Fotografie gleichermaßen unterworfen wie den sich kaum unterscheidenden Malzyklen Salomés. Vieles ist originell, nichts mehr originär. Das ist nicht – wie es sich mit der Namensgebung „Neue Wilde“ mitlesen lässt – ein Makel, sondern eine Qualität der Berliner Neuen Wilden. Sie an den Maßstäben der Begriffe der Moderne zu messen, erscheint irreführend, wenngleich die Moderne von ihnen üppig zitiert wird. Jedoch wird sie dies auf eine kritische Weise – und vor allem auf eine queere. Die Bedeutung der Neuen Wilden ist daher nicht nur innerhalb des Systems Kunst neu zu bewerten, sondern auch für die Geschichte einer sich vom Alltag, aber auch von der Ästhetik inspirieren lassenden queeren Theorie seit Anfang der 1990er-Jahre.

Christian Höller
While the Guinea Fowl Gently Weeps
Über Maler-Musik und Künstler-Bands, 1979–1984

Christian Höller
While the Guinea Fowl Gently Weeps
On Painters' Music and Artists' Bands, 1979–1984

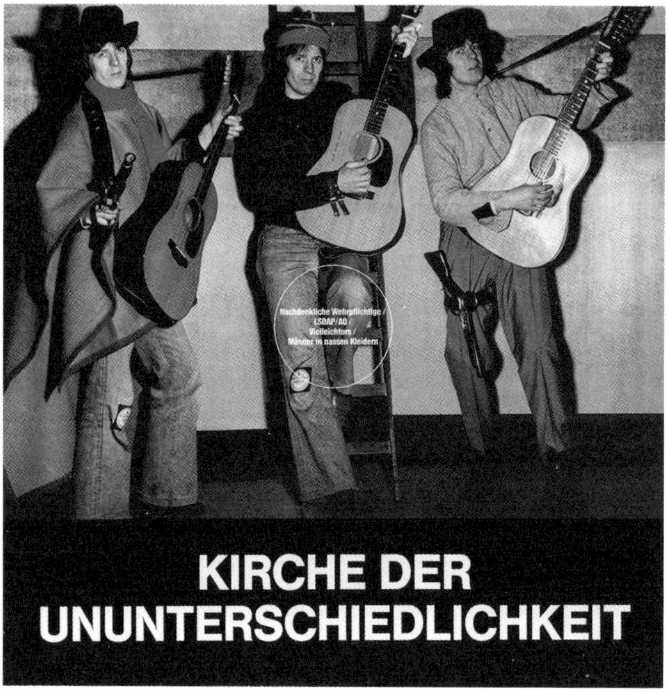

Nachdenkliche Wehrpflichtige, LSDAP/AO, Vielleichtors, Männer in nassen Kleidern, ***Kirche der Ununterschiedlichkeit,*** 1982
Doppel-LP / double LP, ZickZack Platten

Dass gegen Ende der 1970er-Jahre, mit dem Aufkommen von Post-Punk in der Musik und der neuen Wertschätzung für abseitige, „abjekte" Materien in der Kunst, ein weites Feld von Wechselwirkungen eröffnet wurde, mag heute weithin bekannt sein. Wie es um diese Wechselwirkungen genau bestellt war, ist hingegen immer noch fraglich. Handelte es sich bei den zahlreichen Künstler*innen, die damals mit dem Musikmachen begannen, in erster Linie um in Richtung Pop drängende Milieuwechsler? Oder waren Kunst- und Musikmachen auf ein und derselben Ebene, ja innerhalb eines gemeinsamen, verbindenden Horizonts angesiedelt? Vielfach scheint es, als hätten viele, auch aus dem Umfeld der neuen wilden Malerei stammende Künstler*innen die Musik als einen verlängerten Arm der Kunst betrachtet. Ja mehr noch: Als seien die damals initiierten Musikprojekte mehr von den vielerorts erkannten Gemeinsamkeiten zwischen Kunst und Musik ausgegangen als von einer ominösen Eigenlogik der einzelnen Felder. Oder davon, dass man diese Eigenlogiken nach Möglichkeit – mit allem, was zur Verfügung stand – unterlaufen wollte. Inwiefern die „Maler-Musik" beziehungsweise die vielen Künstler-Bands der damaligen Zeit tatsächlich derlei Subversion praktizierten, soll im Folgenden anhand einiger ausgewählter Musikprojekte besprochen werden.

Einer, der Aspekte der Gegenwartsmusik ebenso in sein bildnerisches Werk einfließen ließ wie er umgekehrt aus diesem ein verqueres Musikschaffen speiste – eines, das nicht groß vorhatte, in Pop- oder Avantgardezirkeln zu reüssieren –, war Martin Kippenberger. Künstler wie Kippenberger oder parallel zu ihm Maler wie Albert Oehlen beziehungsweise Walter Dahn wurden nicht deshalb musikalisch aktiv, weil sie „echten" Bands Paroli bieten wollten, auch nicht, um ein klandestines „Doppelleben" zu führen,[1] sondern um ganz selbstverständlich Haltungen, Ideen und künstlerische Parameter zwischen den Feldern auszutauschen oder „bereichsfremde" Testläufe damit zu veranstalten. So war jedenfalls Kippenbergers erstes Bandprojekt namens Luxus stark von künstlerischen Kriterien der damaligen Zeit geprägt. Appropriation, „Deskilling", ein Faible für anti-ästhetisches Dilettieren, dazu das provokante Ausagieren von bewussten Geschmacksverfehlungen – all das lässt sich an den vier Stücken der 1979 erschienenen Doppel-7"-Single der Gruppe Luxus ablesen.[2] Die Achse New York-Berlin spielte dabei eine nicht unwesentliche Rolle: Kippenberger hatte

1 *Doppelleben. Bildende Künstler_innen machen Musik* ist der Titel einer aktuellen groß angelegten Themenausstellung im mumok Wien, die den Verbindungen zwischen Kunst und Musik quer durch das 20. Jahrhundert nachgeht; vgl. doppelleben.mumok.at/de/ (abgerufen am 11.09.2018).

While it may be widely known today that, toward the end of the 1970s, the advent of post-punk in music and the new appreciation of odd and "abject" materials in visual art opened up a broad field of interaction, it still remains unclear exactly how this interaction was structured. Were the numerous artists who started playing music at the time pressing for a change in milieu, primarily in a pop direction? Or was making art and making music on the same level, situated on a common, unifying horizon? It often seems as if many artists, including the circle of Neue Wilde painting, regarded music as an extension of art. Indeed, moreover, as if the music projects initiated at that time were based more on the widely perceived commonalities between art and music rather than on an ominous logic inherent to the individual fields, or on a desire to subvert these logics—using everything at one's disposal. To what extent the "painters' music" of the many artist bands of that time actually practiced such subversion will be explored here using a few selected music projects as examples.

One artist who incorporated aspects of contemporary music into his visual work that, conversely, fed back into his twisted musical creations—someone who was not seeking success in either pop or avant-garde circles—was Martin Kippenberger. Artists such as Kippenberger or, concurrently, painters like Albert Oehlen and Walter Dahn didn't become active musicians because they wanted to pit themselves against "real" bands or lead a clandestine "double life,"[1] but rather to quite naturally exchange attitudes, ideas, and artistic parameters between the fields, or to use them to conduct test runs "alien" to the respective field. At any rate, Kippenberger's first band project named Luxus was strongly influenced by the artistic criteria of the times. Appropriation, deskilling, a preference for anti-aesthetic dilettantism, along with the provocative acting out of deliberate transgressions against good taste, can all be found on the four tracks of the double 7″ single by Luxus from 1979.[2] The New York–Berlin axis played a crucial role here: Kippenberger had just opened Kippenbergers Büro, a sort of Factory, and was co-proprietor of the music club

1 *Doppelleben. Bildende Künstler_innen machen Musik* (Double Lives: Visual Artists Making Music) is the title of a current large-scale thematic exhibition at mumok in Vienna retracing the connections between art and music throughout the twentieth century; see https://www.mumok.at/en/events/double-lives.

2 On Kippenberger's music projects, see the compilation *Martin Kippenberger – Musik 1979–1995*, Berlin 2010, and the texts in the accompanying booklet.

zu dem Zeitpunkt in Berlin gerade „Kippenbergers Büro“, eine Art Factory, eröffnet und war Ko-Betreiber des Musikclubs S.O.36 geworden, als er den New Yorker No-Wave-Filmemacher Eric Mitchell und die Musikerin Christine Hahn – sie spielte unter anderem in Glenn Brancas Band The Static – kennenlernte. Gemeinsam nahmen sie im April 1979 die besagte Doppelsingle auf, die eingepackt in ein selbst hergestelltes sechsseitiges Heftchen erschien (Abb. S. 220–221). Wie abgeschmackt und streitbar-witzelnd das Ensemble agierte, lässt sich gleich am ersten Stück, *New York-Auschwitz*, ermessen. Zu Straßenlärm hört man Gesprächsfetzen, in denen genussvoll deutsch-amerikanische Sprachbarrieren und gewollte Missverständnisse ausgekostet werden: „[Kippenberger:] Die Hose. Lederhose. – [Hahn:] Lederhose? – [K:] Mein Arsch schwitzt. – [H:] Auschwitz?“ Im Stück *Love Song* wird mit gepresster Stimme a cappella stur die Zeile „Can't Buy Me Love“ wiederholt (die gezielte Beatles-Verunstaltung hat Eric Mitchell im Alleingang aufgenommen). Dagegen geht es in *Pretty Good* instrumental – zackig-schrummelnd – schon heftiger zur Sache – das aus heutiger Sicht wohl dauerhafteste Stück der EP. Schließlich wird am Ende, in *Falsch verbunden,* noch das Kinderlied *Alle meine Entchen* zerschrammt.

Kippenberger, der mit dieser Formation – später gehörte ihr auch noch sein S.O.36-Kompagnon Achim Schächtele an – mehrfach auftrat, sah im Musikmachen zweifellos eine Art verlängerten Arm seiner Malerei. Keinen Schauplatzwechsel oder eine abgekoppelte Parallelaktion, sondern vielmehr ein Ausagieren von Motorik, Show-gehabe und nicht zuletzt unverhohlener Peinlichkeit, wie sie auch seine Malerei kennzeichneten. Als selbstverständlicher „Teil der künstlerischen Produktion“ war die Musik ebenso „wie die Einladungskarten, Plakate und Kataloge“[3] – und Kippenberger sollte in unterschiedlichen Ensembles mit diversen stilistischen Vorlieben von Jazz bis Schlager immer wieder darauf zurückkommen – den übrigen Bereichen seiner Arbeit weder vor- noch nachgeordnet. „Genuss und Ausbau der eigenen Entfremdung und [deren] Umlenkung in eine Stärke“[4], wie dieser Modus der Selbstaufspaltung in vielfältige Experimentierstadien treffend genannt wurde, fanden sich zeitgleich auch bei vielen anderen Maler*innen/Musiker*innen. Mag deren künstlerische Priorität auch im visuellen Medium gelegen haben (oder

2 Zu Kippenbergers Musikprojekten vgl. die Compilation *Martin Kippenberger – Musik 1979–1995,* Edition Kröthenhayn, Berlin 2010, beziehungsweise die im begleitenden Booklet enthaltenen Beiträge.

3 Susanne Kippenberger, *Kippenberger. Der Künstler und seine Familien,* Berlin 2007, S. 174.

S.O.36 in Berlin when he met the New York-based No Wave filmmaker Eric Mitchell and the musician Christine Hahn, who played in Glenn Branca's band The Static, among others. They recorded the double single in April 1979 and released it packaged in a six-page self-produced booklet (figs. pp. 220–221). The first piece, "New York – Auschwitz," already demonstrates the tasteless and pugnaciously joking manner in which the ensemble performed. Accompanied by street noise, one hears fragments of a conversation delighting in the barriers between the German and American languages and deliberate misunderstandings: "[Kippenberger:] Die Hose. Lederhose.—[Hahn:] Lederhose?—[K:] Mein Arsch schwitzt [My ass sweats].—[H:] Auschwitz?" In "Love Song," the line "Can't buy me love" is obstinately repeated in a strained voice (Eric Mitchell recorded the deliberate Beatles defacement alone). The snappily strummed instrumental "Pretty Good," on the other hand, is quite powerful and is probably the piece from the EP that stands up best today. The last track, "Falsch verbunden" (Wrong Number), shreds the German children's song "Alle meine Entchen" (All My Little Ducklings).

Kippenberger, who appeared several times with this formation that later included his S.O.36 partner Achim Schächtele, undoubtedly regarded making music as a kind of extension of his painting. Neither a change of scene nor a detached parallel endeavor, but rather an act of motor skills, showmanship, and not least flagrant embarrassment, which also characterized his painting. As a natural "part of artistic production," music, "like the invitation cards, posters, and catalogues"[3]—and Kippenberger returned to music again and again in different ensembles with diverse stylistic preferences, from jazz to the cheesy pop of Schlager—was neither super- nor subordinate to his other fields of activity. "Relishing and pursuing one's own alienation and turning it into a strength,"[4] as this mode of self-fragmentation into diverse stages of experimentation was aptly described, could

3 Susanne Kippenberger, *Kippenberger. Der Künstler und seine Familien*, Berlin 2007, p. 174.

4 Diedrich Diederichsen, "'Selbstdarsteller': Martin Kippenberger between 1977 and 1983," in *Nach Kippenberger*, ed. Eva Meyer-Hermann and Susanne Neuburger, exh. cat. Museum Moderner Kunst Stiftung Ludwig Wien, Vienna 2003, p. 57. It is telling that in the first, highly extensive article on the Neue Deutsche Welle (New German Wave) published by the music magazine *Sounds*, Alfred Hilsberg mentioned the "notorious self-promoter Kippenberger already known from Hamburg"; see "Aus grauer Städte Mauern" (parts 1 to 3), *Sounds*, October/November/December 1979.

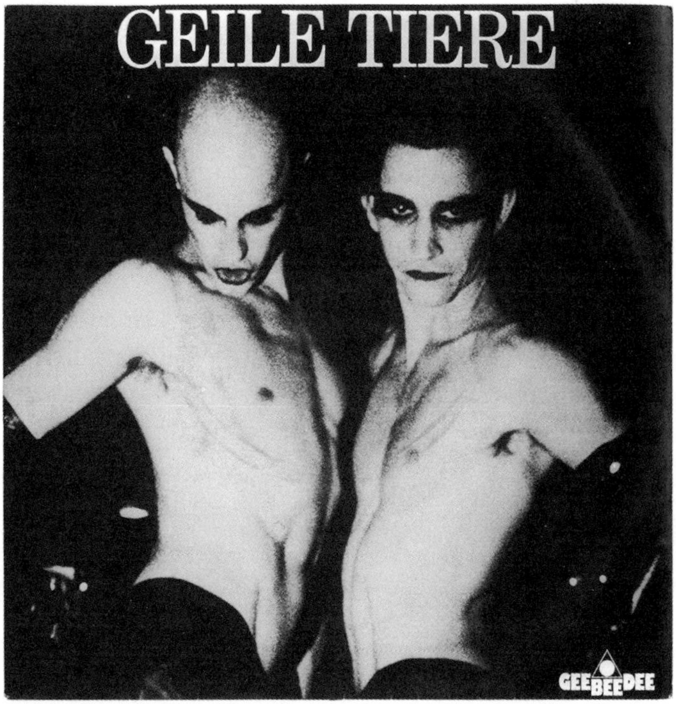

Geile Tiere, *Geile Tiere*, 1982
Single, GeeBeeDee

sich mit der Zeit einseitig darin verfestigt haben), so bewegten sich Malerei und Musik in den Jahren 1979 bis 1984 größtenteils auf ein und derselben Ebene – oder vielleicht besser: innerhalb eines gemeinsamen Horizonts, in dem gezielte Drastik, konfrontative Haltung und unverhohlene Antivirtuosität als Teil einer selbstermächtigenden Praxis mehr als jede Medien- oder Materialspezifik dominierten.

Jedenfalls lässt sich das Austauschverhältnis, in dem Mal- und Musikpraxis im deutschen Post-Punk-Kontext standen, an vielerlei Bandprojekten der Zeit ablesen: an Der Plan etwa (dessen Bühnendekorationen und Coverbilder häufig die an Milan Kunc erinnernden Großformate des Bandgründers Moritz Reichelt bildeten), am Electronic-Duo Geile Tiere, das die beiden Berliner „Wilden" Salomé

4 Diedrich Diederichsen, „Der Selbstdarsteller. Martin Kippenberger zwischen 1977 und 1983", in: Eva Meyer-Hermann und Susanne Neuburger (Hg.), *Nach Kippenberger*, Ausst.-Kat. Museum Moderner Kunst Stiftung Ludwig Wien, Wien 2003, S. 56. Bezeichnend ist, dass bereits in der ersten, äußerst eindrücklichen „Neue Deutsche Welle"-Reportage von Alfred Hilsberg im Musikmagazin *Sounds* von dem „auch schon von Hamburg her berüchtigte[n] Selbstdarsteller Kippenberger" die Rede ist. Vgl. „Aus grauer Städte Mauern" (Teil 1 bis 3), in: *Sounds*, Oktober/November/Dezember 1979.

simultaneously be found with other painters/musicians. Even if their artistic priority was placed on the visual medium (or it unilaterally consolidated as such over time), between 1979 and 1984 painting and music mostly operated on the same level, or perhaps better, within a common horizon that was dominated more by targeted exaggeration, a confrontational stance, and blatant anti-virtuosity as components of a self-empowering praxis than by any media- or material-specificity.

Be that as it may, the relationship of exchange, in which the praxis of painting and making music stood in the German post-punk context, can be discerned in many band projects at the time, with examples including Der Plan (whose stage decorations and album covers were often the large formats, reminiscent of Milan Kunc, painted by band founder Moritz Reichelt); the electronic duo Geile Tiere (Horny Animals) founded by the two Berlin-based Wilde artists Salomé (Wolfgang Ludwig Cihlarz) and Luciano Castelli; the band Freiwillige Selbstkontrolle (F.S.K., Voluntary Self-Regulation) that originated in the context of the Akademie der bildenden Künste in Munich; or Minus Delta t, the performance group initiated as early as 1978 in Düsseldorf, for whom music (if it can be called that) was one component among many others (and whose painting, if it was that at all, was carried out in situ on stage mainly with tar, feathers, and similar materials).[5]

Churchgoers and Soldiers

In Hamburg, the group Nachdenkliche Wehrpflichtige (Pensive Conscripts) was formed in 1980 around Diedrich Diederichsen, then editor of the music magazine *Sounds*, and Albert Oehlen, a student at the Hochschule für bildende Künste. Original members of the group were Frieder Butzmann and Bettina Köster, later a member of Mania D. and Malaria!, as well as F.M. Einheit, who also played with Abwärts (Downwards) and joined Einstürzende Neubauten (Collapsing New Buildings) a short while later. Oehlen's painting for the cover of their EP *Politik für junge Leute* (Politics for Young People, 1980) indicated the kind of confrontation they

5 On the artistic background of these (and other) groups, see the now canonic oral history by Jürgen Teipel, *Verschwende deine Jugend,* Frankfurt am Main 2001, and the associated exhibition *Zurück zum Beton. Die Anfänge von Punk und New Wave in Deutschland 1977–'82* (Back to Concrete: The Beginnings of Punk and New Wave in German 1977–'82), Kunsthalle Düsseldorf, July – September 2002.

(Wolfgang Ludwig Cihlarz) und Luciano Castelli gegründet hatten, an der Band Freiwillige Selbstkontrolle (F.S.K.), die im Umfeld der Münchner Akademie der bildenden Künste entstanden war, oder an Minus Delta t, der bereits 1978 in Düsseldorf initiierten Perfomance-Gruppe, für die Musik (wenn man sie so nennen konnte) ein Bestandteil unter vielen war (und die Malerei, wenn sie das überhaupt noch war, vorwiegend mit Teer und Federn oder ähnlichen Materialien in situ auf der Bühne praktizierte).[5]

Kirchgänger und Soldaten

In Hamburg hatte sich 1980 rund um Diedrich Diederichsen, damals Redakteur bei der Musikzeitschrift *Sounds*, und Albert Oehlen, Student an der Hochschule für bildende Künste, die Formation Nachdenkliche Wehrpflichtige zusammengefunden. Anfangs gehörte der Gruppe neben Frieder Butzmann und Bettina Köster, später bei Mania D. und Malaria!, auch FM Einheit an, der gleichzeitig auch Mitglied von Abwärts war und kurze Zeit später bei den Einstürzenden Neubauten einsteigen sollte. Oehlens Malerei für das Cover der Wehrpflichtigen-EP *Politik für junge Leute* (1980) deutete an, auf welche Art von Konfrontation man mit dieser Form des Musikmachens aus war: Man sieht eine fetzig hingemalte, verschmitzt lachende Gruppe Soldaten, die den Betrachter*innen gleichsam aus dem Bild heraus ihre Stiefel entgegenstreckt. Einziger Farbtupfer in dem fahrigen Schwarz-Weiß-Bild ist ein rotes „Y“, das in grafischer Mimikry den Titel der 1979 erschienenen ersten LP der englischen Band The Pop Group zitiert.

Die mit drei Saxofonen operierende Gruppe macht sich auf den fünf Stücken der EP an einem Mix aus Schlagern, Soldaten-, Fußballer- und Arbeiterliedern (*Hundert Mann und ein Befehl, Er steht im Tor, Arbeitereinheitsfrontlied*) zu schaffen – und atmet damit jenen Geist dezidierter Disharmonie, der auf populärem Allgemeingut aufbaut, dieses aber mit den verfügbaren musikalischen Mitteln weitestmöglich gegen den Strich bürstet. Wie Oehlen dieses Prinzip später einmal für seine Malerei formulierte: „Bilder sollen nicht authentisch sein, sondern taktisch richtig.“[6] Wobei das taktisch Richtige hier darin bestand, vor

5 Zum künstlerischen Background dieser (und anderer) Gruppen vgl. die inzwischen kanonische *Oral History* von Jürgen Teipel, *Verschwende deine Jugend*, Frankfurt am Main 2001 sowie die daran anknüpfende Ausstellung *Zurück zum Beton. Die Anfänge von Punk und New Wave in Deutschland 1977–'82*, Kunsthalle Düsseldorf, Juli bis September 2002.

6 Zit. n. Jutta Koether, „Schlimme Zeiten sind immer zu lang. Werner Büttner und Albert Oehlen“, in: *Spex*, 11, November 1983, S. 29.

were seeking with this form of music-making: it shows a wildly painted group of mischievously smiling soldiers stretching their boots toward the viewer. The only element of color in the erratic black-and-white painting is a red *Y* graphically mimicking the title of the first album of the British band The Pop Group from 1979.

The group featuring three saxophones tackles a mix of Schlager and soldiers', footballers', and workers' songs on the five-track EP ("Hundert Mann und ein Befehl" [One Hundred Men And One Command], "Er steht im Tor" [He's A Goalkeeper], "Arbeitereinheitsfrontlied" [Workers' United Front Song]), and in doing so breathes the spirit of decisive disharmony that builds upon popular common property, but brushes it against the grain as vehemently as possible with the musical means at hand. As Oehlen later formulated this principle for his painting, "Pictures should not be authentic, but tactically correct."[6] In this case, tactical correctness consisted in countering mainstream musical tastes in terms of gesture and attitude—without completely severing the reference to the "popular" (or what was deemed as such).

A similar underlying concept can be found in the record project *Kirche der Ununterschiedlichkeit* (Church of Non-Differentiation, 1982), a double album with one side each by Nachdenkliche Wehrpflichtige, the formation LSDAP/AO,[7] Vielleichtors (Perhaps Gates; the band project of Markus Oehlen), and Männer in nassen Kleidern (Men in Wet Clothes; Albert Oehlen and Bettina Semmer). "Meine Lehrzeit in und außerhalb der Masse ist gründlich gewesen, meine Meinungen habe ich nicht irgendwo aufgelesen" (My apprenticeship inside and outside the masses was thorough, I didn't pick up my opinions from just anywhere), are the first words by Diederichsen in the recitative "Svengali Joe" that reveals a musical makeover of Wehrpflichtige, complemented by his brother Detlef Diederichsen playing "real" guitar. Diederichsen "recites" an excerpt from the memoires of the director Josef von Sternberg accompanied by a relaxed, funky beat that for more than ten minutes loses nothing of its self-assured calmness.

6 Cited in Jutta Koether, "Schlimme Zeiten sind immer zu lang. Werner Büttner und Albert Oehlen," *Spex*, no. 11, November 1983, p. 29.

7 The name merges LSD with NSDAP (National Socialist German Workers' Party), adding AO (Aufbauorganisation, or Establishing Organization) taken from the 1970s German Maoist party KPD/AO.

allem gestisch beziehungsweise haltungsmäßig weit verbreiteten musikalischen Vorlieben entgegenzutreten – ohne den Bezug zum „Populären“ (oder was man dafür hielt) vollends zu kappen.

Ein ähnliches Konzept verfolgte das Plattenprojekt *Kirche der Ununterschiedlichkeit* (1982) – eine Doppel-LP, auf der neben den Nachdenklichen Wehrpflichtigen die Formationen LSDAP/AO, Vielleichtors (das Bandprojekt von Markus Oehlen) und Männer in nassen Kleidern (Albert Oehlen und Bettina Semmer) je eine Plattenseite füllen. „Meine Lehrzeit in und außerhalb der Masse ist gründlich gewesen, meine Meinungen habe ich nicht irgendwo aufgelesen“, heißt es eingangs in dem von Diederichsen vorgetragenen Rezitativ des Stückes *Svengali Joe,* für das die Wehrpflichtigen ein musikalisches *makeover,* ergänzt um den „wirklich“ Gitarre spielenden Bruder Detlef Diederichsen, erfahren haben. Diederichsen „sprechsingt“ einen Auszug aus den Memoiren des Regisseurs Josef von Sternberg, unterlegt von einem relaxt-funkigen Beat, der mehr als zehn Minuten lang nichts von seiner selbstbewussten Entspanntheit einbüßt.

Seite zwei wird von der Wehrpflichtigen-Splittergruppe LSDAP/AO (unter anderem ergänzt um Heiner Goebbels, Markus Oehlen und Rotraut Pape) mit einem Live-Mitschnitt aus dem Hamburger Dankerrt (1981) bestritten. Neben einer mit vielen Bläsern aufgestockten Coverversion des Blues-Klassikers *Tobacco Road* findet sich hier unter anderem auch ein Retake des Soft-Machine-Songs *Dedicated to You But You Weren't Listening.* Die „Ununterschiedlichkeit“ des LP-Titels, sprich das augenzwinkernde Zelebrieren von Nicht-Differenz, zeigt sich hier darin, dass historisch Entlegenes, so disparat es auf Anhieb scheinen mag, auf ein gemeinsames affirmativ-feierliches Plateau gehievt wird – was in der Coverversion von *Dedicated to You* durch die besondere Art der Textmontage bewerkstelligt wird: „Links, links, links, die Trommeln werden gerührt“, heißt es zu Beginn, und am Ende „Kameraden, erkämpft euch die Macht!“ So endet der Originaltext des Liedes *Der rote Wedding,* 1929 verfasst von Erich Weinert in Reaktion auf die gewalttätige Unterbindung des kommunistischen Maiaufmarsches. In der Version von LSDAP/AO wird dieses Fundstück mit der Melodie von Soft Machines *Dedicated to You* gekoppelt (überwiegend a cappella). Hier kommt jene Brückenfunktion zum Tragen, von der gute Popsongs zumeist geprägt sind, die in ihrer Wirkung stets ein wenig über sich „hinausschießen“ beziehungsweise auf etwas anderes, jenseits ihrer selbst Liegendes hin verlinkt sind.

Albert Oehlens Wirken an Saxofon, Violine und Xylofon zieht sich gleich über drei Plattenseiten von *Kirche der Ununterschiedlichkeit.*

Side two features a live recording of the Wehrpflichtige splinter group LSDAP/AO (with Heiner Goebbels, Markus Oehlen, and Rotraut Pape, among others) at Dankerrt in Hamburg (1981). Alongside a cover version of the blues classic "Tobacco Road" augmented by an array of horns, there is also a cover of the Soft Machine song "Dedicated To You But You Weren't Listening." The "Non-Differentiation" of the LP title, in other words, the tongue-in-cheek celebration of non-difference, shows itself in the elevation of historically remote things, as disparate as they may appear at first sight, to a common, affirmative-celebratory plateau—achieved in the cover version of "Dedicated To You" by a special kind of text montage that starts with "Links, links, links, die Trommeln werden gerührt" (Left, left, left, the drums are being beaten) and ends with "Kameraden, erkämpft euch die Macht!" (Comrades, struggle for power!), the original lyrics of the song "Der rote Wedding" (Red Wedding) written by Erich Weinert in 1929 in response to the violent suppression of the communist May Day demonstrations. In the version by LSDAP/AO, this relic is combined with the melody of Soft Machine's "Dedicated To You" (predominantly sung a cappella). The bridge that typically characterizes a good pop song comes into play here, the effect of which is to slightly "overreach" itself and establish a link to something lying beyond it.

Albert Oehlen plays saxophone, violin, and xylophone on three of the four sides of *Kirche der Ununterschiedlichkeit*, with his anti-individualistic albeit "solo-esque" style most prominent on Männer in nassen Kleidern's side. The hallmark of the tracks recorded with Bettina Semmer—leaning heavily toward noise or rhythm improvisation—is the choice of ironic, pun-like titles such as "Eine Frau, die Karate kann, hat keine Chance gegen einen Mann mit einem Wagenheber von einem Toyota" (A Woman Who Can Do Karate Doesn't Stand A Chance Against A Man With A Jack From A Toyota) or "Als hätte man mir die Muschel ausgedreht" (As If Someone Had Screwed Off My Shell). The duo scrapes and scrubs and trumpets on instruments not necessarily made for this purpose, always seeking to create a rhythmic tension that unfolds its appeal precisely in the way it simply spews forth. In the end, there is a spoken-word piece featuring Werner Büttner's strained theatrical voice—"Strenge ohne Liebe" (Severity Without Love), a parable on the mercilessness of the world, accompanied by ominous keyboard and xylophone swells. Oehlen's

Dabei kommt sein anti-individualistischer, wiewohl „solo-esker“ Gestus am stärksten auf der LP-Seite von Männern in nassen Kleidern zum Tragen. Markenzeichen der stark in Richtung Noise- beziehungsweise Rhythmus-Improvisation gehenden, gemeinsam mit Bettina Semmer aufgenommenen Stücke sind ironisch-kalauerhafte Titel wie *Eine Frau, die Karate kann, hat keine Chance gegen einen Mann mit einem Wagenheber von einem Toyota* oder *Als hätte man mir die Muschel ausgedreht*. Dazu schabt und schrubbt und trötet das Duo auf allerlei nicht unbedingt dafür gemachten Instrumenten herum, stets um rhythmische Spannung bemüht, die gerade in ihrer legeren Hingerotztheit ihren Reiz entfaltet. Am Ende gibt es noch ein von Werner Büttner mit gepresster Theaterstimme vorgetragenes Sprechstück – *Strenge ohne Liebe*, eine Parabel auf die Unbarmherzigkeit der Welt, untermalt von unheilvollen Keyboard- und Xylofon-Schwaden. Oehlens damals geäußertes Credo, dass „das Destruktive Konsumierbarkeit [verhindere], aber nicht den Markterfolg“[7], trieb hier bereits pittoreske Blüten. Und wiewohl diesem Musikmachen erwartungsgemäß kein kommerzieller Erfolg beschieden sein sollte, war hier doch der Gestus des Sich-um-jeden-Preis-behaupten-Wollens (wenn es sein muss auch auf dem Kunstmarkt, wie dies später bekanntlich der Fall sein sollte) mit Nachdruck artikuliert.[8]

Wie sich herausstellte, fand das unkultiviert Hässliche und betont „Fehlfarbene“ von Oehlens frühen Bildern bald schon höchst positive Resonanz. Jutta Koether brachte dies in einer frühen Besprechung auf den Punkt, wobei sie eine gewisse Latenz des Unverdaulichen nicht in Abrede stellte: „Der unappetitliche Geschmack mag verschwunden sein, mit den Hässlichkeiten versöhnt man sich einige Tage später, auch wenn es – tief im Bauch – leise gärt und brodelt, da gewisse Rückstände

7 Ebd.

8 Dies sollte sich in den ab 1984 gemeinsam mit Martin Kippenberger verfolgten Musikprojekten wie The Alma Band, Weiß und Doof oder The Knowhow Knockers fortsetzen. 1987 fand das bewusste Verwirrspiel um Identitäten und Stil-Aneignungen Ausdruck in der LP *The Golden Kot Quartett*, worauf Swing-Jazz, eingespielt von einer Gruppe rund um Rüdiger Carl, zu hören ist, wohingegen sich Oehlen und Kippenberger gemeinsam mit Günther Förg und Hubert Kiecol als die vermeintlich echten Musiker ausgaben. Oehlen war zu Beginn der 1990er-Jahre kurzzeitig Mitglied der dritten Reinkarnation von The Red Krayola und Mitte der 1990er Teil von Jailhouse (zusammen mit Rüdiger Carl und seinem Bruder Markus Oehlen), bevor er, erneut mit seinem Bruder Markus, das Projekt Van Oehlen startete. Deren CDs *We Are Eggsperienced* (1998) und *Rock and Roll Is Here to Die* (2003) bürsteten Jazz- und Rock-Vorlagen bewusst gegen den Strich des inzwischen elektronisch Möglichen. Weitere Gemeinschaftsprojekte von Oehlen waren Titankatzen, Euphrat und Tigris beziehungsweise in jüngerer Zeit Luke & Wendy, die 2017 eine Hommage an den kurz zuvor verstorbenen Künstler, Musiker und Filmemacher Tony Conrad herausbrachten.

credo at the time, that "destructiveness [prevents] consumability but not market success,"[8] yielded picturesque effects here. And although this type of music making was, expectably, not commercially successful, it resolutely articulated the gesture of self-assertion at any price (if need be, on the art market, as was later famously the case).[9]

It turned out that the uncultivated ugliness and emphatic "erroneous colors" of Oehlen's early paintings soon met a highly positive response. This was summed up by Jutta Koether in an early review, while not denying a certain latency of the indigestible: "The unappetizing taste may have disappeared, days later one is reconciled with the ugliness, even if—deep in one's gut—it continues to seethe and bubble because certain residues again join forces."[10] Precisely this confrontational joining of forces played a key role in Oehlen's painting as well as in his diverse music projects—the apodictically rendered, basically cacophonic impetus that sought to undermine any tonal balance, (acoustic-)color harmony, or formal consistency.[11] The extent to which this principle took effect in the following years is already demonstrated by exhibition titles such as *Die Feinde unserer Feinde sind auch unsere Feinde* (The Enemies of Our Enemies Are Also Our Enemies, Galerie Rudolf Zwirner, Cologne, 1983) or the motto borrowed from the British post-punk band Blurt, *My Mother Was a Friend of the Enemy of the People* (Galerie Peter Pakesch, Vienna, 1984).

8 Koether 1983 (see note 6).

9 This was continued from 1984 with Martin Kippenberger in music projects such as The Alma Band, Weiß und Doof, or The Knowhow Knockers. In 1987, the deliberate confusion regarding identities and stylistic appropriations was expressed in the album *The Golden Kot Quartett,* featuring swing jazz played by a group headed by Rüdiger Carl, while Oehlen and Kippenberger along with Günther Förg and Hubert Kiecol posed as the real musicians. In the early 1990s, Oehlen was briefly a member of the third reincarnation of The Red Krayola, and in the mid-1990s a member of Jailhouse (with Rüdiger Carl and his brother Markus Oehlen), before launching the project Van Oehlen, again with his brother Markus. Their CDs *We Are Eggsperienced* (1998) and *Rock and Roll Is Here to Die* (2003) consciously brushed against the grain of jazz and rock templates with what was then possible electronically. Other joint projects by Oehlen include Titankatzen, Euphrat und Tigris, and, more recently, Luke & Wendy, who in 2017 released an homage to the recently deceased artist, musician, and filmmaker Tony Conrad.

10 Koether 1983 (see note 6).

11 Diedrich Diederichsen also emphasizes the common foundation of music and painting in the German post-punk context; see "Intensität – Negation – Klartext," in *Zurück zum Beton. Die Anfänge von Punk und New Wave in Deutschland 1977–'82,* ed. Ulrike Groos et al., exh. cat. Kunsthalle Düsseldorf, Cologne 2002, esp. pp. 143–44.

erneut Front machen.“[9] Genau dieses Frontmachen war dasjenige, was in Oehlens Malerei und seinen diversen Musikprojekten gleichermaßen zentral am Werk war – als jener apodiktisch vorgetragene, vom Ansatz her kakophone Impetus, der jede tonale Balance, (klang-)farbliche Harmonie und formelle Stimmigkeit zu unterlaufen trachtete.[10] Wie sehr dieses Prinzip in den folgenden Jahren zum Tragen kommen sollte, zeigen allein schon Ausstellungstitel wie *Die Feinde unserer Feinde sind auch unsere Feinde* (Galerie Rudolf Zwirner, Köln, 1983) oder das von der britischen Post-Punk-Band Blurt entlehnte Motto *My Mother Was a Friend of the Enemy of the People* (Galerie Peter Pakesch, Wien, 1984).

Perlhühner und Hornissen

Alberts Bruder Markus Oehlen hatte zum Zeitpunkt von *Kirche der Ununterschiedlichkeit* schon eine ungleich bewegtere Musikvergangenheit hinter sich. Er war 1978 bei der Ad-hoc-Formation Deutschland Terzett für die „Trommlung“ zuständig und fungierte danach bei der bahnbrechenden Punkband Mittagspause als Schlagzeuger, die zwei Singles herausbrachte (1979), die heute noch als Meilensteine gelten. Danach verfolgte Markus Oehlen verschiedene Musikprojekte zumeist solo oder in wechselnder Mini-Besetzung. Mit den Vielleichtors, wo er neben Schlagzeug auch Gitarre und Keyboards spielte, erging er sich in schleppenden, bisweilen wild aus der Spur mäandernden New-Wave-Grooves. Auf *Kirche der Ununterschiedlichkeit* bestechen die Vielleichtors durch ihre beherzt in Kauf genommene Schwerfälligkeit, punktiert von bewusst kruden Track-Titeln wie „Fantasie in Alkohol“, „Sauaas“ oder „Do you fick?“. Oehlens Vielleichtors waren 1981 auch auf dem programmatischen Sampler *Lieber zuviel als zuwenig* des Hamburger ZickZack-Labels vertreten und gehörten zu jener Riege deutscher „Happy New Wave“-Bands, die der Tausendsassa Xaõ Seffcheque auf seiner Fake-Compilation *Sehr gut kommt sehr gut* (1981) parodierte. *Bring deinen Körper auf die Party, etwas anderes hast du nicht,* so der entsprechende Titel, setzte – ironischerweise – ein schlagkräftiges Funk-Ausrufezeichen und erging sich in jener Groove-

9 Koether 1983 (wie Anm. 6).

10 Die gemeinsame Basis von Musik und Malerei im deutschen Post-Punk-Kontext betont auch Diedrich Diederichsen, „Intensität – Negation – Klartext“, in: Ulrike Groos, Peter Gorschlüter und Jürgen Teipel (Hg.), *Zurück zum Beton. Die Anfänge von Punk und New Wave in Deutschland 1977–’82,* Ausst.-Kat. Kunsthalle Düsseldorf, Köln 2002, vor allem S. 143f.

Guinea Fowl and Hornets

Albert's brother Markus Oehlen could already look back on a far more eventful musical past at the time when *Kirche der Ununterschiedlichkeit* was released. In 1978, he was responsible for the "drumming" in the ad hoc formation Deutschland Terzett (Germany Trio) and was then the drummer of the groundbreaking punk band Mittagspause (Lunch Break) that released a double 7″ and a single (1979), which are still considered milestones today. Markus Oehlen subsequently pursued various music projects, usually solo or with alternating small ensembles. The Vielleichtors, with whom he played guitar and keyboard in addition to drums, performed sluggish, at times wildly meandering new-wave grooves. On *Kirche der Ununterschiedlichkeit,* the Vielleichtors captivate with their boldly sustained ponderousness, punctuated by deliberately crude track titles such as "Fantasie in Alkohol" (Fantasy in Alcohol), "Sauaas" (Bitch), or "Do You Fick?" In 1981, Oehlen's Vielleichtors were also included on the programmatic sampler *Lieber Zuviel Als Zuwenig* (Better Too Much Than Too Little) from the Hamburg-based ZickZack label, and featured among the German "Happy New Wave" bands that the jack-of-all-trades Xaõ Seffcheque parodied on his fake compilation *Sehr gut kommt sehr gut* (Very Good, Sounds Very Good, 1981). "Bring Deinen Körper Auf Die Party!" (Bring Your Body To The Party!), the fitting title, ironically set a powerfully funky exclamation mark and followed the groove blueprint from US disco funk that was to significantly rattle the post-punk scene. It was so successful in this that it was later included in the repertoire of Seffcheque and Peter Hein's band Family 5, which, however, had little to do with the Vielleichtors anymore. At any rate, Markus Oehlen's penchant for cross-stylistic multi-instrumentalism, alternately on keyboards, drums, and various guitars, was also expressed in his participation in the all-star projects LSDAP/AO and The Flying Klassenfeind (The Flying Class Enemy), active from 1981, following after Nachdenkliche Wehrpflichtige.[12]

12 In 1985, Markus Oehlen released his first single recorded entirely by himself, "Beer Is Enough," which was followed by further solo releases under the pseudonym Don Hobby (1998), and the electronic composition *Wanne 4* (2015). As "Kurt Striebe," he and Werner Büttner (alias Ferdinant Fux) recorded the LP *Lousy days are here to stay* (1987).

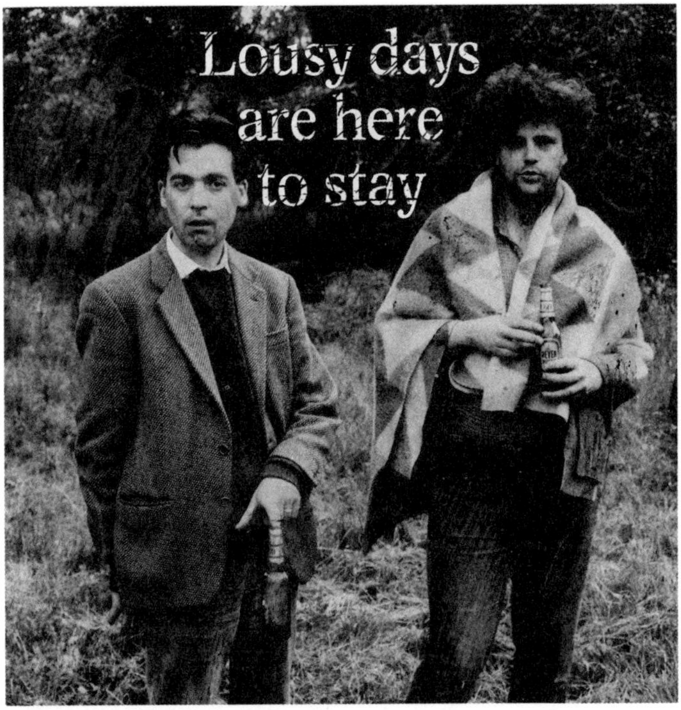

Ferdinant Fux, Kurt Striebe [Werner Büttner, Markus Oehlen],
***Lousy days are here to stay*, 1987**
LP, Hurrah Records, Design: Martin Kippenberger

Blaupause, die damals – vom US-Discofunk herkommend – großräumig die Post-Punk-Szene aufmischen sollte. So gut, dass das Stück später im Repertoire von Seffcheques und Peter Heins Family 5 landete, was allerdings mit den Vielleichtors nichts mehr zu tun hatte. Jedenfalls bekundete sich Markus Oehlens Hang zum stilübergreifenden Multi-Instrumentalismus, mal an den Keyboards, mal am Schlagzeug, mal an diversen Gitarren, auch in seiner Beteiligung an den All-Star-Projekten LSDAP/AO oder The Flying Klassenfeind, die ab 1981 im Gefolge der Nachdenklichen Wehrpflichtigen aktiv waren.[11]

The Flying Klassenfeind entstanden, wie Diedrich Diederichsen erklärt, aus der Idee, Coverversionen von im Post-Punk-Umfeld nur spärlich präsenten Sixties- und Seventies-Bands zu spielen, und zwar mit möglichst vielen des Gitarrenspiels nicht unbedingt mächtigen

11 Markus Oehlen brachte 1985 mit *Beer Is Enough* seine erste komplett im Alleingang eingespielte Single heraus, der später in unregelmäßigen Abständen unter dem Pseudonym Don Hobby (1998) oder mit der Electronic-Komposition *Wanne 4* (2015) weitere Solo-Releases folgen sollten. Als „Kurt Striebe" nahm er gemeinsam mit Werner Büttner (alias Ferdinant Fux) die LP *Lousy days are here to stay* (1987) auf.

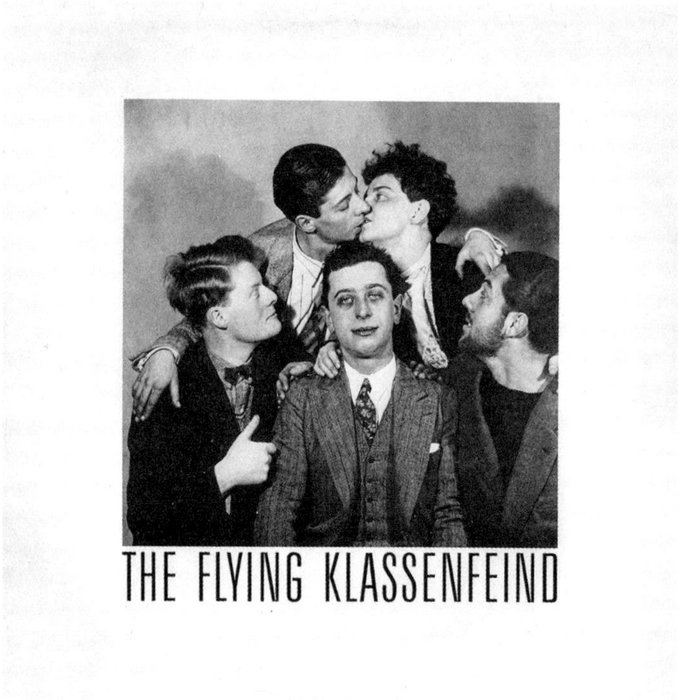

The Flying Klassenfeind, *The Flying Klassenfeind*, 1982
Mini-LP, Line Records

As Diedrich Diederichsen explains, The Flying Klassenfeind originated from the idea of playing cover versions of bands from the 1960s and 1970s that were then barely present in the post-punk scene, with as many guitarists, and not necessarily strong ones, as possible.[13] The band name was itself a combination of The Flying Burrito Brothers (one of the country rock bands covered) and the affronting SozArt (Socialist Art) or Bolshevik chic that had crucially determined the para-musical approach of Nachdenkliche Wehrpflichtige. And that is just how the four tracks of the mini-LP released in 1982 sound—as if in a meeting of the Central Committee taking much too long and involving too much vodka the members suddenly began to furtively sing pop pearls by the Western class enemy. The self-composed "Ulan Bator," however, does stand out: a list of Asian and African city names embedded in a swirling vortex that condenses into an increasingly hypnotic,

13 See the conversation with Diedrich Diederichsen in this volume, pp. 251–267.

Gitarristen.[12] Der Bandname allein ist ein Verschnitt aus Flying Burrito Brothers (dem Namen einer der gecoverten Country-Rock-Bands) und jener möglichst vor den Kopf stoßenden SozArt- beziehungsweise Bolshevik-Chic-Attitüde, die schon den paramusikalischen Wehrpflichtigen-Ansatz zentral bestimmt hatte. Und genau so klingen auch die vier Tracks der 1982 veröffentlichten Mini-LP, nämlich als seien im ZK nach einer zu langen Sitzung und zu viel Wodka plötzlich heimlich Pop-Perlen des westlichen Klassenfeinds angestimmt worden. Wobei die Eigenkomposition *Ulan Bator* aus dem Repertoire heraussticht: Eine Aufzählung von asiatischen und afrikanischen Städtenamen verdichtet sich, in einen malstromartigen Wirbel eingebunden, zu einem immer hypnotischeren, post-psychedelischen Chant, der vom Anspruch her weltumspannend sein will. Noch besser auf den Punkt kommt diese Global-Groove-Ambition in der Bearbeitung, die unter dem Titel *Ulan Bator Dub* auf dem 1982 veröffentlichten Cassetten-Sampler *Klar und wahr – Sounds rettet Deutschland* enthalten ist: Darin wird, gewissermaßen *avant la lettre*, ein wahrer „ocean of sound“[13] entfacht und in all seiner Aufgewühltheit souverän gebändigt. Aber hier war die Kunst, zumal die Malerei, als Sprungbrett in Richtung Musik nicht mehr wirklich maßgeblich; Ansätze wie der von The Flying Klassenfeind zeigten sich stärker von einem erweiterten Sound- und Musikgeschichtsverständnis geprägt als die zeitgleich anhebenden Versuche einer dezidierten „Maler-Musik“.

Diesbezüglich lässt sich nicht nur für Hamburg, sondern auch für Düsseldorf, Köln, München, Berlin und anderswo ein spezifisches Naheverhältnis zwischen Post-Punk und der ab 1980 aufkeimenden „wilden“ Malerei attestieren. Vielfach waren dies externe Beziehungen – beispielhaft repräsentiert etwa von Imi Knoebels kongenialem Coverbild für die Platte *Pst* (1980) der Gruppe S.Y.P.H., eine LP, auf der alle Musikalität zu einer Frage des Gestischen wird, so wie dies auch Knoebels Malerei knappestmöglich zur Schau stellt. Oder man denke an die durchaus humorigen Malereien von Jiří Georg Dokoupil für die Releases der Gruppe The Wirtschaftswunder, in der sein Bruder Tom Dokoupil zugange war. Mit Tom Dokoupil, der auch als „Siluetes 61“ firmierte, nahm Walter Dahn 1981 die Platte *La Freiheit des Geistes* auf, veröffentlicht unter dem Bandnamen Die Partei. Dahn hatte 1980 gemeinsam mit der Malergruppe Mülheimer Freiheit

12 Vgl. das Gespräch mit Diedrich Diederichsen im vorliegenden Katalog, S. 251–267.

13 Vgl. David Toop, *Ocean of Sound. Aether Talk, Ambient Sound and Imaginary Worlds*, London 1995.

post-psychedelic chant with pretensions of globality. This global groove ambition is encapsulated even better on the remix entitled "Ulan Bator Dub" on the cassette sampler *Klar und wahr – Sounds rettet Deutschland* (Clear and True—*Sounds* Saves Germany) of 1982: it gives rise, avant la lettre, as it were, to a true "ocean of sound"[14] that is masterfully tamed in all its turbulence. But in this case, art, especially painting, was no longer really decisive anymore as a springboard to music; approaches like those taken by The Flying Klassenfeind were more influenced by an expanded understanding of the history of sound and music than by the contemporaneous attempts at a determined "painters' music."

In this respect, one can find a uniquely close relationship between post-punk and the burgeoning "wild" painting after 1980, not only in Hamburg but also in Düsseldorf, Cologne, Munich, Berlin, and elsewhere. These were, in many cases, external relationships—exemplarily represented by Imi Knoebel's congenial cover image for the album *Pst* (1980) by the group S.Y.P.H., on which all musicality is reduced to a question of gestures, demonstrated most succinctly by Knoebel's painting. Or the indeed humorous paintings of Jiří Georg Dokoupil for the releases of the group The Wirtschaftswunder (The Economic Miracle), in which his brother Tom Dokoupil played. With Tom Dokoupil, who also performed as Siluetes 61, Walter Dahn recorded the record *La Freiheit des Geistes* (La Freedom of the Mind) in 1981, released under the name Die Partei (The Party). In 1980, Dahn had exhibited with the painters' group Mülheimer Freiheit at Hahnentorburg in Cologne, in a show entitled *Auch wenn das Perlhuhn leise weint* (While the Guinea Fowl Gently Weeps), which would prove to be groundbreaking for the Neue Wilde. From then on, the painting of Dahn, Dokoupil, Peter Bömmels, Hans Peter Adamski, and the other "Mülheimers" virtually went through the roof.[15] The Neo-Expressionist "Hunger nach Bildern" (hunger for pictures), as spontaneous and concept-free as possible but with the greatest possible visual impact, found its counterpart in rather conceptual music projects that, in spite of a superficial impetus of just playing out, possessed a far more thought-out foundation than is often assumed.

14 See David Toop, *Ocean of Sound: Aether Talk, Ambient Sound and Imaginary Worlds*, London 1995.

15 See Jutta Koether, "Köln. Der Fällt-Auf-Schwung," *Kunstforum International* 68 (1983).

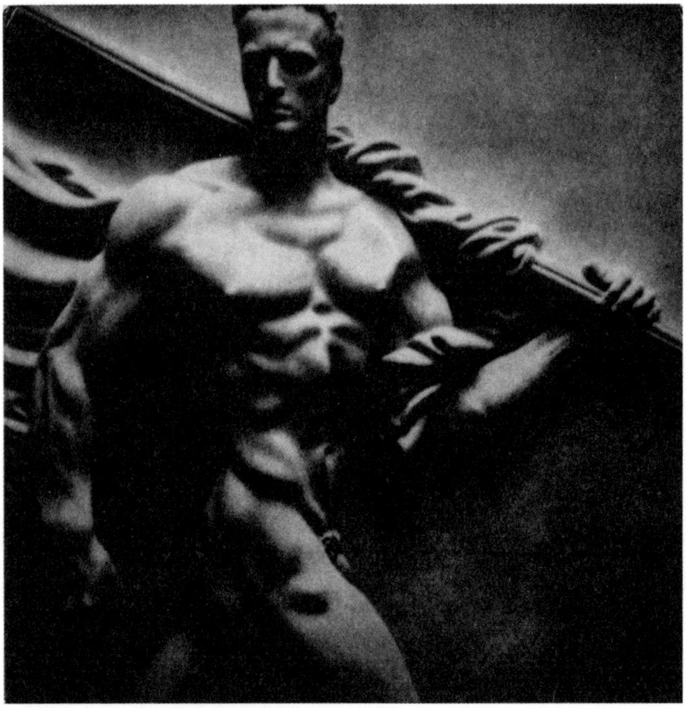

Die Partei, *La Freiheit des Geistes*, 1981
LP, Tausend Augen

in der Kölner Hahnentorburg ausgestellt – in einer Schau mit dem Titel *Auch wenn das Perlhuhn leise weint*, die bahnbrechend für die „Neuen Wilden“ werden sollte. Von da an schoss die Malerei von Dahn, Dokoupil, Peter Bömmels, Hans Peter Adamski und den weiteren „Mülheimern“ regelrecht durch die Decke.[14] Ihr neo-expressionistischer „Hunger nach Bildern“, möglichst spontan und konzeptfrei, dafür aber mit größtmöglicher visueller Wucht, fand sein Pendant in durchaus konzeptuell angelegten Musikprojekten, denen zwar der vordergründige Impetus des Drauflosmusizierens anhaftete, tatsächlich aber eine viel durchdachtere Grundlage eignete als gemeinhin angenommen.

Ähnlich wie Salomés und Castellis Geile Tiere in Berlin 1980/81 ein durchaus formidables Konzept (queerer Schepper-Electro mit hysterisch-sexualisierten Texten) verfolgten, so war auch Walter Dahns und Tom Dokoupils Bandprojekt Die Partei einer forschen, diverse Klanggeografien einbeziehenden Synthie-/Electro-Machart verpflichtet.

14 Vgl. Jutta Koether, „Köln. Der Fällt-Auf-Schwung“, in: *Kunstforum International*, Bd. 68, 1983.

Similar to the way in which Salomé and Castelli's Geile Tiere followed a formidable concept (queer, wonky electro with hysterically sexualized lyrics) in Berlin in 1980–81, Walter Dahn and Tom Dokoupil's band project Die Partei was also dedicated to a perky synth-electro style incorporating diverse sound geographies. The mostly instrumental spectrum of sounds on their LP *La Freiheit des Geistes* ranges from "Ostafrika" (East Africa) and "Föhn in den Bergen" (Foehn in the Mountains) to "Tage an der Grenze" (Days at the Border) and "Strahlsund" (a pun combining *Strahl*, or ray, with the town of Stralsund)—tracks that were for the most part built on upbeat, slightly dubby synth lines repeatedly interspersed with sampled voices ("Ihr meint, ihr seid schon im automatischen Zeitalter? So weit ist es noch nicht." [You think you're already in the automatic age? We're not there yet.]). One often senses the proximity to Düsseldorf as the mecca of electronic music (Kraftwerk, Neu!, Harmonia, etc.) when listening to the pieces, while "Rote Schuhe" (Red Shoes), for example, with its elegantly staggered audio tracks, counts as a classic of the minimal wave movement that evolved three decades later.

In a metaphorical sense, one could say that though the guinea fowl may have wept only gently, it was widely heard despite this restraint. And even if this rather intricate musical style only partially matched the impasto explosiveness of the paintings, two loose ends that originated from the same maker did meet somewhere in the medial infiniteness. Dahn went on to found together with Detlev Kühne Die Hornissen (The Hornets), which scored a minor hit in 1982 with their cover version of the Velvet Underground's "Pale Blue Eyes"; and in 1984, with their album *Zwei Jahre / Two Years*, they attempted to dig a today much sought-after "Time Tunnel / Zeittunnel" (the title of one of the tracks) to all kinds of historically remote pop moments.[16]

Meanwhile, the Hamburg guinea fowl was not idle either, and in 1984—under the title *Die Rache der Erinnerung* (The Revenge of Memory)—tackled an array of pop classics from the 1960s, 1970s, and early 1980s. The alliance of Martin Kippenberger, Werner Büttner, and the Oehlen brothers with members of the then somewhat older generation, Jörg Immendorff and A. R. Penck,

16 Or they remained strictly rooted in the present, as demonstrated by the project Slinky Gym School, in which Dahn, Kühne, Dokoupil, and Robert Crash recorded the electro-hip hop track "Crazy Sneaker" with the New York rapper Rammellzee in fall 1983.

Der weitgehend instrumentale Klangbogen der LP *La Freiheit des Geistes* spannt sich von *Ostafrika* über *Föhn in den Bergen* und *Tage an der Grenze* bis nach *Strahlsund* – Stücke, die auf flotten, zumeist leicht „dubbigen" Synthie-Lines errichtet sind und immer wieder von gesampelten Stimmen interpunktiert werden. („Ihr meint, ihr seid schon im automatischen Zeitalter? So weit ist es noch nicht.") Man merkt den Tracks vielfach ihre Nähe zum Electronic-Mekka Düsseldorf (Kraftwerk, Neu!, Harmonia etc.) an, zugleich gelten Titel wie *Rote Schuhe* mit seinen elegant gegeneinander versetzten Spuren drei Jahrzehnte später als Klassiker der Minimal-Wave-Bewegung.

Das Perlhuhn, könnte man im übertragenen Sinne sagen, hat zwar nur leise geweint, gehört wurde es aber trotz dieser Verhaltenheit weithin. Und selbst wenn dieser eher feingliedrige musikalische Duktus nur bedingt der pastosen Fulminanz der Malereien entsprach, trafen sich hier doch zwei lose Enden, die vom gleichen Macher ausgingen, irgendwo in der medialen Unendlichkeit. Dahn gründete in der Folge gemeinsam mit Detlev Kühne Die Hornissen, die 1982 durch ihre Coverversion des Velvet-Underground-Songs *Pale Blue Eyes* einen Mini-Hit landeten und 1984 mit der LP *Zwei Jahre / Two Years* einen heute gesuchten *Zeittunnel* (so der Titel eines der darauf enthaltenen Stücke) hin zu allerlei entlegenen historischen Pop-Momenten zu graben versuchten.[15]

Währenddessen war aber auch das Hamburger Perlhuhn nicht untätig und machte sich 1984 – unter dem Titel *Die Rache der Erinnerung* – über einen Schwung Pop-Klassiker aus den 1960er-, 70er- und frühen 80er-Jahren her. Der Zusammenschluss von Martin Kippenberger, Werner Büttner und den Gebrüdern Oehlen mit Vertretern der schon etwas älteren Generation wie Jörg Immendorff und A. R. Penck brachte diesen seltsamen Vogel – „Retro" war damals noch nicht in aller Munde – stilgerecht zum Weinen, wenn nicht gar zum Winseln. Mit einer Reihe von Gastmusikern knöpfte man sich Canned Heats *Going Up the Country*, den Stones-Klassiker *Sympathy for the Devil* oder Michael Jacksons *Beat It* vor und nagte die Vorlagen teilweise bis auf die Knochen ab. Was dem Konzept dieser Platte bestens entsprach, präsentierte sich die Künstlerriege auf dem Innencover doch nackt in der Sauna. Zu Markus Oehlens Version des Medicine-Head-Songs *One & One Is One* wurde sogar ein Videoclip

15 Oder auch strikt in der Gegenwart verankert blieben, wie das Projekt Slinky Gym School beweist, bei dem Dahn, Kühne, Dokoupil und Robert Crash im Herbst 1983 gemeinsam mit dem New Yorker Rapper Rammellzee das Electro-HipHop-Stück *Crazy Sneaker* aufnahmen.

made the strange bird—the term "retro" was then not yet on everyone's lips—weep, if not whimper, with style. With a number of guest musicians, they explored Canned Heat's "Going Up The Country," the Rolling Stones classic "Sympathy For The Devil," or Michael Jackson's "Beat It" and gnawed the templates partially to the bone. Corresponding perfectly to the album's concept, the inside cover featured the group of artists naked in the sauna. A video clip was even produced for Markus Oehlen's version of the Medicine Head song "One & One Is One," although it received little airplay on the then still fledgling music television.

The most well-known songs over the years were, understandably, the two sung by Kippenberger: Adriano Celentano's "Yuppi du," and "Bang Bang," originally performed by Cher and Nancy Sinatra. In "Yuppi du," Kippenberger satirizes the budding yuppie culture with his typical duplicity; and "Bang Bang" anticipates, as it were, the rediscovery of the song twenty years later when it was used in Quentin Tarantino's movie *Kill Bill*. The "luxury" of the artists' music that in the late 1970s took painting as its point of departure had already been differentiated in numerous subfields. The big "bang" was hardly repeatable with the force it had possessed twenty years earlier. The guinea fowl, if you like, had to weep all the more loudly from then on.

produziert, dessen Einsatz im damals noch jungen Musikfernsehen jedoch bescheiden blieb.

Am bekanntesten wurden im Laufe der Zeit, nachvollziehbarerweise, die beiden von Kippenberger gesungenen Stücke – Adriano Celentanos *Yuppi du* und das ursprünglich von Cher beziehungsweise Nancy Sinatra gesungene *Bang Bang*. In *Yuppi du* nimmt Kippenberger mit der für ihn typischen Doppelzüngigkeit die zu der Zeit gerade anhebende Yuppie-Kultur aufs Korn; und *Bang Bang* antizipiert gleichsam jene Wiederentdeckung, die dem Stück zwanzig Jahre später durch den Einsatz in Quentin Tarantinos *Kill Bill* beschert sein sollte. Der „Luxus" der Künstler-Musik, die in den späten 1970er-Jahren in der Malerei ihren Ausgang genommen hatte, war da schon in zahlreiche Subbereiche ausdifferenziert. Der große „Bang" sollte mit jener Wucht, die er zwanzig Jahre zuvor hatte, kaum noch wiederholbar sein. Das Perlhuhn, wenn man so will, musste fortan umso lauter weinen.

Catherine Dossin
Die Rückkehr zur Malerei und das europäische Comeback der 1980er-Jahre: Jenseits von Marketing und Zeitgeist

Catherine Dossin
The Return to Painting and the European Comeback of the 1980s: Beyond Marketing and Zeitgeist

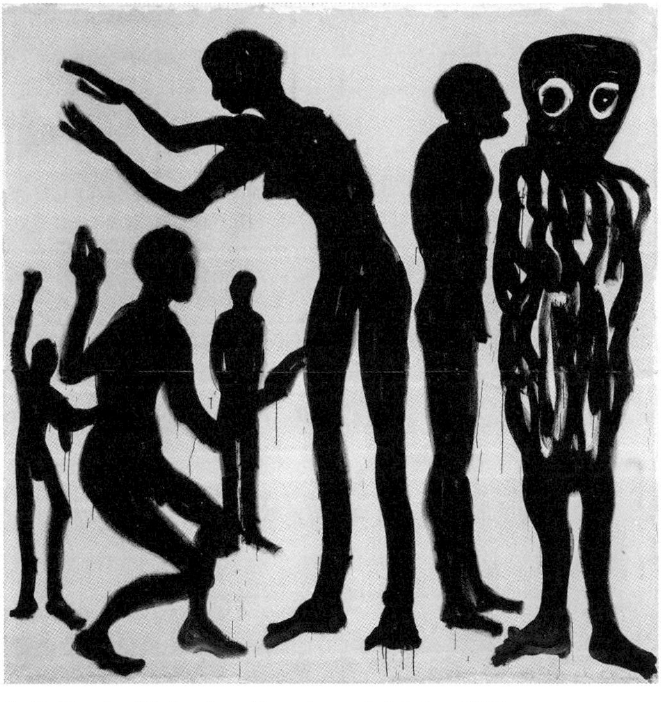

A. R. Penck, ***Hinter Leo Berrybora dahinter,*** **1975**
Öl auf Leinwand / oil on canvas, 285 × 285 cm

Im Jahr 1981 eröffnete an der Royal Academy of Arts in London die Ausstellung *A New Spirit in Painting* unter der Prämisse, dass nun, da „Künstler*innen sich wieder mit der Malerei befassen, diese ganz entscheidend für sie wurde und das neue Bewusstsein für die aktuelle Bedeutung der ältesten Form ihrer Kunst greifbar in der Luft liegt, wo immer Kunst entsteht".[1] Da die Ausstellung zum großen Teil europäische Künstler zeigte, wurde sie auch als Proklamation von deren Comeback nach Jahren der US-amerikanischen Vorherrschaft aufgefasst.[2] Die Rückkehr zur Malerei und das europäische Comeback waren in zeitgenössischen Darstellungen so eng miteinander verwoben, dass sie nahezu synonym wurden. Westeuropäische Kunst wurde infolgedessen mit Malerei in Verbindung gebracht, während die US-amerikanische Kunst mit Konzeptkunst gleichgesetzt wurde. Da man die Rückkehr zur Malerei entweder wohlwollend als notwendige Normalisierung künstlerischer Praktiken ansah oder als kommerzielle Gegenreaktion auf die Konzeptkunst ablehnte, wurde das europäische Comeback entweder als kreative Wiedergeburt porträtiert oder als kommerzieller Schachzug abgetan.

In den Vereinigten Staaten konzentrierte sich die lebhafte Debatte über die neue Malerei auf die ontologische Natur des Mediums sowie die philosophischen Implikationen, die mit seiner Nutzung am Ende des 20. Jahrhunderts einhergingen, statt auf die historischen Umstände, unter denen es in den 1980er-Jahren eine Renaissance erlebte, insbesondere in Westeuropa.[3] Europäische Berichte aus jener Zeit helfen genauso wenig dabei, die neue Malerei zu verstehen. Sie erklären sie schlicht zum Ausdruck eines neuen Zeitgeists – zu etwas, das „in der Luft" lag, wie Christos Joachimides, der Kurator von *A New Spirit in Painting*, es formulierte. Doch die Idee einer spontanen Regeneration der europäischen Malerei nach Jahren der kreativen Apathie scheint wenig glaubhaft. Das Problem bestand nicht darin, dass es Westeuropa an guten Künstler*innen mangelte, sondern vielmehr darin, dass sie unsichtbar waren und ihre Fähigkeiten somit nicht erkannt werden konnten. Dieser Essay untersucht jenseits vereinfachender, gelungenes Marketing oder den Zeitgeist ins Feld führender Erklärungen die materiellen und historischen Voraussetzungen, die es Künstler*innen in Westeuropa ermöglichten, wieder geschätzt zu werden. Ausgangspunkt dafür war

1 Christos M. Joachimides und Norman Rosenthal (Hg.), *A New Spirit in Painting*, Ausst.-Kat. Royal Academy of Arts, London 1981, S. 15.

2 Es wurden 26 europäische und 11 US-amerikanische Künstler gezeigt.

3 Zu diesen Diskussionen siehe Alison Pearlman, *Unpackaging Art of the 1980s*, Chicago 2003.

In 1981, *A New Spirit in Painting* opened at the Royal Academy of Arts in London on the premise that "artists are involved in painting again, it has become crucial to them, and the new consciousness of the contemporary significance of the oldest form of their art is in the air, tangibly, wherever art is being made."[1] Featuring a large majority of European artists, the show was also received as proclaiming their comeback, after years of American domination.[2] The return to painting and the European comeback were so entangled in contemporary accounts that they became almost interchangeable. Western European art was consequently associated with painting, while American art was identified with Conceptualism. As one either welcomed the return to painting as a necessary normalization of artistic practices or rejected it as a commercial backlash against Conceptual Art, the European comeback was accordingly either portrayed as a creative renaissance or dismissed as a commercial move.

In the United States, the vivid debate about the new painting focused on the ontological nature of the medium and the philosophical implications of using it at the end of the twentieth century rather than on the historical circumstances of its return in the 1980s, and in Western Europe in particular.[3] Contemporary European accounts are no more useful in understanding the new painting. They simply explain it as the expression of a new zeitgeist—something "in the air," as Christos Joachimides, the curator of *A New Spirit in Painting*, suggested. Yet the idea of a spontaneous regeneration of European painting after years of creative apathy does not seem credible. The problem was not that Western Europe lacked good artists, but rather that they were invisible and thus could not be recognized as great. Moving beyond simplistic marketing or zeitgeist explanations, this essay examines the material and historical conditions that made it possible for Western European artists to be regarded as great once again, starting with the strength of the Western European art worlds that had been thriving in the shadow of New York since the 1960s.[4]

1 *A New Spirit in Painting*, ed. Christos M. Joachimides and Norman Rosenthal, exh. cat. Royal Academy of Art, London 1981, p. 15.

2 It featured twenty-six Europeans and eleven Americans.

3 On these debates, see Alison Pearlman, *Unpackaging Art of the 1980s*, Chicago 2003.

die starke westeuropäische Kunstszene, die bereits seit den 1960er-Jahren im Schatten von New York aufblühte.[4]

Im Jahr 1980, als das europäische Comeback stattfand, konnte Westeuropa mit einem lebendigen Fördersystem für die Künste aufwarten, das auf großzügigen Staatsausgaben, großem Enthusiasmus der Kunstgemeinde und anhaltender öffentlicher wie privater Sammeltätigkeit beruhte. Dies war eine fruchtbare Zeit für die Fachpresse, die Museen und selbst die Kunstgalerien. Beginnend mit dem Erfolg der US-amerikanischen Pop-Art sprossen die Galerien seit Mitte der 1960er-Jahre in dem Maße aus dem Boden, in dem sich um jede aus den USA kommende Tendenz neue Netzwerke bildeten. Die neu ins Leben gerufenen Kunstmessen – der Kölner Kunstmarkt, die Art Basel und so weiter – entwickelten sich neben der bereits etablierten documenta und der Biennale von Venedig schnell zu beliebten Treffpunkten der internationalen Kunstszene. Dieses engmaschige System aus Einzelpersonen und Institutionen vereinfachte den Austausch zwischen den Westeuropäer*innen, die so die neuesten künstlerischen Strömungen schnell und effizient in der westlichen Welt bewerben konnten. Obwohl New York noch immer als Zentrum der internationalen Kunstwelt angesehen wurde, verfügte Westeuropa über Macht und Einfluss in beträchtlichem Maße.

Die westeuropäischen Künstler*innen waren zur Zeit ihres sogenannten Comebacks allerdings keinesfalls von der Bildfläche verschwunden. Obwohl es scheinbar niemand bemerkte, waren sie in den europäischen Galerien, in privaten und öffentlichen Sammlungen und sogar in den Vereinigten Staaten gut vertreten. Museen in Westeuropa hatten während der sogenannten Vorherrschaft der US-amerikanischen Kunst nie damit aufgehört, europäische Künstler*innen zu unterstützen und ihre Werke zu zeigen. Das Moderna Museet in Stockholm und das Stedelijk Museum in Amsterdam wurden zwar oft beschuldigt, lokale und europäische zugunsten US-amerikanischer Künstler*innen zu vernachlässigen, dabei sammelten und zeigten sie jedoch überwiegend europäische Kunst – genau wie alle anderen europäischen Museen.[5] Als öffentliche Institutionen mussten sie Kunst

4 Für eine detailliertere Antwort und eine umfassende Bibliografie siehe Catherine Dossin, *The Rise and Fall of American Art, 1940s–1980s: A Geopolitics of Western Art Worlds*, New York 2015, S. 229–275.

5 Siehe Pontus Hultén (Hg.), *Catalogue of the Modern Museums Collection of Swedish and International 20th Century Art*, Moderna Museet, Stockholm 1976; und Joop M. Joosten (Hg.), *20 Years of Art Collecting: Acquisitions Stedelijk Museum Amsterdam, 1963–1984*, Amsterdam 1984.

By 1980, when the European comeback took place, Western Europe boosted a dynamic support system for the arts that rested on generous public spending, wide community enthusiasm, and sustained private and public collecting. Those were prosperous years for the specialized press, the museums, and even the art galleries. Feeding on the success of American Pop Art, the number of European galleries had kept on growing from the mid-1960s onward as new networks emerged devoted to each of the new trends coming from the United States. The newly launched international art fairs—Cologne's Kunstmarkt, Art Basel, and so on—had quickly become major rendezvous for the international community, as were already Documenta and the Venice Biennale. This dense system of individuals and institutions allowed Western Europeans to communicate easily among themselves quickly and efficiently to promote the newest artistic developments throughout the Western world. Even though New York continued to be regarded as the center of the international art world, Western Europeans' power and influence were significant.

As for Western European artists, by the time of their purported comeback they had all but disappeared. Although nobody seemed to take notice, they were well represented in European galleries, private and public collections, and even in the United States. Western European museums never stopped supporting and featuring European artists during the so-called domination of American art. The Moderna Museet of Stockholm and the Stedelijk Museum of Amsterdam, which were often accused of neglecting local and European artists in favor of the Americans, were exhibiting and collecting predominantly European art, as were all the other European museums.[5] As public institutions, they were required to buy art from local artists, and American artists were rather expensive for their limited budgets.

Western European collectors—even the ones most dedicated to American art—likewise remained faithful to European art. Karl Ströher, a strong supporter of American art, was equally committed to German art. German Expressionism, postwar

4 For a more detailed answer and a comprehensive bibliography, see Catherine Dossin, *The Rise and Fall of American Art, 1940s–1980s: A Geopolitics of Western Art Worlds*, New York 2015, pp. 229–75.

5 See *Catalogue of the Modern Museums Collection of Swedish and International 20th Century Art*, ed. Pontus Hultén, Moderna Museet, Stockholm 1976; and *20 Years of Art Collecting: Acquisitions Stedelijk Museum Amsterdam, 1963–1984*, ed. Joop M. Joosten, Stedelijk Museum, Amsterdam 1984.

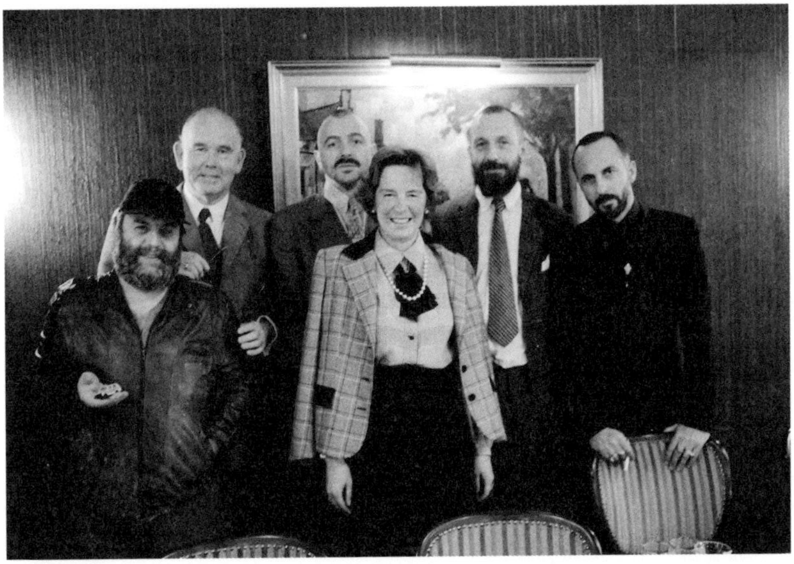

A. R. Penck, Peter Ludwig, Markus Lüpertz, Irene Ludwig, Georg Baselitz, Jörg Immendorff
Empfang zur Ausstellung / Reception to the exhibition *Georg Baselitz*, Galerie Michael Werner, Köln / Cologne, 1984

von lokalen Künstler*innen ankaufen, und Künstler*innen aus den USA waren angesichts ihrer limitierten Budgets ziemlich teuer.

Westeuropäische Sammler*innen – sogar diejenigen, die sich am meisten für die US-amerikanische Kunst begeisterten – blieben ebenfalls der europäischen Kunst treu. Karl Ströher, ein großer Förderer US-amerikanischer Kunst, widmete sich ebenso intensiv der deutschen Kunst. Der deutsche Expressionismus, die Abstraktion der deutschen Nachkriegszeit und Joseph Beuys machten daher einen großen Anteil seiner Sammlung aus. Peter Ludwig, *der* Sammler der US-amerikanischen Pop-Art und Leo Castellis bester Kunde, sammelte ebenfalls deutsche und europäische Kunst.[6] Auch Giuseppe Panza unterstützte sowohl die US-amerikanische als auch die deutsche Kunst. Wer nach Varese fuhr, um sich seine Sammlung anzusehen, entdeckte dort Minimal Art und Konzeptkunst von beiden Seiten des Atlantiks.[7]

Dasselbe galt für europäische Kunstgalerien: Selbst diejenigen, die sich angeblich der US-amerikanischen Kunst verschrieben hatten, zeigten europäische Künstler*innen. Konrad Fischer, *der* europäische

6 Zu diesem Aspekt der Sammlung Ludwig siehe zum Beispiel Wolfgang Becker (Hg.), *La nouvelle peinture allemande dans la Collection Ludwig Aix-la-Chapelle*, Ausst.-Kat. Goethe-Institut, Lyon 1986.

7 Giuseppe Panza di Biumo, *Giuseppe Panza: Memories of a Collector*, New York 2007.

German abstraction, and Joseph Beuys thus constituted major portions of his collection. Peter Ludwig, *the* collector of American Pop Art and Leo Castelli's best client, also collected German and European art.[6] Giuseppe Panza was also supporting both American and European art. Those who went to Varese to see his collection discovered both Minimal and Conceptual Art from both sides of the Atlantic.[7]

And the same was true in European art galleries: even those supposedly dedicated to American art featured European artists. Konrad Fischer, *the* European dealer of American Conceptual Art, represented many of them, and his gallery featured a number of German artists, including his friends Gerhard Richter and Sigmar Polke. Kasper König, who helped Fischer define the program of the gallery, explained, "The exhibitions were orchestrated in such a way that American and European artists alternated."[8] Gian Enzo Sperone, whose gallery had become famous for its exhibitions of American Pop Art, remained likewise committed to Italian artists, whom he exhibited along with the Americans.[9] As for Paul Maenz, thanks to whom American Minimal and Conceptual Art first came to West Germany, he was the first to bring together European Conceptual artists during *Dies alles Herzchen wird einmal dir gehören* (All These, Little Darling, Will One Day Be Yours), which he staged in September 1967.[10] When he opened his own space in Cologne in the 1970s, Maenz took on Conceptual artists from both the United States and Europe, launching the gallery with an exhibition of Hans Haacke.

Even Ileana Sonnabend, who had orchestrated the Pop invasion of Europe from her Paris gallery, was not just a dealer of American art; she also represented European artists. The exchanges with her European partners were not as unidirectional

6 On this aspect of the Ludwig Collection, see for instance *La nouvelle peinture allemande dans la Collection Ludwig Aix-la-Chapelle*, ed. Wolfgang Becker, exh. cat. Goethe-Institut, Lyon 1986.

7 Giuseppe Panza di Biumo, *Giuseppe Panza: Memories of a Collector*, trans. Michael Haggerty, New York 2007.

8 Kasper König, "Two-Women Show as Good as One-Man Show: A Conversation with Kasper König," in *Konrad Fischer: Okey Dokey*, ed. Brigitte Kölle, Cologne 2007, p. 86.

9 Anna Minola et al., *Gian Enzo Sperone: Torino—Roma—New York. 35 anni di mostre tra Europa e America*, 2 vols., Turin 2000.

10 Suzaan Boettger, "The Lost Contingent: Paul Maenz's Prophetic 1967 Event and the Ambiguities of Historical Priority," *Art Journal* 62, no. 1 (Spring 2003), pp. 34–47.

Kunsthändler für US-amerikanische Konzeptkunst schlechthin, vertrat viele von ihnen, und seine Galerie zeigte die Arbeiten einer ganzen Anzahl deutscher Künstler*innen, darunter die seiner Freunde Gerhard Richter und Sigmar Polke. Kasper König, der Fischer dabei half, das Programm seiner Galerie festzulegen, erklärte dazu: „Die Ausstellungen waren so orchestriert, dass sich amerikanische und europäische Künstler abwechselten."[8] Gian Enzo Sperone, dessen Galerie sich für ihre Ausstellungen der US-amerikanischen Pop-Art einen Namen gemacht hatte, blieb den italienischen Künstler*innen ebenso verbunden, die er zusammen mit den US-Amerikaner*innen ausstellte.[9] Was Paul Maenz betrifft, dem zu verdanken war, dass die US-amerikanische Minimal Art und Konzeptkunst überhaupt nach Westdeutschland gekommen war, so brachte er in seiner Ausstellung *Dies alles Herzchen wird einmal Dir gehören* im September 1967 erstmals europäische Konzeptkünstler*innen zusammen.[10] Als er in den 1970er-Jahren in Köln eigene Räumlichkeiten aufmachte, nahm er Konzeptkünstler*innen sowohl aus den USA als auch aus Europa auf und eröffnete die Galerie mit einer Hans-Haacke-Ausstellung.

Sogar Ileana Sonnabend, die die Pop-Invasion in Europa von ihrer Pariser Galerie aus mit gesteuert hatte, handelte nicht ausschließlich mit US-amerikanischer Kunst, sondern repräsentierte auch europäische Künstler*innen. Der Austausch mit ihren europäischen Partner*innen war nicht so einseitig, wie man glauben mag: Sie schickte ihnen US-amerikanische Künstler*innen, umgekehrt schickte man ihr aber auch die eigenen Künstler*innen. Sonnabend stellte daher regelmäßig italienische und westdeutsche Künstler*innen in Paris aus und sie eröffnete in den 1970er-Jahren einen Raum in New York, um sie zu fördern.[11] „Eine Galerie in New York aufzumachen war wirklich das Gegenteil meiner Situation in Paris, teils auch, weil ich wollte, dass dort Europäer*innen zu sehen sind"[12], erklärte sie einmal.

Der Anerkennung westeuropäischer Künstler*innen stand vieles im Wege. Dazu zählte auch die Vorherrschaft des US-amerikanischen

8 Kasper König, „Two-Women Show as Good as One-Man Show: Ein Gespräch mit Kasper König", in: Brigitte Kölle (Hg.), *okey dokey Konrad Fischer*, Köln 2007, S. 73.

9 Anna Minola u. a., *Gian Enzo Sperone: Torino – Roma – New York. 35 anni di mostre tra Europa e America*, 2 Bde., Turin 2000.

10 Suzaan Boettger, „The Lost Contingent: Paul Maenz's Prophetic 1967 Event and the Ambiguities of Historical Priority", in: *Art Journal*, 62, Nr. 1, Frühling 2003, S. 34–47.

11 Michel Bourel, „Les Galeries d'Ileana Sonnabend", in: *Collection Sonnabend. 25 années de choix et d'activités d'Ileana et Michael Sonnabend*, CAPC Musée d'art contemporain, Bordeaux 1988, S. 11–80.

12 Ileana Sonnabend, zit. in: Laura de Coppet und Alan Jones, *The Art Dealers: The Powers Behind the Scene Tell How the Art World Really Works*, New York 1984, S. 114.

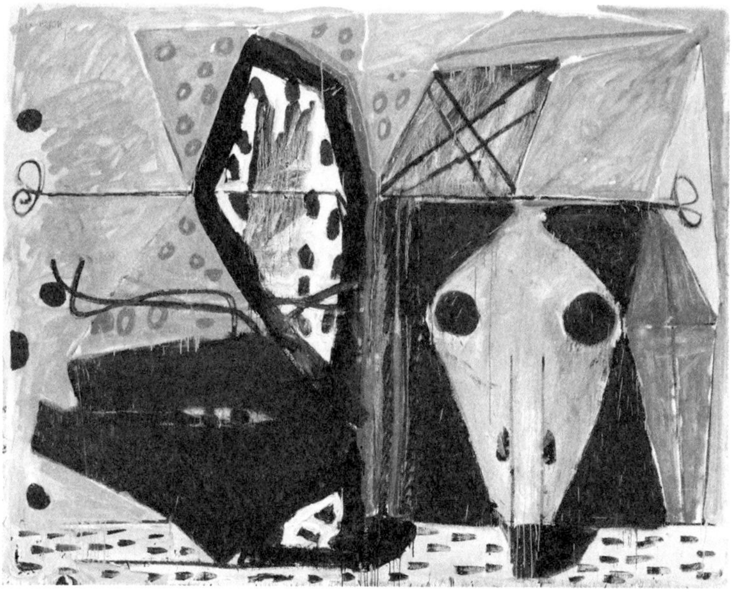

Markus Lüpertz, *Stil-Tod des Schauspielers*, 1978
Öl und Mischtechnik auf Leinwand / oil and mixed media on canvas, 190 × 245 cm

as one might think: she sent them American artists, but they also sent her their artists. Sonnabend Paris thus regularly exhibited Italian and West German artists, and in 1970 she opened a space in New York to promote them.[11] "Opening a gallery in New York," she explained, "was really the reverse of my Paris situation, partially because I wanted Europeans to be seen there."[12]

There were then many obstacles to Western Europeans' recognition, including the domination of the American model of art history, one based on the idea of a progression of modern art toward an always greater reduction of its means. This model, exemplified by Alfred Barr, Jr.'s diagrams and Clement Greenberg's writings, had played a very important role in shaping the narrative of the supremacy of American art, and the shift from Paris to New York. Artistic developments outside this American modernist canon were considered provincial and retrograde, and dismissed

11 Michel Bourel, "Les galeries d'Ileana Sonnabend," in *Collection Sonnabend. 25 années de choix et d'activités d'Ileana et Michael Sonnabend*, CAPC Musée d'art contemporain, Bordeaux 1988, pp. 11–80.

12 Ileana Sonnabend, cited in Laura de Coppet and Alan Jones, *The Art Dealers: The Powers Behind the Scene Tell How the Art World Really Works*, New York 1984, p. 114.

Modells der Kunstgeschichtsschreibung, das auf der Idee des Fortschritts der modernen Kunst in Richtung einer immer umfassenderen Reduktion ihrer Mittel beruhte. Dieses Modell, das durch Alfred Barr Jr.s Diagramme und Clement Greenbergs Schriften beispielhaft belegt ist, hatte eine entscheidende Rolle dabei gespielt, das Narrativ der Überlegenheit der US-amerikanischen Kunst sowie die Verlagerung von Paris nach New York zu entwickeln. Künstlerische Formen außerhalb dieses modernistischen US-amerikanischen Kanons wurden als provinziell und rückschrittlich angesehen und daher abgelehnt. Mit diesem „provinziellen“ Ansatz wurden auch Georg Baselitz, Eugen Schönebeck, A. R. Penck und Markus Lüpertz in Verbindung gebracht, eine Gruppe deutscher Maler, die sich Wols, Jean Dubuffet, Antonin Artaud und weitere außerhalb des Kanons stehende Künstler zum Vorbild nahmen. Diese Berliner Künstler waren mit dem Schweizer Kunsthistoriker Johannes Gachnang und mit Michael Werner befreundet, der damals Praktikant in der Galerie Rudolf Springer war. Ebenfalls mit der Springer-Gruppe assoziiert war der oben erwähnte griechische Kunsthistoriker Christos Joachimides, der damals in Berlin studierte.

Über die Jahre versuchten Werner und Gachnang ihr Möglichstes, um die untypischen Werke ihrer Freunde bekannt zu machen. Gachnang, der zuerst am Goethe-Institut in Amsterdam arbeitete und dann Direktor der Kunsthalle Bern war, organisierte viele Ausstellungen mit Baselitz, Lüpertz, Penck und Anselm Kiefer, der sich der Gruppe kurz zuvor angeschlossen hatte. Entscheidender war, dass er eine Theorie des Provinzialismus entwickelte, die eine Alternative zu dem Mythos bot, mit dem der Formalismus als universelle Sprache der Kunst untermauert wurde, und so für einen konzeptuellen Rahmen sorgte, in dem die Arbeiten seiner Freunde – und auch die anderer nicht-konformistischer Künster*innen – als ebenso relevant angesehen wurden wie die Mainstream-Kunst aus den USA. Statt provinzielle Besonderheiten abzutun, feierte Gachnang sie als positive und anregende Andersartigkeiten. Seiner Lesart nach stellte die US-amerikanische Kunst nur *eine* Kunstprovinz dar, weshalb er in der von ihr gesprochenen Sprache nur einen Dialekt und nicht die einzige authentische Ausdrucksform der modernen Kunst sah.

Im Verlauf der 1970er-Jahre fanden Gachnangs Ideen unter den Entscheidungsträger*innen der europäischen Kunstszene zunehmend Verbreitung. Rudi Fuchs, der 1982 künstlerischer Leiter der documenta 7 war, erinnert sich:

as such. Among those "provincial" approaches was a group of German painters—Georg Baselitz, Eugen Schönebeck, A. R. Penck, and Markus Lüpertz—who had for models Wols, Jean Dubuffet, and Antonin Artaud, among other noncanonical artists. These Berlin artists were friends with Johannes Gachnang, a Swiss art historian, and Michael Werner, then a trainee at Rudolf Springer's gallery. Also associated with the Springer group was Christos Joachimides, the Greek art historian who was then studying in Berlin.

Over the years, Werner and Gachnang tried their hardest to promote the atypical works of their friends. Working at the Goethe-Institut of Amsterdam and then as director of the Kunsthalle Bern, Gachnang organized many exhibitions with Baselitz, Lüpertz, Penck, and Anselm Kiefer, who had recently joined the group. More importantly, he elaborated a theory of provincialism that offered an alternative to the myth that underpinned formalism as a universal language of art and provided a conceptual framework under which the works of his friends—as well as those of other nonconforming artists—were considered as pertinent as mainstream American art. Instead of dismissing provincial particularities, Gachnang celebrated them as positive and stimulating differences. In his reading, American art was just *one* province of art, and the language it spoke was just one dialect and not *the only* authentic expression of modern art.

Throughout the 1970s, Gachnang's ideas gained currency among other European art players. As Rudi Fuchs, artistic director of Documenta 7 in 1982, recalled:

> Although at first their work was disturbing for its lack of affinity to American art, its quality became increasingly obvious and *irresistible.* It could not be ignored; and that simple fact led to the realization that American art, programmatically pushing toward the limits of its adopted morphology, was just a style, or even just another dialect in the great diversity of artistic expression. Almost overnight, I found myself *defending* European art and artists, "who had to worry a lot before they could make something," against what we perceived as the haughtiness of American style.[13]

13 Rudolf Hermann Fuchs et al, eds., *Views from Abroad: European Perspectives on American Art,* vol. 1, exh. cat. Whitney Museum of American Art, New York 1995, p. 25.

> „Obwohl ihre Arbeiten zunächst aufgrund des fehlenden Bezugs zur US-amerikanischen Kunst verstörten, wurde ihre Qualität immer augenscheinlicher und *unwiderstehlich*. Das konnte man nicht ignorieren, und diese Tatsache allein führte zu der Erkenntnis, dass die US-amerikanische Kunst, die programmatisch an die Grenzen der von ihr aufgegriffenen Morphologie stieß, letztlich nur einen Stil darstellte – oder sogar bloß einen weiteren Dialekt innerhalb der enormen Diversität künstlerischer Ausdrucksformen. Fast über Nacht begann ich plötzlich die europäische Kunst und ihre Vertreter*innen, ‚die sich jede Menge Sorgen machen mussten, bevor sie überhaupt etwas machen konnten', zu *verteidigen* gegen das, was wir als Überheblichkeit des US-amerikanischen Stils wahrnahmen."[13]

In Italien eröffnete Achille Bonito Oliva auf ähnliche Weise einen regionalistischen/pluralistischen Diskurs, der sich dem modernistischen universalistischen/monistischen (US-amerikanischen) Modell entgegenstellte – zuerst in *Flash Art* und dann in mehreren Büchern, darunter *Europe/America: The Different Avant-gardes* (1976) und *La Transavanguardia internazionale* (1982), wo er zwischen der europäischen und der US-amerikanischen Kunst unterschied. Erstere sah er durch Joseph Beuys verkörpert – eine in Geschichte, Kultur und Spiritualität wurzelnde Kunst –, während Letztere für ihn in Andy Warhol ihren Ausdruck fand, dargestellt als auf Gegenwart und Technologie fokussierte Kunst.

In Italien wurde die Malerei Teil eines regionalistischen Diskurses, als die Generation, die den Künstler*innen der Arte povera nachfolgte (und oft bei ihnen gelernt hatte, wobei sie mit Fotografie und Zeichnung begonnen hatte), sich schließlich der Malerei zuwandte – einem Medium, welches ihre Vorgänger*innen nicht besonders stark geprägt hatten und das daher neue Möglichkeiten versprach. Zwischen den Künstler*innen der Arte povera und ihren Nachfolger*innen – Francesco Clemente, Sandro Chia und so weiter – gab es keinen Bruch, sondern nur eine kontinuierliche Entwicklung.[14] Die Verbindung zwischen beiden wurde durch die Tatsache gestärkt, dass Sperone beide Generationen

13 Rudolf Hermann Fuchs u. a. (Hg.), *Views from Abroad: European Perspectives on American Art*, Bd. 1, Ausst.-Kat. Whitney Museum of American Art, New York 1995, S. 25.

14 Zur Verbindung zwischen Arte povera und Transavanguardia siehe Marcia E. Vetrocq, „Utopias, Nomads, Critics: From Arte Povera to the Transavanguardia", in: *Arts Magazine*, April 1989.

In Italy, Achille Bonito Oliva similarly developed a regionalist/pluralist discourse against the modernist universalist/monist (American) model, first in *Flash Art* and then in several books, including *Europe/America: The Different Avant-Gardes* (1976) and *La Transavanguardia internazionale* (1982), in which he distinguished between European art, embodied by Joseph Beuys and rooted in history, culture, and spirituality, and American art, embodied by Andy Warhol, which was portrayed as focusing on the present time and technology.

In Italy, painting became part of the regionalist discourse as the generation that came after the Arte Povera artists (and often studied under them, first working in photographs and drawings) came to embrace painting as a medium on which their predecessors had not left a strong mark and which thus offered new opportunities. Between Arte Povera artists and their successors—Francesco Clemente, Sandro Chia, and so on—there was no rupture, only consistent development.[14] The link between the two was reinforced by the fact that Sperone exhibited both generations together. Another artist from Sperone's gallery who made the transition between Conceptual photography and Conceptual painting was Salvo (Salvatore Mangione). Salvo's use of painting as a Conceptual tool was important, since it legitimized the use of painting and opened the door for other Conceptual painters, like Carlo Maria Mariani, whose work also blurred the distinction between Conceptual Art and figurative painting. When Maenz discovered Mariani's meta-paintings, he was seduced and immediately bought one for his personal collection.

In 1978, Maenz decided to devote his entire program to these new Italian developments. While they were challenging to someone whose aesthetic was grounded in 1960s Minimal and Conceptual Art, he felt the new generation was doing something important. At the time, Maenz's Italian year was regarded as a betrayal of the Conceptual cause—a commercial move from difficult art to pretty paintings. However, the gallery's archives offer evidence that Maenz had difficulty selling their works to a clientele accustomed to seeing Conceptual Art in his gallery.[15] Far from being a commercial move, the transition from Conceptual

14 On the connection between Arte Povera and Transavanguardia, see Marcia E. Vetrocq, "Utopias, Nomads, Critics: From Arte Povera to the Transavanguardia," *Arts Magazine,* April 1989, pp. 49–54.

gemeinsam ausstellte. Ein weiterer Künstler aus seiner Galerie, der den Übergang von der konzeptuellen Fotografie zur konzeptuellen Malerei mitgemacht hatte, war Salvo (Salvatore Mangione). Salvos Nutzung der Malerei als konzeptuelles Werkzeug war deshalb wichtig, weil sie der Malerei Legitimation verschaffte und anderen Konzeptkünstler*innen, deren Œuvre ebenfalls die Unterscheidung zwischen Konzeptkunst und figurativer Malerei verwischte, wie etwa bei Carlo Maria Mariani der Fall, neue Türen öffnete. Als Maenz Marianis Meta-Gemälde entdeckte, war er von ihnen fasziniert und kaufte sofort eines für seine persönliche Sammlung.

1978 beschloss Maenz, sein gesamtes Programm diesen neuen Entwicklungen in Italien zu widmen. Für die Betrachter*innen, deren Auffassung von Ästhetik in der Minimal Art und der Konzeptkunst der 1960er-Jahre verwurzelt war, stellten sie zwar eine Herausforderung dar, doch spürte er, dass diese neue Generation einen wichtigen Weg einschlug. Damals wurde Maenz' italienisches Jahr als Betrug an der konzeptuellen Sache angesehen – als kommerzieller Schachzug weg von schwieriger Kunst und hin zu hübschen Gemälden. Die Archive der Galerie zeigen jedoch, dass Maenz Schwierigkeiten beim Verkauf der Arbeiten an eine Klientel hatte, die daran gewöhnt war, in seiner Galerie Konzeptkunst anzutreffen.[15] Seine Entscheidung war weit entfernt davon, eine rein kommerzielle zu sein, vielmehr resultierte der Übergang von der Konzeptkunst zur figurativen Malerei daraus, dass Maenz die Vorstellung einer regionalen Identität und künstlerischer Vielfalt anzunehmen und zu propagieren versuchte.

Während des italienischen Jahres traf Maenz junge deutsche Künstler*innen, die in einer ähnlichen Richtung arbeiteten – beispielsweise die Künstler*innen der Galerie am Moritzplatz in Berlin und die Gruppe Mülheimer Freiheit aus Köln. Wie die Italiener hatten diese deutschen Kunstschaffenden bei Konzeptkünstlern studiert und versuchten nicht so sehr ihre Vorgänger zu boykottieren als vielmehr ihre eigene Stimme zu finden. Walter Dahn etwa hatte bei Beuys studiert und Jiří Georg Dokoupil bei Hans Haacke. Doch als Maenz 1980 *Mülheimer Freiheit & Interessante Bilder aus Deutschland* zeigte, bestand er beim Bewerben der Ausstellung darauf, dass hier eine *neue* Generation in Erscheinung trete. Damit wurde die Verbindung zwischen den Neuen Wilden – dies war der Name, unter dem die

15 Dies lässt sich an Maenz' Briefen und Berichten aus jener Zeit ablesen. Siehe Galerie Paul Maenz Köln Records, 1956–1991, The Getty Center for the History of Art and the Humanities Special Collections and Visual Resources, Los Angeles, 910066.

Art to figurative painting was the result of Maenz's accepting and promoting the ideas of regional identity and artistic pluralism.

During the Italian year, Maenz met young Germans who were working in a similar vein, including the artists from Galerie am Moritzplatz in Berlin and the Mülheimer Freiheit group from Cologne. Like the Italians, these German artists had studied with Conceptual artists and were not trying to undermine their predecessors so much as they were aiming to find their own voices. Walter Dahn, for instance, had studied with Beuys, and Jiří Georg Dokoupil with Haacke. Yet, when Maenz presented *Mülheimer Freiheit & Interessante Bilder aus Deutschland* (Mülheimer Freiheit & Interesting Pictures from Germany) in 1980, the insistence in its promotion on the emergence of a *new* generation concealed the links between the Neue Wilde—the name by which the young Germans became known—and their predecessors, and Maenz was again accused of having opportunistically betrayed Conceptual Art.

Even though the evolution of Conceptual Art into figurative painting was not followed by—or even visible to—the public, its story is important for us because it shows that the reemergence of painting, like the stylistic diversity and historical references of much art in the early 1980s, was not simply the result of a change in taste or of commercial calculations; rather, it evidences the continuation of projects and discussions that had started in the 1970s but became public only in the early 1980s, when they entered the international art field and came to the attention of the American scene.

Joseph Beuys's international rise to fame that culminated with his 1979 retrospective at the Guggenheim Museum in New York was key to the European comeback. Through the 1970s, he slowly overturned the taboo surrounding German art by creating works that addressed German history without alienating the international (American) public, who appreciated them as a metaphor of the human condition and did not dismiss them as "too German." In 1980, Baselitz and Kiefer were selected to represent Germany at the Venice Biennale. The Biennale marked a turning point in Baselitz's career, not because his work had changed but because the attitude of the art worlds toward him had changed. Sonnabend, who had been among the few visitors

15 This can be seen in Maenz's letters and reports from that period. Galerie Paul Maenz Köln Records, 1956–1991, The Getty Center for the History of Art and the Humanities Special Collections and Visual Resources, Los Angeles, 910066.

jungen Deutschen bekannt wurden – und ihren Vorgängern verschleiert, woraufhin Maenz erneut beschuldigt wurde, die Konzeptkunst auf opportunistische Weise betrogen zu haben.

Obwohl die Weiterentwicklung der Konzeptkunst hin zur figurativen Malerei nicht von der Öffentlichkeit verfolgt wurde – oder sogar für sie nicht einmal sichtbar war –, ist ihre Geschichte wichtig für uns, da sie zeigt, dass das Wiederaufkommen der Malerei wie auch der stilistischen Diversität und der Geschichtsbezüge eines Großteils der Kunst Anfang der 1980er-Jahre nicht bloß das Resultat eines veränderten Geschmacks oder kommerziellen Kalküls war. Vielmehr belegt sie die Fortdauer von Projekten und Diskussionen, die in den 1970er-Jahren einsetzten, aber erst Anfang der 1980er-Jahre öffentlich wahrgenommen wurden, als sie Eingang in die internationale Kunstszene fanden und die US-amerikanische Kunstwelt darauf aufmerksam wurde.

Entscheidend für das europäische Comeback war, dass Joseph Beuys internationale Anerkennung erlangte, die 1979 in einer Retrospektive seines Werks im Guggenheim Museum New York gipfelte. In den 1970er-Jahren überwand er langsam das Tabu, mit dem deutsche Kunst belegt war, indem er Werke schuf, welche die deutsche Geschichte adressierten, ohne die internationale (US-amerikanische) Öffentlichkeit zu befremden, die sie als Metaphern des menschlichen Daseins im Allgemeinen schätzte und nicht als „zu deutsch" ablehnte. 1980 wurden Georg Baselitz und Anselm Kiefer für den deutschen Beitrag zur Biennale von Venedig ausgewählt. Die Biennale stellte einen Wendepunkt in Baselitz' Karriere dar – nicht nur, weil seine Arbeiten sich verändert hatten, sondern auch, weil sich die Haltung der Kunstwelt ihm gegenüber verändert hatte. Ileana Sonnabend, die unter den wenigen Besucher*innen von Baselitz' erster Ausstellung 1963 in Berlin war, zeigte sich sehr beeindruckt. Xavier Fourcade, der ihn ebenfalls seit Langem kannte, erinnert sich: „Im Jahr 1980 zeigte er dann bei der Biennale von Venedig eine Skulptur, die ganz allein in der großen Halle des Deutschen Pavillons stand. Das war fantastisch – so stark, so neuartig, so originell, dass ich realisierte, dass wir es hier tatsächlich mit einem erstrangigen Künstler zu tun hatten, der Skulpturen derselben Qualität erstellen konnte, wie sie auch seine unglaublich beeindruckenden Bilder auszeichnete."[16] Das Deutsche in Baselitz' Arbeiten, das ihn lange auf Nebenschauplätze der zeitgenössischen Kunstszene verbannt hatte, wurde nun als ihre Stärke und Originalität angesehen.

16 Xavier Fourcade, zit. in: Coppet/Jones 1984 (wie Anm. 12), S. 184.

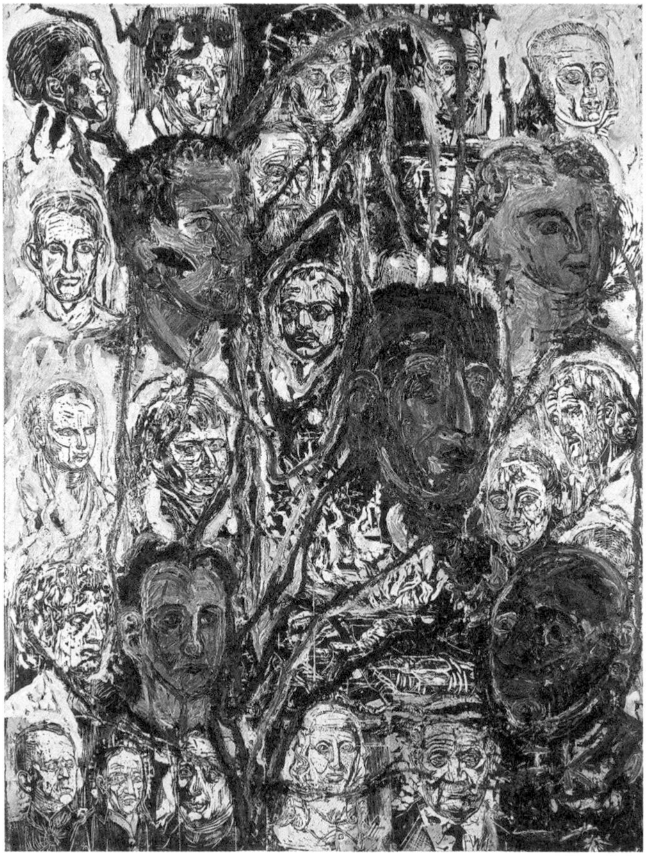

Anselm Kiefer, *Wege II*, 1977
Öl auf Holzschnitt auf Bütten, auf Leinwand kaschiert / oil on woodcut on handmade paper, mounted on canvas, 270 × 210 cm

to Baselitz's first exhibition in 1963 in Berlin, was very impressed. Xavier Fourcade, who had also known him for a long time, remembered, "Then in 1980 he showed a sculpture at the Venice Biennale which was placed alone in the big hall of the German pavilion. It was amazing—so strong—so fresh, so original, that I realized that here was really a first-rate artist, who could make sculpture of the same quality as his immensely impressive paintings."[16] The Germanness of Baselitz's work, which had long kept him on the sidelines of the contemporary art scene, now was seen as its strength and originality.

The Biennale was followed by *A New Spirit in Painting*, which further gave international exposure to Baselitz, Kiefer,

16 Xavier Fourcade, cited in Coppet and Jones 1984 (see note 12), p. 184.

Auf die Biennale folgte *A New Spirit in Painting,* was Baselitz, Kiefer und der restlichen Werner-Gruppe sowie einigen von Maenz' neuen italienischen Künstlern noch mehr internationale Aufmerksamkeit einbrachte. In den Wochen und Monaten nach der Londoner Ausstellung konnte man allgemein ein erhöhtes Tempo feststellen, was sich darin zeigte, dass Kunsthändler*innen miteinander um Verträge mit diesen Kunstschaffenden konkurrierten und sie unbedingt als Erste ausstellen wollten. Innerhalb weniger Wochen hatten alle deutschen und italienischen Kunstschaffenden Ausstellungen in New York. Die schnelle Abfolge dieser Ausstellungen hinterließ bei den New Yorker*innen einen starken Eindruck, die sich von so vielen europäischen Gemälden geradezu überrannt fühlten. William Zimmer, der im Dezember 1981 in der *SoHo News* die New Yorker Ausstellungen deutscher Künstler besprach, betitelte seinen Artikel mit „Blitzkrieg Bopped“[17] (auf Deutsch etwa: „abgerockter Blitzkrieg“). Wenn schon das Schreckgespenst des Faschismus die Rezeption deutscher – und in geringerem Maße auch italienischer – Künstler*innen in den USA trübte, so war der häufigste Vorwurf, den sie sich gefallen lassen mussten, der, dass sie bloß Teil einer kommerziellen Masche waren, eines Tricks der Händler*innen, die sich leicht verkäuflichen europäischen Gemälden zugewandt hätten, nachdem sie sich nicht in der Lage sahen, die schwierigen Werke der Konzeptkünstler*innen zu verkaufen.

Der Wirtschaftsboom der 1980er-Jahre verstärkte diese Fehlinterpretation, warum sich US-amerikanische Galerien der europäischen Kunst zuwandten – eine Tendenz, die deshalb mit Reaganomics und dem Aufkommen der Yuppies in Zusammenhang gebracht wurde. Doch dieses Comeback fand zwischen 1979 und 1982 statt und damit zu einer Zeit, als die US-Wirtschaft nach der zweiten Ölkrise von 1979 eine Rezession durchmachte. Diejenigen New Yorker Galerien, die 1981 und 1982 europäische Maler*innen ausstellten, versuchten nicht etwa vom Wirtschaftswachstum zu profitieren, denn dieses setzte erst 1983 ein, als das europäische Comeback bereits vollzogen war. Auch bedienten sie nicht habgierig den Geschmack der Yuppies, indem sie expressionistische und figurative Bilder zeigten, denn zu dieser Zeit gab es noch gar keine Yuppies.[18]

Vielmehr wurden die US-amerikanischen Kunsthändler*innen durch ihre engen Verbindungen zur und ihre Abhängigkeit von der

17 William Zimmer, „Blitzkrieg Bopped“, in: *The SoHo News,* 22. Dezember 1981, S. 61.

18 Sie tauchten erst 1984 auf. Siehe „The Year of the Yuppie“, in: *Newsweek,* 31. Dezember 1984.

and the rest of Werner's group, as well as to some of Maenz's new Italian artists. In the weeks and months following the London exhibition, everything accelerated, as dealers competed against one another to secure contracts with those artists and rush to be the first to exhibit them. In a few weeks, all the Germans and Italians had shows in New York. The rapid scheduling of these exhibitions made a strong impression on the New Yorkers who felt assaulted by so many European paintings. Reviewing the exhibitions of German artists taking place in New York in December 1981 for the *Soho News*, William Zimmer titled his article "Blitzkrieg Bopped."[17] If the specter of fascism clouded the reception of German—and to a lesser extent Italian—artists in the United States, the most common accusation thrown at them was that they were nothing but a commercial fad, a trick of dealers who, unable to sell the difficult works of the Conceptual artists, had been picking up easy-to-sell paintings in Europe.

The economic boom of the 1980s reinforced this misinterpretation of American galleries' embrace of European art, which was consequently associated with Reaganomics and the Yuppies phenomenon. Yet that comeback took place between 1979 and 1982, when the US economy was going through a recession following the second oil crisis of 1979. The New York galleries that gave shows to the European painters in 1981 and 1982 were not trying to profit from the economic growth, because it started only in 1983, when the European comeback was a fait accompli. Likewise, by showing expressionist, figurative paintings, they were not greedily catering to the tastes of the Yuppies because they did not yet exist.[18]

Rather, American dealers were encouraged to take on European artists by their close links to and dependence on the Western European art worlds. On the one hand, they were informed and connected to the European art scene through their colleagues and clients, and, like them, they came to believe that European artists were creating important works that ought to be shown in the United States. On the other hand, they realized that Europeans were directing their attention and purchases to those artists. Unless they started representing them, they would lose their best clients or at least part of their purchases. When Fourcade presented

17 William Zimmer, "Blitzkrieg Bopped," *The Soho News*, December 22, 1981, p. 61.

18 They emerged in 1984. See "The Year of the Yuppie," *Newsweek*, December 31, 1984.

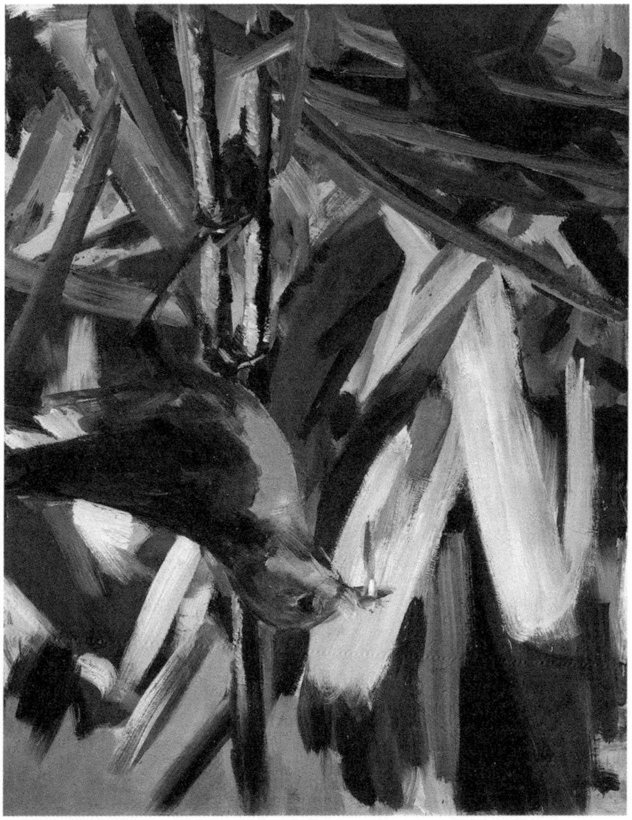

Georg Baselitz, *Singvogel*, 1971
Öl auf Leinwand / oil on canvas, 162 × 130 cm

Kunstszene Westeuropas dazu ermutigt, europäische Künstler*innen in ihr Programm aufzunehmen. Einerseits wurden sie durch ihre Kolleg*innen und Kund*innen informiert und mit der europäischen Kunstszene vernetzt und kamen – wie diese – zu der Überzeugung, dass europäische Künstler*innen wichtige Arbeiten schufen, die auch in den USA gezeigt werden sollten. Andererseits realisierten sie, dass Europäer*innen ihre Aufmerksamkeit diesen Künstler*innen zuwandten und ihre Werke kauften. Wenn man also nicht auch damit anfing, sie zu vertreten, würde man seine beste Kundschaft oder zumindest einen Teil der Verkäufe verlieren. Als Fourcade im Jahr 1981 Baselitz zeigte, verkaufte er zwei Gemälde: eines an die Tate Gallery und eines ans Centre Pompidou.[19] Als Mary Boone ihn dann 1984 ausstellte, verkaufte sie ihrerseits eine Arbeit ans Stedelijk Museum Amsterdam.[20]

19 Paul Taylor, „Boone's Groom: The Brilliant Match of Mary Boone and Michael Werner Could Make Art History", in: *Manhattan, Inc.*, Juni 1986, S. 91.

20 Joosten 1984 (wie Anm. 5), S. 321.

Baselitz in 1981, he sold two paintings: one to the Tate Gallery and one to the Centre Pompidou.[19] Likewise, when Mary Boone showed him in 1984, she sold a work to the Stedelijk Amsterdam.[20]

Despite all the misunderstandings that surrounded the different aspects of the European comeback, by the mid-1980s Western European artists had moved from the shadows to the spotlight. In 1986, the Venice Biennale reinstituted the grand prizes, which had been eliminated after the events of 1968, under the new name "Golden Lion." That year the prize went to Sigmar Polke. To be sure, this victory did not have the same impact as Rauschenberg's in 1964, but it was a very symbolic moment for Western European art in terms of its prestige and for German art in particular. Western European artists were back on the map, but what the consequences of their comeback would be on the narrative of twentieth-century art remained uncertain.[21]

19 Paul Taylor, "Boone's Groom: The Brilliant Match of Mary Boone and Michael Werner Could Make Art History," *Manhattan, Inc.*, June 1986, p. 91.

20 Joosten, *20 Years of Art Collecting*, p. 321.

21 On this question, see Dossin 2015 (see note 4), pp. 277–87.

Trotz aller Missverständnisse, die verschiedene Aspekte des europäischen Comebacks umgaben, hatten es bis Mitte der 1980er-Jahre verschiedene westeuropäische Künstler*innen vom Schattendasein ins Rampenlicht geschafft. 1986 verlieh die Biennale von Venedig wieder die großen Preise, die nach den Ereignissen von 1968 abgeschafft worden waren, unter dem neuen Namen „Goldener Löwe“. In diesem Jahr erhielt Sigmar Polke den Goldenen Löwen. Sicherlich hatte dieser Triumph nicht dieselbe Wirkung wie der von Rauschenberg im Jahr 1964, aber es war dennoch ein wichtiger symbolischer Moment für das Prestige der Kunst Westeuropas und insbesondere Deutschlands.
Die Künstler*innen aus Westeuropa erschienen erstmals wieder auf der Landkarte, aber es blieb ungewiss, welche Konsequenzen ihr Comeback für das Narrativ der Kunst des 20. Jahrhunderts haben würde.[21]

21 Zu dieser Frage siehe Dossin 2015 (wie Anm. 4), S. 277–287.

1. außerordentliche Veranstaltung in Bild und Klang zum Thema der Zeit: Elend
Poster, Kippenbergers Büro, Berlin, 1979, Design: Martin Kippenberger

Auch wenn das Perlhuhn leise weint
Poster, BBK Hahnentorburg, Köln / Cologne, 1980, Design: Jiří Georg Dokoupil

Finger für Deutschland
Flyer, Atelier Jörg Immendorff, Düsseldorf, 1980, Design: Martin Kippenberger

Tunten Television
Flyer, Galerie am Moritzplatz, Berlin, 1977

New York Narrative Film Fest
Poster, S.O.36, Berlin, 1979, Design: Martin Kippenberger, Uli Kukulies, Andreas Rohé

Programm / Program
Flyer, S.O.36, Berlin, Mai / May 1979, Design: Martin Kippenberger

Programm / Program
Flyer, S.O.36, Berlin, März–April / March–April 1979, Design: Martin Kippenberger

Programm / Program
Flyer, S.O.36, Berlin, Oktober / October 1978, Design: Uli Kukulies, Andreas Rohé

1. außerordentliche Veranstaltung
in Bild und Klang zum Thema der Zeit:

ELEND

mit Ina Barfuss, Werner Büttner, Walter Dahn,
Michael Deissler, Achim Duchow, Uwe Gabriel,
Georg Herold, Kippenberger, Joachim Krüger,
Meuser, Albert Oehlen, Marcus Oehlen,
Brigitta Rohrbach, Thomas Wachweger

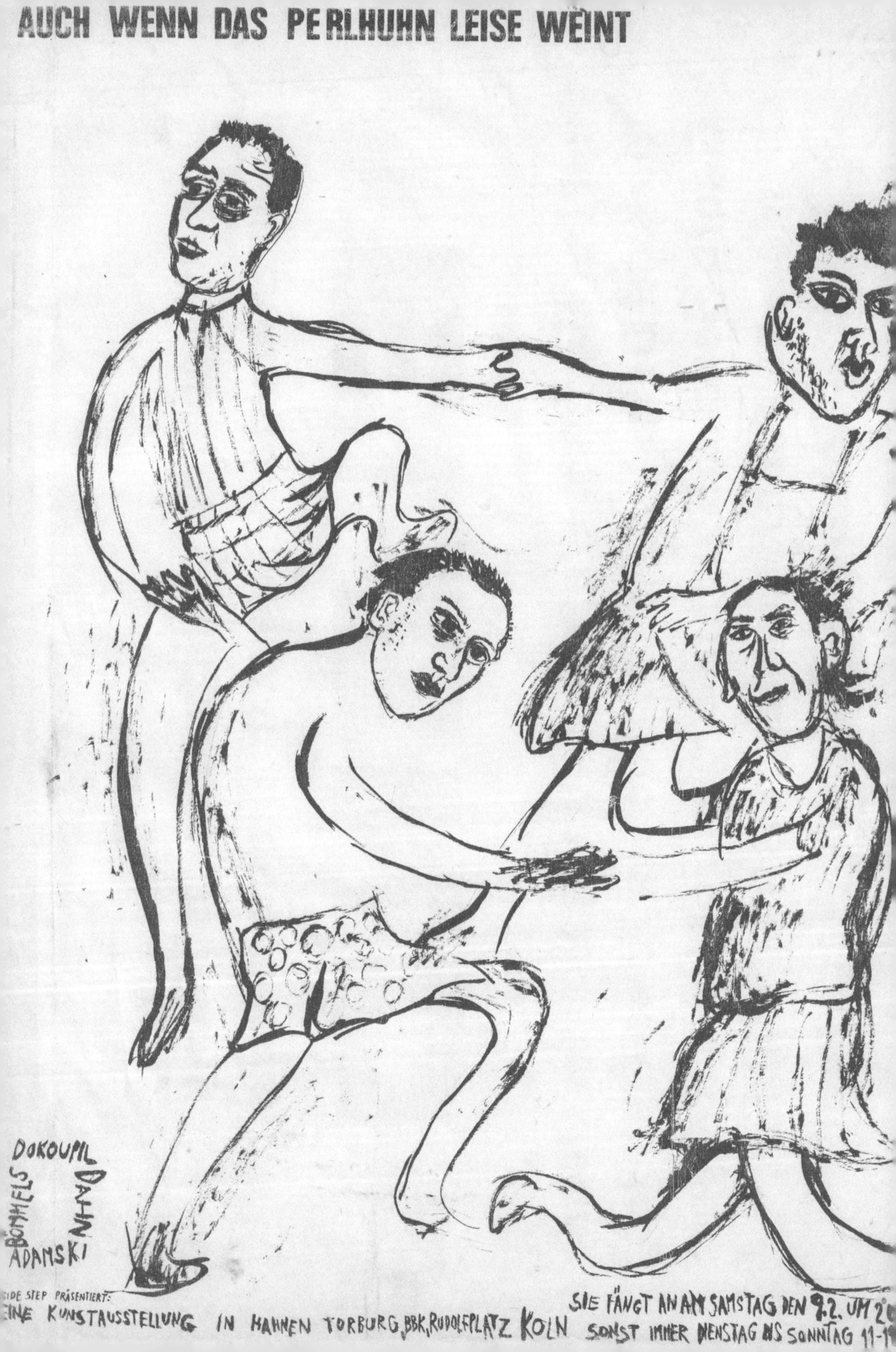
AUCH WENN DAS PERLHUHN LEISE WEINT
DOKOUPIL
DAHN
BOMMELS
ADAMSKI
IDE STEP PRÄSENTIERT:
INE KUNSTAUSSTELLUNG IN HAHNEN TORBURG, BBK, RUDOLFPLATZ KOLN
SIE FÄNGT AN AM SAMSTAG DEN 9.2. UM 2
SONST IMMER DIENSTAG BIS SONNTAG 11-1

Finger für Deutschland

Peter Adamski   Elvira Bach   Ina Barfuß

Uwe Gabriel   Georg Herold   Walter Dahn

Albert Oehlen   Markus Oehlen   Brigitta Rohrbach

Martin Kippenberger   Elviera Wersche

Jörg Immendorff   Peter Bömm   Christa Näher

Günther Tuzina   Michael Bauch   Gerd Klever

Werner Büttner   Gerhard Naschberger

Georg Dokupil   Thomas Wachweger

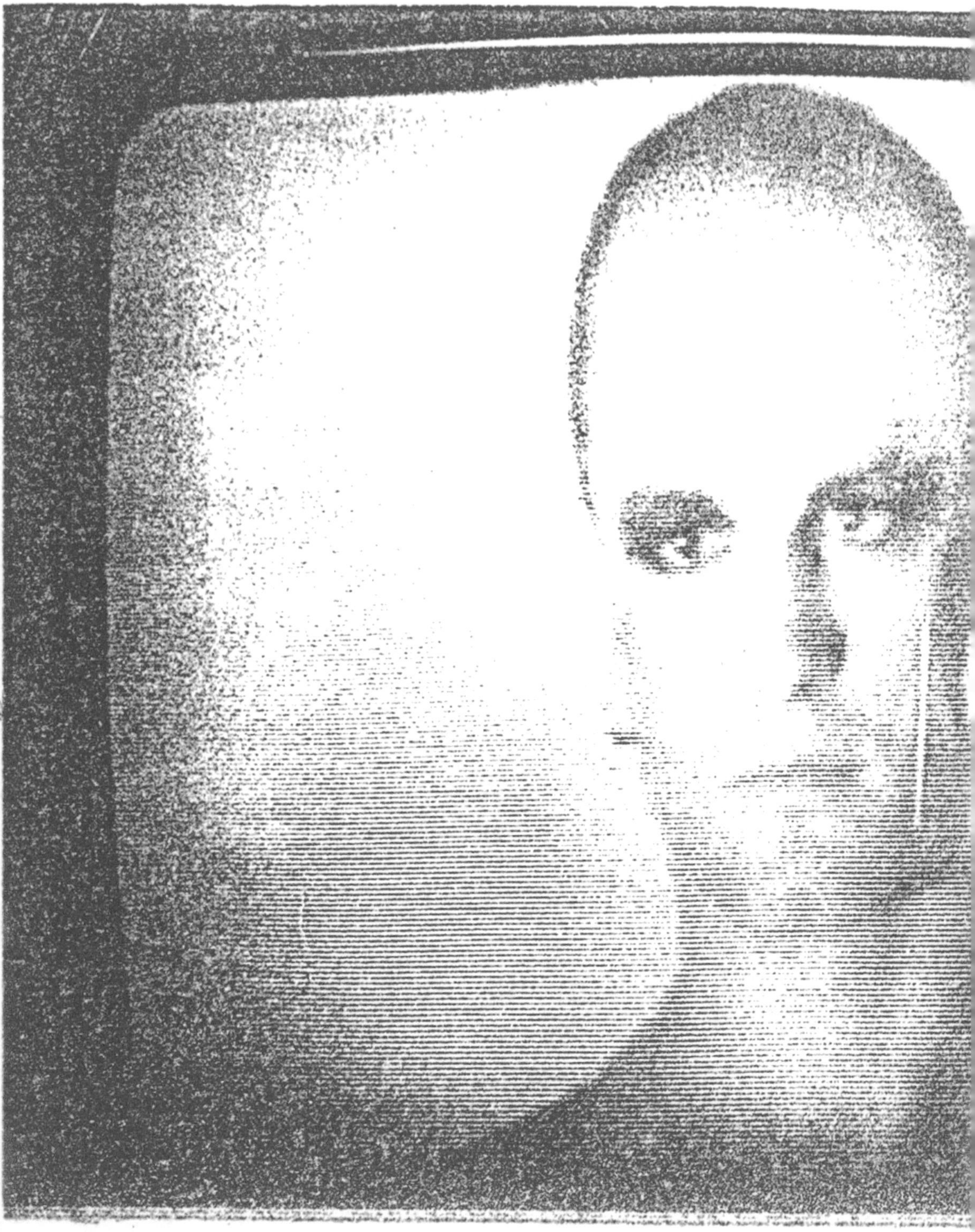

NEW YORK NARRATIVE FILM FEST
im S.O. 36 · Oranienstr. 190 · 12. 6. – 23. 6.

Di 12. 6.
21.00 Uhr **Shame**
von John Aheaern 15 min, 16 mm, Ton, Farbe
Beklemmende Grossaufnahmen in Limonengruen und scharfem Pink
Volkommener Wandel der beiden Charactere – Herrschaft wird Unterwuerfigkeit, aus der theatralischen Pose werden persoenliche Bekenntnisse
„Ihre Freude naehrt unsere Schande"

The Deadly Art Of Survival
von Charley Ahearn 82 min, Super 8
Liebe und Gewalt im Ghetto
Sie entfuehren Nathans kleinen Sohn
Der schoene Harry aus der Disco
Nathans Rache & der Kampf am Pier

Do. 14. 6.
21.00 Uhr **Black Box**
von Beth B. & Scott B. 30 min, Super 8
Unschuldige Jugend in der Folterkammer.
In der Kanalzone, am Potomac Fluss in Texas und in Brunswick, Texas unterhaelt die Regierung der USA Ausbildungsstaetten an denen Verhoerstechniken vermittelt werden. Diese Schulen vergeben Foltertechniken an bestimmte totalitaere Regierungen um deren Macht aufrecht zu erhalten.

22.00 Uhr **Bored**
von Karin Luner N.Y. 30 min, Super 8
Das Leben ist so langweilig oder ich will mich verlieben.
New York scene – picture shooting – going out for concerts – hangouts – make up & fucked up. Ich suche einen Liebhaber – buy a man for 25 dollar . . . use it & throw away Kleinkind, ich bin immer noch gelangweilt. Suicide in a foto-machine.

23.00 Uhr **Rome '78**
von James Nares 90 min, Super 8
Moderne Menschen verschwoeren sich gegen Caesar.
Ein todbringender Machtkampf.
Wir haben Koenigreich gespielt, genau wie wir es als Kinder taten, bloss dass es jetzt jemand gefilmt hat. Wir brauchten kein Drehbuch, da wir wussten wer wir waren. Wir habens einfach gemacht.

Di 19. 6.
21.00 Uhr **Red Italy**
von Eric Mitchel Video
Der bislang wohl unterhaltendste Punk Film ueberhaupt. Eine gelangweilte Reiche greift sich einen schwarzen GI. Sie nimmt ihn mit in ihr Appartment. Waehrend er sie auszieht beschwoert er sie, dass er nicht vorhat sie zu ficken. Allein das wird ausreichen das gesunde Volksempfinden zu erregen.

22.30 Uhr **Kidnapped**
von Eric Mitchel 60 min, Video
Ein Untergrundfilm aus den 60igern von heute. Sex & Politik an einem Amphetamintag in einer Wohnung im East Village.

Mi 20. 6.
21.00 Uhr **Rund um USA**
von Colen Fitzgibbon 15 min, Video
Ein Film aus Nachrichten ueber Deutschland und den USA.
Die Wahrscheinlichkeit dass du entfuehrt wirst ist groesser als dass du bei einem Flugzeugabsturz drauf gehst.

21.30 Uhr **Slow Scan Transmissions**
von Liza Bear Video
Die Schluesselfunktion des Kreislaufes ist ein Videosignal in ein akustisches zu uebertragen, das im Ukw-Bereich liegt, und zwar innerhalb des vorhandenen Telefonnetzes.
Der Empfaenger transformiert die akustischen Signale wieder in optische mit Hilfe des gleichen Geraetes. Das Bild wird sichtbar auf jedem handelsueblichen TV-Bildschirm, dieser Vorgang ist umkehrbar.
Das hat natuerlich den Vorteil, dass jeder jedem sein eigenes Material senden kann. Wir waeren nicht mehr die passiven Empfaenger.

22.00 Uhr **Policeband Loop Tape**
von Diego Cortes 60 min, Farbe, Video, 1979
Eine Studioaufnahme der Policeband (Boris Gladstone) vom Februar 1979 in New York City. Das Band ist eine Serie von 20 fuenf Minuten Sequencen, die sich staendig wiederholen. Die Originalsequenz ist ein Mitschnitt aus einer Diskussion, die Mitglieder der „Collaborative Projects, Inc." mit Hanns Magnus Enzensberger ueber juengste politische Ereignisse in der

Sa 23. 6.
21.00 Uhr **Brooklyn 11238**
von Rainer Fetting 1978/1979
90 min, color, Magnetton Super 8

Darst.: Bergmann, Krey, Middendorf, Salomé, Zimmer u. a.

Inhalt:
Junger Maler geht nach New York, verliebt sich kurz vor seiner Abreise in Berlin und flippt schließlich aus.
In New York erlebt er ungewohnte Dinge: Punkgruppen in C.B.G.B., Brooklyn und die Schwarzen, Deutsche, die sich vergittern, Einbrueche, Cockroaches, explodierende Briefkaesten . . .
An Sylvester faehrt er mit einem Mietwagen Amok durch Manhattan.
Das alles endet mit einer Vergewaltigung.

Live in New York:
Richard Hell and the Voidoids
the Police
B-52

Filmmusik: Günter Schickert

22.45 Uhr **Burning Desire**
von Robin Winters 12 min, Ton, Super 8
Der tiefe Glaube eines umherirrenden Kindes, unbefriedigt in seinem Verlangen nach Liebe. Es verbrennt Gegenstaende – Haeuser, Betten, Autos und Fabriken.
Der Film zeigt die Qual der Ablehnung, und dessen Darstellung aus der Sicht eines Pyromanen.

23.15 Uhr **Beauty Becomes The Beast**
von Vivienne Dick 40 min, Super 8
Daemonen der Kindheit und der Paranoia, Kalter Sex, Kurzschluesse, Vergeltung, Verwesung der Normen.
Der Film zeigt die psycho-sexuellen Drohgebaerden zwischen Mann und Frau. Die Erziehung eines Maedchens und die Funktion der Unterdrueckung bei ihrer Einfuehrung in Sexualitaet.

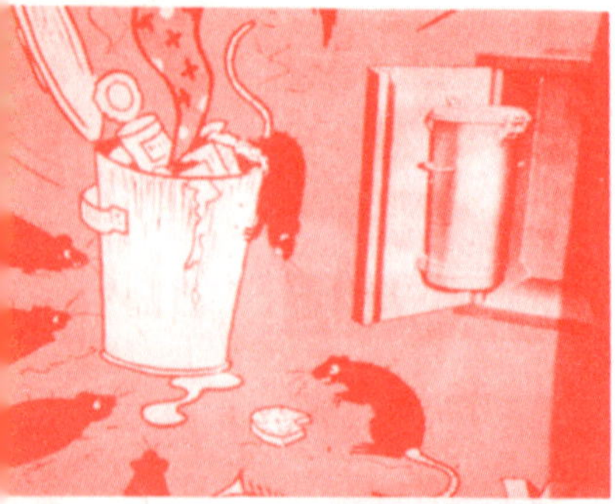

ASCHA MATTA

Laufende Bilder
Bericht über die Jugend aller Länder und deren Problem jung zu sein

Super 8 Normal 8 dreifach Kodak-Projektion

MI 9. 5.

Bringt eure Fotos mit

NICKY & THE DOTS

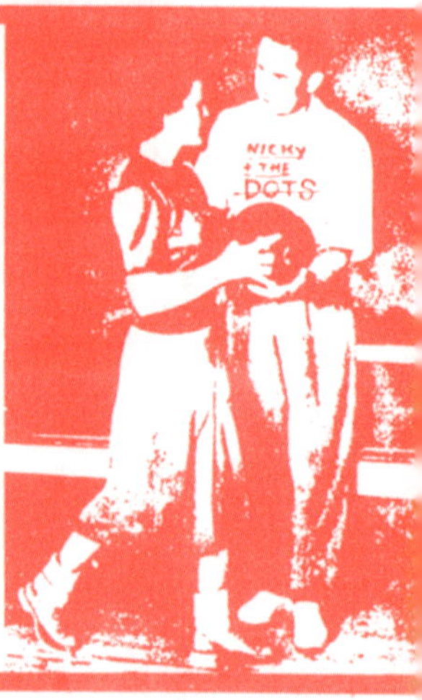

Neben der Rockmetropole London entwickelt sich in Brighton — beinahe unbeachtet — eine eigenstädige Musikszene. Neben den „Vitamins" und den „Piranhas" sind „Nicky & The Dots" die Spitzenvertreter dieser Richtung. In ihrer Musik lassen sie Einflüsse der Mods und Mersybeat-Gruppen der frühen 60er Jahre erkennen.

Besetzung: Nick Dwyer (main voc.), Dave Williams (bass, voc.), Paul Clark (org.), Ken Hogg, the nasty wee man (dr.)

FR 11. 5. / SA 12. 5.

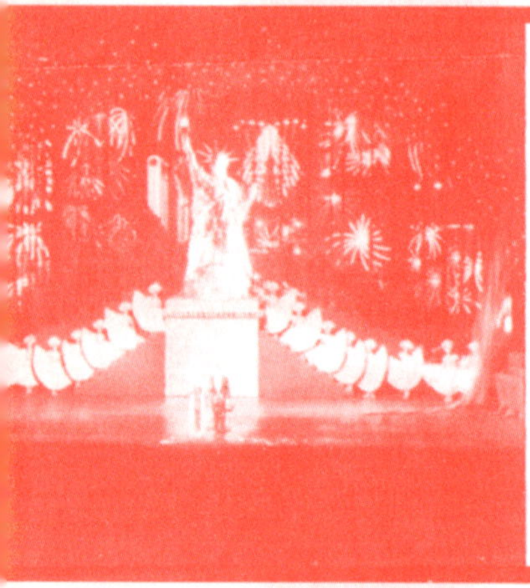

LIBERTY 3 ×

Freiheit zum Angucken für Ausländer

„New York im letzten Jahr! Da stehst Du nun zwischen allem Glitter und Mist und immer wieder: LIBERTY! Schwarz über weiß oder weiß über schwarz? Fragezeichen!"

Helmut Metzner

Bilder in 160 × 200 Graphit auf Papier

DI 15. 5.

KUCKI LUCKI

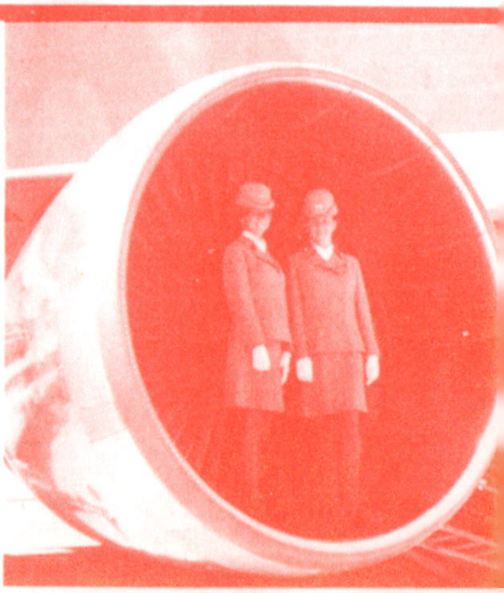

Filmnacht
u. a. wird geboten:
Do you like snow
Der Besenbinder von Kentucky
Durchquerung des Panamakanals
Mutti bei Dreharbeiten
Charlton Heston öffnet die Türen hinter den Kulissen
Etwas über John F. und Robert Kennedy's Beerdigung

MI 16. 5.

FREITAG, 22 - 3 - 1979
Rock 'n' Roll Nacht
Mit: *Fredy Fingers Lee* (England) und Preistanz
PS. Anmeldung und Schallplattenwünsche bis 22 Uhr an der Kasse!

DONNERSTAG, 29 - 3 - 1979
Text am Bild 2-fach Projektion
Mit: *Werner Büttner, Claus Bömler, Andi Hertel, Joachim Krüger, Thomas Wachweger* u. a.

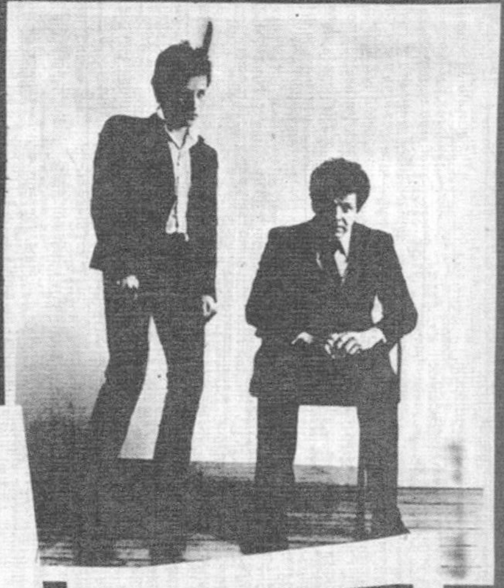

SAMSTAG 7 - 4 - 1979
Red Crayola & Scritti Politi im Doppelprogramm Live!
Rockmusik aus New York

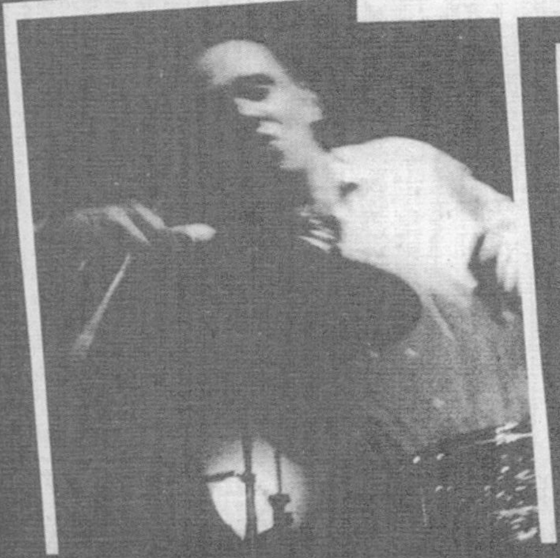

DIENSTAG 10 - 4 - 1979 und
DONNERSTAG 12 - 4 - 1979
In Vorbereitung:

Nordeuropäisches Improvisations- und Klangorchester,
Mit: *Rüdiger Carl*, Tenorsax cl., BRD; *Ernst-Ludwig Petrowski*, Alt sax. cl., DDR; *Wolfgang Fuchs*, Sopranino, b.cl., W-B; *Radu Malfatti*, posaune, Ö; *Thomas Wiedermann*, posaune, W-B; *Hans Reichel*, gitarre, BRD; *Norbert Eisbrenner*, gitarre, BRD; *Maarten van Regferen*, Altena b., Holland; *Sven Ake Johansson*, dr, Schweden.

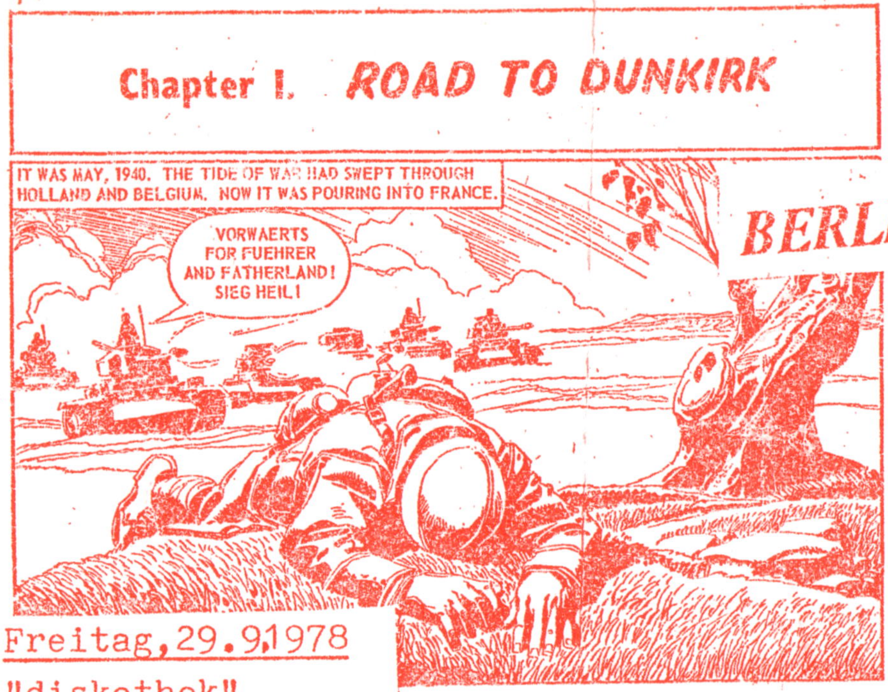

SC

BERLIN IST D

MI,FR,SA

Freitag,29.9.1978
"diskothek"
Eintritt: DM 2.-

Samstag,30.9.1978
Sonntag,1.10.1978
DEUTSCHER TOUR 78
ADAM AND THE ANTS
DIE "JUBILEE" SENSATION AUS ENGLAND
Eintritt: DM 7.-

Mittwoch,4.10.1978
Halbautomatische Klänge
im Zeitalter der Wechselschicht.
Mittagspause
Eintritt: DM 4.-

„HASTE SCHON JEHÖRT?"
"WALL CITY", WA?

Freita
"disko
Raritä
und In

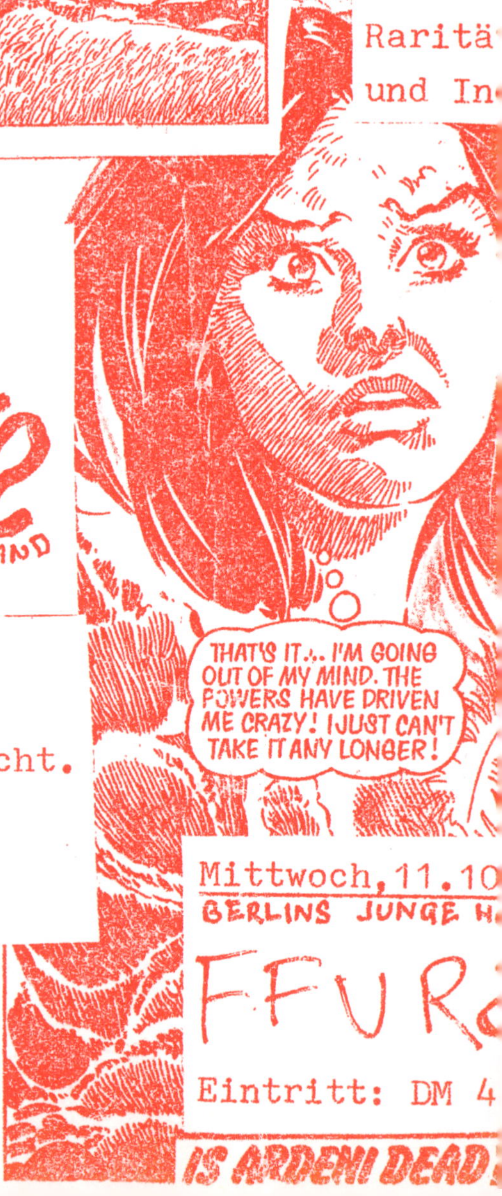

Mittwoch,11.10
BERLINS JUNGE H
FFURa
Eintritt: DM 4

6

NTRALISIERT!

…ns Zeit SO 21⁰⁰-5⁰⁰

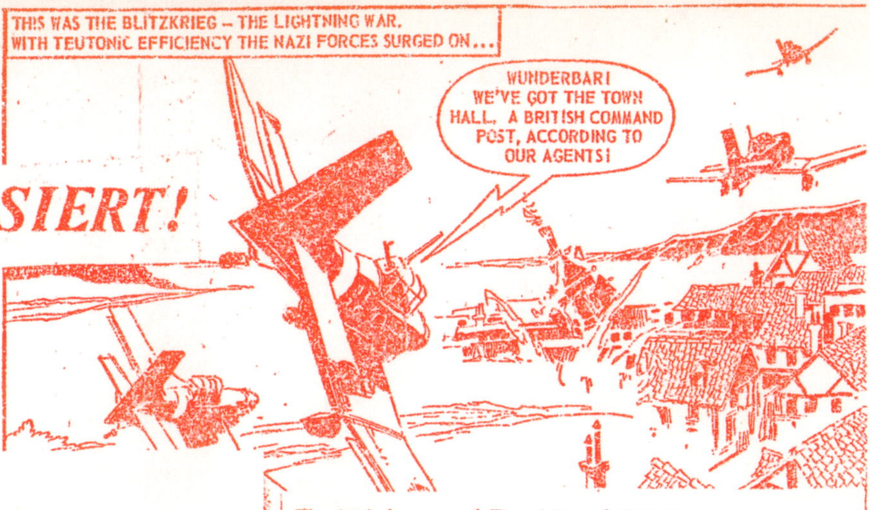

).1978
Die schräge Konserve.
ıs der Welt der Technik
.e. Eintritt: DM 2.-

Freitag, 13.10.1978 "disko"
Eintritt: DM 2.-

Samstag, 14.10.1978
Sonntag, 15.10.1978
EX 'COCKNEY REBELS'
The Warm Jets
AUS LONDON
Eintritt: DM 7.-

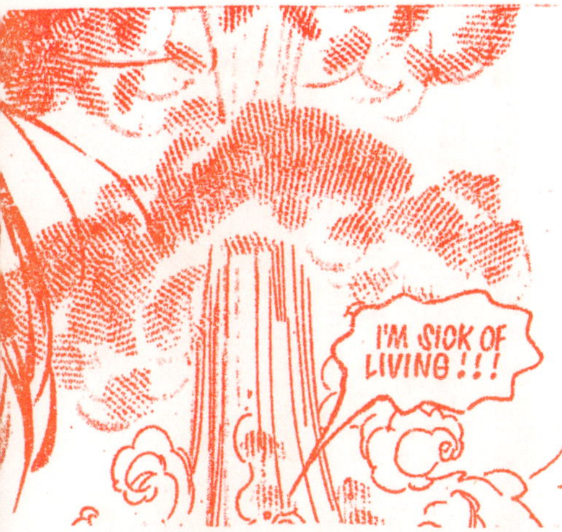

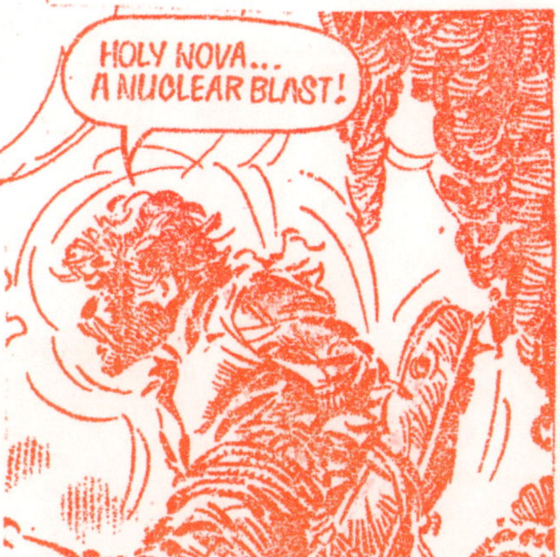

Samstag, 7.10.1978
Sonntag, 8.10.1978

AUTOMATICS

Eintritt: DM 7.-

Mittwoch, 18.10.1978
MULTI-SLIDE-SHOW
BUENOS DIAS-KIPPENBERGER

Eintritt: DM 3.-

OUT IN NEXT WEEK'S CONCLUDING EPISODE!

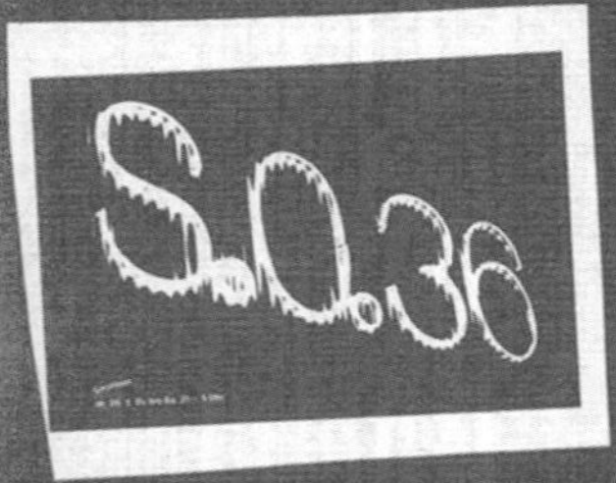

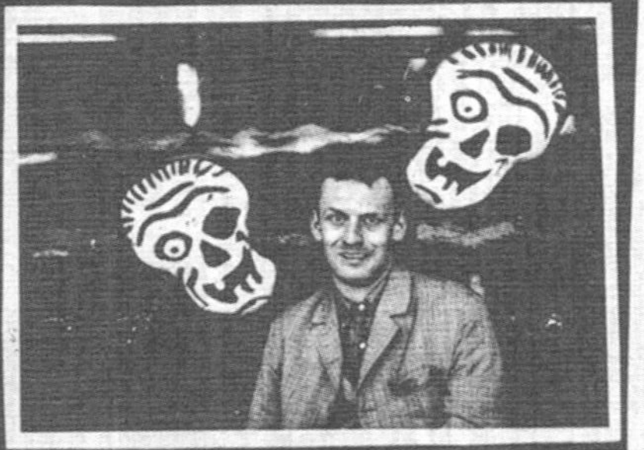

FREITAG, 2 - 3 - 1977
1/4 Jahrhundert
Einer von Euch – mit Euch – unter Euch

Mit: *Tabea Blumenschein:* Filmuraufführung **Die Dollarprinzessin;**

Klippenberger Junior: Video, Normal 8, 3-fach Tonbildschau, Tanz und Spaß;

Klippenberger Senior: Übertage/Untertage, Zandvoort an Zee, 2-fach Projektion;

RCB = Rocking Club Berlin: Rock 'n' Roll Akrobatik;

The Warm Jets: Musik aus London.

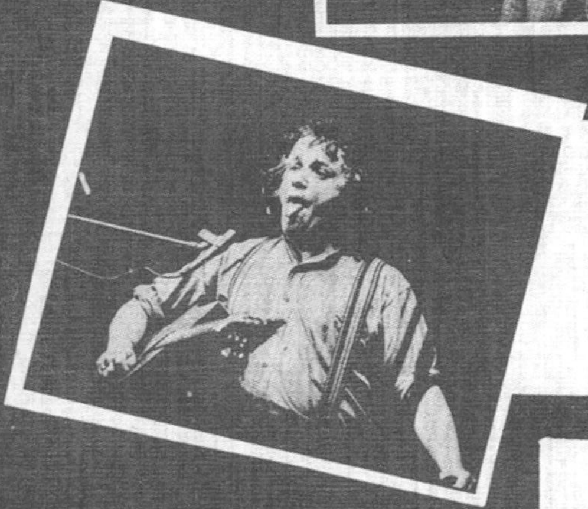

MITTWOCH 7 - 3 - 1979
Kevin Coyne,
ist 35 Jahre alt, verheiratet, hat 2 Kinder. Er stammt aus der mittelenglischen Stadt Derby, die ungefähr auf halbem Weg zwischen Birmingham und Sheffield in den reizlosen Midlands liegt. Er kommt mit Band.

DIENSTAG, 13 - 3 - 1979
Elvira Bach,
Jahrgang 51 (Frankfurt/M), zeigt Badewannenbilder.

FREITAG, 16 - 3 - 1979
Kleenex
Frauenband aus der Schweiz.

DIENSTAG, 20 - 3 - 1979
Die Abfahrer
LKW-Film von Adolf Winkelmann

SUICIDE

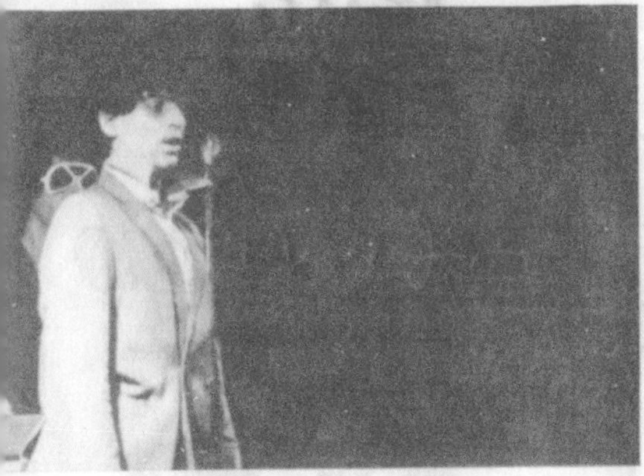

Nach langen Bemühungen ist es uns endlich gelungen, Suicide nach Berlin zu verpflichten. Diese Zwei-Mann-Formation aus New York besteht seit sieben Jahren. Als Pioniere der modernen Elektronik haben sie Musiker wie Brian Eno, Robert Rental und Schneider-Essleben (Kraftwerk) entscheidend beeinflußt. Die visuelle und musikalische Dynamik dieser Gruppe kommt insbesondere bei Live Auftritten zur Geltung, und ist auf Platte nur ansatzweise konservierbar. In Deutschland erschienene Platten: Single: Cheree (Red Star 78) Album: Suicide (Red Star 78) und Rocket USA auf dem Sampler „Live At Max's Kansas City" (CBS 78).

SA 19. 5. / DI 22. 5.

SONNENUNTERGANG

olossalgemälde vor Ort
usführung Middendorf und Fetting

lme von Scodelmeier, Fetting,
iddendorf,

avid am Piazale Mikel Angelow

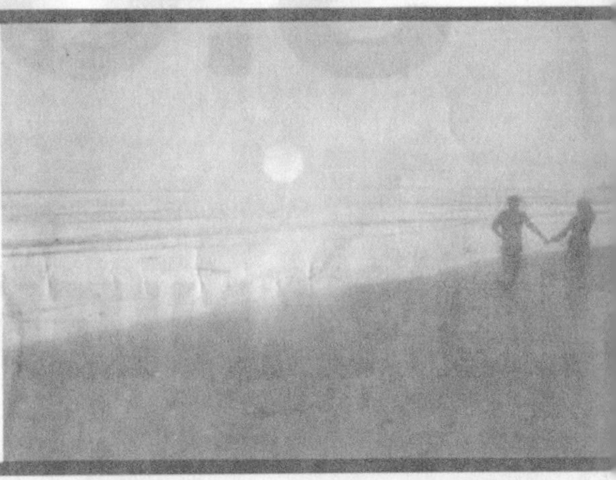

MI 23. 5.

THE NORMAL / ROBERT RENTAL

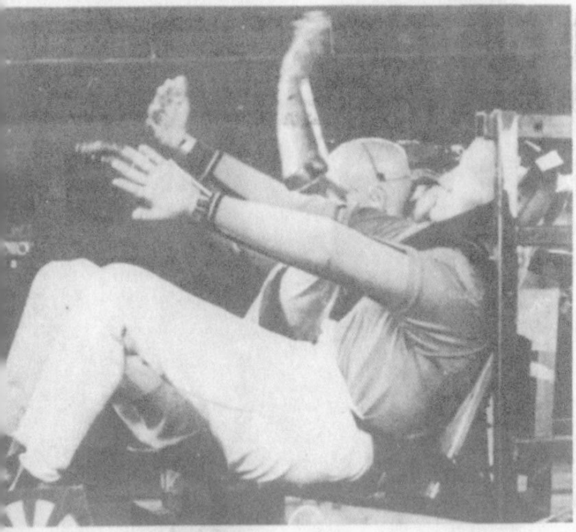

Diese Londoner Gruppe Daniel Miller (synth., voc.) produzierte im Mai 78 eine der ersten Platten der Neuen Elektronik: T.V.O.D./warm leatherette (Mute Rec. 78). Ihre Musik beschreibt das von Technik bestimmte Leben unseres Digitalzeitalters oder den schnellen Sex im gestohlenen Wagen mit attraktiver Kälte und Distanz.
Robert Rental, der am selben Abend mit seinem eigenen experimentellen elektronischen Programm auftritt, arbeitet seit einiger Zeit eng mit The Normal zusammen. Seine bisherige Plattenveröffentlichung: A.C.C./Paralysis (Regular Rec 78). Diese Doppelveranstaltung bietet erstmals die Möglichkeit, Vertreter der Neuen Lodoner Elektronic kennenzulernen.

MI 30. 5.

Adele Bertei & Her Assasins

Sa 16. 6. **G-man**
22.00 Uhr von Beth B. & Scott B. 70 min, Super 8
Das private und oeffentliche Leben des Max Karl, Chef des „Arson Explosive Squad“ (am. Spezialeinheit zur Terrorbekaempfung)
Sein Leben spielt zwischen seiner Perversitaet und dem Bild, dass er in den Medien als befehlshabender Offizier darstellt.
Der Terror ist fuer ihn die Chance endlich mal gross raus zukommen.
& No New York Wave Music:
Doppelkonzert
Teenage Jesus & The Jerks
Adele Bertei & Her Assasins

von Cara Perlman 16 min, Color-Video
Farbvideo ueber eine New Yorker Oben-Ohne-Taenzerin waehrend der Arbeit. Wie sie es macht, wer in die Bars geht, und was die Angestellten darueber denken.

24.00 Uhr Men In Orbit
von John Lurie 45 min, Video
Kontrollzentrum in der Kueche.
Monitore, Digitalanzeiger, kaputte Fernseher.
Ein Autositz, etwas Pappe, ein Buendel Kabel
Astronauten im Raum
Bedraengnis und Hektik, eine Reise ins Ungewisse
„Voll auf Acid, dachten wir echt wir waeren im Weltraum.“

von Rainer Fetting 1978/79
30 min, Super 8, color, magnetton
mit viel Musik, the dictators und Musik von Günter Schickert

S.O. 36: Fetting und Zimmer malen New York.

Und Fetting und Middendorf echt in New York.
Und junge go-go-girls, die ihre Badehose zeigen.

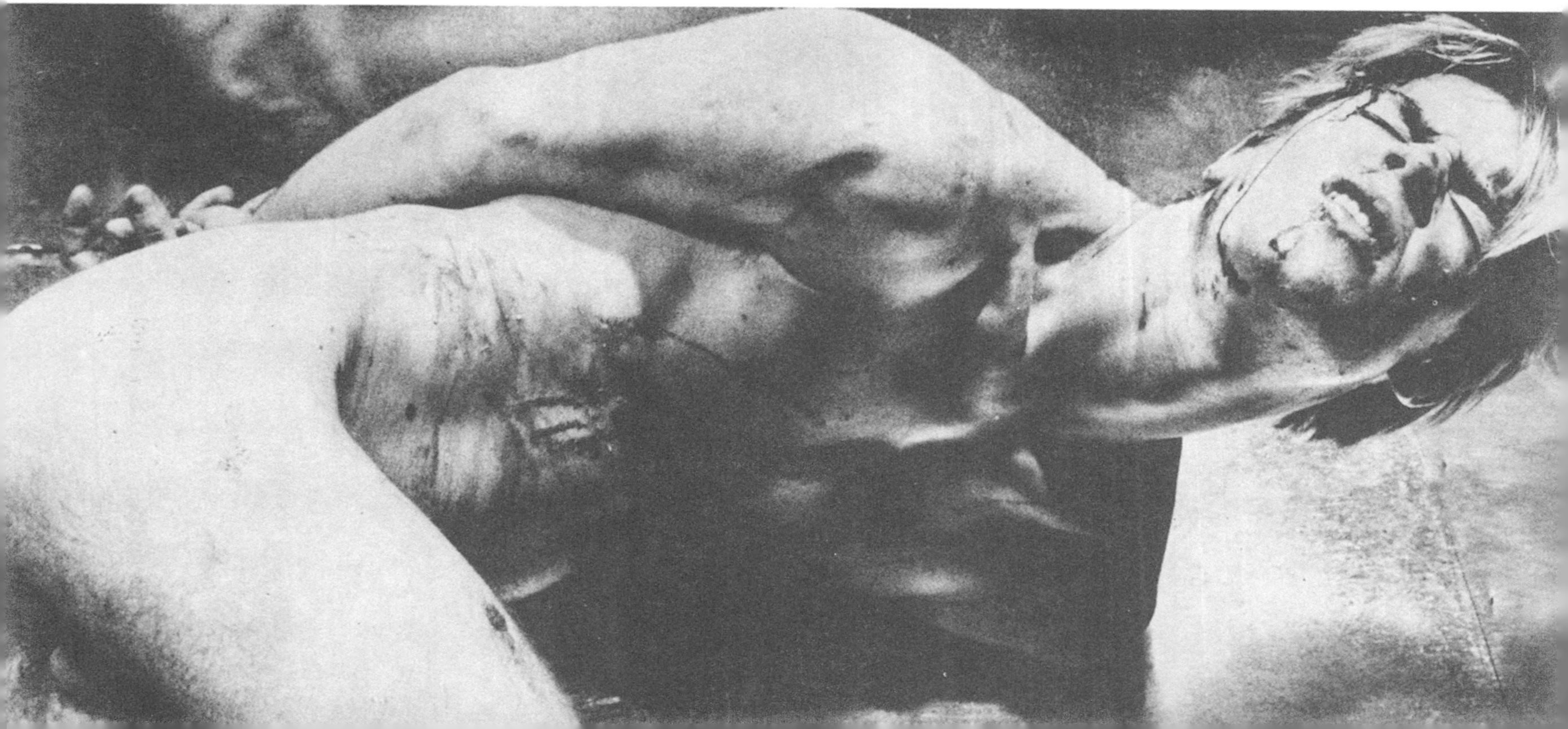

TUNTEN TELEVISION TUNTEN TELEVISION TUNTEN TELEVISION TUNTEN TELEVISION TUNTEN

WIR MACHEN EINEN RERNSEHABEND MIT EIGENEN PRODUKTIONEN

GALERIE AM MORITZPLATZ Oranienstr.58 Fabrik 1000 Berlin 61
U-Moritzplatz A29;75 Tel.6148618

SAMSTAG 5.11.77 19.00 Uhr

Hilka Nordhausen   Jürgen Drescher   Berger

Eintritt DM 10.-   Die Eintrittskarte ist ebenfalls gültig
für das Konzert am 5. Oktober im Ratinger Hof
Eröffnung 27. September 80, 18 Uhr   Öffnungszeiten 15   19 Uhr

Atelier Jörg Immendorf
Gustav Poensgen Straße 29   4000 Düsseldorf   Telefon 375643

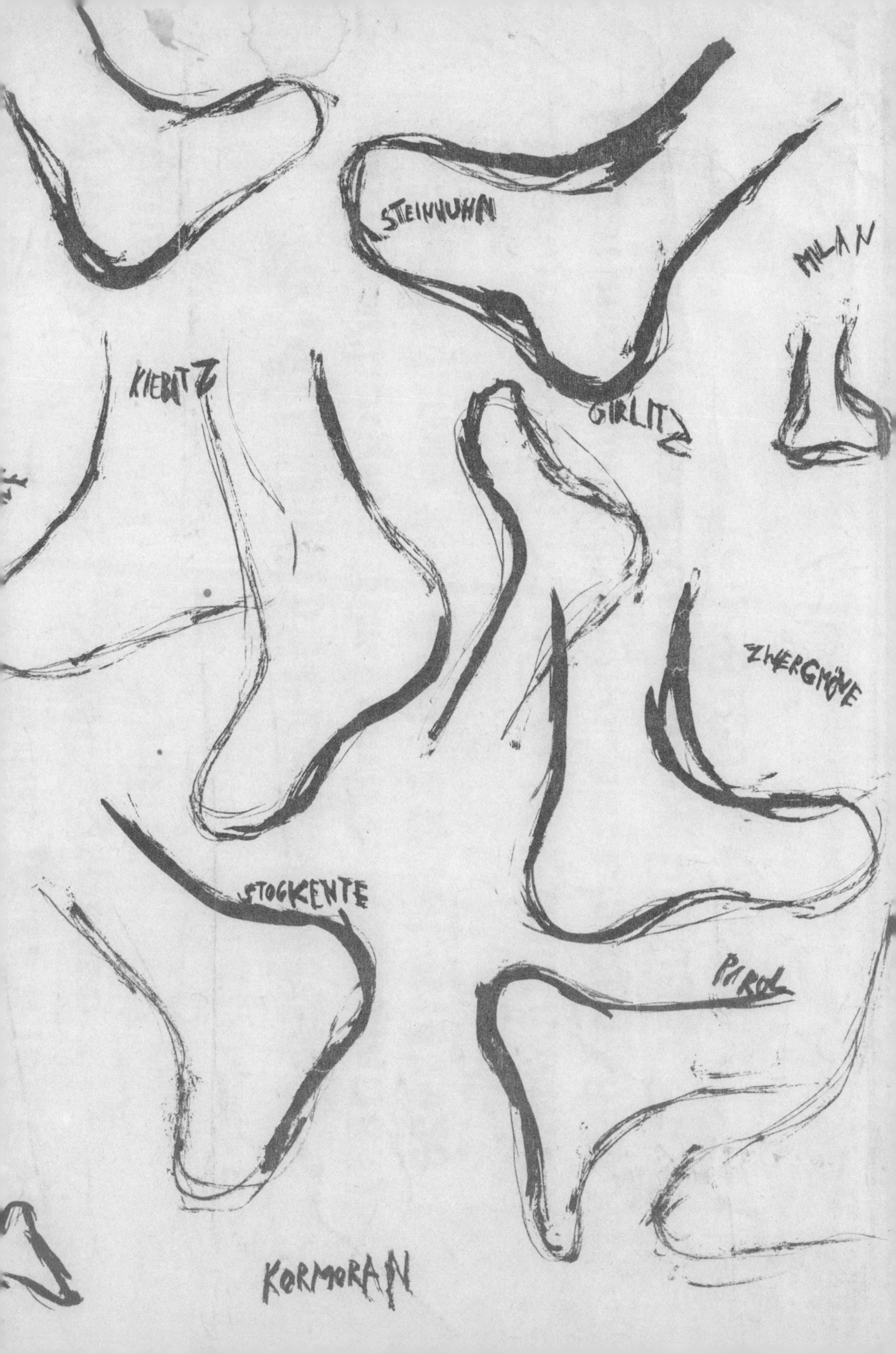
STEINHUHN
MILAN
KIEBITZ
GIRLITZ
ZWERGMÖVE
STOCKENTE
PIROL
KORMORAN

Musik: **White Russia (ex PVC)**
Mania D. **Mittagspause**
Luxus **Syph**

Eröffnungsveranstaltung

in Kippenbergers Büro am 17. Nov. um 18 Uhr
Segitzdamm 2-4, Berlin 61, Tel. 6147928

Geöffnet Do, Fr, Sa 17-20 Uhr und nach Vereinbarung. Ausstellungsdauer bis zum 18. Dez.
Kartenvorverkauf bei Zensor Belziger Str. 23
Tel. 7812698

Salomé
Es ging um das Einbringen des Andersseins in die Kunst

Salomé
I wanted to inject otherness into art

Auszüge aus einem Gespräch mit den Herausgeber*innen /
Excerpts from a conversation with the editors, Berlin, April 2018

I arrived in Berlin in 1973 and immediately joined the Homosexuelle Aktion Westberlin to be active in politics. There I was part of the faggot faction, and even within the HAW we were the subject of heated discussions. The HAW recruited mainly from the students and they were split into countless leftist groups, and the Marxists were adamant that the main contradiction needed to be eradicated first, namely capitalism. And we faggots replied, well if that's the case, then we'll have to wait an eternity, we'll never have a chance to gain liberation. But we want liberation now, we can get rid of capitalism afterwards. And continuously that led to arguments about how we should create a public presence. We faggots always said that we had to get out in the subways, distribute leaflets, we have to strike up conversations with ordinary people. The others wanted to debate at some political party event or wanted to march at the May Day demo with the SED [Socialist Unity Party of Germany], armed with a small banner. And we said: No, either we march with a large banner solely for ourselves, or we don't march at all with those kind of people. You need to remember that most of these groups were scared that the whole left-wing movement could be vilified as being gay, and that's why the gays weren't that welcome. The liberated women had very similar problems. But faggots know no fear, we were always loud and aggressive in our political demands. For us it was all about attracting attention, we weren't about the normal, inhibited homo yet to come out of the closet. That's why huge clashes took place at these HAW meetings quite often. [...]

I then tried to use art to press ahead with liberation. And that only works if you paint provocative pictures, and preferably as self-portraits. At the intake interview for the Hochschule für bildende Künste, today the Berlin University of the Arts, Professor Hödicke asked what I wanted to paint, and I said "myself"—and he admitted me. I really pushed it with the figural on myself in provocative gestures and poses. First using mirrors, then photos, from which I then developed the paintings. The works were always both. Self-portraits and the representation of an artistic figure. I wanted to inject otherness into art. That was a political act back then and extremely provocative, for the motifs I painted hardly existed in art and the public domain, in painting even less so. One important impulse for these works was the catalogue of the exhibition *Transformer – Aspekte der Travestie* [Transformer—Aspects of Travesty], held at the Kunstmuseum Luzern in 1974. There mainly photography was shown and painting actually only in the form of works on paper. I was intrigued by these stories of self-representation, the photographic work of Pierre Molinier had left a deep impression on me. And Luciano Castelli was also part of this exhibition. This had given me the first push, so to speak, for my own art; I then reformulated this into painting during my studies. [...]

Ich bin 1973 nach Berlin gekommen und gleich in die Homosexuelle Aktion Westberlin gegangen, um politisch aktiv zu werden. Da war ich Teil der Tuntenfraktion, die selbst innerhalb der HAW für Diskussionen sorgte. Die Studentenschaft, aus der sich die HAW maßgeblich rekrutierte, war ja aufgesplittet in unzählige linke Gruppierungen, und die Marxisten haben immer gesagt, zuerst muss der Hauptwiderspruch beseitigt sein, das Kapital. Und da haben wir Tunten eben gesagt, na da können wir ja ewig warten, dann kommen wir ja nie dran mit unserer Emanzipation. Wir wollen die Emanzipation aber jetzt, danach können wir das Kapital abschaffen. Und das führte immer wieder zu Streitereien darüber, wie man sich in der Öffentlichkeit präsentieren sollte. Wir Tunten haben immer gesagt, wir müssen in die U-Bahnen, wir müssen Flyer verteilen, wir müssen ins Gespräch mit den Leuten kommen. Die anderen wollten eher auf irgendwelchen Parteiveranstaltungen debattieren oder wollten auf der Demo zum 1. Mai bei der SED mitlaufen, mit 'nem kleinen Banner. Und wir haben gesagt: Nein, entweder wir laufen mit einem großen Banner für uns alleine, oder wir laufen bei keinem dieser Leute mit. Man darf nicht vergessen, dass die meisten dieser Gruppierungen Angst hatten, die ganze linke Bewegung könne als schwul diffamiert werden, deswegen waren die Schwulen gar nicht so gerne gesehen. Die emanzipierten Frauen hatten dort ganz ähnliche Probleme. Aber Tunten sind ja angstlos, wir waren immer laut und offensiv in unseren politischen Forderungen. Uns ging's immer darum, Aufmerksamkeit zu erregen, und es ging nicht um den normalen, verklemmten Homo, der noch im Schrank lebte. Das hat dann oft gekracht bei diesen Sitzungen in der HAW. [...]

Ich habe dann versucht, die Emanzipation über die Kunst weiterzutreiben. Und das geht nur, wenn man provokante Bilder malt, und am besten mit Selbstdarstellungen. Beim Bewerbungsgespräch an der Hochschule für bildende Künste, der späteren UDK, hat mich Professor Hödicke gefragt, was ich malen will, und ich sagte „mich selbst" – daraufhin hat er mich aufgenommen. Ich habe das Figürliche an mir selbst in provozierenden Gesten und Haltungen forciert. Zuerst über Spiegel, später über Fotos, aus denen ich dann die Bilder entwickelt habe. Die Werke waren immer beides, Selbstporträts und die Vorstellung einer Kunstfigur. Es ging um das Einbringen des Andersseins in die Kunst. Das war damals ein politischer Akt und ausgesprochen provokativ, denn die Motive, die ich malte, waren in der Kunst und der Öffentlichkeit kaum vorhanden, in der Malerei schon gar nicht. Ein Impuls für diese Arbeiten war der Katalog zu der Ausstellung *Transformer – Aspekte der Travestie* im Kunstmuseum Luzern 1974. Da wurde hauptsächlich Fotografie gezeigt und Malerei eigentlich nur in Form von Papierarbeiten. Ich fand diese Selbstdarstellungsgeschichten interessant, beeindruckt hat mich zum Beispiel das fotografische Werk von Pierre Molinier. Und Luciano Castelli war bei dieser Ausstellung auch schon dabei. So habe ich sozusagen den ersten Push bekommen für meine eigene Kunst, ich habe das dann während meines Studiums in Malerei umformuliert. [...]

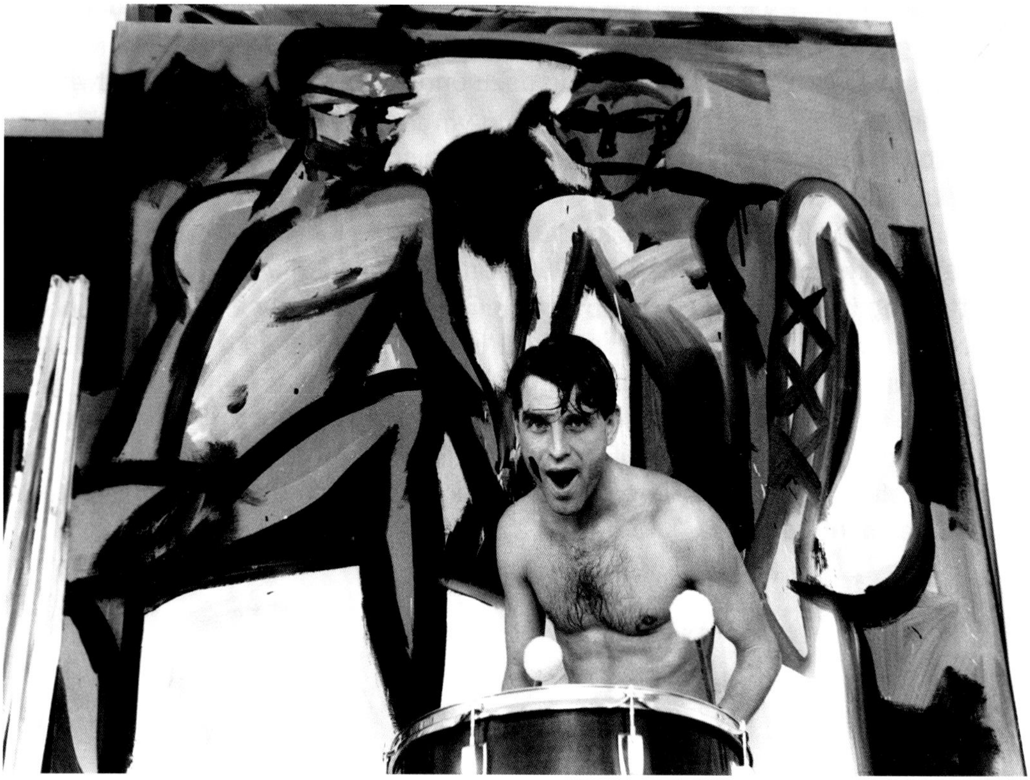

Rolf von Bergmann, *Rainer Fetting*, 1982, Silbergelatineabzug / gelatin silver print, 23,6 × 34,8 cm

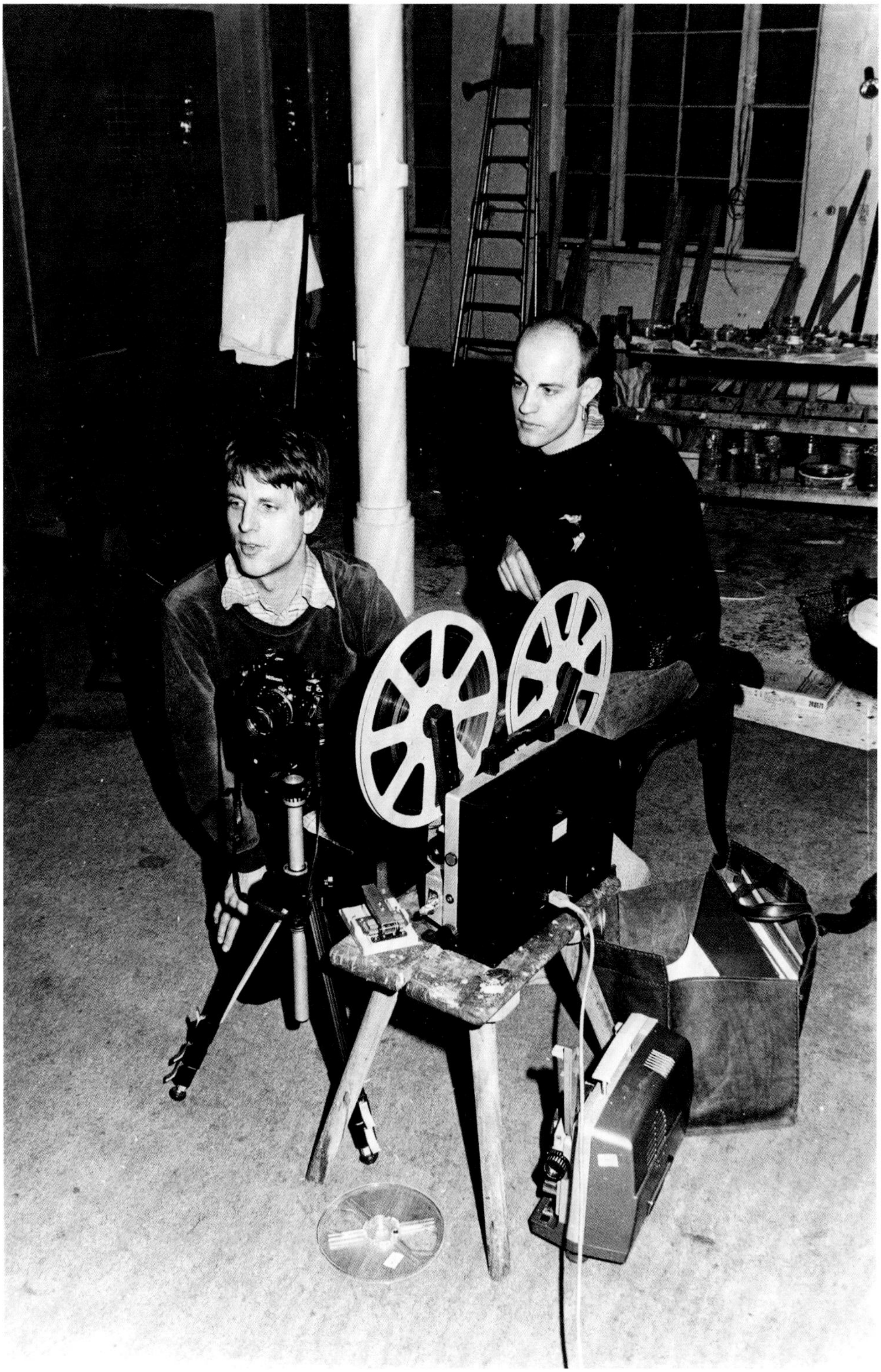

Rolf von Bergmann, *Rainer Fetting und Salomé*, 1977, Silbergelatineabzug / gelatin silver print, 34,7 × 23,2 cm

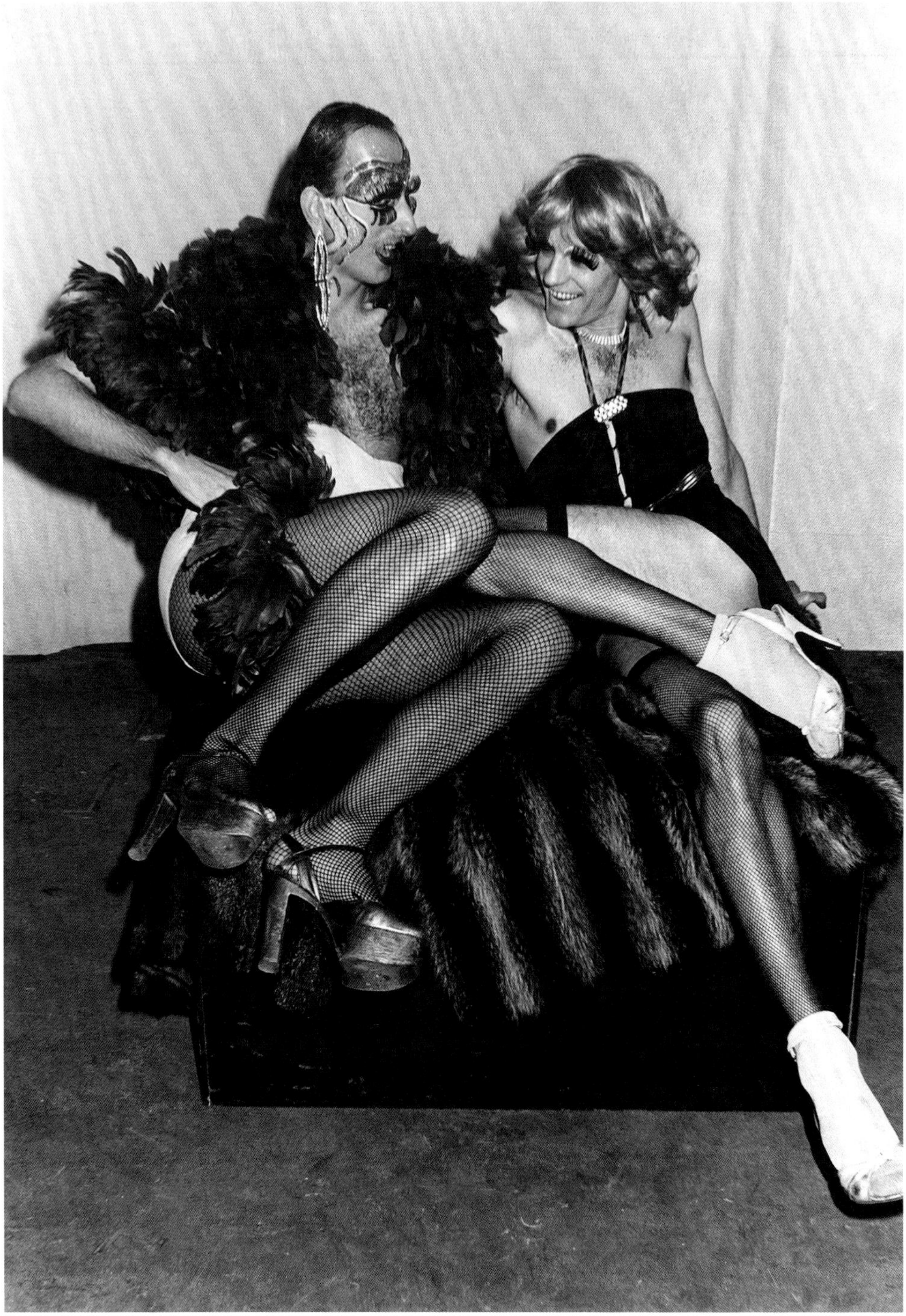

Rolf von Bergmann, *Ohne Titel (Selbstporträt, mit Salomé)*, 1977,
Silbergelatineabzug / gelatin silver print, 30,1 × 21,4 cm

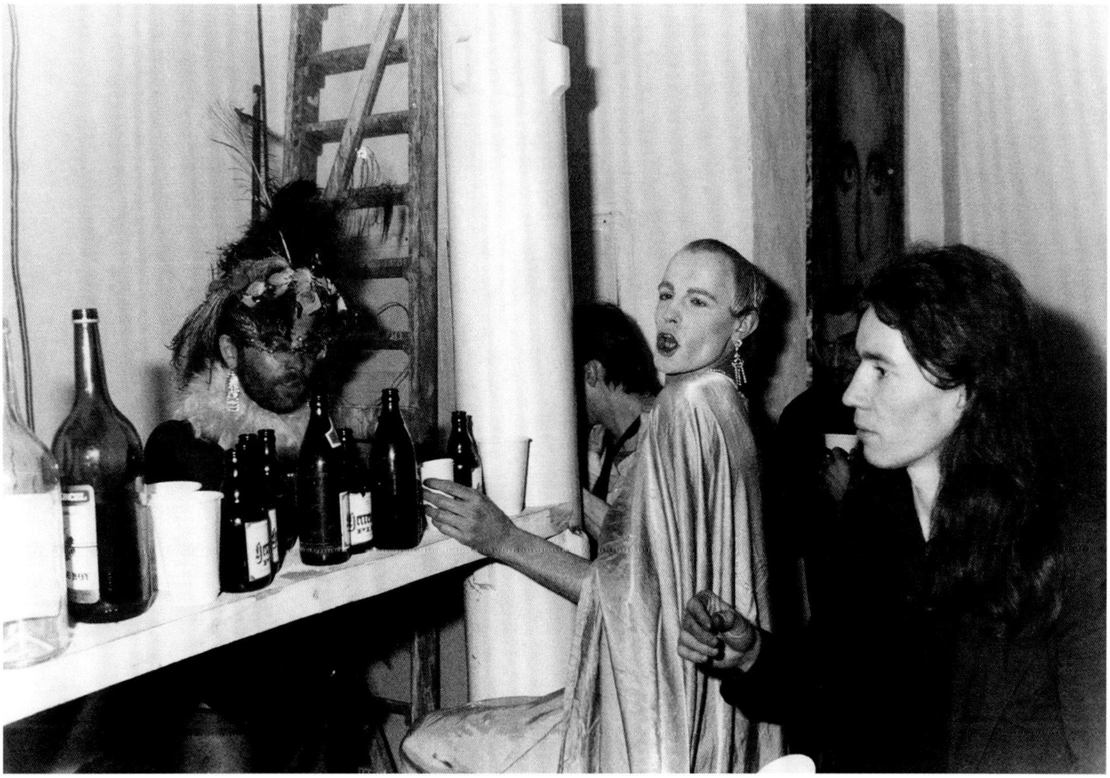

Rolf von Bergmann, *Gerd Kropp, Salomé, Helmut Middendorf,* 1978,
Silbergelatineabzug / gelatin silver print, 23,6 × 34,8 cm

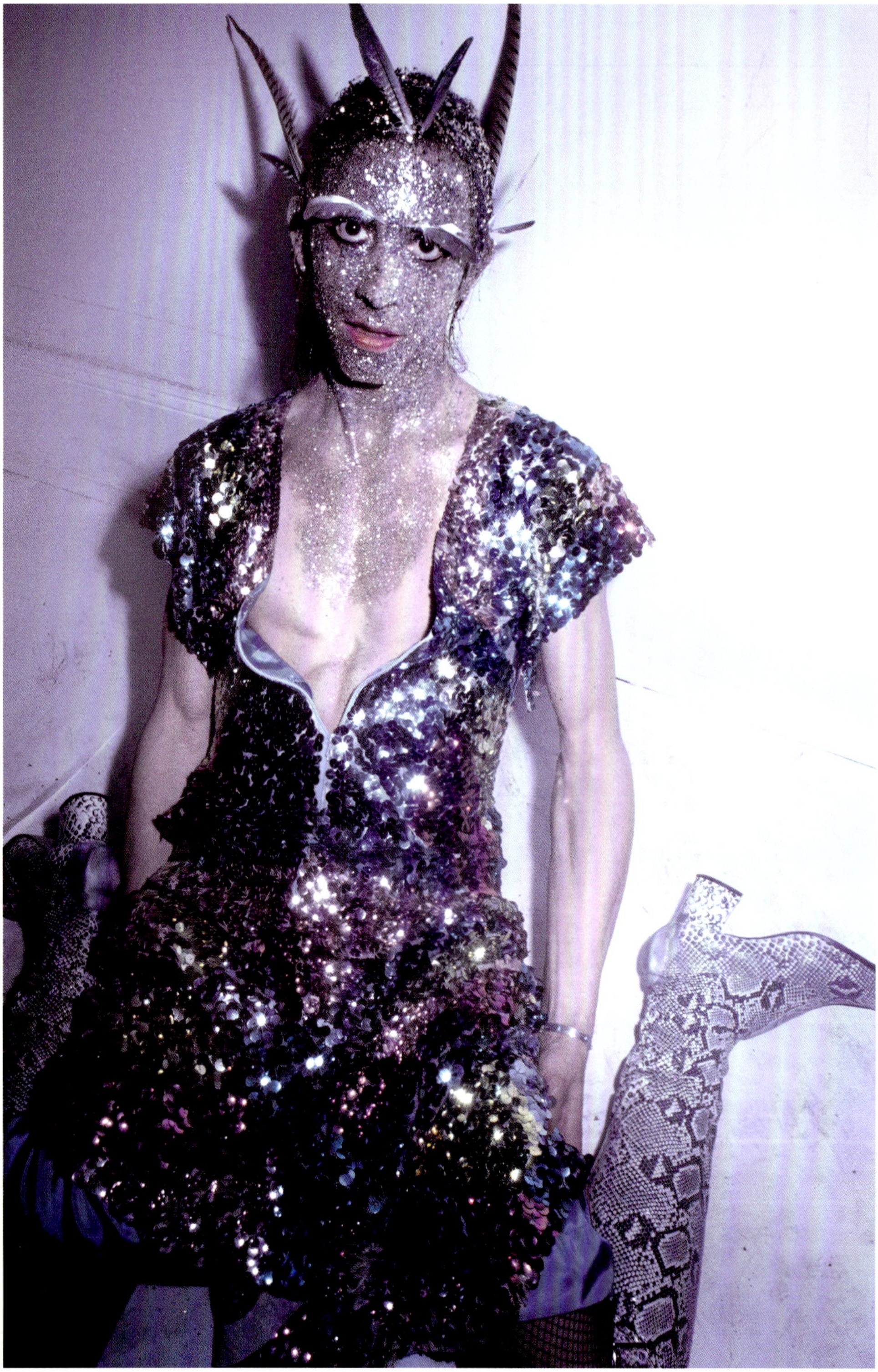

Luciano Castelli, *His Majesty the Queen*, 1973/2018, Farbfotografie / color photograph, 100 × 70 cm

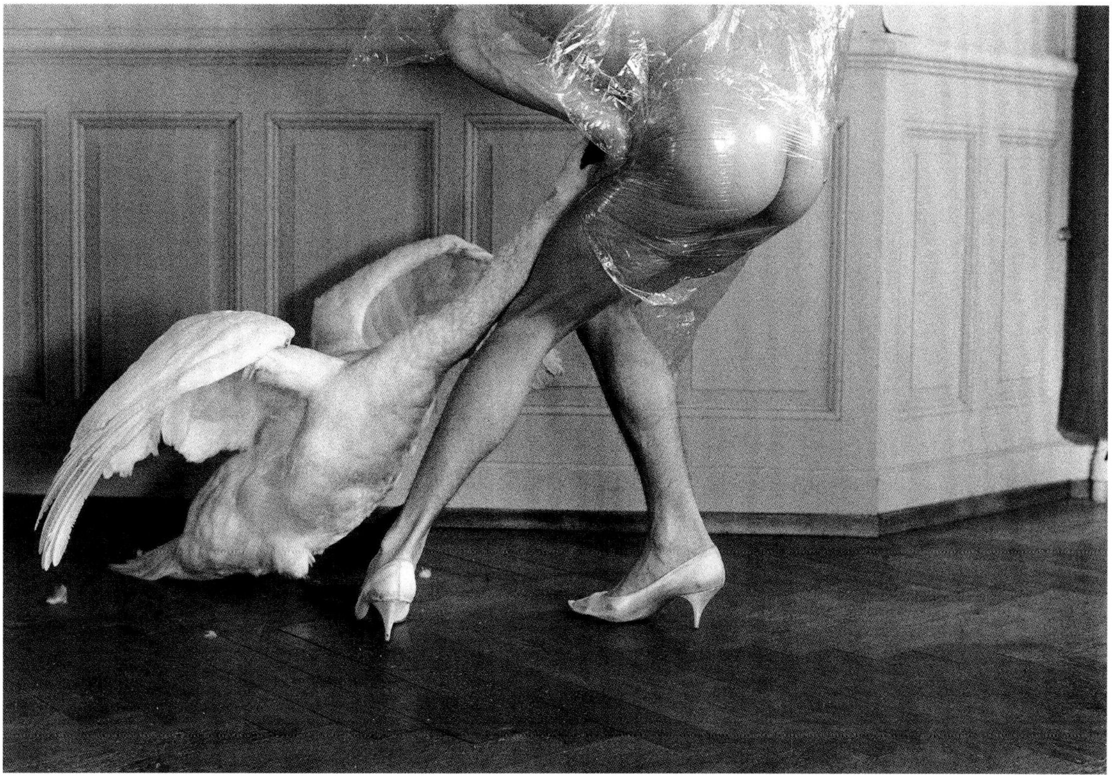

Luciano Castelli, *Luciano und der Schwan (self-portrait)*, 1976/2018, Schwarz-Weiß-Fotografie / b/w photograph, 30 × 40 cm

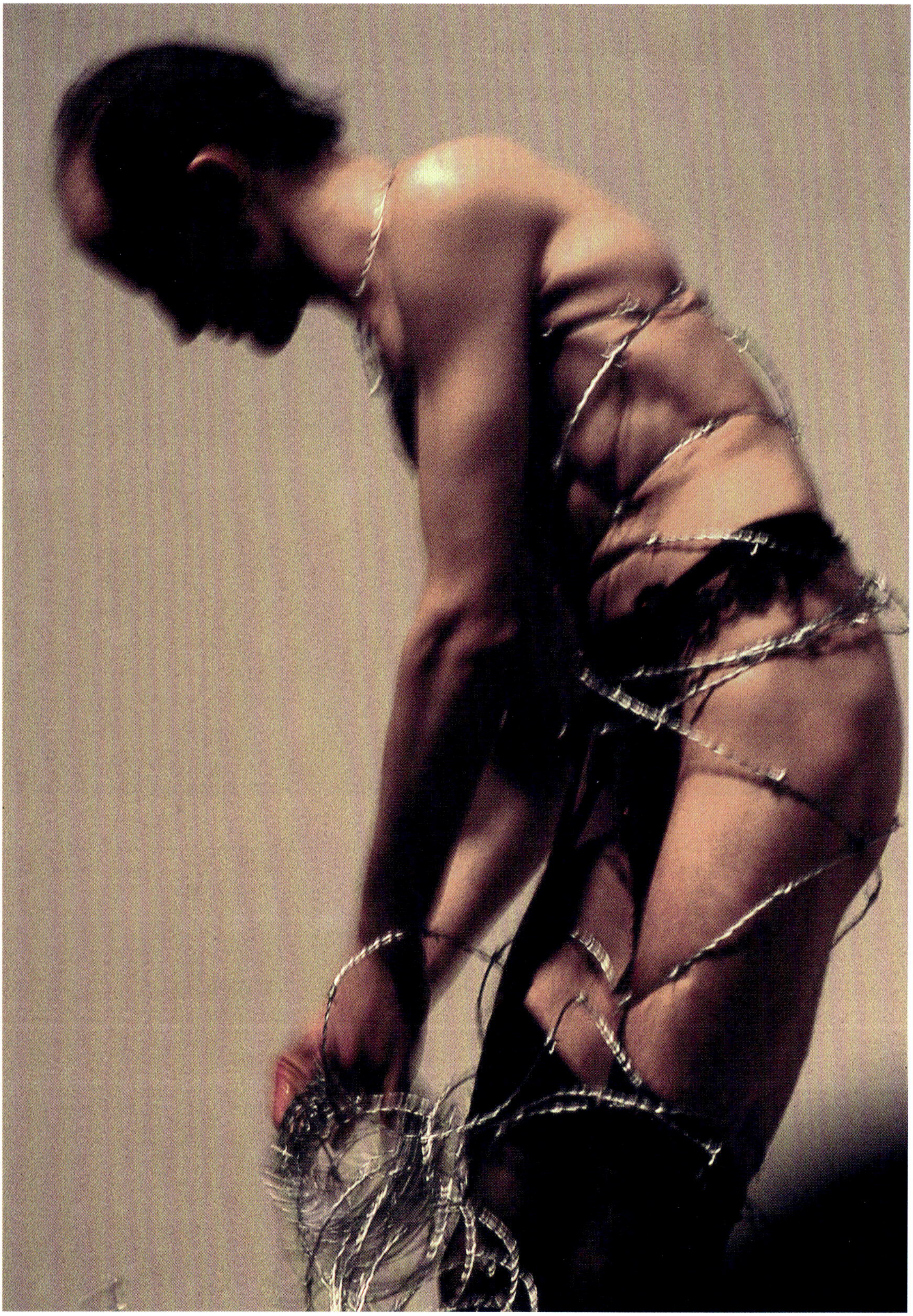

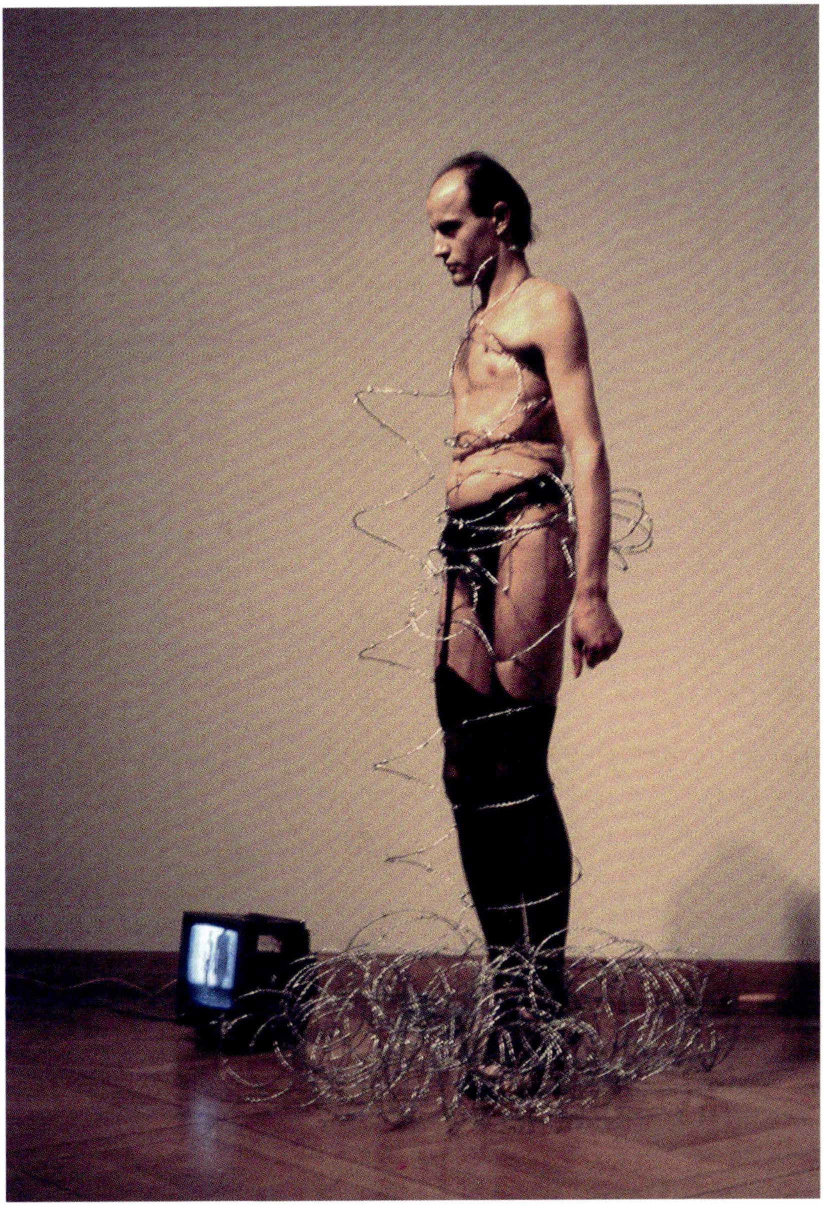

Salomé bei seiner Performance / during his performance *Für meine Schwestern in Österreich*, Neue Galerie – Sammlung Ludwig, Aachen, 1978

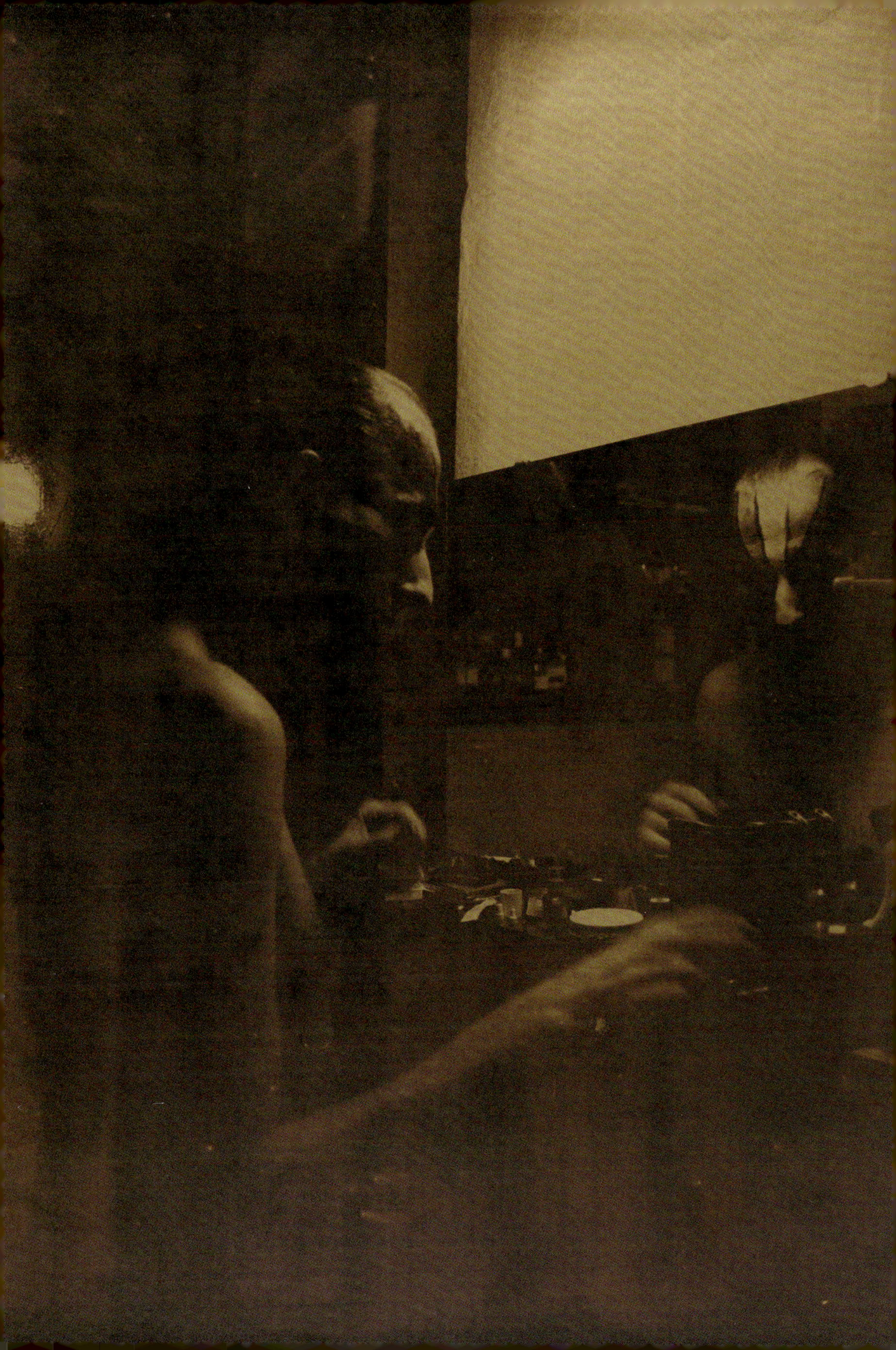

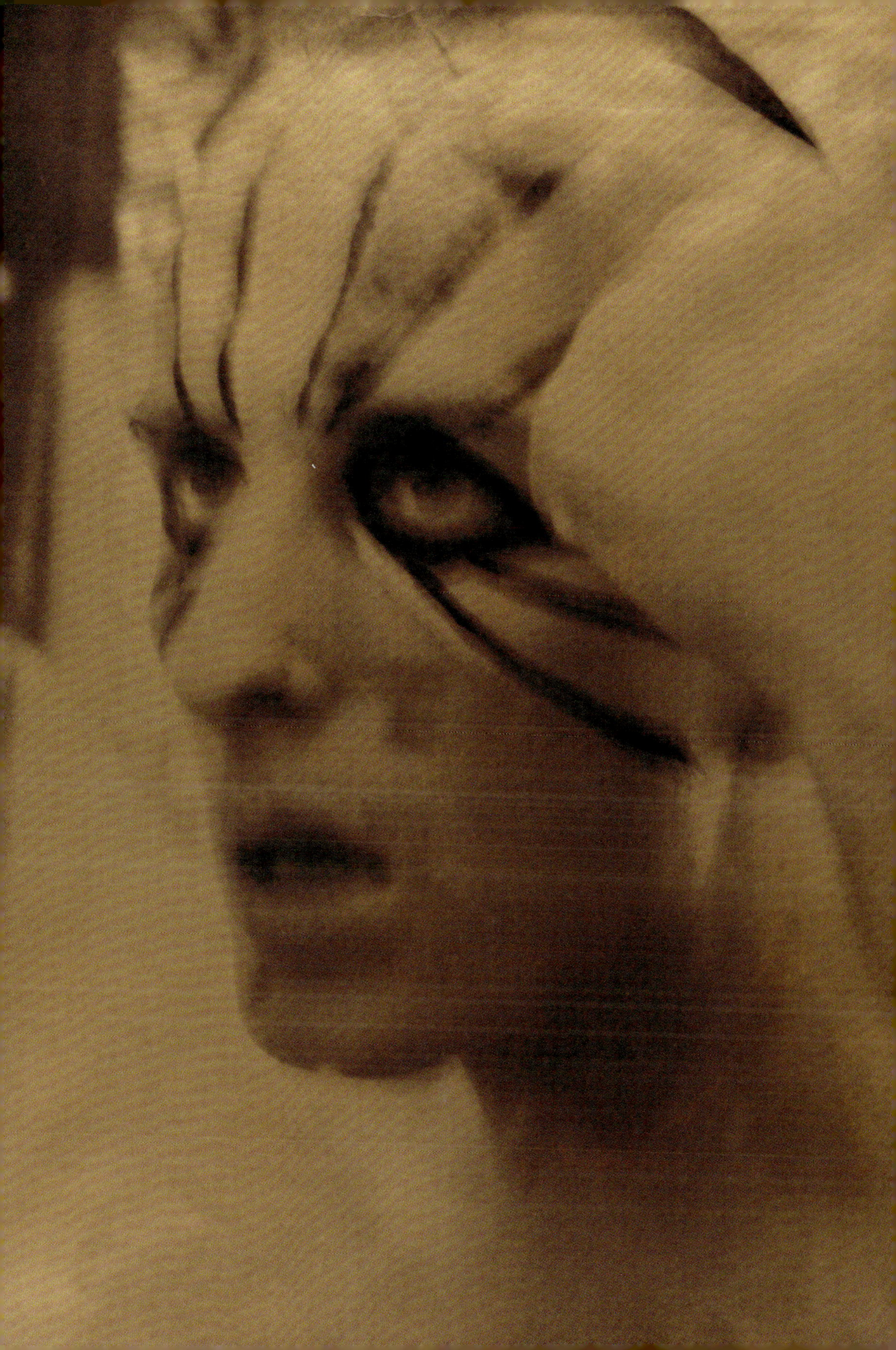

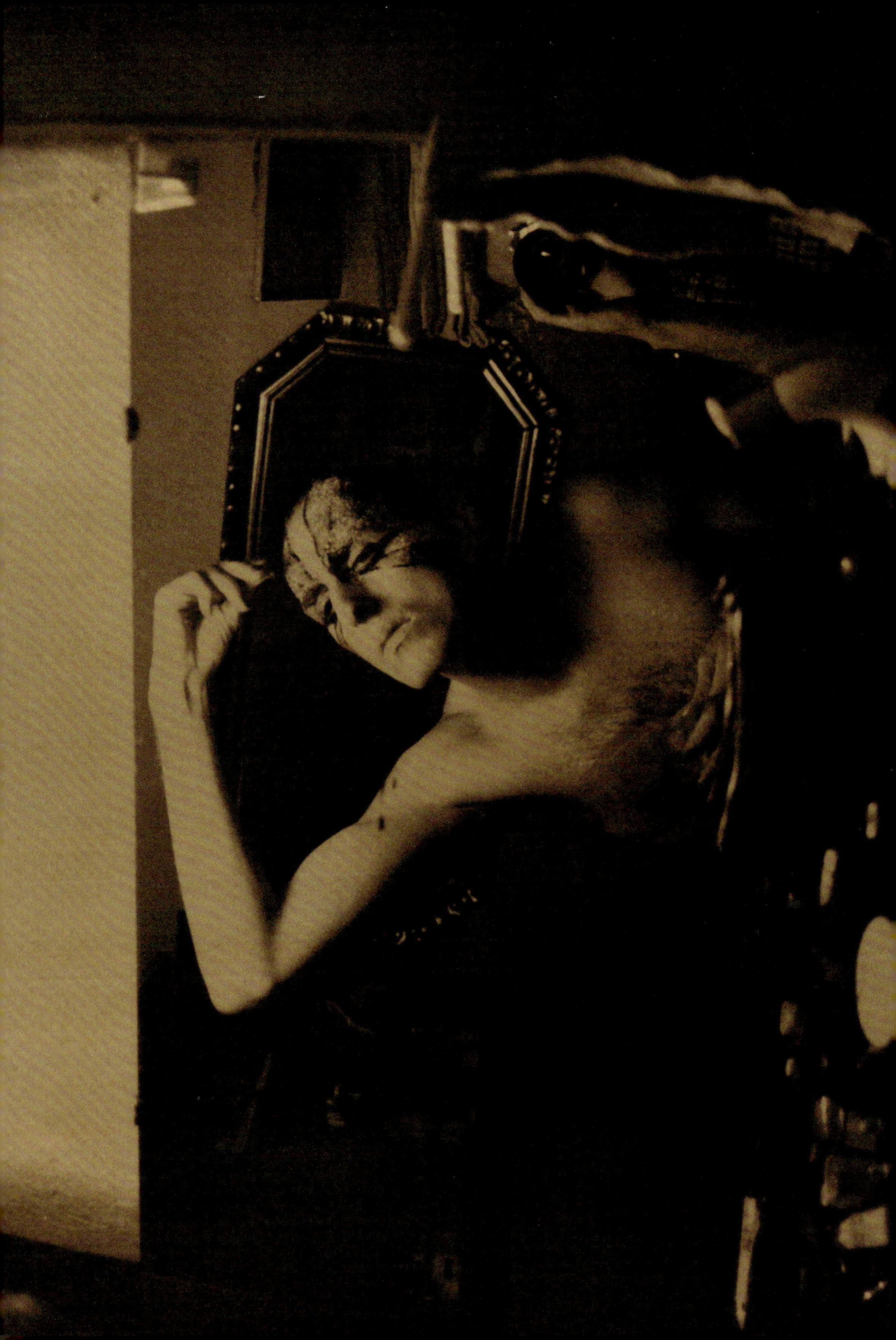

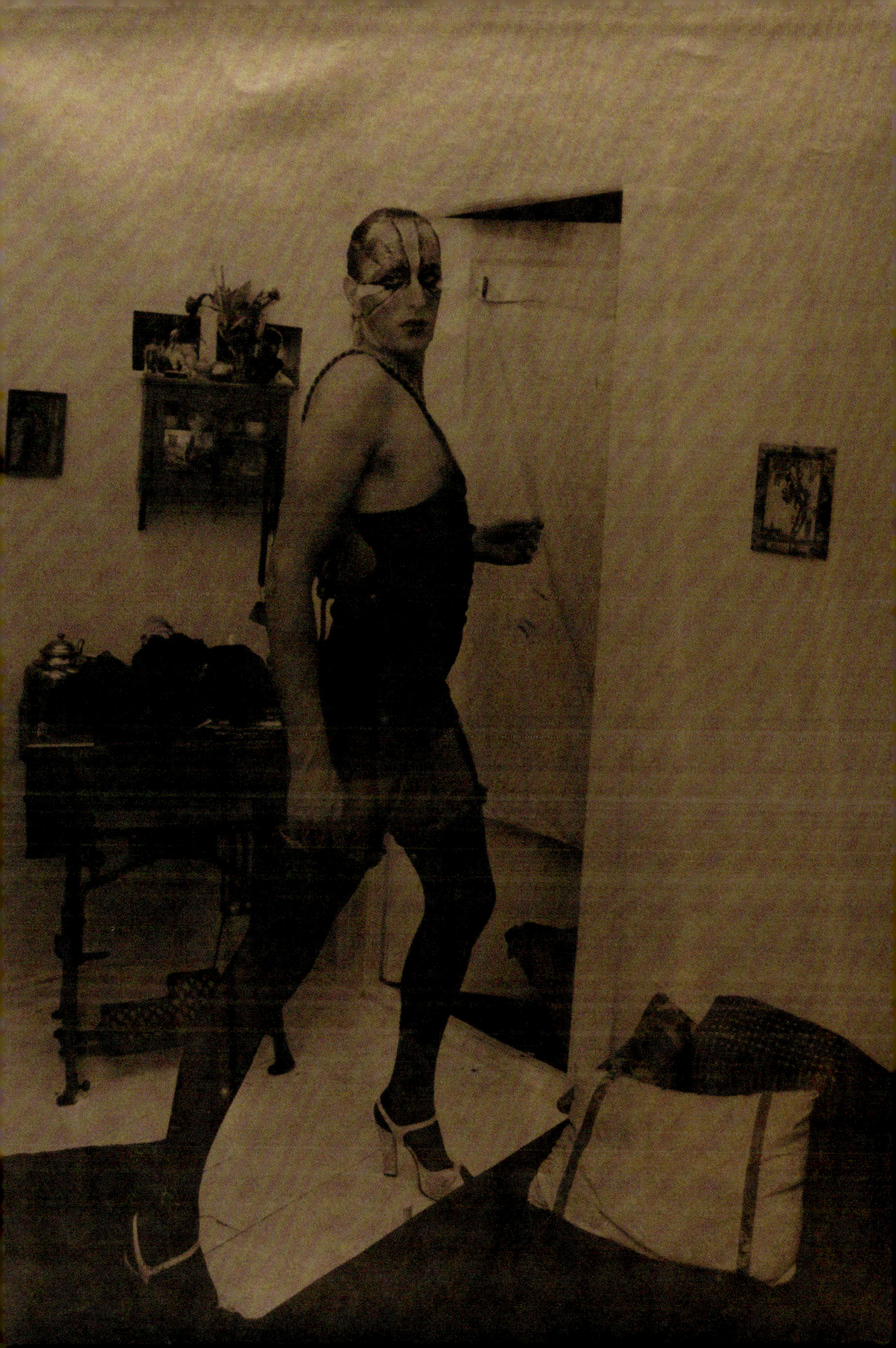

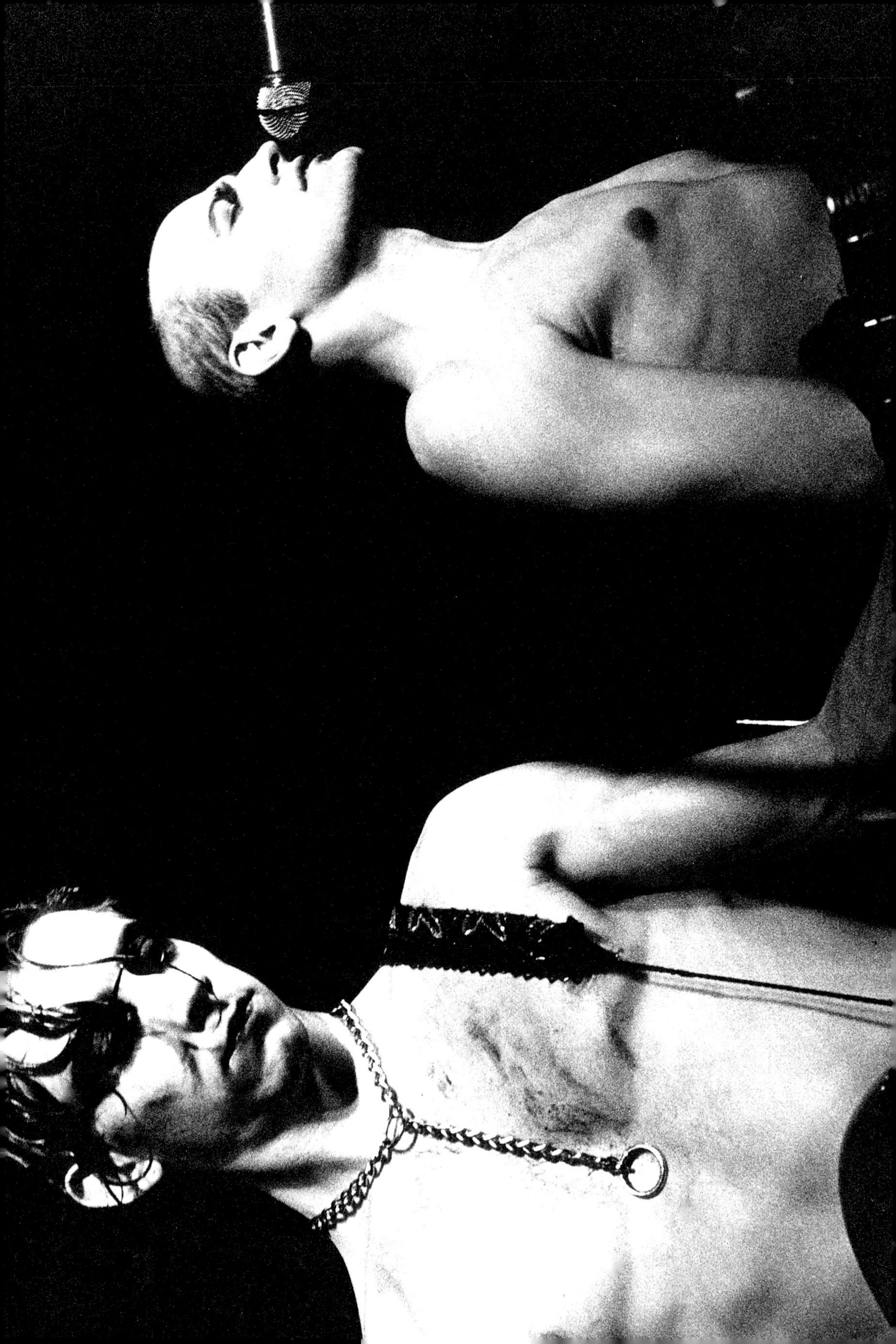

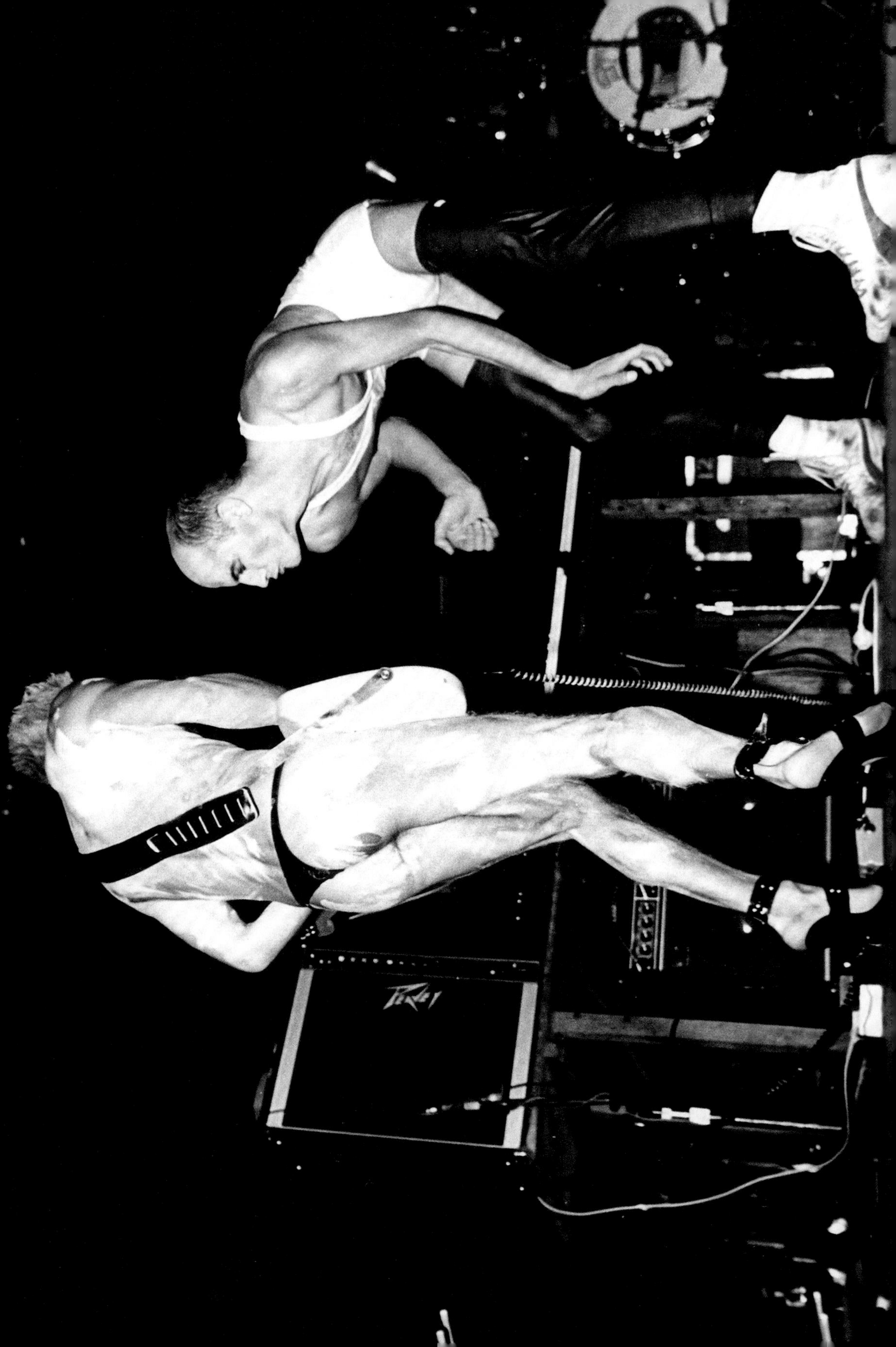

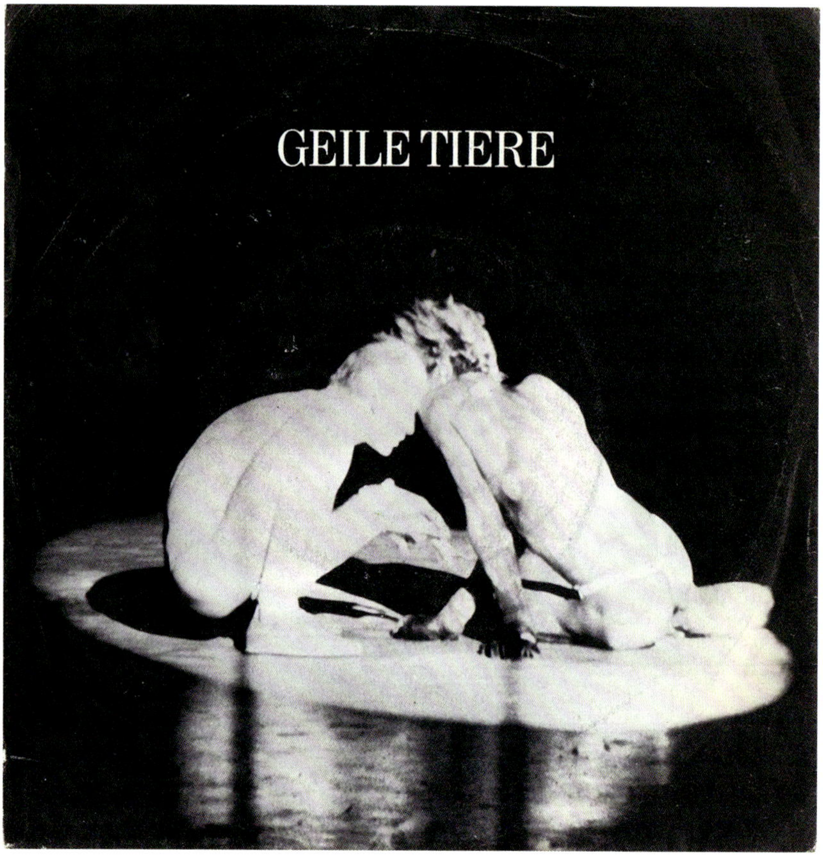

Geile Tiere, *Geile Tiere*, 1980, Single, Eigenverlag / self-released

(166–169) Rolf von Bergmann, *Ohne Titel ((Selbst-)Porträt)*, ca. 1978, Silbergelatineabzug / gelatin silver print, 40,5 × 30,5 cm
(170) Geile Tiere, Konzert / concert, Dschungel, Berlin, 1981, Foto / photo: Helmut Metzner
(171) Geile Tiere, Konzert / concert, Deutschlandhalle, Berlin, 1982, Foto / photo: Helmut Metzner

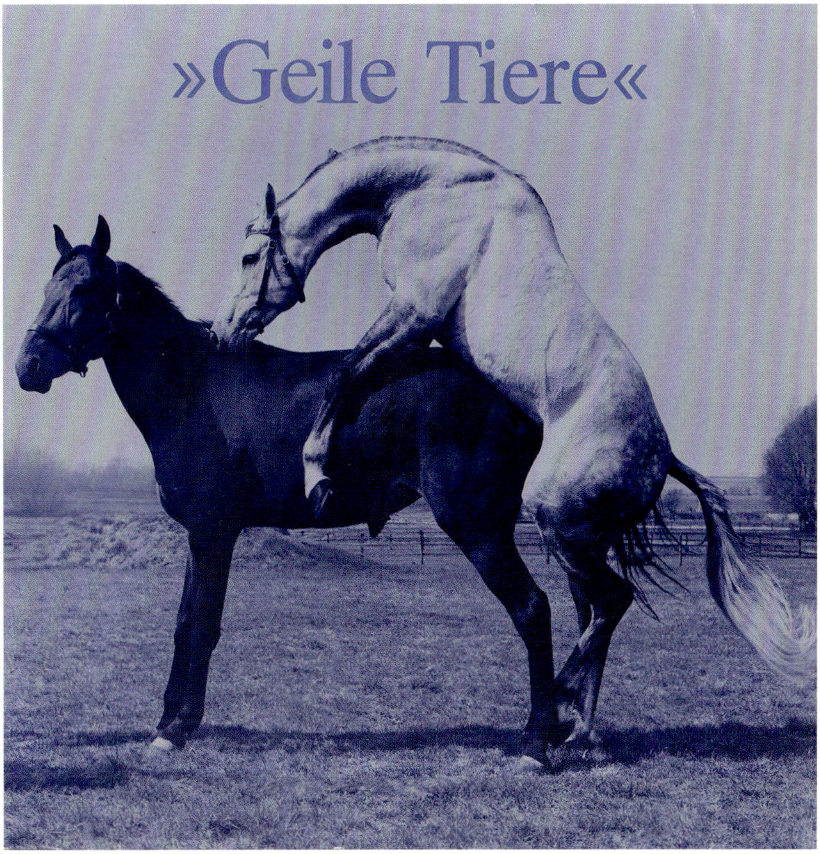

Geile Tiere, *»Geile Tiere«*, 1981, LP, GeeBeeDee

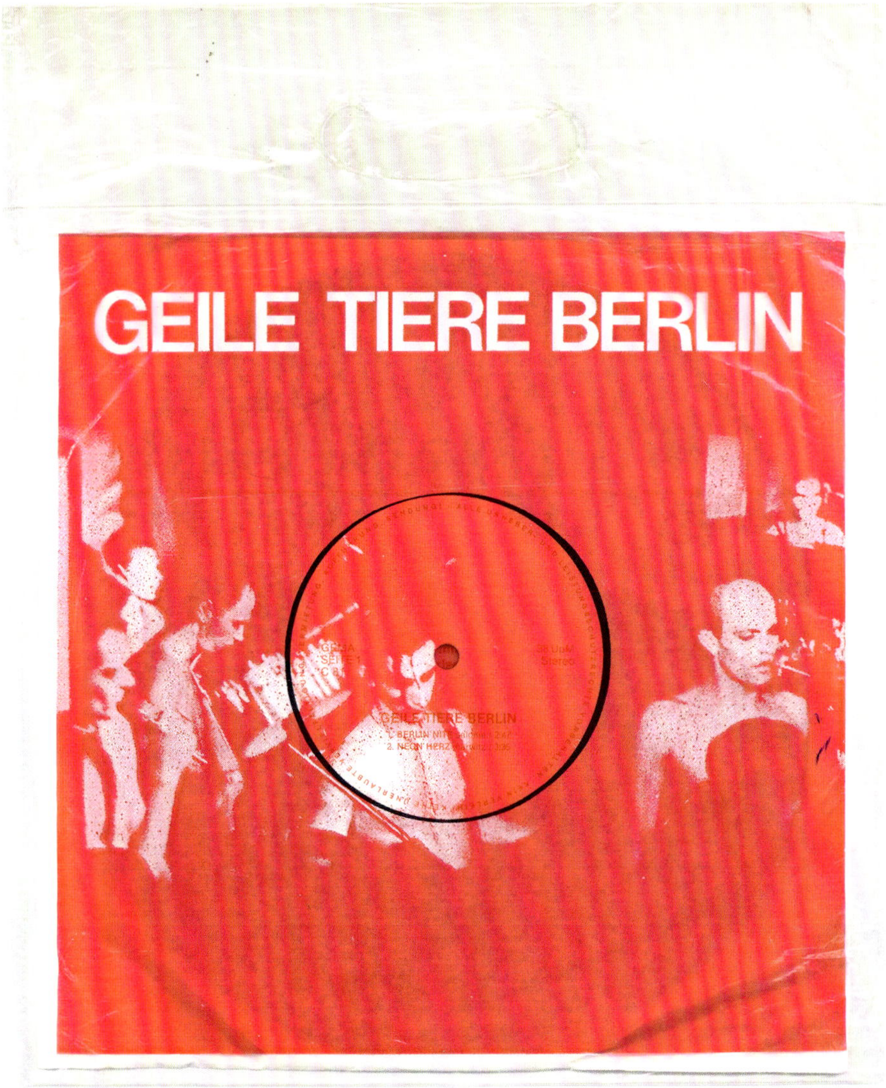

Geile Tiere, *Geile Tiere Berlin*, 1980, EP, Eigenverlag / self-released

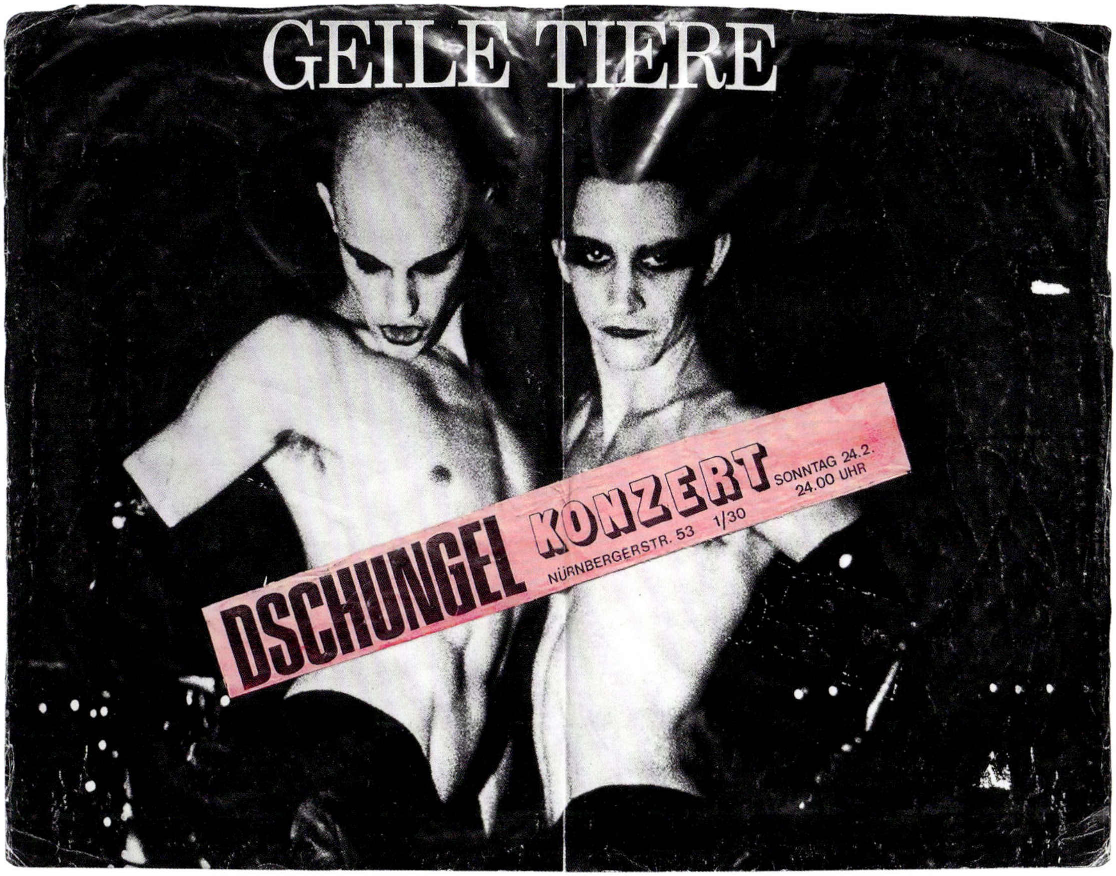

Geile Tiere, Poster, Dschungel, Berlin, 1981

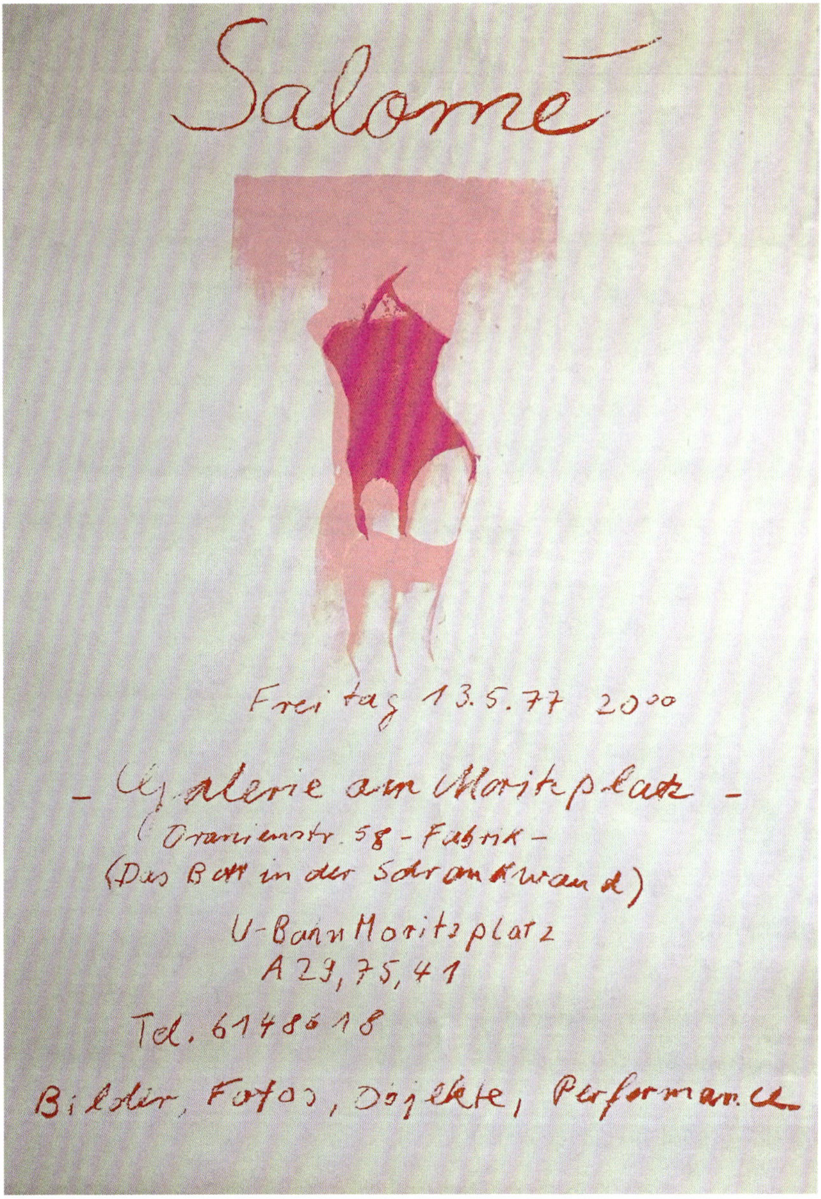

Salomé, Poster, Galerie am Moritzplatz, Berlin, 1977

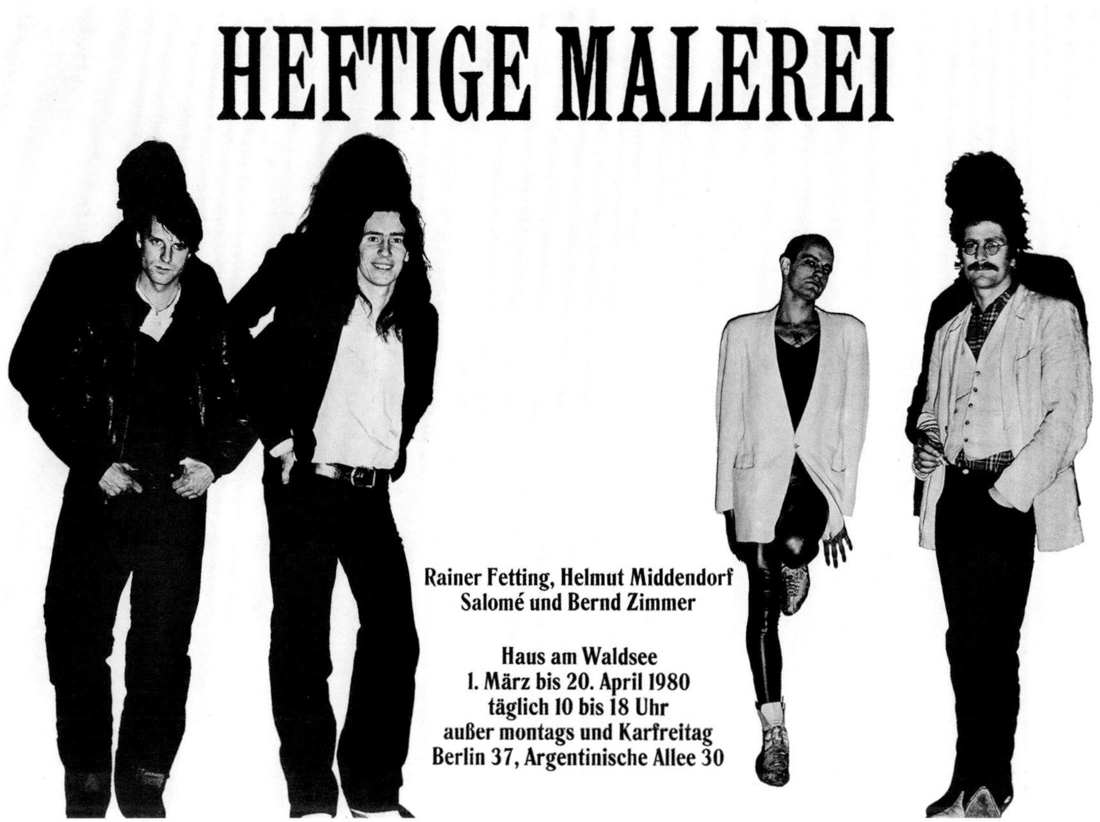

Heftige Malerei, Poster, Haus am Waldsee, Berlin, 1980

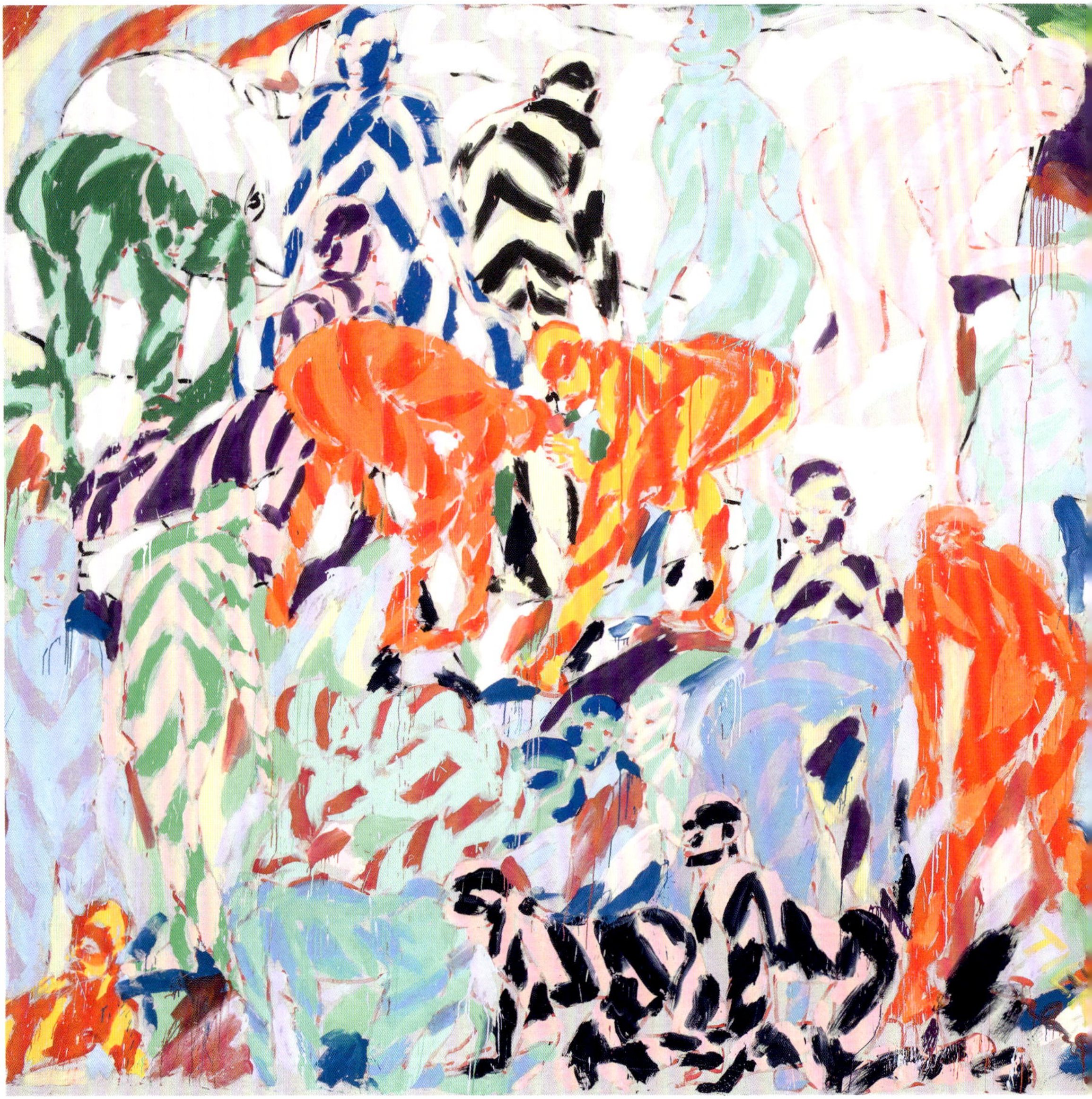

Salomé, Luciano Castelli, *Tiere*, 1981, Dispersion auf Nessel, 2-teilig / dispersion paint c

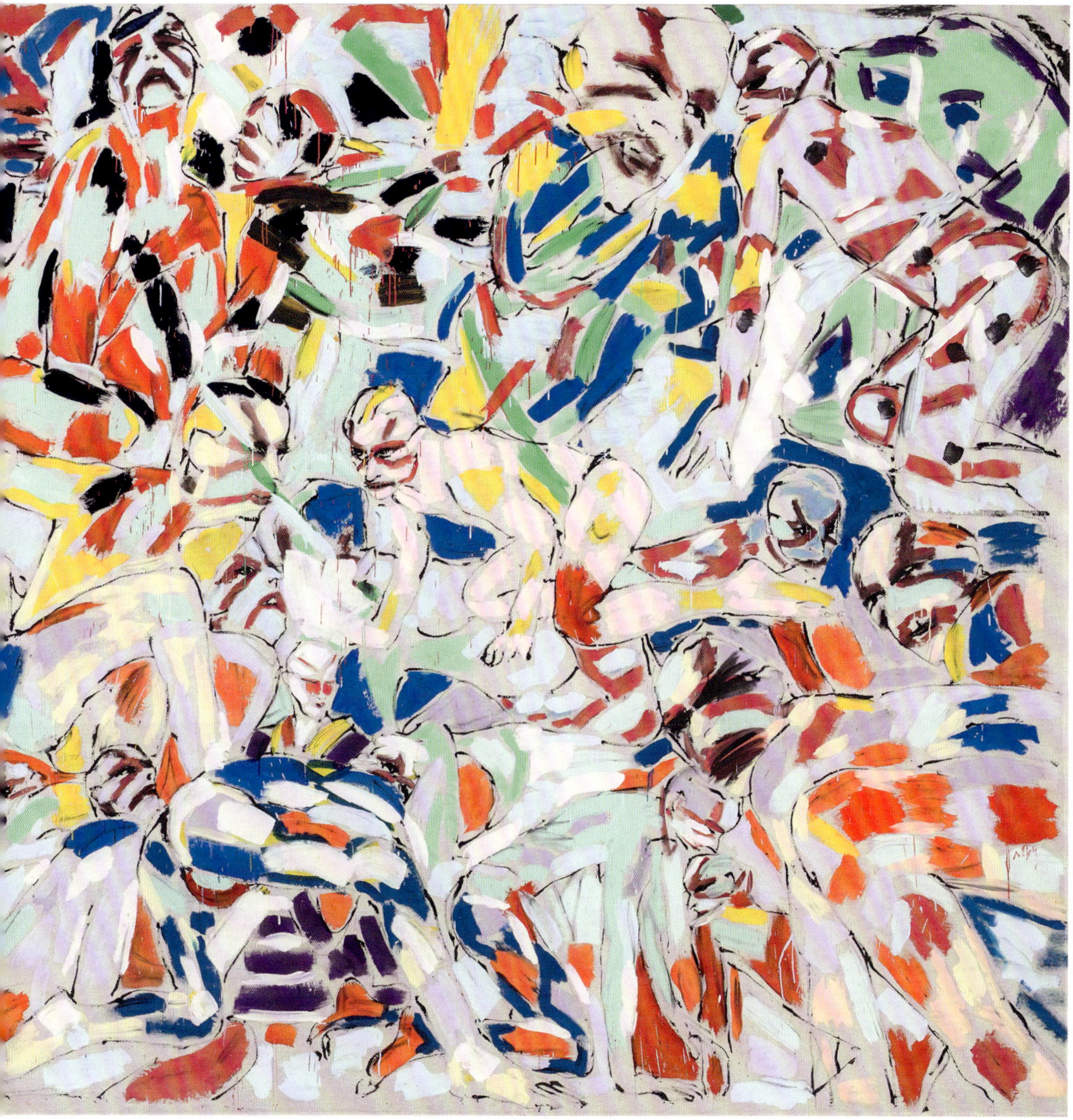

tton canvas, 2 parts, 400 × 430 cm, 400 × 415 cm

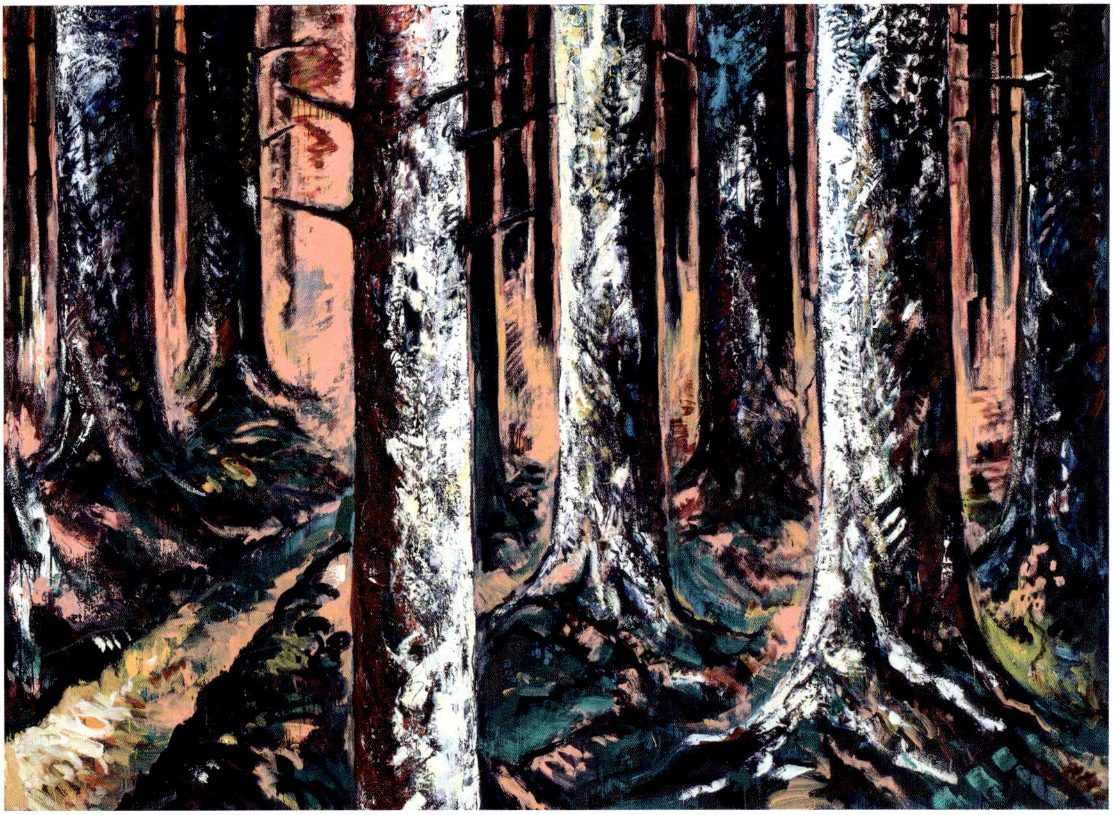

Bernd Zimmer, *Fichtenwald*, 1986, Dispersion und Öl auf Leinwand / dispersion paint and oil on canvas, 240 × 320 cm

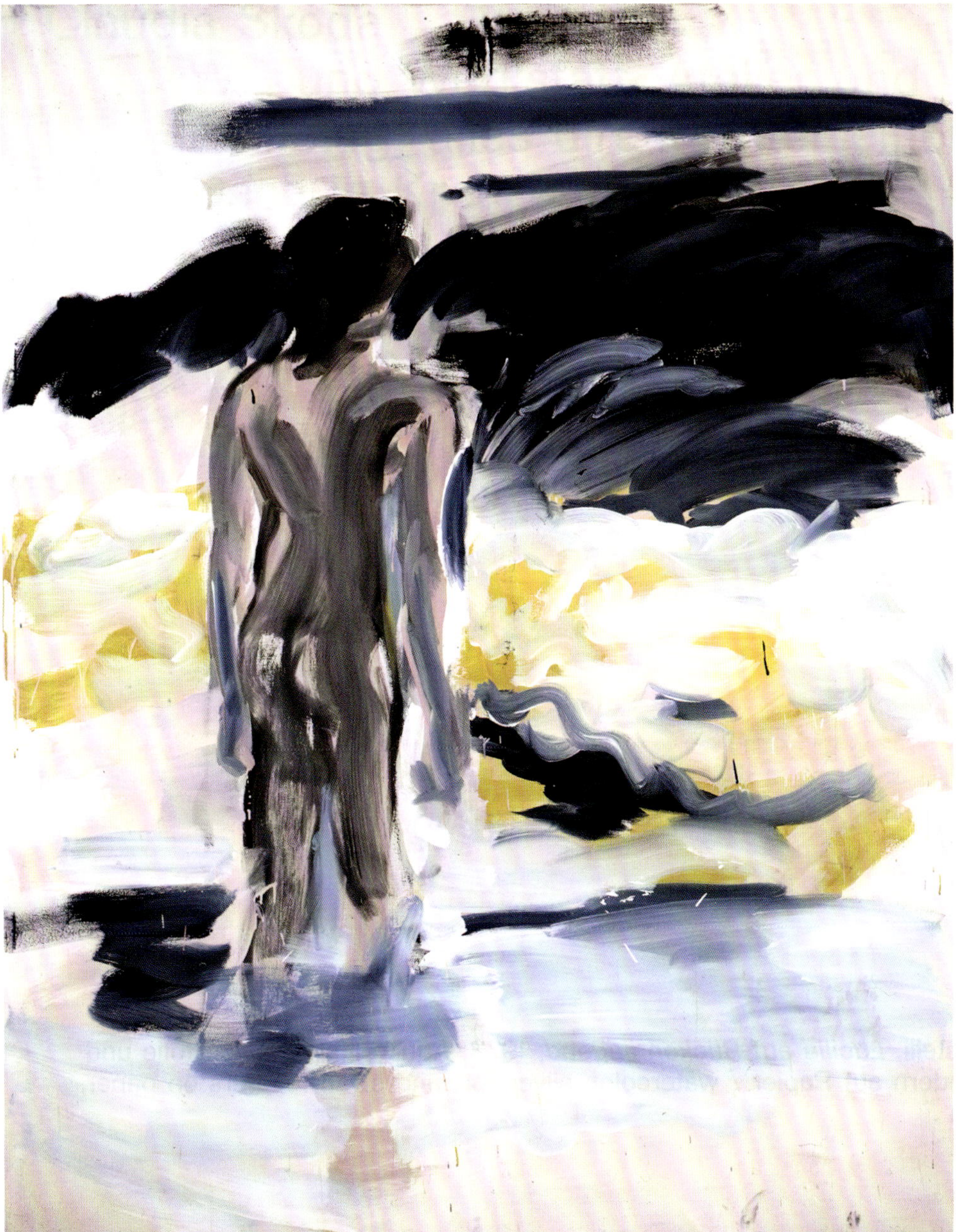

Rainer Fetting, *Mann in Brandung*, 1980, Mischtechnik auf Nessel / mixed media on cotton canvas, 250 × 200 cm

For me it all first really got going with fashion, when we founded the Fabrikneu [Factory New], that's where my first Berlin shows took place, and it was soon a great success. My ex-husband Jürgen Skoda was a sculptor back then, and he knew Edgar Froese from Tangerine Dream and Georg Baselitz. They were the same generation. Jürgen Skoda helped me to organize everything. We'd already lived together with Jenny Capitain and Klaus Krüger and a bunch of other people on a factory floor, but we didn't really get on with the others and we started looking for a new factory. And that's how Fabrikneu was founded in 1973. There were six of us to begin with: the painter Angelik Riemer; Reinhard Bock, he was a Super-8 filmmaker; Klaus Krüger, he was a drummer and later played in Iggy Pop's band; Jenny Capitain, later Helmut Newton's stylist and herself a model; Jürgen Skoda; and myself. The first six of the Fabrikneu. It was a living community and workshop, atelier and catwalk, everything directly under one roof in Kreuzberg. [...]

Fabrikneu was one large space, with seating only along the edges. Jürgen Skoda had built podiums where one could sleep, lie down, and sit, while there was a free space in the middle. We painted the motto of the fashion show on the floor. For example, there was *Shake Your Hips*, and it was as if everything was in seawater, and then we placed a palm tree in the middle. The next show was *Neues Spiel* [New Game]; we had a kind of casino on the floor, and Kippenberger was involved as a guest. He had designed the invitation, a playing card, the Queen of Hearts, with a portrait of me and one of himself. I'd met Kippenberger at my first-ever show on Ibiza. He spent a lot of time in the Fabrikneu, even lived there with us, and photographed our entourage the whole day. Then he had the idea to use the photos as a floor and he shot over a thousand photos within a week. At the time Jürgen Skoda was working a lot with acrylic glass. Martin arranged all the photos on the ground and my ex-husband then laid an acrylic glass floor over them so that one could walk on top. The opening was then called *Fotos von Martin* [Photos by Martin], or something like that—that was the subject. The floor then actually stayed that way for the next ten years, until we couldn't stand it anymore and covered it. It was first uncovered again in 2000. [...]

Kippenberger had yet to make a name for himself back then. And then there were the painters from Moritzplatz; I knew them from Fabrikneu, they were there quite often. We all just met up somewhere, mainly in Dschungel. Salomé was working at the bar, everyone was there all the time. Luciano Castelli lived with us for a while and photographed the fashion as well, often in the run-up to a show. He made slide projections, placed the models in them, and photographed them. Many of the photos were then a source of inspiration for his paintings. [...]

I'd say that Berlin became really exciting around 1975, Iggy Pop and David Bowie were here and that played a role. There were also a lot of New

So richtig los ging das bei mir mit der Mode, als wir die Fabrikneu gegründet haben, dort waren meine ersten Berliner Shows, und das wurde dann auch schnell sehr erfolgreich. Mein Ex-Mann Jürgen Skoda war damals Bildhauer, und er war wiederum bekannt mit Edgar Froese von Tangerine Dream und Georg Baselitz. Das war eine Generation. Jürgen Skoda hat mir geholfen, alles aufzubauen. Wir hatten damals schon gemeinsam mit Jenny Capitain und Klaus Krüger und weiteren Leuten in einer Etage gewohnt, aber wir haben uns mit den anderen dort nicht so gut verstanden und deshalb eine neue Fabrik gesucht. So wurde 1973 die Fabrikneu gegründet. Am Anfang waren wir zu sechst: die Malerin Angelik Riemer, Reinhard Bock, er war Super-8-Filmer, Klaus Krüger, er war Schlagzeuger und hat später bei Iggy Pop gespielt, Jenny Capitain, später Stylistin von Helmut Newton und auch selber Model, Jürgen Skoda und ich. Das waren die ersten sechs von der Fabrikneu. Der Ort war WG und Werkstatt, Atelier und Laufsteg, alles direkt unter einem Dach in Kreuzberg. [...]

Die Fabrikneu war ein großer Raum, Sitzmöglichkeiten gab es nur am Rand. Jürgen Skoda hatte Podeste gebaut, da konnte man auch schlafen, liegen, sitzen, und in der Mitte war alles frei. Wir haben damals mit Farbe das Motto der Modenschau auf den Boden gemalt. Da gab es dann zum Beispiel *Shake Your Hips*, da war alles so bemalt, als wäre es Meerwasser, und in der Mitte gab's ne Palme. Die nächste Show war *Neues Spiel*, da hatten wir dann eine Art Casino auf dem Boden, und da war dann auch Kippenberger zu Gast. Die Einladung hat er gestaltet, in Form einer Spielkarte, Herz-Dame, mit einem Porträt von mir und einem von ihm selbst. Kennengelernt habe ich Kippenberger bei meiner allerersten Show auf Ibiza. Er war viel in der Fabrikneu, hat auch bei uns gewohnt und den ganzen Tag unser Umfeld fotografiert. Irgendwann hatte er die Idee, mit den Fotos einen Boden zu gestalten, er hat dann innerhalb von einer Woche tatsächlich über tausend Fotos geschossen. Jürgen Skoda hat damals viel mit Acrylglas gearbeitet. Martin hat die Fotos alle verlegt und mein Ex-Mann hat dann einen Acrylglasboden drübergelegt, sodass man drüberlaufen konnte. Die Eröffnung des Ganzen hieß dann *Fotos von Martin* oder so ähnlich – das war das Thema. Den Boden hatten wir dann tatsächlich zehn Jahre lang, bis wir ihn nicht mehr sehen konnten und ihn verdeckt haben. Anfang 2000 wurde er schließlich wieder freigelegt. [...]

Kippenberger hatte sich damals noch keinen Namen gemacht. Parallel gab es ja schon die Maler vom Moritzplatz, die kannte ich aus der Fabrikneu, die waren oft zu Gast. Man hat sich eben so getroffen, hauptsächlich im Dschungel. An der Bar arbeitete Salomé, da waren alle ständig da. Luciano Castelli hat ja auch eine Zeit bei uns gewohnt und auch Mode für uns fotografiert, oft im Vorfeld der Shows. Er hat Diaprojektionen gemacht und da dann Models reingestellt und fotografiert. Dabei sind auch viele Fotos als Inspiration für seine Bilder entstanden. [...]

Ich würde sagen, um 1975 wurde Berlin spannend, da war ja auch noch parallel die Anwesenheit von Iggy Pop und David Bowie, diese spielt da auch mit rein. Es waren ganz viele New Yorker*innen hier und Künstler*innen wie die Filmemacherin

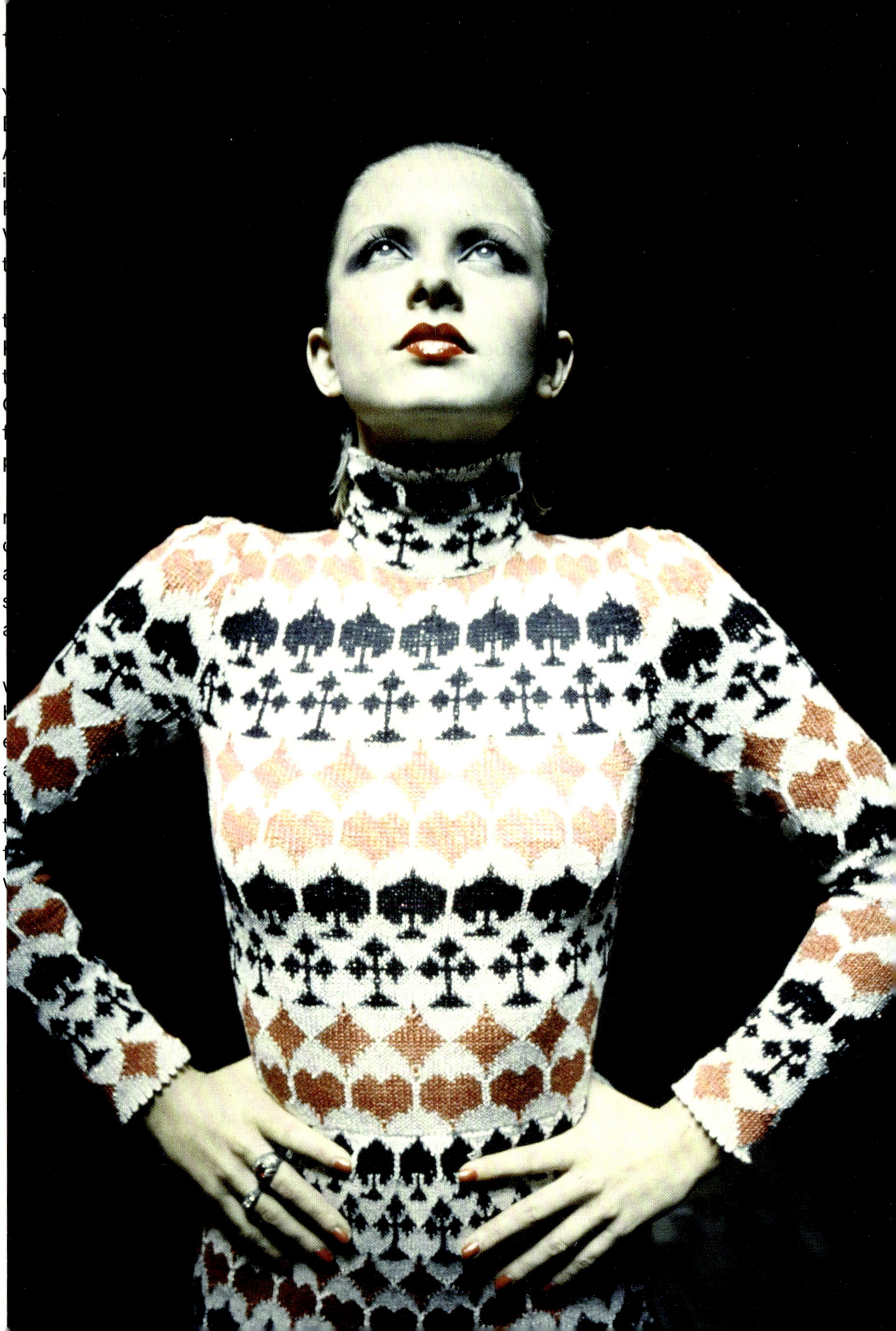

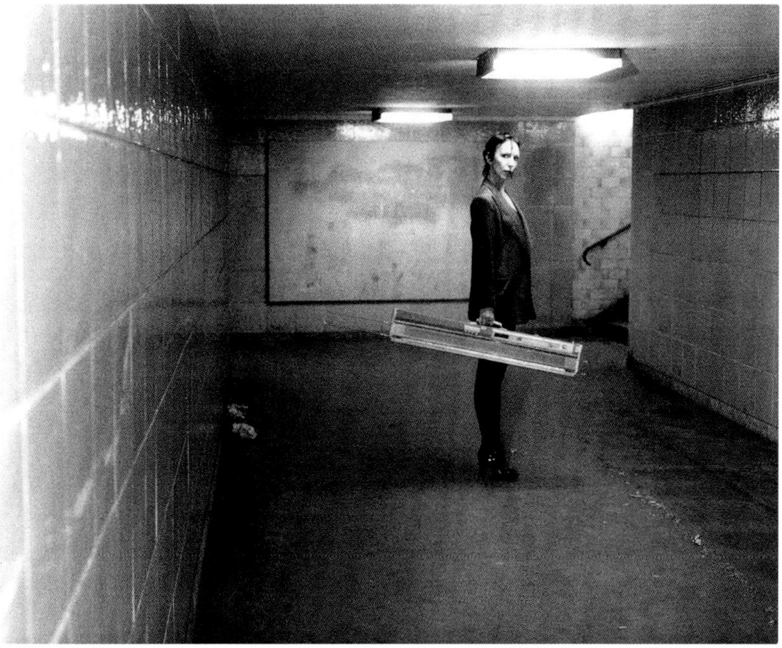

Claudia Skoda mit Strickmaschine im U-Bahnhof Kottbusser Tor / with a knitting machine at Kottbusser Tor subway station, Berlin, 1976, Foto / photo: Martin Kippenberger

Model mit Entwurf von Claudia Skoda aus ihrer Kollektion *Neues Spiel* / Model wearing a design by Claudia Skoda from her *Neues Spiel* collection, ca. 1977, Foto / photo: Martin Kippenberger

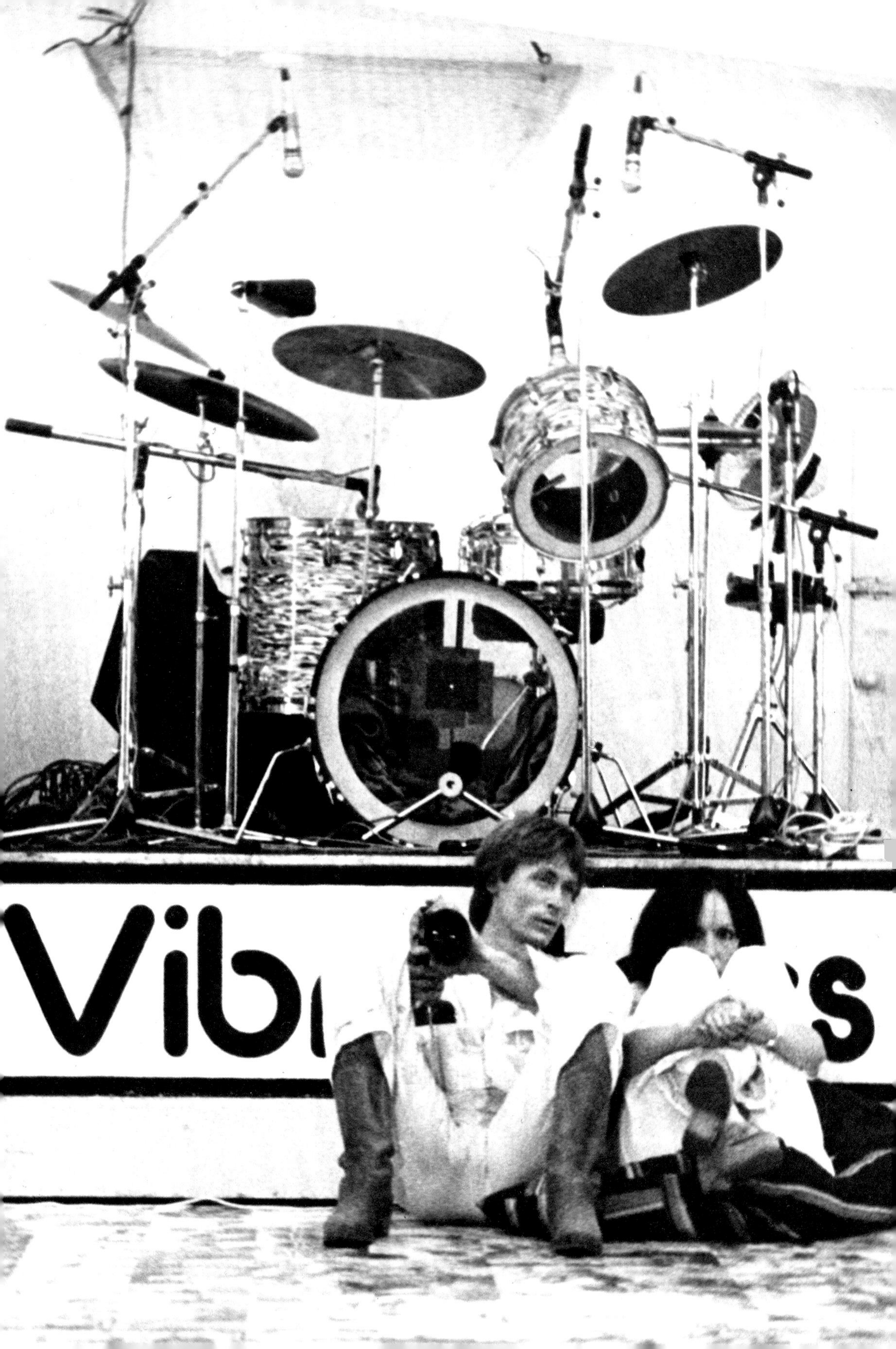
Vib
s

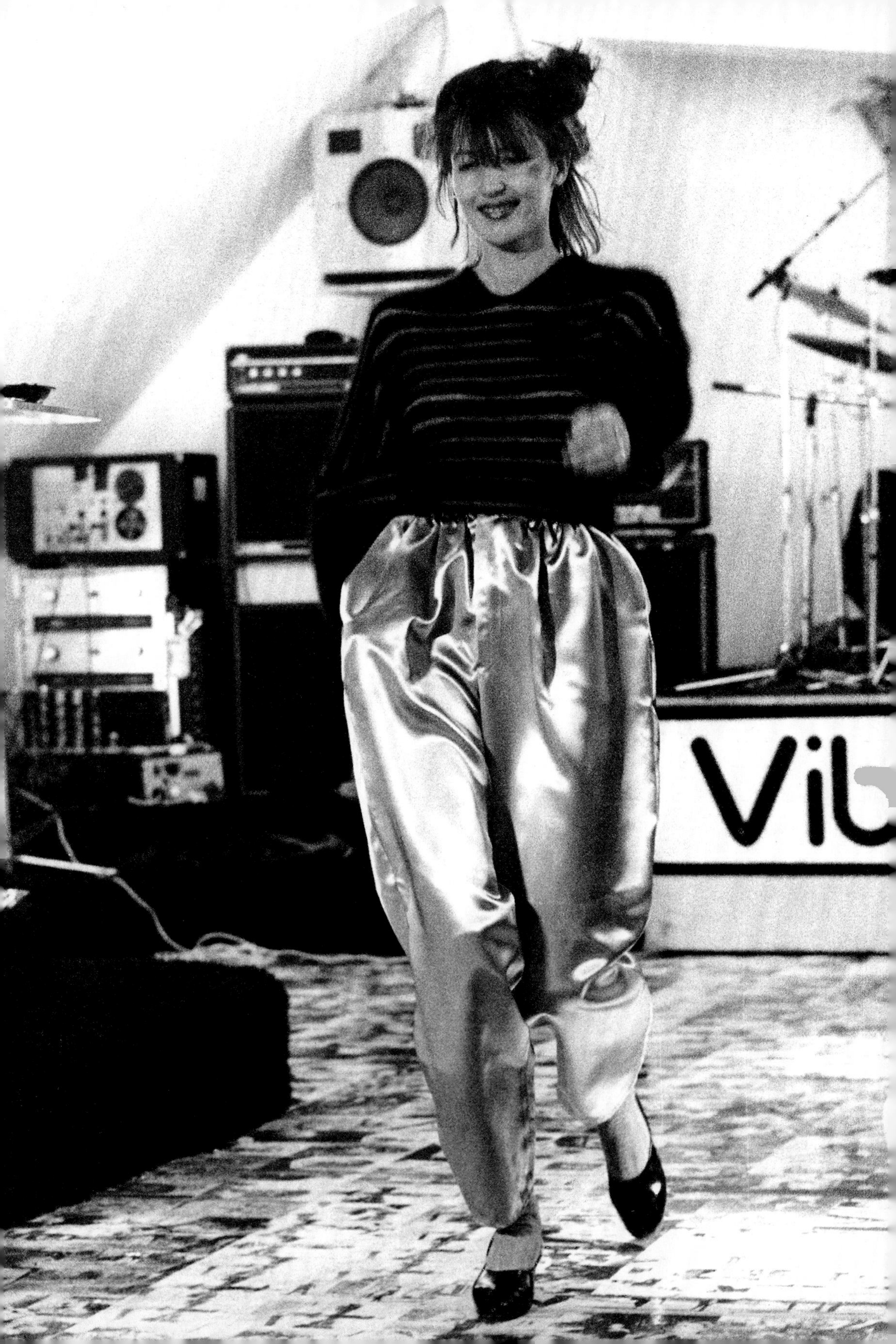
Vi

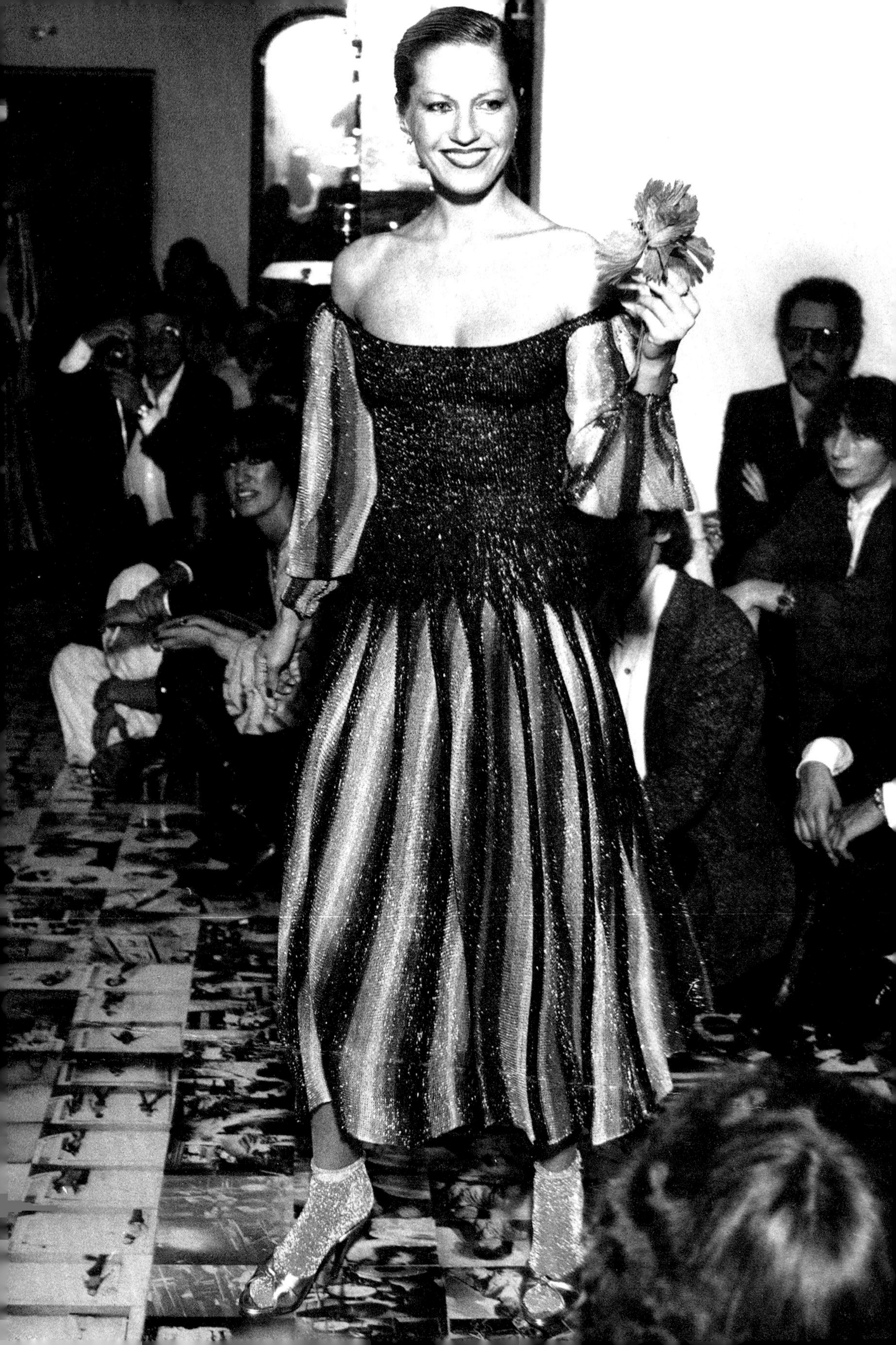

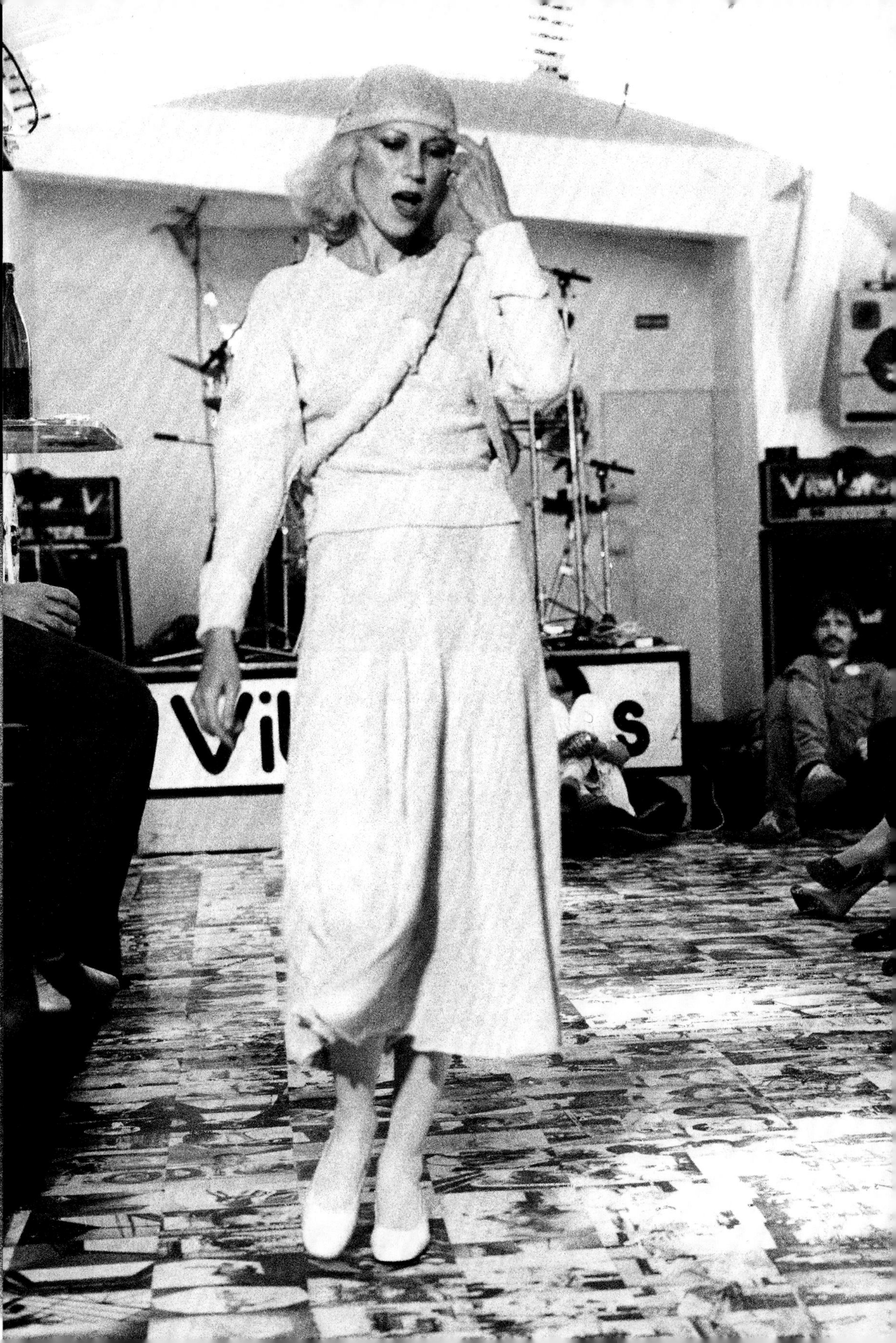

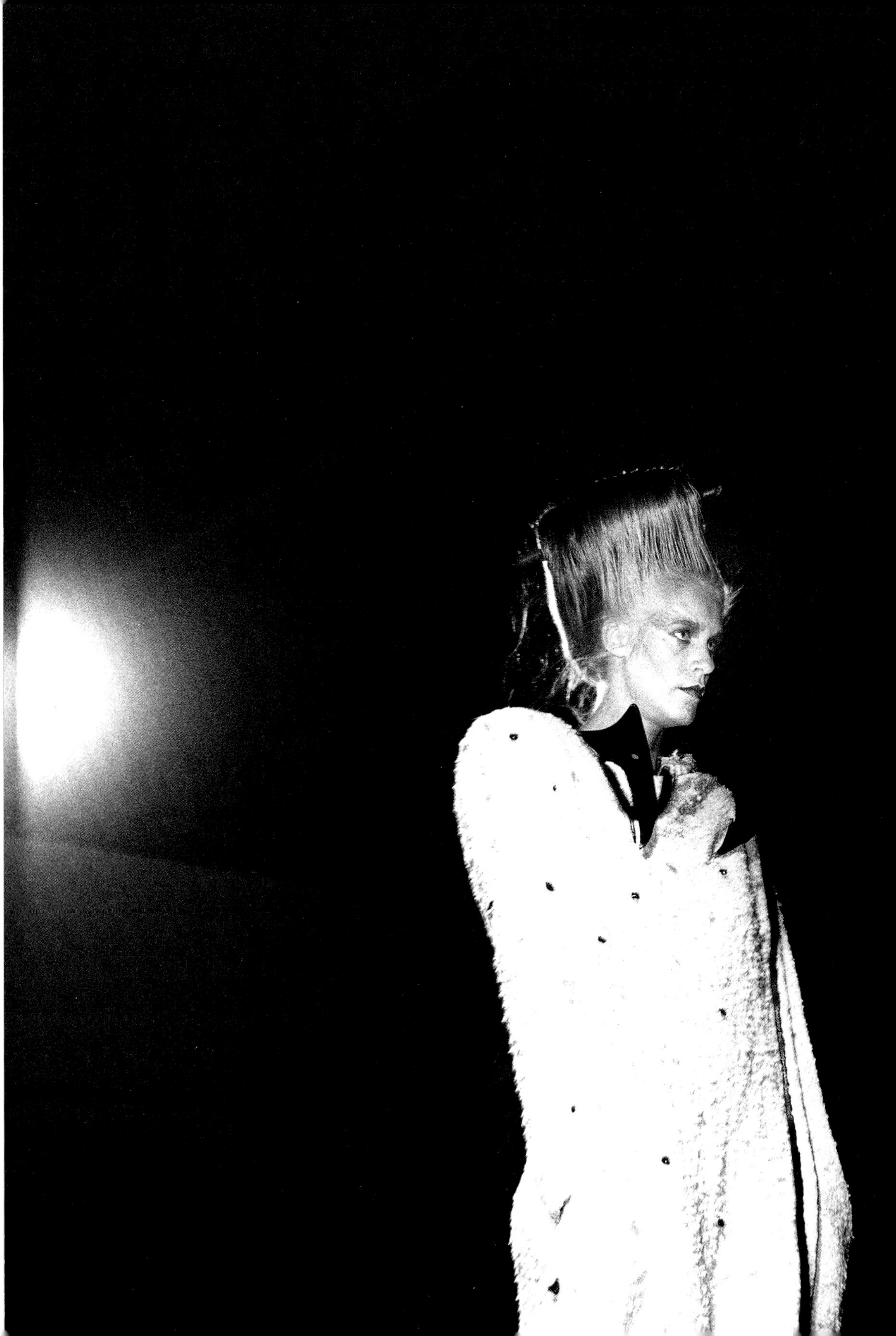

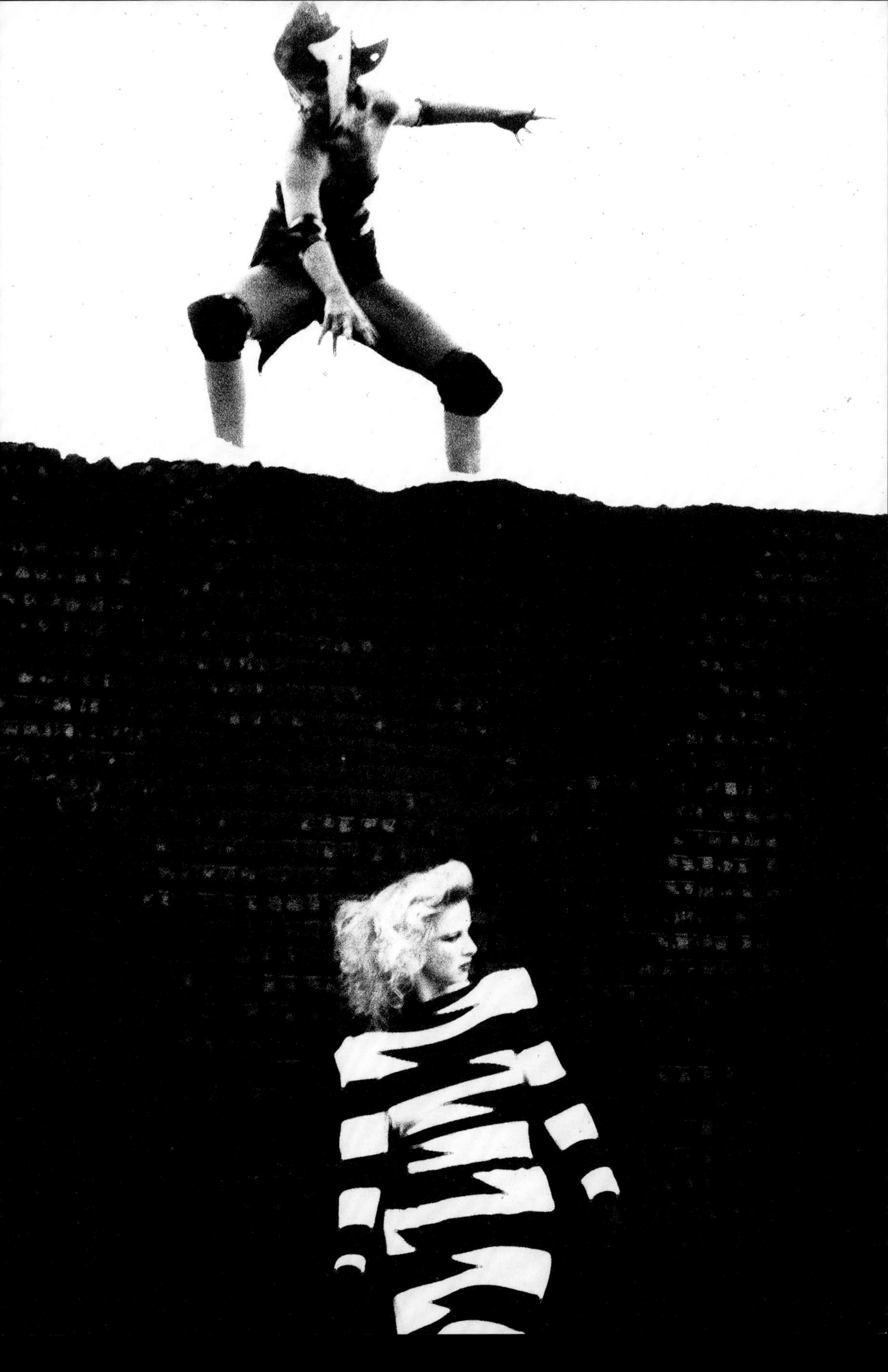

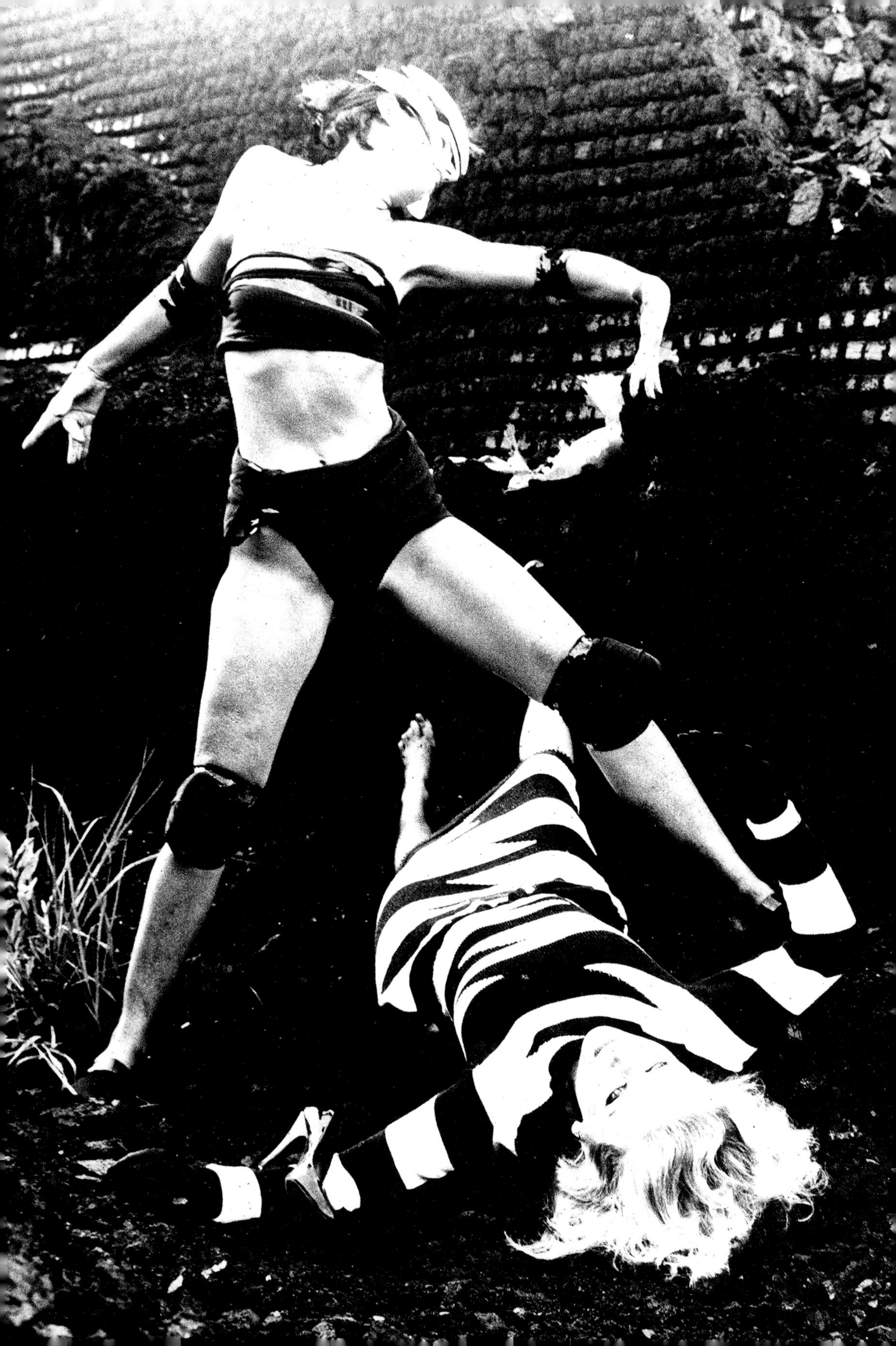

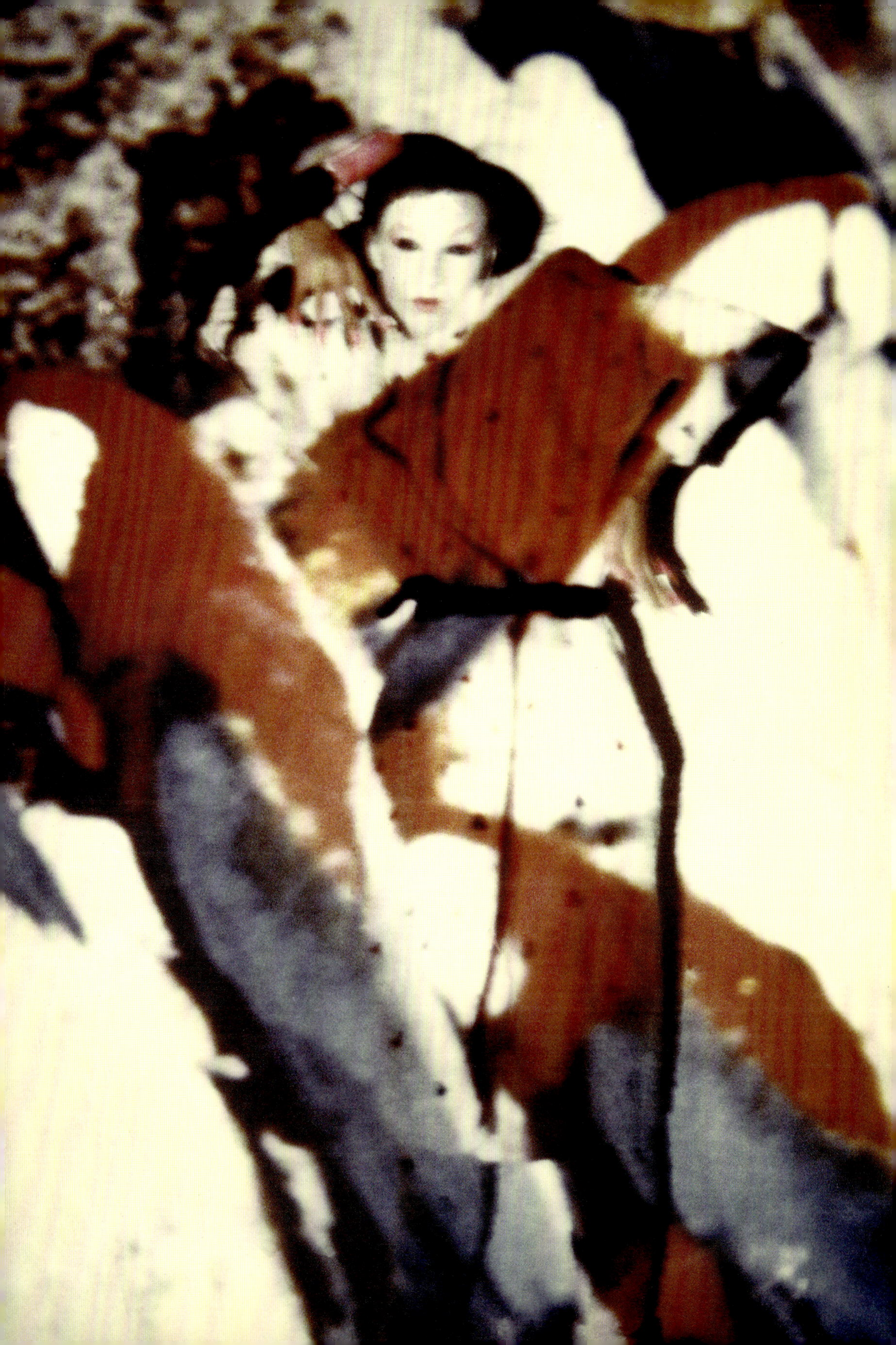

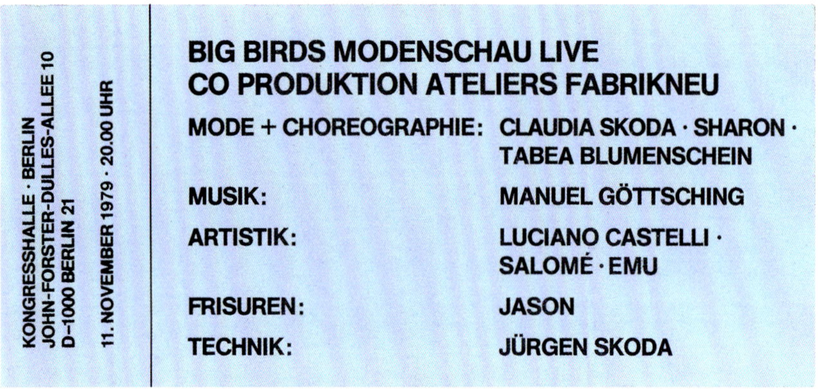

Big Birds, Flyer, Kongresshalle, Berlin, 1979

(195–196) *Big Birds*, Modenschau / fashion show, Kongresshalle, Berlin, 1979, Fotos / photos: Helmut Metzner
(197–198) Promoaufnahmen für das Plakat zur Modenschau *Big Birds* von Claudia Skoda / Promo photographs for the poster of the *Big Birds* fashion show by Claudia Skoda, 1979, Fotos / photos: Luciano Castelli
(199) Modefotografie für Claudia Skodas Kollektion *Big Birds* / Fashion photograph for Claudia Skoda's *Big Birds* collection, 1979, Foto / photo: Luciano Castelli

Achim Schächtele
Der Plan war, ohne Plan zu arbeiten

Achim Schächtele
The plan was to work without a plan

Auszüge aus einem Gespräch mit den Herausgeber*innen /
Excerpts from a conversation with the editors, Berlin, April 2018

Kippenberger moved to Berlin from Hamburg because of his friendship with Ina Barfuss and Thomas Wachweger. He'd given up painting and founded, with Gisela Capitain, who was working as a primary school teacher in Berlin-Schöneberg at the time, his office, where exhibitions and events were held. Basically he was doing the same thing as we were: self-organization. It was crystal clear, something like this was begging to be done. He produced copious quantities of stuff in his office, the graphics cabinet was full of flyers, stickers, and the like. And posters. The paintbrush was left alone, it was about much more. [...]

Eventually we noticed that our money was evaporating. The whole undertaking had nothing to do with common business sense, we wanted to save our necks. At the same time Kippenberger was set on celebrating his birthday in S.O.36. He bought Brennecke's share and pumped an additional 30,000 marks in as a loan, and the club got going again. We kept it going for a couple of more months, and by then it was obvious that we'd be closing the bunker. The finale was the *New York Narrative Film Fest.* Kippenberger had traveled to New York to get some new ideas and proposed the program. Films were shown by people who we rated. Then came *Die letzte Nacht im S.O.36* [The Last Night in S.O.36], and Lydia Lunch and others played. That was the climax, and then it was over. [...]

Kippenberger himself also took the stage of S.O.36 now and then, liked to recite poems, accompanied by a touch of rhythm or beat. It actually went down quite well, but never longer than five minutes. The band Luxus was naturally Kippenberger's baby. Because it was a "luxury" to do something like that. There was a national and an international formation. In Germany we played with Uli Kukulies. A typical performance went like this: the instruments were standing around, so we picked them up and started to play. The plan was to work without a plan. Because Kukulies was a pro, no one ever doubted that we knew what we were doing. But I could only just about plug in a guitar and otherwise didn't have the foggiest. In New York, Luxus then gave a concert with Eric Mitchell and Christine Hahn. [...]

Kippenberger and I traveled to the United States after S.O.36 was closed, in June 1979. We called ourselves the "vassals of tourism," photographing incessantly and recording with our cassette recorder, making music ourselves and printing posters—we wanted to push the limits and then perhaps sell it all to rake in the cash again for S.O.36. Kippenberger later took up some of the motifs again in his painting. We considered the whole trip as a kind of action. Back in Berlin we gave a concluding presentation at Café Einstein, which was actually a financially successful evening, but of course never racked up enough to cover the costs of the whole thing. We assembled all the things we had done and collected during the trip into a huge installation and put on a performance ourselves. Permanent action, that was always our way.

Kippenberger war aus Hamburg nach Berlin gekommen, bedingt durch die Freundschaft mit Ina Barfuss und Thomas Wachweger. Er hatte das Malen aufgegeben und mit Gisela Capitain, die damals als Grundschullehrerin in Berlin-Schöneberg arbeitete, sein Büro gegründet, wo Ausstellungen und Veranstaltungen liefen. Im Grunde machte er das Gleiche wie wir: sich selbst organisieren. Das war klar wie Kloßbrühe, so etwas musste gemacht werden. Er produzierte Unmengen an Zeug in seinem Büro, der Grafikschrank war voll mit Flyern, Aufklebern und so weiter. Und Plakaten. Der Pinsel wurde liegen gelassen, da ging's um mehr. [...]

Wir merkten irgendwann, dass unser Geld schwindet. Das Ganze hatte mit kaufmännischer Führung nichts zu tun, wir wollten den Kopf aus der Schlinge ziehen. Zugleich wollte Kippenberger unbedingt seinen Geburtstag im S.O.36 feiern. Er kaufte Brennecke dessen Anteile ab und schoss zusätzlich 30 000 DM als Darlehen rein, der Club konnte wieder Fahrt aufnehmen. Wir machten es noch ein paar Monate, und dann war sowieso klar, dass wir den Bunker dichtmachen. Der Abschluss war das *New York Narrative Film Fest*. Kippenberger war nach New York gefahren, um neue Ideen zu bekommen, und schlug das Programm vor. Da waren Filme zu sehen von Leuten, die wir gut fanden. In der *Letzten Nacht im S.O.36* spielten dann Lydia Lunch und andere. Das war der Höhepunkt, dann war Schluss. [...]

Auch Kippenberger stand natürlich hin und wieder auf der Bühne des S.O.36, hat gerne Gedichte vorgetragen mit ein bisschen Rhythmus oder Beat. Das kam eigentlich ganz gut an, aber nie länger als fünf Minuten. Die Band Luxus war natürlich die Erfindung von Kippenberger. Weil es eben „Luxus" war, so etwas zu tun. Es gab eine nationale und eine internationale Formation. In Deutschland haben wir mit Uli Kukulies gespielt. Ein klassischer Auftritt sah so aus, dass, wenn Instrumente rumstanden, wir einfach drauflos spielten. Der Plan war, ohne Plan zu arbeiten. Dadurch, dass Kukulies Profi war, hat auch keiner angezweifelt, dass wir wissen, was wir tun. Dabei wusste ich gerade mal, wie man eine Gitarre einstöpselt, und hatte sonst keinen blassen Schimmer. In New York hatte Luxus dann einen Auftritt mit Eric Mitchell und Christine Hahn. [...]

Die Reise in die USA haben Kippenberger und ich nach der Schließung des S.O.36 im Juni 1979 gemacht. Wir nannten uns „Knechte des Tourismus" und haben ständig fotografiert und mit unserem Kassettenrekorder aufgezeichnet, auch selbst Musik gemacht und Plakate gedruckt – wir wollten einfach alles ausreizen und das dann vielleicht später verkaufen, um die Kohle für das S.O.36 wieder reinzukriegen. Kippenberger hat einzelne Motive später wieder in der Malerei aufgegriffen. Die gesamte Reise haben wir als Aktion betrachtet. Zurück in Berlin haben wir im Café Einstein eine Abschlusspräsentation gegeben, das war wirtschaftlich tatsächlich ein erfolgreicher Abend, aber der hat natürlich nicht die Kosten der ganzen Sache reingeholt. Wir haben da sämtliche Dinge, die wir während der Reise gemacht und gesammelt hatten, zu einer riesigen Installation zusammengefügt und sind selbst noch aufgetreten. Permanente Aktion, das war immer unser Ansatz.

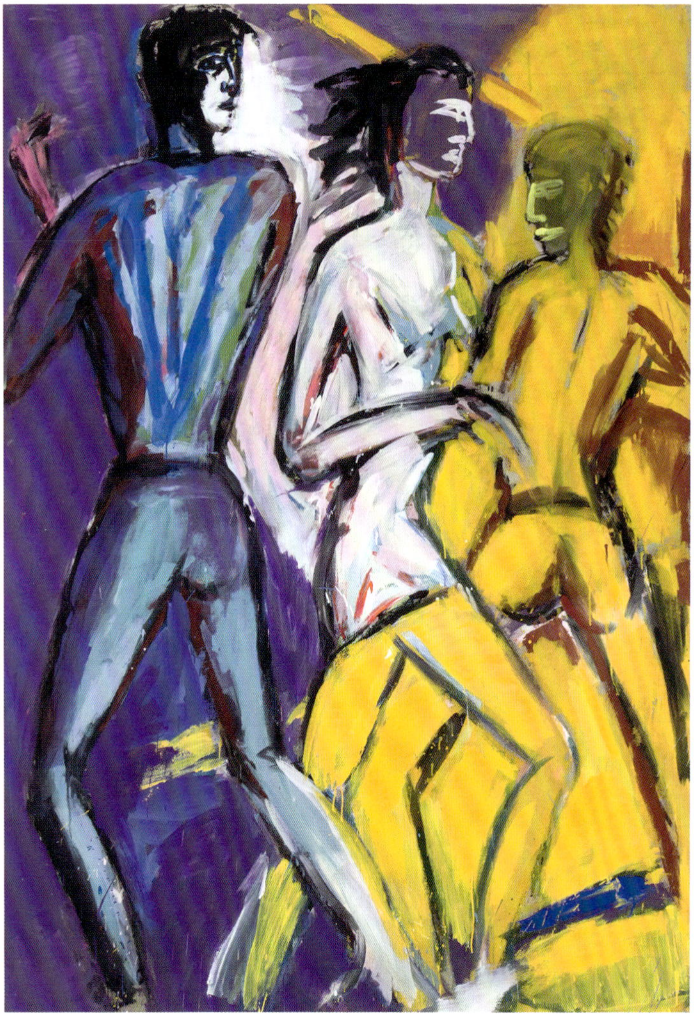

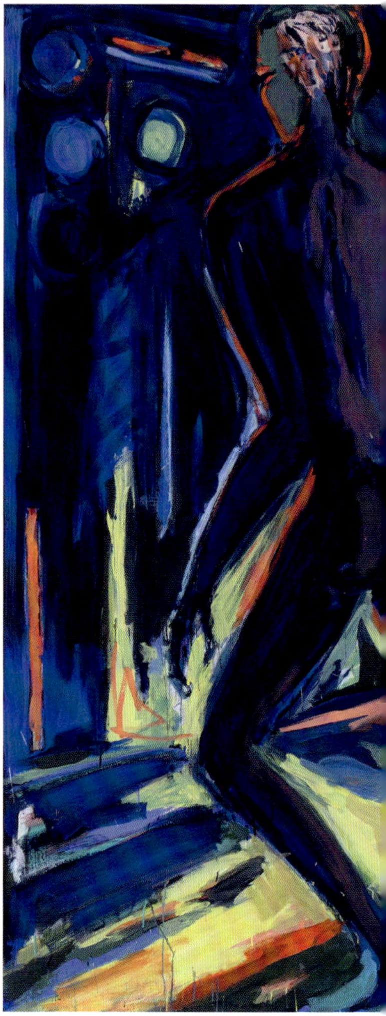

Helmut Middendorf, *Reise ans Ende der Nacht*, 1981, Öl und Mischtechnik auf Leinwan
250 × 175 cm, 250 × 170 cm, 250 × 175 cm

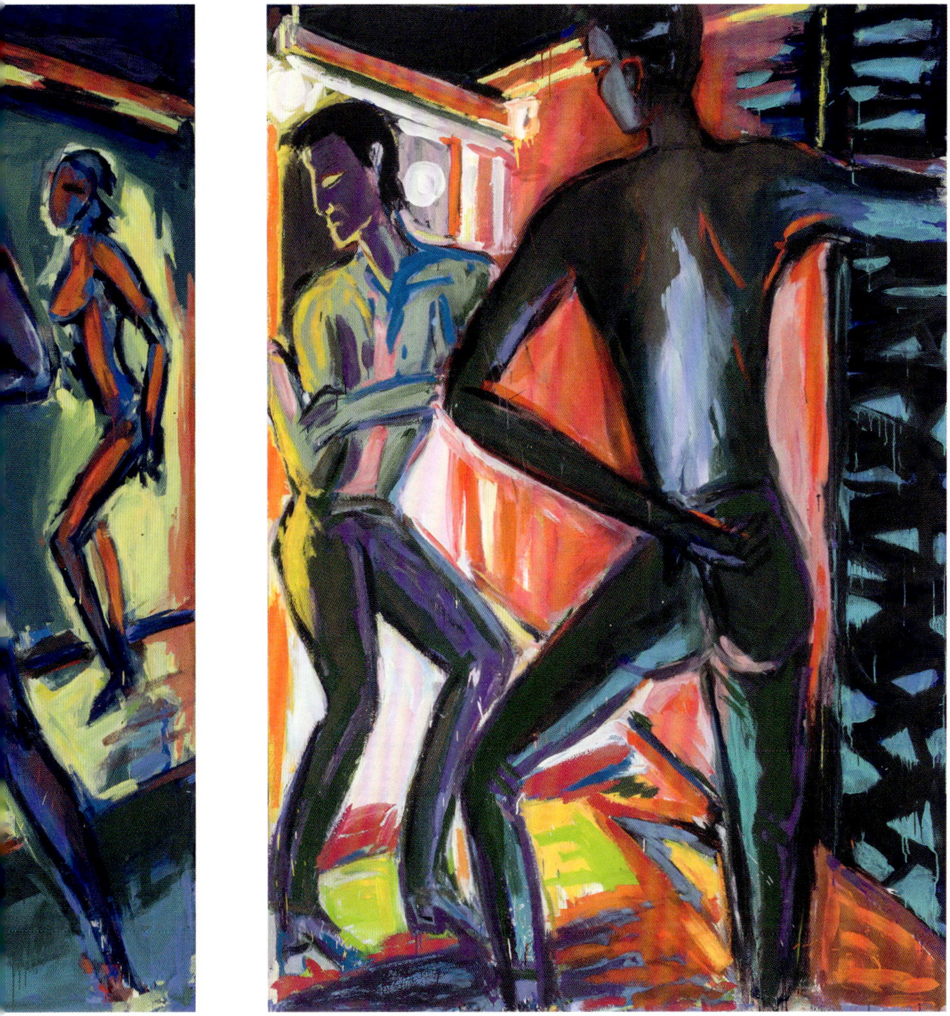

-teilig / oil and mixed media on canvas, 3 parts,

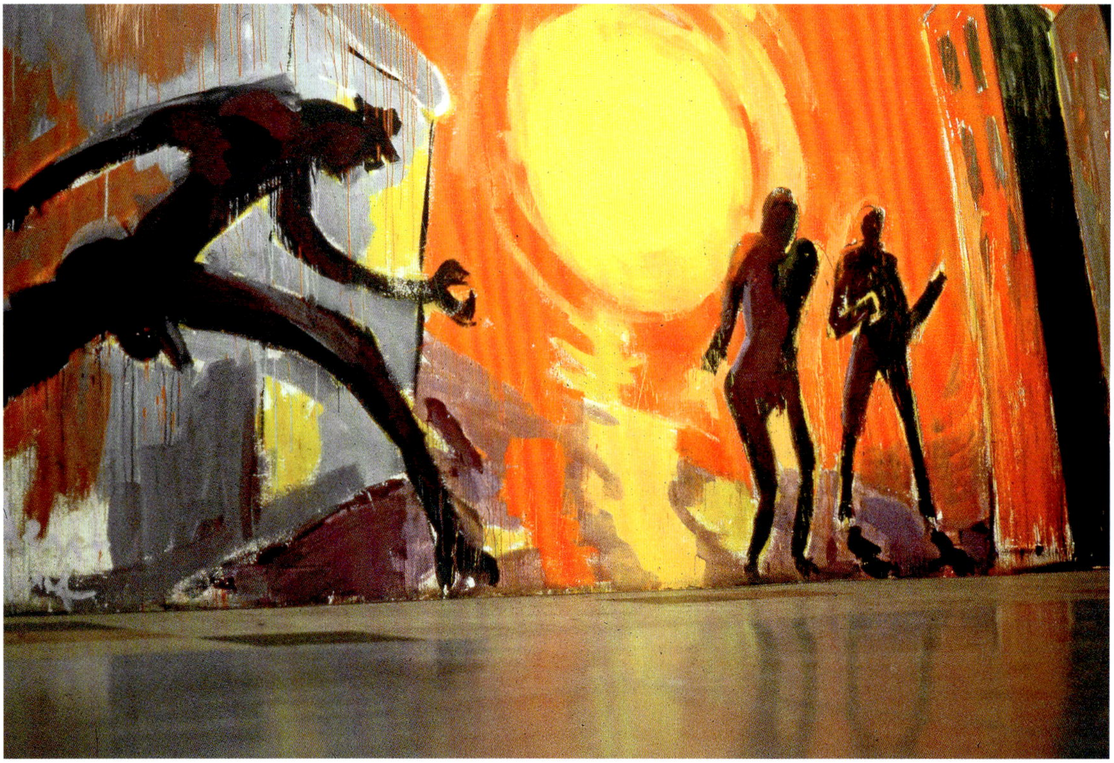

Rainer Fetting, Helmut Middendorf, *Sonnenuntergang*, Wandarbeit / mural, S.O.36, Berlin, 1978

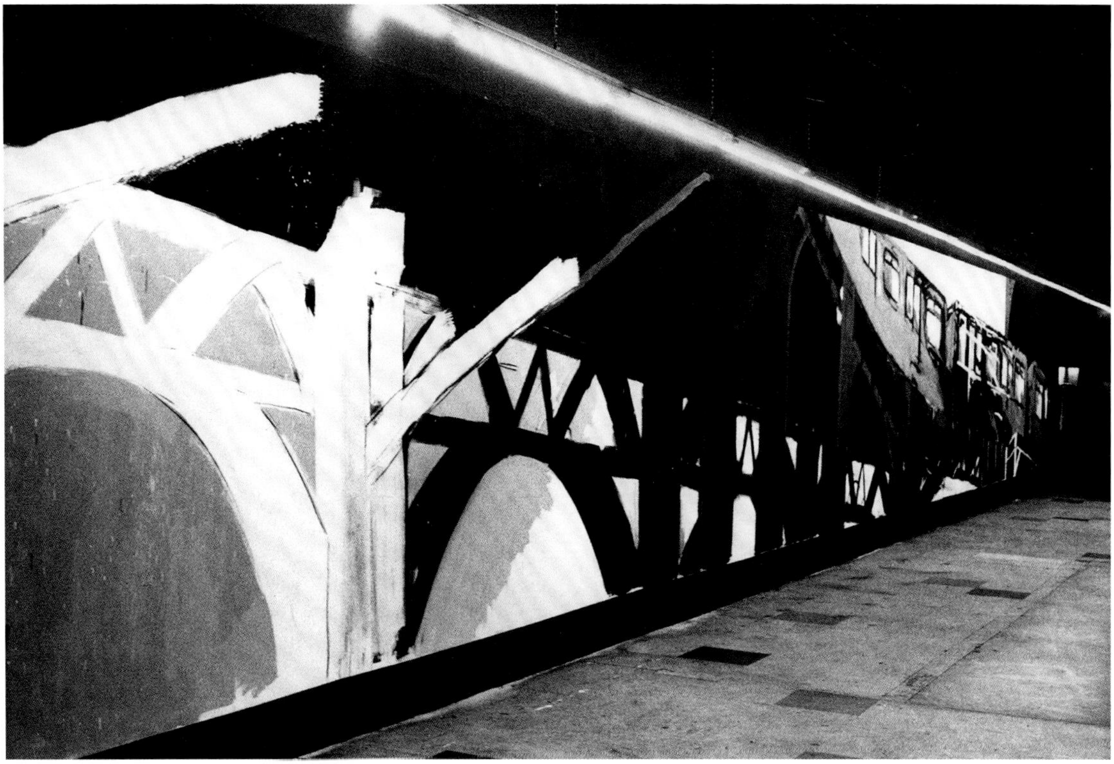

Bernd Zimmer, *U-Bahn (1/10 Sekunde auf der Warschauer Brücke, Stadtbild 3/28)*, 1978, Dispersion und Leimfarbe auf Nessel / dispersion paint and distemper on cotton canvas, 300 × 280 cm, Installation: S.O.36, Berlin, 1978

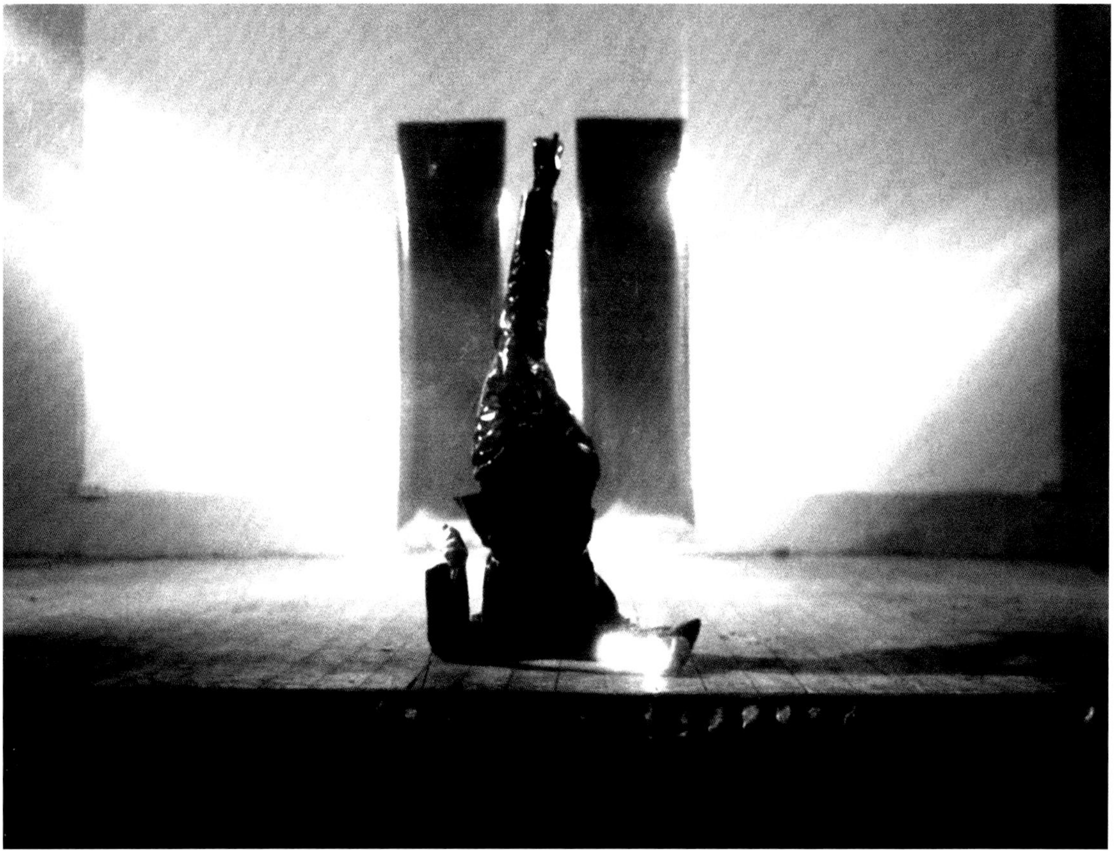

Anne Jud, *eingeschlossen (allein) S.O.36* (Detail), 1979, 36-teilige Fotoserie / 36-part photo series, je / each 20,5 × 29,5 cm

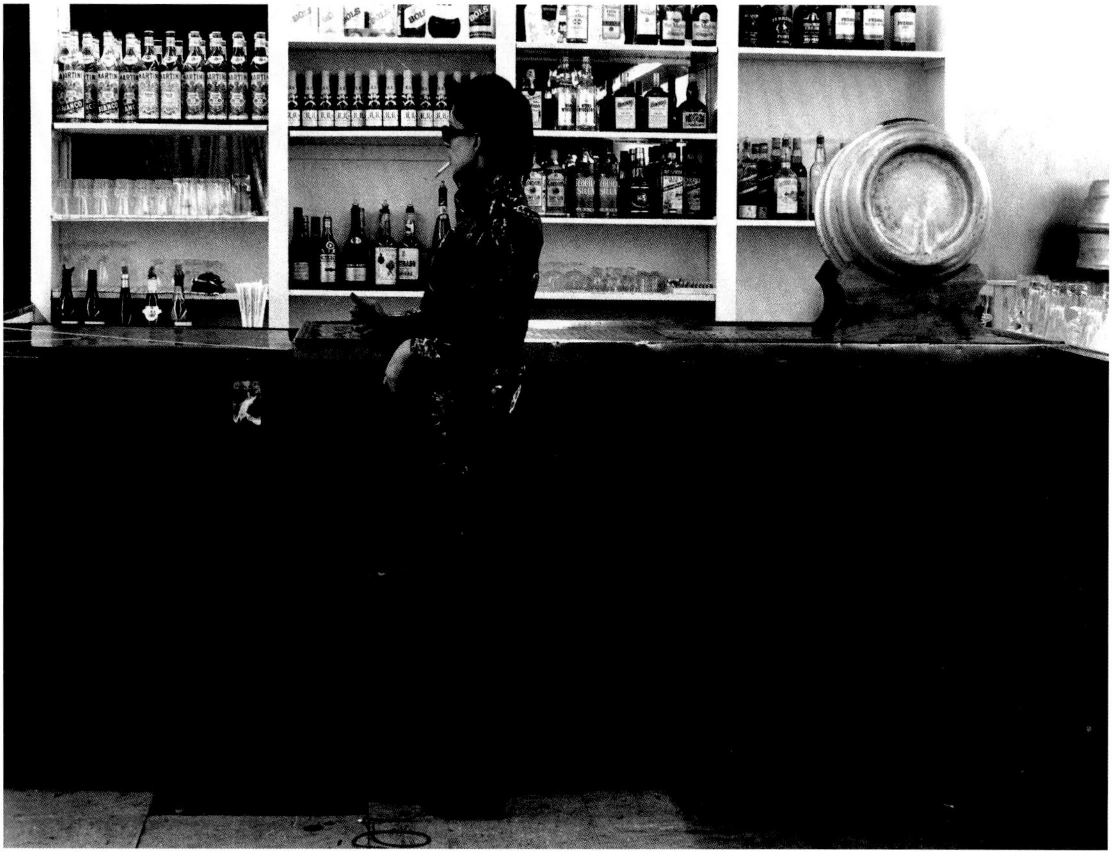

Anne Jud am Tresen / at the bar, S.O.36, Berlin, 1979, Foto / photo: Selbstauslöser / self-timer

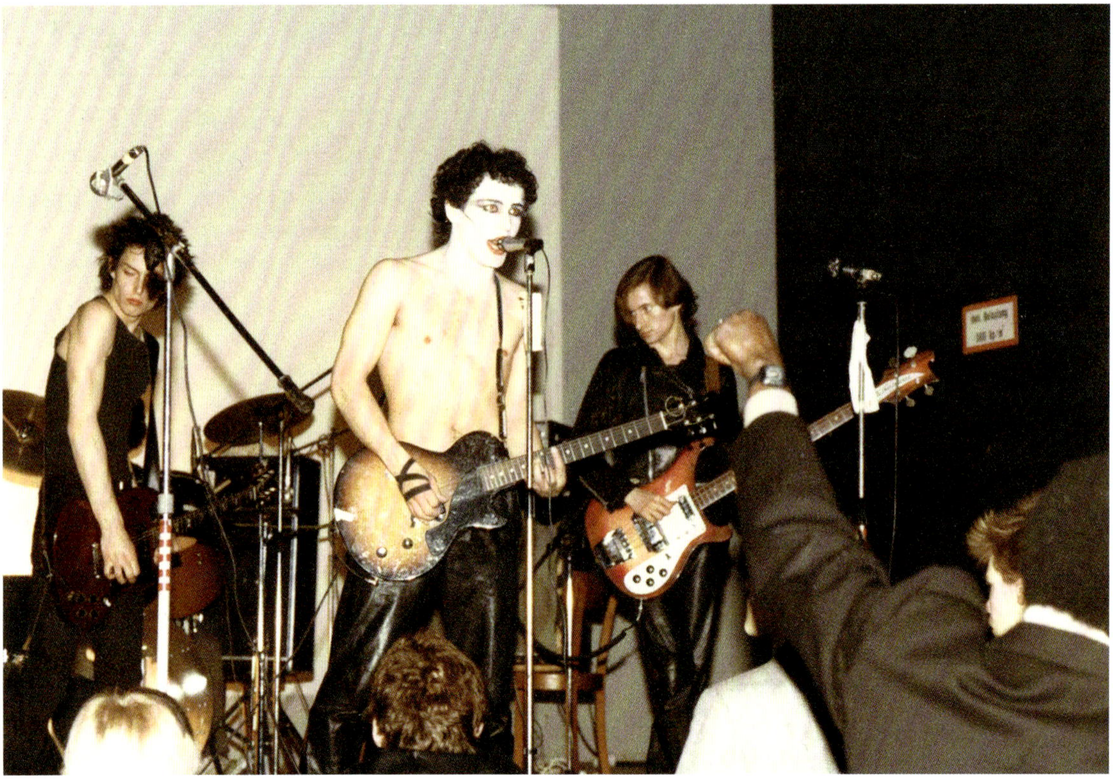

Adam and the Ants, Konzert / concert, S.O.36, Berlin, 1979,
Foto / photo: Achim Schächtele

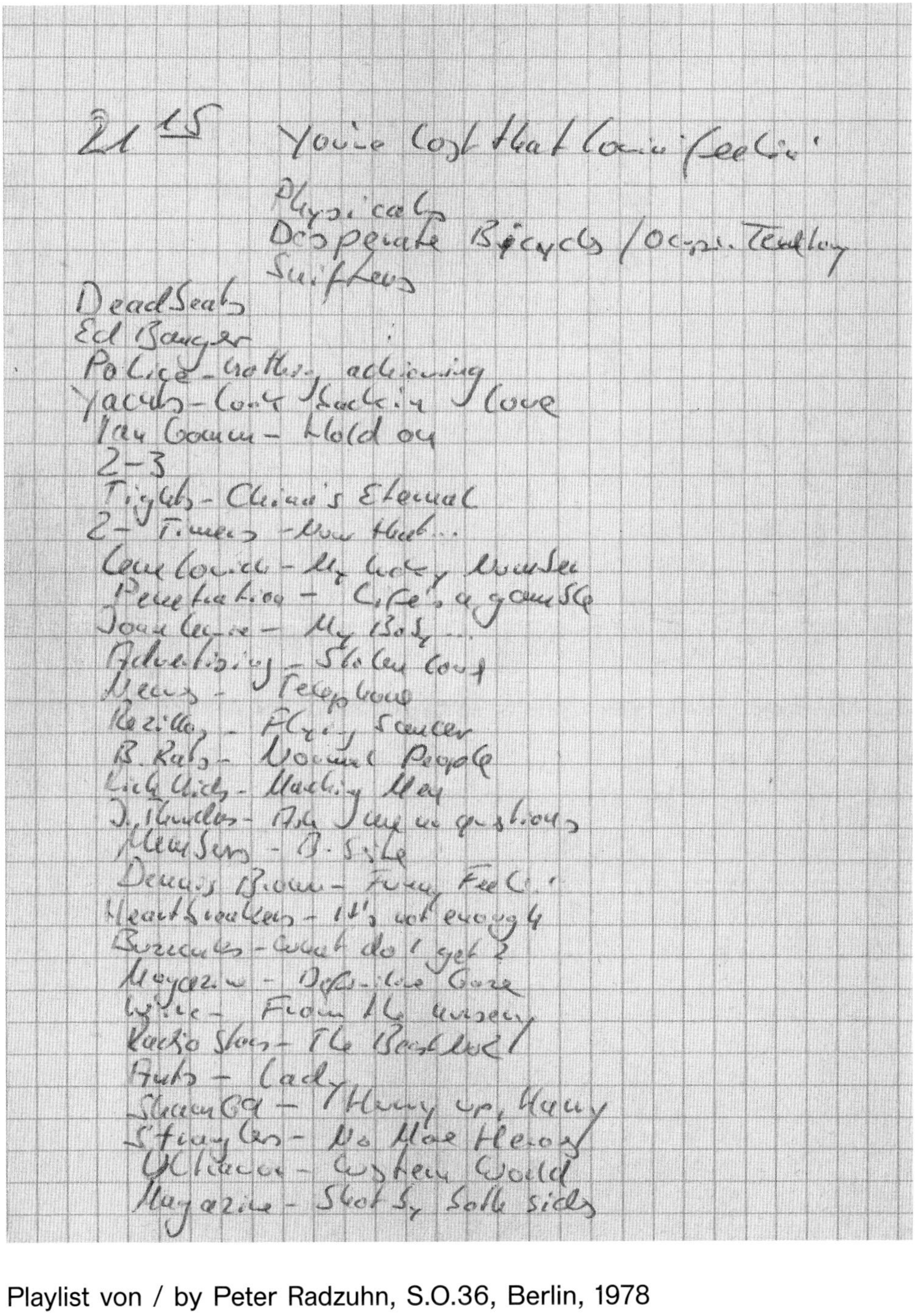

Playlist von / by Peter Radzuhn, S.O.36, Berlin, 1978

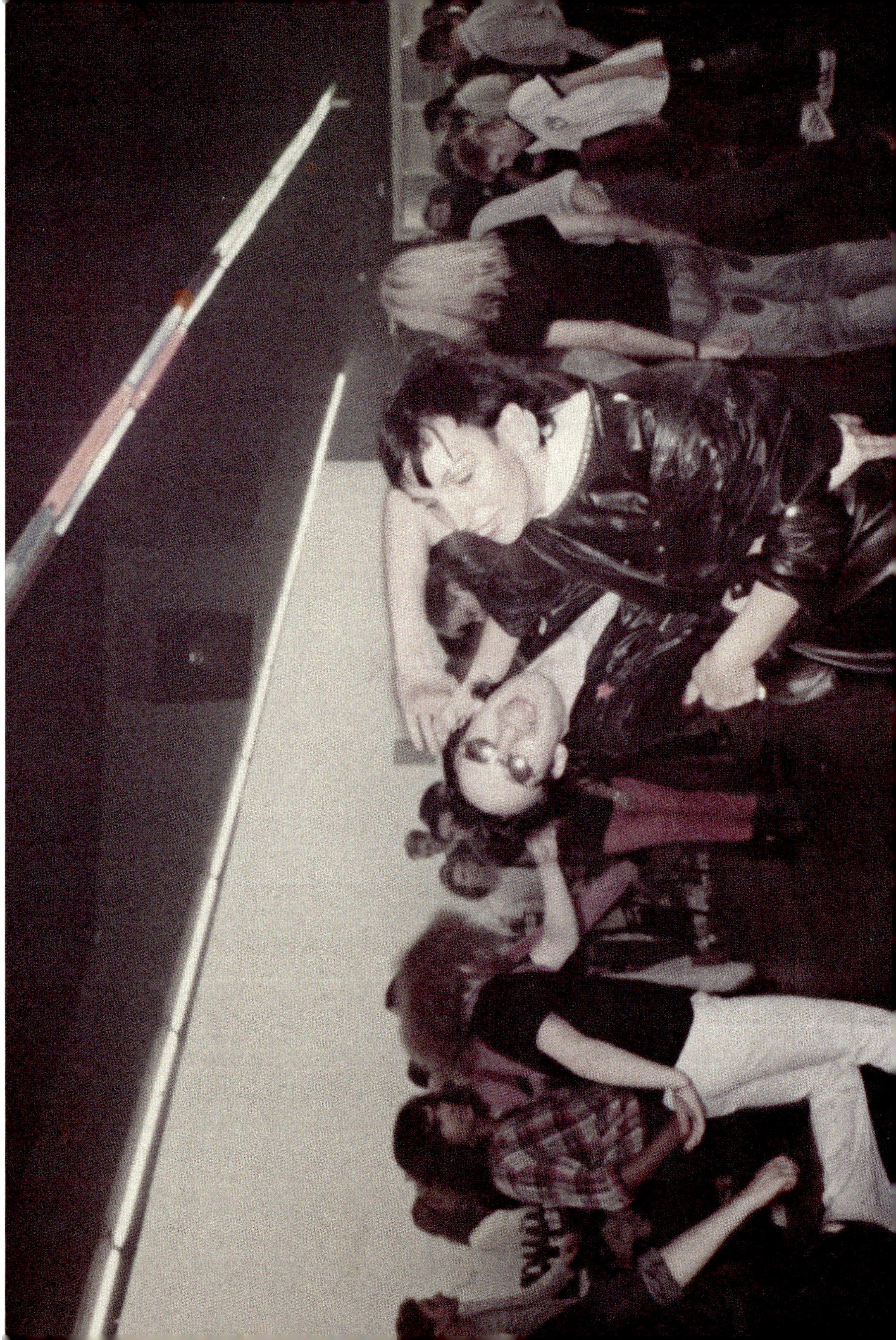

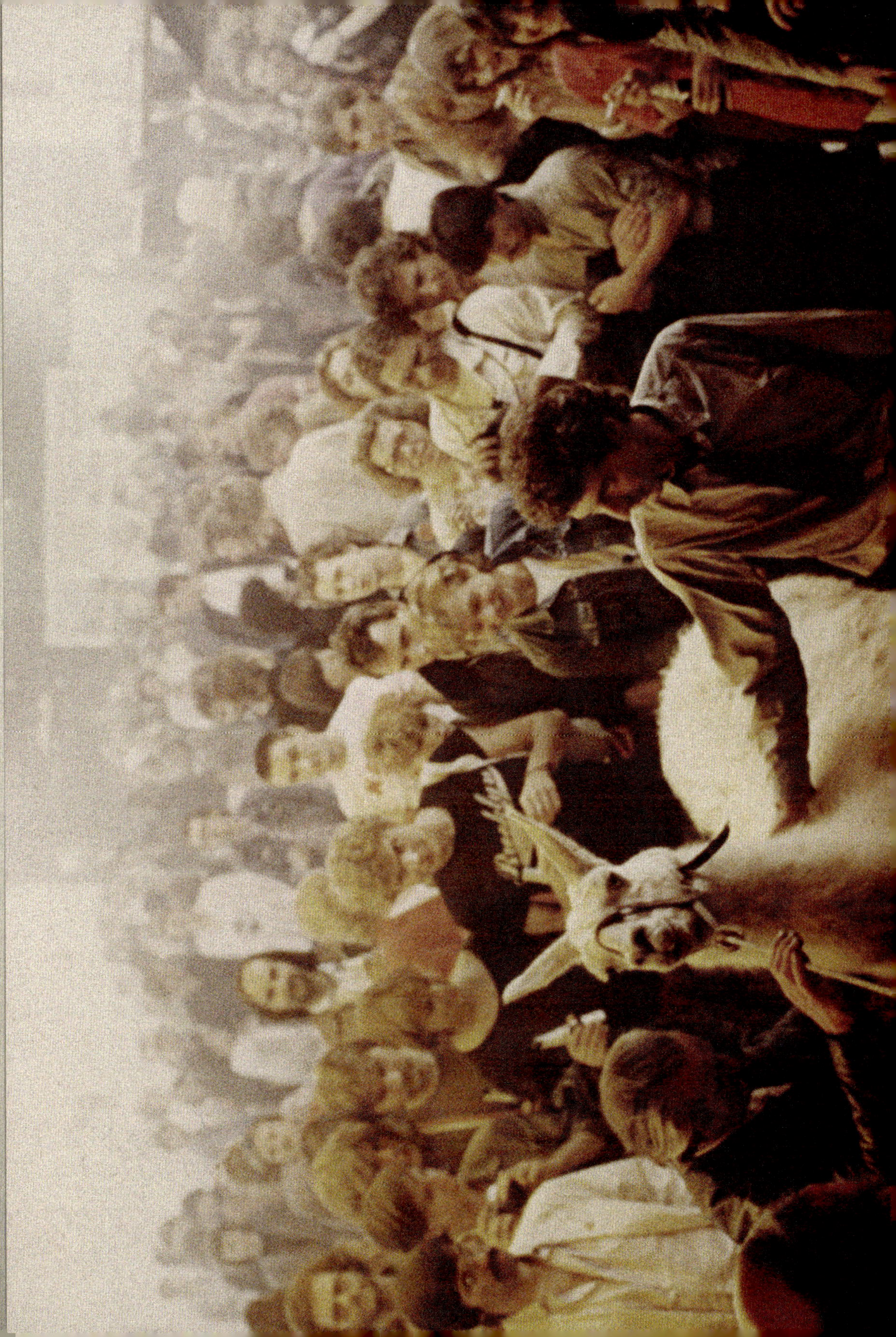

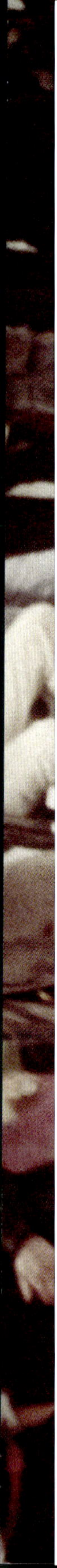

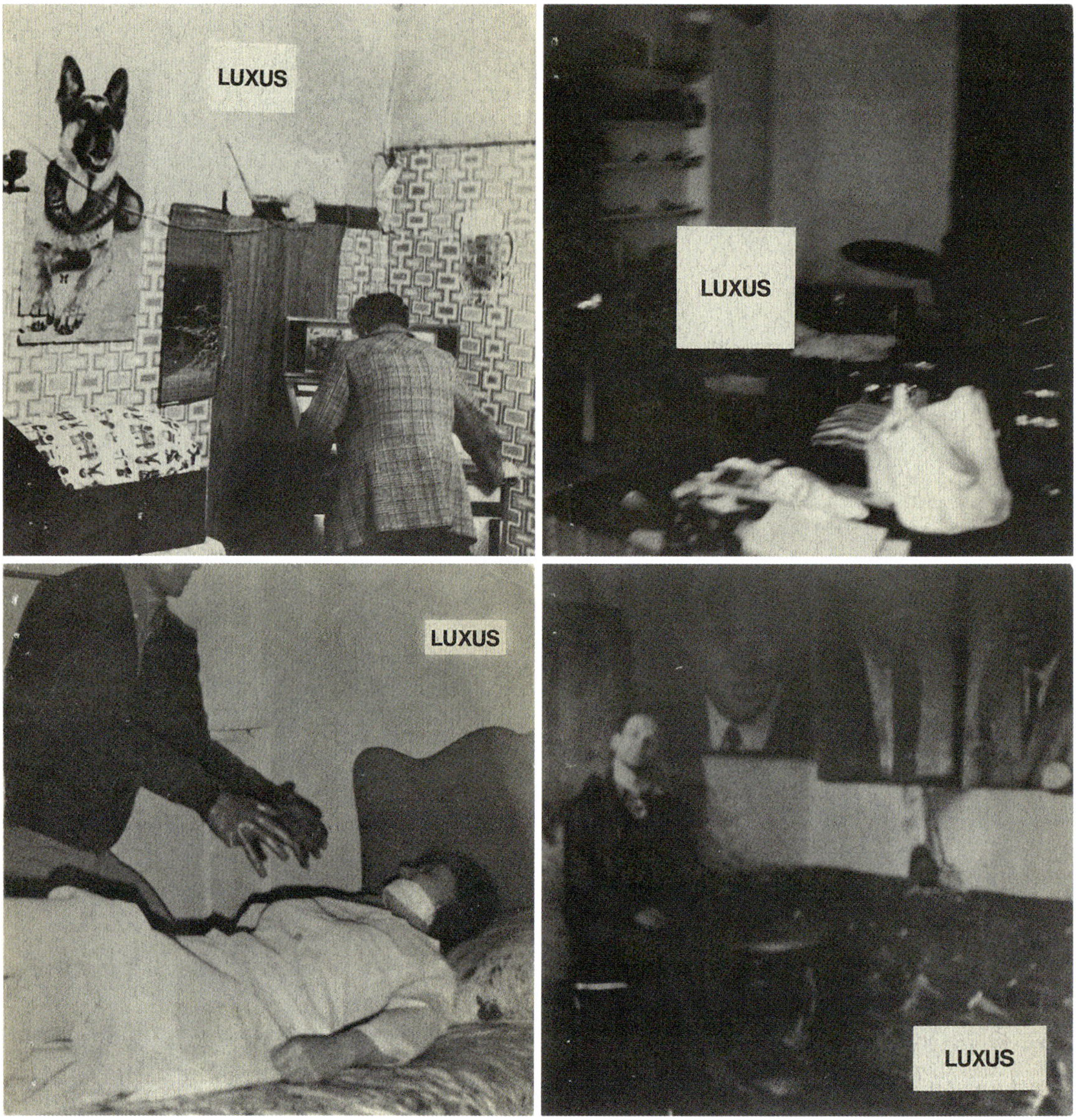

Luxus, *Luxus*, 1979, Doppel-Single mit 6-seitigem Booklet / double single with 6-page booklet, S.O.36 Records, Design: Christine Hahn, Martin Kippenberger, Eric Mitchell

(215 – 219) *Die letzte Nacht im S.O.36*, Berlin, 1979, Martin Kippenberger (215), Claudia Skoda (216 r.), Anne Jud (218 r.), Fotos / photos: Achim Schächtele

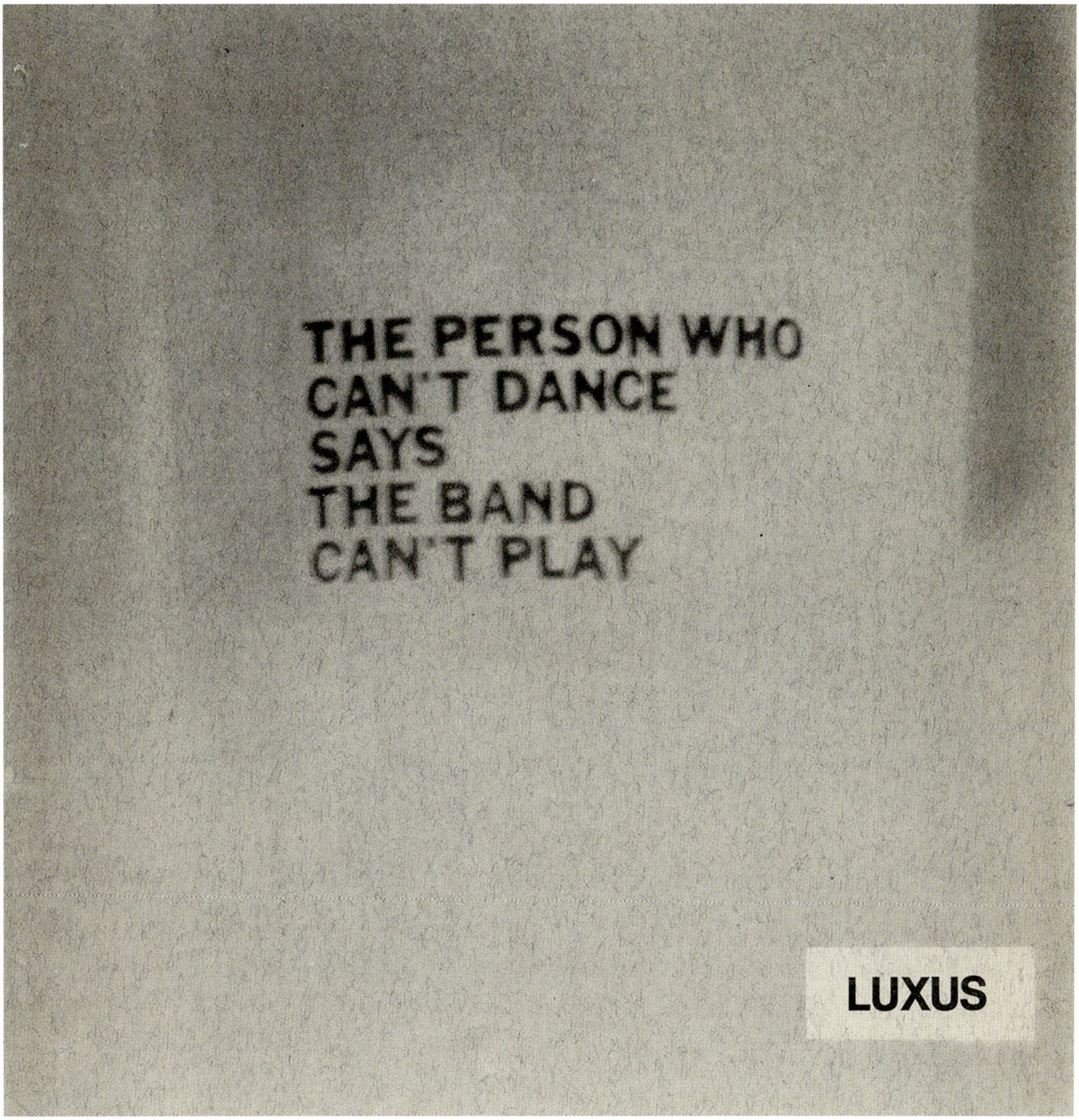
THE PERSON WHO
CAN'T DANCE
SAYS
THE BAND
CAN'T PLAY
LUXUS

THIS BAND IS PLAYING ON LUXUS

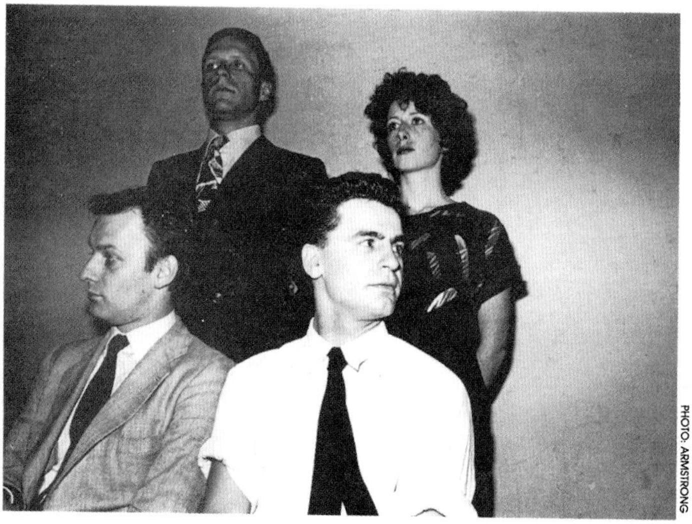

PHOTO: ARMSTRONG

S.O.36 RECORDS

Martin Kippenberger, *This Band is Playing on Luxus*, 1979, Offset, 35,5 × 21,6 cm, S.O.36 Records, Berlin

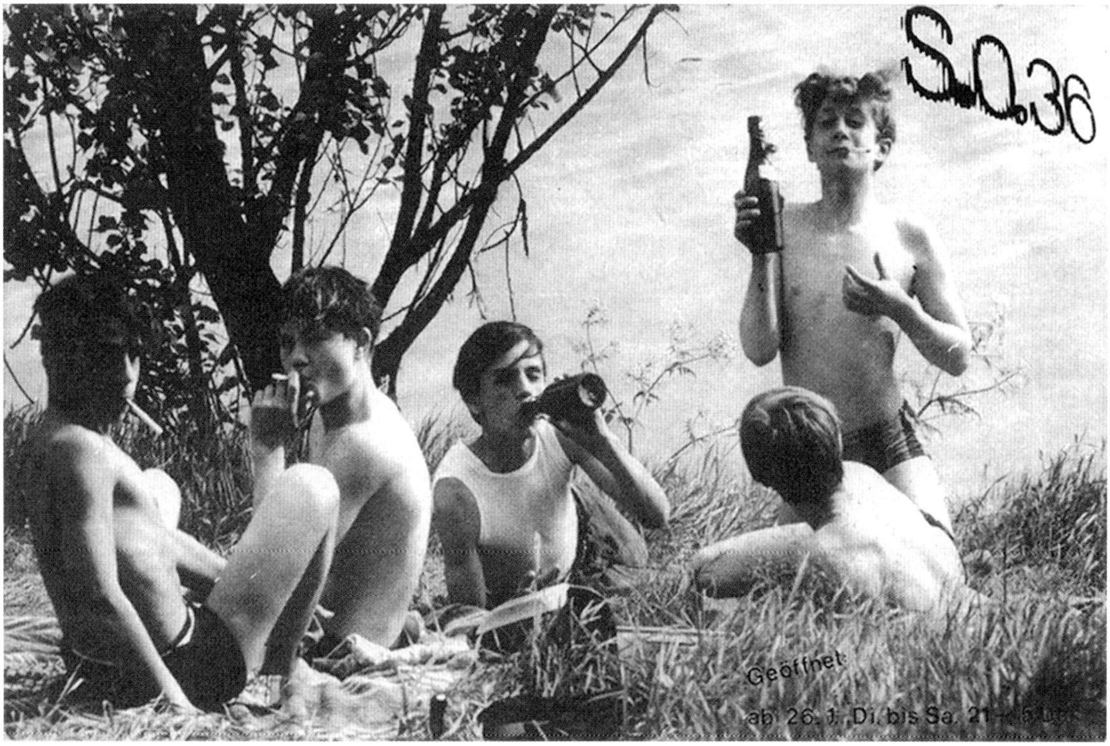

Sticker, S.O.36, Berlin, 1979, Design: Martin Kippenberger

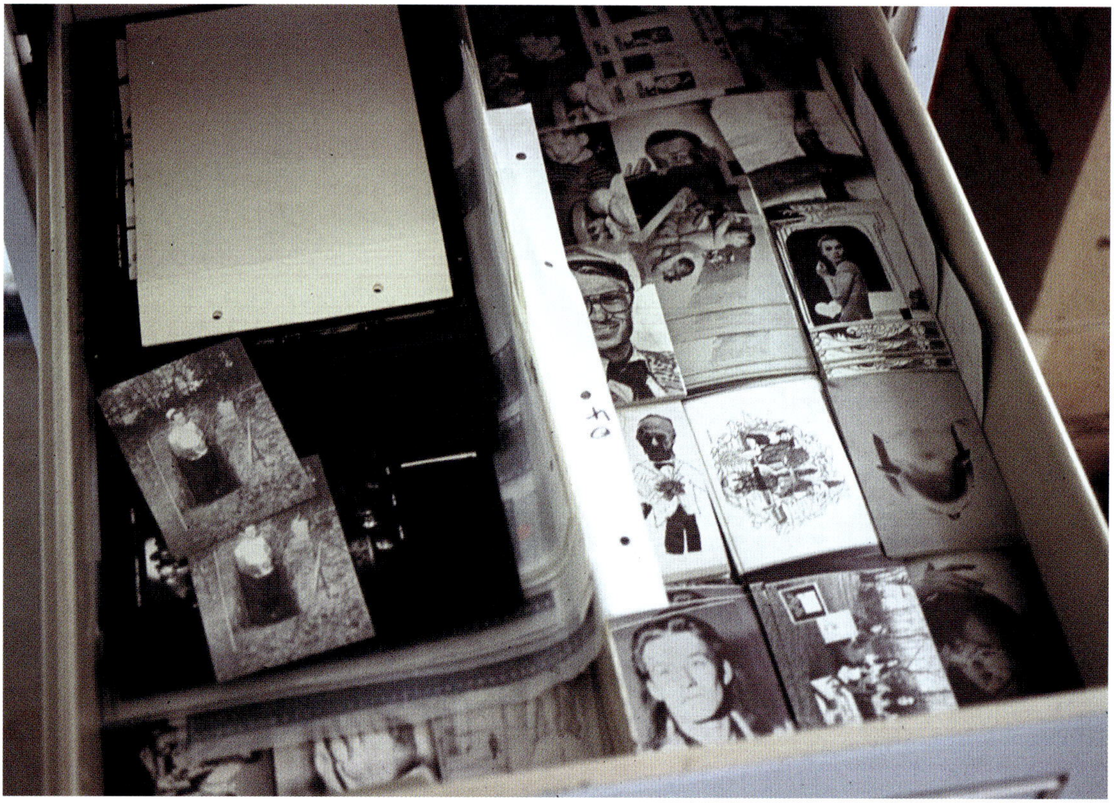

Schublade mit Stickern von Martin Kippenberger / Drawer with stickers by Martin Kippenberger, Kippenbergers Büro, Berlin, ca. 1979, Foto / photo: Achim Schächtele

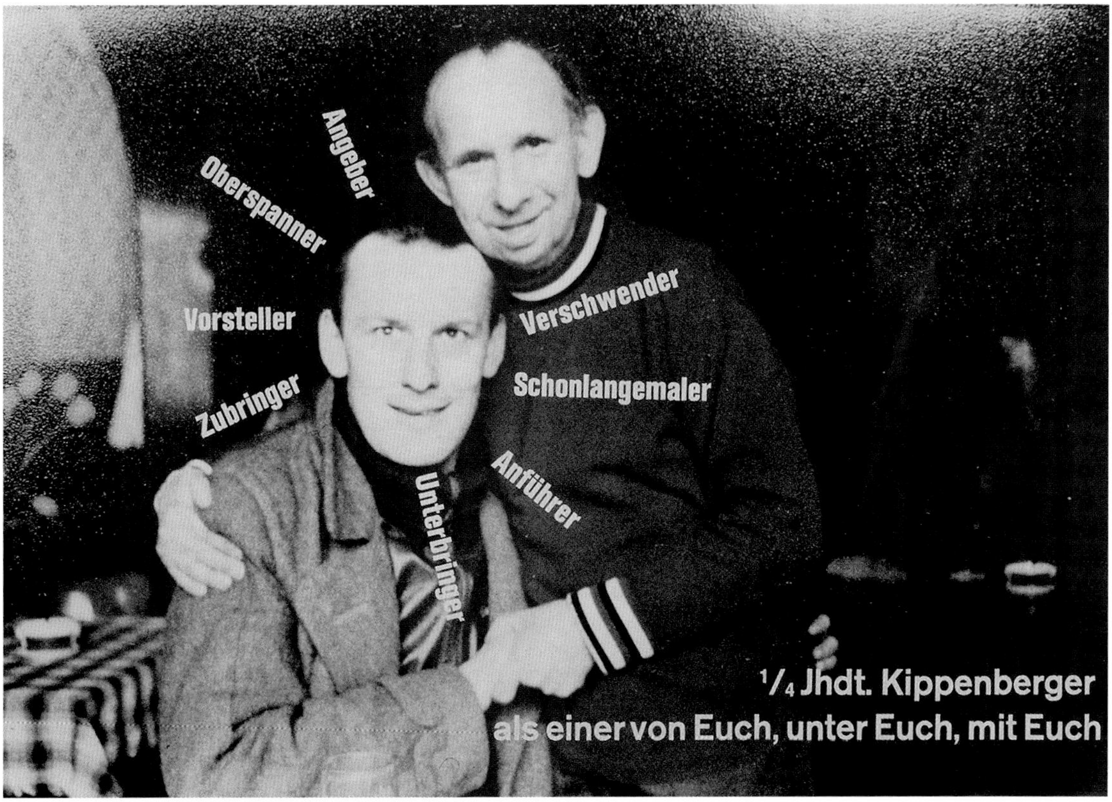

Martin Kippenberger, *¼ Jhdt. Kippenberger als einer von Euch, unter Euch, mit Euch*, 1978, Offset, 59 × 85 cm

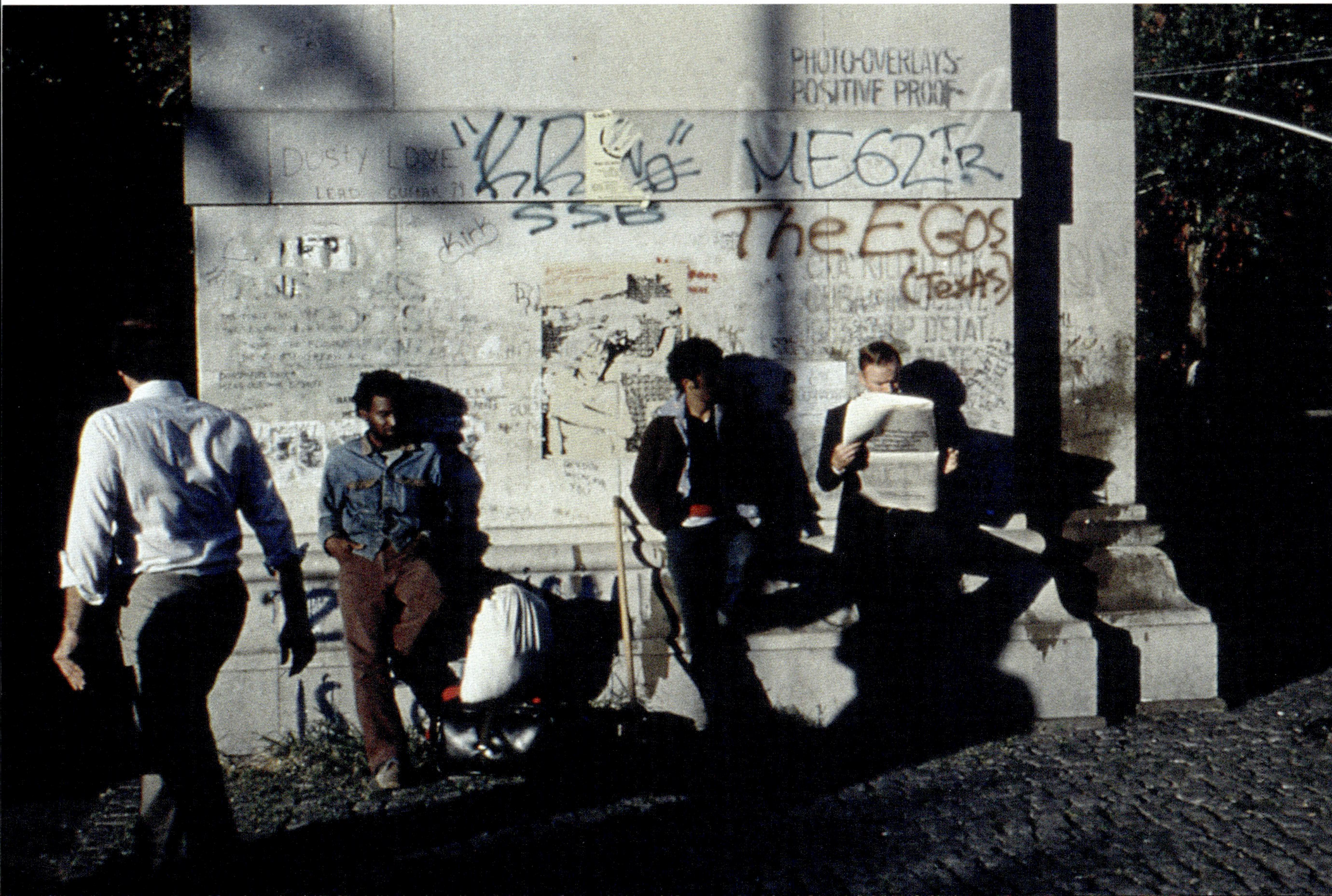
PHOTO-OVERLAYS
POSITIVE PROOF
The EGOS
(TEXAS)

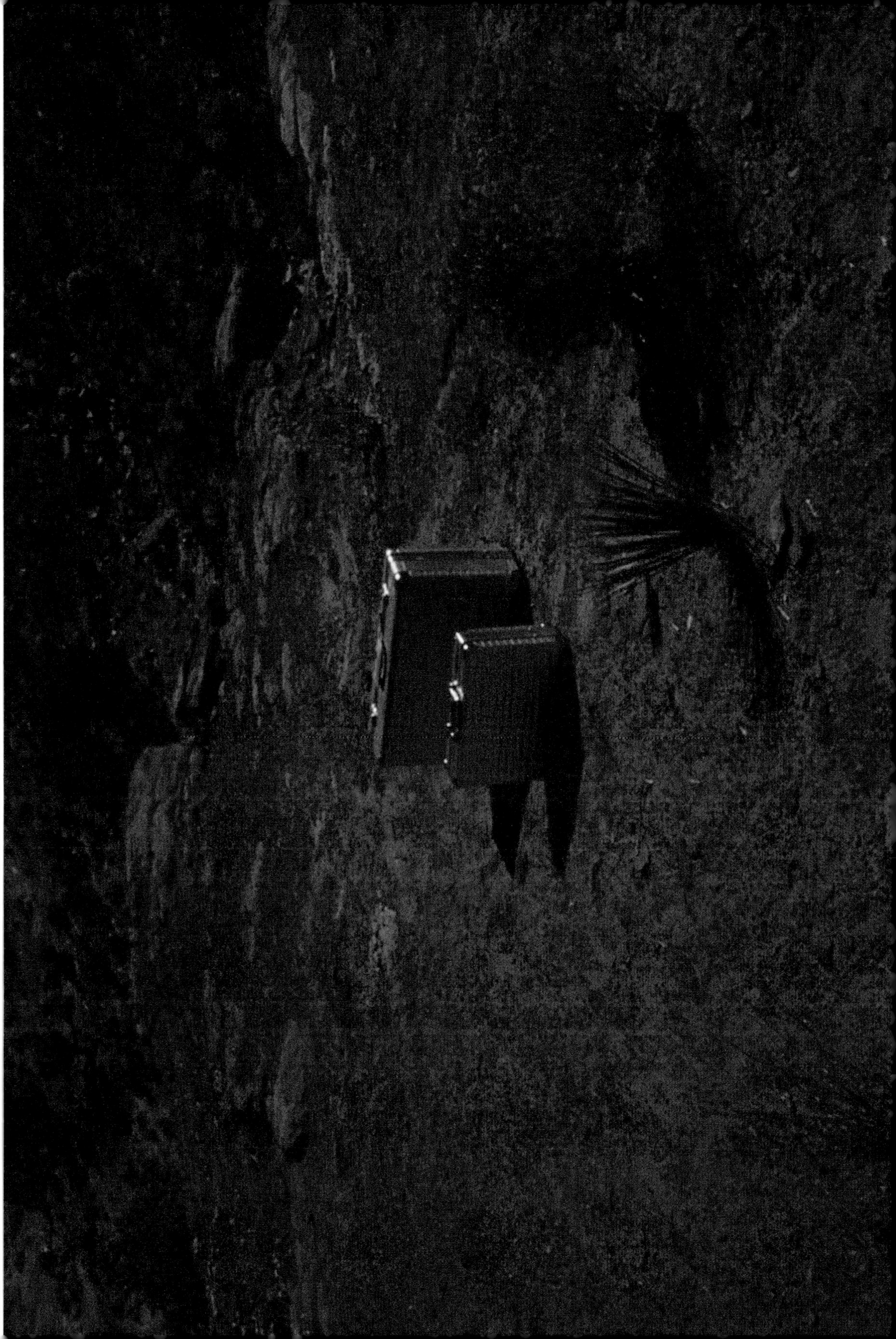

It all started with the idea of a man (his name doesn't matter) to make extensive use of his open-plan office in Berlin before moving out. Selflessly (as we must assume until there is proof to the contrary), he decided to initiate a quite unique cultural event. No sooner said than done. A couple of phone calls assured the participation of numerous befriended and known (to him) freelance artists. A date was fixed, a poster was printed. The party was set to begin. On a wall surface of more than four hundred square meters, the works of fourteen artists dedicated to the vaguely formulated theme of *Elend* [Misery] were on display. None were off-topic. In the evening, several punk bands performed in front of up to two hundred (mostly paying) guests. The mood was good. There was only one altercation when a phone was torn from the wall. An apparently innocent person was tousled by the host for this reason. No further human or material damages were registered. A lot of attention was paid to the pictures and the music. At the end, a few (three) artists from Hamburg switched on their smoke machine. The machine was supposed to suck in the smoke of a smoke grenade and slowly emit it again through its slits. Unfortunately, they had installed the vacuum motor the wrong way. Instead of sucking the smoke in, it was instantly blown into the space. The pictures and people were obscured in white clouds of smoke thus lending a further special appeal. The evening came to an end. The nice evening came to an end.

It was decided from the onset that this was not to remain a nice one-off. Since the artists were from three cities, it suggested itself to organize an event of this kind in all three cities. So now it was Hamburg's turn. Hamburg, it must be said, is a city with special difficulties. Full of small-minded people and precisely refurbished, it places agitating obstacles in the way of cultural producers seeking appropriate spaces. But a factory space with the usual dimensions was also found here. Around the same number of artists presented their works on a new theme, this time: *Aktion Pisskrücke. Geheimdienst am Nächsten* [Action Piss-Crutch: Secret Service on Your Neighbor]. None of the pieces were off-topic with regard to the somewhat mysterious title either. The opening evening saw the performance of free music: Sven-Åke Johansson on drums in conjunction with contemporary visual art will remain an unforgettable experience for those who attended. The conspicuous lack of glamour à la Berlin was interpreted by some malicious tongues as the sign of an unsuccessful evening. This is wrong, with reservations. One has to take the peculiarities of the Hanseatic City into account. On this evening, it was possible to at least get a foot in the door, and lying dormant in this city are cultural potencies that can be good for surprises.

This is now the result of the events in Berlin and Hamburg. Off the well-trodden cultural paths, a new routine has emerged that comes to a preliminary end in Düsseldorf. In the spaces of a conditionally successful artist, a group of artists that had suddenly, abruptly, and unexpectedly doubled (twenty-seven)

Alles fing damit an, dass in Berlin ein Mann (sein Name tut nichts zur Sache) auf die Idee kam, vor dem ins Haus stehenden Auszug sein Grossraumbüro noch einmal ausgiebig zu nutzen. Uneigennützig (so müssen wir bis zum Beweis des Gegenteils vermuten) beschloss er, eine Kulturveranstaltung ganz eigener Art ins Leben zu rufen. Gesagt – getan. Ein paar Telefonate versicherten ihn der Teilnahme zahlreicher befreundeter und bekannter (ihm bekannter) freischaffender Künstler. Ein Termin ward festgesetzt, ein Plakat gedruckt. Die Party konnte beginnen. Auf über 400qm Wandfläche hingen die Beiträge von 14 Künstlern zum vage formulierten Thema „Elend". Es gab keine Themaverfehlungen. Mehrere Punkgruppen spielten während des Abends für teilweise bis zu 200 (zum grössten Teil zahlende) Besucher. Die Stimmung war gut. Es gab nur einen Eklat, als ein Telefon aus der Wand gerissen wurde. Ein offensichtlich Unschuldiger wurde deswegen vom Hausherren gezaust. Weitere Beschädigungen an Menschen und Material wurden nicht verzeichnet. Bildern und Musik wurde viel Aufmerksamkeit gewidmet. Zum Schluss warfen ein paar (3) Künstler aus Hamburg ihre Nebelmaschine an. Diese Maschine sollte den Rauch einer Nebelkerze in sich aufsaugen und ihn langsam durch ihre Ritzen wieder abgeben. Leider hatten sie den Staubsaugermotor falsch eingebaut. Statt den Nebel aufzusaugen, blies sie ihn ohne Verzögerung in den Raum. Bilder und Menschen versanken in weissen Dunstschwaden und bekamen auf diese Weise noch einmal einen besonderen Reiz. Der Abend klang aus. Der schöne Abend klang aus.

Es war von Anfang an beschlossene Sache, dass es bei diesem schönen Einmal nicht bleiben sollte. Da es sich um Künstler aus drei Städten handelte, bot es sich an, in allen drei Städten eine Veranstaltung dieser Art durchzuführen. So war nun die Reihe an Hamburg. Hamburg, so muss man sagen, ist eine Stadt mit besonderen Schwierigkeiten. Voller Krämerseelen und präzise saniert, legt sie Kulturschaffenden beim Auffinden geeigneter Räume erregende Hindernisse in den Weg. Doch es fand sich auch hier ein Fabrikraum von gewohnten Dimensionen. Annähernd dieselbe Anzahl Künstler zeigte diesmal Arbeiten zu einem neuen Thema: Aktion Pisskrücke / Geheimdienst am Nächsten. Auch zu diesem etwas geheimnisvoll klingenden Titel gab es keine Themaverfehlungen. Musikalisch wurde der Eröffnungsabend von der Free Music bestritten. Sven-Åke Johanssons Performance am Schlagzeug, verbunden mit zeitgenössischer bildender Kunst, wird denen, die dabei waren, ein unvergessliches Erlebnis bleiben. Das auffällige Fehlen von Glamour à la Berlin wurde von böswilligen Zungen als ein Misslingen des Abends ausgelegt. Dies ist mit Einschränkung falsch. Man muss hier den Besonderheiten der Hansestadt Rechnung tragen. An diesem Abend wurde zumindest ein Fuss in die Tür gebracht und es schlummern in dieser Stadt kulturelle Potenzen, die noch für Überraschungen sorgen können.

Dies ist nun das Ergebnis der Veranstaltungen von Berlin und Hamburg. Abseits der ausgetretenen Kulturpfade hat sich eine neue Routine entwickelt, die in Düsseldorf ihr vorläufiges Ende findet. In den Räumen eines mit Einschränkung arrivierten Künstlers zeigt eine diesmal plötzlich, jäh und unerwartet auf das

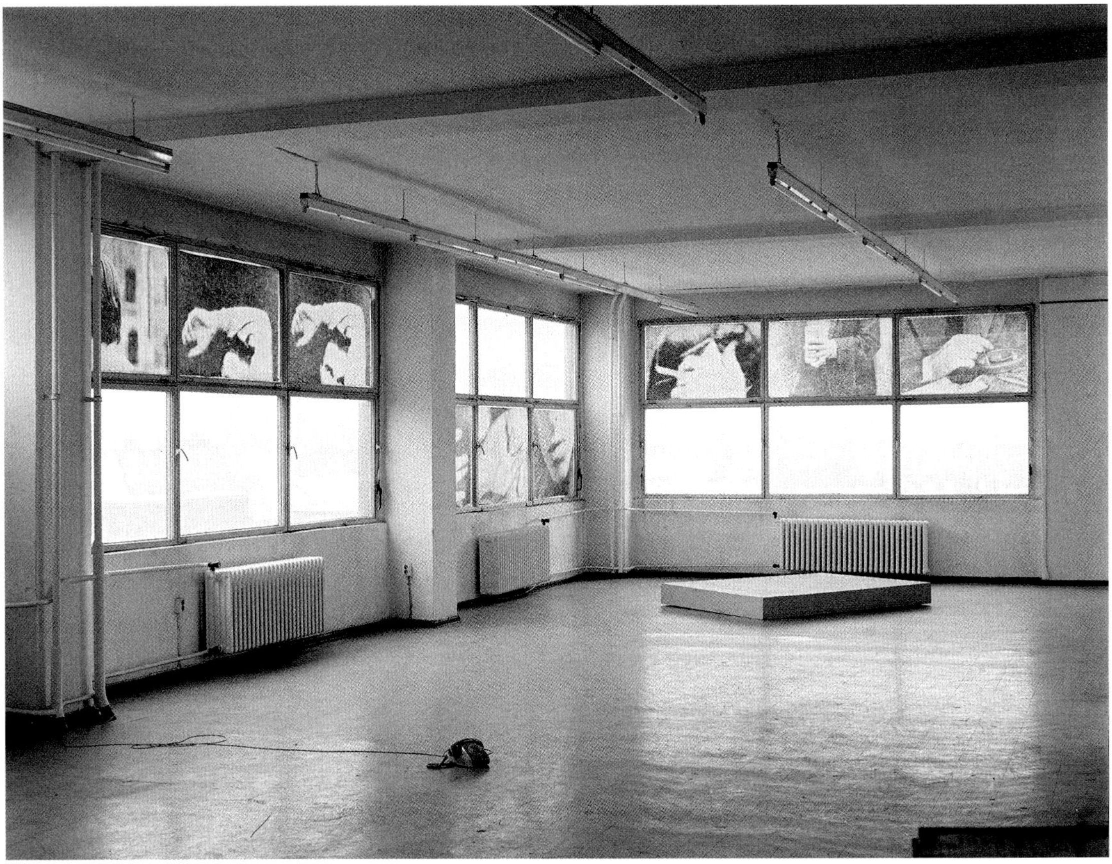

Brigitta Rohrbach, *Ausschnitte 79-3 I–VI*, 1979, 6 Gruppen à 3 Schwarz-Weiß-Fotografien, oben je 86 × 146 cm, unten je 98 × 146 cm / 6 groups of 3 b/w photographs, top: 86 × 146 cm each, bottom: 98 × 146 cm each, Installation: Kippenbergers Büro, Berlin, 1979, Fotos / photos: Jutta Henglein

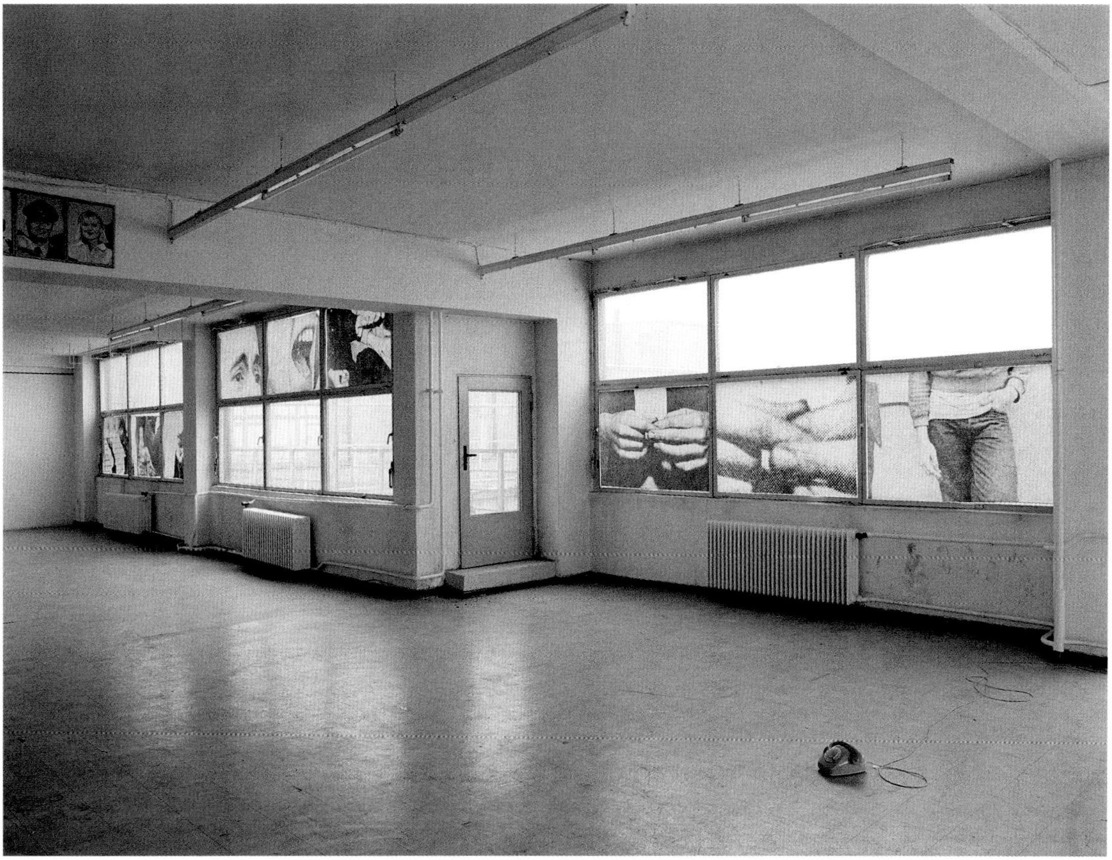

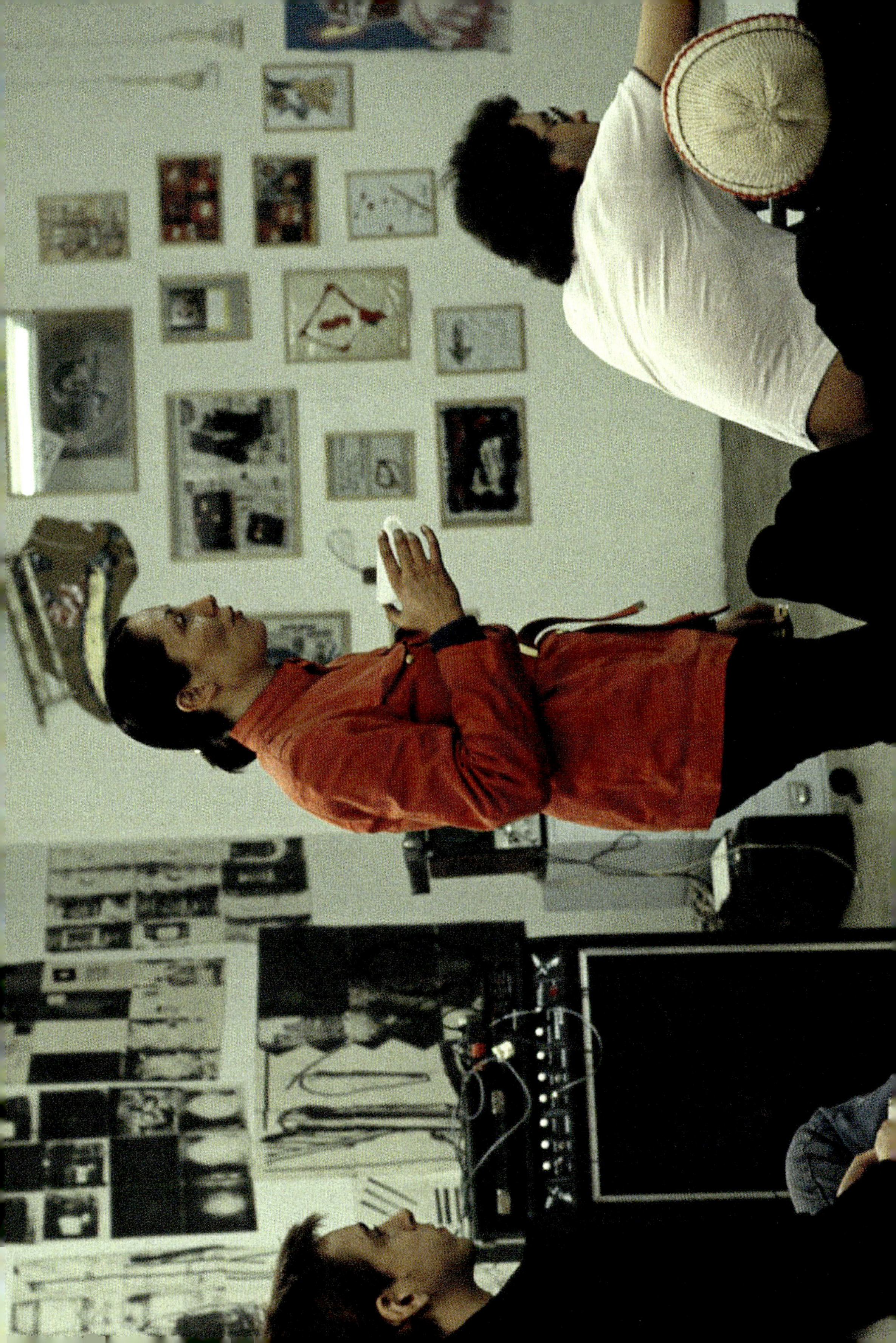

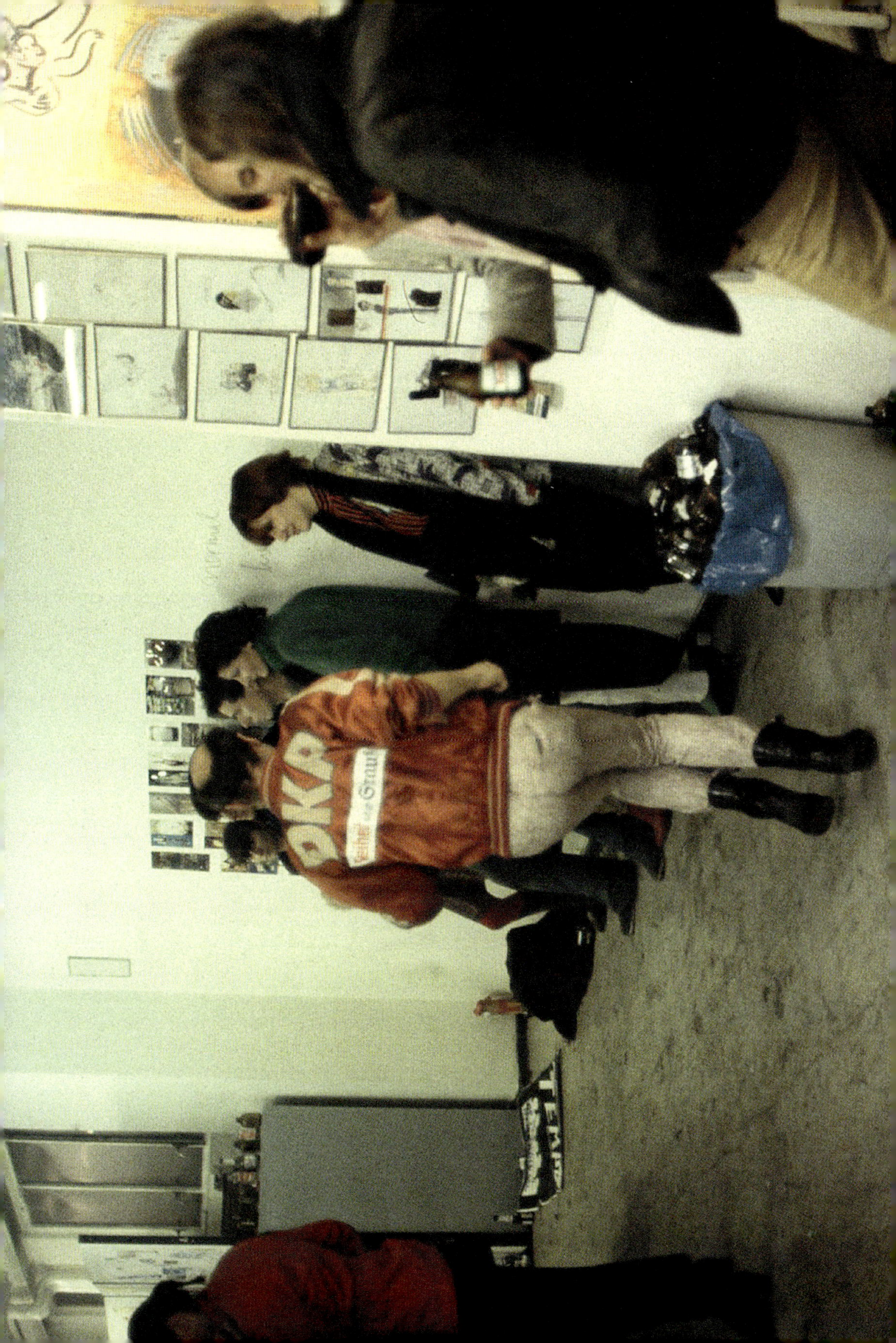

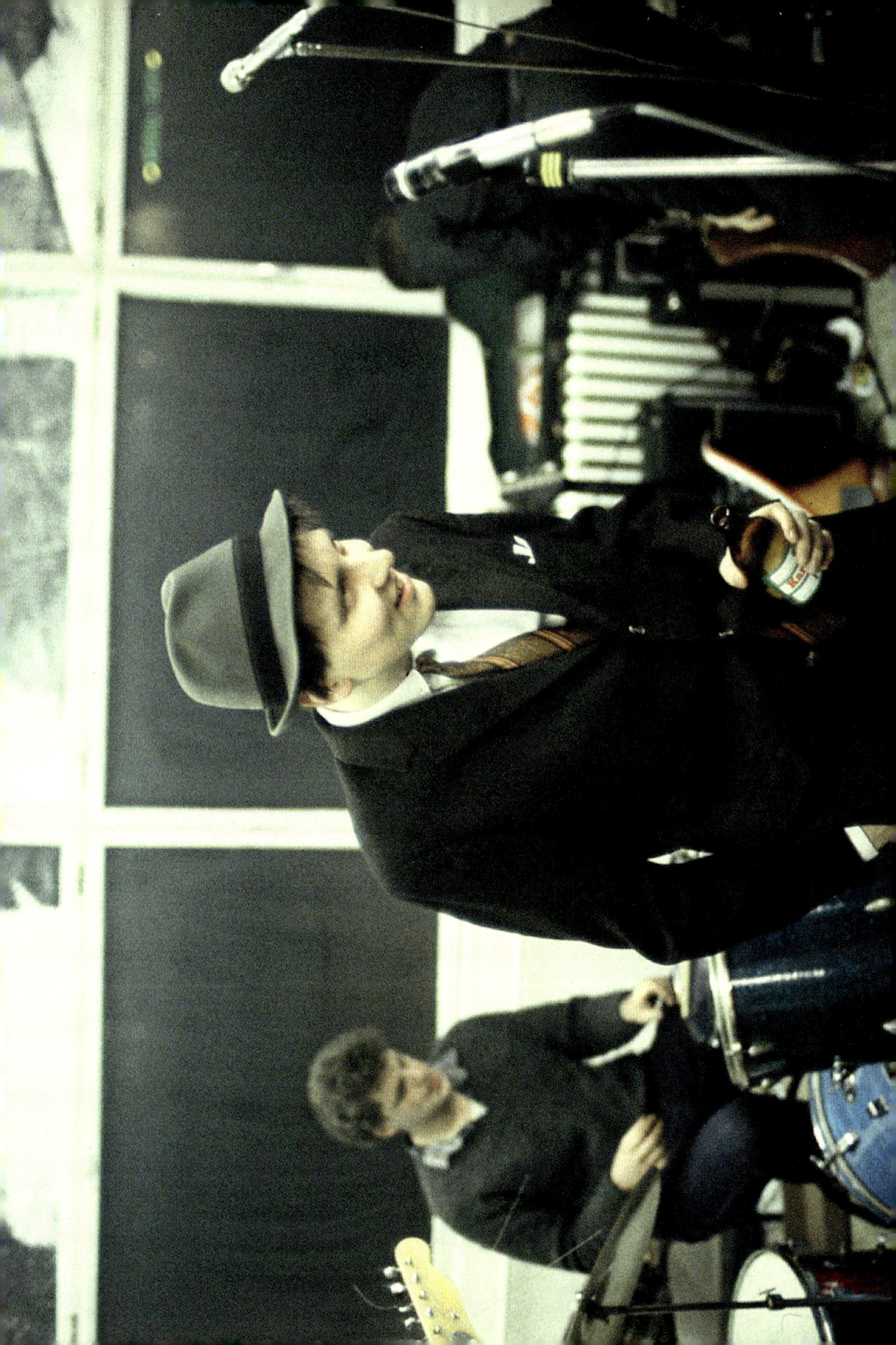

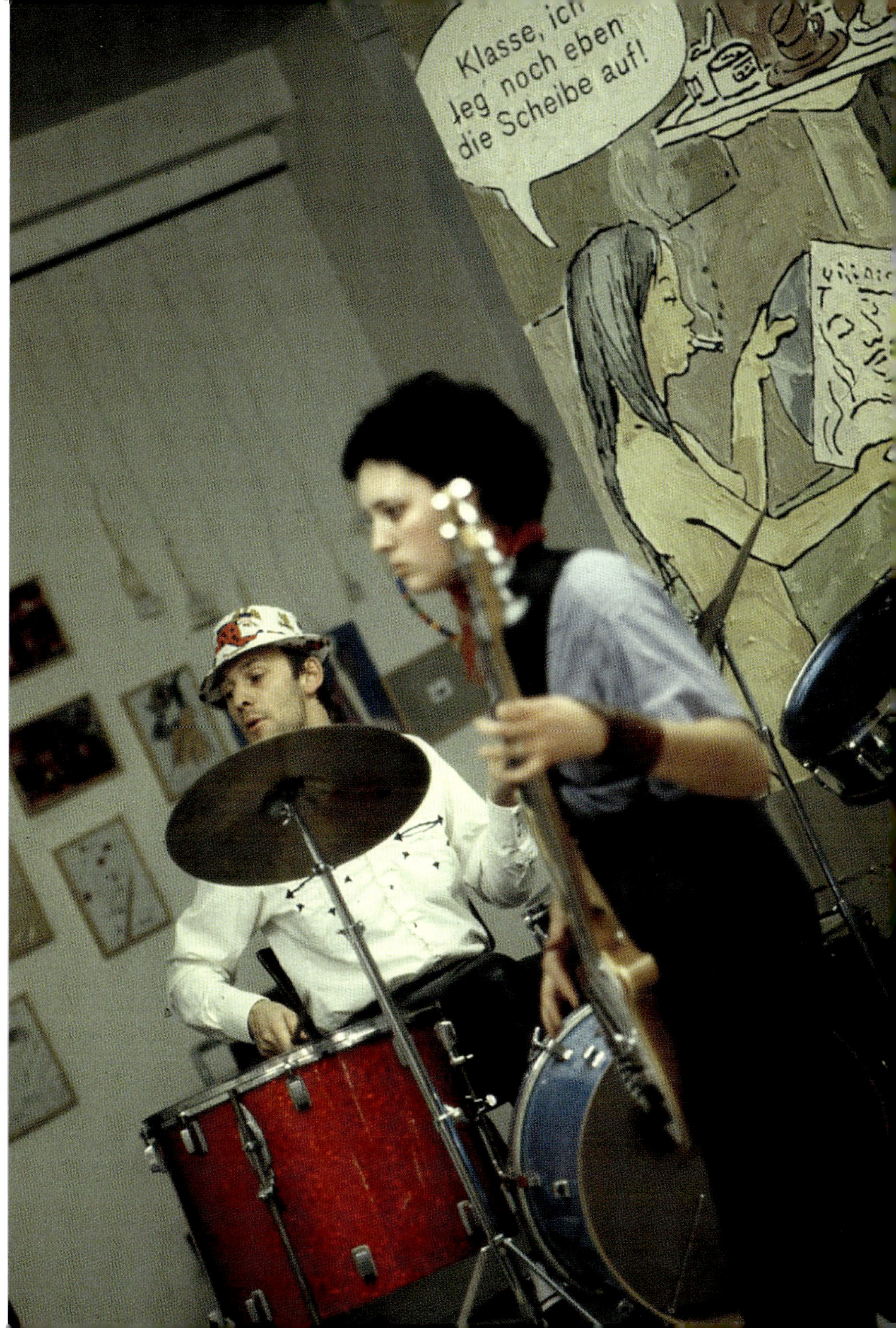
Klasse, ich leg' noch eben die Scheibe auf!

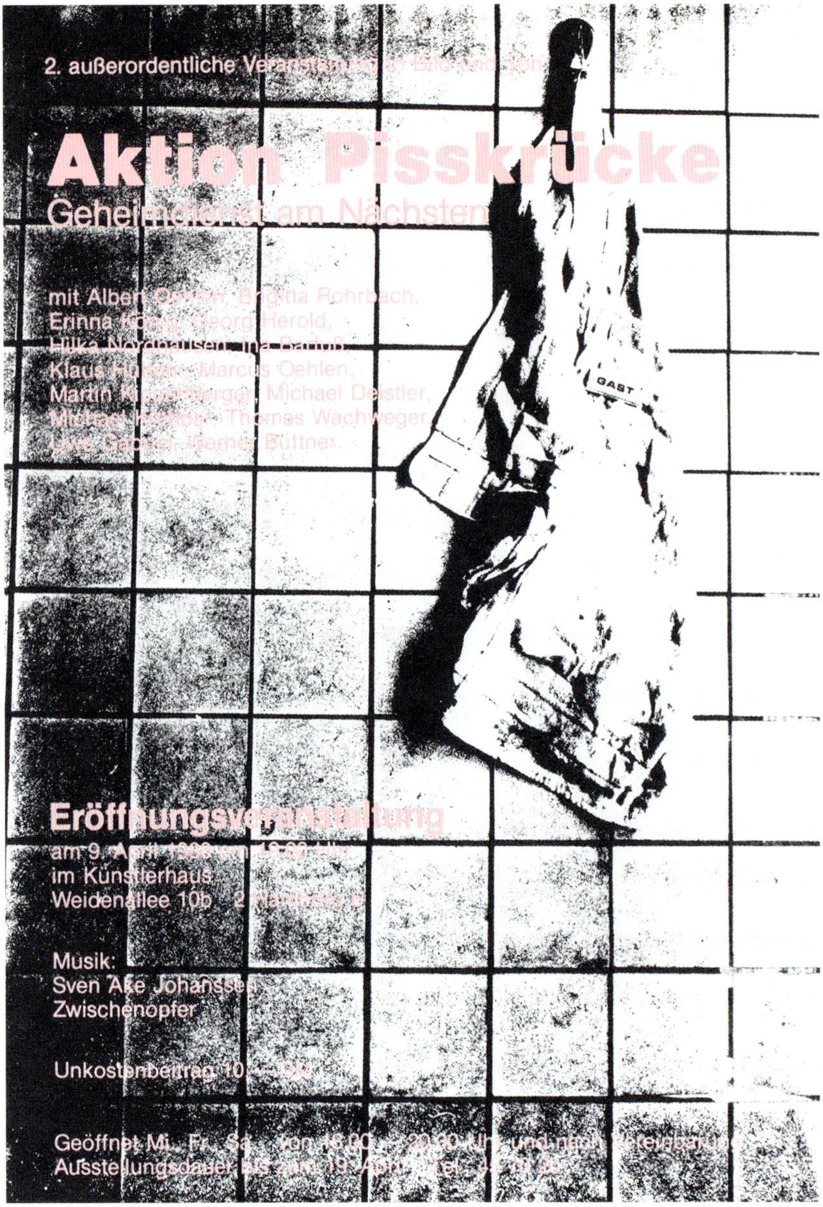

Poster, Design: Hubert Kiecol

2. außerordentliche Veranstaltung in Bild und Ton: Aktion Pisskrücke. Geheimdienst am Nächsten, Künstlerhaus Hamburg e. V., Hamburg, 1980, Fotos / photos: Uwe Gabriel

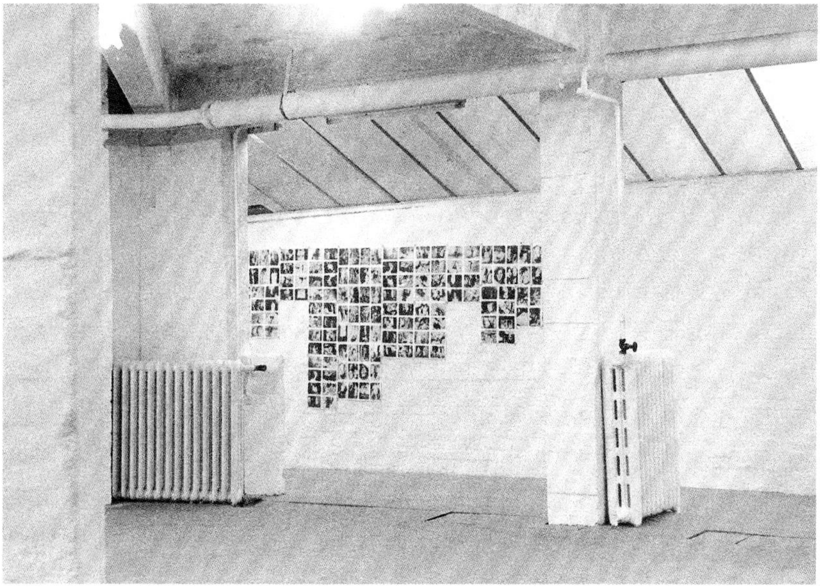

Werk von / Work by Martin Kippenberger

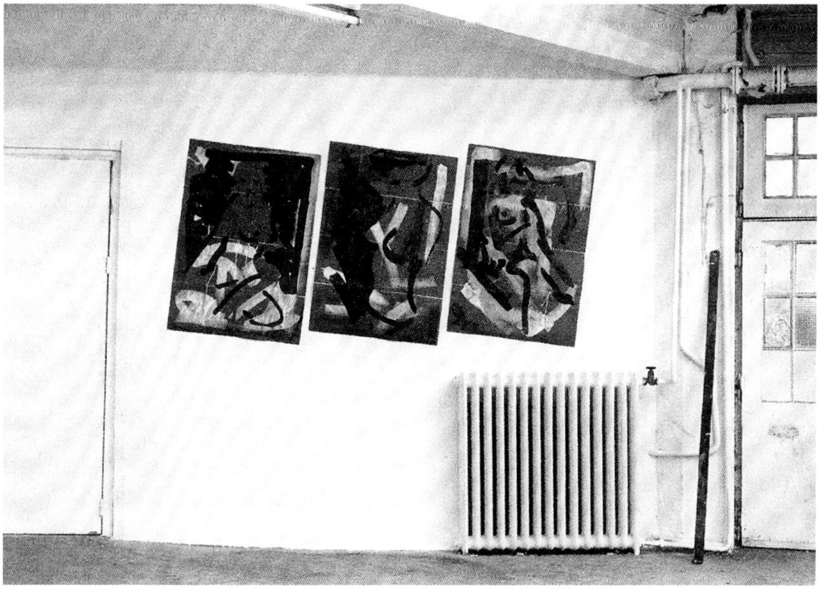

Werk von / Work by Markus Oehlen

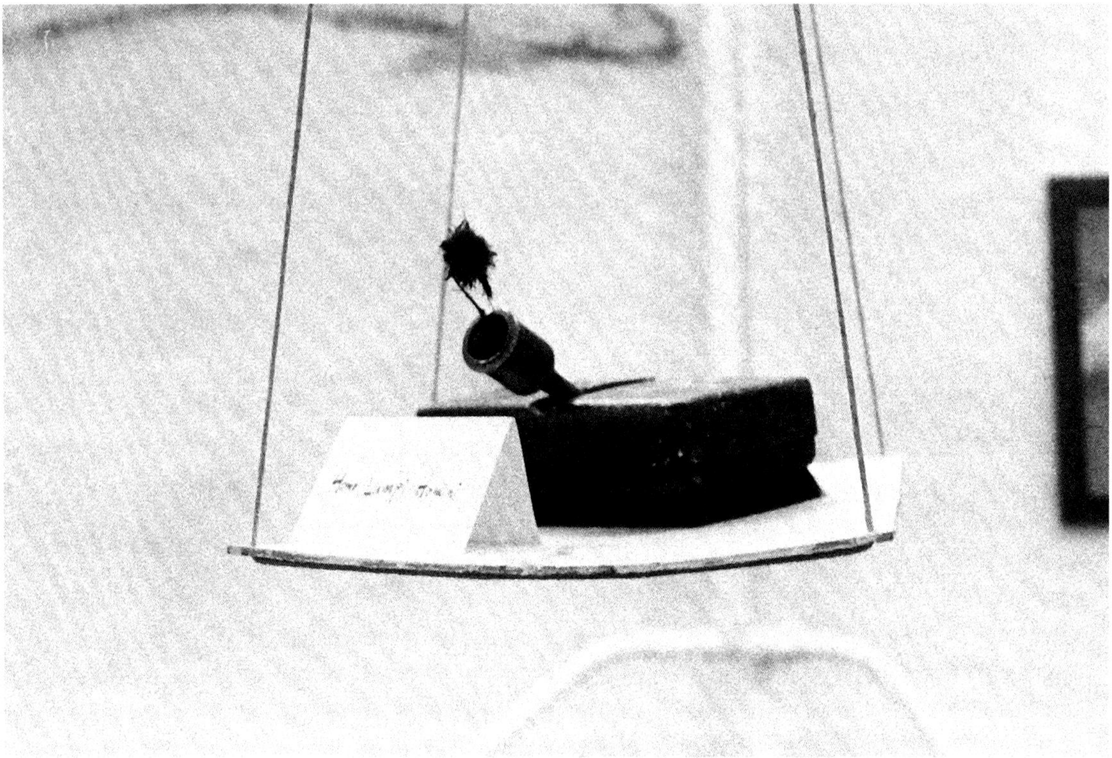

Werk von / Work by Werner Büttner, Albert Oehlen

2. außerordentliche Veranstaltung in Bild und Ton: Aktion Pisskrücke. Geheimdienst am Nächsten, Künstlerhaus Hamburg e. V., Hamburg, 1980, Fotos / photos: Uwe Gabriel

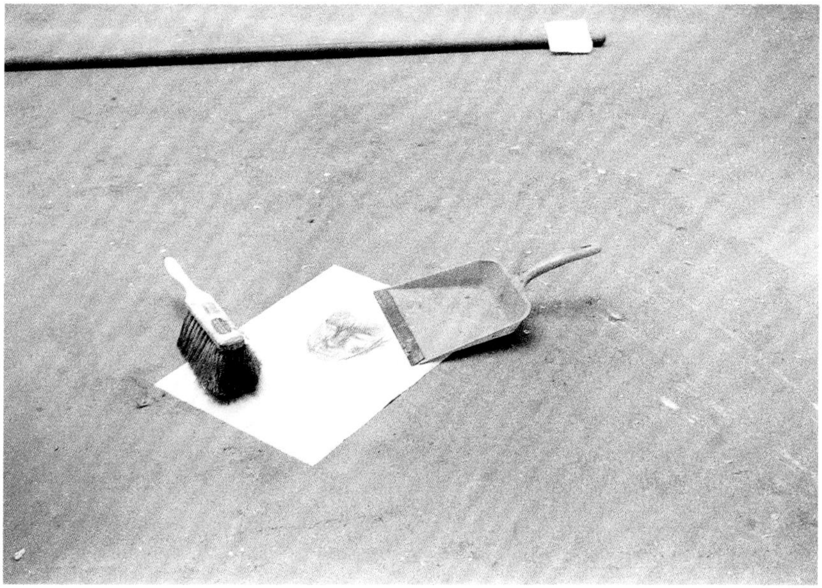

Werk von / Work by Werner Büttner, Albert Oehlen

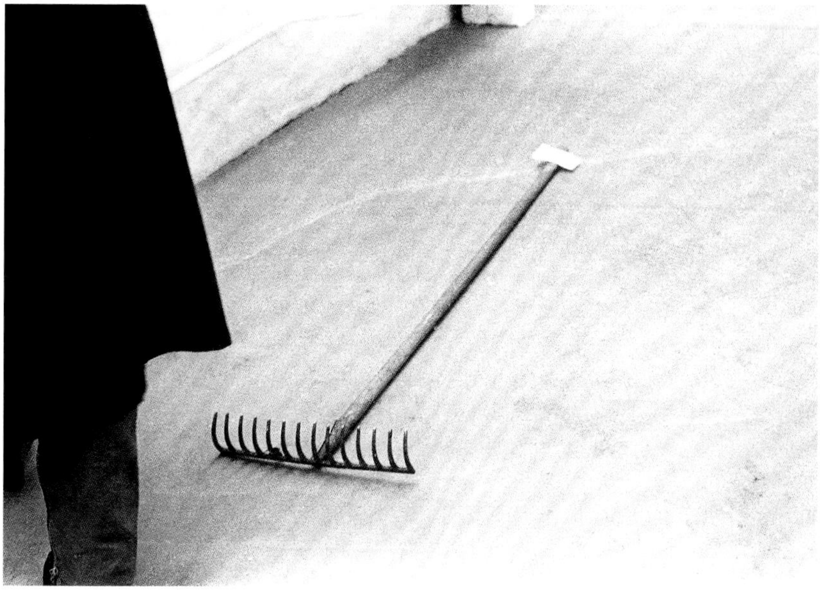

Werk von / Work by Georg Herold

Benjamin Dodenhoff:
In the mid- to late 1970s, you were in Hamburg, where you got to know Albert Oehlen and Werner Büttner.

Diedrich Diederichsen:
Yes, both of them had just come from Berlin. At first, I only knew them from nightlife. They were pretty striking, pretty dressed up by the standards back then. Albert had a sort of rockabilly thing going on and used to play saxophone in a rockabilly band. And Büttner, he used to have a mohawk for a while. Sometime toward the end of 1979, Albert struck up a conversation with me about a text I'd written in *Sounds*—we were standing next to each other in the Marktstube, which was pretty cramped. The text was a review of George A. Romero's *Zombie.* He thought it was good that the film was being written about.

B.D.:
There's a statement Oehlen once made in an interview, before you started making music together with him. When an interviewer declared, "You can't even sing," he responded, "Nah, but I can make a record." The remark evoked the DIY spirit, which is also connected to the idea of doing things as a dilettante. Was that the driving force?

D.D.:
It wasn't just about being a dilettante, along the lines of "we don't know how to do it, but we're gonna do it anyway out of rebellion," rather it was about finding a different way to set the parameters of what you're doing. The idea was that what was important about music and records wasn't necessarily the mastery of instruments, which is usually a given: the traditions of using instruments that have survived relatively unscathed in all the avant-garde currents. Instead, everything should be subject to negotiation, but not just in the predictable avant-garde logic of expanding, dissolving, etcetera, but rather by first realizing that everything you do is based on important ideological decisions, which aren't just self-evident. They're our decisions: we decide to use this or that instrument, this or that title and text, photos, and so on. That was what the conversations about music and art had in common: everything was available to you. All the parameters of a work have to be controlled; you have to make decisions about them, and they should be recognizable. That was the main point. One of those parameters was traditional skill, or a lack thereof. But the emphasis on this question, the fixation with the idea of dilettantism came later on, and maybe it manifested in the notion of "Geniale Dilletanten" [Brilliant Dilettantes] that started popping up in Berlin around 1981. But interpreting it to mean "everyone can just do what they want" is a bit of a simplification, even if it's the dominant one today. I think it was more about insisting that all these given conditions had to be discussed, and at the same time it was clear that pure refusal was just too simple.

Benjamin Dodenhoff:
Sie waren Mitte/Ende der 1970er-Jahre in Hamburg und haben dort Albert Oehlen und Werner Büttner kennengelernt.

Diedrich Diederichsen:
Ja, die beiden waren gerade aus Berlin gekommen. Ich hatte die zunächst nur im Nachtleben gesehen. Sie waren sehr auffällig, sehr gestylt für damalige Verhältnisse. Albert war so ein bisschen Rockabilly-mäßig unterwegs und spielte auch Saxofon in einer Rockabilly-Band. Und Büttner, der hatte eine Zeit lang einen Irokesen. Albert hat mich irgendwann Ende 1979 auf einen Text in *Sounds* angesprochen – wir standen in der sehr engen Marktstube nebeneinander. Es ging um eine Rezension von George A. Romeros *Zombie*. Er fand gut, dass man über den Film schreibt.

B.D.:
Es gibt eine Interviewaussage von Albert Oehlen, mit dem Sie dann ja auch zusammen Musik gemacht haben. Auf die Feststellung der Interviewerin, „Sie können doch gar nicht singen“, antwortet er: „Nö, aber ich kann eine Platte machen.“ Darin scheint der DIY-Geist der Zeit zu stecken, der ja auch eng verknüpft ist mit der Idee, gerade auch als Dilettant*in etwas zu machen. War das eine Triebfeder?

D.D.:
Es ging nicht nur darum, als Dilettant*in was zu machen, im Sinne von „wir können das nicht, wir machen es aber trotzdem aus lauter rebellischem Geist“, sondern es ging darum, die Parameter anders zu bestimmen, mit denen man was machte. Die Idee war: Was an Musik und an Schallplatten wichtig ist, ist nicht das, was mit dem Beherrschen von Instrumenten einhergeht, was also quasi gegeben ist: durch die Tradition der Benutzung von Instrumenten, die es ja noch nahezu in alle Avantgarden unbeschadet geschafft hatte. Vielmehr sollte alles zur Disposition stehen, aber nicht in der vorhersehbar avantgardistischen Logik der Erweiterung, Auflösung et cetera, sondern zunächst, indem man sich klarmachte, dass allem, was man macht, bedeutsame ideologische Entscheidungen zugrunde liegen, die sich nicht von selbst verstehen. Es sind unsere Entscheidungen: Wir setzen die und die Instrumente ein oder die und die Titel und Texte, Fotos und so weiter. Das war ja auch das Gemeinsame im Diskurs, wie man über bildende Kunst und Musik sprach: Es steht einem alles zur Verfügung. Alle Parameter einer Arbeit müssen kontrolliert werden und dazu muss es Entscheidungen geben und die müssen erkennbar sein. Das war der Hauptpunkt. Einer der Parameter war traditionelles Können oder eben Nichtkönnen. Aber die Verengung auf diese Frage und die Fixierung auf den Dilettantismus-Begriff kam später und schlug sich vielleicht auch in Konjunkturen wie dem Begriff der „Genialen Dilletanten“ nieder, die 1981 in Berlin aufkamen. Die Lesart, dass jeder darf, war aber schon eine Vereinfachung, auch wenn sie heutzutage die dominierende Lesart ist. Ich denke, es ging darum, dass alles Gegebene diskutiert werden muss, klar war aber auch, dass reine Ablehnung zu einfach ist.

Ramona Heinlein:
In 1985, you wrote that Albert Oehlen's and, I assume, also Werner Büttner's work was a "totality of strategic actions."[1] Does that relate to this way of thinking in terms of parameters?

D.D.:
Yeah, it sounds like something I'd say. The word "strategic" was pretty popular back then. It was a way of expressing what I've just tried to describe, though I think the way I describe it now is a bit more accurate. "Strategy," of course, is also a political metaphor. It all has to do with conquest, with military metaphors. You're fighting against the others. That's how people saw it back then. A lot of the decisions were decisions *against* something, and not so much decisions *for* oneself. And it was often against the people that you might get mistaken for, the people actually closest to you. Classic K-Gruppe logic:[2] the worst K-Gruppe is the one who wants almost the exact same things as you do.

R.H.:
The military metaphors you've brought up, these can also be found in the music projects coming out of the artists' milieu, for example the band Nachdenkliche Wehrpflichtige [Pensive Conscripts]. On the cover of the EP, which you were involved in alongside Albert Oehlen and Frieder Butzmann, there's an Albert Oehlen painting showing a group of soldiers.

D.D.:
The Nachdenkliche Wehrpflichtige thing was of course a joke about the antiwar movement. But the idea wasn't to be like, oh, we're more clever than they are, they're reformists and we want more. That would have been the classical radical leftist position. Ours was more along the lines of, they're completely ridiculous, but we still have solidarity with them. If someone's pensive and keeps congratulating themselves about it, well it's a pretty sickening attitude. And that was the most obnoxious side of this milieu. On the other hand, I was also a conscript and didn't want to do military service.

But nonetheless, I'd still say yes, it's true that most people eventually fell out of touch with whichever political organizations they were once involved with. Either they didn't exist anymore, or you just thought they were silly after a while. Nonetheless, you still found yourself trying to keep up the rhetoric, that you were in a conflict-laden situation, that you hadn't deserted to the "inwardness" camp. Also in order not to be confused with those people who made fantasy their program. We thought fantasy was shit. At the same time, we didn't want to just hop on the bandwagon of the stuff the zeitgeist magazines were writing. The diagnosis in the feuilletons was, "The decade of the left is over, now postmodernism is coming, anything goes." And in order to demonstrate that we still wanted to engage with the recently discredited, aggressive, dissociative jargon of K-Gruppe culture, we continued using their language.

Ramona Heinlein:
Sie schreiben dementsprechend 1985, dass die Arbeit von Albert Oehlen und wohl auch Werner Büttner „eine Gesamtheit strategischer Maßnahmen“ sei.[1] Knüpft das an dieses Parameter-Denken an?

D.D.:
Ja, die Formulierung klingt nach mir. Das Wort „strategisch“ war damals weitverbreitet. Das war eine Formel für das, was ich eben beschrieben habe, aber so, wie ich es jetzt beschreibe, finde ich es eigentlich passender. „Strategie“ ist natürlich auch eine politische Metapher gewesen. Das Ganze hat zu tun mit Eroberung, eben mit Kriegsmetaphern. Man kämpft gegen andere. Das war ja auch das Selbstverständnis damals. Viele Entscheidungen waren sozusagen Entscheidungen *gegen* andere und nicht nur *für* einen selbst. Und zwar oft gegen die, mit denen man verwechselt hätte werden können, also die, die einem eigentlich nahestehen. Klassische K-Gruppen-Logik: Am schlimmsten ist die K-Gruppe, die eigentlich fast genau dasselbe will.

R.H.:
Diese Kriegsmetaphorik, die Sie ansprechen, ist ja auch in den Musikprojekten im Umfeld der Künstler zu finden. Zum Beispiel bei der Band Nachdenkliche Wehrpflichtige. Auf der EP, an der neben Albert Oehlen auch Sie und Frieder Butzmann beteiligt waren, ist zum Beispiel eine – von Albert Oehlen gemalte – Gruppe von Soldaten zu sehen.

D.D.:
Das mit den Nachdenklichen Wehrpflichtigen war natürlich ein Witz über die Friedensbewegung. Aber die Position sollte nicht sein: Wir sind jetzt schlauer als die, also, das sind Reformist*innen und wir wollen mehr. Das wäre die klassische linksradikale Position gewesen. Unsere Position war: Die sind total lächerlich, aber wir sind trotzdem doch auch solidarisch mit denen. Dass jemand nachdenklich ist und sich das selbst zum Lob macht, ist eine extrem scheußliche Haltung. Das ist die richtig widerliche Seite dieses Milieus gewesen. Auf der anderen Seite war ich selbst ein Wehrpflichtiger und wollte keinen Wehrdienst leisten.

Aber trotzdem würde ich auch sagen: Ja es stimmt, es war so, dass bestimmte politische Organisationen, mit denen die verschiedenen Leute vorher etwas zu tun hatten, einem mehr oder weniger verloren gegangen sind. Entweder existierten sie nicht mehr oder man fand sie zu doof. Aber man versuchte irgendwie durch seine ganze Rhetorik weiterhin aufrechtzuerhalten, dass man sich in einer konflikthaltigen Situation befand, dass man jetzt nicht zur Innerlichkeit übergelaufen war. Auch um nicht verwechselt zu werden mit der Position, die sich die Fantasie auf die Fahnen schreibt. Fantasie fanden wir scheiße. Gleichzeitig war da die Idee, sich eben nicht einfach dem anzuschließen, was damals die Zeitgeist-Zeitschriften schrieben. Die feuilletonistische Diagnose war ja: „Das linke Jahrzehnt ist vorbei, jetzt kommt die Postmoderne, anything goes.“ Um zu demonstrieren, dass man gerade mit dem nun diskreditierten, aggressiven, sich abgrenzenden Jargon der ganzen

B.D.:
Of course you're coming out of an extremely politicized time. How would you describe it? Were politics actually important to the artists?

D.D.:
Of course it depends on the individual artist. It varied from person to person. I think Kippenberger, for example, wasn't so interested in political rhetoric. He was never interested in all the reasons for getting political. He thought it was just a funny phase or an excuse for people to get together. It was different with Albert. The political positions he got involved with were fairly important to him, and to some extent he'd been politicized through Immendorff. Immendorff was *the* politicized artist of the previous generation and was a pretty isolated figure in the art world in that sense. Apart from him, there were hardly any artists who were as political while at the same time operating in the heart of the art market, showing at Galerie Michael Werner and so on.

But to get back to your question, I think the problem was that everyone in our generation who got politicized, a generation slightly younger than the real 1968 generation, simultaneously got to know an interesting milieu alongside interesting ideas, but we were quickly disciplined, and the milieu itself quickly became problematic for everyone involved. In other words, there was a sense of disappointment with political culture, but not so much with the ideas themselves. We continued to find them plausible. It was just that the milieus that expressed them became unbearable.

R.H.:
So you were distancing yourself on two fronts: from the old left, and from the conservatives of course. And then when you start singing the "Einheitsfrontlied" [United Front Song] like on the Nachdenkliche Wehrpflichtige record...

D.D.:
...then you think it's good again. There were also versions of the "Einheitsfrontlied" by Peter Brötzmann... and by Ton Steine Scherben. That was the good part of the tradition we wanted to be engaged with.

R.H.:
There are a lot of different things happening on that record. You also sang a Schlager song by Wencke Myhre, for example.

D.D.:
Yeah, Schlager, that was a long time before people started seeing it as a possibility again. At the time, Wencke Myhre was seen as the dullest thing to ever exist. "Er hat ein knall... – ...rotes Gummiboot" [He has a bright red rubber boat] and "Er steht im Tor und ich dahinter..." [He's standing at the goal and I'm behind him]. It was the worst thing you could imagine. And finding exactly that good, well, it helped get rid of a lot of people.

K-Gruppen-Kultur durchaus noch etwas zu tun haben wollte, haben wir weiter diese Sprache verwendet.

B.D.:

Man kam natürlich aus einer extrem politisierten Zeit. Wie würden Sie das beschreiben? War das Politische tatsächlich wichtig für die Künstler*innen?

D.D.:

Das kommt natürlich auf den Künstler oder die Künstlerin an, das ist unterschiedlich bei denen. Ich glaube, die politische Rhetorik interessiert zum Beispiel Kippenberger nicht sehr. Der hat sich nie für die Gründe interessiert, warum man sich politisiert. Der fand das auch nur eine lustige Phase oder einen Grund für Leute, zusammenzukommen. Anders als zum Beispiel bei Albert, dem die politischen Positionen, mit denen er zu tun hatte, schon wichtig waren und der ja auch bis zu einem Grade über Immendorff politisiert wurde. Immendorff war ja *der* politisierte Künstler einer Generation früher, aber in der Kunstwelt weitgehend alleinstehend damit. Es gab ja außer ihm fast keine Künstler*innen, die so politisch waren und trotzdem im Herzen des Kunstmarktes agierten und bei der Galerie Werner ausstellten.

Aber um nochmal darauf zurückzukommen: Ich glaube, das Problem war ja für alle, die politisiert wurden in unserer Generation, die also etwas jünger waren als die richtigen Achtundsechziger, dass wir das zugleich als ein interessantes Milieu und als interessante Inhalte kennenlernten, aber dass man sehr schnell diszipliniert wurde und das Milieu so sehr schnell problematisch wurde für alle Beteiligten. Das heißt, es gab sozusagen eine Enttäuschung von der politischen Kultur und nicht so sehr von den Inhalten, die fand man weiterhin plausibel. Nur die Milieus, die sie trugen, waren unerträglich geworden.

R.H.:

Also man grenzt sich zu beiden Seiten hin ab, zu den Altlinken, und zu den Konservativen sowieso. Und wenn man dann, wie auf der Platte der Nachdenklichen Wehrpflichtigen, das *Einheitsfrontlied* singt…

D.D.:

…findet man das wieder gut. Das *Einheitsfrontlied* gab es ja auch in der Fassung von Peter Brötzmann… und von Ton Steine Scherben. Das war ja der gute Teil der Tradition, mit dem wir zu tun haben wollten.

R.H.:

Auf dieser Platte kommen sehr unterschiedliche Sachen vor. Sie singen zum Beispiel auch einen Schlager von Wencke Myhre.

D.D.:

Ja, Schlager, das war noch lange, bevor das als Möglichkeit wiedergesehen wurde. Wencke Myhre galt als das Stumpfeste, was es überhaupt gibt. „Er hat ein knall… – … rotes Gummiboot" und „Er steht im Tor und ich dahinter…". Das war das Schlimmste, was man sich nur irgendwie vorstellen konnte. Und genau das gut zu finden, damit hat man sich natürlich auch wieder viele Leute vom Hals geschafft.

B.D.:
You're saying Schlager was totally out, so of course it's the first thing you do. Was it about intentionally transgressing the boundaries of good taste, or was it about being embarrassing?

D.D.:
No, just doing the opposite of what's allowed would be stupid. We saw potential in Wencke Myhre, and there was a concrete kind of fun you could have with such gaudy truisms, to spite the tortured sensitive souls. Finding precisely those blunt and loud aspects good, it's the same thing as Kippenberger's motto "known from film, radio, television, and emergency telephones"—finding yellow-press culture good, it was more about the yellow press than Schlager, people had already forgotten about Schlager. There wasn't anyone interested in it, not even in a critical sense, and that fact itself was what made it so jarring and interesting. Of course it didn't last very long, and just a few years later that kind of tongue-in-cheek endorsement of regressiveness would become standard fare at student parties.

R.H.:
Let's talk about The Flying Klassenfeind [The Flying Class Enemy] record. Markus Oehlen was also involved alongside yourself.

D.D.:
About The Flying Klassenfeind group: well, with Nachdenkliche Wehrpflichtige the idea was to recruit as many saxophonists as possible for the live performances. Saxophones pretty much didn't exist in the punk scene. That was before Spandau Ballet and new wave, before saxophones made a comeback and people started liking jazz again. It was really directed against the punk scene—as many horns as possible, free jazz, noise, and generally being annoying. And at some point, it'd been exhausted. Then Nachdenkliche Wehrpflichtige decided to try out other things, a different concept each time. Then there were people involved who could actually play instruments, like my brother Detlef or Holger Hiller from Palais Schaumburg, for example. And then that also went as far as it could go, and we thought it would be good to just strum electric guitars as simply as possible. At some point, that turned into the idea of starting a band that only had guitarists, six of them, and not a single one who could play. It looked a bit like Glenn Branca and even sounded like him sometimes [*laughs*]. But the difference is that we then taught ourselves the dullest chord progressions, "Smoke on the Water" and "Sweet Jane." The first things that any guitar student learns. And then we started playing concerts with these lineups. One guy, Chris Lunch, would cross the guitar strings over each other when he restrung them, and others just played. The concerts weren't very long. And then when we wanted to do a record, we had to come up with a new idea, because it wasn't the kind of thing you could do on a record. So we decided to

B.D.:
Sie sagen, Schlager ging überhaupt nicht, also macht man es natürlich direkt. Geht's da um das bewusste Brechen von Geschmacksgrenzen oder darum, gezielt peinlich zu sein?

D.D.:
Nein, einfach nur das Gegenteil vom Erlaubten zu machen wäre blöde. Wir sahen ja Potenzial in Wencke Myhre und man konnte einen sehr konkreten Spaß haben mit solchen grellen Wahrheiten, gegen verquälte Sensibilisten. Das Stumpfe und Laute daran gut zu finden, das ist genau dasselbe wie Kippenbergers Motto „Bekannt durch Film, Funk, Fernsehen und Polizeirufsäulen" – Boulevard gut finden, eher Boulevard als Schlager. Schlager war auch in Vergessenheit geraten, es gab niemanden, der sich auch nur kritisch dafür interessierte, allein das war also schon schrill und interessant. Hielt natürlich nicht lange, augenzwinkerndes Einverständnis mit dem Regressiven war schon ein paar Jahre später Common Sense von Studentenpartys.

R.H.:
Lassen Sie uns noch über die Flying-Klassenfeind-Platte sprechen. Hier war ja neben Ihnen zum Beispiel auch Markus Oehlen beteiligt.

D.D.:
Zu der Gruppe Flying Klassenfeind: Also bei den Nachdenklichen Wehrpflichtigen war die Idee, live immer so viele Saxofone wie möglich zu rekrutieren. In der ganzen Punk-Welt gab es Saxofone überhaupt nicht, das war noch vor Spandau Ballet und New Wave, bevor dann Saxofone wiederkamen und auch Jazz wieder gut gefunden wurde. Das war also richtig gegen die Punkszene gerichtet – möglichst viele Bläser, Free Jazz, Geräusch, nerven und so. Und das verbrauchte sich irgendwann. Dann haben die Nachdenklichen Wehrpflichtigen andere Sachen ausprobiert, also jedes Mal ein anderes Konzept. Es waren dann auch Leute dabei, die spielen konnten, mein Bruder Detlef oder Holger Hiller von Palais Schaumburg zum Beispiel. Und dann ging auch das nicht weiter und dann fanden wir es gut, mit elektrischen Gitarren möglichst simpel rumzuschrummen. Und daraus wurde dann irgendwann die Idee, eine andere Band zu gründen, die nur aus Gitarristen besteht, so sechs Stück, die alle nicht spielen können. Das sah ein bisschen so aus wie Glenn Branca und hörte sich teilweise auch so an [*lacht*]. Aber mit dem Unterschied, dass wir uns dann ganz stumpfe Songs beibrachten, also *Smoke on the Water* und *Sweet Jane*. So Sachen, die jede Gitarrenschüler*in als Erstes lernt. Und dann haben wir in diesen Besetzungen Konzerte gegeben. Einer, Chris Lunch, hat seine Saiten über Kreuz aufgespannt und andere haben einfach nur gespielt. Die dauerten nicht besonders lange, diese Konzerte. Und als wir dann 'ne Platte machen wollten, brauchten wir eine neue Idee dafür, weil das nichts für eine Platte war. Es ging dann darum, dass wir Sachen spielen, die wir gut finden und die in der ganzen Punk- und New-Wave-Welt überhaupt nicht vorkommen. Zum Beispiel die Flying Burrito Brothers, die fanden wir immer gut, und dazu musste man sich jetzt mal bekennen. Und das Zweite war: Die Platte

play the stuff we thought was good but wasn't being received in the punk and new wave scenes at all. Like the Flying Burrito Brothers, for example, we always liked them, and that was the time to profess it. The second thing was that we decided to dedicate the record exclusively to the second-place or third-place figures in other bands, like Ken Weaver [The Fugs] and Chris Hillman [The Flying Burrito Brothers].

R.H.:

So there was this allusive concept of the record. Was it also important to perform live?

D.D.:

Yes, we played at all these festivals that used to be around back then. Nothing else. I don't think there was a single performance that wasn't at a festival, except for a Flying Klassenfeind gig at Dankerrt, together with Faust. Then we also had our own gig at Dankerrt with another group we started—LSDAP/AO. Otherwise, it was always these band tours that Alfred Hilsberg organized, to Berlin, or Düsseldorf, or wherever, with four to six bands. "Better too much than too little" was the motto.

R.H.:

In 1979–80, there was a series of self-organized group shows with artists like Martin Kippenberger, Werner Büttner, Georg Herold, Brigitta Rohrbach, Meuser, Thomas Wachweger, and Ina Barfuss. It's noteworthy that the exhibitions were usually accompanied by concerts. So the likes of Markus and Albert Oehlen weren't just exhibiting but also playing the stage as musicians. The opening concert for the third of these exhibitions, *Finger für Deutschland* [Finger for Germany], took place at Ratinger Hof in Düsseldorf, and you also played there.

D.D.:

Yeah, it was the first live performance for Nachdenkliche Wehrpflichtige.

B.D.:

Do you remember the exhibition in Jörg Immendorff's studio?

D.D.:

I remember that it was really big with an insane amount of stuff, and I knew the artists. I mostly remember the event at Ratinger Hof. It was election day, and Immendorff got arrested for wearing a police uniform. Beuys was also there. Kippenberger did a performance with his poet friend from Stuttgart.

R.H.:

Were you also at the second group show *2. außerordentliche Veranstaltung in Bild und Ton: Aktion Pisskrücke. Geheimdienst am Nächsten* [Second Extraordinary Event in Pictures and Sound: Action Piss-Crutch: Secret Service on Your Neighbor] in Hamburg? What kind of music did they have there?

D.D.:

Yes, there was the group Zwischenopfer. It was Albert's idea. They played

haben wir lauter Leuten gewidmet, die immer nur die Nummer zwei oder die Nummer drei einer Band waren, zum Beispiel Ken Weaver [The Fugs] und Chris Hillman [The Flying Burrito Brothers].

R.H.:

Es gab also dieses anspielungsreiche Konzept der Platte. War es denn auch wichtig aufzutreten?

D.D.:

Ja, wir haben bei all diesen Festivals gespielt, die es damals gab. Sonst nicht. Ich glaube es gibt keinen einzigen Auftritt, der nicht auf einem Festival war, außer einem Gig mit Flying Klassenfeind im Dankerrt mit Faust zusammen. Und dann gibt es noch einen anderen eigenen Gig im Dankerrt von einer weiteren Gruppe, die wir auch noch hatten – LSDAP/AO. Ansonsten immer diese Bandtourneen, die Alfred Hilsberg dann so organisierte, nach Berlin, Düsseldorf oder sonstwo mit vier bis sechs Bands. „Lieber zu viel als zu wenig", so lautete meistens das Motto.

R.H.:

Es gab ja 1979/80 eine Reihe von selbst organisierten Gruppenausstellungen, an denen Künstler*innen wie Martin Kippenberger, Werner Büttner, Georg Herold, Brigitta Rohrbach, Meuser, Thomas Wachweger oder Ina Barfuss beteiligt waren. Bemerkenswert ist, dass die Schauen von Konzerten begleitet waren. Da stellten dann zum Beispiel Markus Oehlen oder auch Albert Oehlen nicht nur aus, sondern standen auch als Musiker auf der Bühne. Das Eröffnungskonzert der dritten dieser Ausstellungen, *Finger für Deutschland*, fand im Ratinger Hof in Düsseldorf statt, hier haben ja auch Sie gespielt.

D.D.:

Ja, das war der erste Liveauftritt der Nachdenklichen Wehrpflichtigen.

B.D.:

Erinnern Sie sich an die Ausstellung bei Jörg Immendorff im Atelier?

D.D.:

Ich weiß noch, dass die sehr groß war, dass da irrsinnig viel Zeugs war, und ich kannte halt die Leute, also die Künstler*innen. Ich kann mich vor allem an die Veranstaltung im Ratinger Hof erinnern. Es war ja eben Wahlabend, und Immendorff ist festgenommen worden, weil er eine Polizeiuniform getragen hat. Beuys war auch da. Kippenberger hat mit einem Stuttgarter Dichter zusammen performt.

R.H.:

Waren Sie auch bei der zweiten Gruppenausstellung *2. außerordentliche Veranstaltung in Bild und Ton: Aktion Pisskrücke. Geheimdienst am Nächsten* in Hamburg zugegen? Was gab es da an Musik?

D.D.:

Ja, da gab es die Gruppe Zwischenopfer. Das war eine Idee von Albert. Die spielten mit Saxofon und anderen Instrumenten mit Eimern überm Kopf und liefen so durchs Publikum. Die Ausstellung war im Künstlerhaus. Und das hat das auch ein bisschen

myself. At some point I asked them to pay me for my work in shares. Anyway, Bömmels was one of the people who hired me in the beginning. At the time, he was no longer working on the actual editing work, but he still wrote for *Spex* and was still very active as an editor. He was one of the people who strongly identified with the magazine.

B.D.:

In another interview, you mentioned something interesting about the writing style at *Spex*. It was notorious and slightly convoluted. You said, "it should be as obscure as possible," while still being just interesting enough to keep you reading.

D.D.:

That sentence from the *Jungle World* interview[3] was trying to talk about the idea of lovingly observing one's own complicated experience of reception, to present the process of reception in its full breadth, since the dreary language of rock criticism that was everywhere else at the time couldn't do justice to the dignity of fandom and the intensive reception of pop music. Obscurity isn't an end in itself, rather it's related to a certain idea about the appropriate way to address music. And that you nonetheless still have to communicate, win over advertising customers and readers, and so on, that's the tension and it leads to conflicts. That's where you have to start talking about boundaries, where it works and where it doesn't. This idea was, of course, borne out differently by the various members of the collective. There were those who, as early as 1985, were saying why don't we just become *Tempo,* and then others who wanted the exact opposite, myself included.

R.H.:

So it was about wholeheartedly engaging with the specific field of pop music, instead of trying to write about it "informatively" from a distanced position.

D.D.:

Exactly, this meant taking one's own experience of reception seriously and being in a sense faithful to it: the things you were contriving in yourself when you listened to music or became interested in it. And I think that was one of the most successful aspects, because a lot of people could recognize themselves in it. Basically it was a way of writing that at the same time also appeared in a certain kind of literature, which was usually about how one receives cultural products, one's own secondary status in the process. It was about showing how one is conditioned by cultural products, and not so much about some supposedly deep true sensations. It was basically a paradigm shift away from the Peter Handke 1970s, where it was all about true or deep perceptions and sentiments, and where one found oneself in the process of experience. In the 1980s, by contrast, it was about observing oneself in the process of receiving prefabricated products.

aber er hat noch geschrieben für *Spex* und als Herausgeber war er schon aktiv. Er gehört zu den Leuten, die sich mit dem Laden stark identifizierten.

B.D.:

Sie haben in einem Interview was Interessantes gesagt, nämlich über den Schreibstil, den es in der *Spex* gab, den berüchtigten, leicht verschwurbelten. Da sagten sie, „es sollte so obskur sein, wie es gerade noch ging", aber gerade noch so, dass es interessant genug ist, reinzulesen.

D.D.:

Dieser Satz, der in einem *Jungle-World*-Interview[2] fällt, meint die Idee, sich bei seiner eigenen komplizierten Rezeption liebevoll zu beobachten. Was zu schwer verständlichen Texten führt, weil es bedeutet, den Rezeptionsvorgang in seiner ganzen Breite und Länge darzustellen, während die öde Sprache der Rock-Kritik, die es sonst so gibt, der Würde des Fantums und der intensiven Rezeption von Popmusik nicht gerecht wird. Die Obskurität ist kein Selbstzweck, sondern hat zu tun mit einer bestimmten Vorstellung davon, was angemessenes Verhalten gegenüber der Musik ist. Und dass man dann trotzdem noch darüber kommuniziert, dass man trotzdem Anzeigenkunden gewinnen und Leser*innen haben muss und so weiter, das ist die Spannung, darüber gibt's dann Konflikte. Und da muss man dann über Grenzen reden, wo geht's noch und wo nicht mehr. Und das wurde natürlich von den Personen in dem Kollektiv unterschiedlich vertreten. Es gab welche, die sagten schon 1985, lass uns doch lieber *Tempo* werden, und es gab andere, die das Gegenteil wollten – ich zum Beispiel.

R.H.:

Es ging also darum, sich auf das spezifische Spiel der Popmusik einzulassen, statt zu versuchen, aus einer distanzierten Position heraus „informativ" über diese Sachen zu schreiben.

D.D.:

Genau, es bedeutete, die eigene Rezeption ernst zu nehmen und ihr eine gewisse Treue entgegenzubringen. Also das, was man selbst da so veranstaltete, wenn man Musik hörte oder wenn man sich dafür interessierte. Und das ist, glaub ich, auch sehr erfolgreich gewesen, weil sich da viele drin wiedergefunden haben. Das ist im Grunde genommen ja eine Art zu schreiben, die sich zur gleichen Zeit auch in einer bestimmten Form von Literatur mitgeteilt hat, in der es oft darum ging, wie man irgendwelche Kulturprodukte rezipiert, die also die eigene Sekundarität, das heißt, das Geprägt-Sein von kulturellen Produkten, ausstellte, und nicht so sehr die wahre Empfindung. Das war im Grunde der Paradigmenwechsel zu den Peter-Handke-Siebzigern, wo es um die wahre Empfindung geht und darum, wo das Selbst in der Erfahrung zu sich findet. Dagegen ging es in den 1980er-Jahren darum, das Selbst beim Vollzug von Rezeption von bereits fertigen Dingen zu beobachten.

R.H.:

Und dabei ging es dann weniger um Theorie als um Poesie?

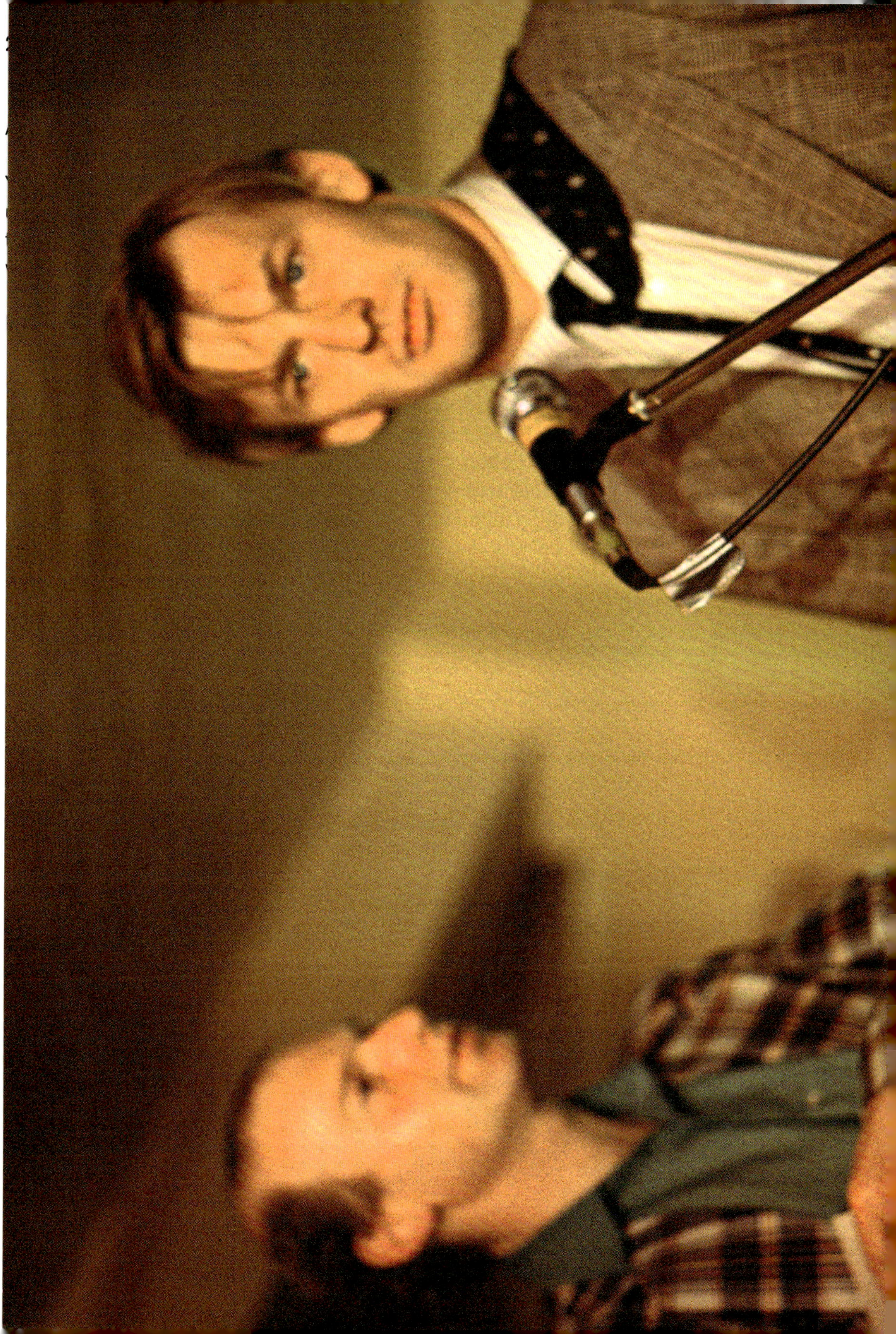

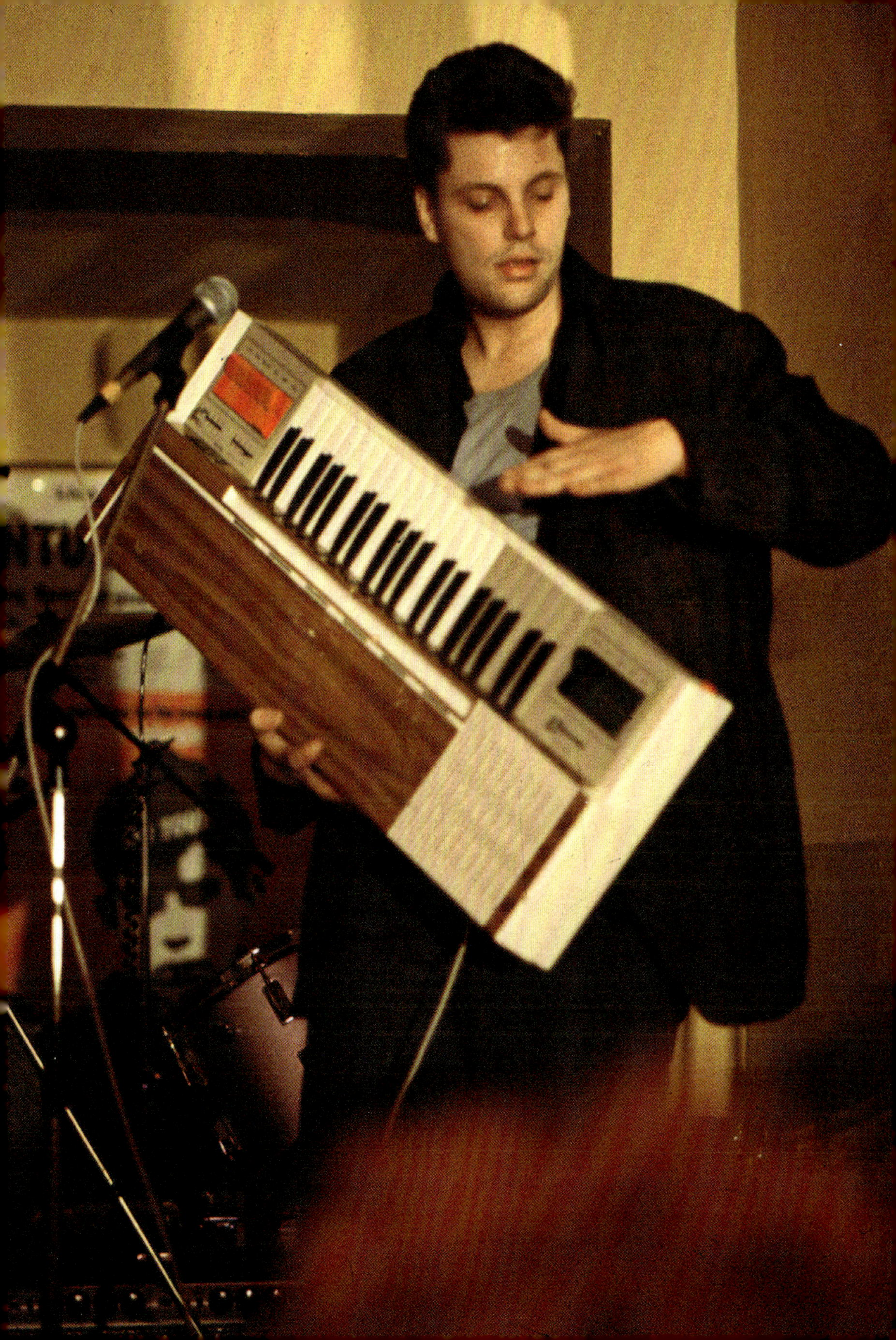

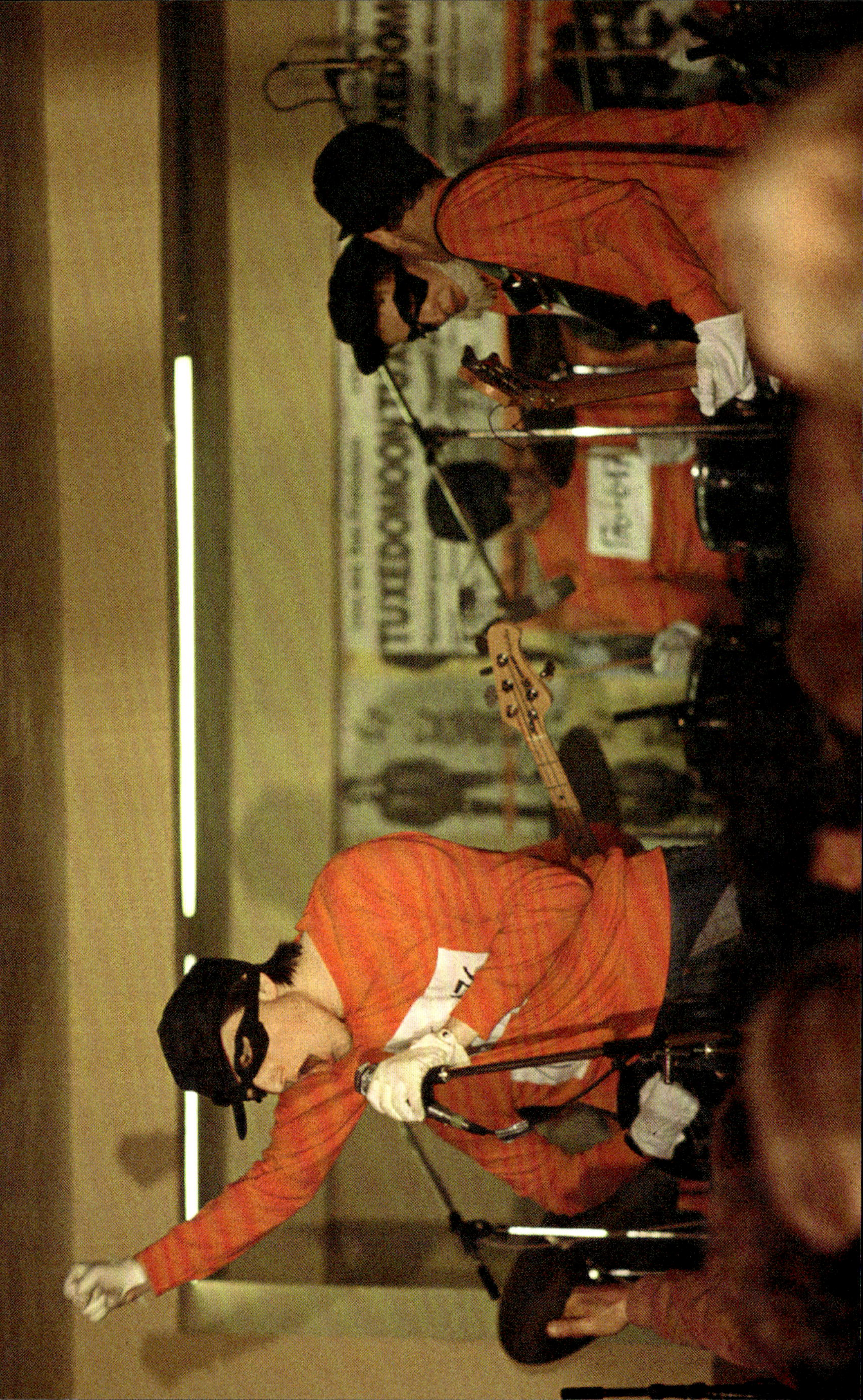

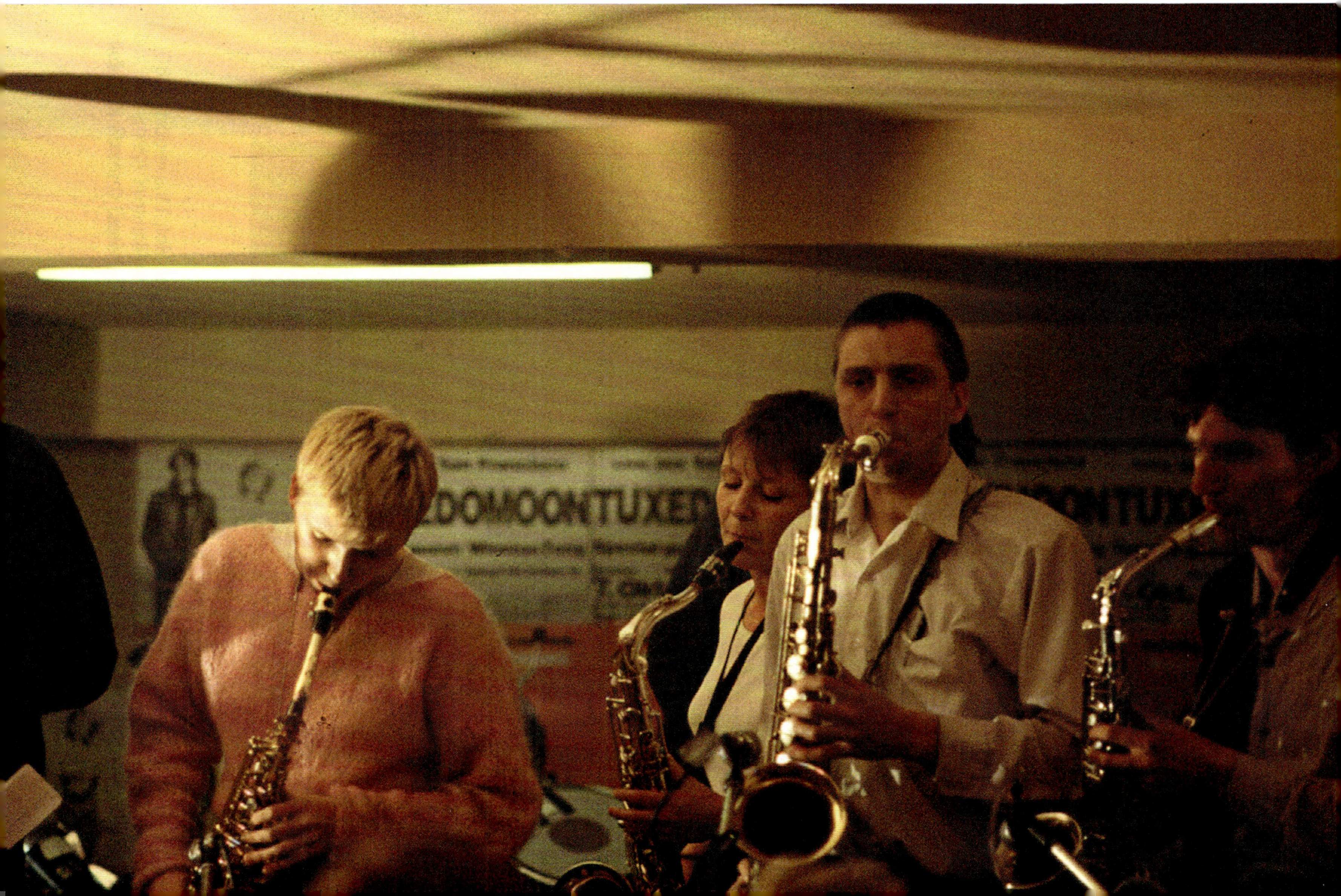

DOMOONTUXED

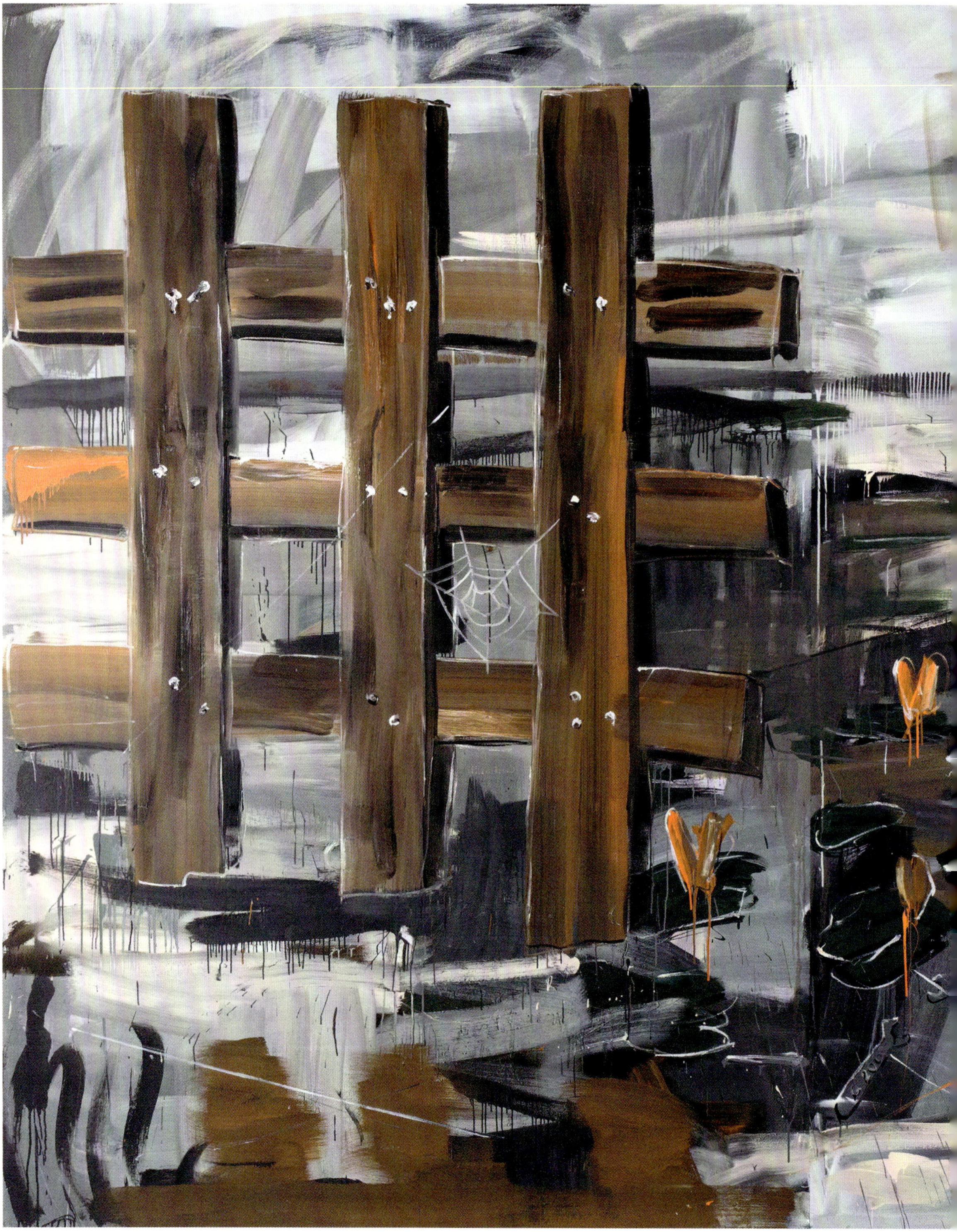

Albert Oehlen, *Ohne Titel (Seerosen)*, 1982, Mischtechnik auf Leinwand, 2-teilig / mixe

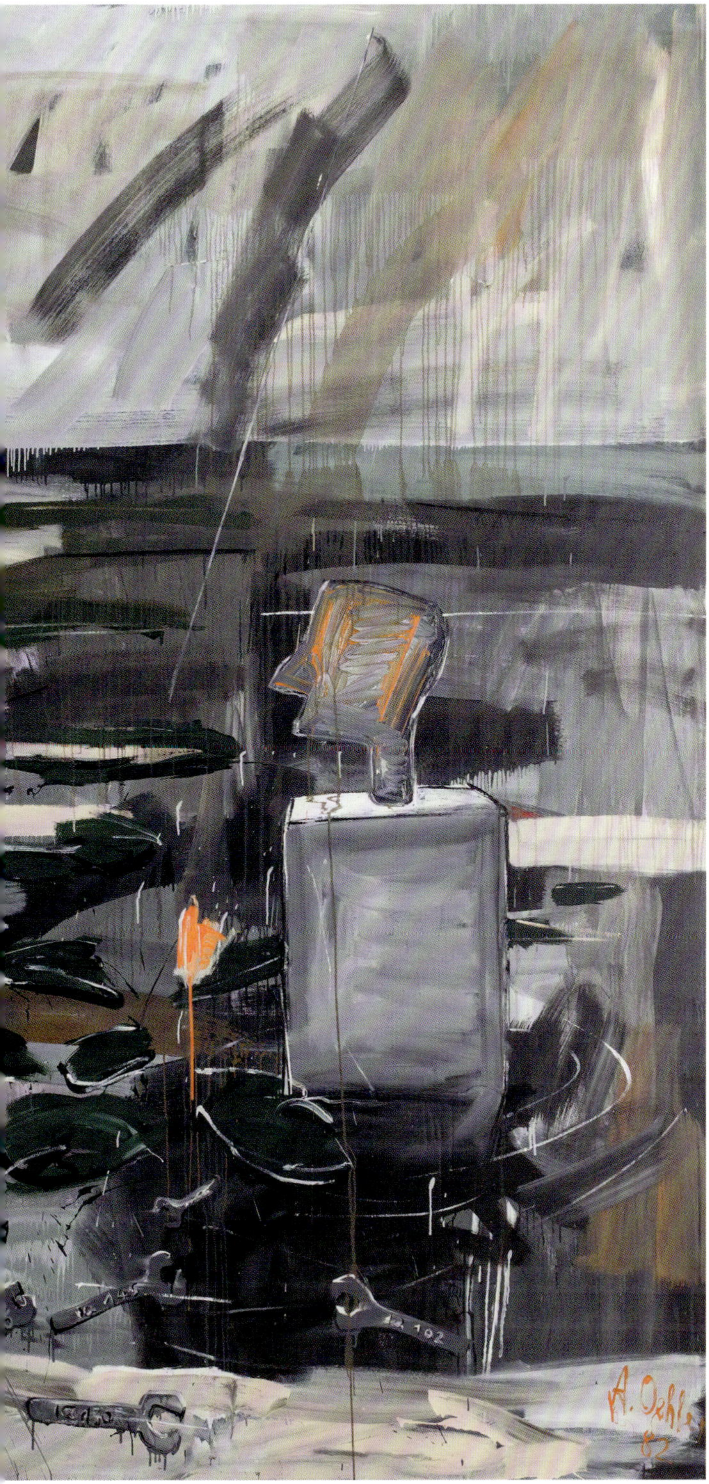

edia on canvas, 2 parts, je / each 260 × 180 cm

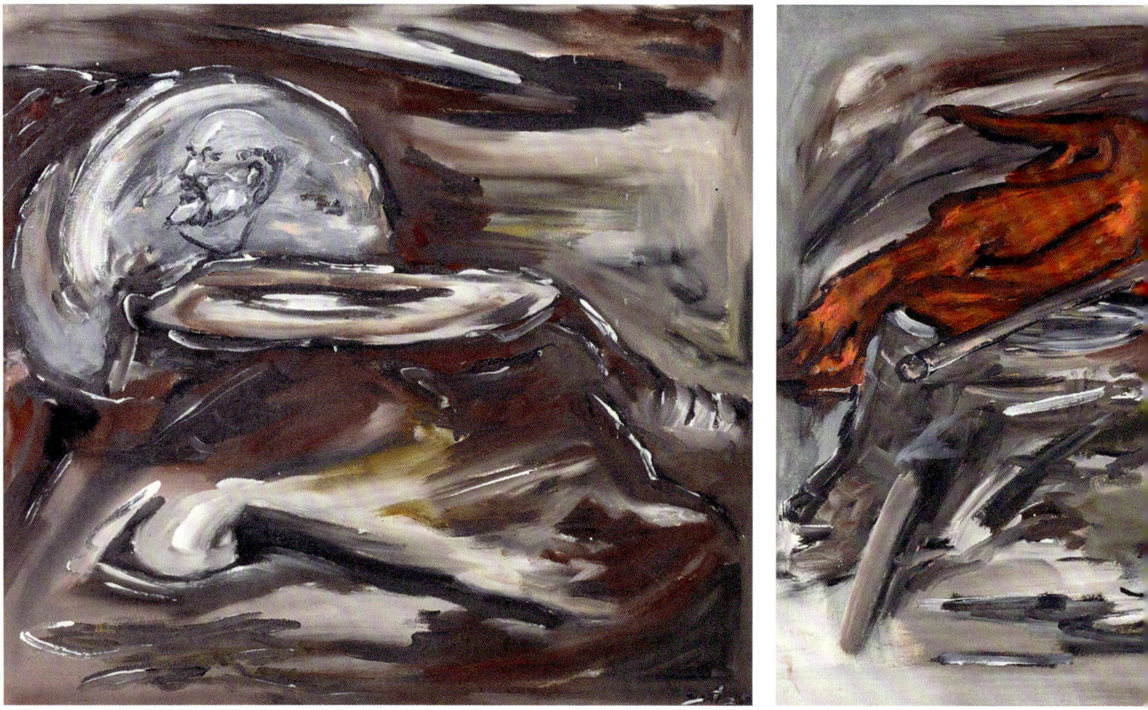

Werner Büttner, *Spuren des Picknicks der KPD/ML-Ortsgruppe Krefeld*, 1981, Öl auf Leinwand, 3-teilig / oil on canvas, 3 parts, 80 × 90 cm, 80 × 100 cm, 80 × 90 cm

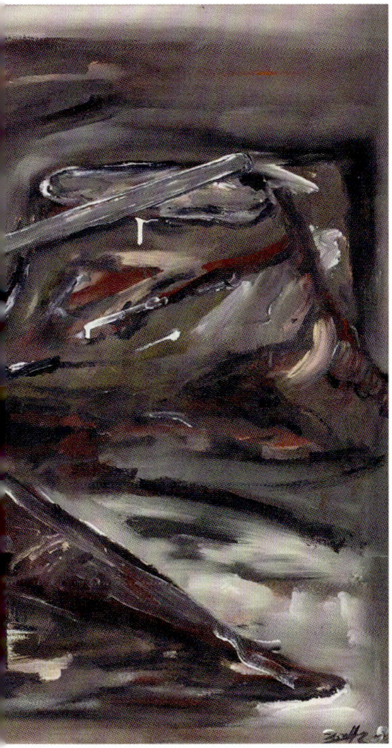

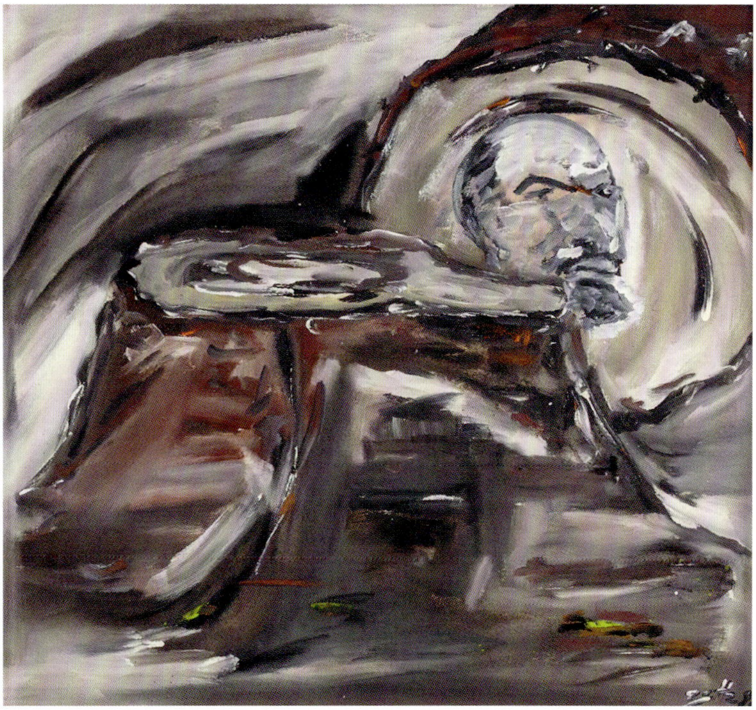

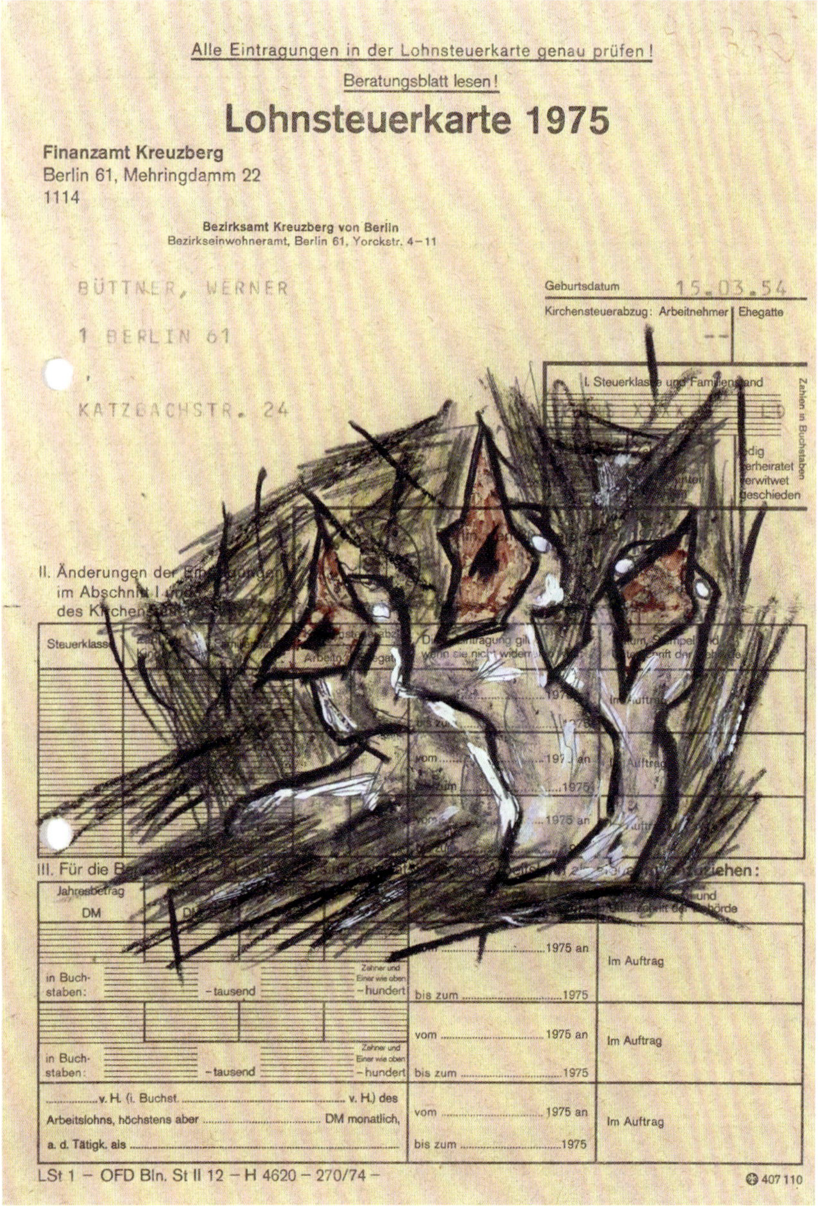

Werner Büttner, *Erste Versuche*, 1980, Mischtechnik auf Lohnsteuerkarte / mixed media on income tax card, 21 × 14,8 cm, aus der gleichnamigen Serie / from the eponymous series, 1980

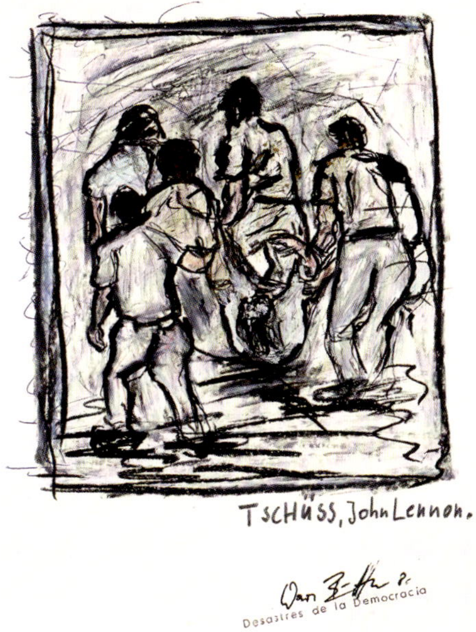

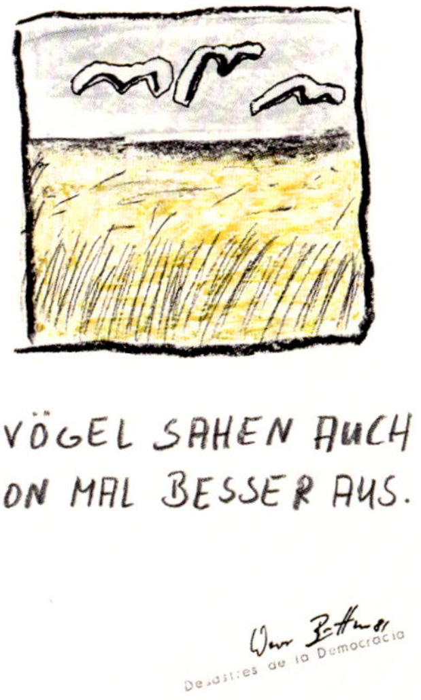

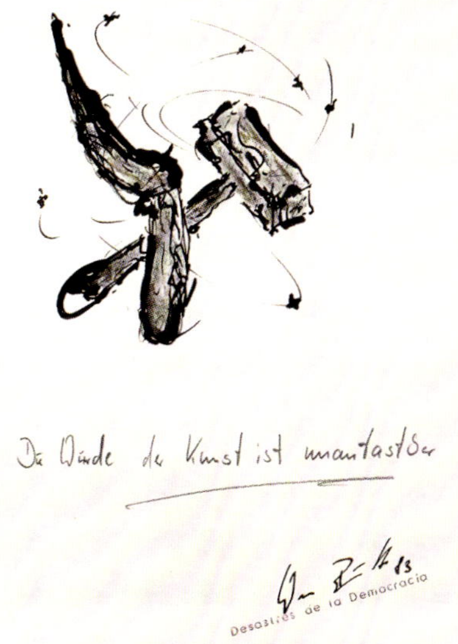

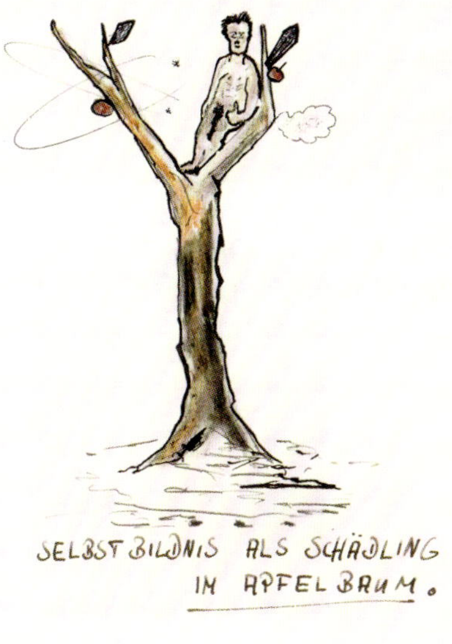

Werner Büttner, *Schrecken der Demokratie*, 1980/1981/1983/1984, Mischtechnik auf Papier / mixed media on paper, je / each 29,5 × 21 cm, aus der gleichnamigen Serie / from the eponymous series, 1979–1999

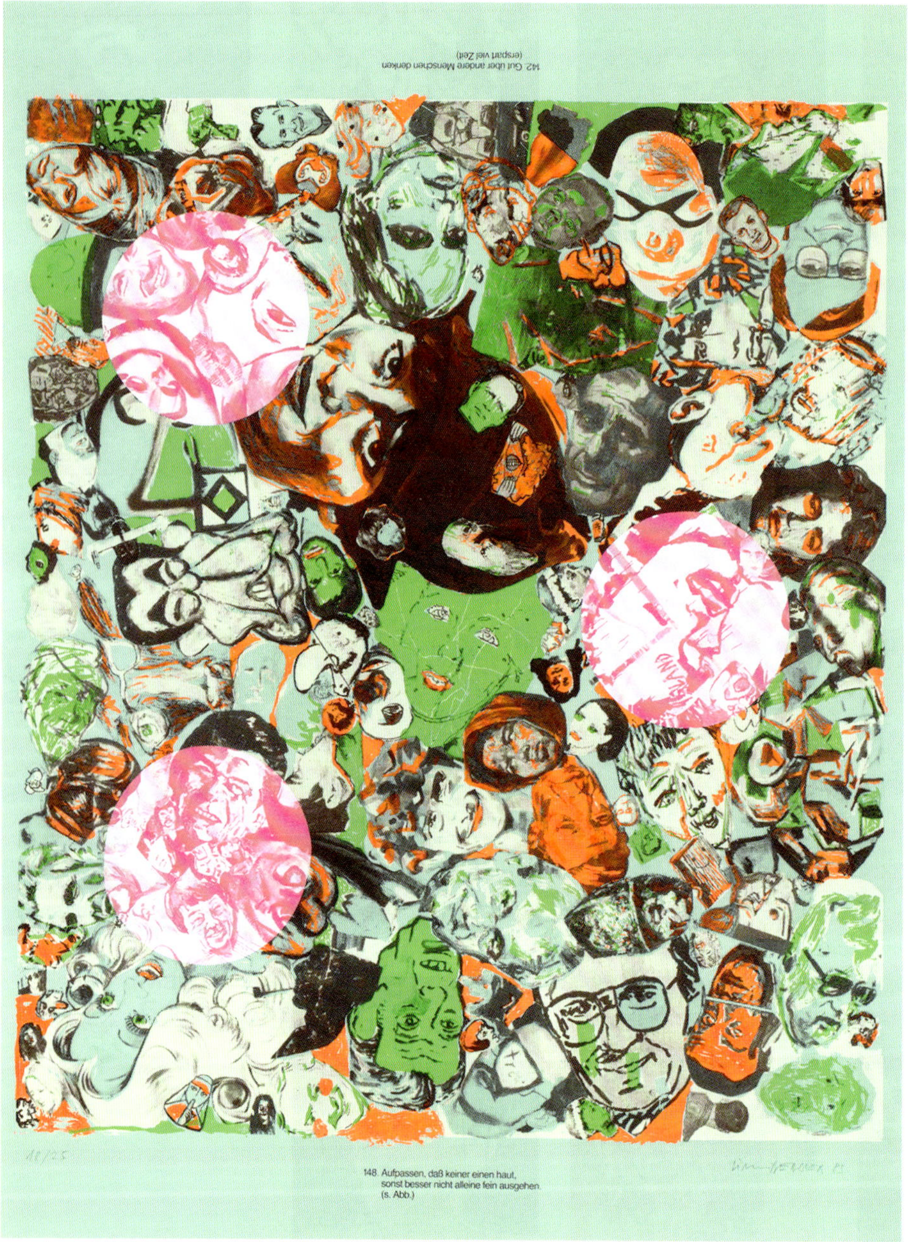

Martin Kippenberger, *Alle Menschen sind gleich*, 1983, Siebdruck auf Chromolux und PVC-Folie / silkscreen on chromolux and PVC foil, 80 × 61 cm, aus der Mappe / from the portfolio *laque des hommes*

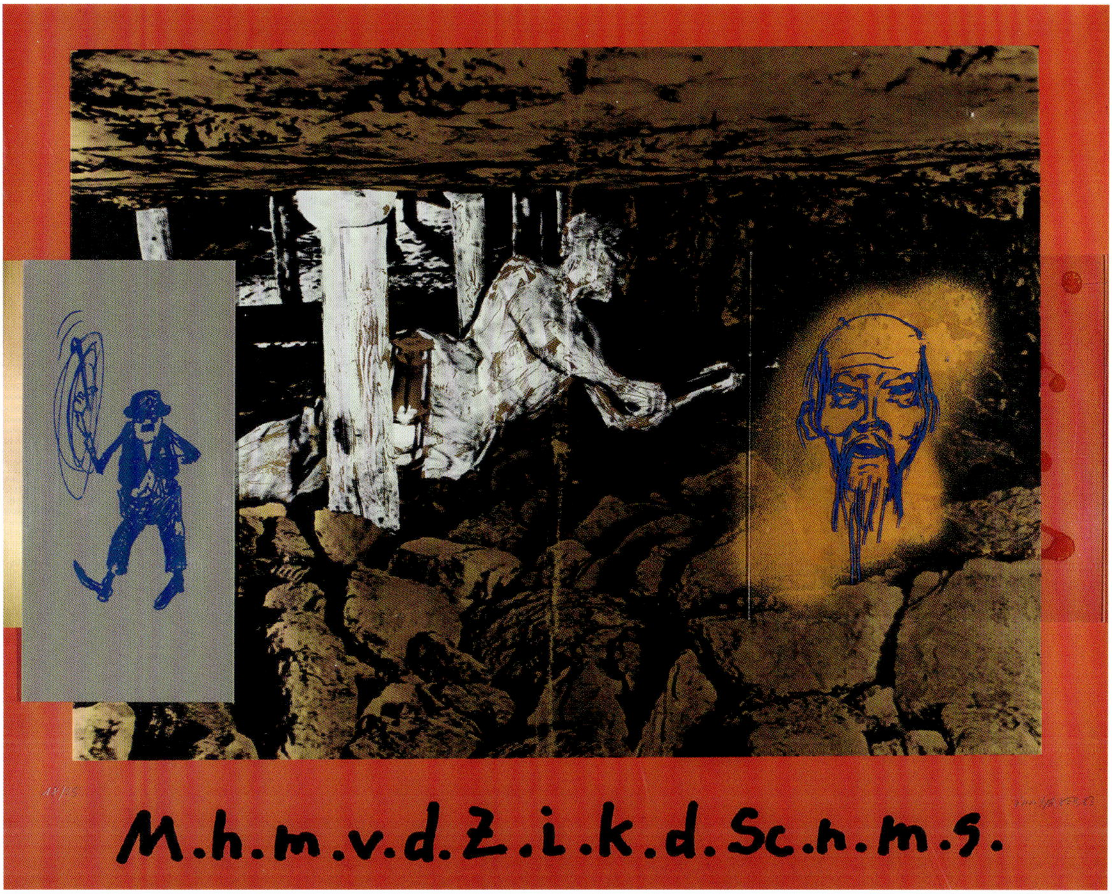

Martin Kippenberger, *Mutti, hol mich von der Zeche, ich kann dat Schwatte nicht mehr sehen*, 1983, Siebdruck auf Plexiglas und Chromolux / silkscreen on plexiglas and chromolux, 61 × 80 cm, aus der Mappe / from the portfolio *laque des hommes*

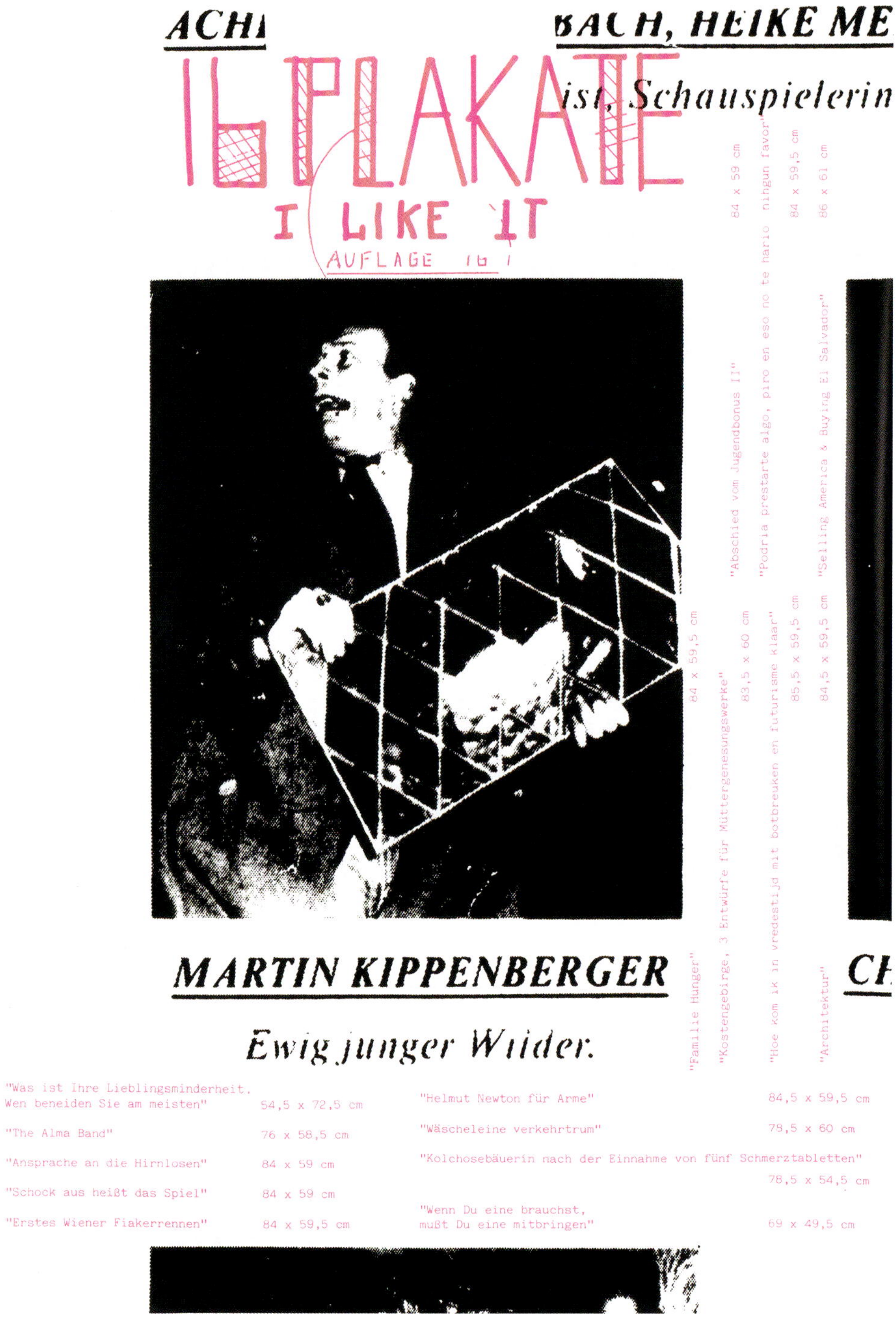

Martin Kippenberger, *I like it – Ewig junger Wilder*, 1984, Siebdruck auf Papier / silkscreen on paper, 85 x 59 cm

Hilka Nordhausen
Buch Handlung Welt. Mein Anschlag auf die Wirklichkeit

Hilka Nordhausen
Buch Handlung Welt: My Attack on Reality

Auszüge aus einem Gespräch mit / Excerpts from a conversation with Bettina Sefkow, Berlin, 1990, zuletzt erschienen in / last published in: Hans-Christian Dany, Ulrich Dörrie und / and Bettina Sefkow (Hg. / eds.), *dagegen dabei. Texte, Gespräche und Dokumente zu Strategien der Selbstorganisation seit 1969*, Hamburg 1998.

I wanted to break that open with the concept of the wall.

Through the wall, the space was declared an artistic situation. It was a public field of experimentation where you could mess around. The invited artist had one week, in the evenings, to do their thing.

It was also about opening art up to painting again. Something different necessarily emerged, because it wasn't a canvas.

And the story with this overly intellectual Conceptual Art, where every art teacher passes his exams with a conceptual work, was downright ridiculous. A photo sequence here, playing with water and sand there. I wanted to kick out at that whole story. No exhibition of individual pieces, but the creation of a work, an oeuvre, a context. That's what it was all about. A wall work, projected onto the space, in which something happens. *Buch Handlung Welt* was not a gallery, not an alternative exhibition venue. The concept of the wall was the expression of a new position. [...]

And then the idea of involving new people. Contacts to the university were good, but there were not enough people in Hamburg who were really interested in these musings. Then in around 1978 I met Albert Oehlen and Werner Büttner in the Marktstube. And with them I knew right away that everything was clear, that they didn't respect anything, I wanted them for the cause. [...]

In 1976, painting was frowned upon. But now the artists wanted to paint with joy... *Buch Handlung Welt* with its wall was a real bridgehead in this development.

That suddenly changed in 1980. The Neue Wilde took the stage. It literally exploded after all those intellectual diktats of Conceptual Art. The wall was thus confirmed in its function as evidence of a new attitude. The new was now there, and basically the wall was to be given a new task. Work continued along these lines for two years, but the approach was now well established and the thrill was gone. That's why the last wall work by Hubert Kiecol—three forms chiseled into the wall—was the statement that the events here, on this wall and in this place, were over.

I was organizer, bookseller, accountant, and bridge builder, all at the same time. The artistic work was in the connecting. Everything I did and strived for in the seven and a half years of *Buch Handlung Welt* was just that: practicing to achieve as much as possible with modest means. It was networking, it was knowing the map in Germany, who is where and what they do. It was about creating an overview, in terms of content but also on the basis of places, places and between the places, that which is still fluid, not yet manifest, still in motion, in the so-called subculture, the avant-garde, the underground. A personal conviction and that it really, here and now, makes sense. *Buch Handlung Welt* is a conviction.

eine Art Falle, der ich mich entziehen wollte. *FLUXUS* war out, Concept Art war in, Ende der Kunstgeschichte. Was nicht präsent ist, ist nicht da.

Das wollte ich aufbrechen mit dem Konzept der Wand.

Durch die Wand war der Raum zu einer künstlerischen Situation erklärt. Es war ein öffentliches, experimentelles Feld, da durfte auch rumgesaut werden. Der eingeladene Künstler hatte eine Woche Zeit, abends, um seine Sache umzusetzen.

Dabei ging es auch darum, die Kunst wieder für Malerei zu öffnen. Da mußte ja notwendigerweise irgend etwas anderes entstehen, weil es keine Leinwand war.

Und die Geschichte mit dieser kopflastigen Konzeptkunst, wo jeder Kunsterzieher sein Examen mit einer Konzeptarbeit machte, das war ja geradezu schon lächerlich. Da noch 'ne Fotosequenz und da noch mal mit Wasser und mit Sand gespielt. Dieser ganzen Geschichte wollte ich einen Tritt versetzen. Keine Ausstellung von Einzelarbeiten, sondern das Erstellen einer Arbeit, eines Werks, eines Zusammenhangs. Darum ging's. Eine Wandarbeit, projiziert auf den Raum, in dem was passiert. *Buch Handlung Welt* war keine Galerie, kein alternativer Ausstellungsort. Das Konzept der Wand war der Ausdruck einer neuen Position. [...]

Und dann der Gedanke, neue Leute zu bringen. Die Kontakte zur Hochschule waren gut, aber es gab wenig Leute in Hamburg, die sich für diese Überlegungen wirklich interessierten. Dann lernte ich Albert Oehlen und Werner Büttner in der Marktstube kennen, so um 1978. Und bei denen wußte ich sofort, alles klar, die hatten vor nichts Respekt, die wollte ich für die Sache haben. [...]

1976 war Malerei verpönt. Nun wollten die Künstler aber fröhlich tuschen... *Buch Handlung Welt* mit ihrer Wand war ein richtiger Brückenkopf in diesem Geschehen.

Das änderte sich schlagartig nach 1980. Die Neuen Wilden rückten ins Feld. Es explodierte förmlich nach all dem kopflastigen Diktat der Konzeptkunst. Damit war die Wand als Beleg für eine neue Haltung in ihrer Funktion bestätigt. Das Neue war nun da, und im Grunde stand es an, der Wand eine neue Aufgabe zu geben. In diesem Sinne wurde zwei Jahre weitergearbeitet, aber diese Haltung war nun eingeführt, der Kitzel war weg. Darum ist die letzte Wandarbeit von Hubert Kiecol – drei Formen, ausgemeißelt bis auf die Mauer – das Statement, daß die Ereignisse hier, auf dieser Wand und an diesem Ort, beendet sind.

Ich war Organisatorin, Buchhändlerin, Buchhalterin und Brückenbauer, alles gleichzeitig. Das Verknüpfen war die künstlerische Arbeit. Alles, was ich in siebeneinhalb Jahren *Buch Handlung Welt* gemacht und angestrebt habe, war das, war üben, mit wenigen Mitteln möglichst viel zu erreichen. Das war Vernetzung, das war in Deutschland die Wege wissen, wo wer sitzt und wo was macht. Das war einen Überblick herstellen, inhaltlich, und zwar auch anhand von Orten, Orten und zwischen den Orten, dem noch Flüssigen, noch nicht Manifestierten, wo es sich bewegt, in der sogenannten Subkultur, der Avantgarde, im Untergrund. Eine persönliche Überzeugung, und daß es wirklich, hier und jetzt, einen Sinn macht. *Buch Handlung Welt* ist eine Überzeugung.

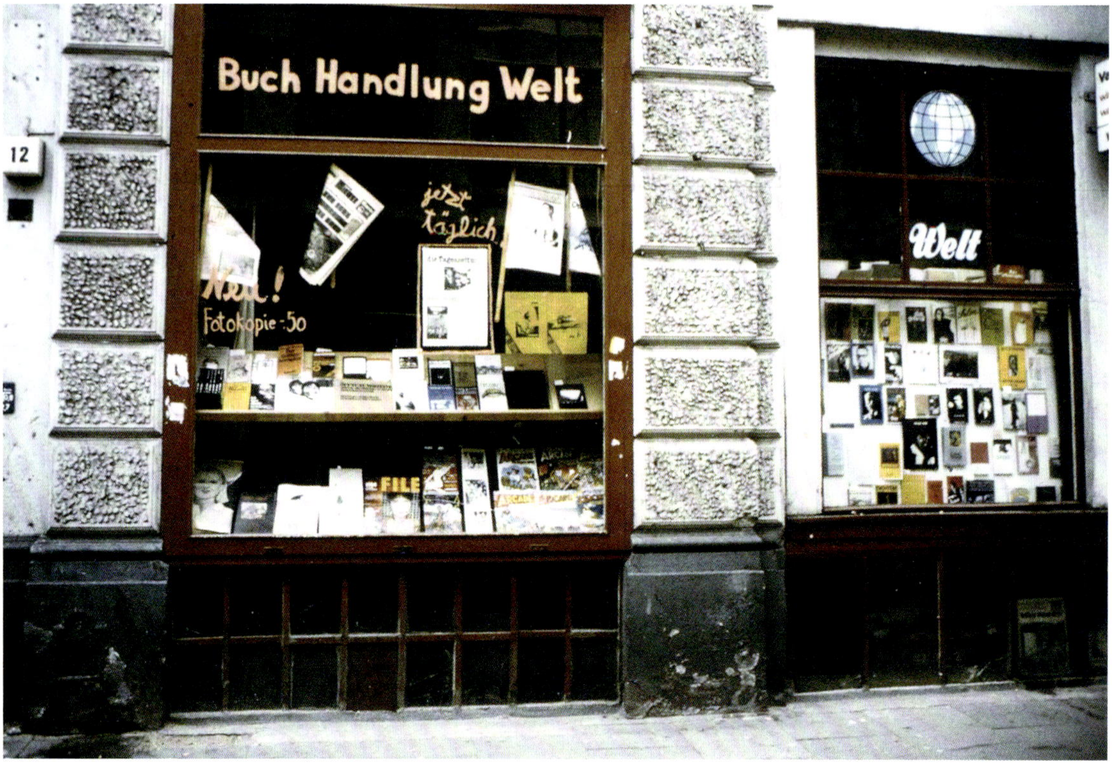

Buch Handlung Welt, Schaufenster / storefront, Hamburg, 1980

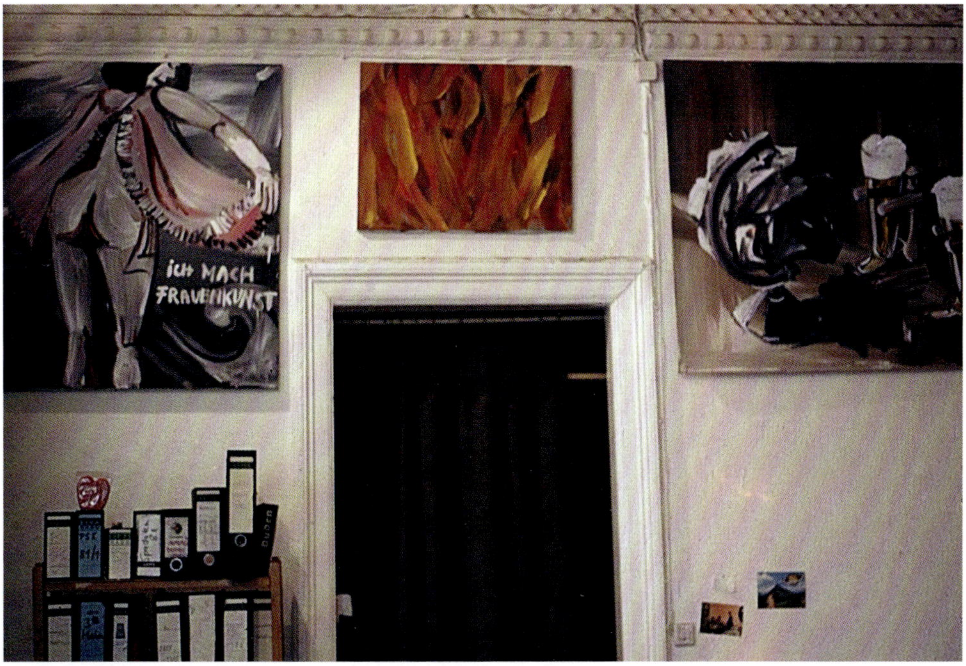

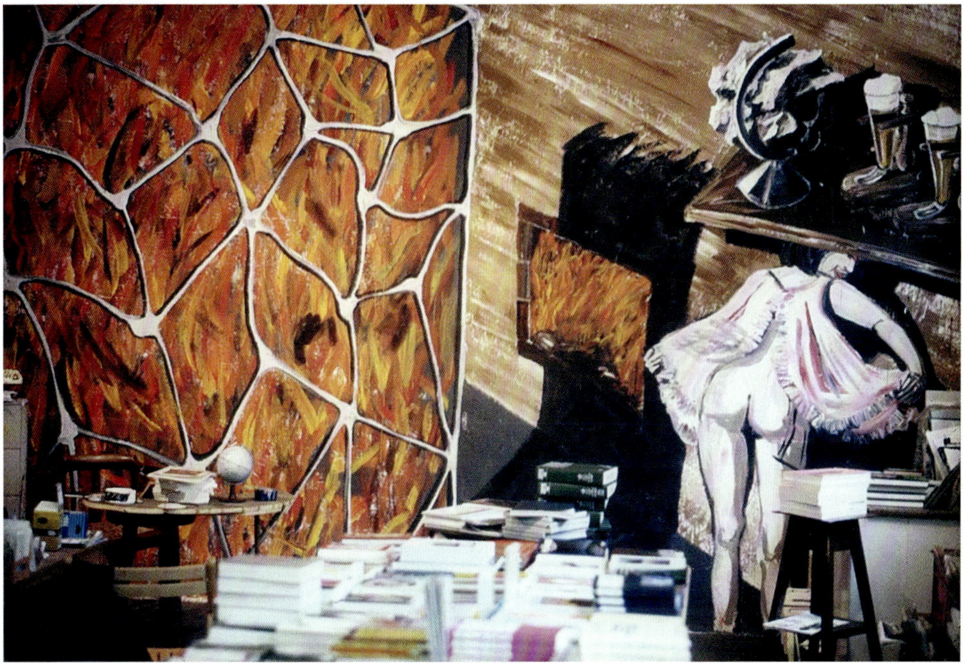

Bettina Semmer, *Ich mach Frauenkunst*, Installation (Detail), Buch Handlung Welt, Hamburg, 1982

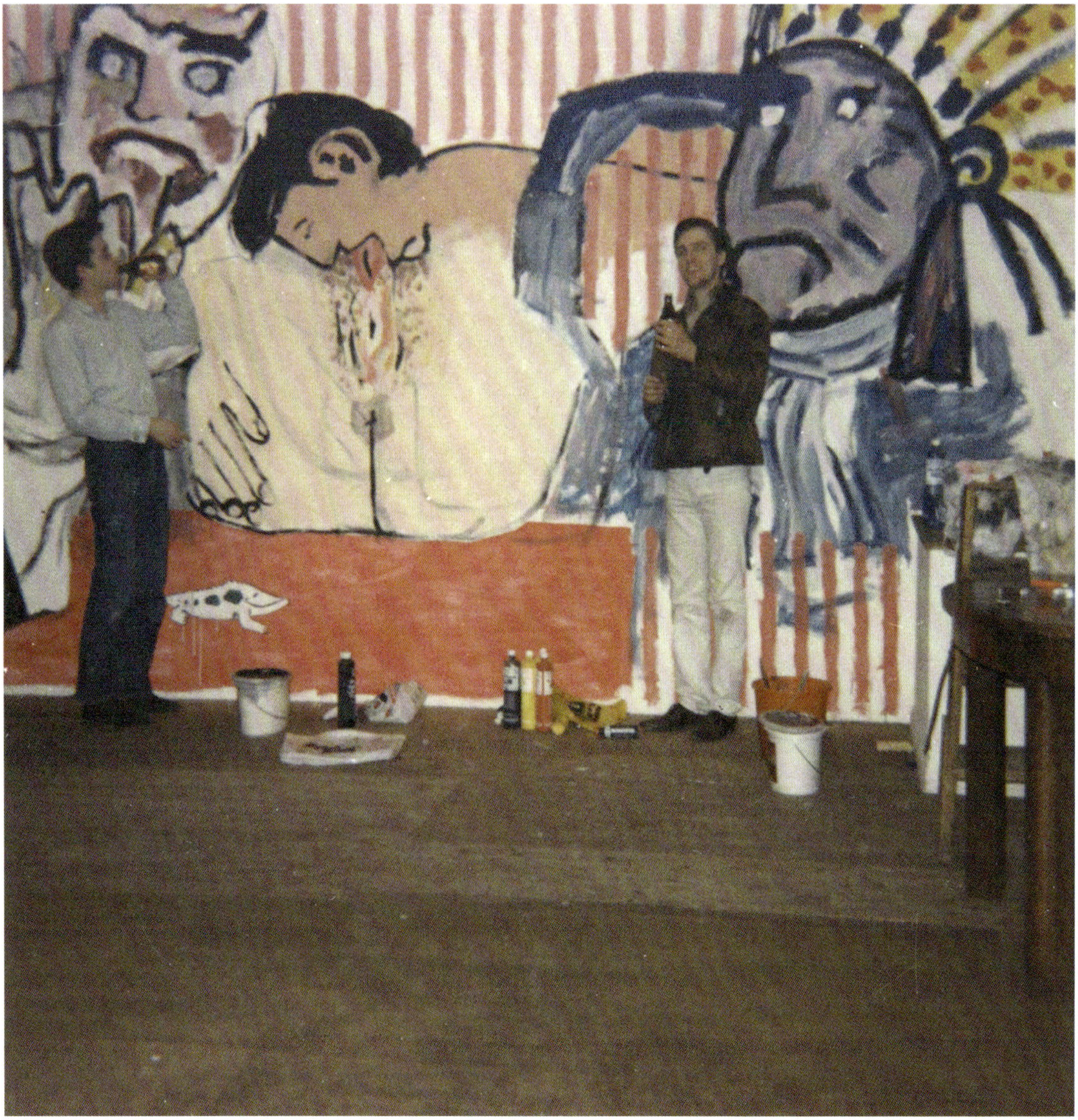

Werner Büttner und / and Albert Oehlen vor ihrer Wandarbeit / in front of their mural *Das Licht von der anderen Seite*, Buch Handlung Welt, Hamburg, 1978

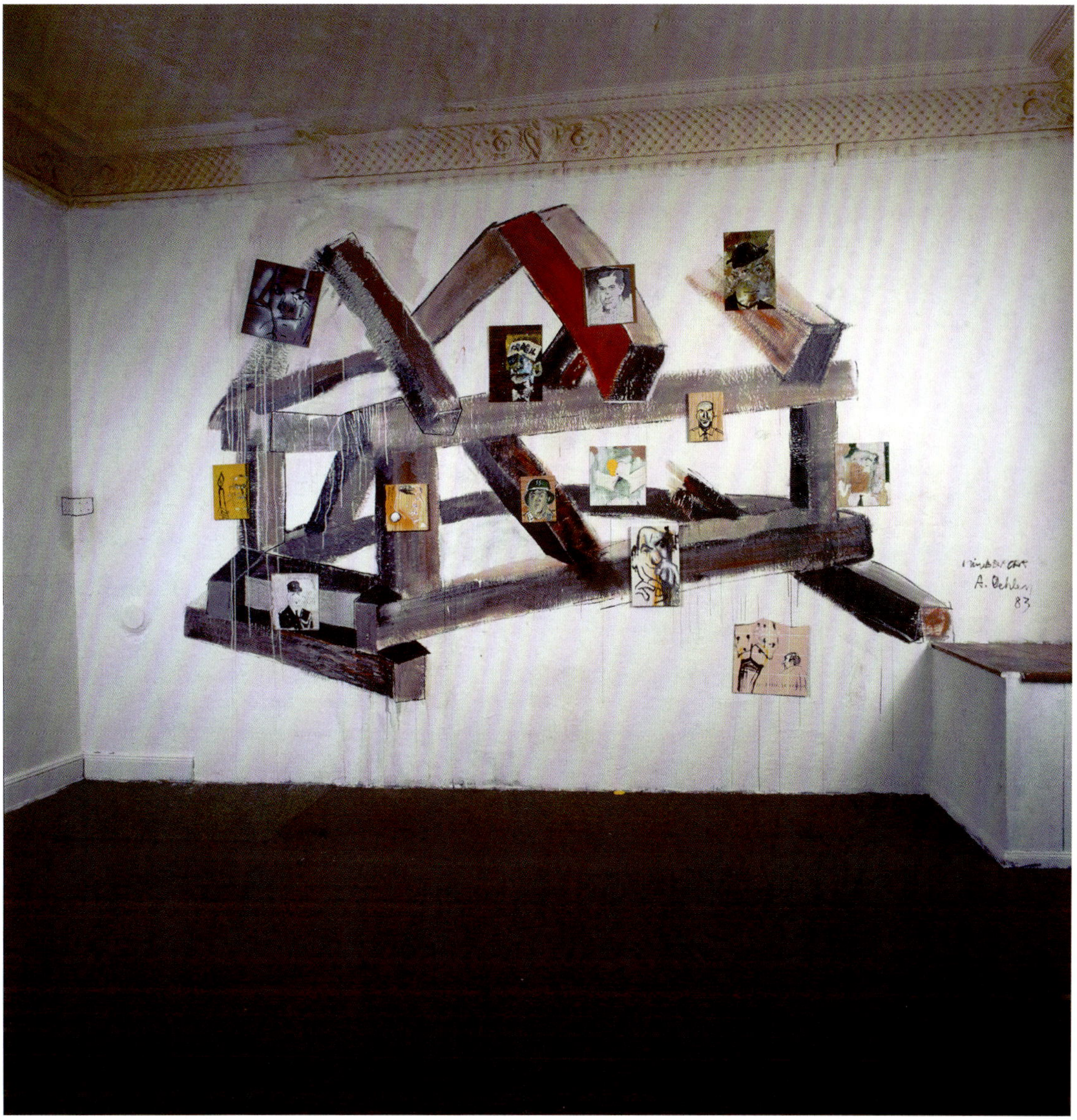

Martin Kippenberger, Albert Oehlen, *James Dean*, Wandarbeit / mural,
Buch Handlung Welt, 1983

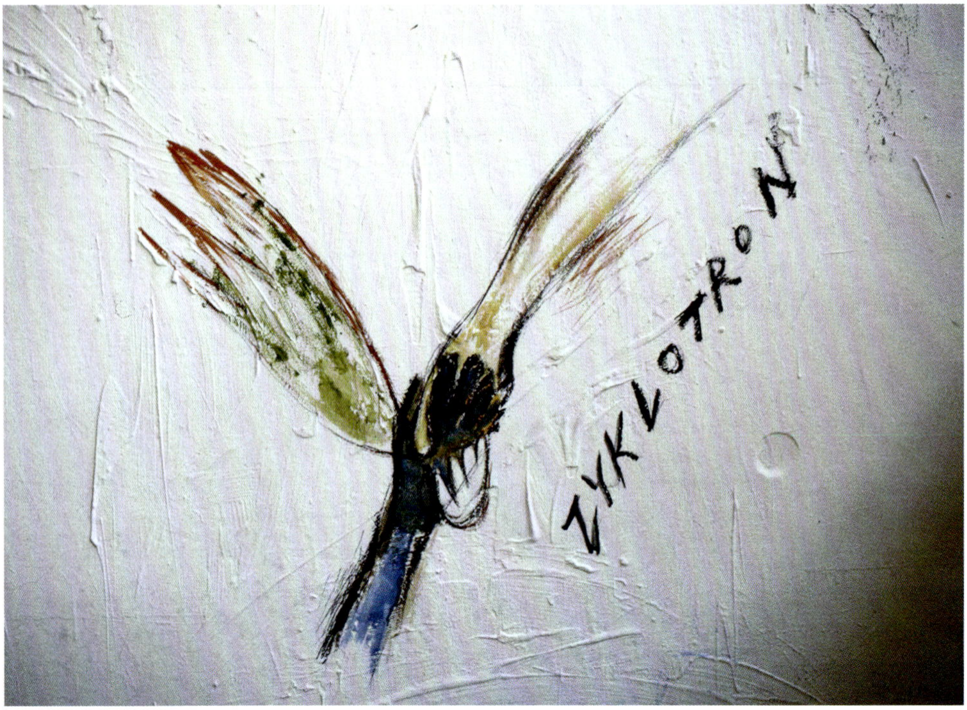

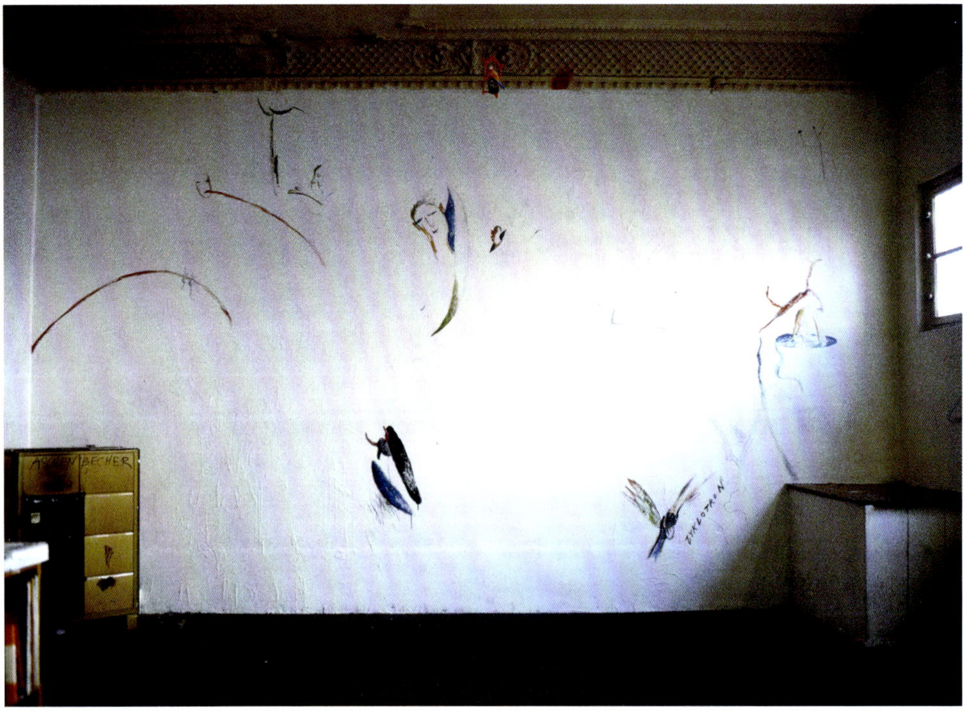

Walter Dahn, Jiří Georg Dokoupil, *Entweder Kirk Douglas oder die Sonne im Nil*, Wandarbeit / mural, Buch Handlung Welt, Hamburg, 1980

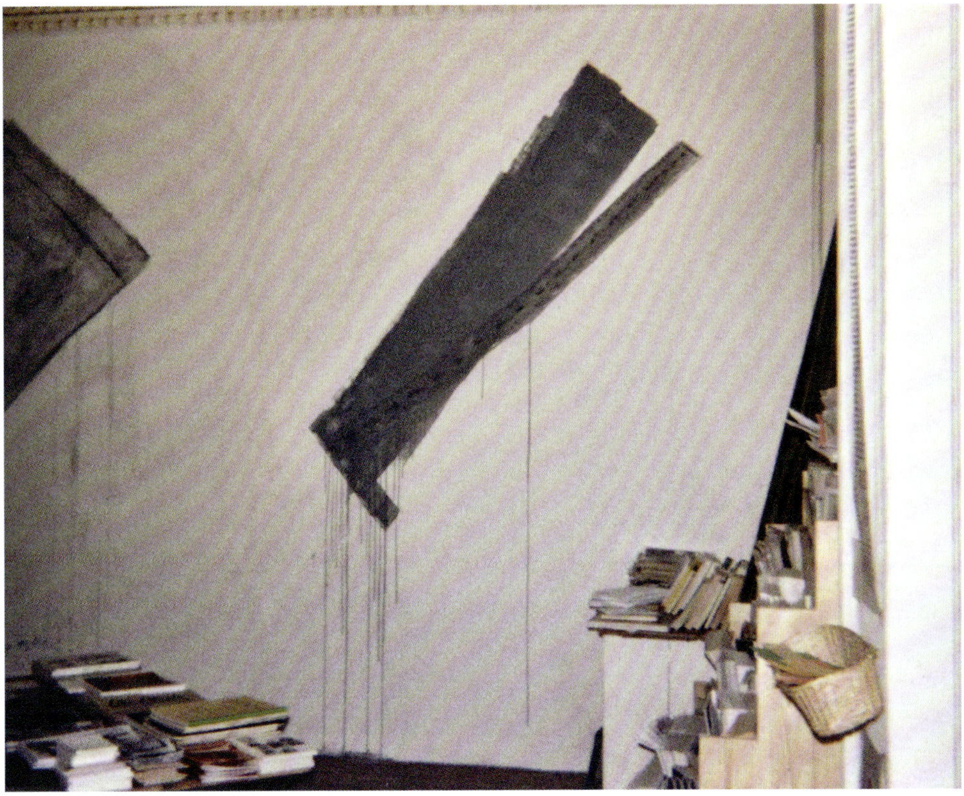

Hilka Nordhausen, *Ach, Malewitsch*, Wandarbeit / mural, Buch Handlung Welt, Hamburg, 1978

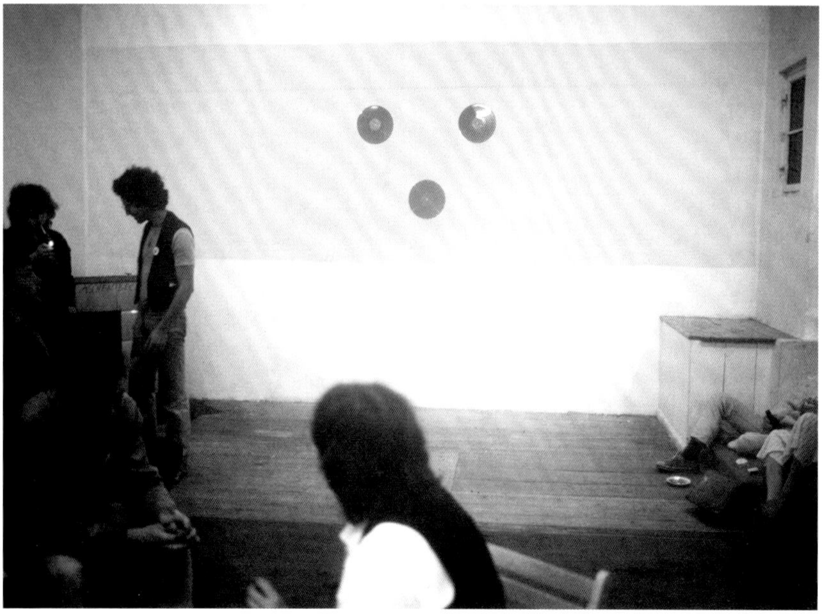

Bettina Sefkow, *Von einem Blinden mit dem Munde gemalen*, Wandarbeit / mural, Buch Handlung Welt, Hamburg, 1978

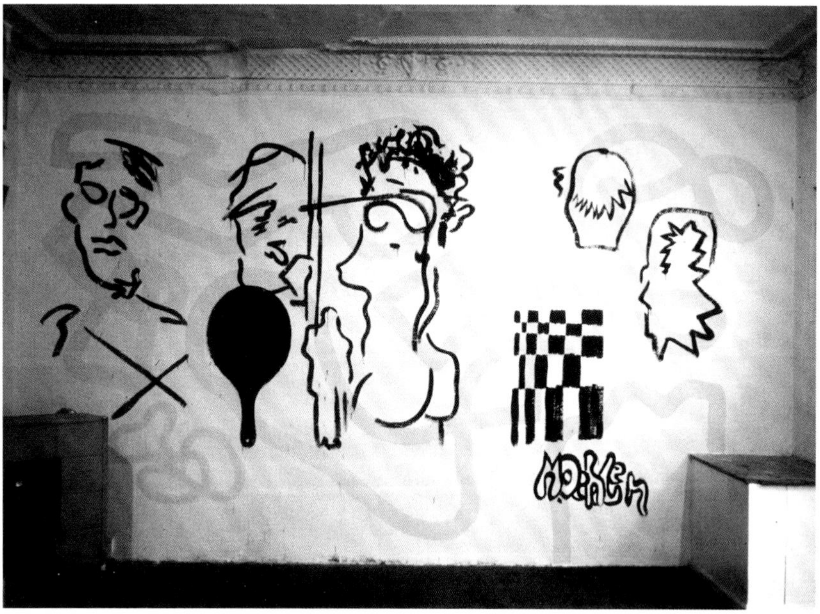

Markus Oehlen, Wandarbeit / mural, Buch Handlung Welt, Hamburg, 1981

Hubert Kiecol, *3 Figuren, ausgemeißelt bis auf d. Mauerwerk, Freilegung d. Schichten von 88 Wandbildern*, Wandarbeit / mural, Buch Handlung Welt, Hamburg, 1983

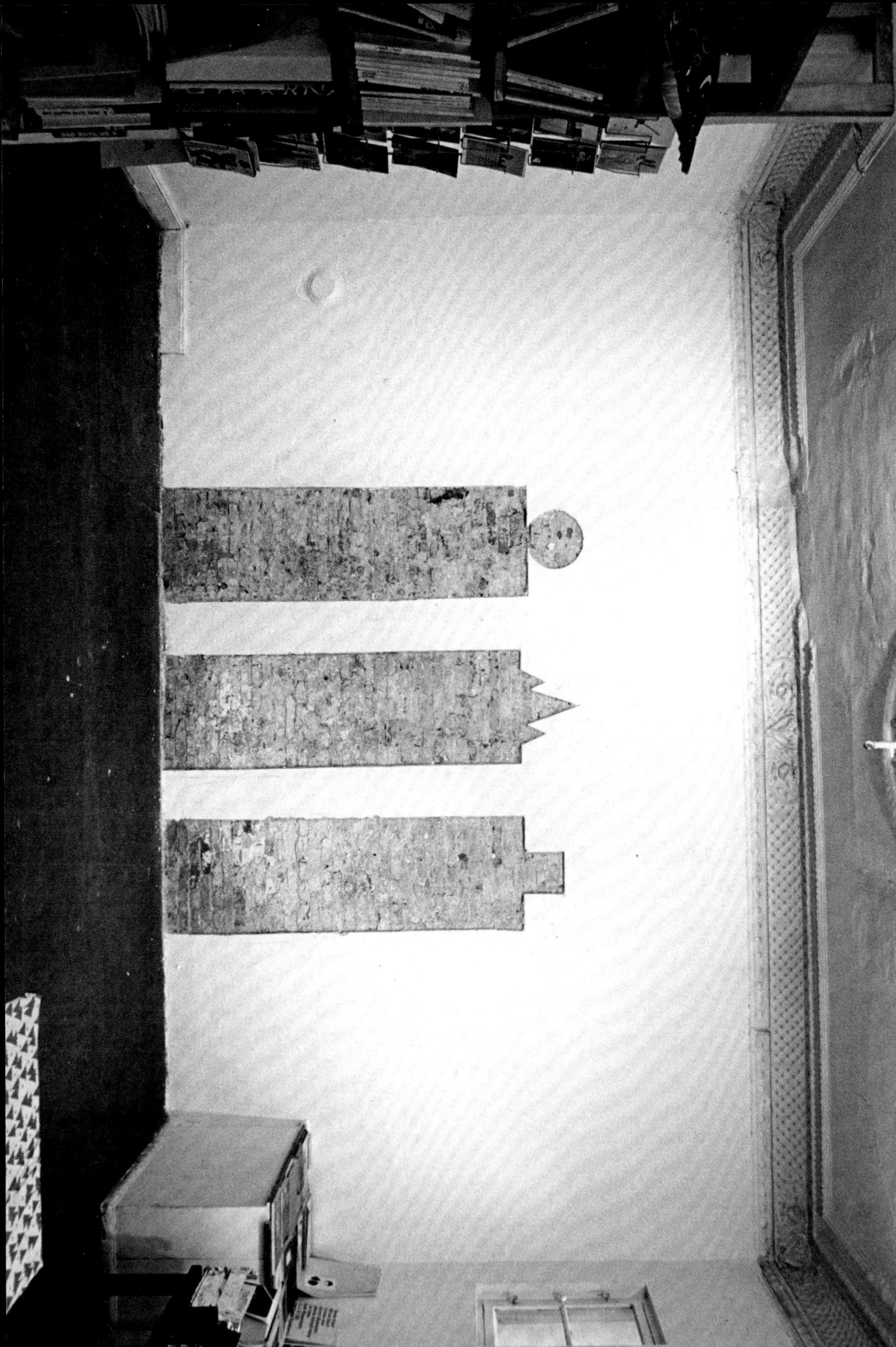

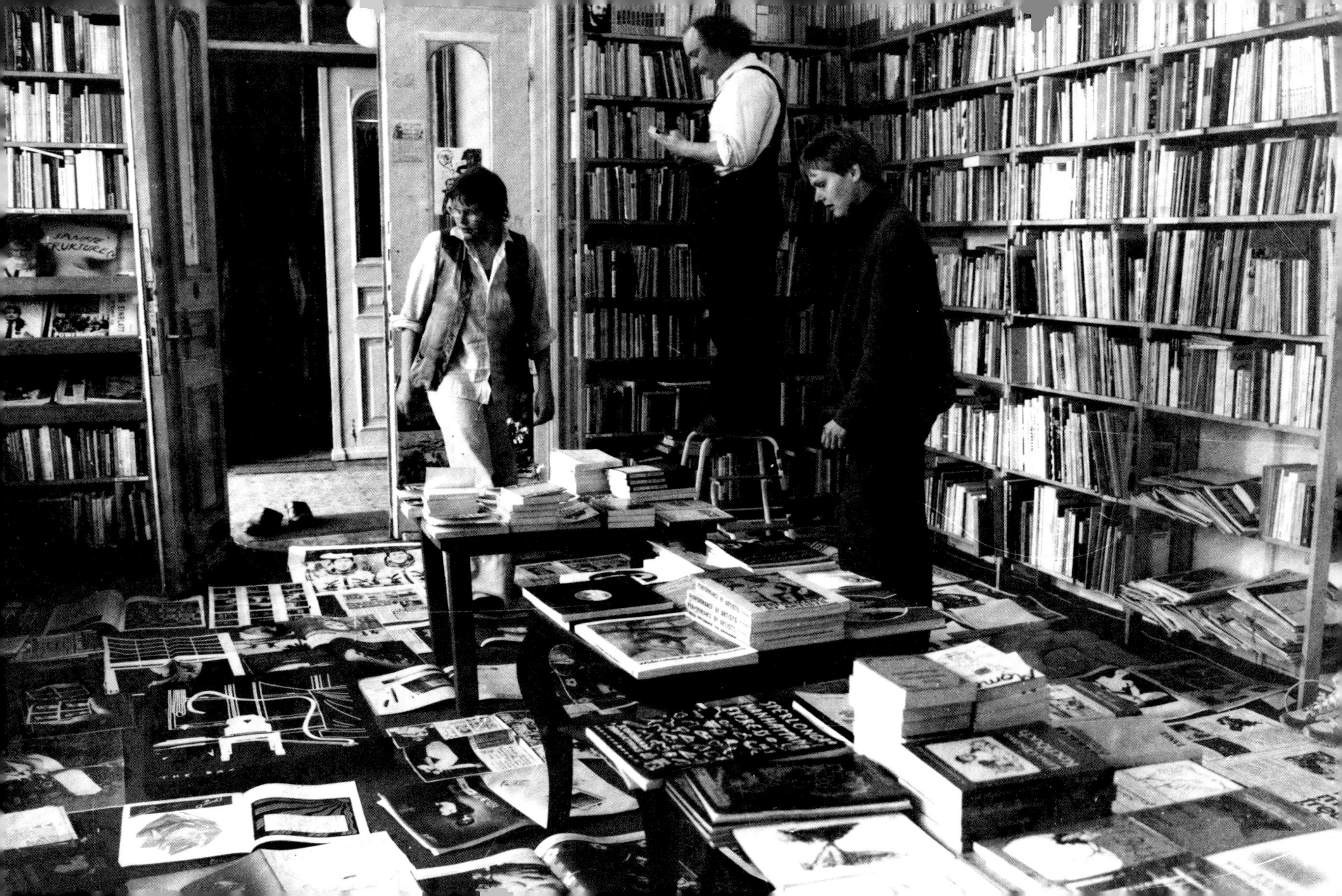
SPERLONGA MANHATTAN EXPRESS
PERFORMANCE BY ARTISTS

Bettina Semmer
Wir konterkarierten die Männerdomäne mit unserer weiblichen Seilschaft

Bettina Semmer
We counteracted the masculine domain with our network of women

Ein Gespräch mit Ramona Heinlein / A conversation with Ramona Heinlein, Berlin, Oktober / October 2018

(300) Hilka Nordhausen, Hans-Jürgen Masch und / and Vera Geiger, Buch Handlung Welt, Hamburg, 1980, Foto / photo: Michael Kellner

Ramona Heinlein:
The subjects of your paintings from the 1980s span from female bodies with cow heads to "street furniture" or apocalyptic scenes and still lifes—some of them seem ironic and absurd, others surreal to the point of feeling oppressive and catastrophic. What got you interested in painting back then? Why did you start painting?

Bettina Semmer:
I had always painted. It wasn't so much a question of getting started, but rather of integrating into the contemporary context. During my first semesters with Lothar Baumgarten in Münster—contrary to the general zeitgeist of Conceptual Art—painting wasn't completely written off, or maybe only halfway. As a Beuys student, he was quick to mouth off his dictum, "The problem already starts when someone gets ready to buy stretchers and canvases." Encouragement on one hand, but also encouraging doubt on the other. After a year I moved on to Hamburg where everything seemed pretty antiquated to me. So I bustled about and studied with Franz Erhard Walther, among others. I also encountered mixed messages about painting here. Franz Erhard Walther would say, "I come from painting," but he didn't paint.

What I was interested in were simply images that I wanted to realize, and the haptic, sensual, tangible immediacy of painting that goes through your whole body, filtered by the content and the will to composition. In the beginning I painted very realistically or naturalistically. But it wasn't until 1980 that I made a conscious decision to start painting. The time in between was more about trying things out, an experiment, small canvases, works on paper, or found supports like wallpaper—this was influenced by Pop Art and Sigmar Polke. I painted analytically, for example with repetitions of one and the same thing, or as commentary, such as a hand-painted Daniel Buren with an omitted zebra. And then there was the guest professor Stanley Brouwn, who commented on everything with a smile. I think most painters' training starts with an initial spontaneity and goes through a phase of insecurity and sarcasm before returning to one's own "voice." That's how it was with me. Getting to know the works of Polke and Gerhard Richter around 1977 was also decisive for my sense of irony and distance as well as technique and pictorial invention.

R.H.:
As you just mentioned, you studied with Franz Erhard Walther and Sigmar Polke. You also studied with Gerhard Richter and Jörg Immendorff. During the early 1980s, were there also established female artists who were important for you? In one interview, for example, you mentioned Meret Oppenheim's guest professorship in Hamburg.

B.S.:
Meret was more of a legend. She appeared and was a "guest." Back then

Ramona Heinlein:
Die Sujets deiner Gemälde aus den 1980er-Jahren reichen von weiblichen Körpern mit Kuhköpfen über „Straßenmöbel" bis hin zu apokalyptischen Szenen oder Stillleben – einige davon wirken ironisch und absurd, andere surreal bis hin zu beklemmend und katastrophisch. Was hat dich damals an der Malerei interessiert? Warum hast du angefangen zu malen?

Bettina Semmer:
Ich hatte immer gemalt, es war keine Frage des Anfangens, sondern eher eine der Einordnung in einen zeitgenössischen Kontext. Das Malen wurde mir zunächst in meinen ersten Semestern in Münster bei Lothar Baumgarten – im Gegensatz zum allgemeinen Zeitgeist der Konzeptkunst – nicht madig gemacht, oder nur so halb, denn als Beuys-Schüler kamen ihm auch schnell dessen geflügelte Worte: „Der Fehler fängt schon an, wenn einer sich anschickt, Keilrahmen und Leinwand zu kaufen" – also einerseits Ermutigung, andererseits Verunsicherung. Nach einem Jahr kam ich dann nach Hamburg, wo mir alles recht verstaubt vorkam. Da bin ich viel rumgeschwirrt und war dann unter anderem bei Franz Erhard Walther. Die Mixed Messages zur Malerei begleiteten mich auch hier. Franz Erhard Walther: „Ich komme aus der Malerei". Er malte aber nicht.

Was mich interessierte, waren zunächst einfach Bilder, die ich verwirklichen wollte, und die haptische, sinnliche, greifbare, durch den Körper gehende Unmittelbarkeit der Malerei, gefiltert durch die Inhalte, den Willen zur Gestaltung. Ich malte anfangs sehr realistisch bis naturalistisch. Bewusst angefangen zu malen habe ich dann erst wieder um 1980 herum, zwischendurch war es mehr ein Ausprobieren, ein Experiment, kleine Leinwände und Arbeiten auf Papier, auf vorgefundenen Untergründen wie Tapeten – das war auch von Pop und von Sigmar Polke beeinflusst. Ich malte analytisch, zum Beispiel Wiederholungen ein und desselben, oder kommentierend, etwa einen handgemalten Daniel Buren mit einem ausgesparten Zebra. Es gab da noch den Gastprofessor Stanley Brouwn, der das alles mit einem Lächeln kommentierte. Ich denke, die Schulung der meisten Maler*innen geht von der Spontaneität über die Verunsicherung und den Sarkasmus wieder hin zur eigenen „Stimme". So war es auch bei mir. Sowohl für Ironie und Distanz als auch für Technik und Bildfindung war dabei, um 1977, die Kenntnis der Arbeiten von Polke und Gerhard Richter entscheidend.

R.H.:
Wie du gerade sagst, hast du bei Franz Erhard Walther und Sigmar Polke studiert, außerdem auch bei Gerhard Richter und Jörg Immendorff. Gab es Anfang der 1980er-Jahre auch arrivierte Künstlerinnen, die wichtig für dich waren? Du erwähnst in einem anderen Interview zum Beispiel die Gastprofessur von Meret Oppenheim in Hamburg.

B.S.:
Meret war mehr so eine Legende, sie erschien und war „Gast". Ich bin damals wegen Polke nach Hamburg gegangen. In Hamburg waren die Meisterschüler weitgehend

R.H.:
The appropriation of preexisting images seems to be an important part of your artistic practice. Previously you'd mentioned that you painted a Buren while you were in Stanley Brouwn's class. In 1986, you painted yourself as Albert Einstein—can you tell us something about this painting.

B.S.:
On one hand, the portrait as Einstein has something to do with transvestism—me as a cross-dresser—on the other, it's partly a series of black paintings: orgies, Einstein, optical illusions—a mishmash of "catastrophic" images realized in black on black, an impossibility, a riddle, a secret. I don't think painting reveals secrets, but rather creates them. I don't understand Einstein's formula. It was simultaneously hubris and comedy. Like the hubris of painting in a blurry Richter style, which I did for a while, or copying a Buren. I was never very consistent about appropriating styles, but it's still a central thought for me to this day that one has to appropriate things, especially the masculine domains, in order to free the feminine domains of their devaluation. Of course there were practical jokes, humor, and irony, but there was also this undertone. Einstein, for example, was together with a very talented physicist. Many scientists were assisted by women, and some of the discoveries were even made by them but not attributed to them. Of course, something similar also happens in painting.

R.H.:
In 1982, at Buch Handlung Welt in Hamburg, which was an art project by Hilka Nordhausen, you showed a painting that bore the sentence "Ich mach Frauenkunst" [I make women's art] alongside a woman in a nightgown. Christa Näher, for example, was similarly offensive and ironic in the way she thematized her role as a female painter, like with the caption "Frauen die malen, drücken sich vor der Arbeit" [Women who paint are copping out of work] on an early invitation card. Was it important to directly and offensively address the marginalization of women in painting? What were the reactions like?

B.S.:
Yeah, also with the woman in the negligee that showed up at Hilka's, it was about an analogy between the "art" of sex work and painting, about advertising one's own body and the representation of the painterly body, which was the theme of the Reeperbahn paintings. I was just looking at some books again about sacred sexuality before it was made an object of shame and criminalization: *Sacred Sex, The Sacred Prostitute, Die Göttin und ihr Heros,* etc.

The reactions were incomprehension, head shaking, and maybe some secret admiration for this courage that was expressed as condemnation. It was a curious mixture; one can hardly describe it. What was good painting at all? What was it about? The men intentionally occupied the position of bad painters, but when a woman did it, it was just bad painting. Today, looking back from a certain

R.H.:
Der Aspekt der Aneignung bereits bestehender Bilder scheint ein wichtiger Teil deiner künstlerischen Praxis zu sein. Eben erwähntest du, dass du in der Klasse von Stanley Brouwn einen Buren gemalt hast. 1986 maltest du dich selbst als Albert Einstein – kannst du etwas zu diesem Bild erzählen?

B.S.:
Das Porträt als Einstein hat einerseits was mit Travestie zu tun – ich als Cross-dresser*in – und andererseits gehört es zur schwarzen Serie: Orgien, Einstein, optische Täuschungen – ein Sammelsurium „katastrophischer" Bilder, die Schwarz auf Schwarz realisiert wurden, ein Ding der Unmöglichkeit, Rätsel, Geheimnis.
Ich denke, die Malerei deckt Geheimnisse nicht auf, sie erfindet sie. Ich verstehe die Formeln von Einstein nicht, es war Anmaßung und Komödie zugleich. Wie auch die Anmaßung, in Richter-Technik verwischt zu malen, was ich zum Beispiel auch eine Zeit lang gemacht habe, oder eben einen Buren zu kopieren. Ich habe diese Appropriationen von Stilen nie mit großer Konsequenz betrieben, aber für mich ist es bis heute ein zentraler Gedanke, dass man sich die Dinge aneignen muss, vor allem die männlichen Domänen, und gleichzeitig die weiblichen Domänen von ihrer Entwertung befreien. Da war natürlich auch Ulk, Humor und Ironie drin, aber eben auch dieser Unterton. Einstein war ja zum Beispiel auch mit einer hochbegabten Physikerin zusammen. Vielen Wissenschaftlern wurde von Frauen assistiert, zum Teil werden die Erfindungen sogar von diesen gemacht, ihnen werden sie aber nicht zugeschrieben. Sowas passiert natürlich auch in der Malerei.

R.H.:
1982 hast du in der Hamburger Buch Handlung Welt, die ein Kunstprojekt von Hilka Nordhausen war, ein Gemälde gezeigt, das die Aufschrift „Ich mach Frauenkunst" trägt, daneben eine Frau im Nachthemd. Ähnlich offensiv und ironisch thematisiert zum Beispiel auch Christa Näher ihre Rolle als Malerin, etwa mit der Aufschrift „Frauen die malen, drücken sich vor der Arbeit" auf einer frühen Ausstellungseinladung. War es wichtig, die Marginalisierung von Frauen in der Malerei ganz direkt und offensiv zu adressieren? Wie waren hier die Reaktionen?

B.S.:
Ja, auch bei der Frau im Negligé, die bei Hilka auftauchte, geht es um eine Analogie zwischen der „Kunst" der Prostitution und der Malerei, also der Anpreisung des eigenen Körpers und der Darbietung des Malereikörpers, wie sie in den Reeperbahn-Gemälden Thema war. Dazu habe ich gerade wieder die Bücher aufgeschlagen, in denen es um eine heilige Sexualität geht, bevor diese der Scham und Kriminalisierung ausgesetzt wurde: *Sacred Sex, The Sacred Prostitute, Die Göttin und ihr Heros* und so weiter.

Die Reaktionen waren Unverständnis, Kopfschütteln, vielleicht heimlich auch Bewunderung für den Mut, ausgedrückt als Verächtlichmachung. Es war eine so kuriose Mischung, man kann es gar nicht beschreiben. Was war gute Malerei

distance, things can be assessed much better. But people's evaluation back then followed different rules. It's always about the evaluation. Positive criticism enabled you to continue; negative criticism made you falter and give up. I think that's the reason why women didn't end up in the exhibitions. Up to 95 percent of the listings of the time are occupied by male names. This was especially the case in Germany, while it was much easier to succeed as a woman in the United States or Great Britain. That's also why my shows in the 1980s were in London, New York, Seville, Zurich, Graz, but not in Cologne.

R.H.:

Yes, that's a decisive point. Young figurative painting from Germany was primarily associated with cliques of male painters. This can also be seen in early group shows like *10 junge Künstler aus Deutschland* by Zdenek Felix or *12 Künstler aus Deutschland* by Jean-Christophe Ammann. There were only male artists shown. Of course there were female artists in the Neue Wilde's milieu, such as G. L. Gabriel-Thieler, who was part of the Galerie am Moritzplatz; Elvira Bach, Christa Näher, and Ina Barfuss, who likewise lived in Berlin in the early 1980s; or Bettina Sefkow, who was active in the milieu around Buch Handlung Welt and studied with both Karl Horst Hödicke and Polke. Some women—albeit only a few—participated in the self-organized shows that came before the institutional group exhibitions; for example, in *Elend* [Misery], *Aktion Pisskrücke. Geheimdienst am Nächsten* [Action Piss Crutch: Secret Service on Your Neighbor], and *Finger für Deutschland* [Finger for Germany], there was Hilka Nordhausen or Brigitta Rohrbach, who didn't paint but showed photographic works. Peter and Irene Ludwig didn't acquire works by any of these artists for their collection in the 1980s. This of course also had to do with the fact that the Ludwigs acquired works of the so-called Neue Wilde through Galerie Max Hetzler and Galerie Paul Maenz, or the older generation—Baselitz, Lüpertz, Penck, Immendorff—through Galerie Werner. None of them represented any of these female painters in their program.

B.S.:

Yes, galleries are an important point. The way I perceived it, the system in Hamburg was such that the teachers and established artists recommended their favorites to their gallerists. So that way, the men usually stuck with each other. Rosemarie Trockel, for example, was able to make it because she worked closely with Monika Sprüth and her gallery in Cologne. Rosemarie was very autonomous and that helped.

R.H.:

Despite their associations with the various groups of painters, the female artists often appeared to adopt individual positions. What was the situation like for you back then—especially given your friendship with Albert Oehlen, Martin Kippenberger, and company? And how did you get to know the artists?

überhaupt noch? Worum ging es? Die Männer besetzten ja bewusst Positionen schlechter Malerei, wenn eine Frau das aber tat, so war es schlechte Malerei. Wobei ja vieles heute, aus einem gewissen Abstand betrachtet, wirklich besser beurteilt werden kann, aber Bewertung lief damals nach anderen Regeln. Es geht immer um Bewertung, und die positive Kritik führte dazu, dass man weitermachen konnte, die negative führte oft zum Stocken und Aufhören. Das ist meines Erachtens der Grund, warum die Frauen nicht in die Ausstellungen kamen, die Listen der Zeit sind zu 95 Prozent von männlichen Namen besetzt. Diese Tendenz gilt besonders für Deutschland, während es in den USA und Großbritannien einfacher war, als Frau zu reüssieren. Weshalb ja auch meine Ausstellungen in den 1980er-Jahren in London, New York, Sevilla, Zürich, Graz stattfanden, aber nicht in Köln.

R.H.:

Ja, das ist ein entscheidender Punkt. Die junge figurative Malerei aus Deutschland war damals in erster Linie mit männlichen Malercliquen verbunden. Das zeigt sich auch in frühen Gruppenausstellungen wie *10 junge Künstler aus Deutschland* von Zdenek Felix oder *12 Künstler aus Deutschland* von Jean-Christophe Ammann. Hier waren ausschließlich männliche Künstler zu sehen. Natürlich gab es Künstlerinnen im Umfeld der Neuen Wilden, zum Beispiel G. L. Gabriel-Thieler, die Teil der Galerie am Moritzplatz war, Elvira Bach, Christa Näher und Ina Barfuss, die Anfang der 1980er-Jahre ebenfalls in Berlin lebten, oder Bettina Sefkow, die sich im Umfeld der Buch Handlung Welt bewegte und sowohl bei Karl Horst Hödicke als auch bei Polke studiert hatte. Auch an einigen selbstorganisierten Schauen, die vor den institutionellen Gruppenausstellungen stattfanden, zum Beispiel *Elend, Aktion Pisskrücke. Geheimdienst am Nächsten* oder *Finger für Deutschland*, nahmen – wenn auch wenige – Künstlerinnen teil, zum Beispiel Hilka Nordhausen oder Brigitta Rohrbach, die allerdings nicht malte, sondern dort Fotoarbeiten zeigte. Von keiner dieser Künstlerinnen haben Peter und Irene Ludwig in den 1980er-Jahren Werke für ihre Sammlung erworben. Das liegt natürlich auch daran, dass die Ludwigs die sogenannten Neuen Wilden bei der Galerie Max Hetzler oder der Galerie Paul Maenz erwarben, oder die ältere Generation – Baselitz, Lüpertz, Penck, Immendorff – bei der Galerie Werner, die eben diese Malerinnen alle nicht im Programm hatten.

B.S.:

Ja, Galerien sind da natürlich ein wichtiger Punkt. Das System in Hamburg habe ich so wahrgenommen, dass die Lehrer oder die schon erfolgreichen Künstler ihren Galeristen ihre Lieblinge empfahlen. Und da blieben die Männer dann eben doch oft unter sich. Rosemarie Trockel zum Beispiel hat es dann geschafft, weil sie mit Monika Sprüth und deren Galerie in Köln eng zusammengearbeitet hat. Rosemarie war sehr autonom, das hat sehr geholfen.

R.H.:

Trotz verschiedener Verbindungen mit den Malergruppen traten die Künstlerinnen also doch eher als Einzelpositionen auf. Wie war die Situation für dich damals –

B.S.:
I first met Kippenberger briefly through his Büro in Berlin in 1978 or 1979. We even danced together at S.O.36. It was through my boyfriend at the time, the filmmaker Klaus Wyborny. I met Albert Oehlen, Werner Büttner, and Georg Herold at the academy in Hamburg. Martin Kippenberger showed up again later on when we visited Max Hetzler in Stuttgart.

The first thing my gallerist Ascan Crone—who I got to know when he was interested in Albert, my boyfriend at the time—asked me was, "Are you also an artist?" I was very pleased. For him I was immediately more than just the "girlfriend of..." and he started exhibiting my work in 1984. Albert and I also painted together: on large sheets of packing paper, the motifs and techniques developed spontaneously.

R.H.:
And how was the support from your male artist colleagues?

B.S.:
You couldn't expect any collegial solidarity. Kippenberger, for example, saw everybody as a buddy to play with, but also as competition. There wasn't any trust at all. Instead, everyone was up against each other, constantly undermining each other and filling each other with doubt. Filling people with doubt was one of Kippenberger's favorite strategies anyway. It was "survival of the fittest." If you could assert yourself in the face of all that, and keep on painting, then you were good. Angelika Oehms and Hilka Nordhausen must also have suffered under this situation. The structural situation was so full of adversities, sexism in every form.

I had to listen to things like, "You're a pretty woman, why do you have to paint pretty pictures too," or, "You've got an amazing painter at your side, why do you want paint as well?" The list could go on endlessly.

R.H.:
Women, however, played a major role as mediators and organizers, such as Monika Sprüth, whom you mentioned earlier, Gisela Capitain, and Hilka Nordhausen. With Buch Handlung Welt, Nordhausen was an important hub for a lot of people. At the same time, she was also an artist.

B.S.:
Yes, Hilka was close friends with the men and was at the center of things. As an artist, she wasn't so well received. She wrote poems, drew, and made pictures. That was difficult for people. They needed things to be clear. Poems and paintings and so on, and then a woman who worked across so many different media, that was too much. Another really good ally was Rosemarie Trockel, who I just mentioned. I met her in Cologne in 1983–84. Kippenberger was a big admirer of hers and introduced us. I can clearly remember him saying, "She makes women's art, vases and such" [*laughs*]. She was allied with Monika

gerade auch durch deine Freundschaft mit Albert Oehlen, Martin Kippenberger und Co.? Und wie hast du die Künstler kennengelernt?

B.S.:

Kippenberger kannte ich zuerst flüchtig aus seinem Büro in Berlin 1978 oder 79, wir hatten sogar mal ein Tänzchen hingelegt im S.O.36, das kam durch meinen damaligen Freund, den Filmemacher Klaus Wyborny. Albert Oehlen und Werner Büttner wie auch Georg Herold lernte ich an der Hochschule in Hamburg kennen, später kam auch Martin Kippenberger wieder dazu, als wir Max Hetzler in Stuttgart besuchten.

Mein Galerist Ascan Crone, den ich kennenlernte, als er sich für Albert, meinen damaligen Freund, interessierte, fragte mich übrigens als Erstes: „Sind Sie auch Künstlerin?" Was mich sehr gefreut hat. Für ihn war ich sofort mehr als nur die „Freundin von...", 1984 begann er mich dann auszustellen. Albert und ich haben übrigens auch gemeinsam gemalt: auf große Bögen Packpapier, die Motive und Techniken entstanden spontan.

R.H.:

Und wie stand es mit der Unterstützung der männlichen Künstlerkollegen?

B.S.:

Da konnte man keine kollegiale Solidarität erwarten. Kippenberger hat einen zum Beispiel als Kumpel, aber immer auch als Konkurrenz gesehen. Es war überhaupt kein Vertrauen, sondern in erster Linie ein Gegeneinander und ein ständiges Untergraben und Verunsichern, Verunsichern war ja sowieso eine von Kippenbergers liebsten Strategien. Es war wie *survival of the fittest*. Wenn man sich dagegen durchsetzen und weitermalen konnte, dann war man gut. Auch Angelika Oehms oder Hilka Nordhausen haben sicherlich unter dieser Situation gelitten. Die strukturelle Situation war einfach so voller Widrigkeiten, Sexismus in jeder Form.

Ich habe Sätze zu hören bekommen wie „Du bist doch 'ne schöne Frau, was willst du auch noch schöne Bilder malen" oder „Du hast doch einen tollen Maler an deiner Seite, was willst du auch noch Bilder malen". Die Liste nimmt kein Ende.

R.H.:

Eine wichtige Rolle spielten Frauen aber durchaus als Vermittlerinnen oder Organisatorinnen, wie zum Beispiel die von dir eben erwähnte Monika Sprüth, Gisela Capitain oder auch Hilka Nordhausen. Mit der Buch Handlung Welt war Nordhausen ja für viele ein wichtiger Knotenpunkt. Gleichzeitig war sie selbst aber auch Künstlerin.

B.S.:

Ja, Hilka war eng befreundet mit den Männern und war da auch im Mittelpunkt. Als Künstlerin wurde sie aber nicht so beachtet, sie hat ja auch Gedichte geschrieben und gezeichnet und Bilder gemacht. Das war schon schwierig für die Leute, es musste immer eindeutig sein. Gedichte und Malerei und so weiter und dann noch eine Frau, die sich so vieler Medien ermächtigte, das war zu viel. Eine wirklich gute Verbündete war auch die eben erwähnte Rosemarie Trockel. Ich lernte sie in Köln 1983/84 kennen,

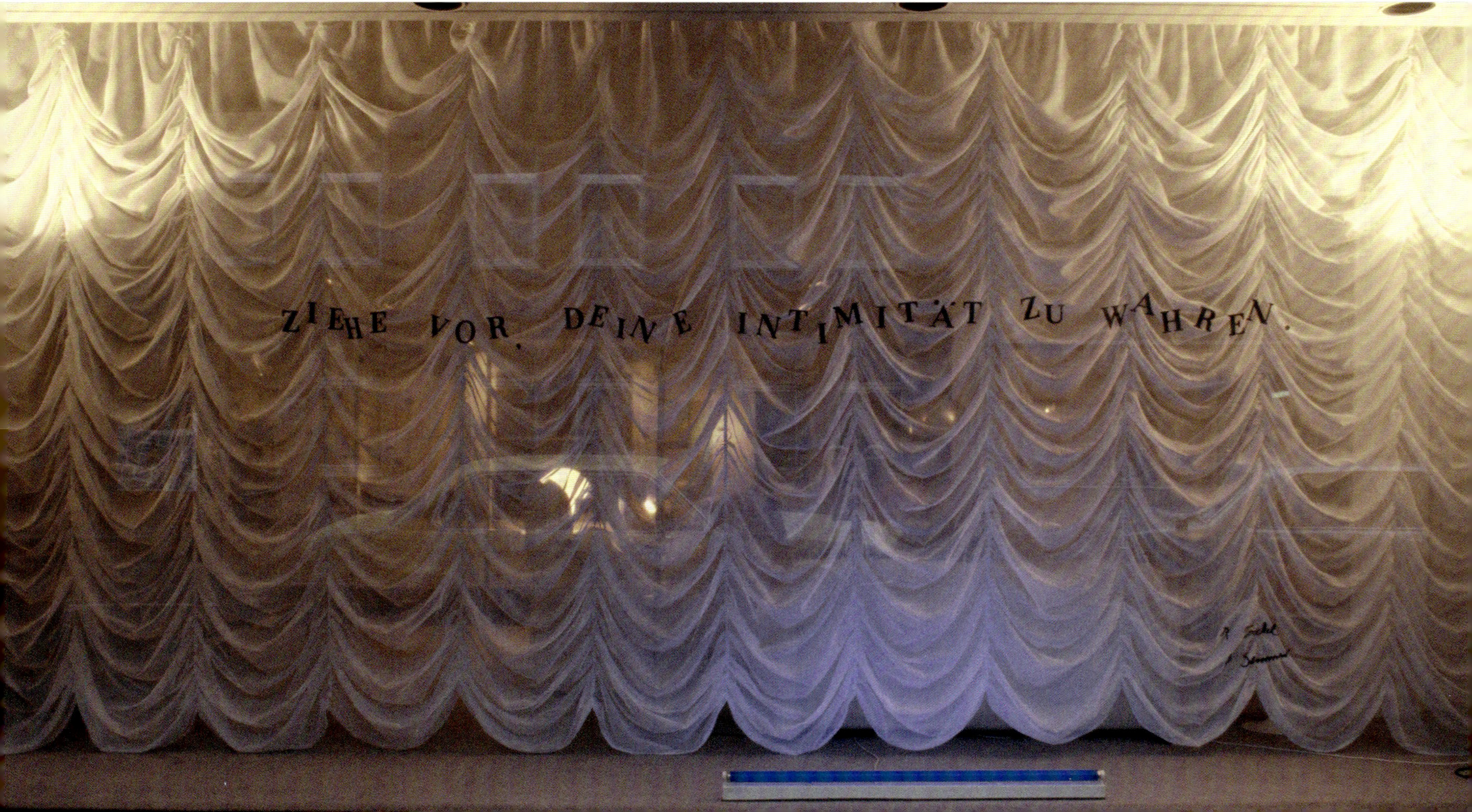
ZIEHE VOR, DEINE INTIMITÄT ZU WAHREN.

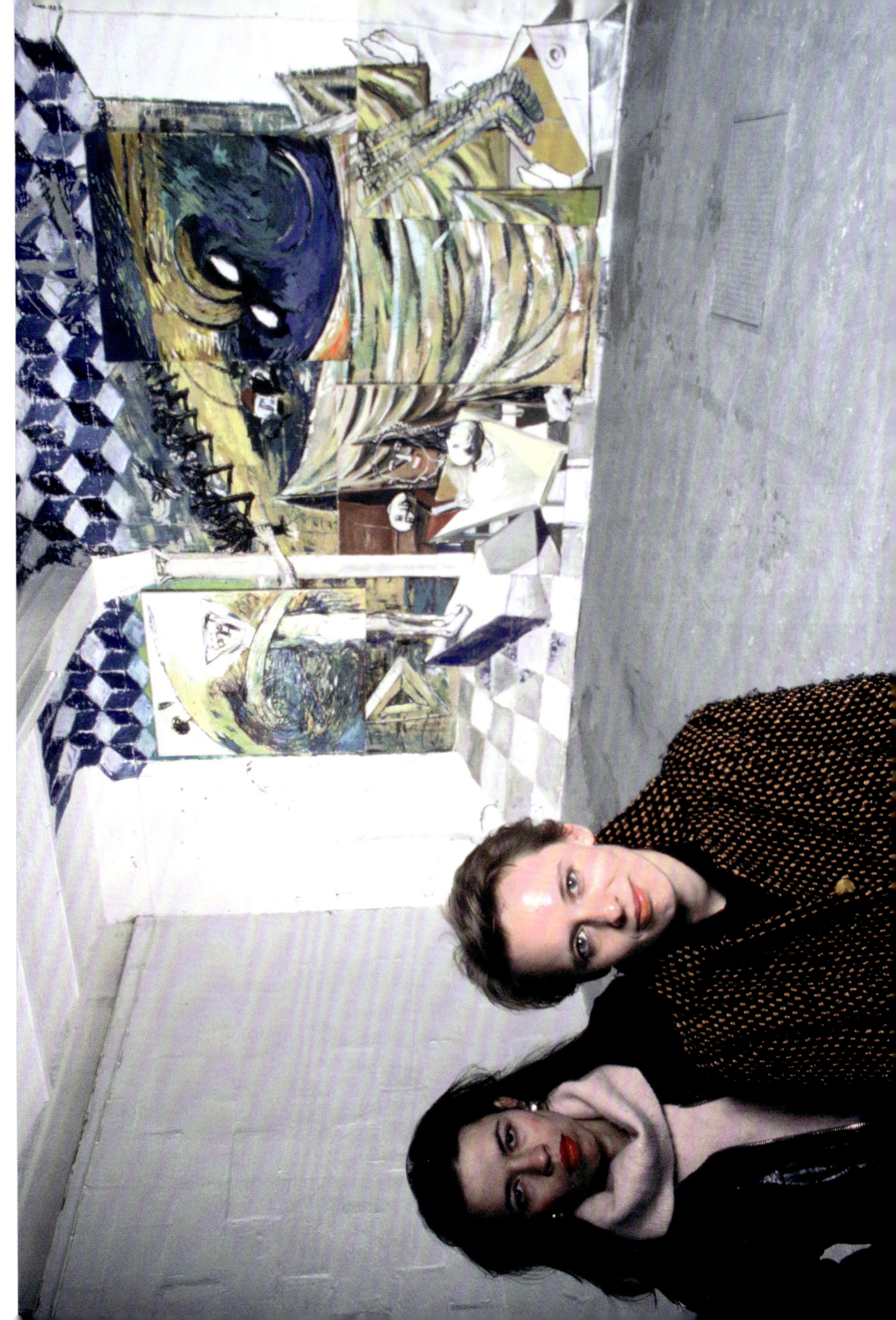

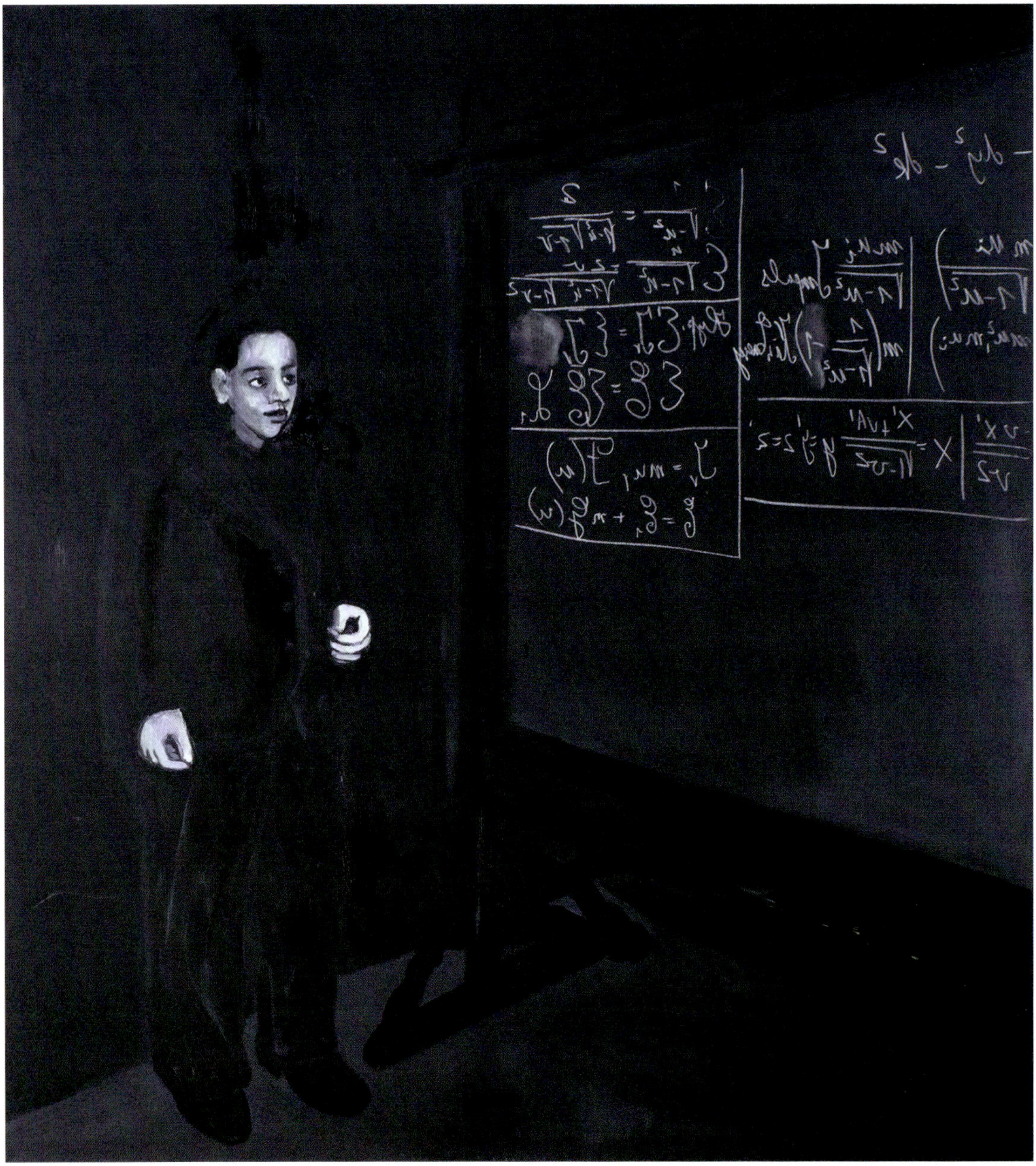

Bettina Semmer, *Einstein*, 1986, Öl und Kreide auf Leinwand / oil and chalk on canvas, 200 × 180 cm

Bettina Semmer, *Straßenmöbel / Poller*, 1985, Haushaltsfarbe und Öl auf Leinwand / household paint and oil on canvas, 190 × 155 cm

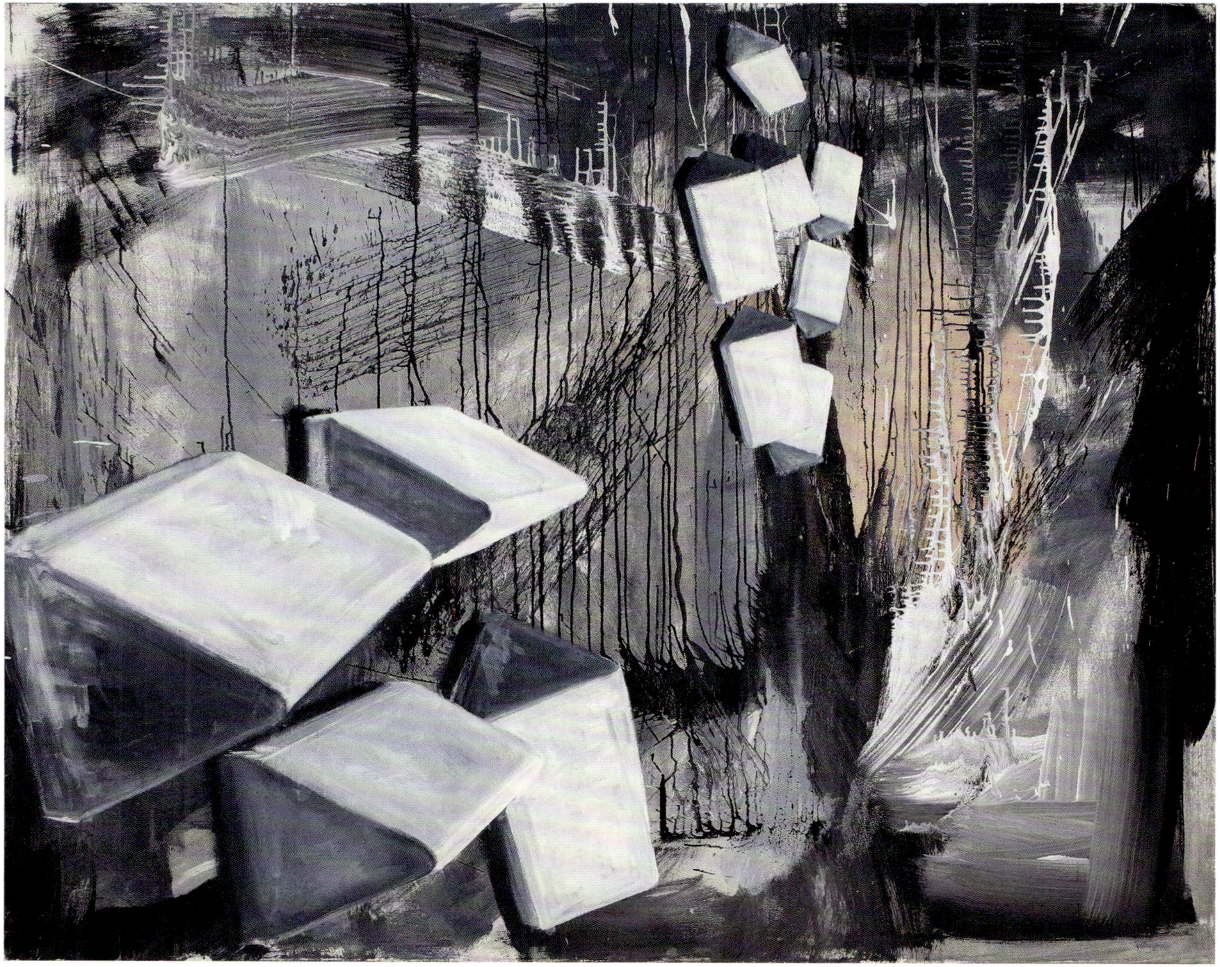

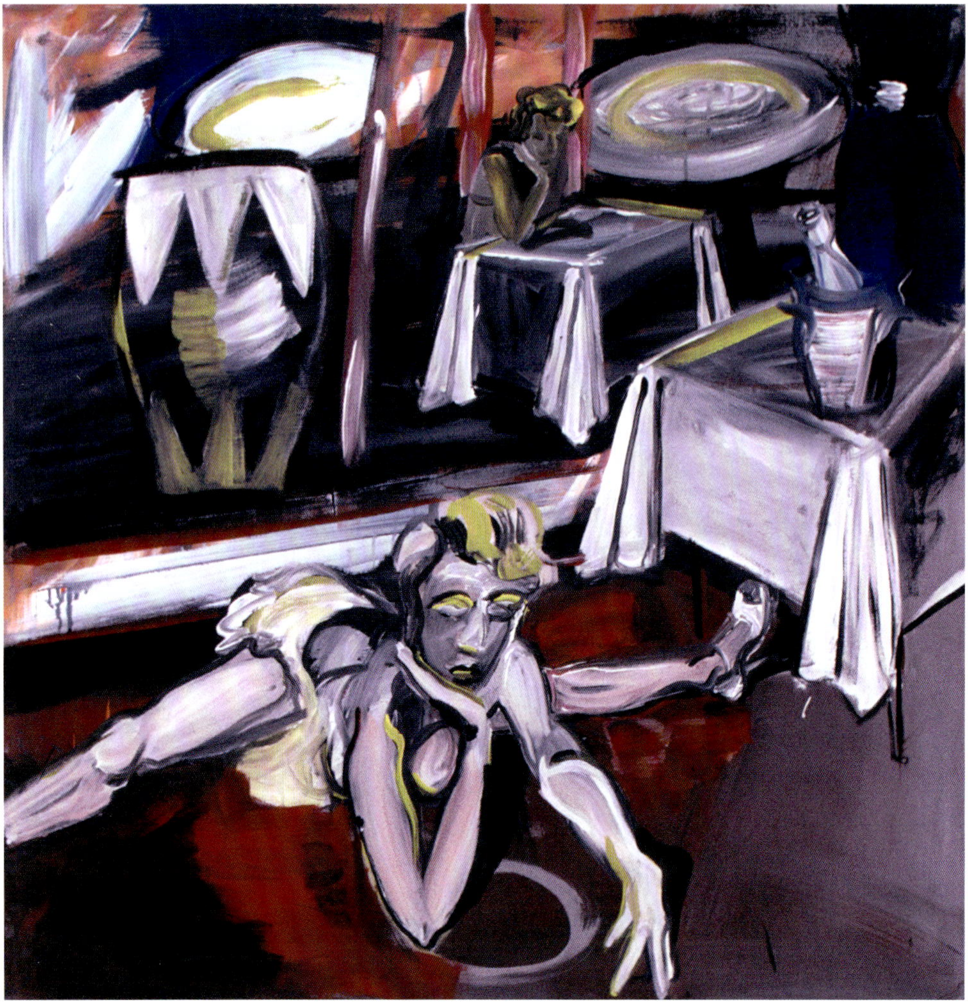

Bettina Semmer, *Reeperbahn Frauenkunst 3*, 1982, Acryl auf Leinwand / acrylic on canvas, 100 × 120 cm

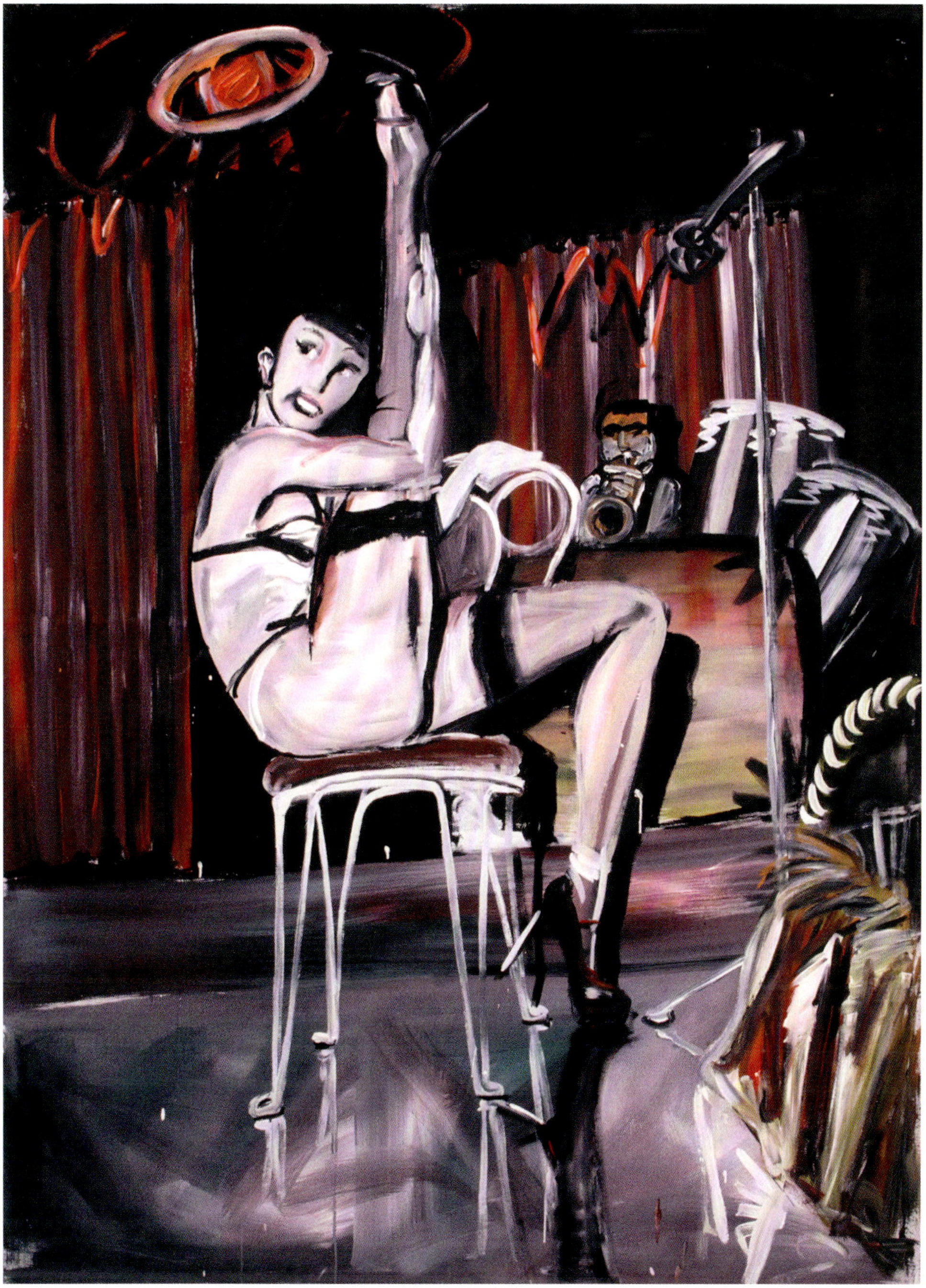

Bettina Semmer, *Reeperbahn Frauenkunst 1*, 1982, Acryl auf Leinwand / acrylic on canvas, 160 × 120 cm

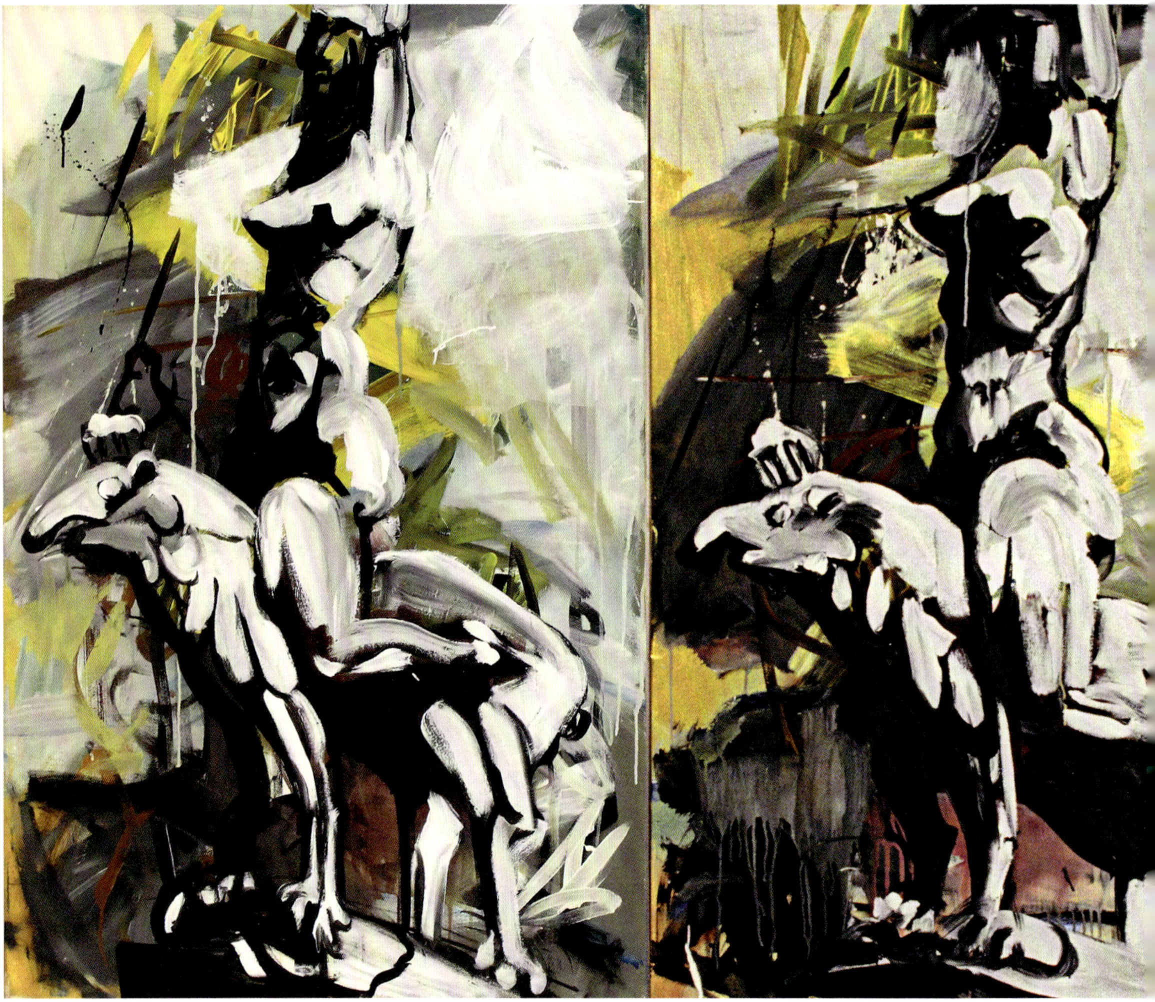

Bettina Semmer, *María Lionza*, 1981, Acryl auf Leinwand, 3-teilig / acrylic on canvas, 3 par

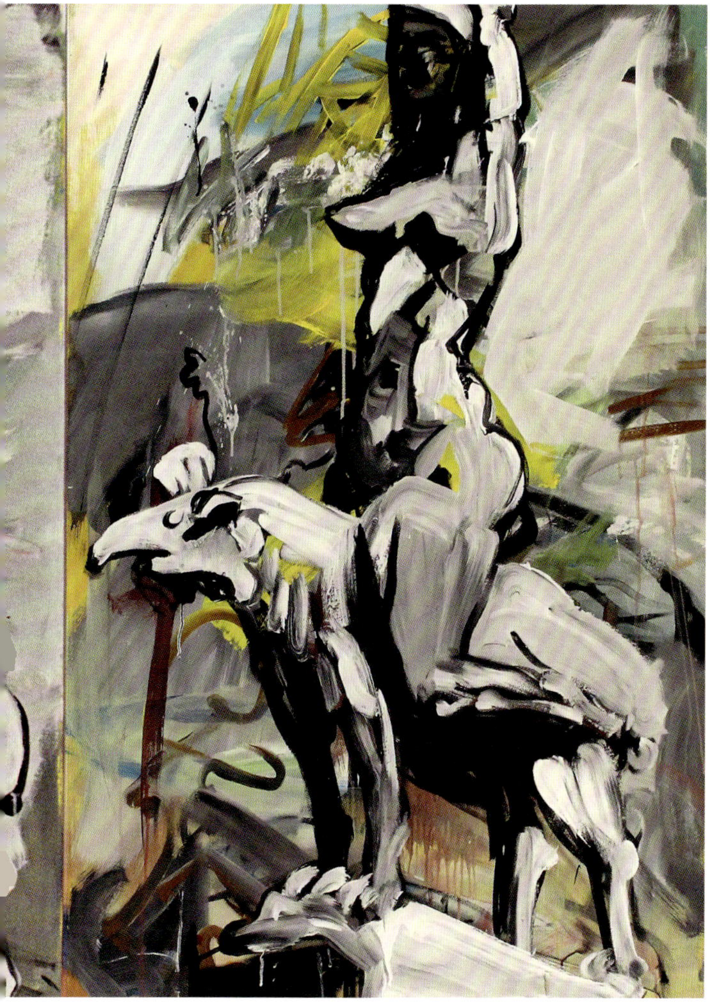

/ each 120 × 75 cm

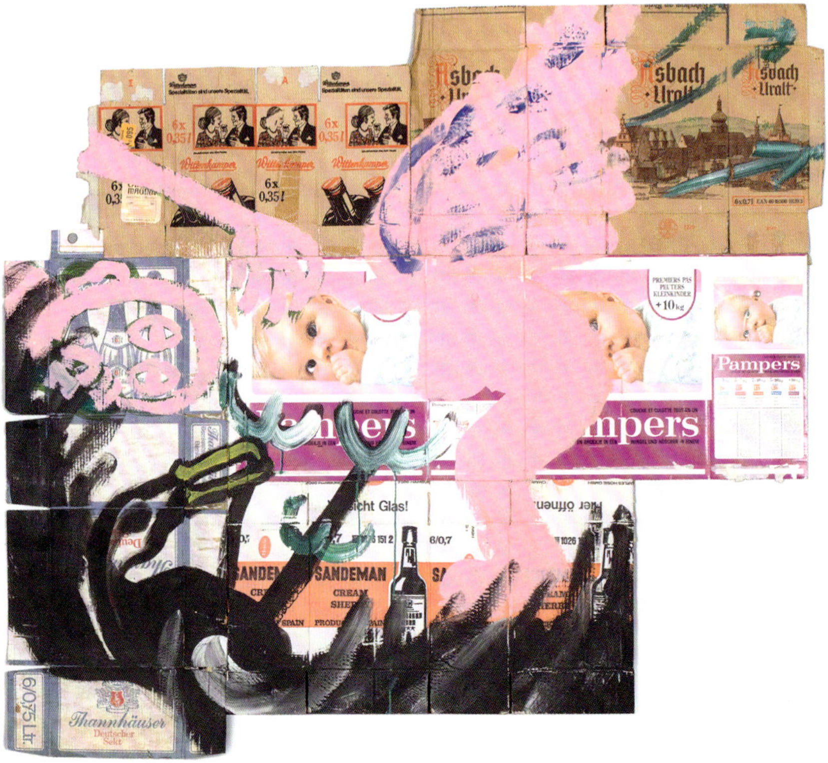

Hilka Nordhausen, *Ohne Titel (Baby Engel)*, 1980, Dispersionsfarbe auf Karton / dispersion paint on cardboard, ca. 150 × 170 cm

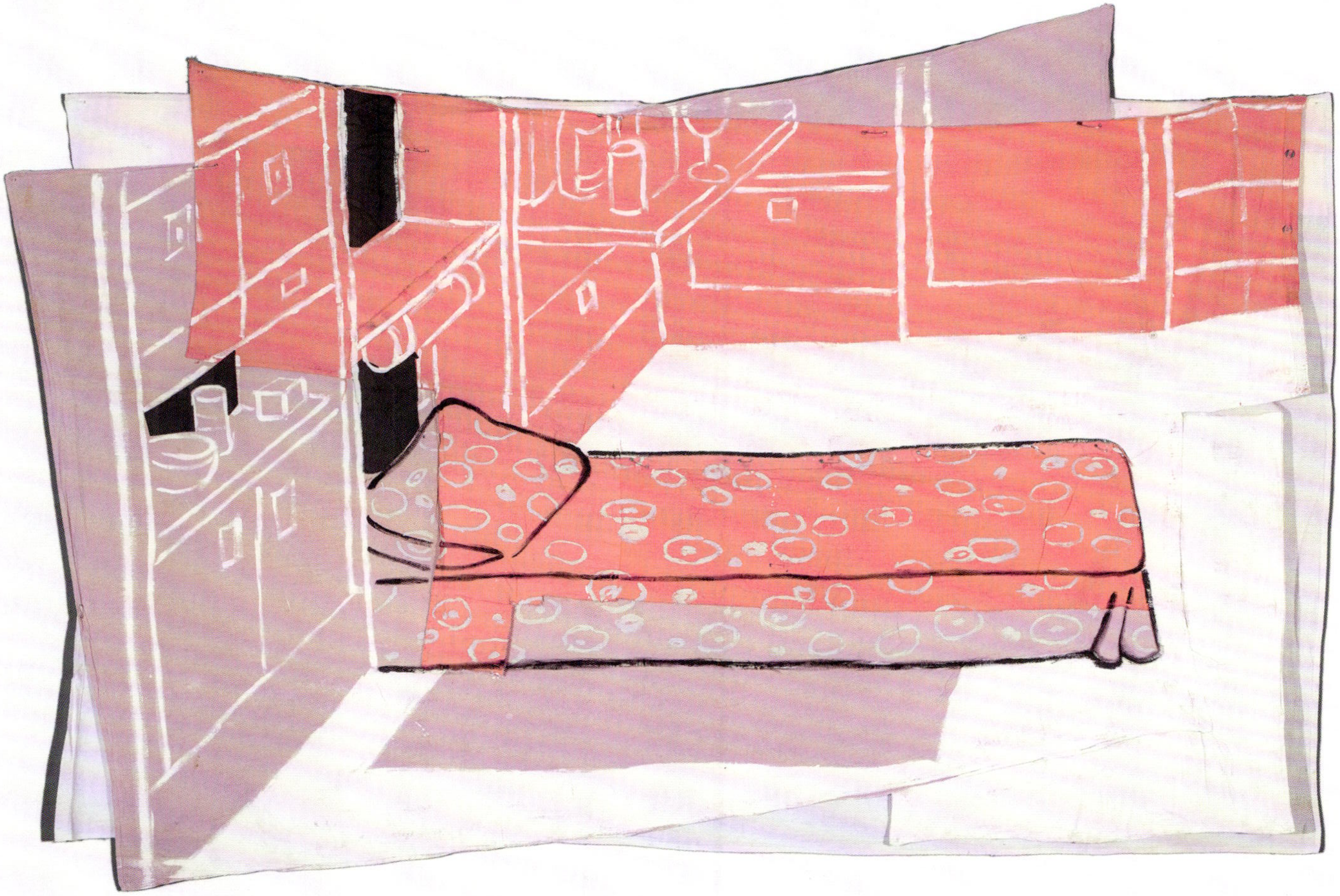

Bettina Semmer (?), *Das Bett*, 1978, Malerei und Collage auf Kommunebettlaken, Stoff, Wandfarbe, Papier / painting and collage on communal bed sheet, cloth, wall paint, paper, ca. 180 × 255 cm

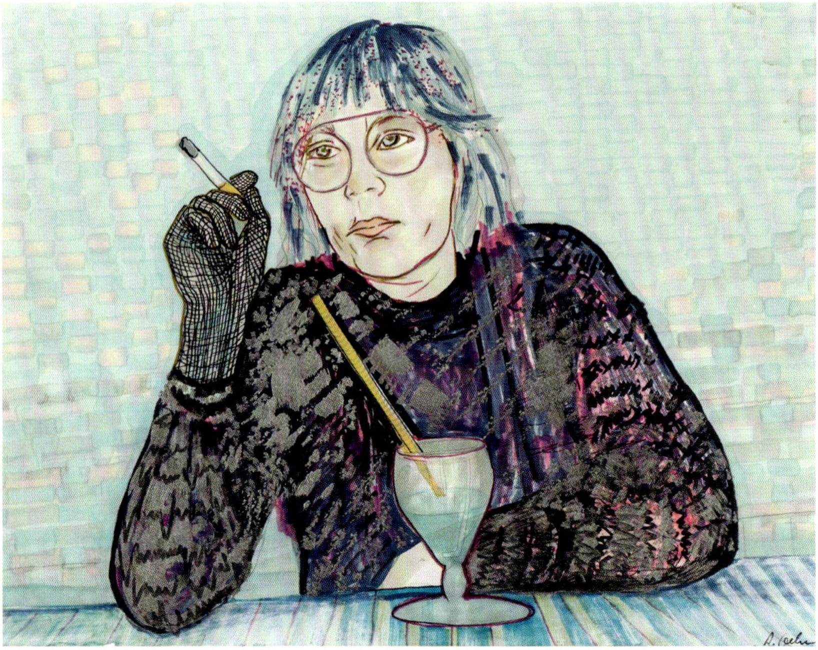

Angelika Oehms, *Hilka Nordhausen*, 1980, Filzstift auf Papier / felt-tip on paper, 29 × 39 cm

Peter Bömmels
Die Voraussetzung von Können ist das Nichtskönnen

Peter Bömmels
The precondition of competence is incompetence

Auszüge aus einem Gespräch mit den Herausgeber*innen /
Excerpts from a conversation with the editors, Berlin, April 2018

be neat and tidy, then it must have been like a slap in the face. [...]

When Paul Maenz and Jean-Christophe Ammann visited the exhibition in 1980, they immediately felt this energy. Maenz wanted a local troop of young artists for his gallery. That was like winning the lottery. Our first exhibition with him was called *Mülheimer Freiheit & Interessante Bilder aus Deutschland* [Mülheimer Freiheit & Interesting Pictures from Germany]. The title was coined by Wolfgang Max Faust, and so the name of our group was born. We thought it was great: the address of our studio, and anything associated with freedom was good in any case. From then on there were six of us, together with Gerard Kever and Gerhard Naschberger. Maenz told us that we needed to put the pictures on stretcher frames to sell them better. At first that was unimaginable for us. You can make money with art? But it was true! We lapped it up like manna from heaven. Suddenly contemporary art was in the headlines again, there was a long article in *Der Spiegel*, and the photographer from *Stern* visited the studio. Other gallerists also paid visits, for example Bruno Bischofberger from Switzerland. There was also resistance of course—in the *Frankfurter Rundschau* Peter Iden called us "light-hearted incompetents." I took it as a great compliment however. I understood that as "showing heart," for the precondition of competence is incompetence. One should always first try things that you can't do, otherwise you just keep going back to doing what you can, and nothing new or exceptional comes about. [...]

It was intoxicating at first, we painted incredible amounts. At the Kunstverein Freiburg we had so many paintings with us that we placed them against one another, like tents, like houses of cards. The whole space was full of pictures, but one couldn't look at them directly, it felt like being in a pinball machine. At the Kunstverein Wolfsburg we then didn't show any canvases at all. We only started thinking about what we were going to do on the way there. We came up with the obvious subject of "Cars and Sex" and painted pictures and texts directly on the walls. Five hours later we were finished and everyone was happy. Except for the Volkswagen managers, who avoided the room. For us it was a test to see if we could still motivate one another, spur each other on, try to outdo each other. A kind of homemade Situationism, you put yourself in an exciting situation and try to make something productive out of the mood. At some point, around 1982–83, Maenz said that he could only keep working with three of us—with Dahn, Dokoupil, and me. At that time the contact between us was no longer as close as it had been, and it was in any case obvious that everyone was going their own way. For me, the dissolving of the group form came too early, but the others thought differently. The friction between the group-ego and the self-ego really appealed to me. [...]

Spex was a "do-it-yourself" political project. Gerald Hündgen and I had the idea to use the punk and new wave movement and our own enthusiasm for

junger Maler haben für seine Galerie. Das war für uns wie ein Sechser im Lotto. Unsere erste Ausstellung bei ihm hieß *Mülheimer Freiheit & Interessante Bilder aus Deutschland*. Der Titel kam von Wolfgang Max Faust, und damit war auch der Name unserer Gruppe geboren. Wir fanden das toll: die Adresse unseres Ateliers, und alles mit Freiheit war sowieso gut. Ab da waren wir zu sechst, zusammen mit Gerard Kever und Gerhard Naschberger. Maenz hat uns damals gesagt, wir sollten die Bilder auf Keilrahmen aufziehen, um sie besser verkaufen zu können. Zunächst war es für uns unvorstellbar, dass man mit Kunst Geld verdienen konnte, aber es war so! Wir nahmen's hin wie Manna. Die bildende Kunst war plötzlich in den Schlagzeilen, im *Spiegel* stand ein langer Artikel, und der Fotograf des *Stern* kam ins Atelier. Uns besuchten andere Galeristen, wie zum Beispiel Bruno Bischofberger aus der Schweiz. Natürlich kam auch Gegenwind – Peter Iden nannte uns in der *Frankfurter Rundschau* „Hochgemute Nichtskönner". Das fand ich allerdings ein tolles Kompliment. Ich habe das als „Mut" verstanden, die Voraussetzung von Können ist ja das Nichtskönnen. Man sollte versuchen, erstmal wieder nichts zu können, sonst kommt man immer nur zu dem zurück, was man kann, da entsteht nichts Neues oder Außergewöhnliches. [...]

Die erste Zeit war wie ein Rausch, wir haben unglaublich viel gemalt. Im Kunstverein Freiburg hatten wir zu viele Bilder mit, da haben wir die einfach gegeneinander gestellt, wie Zelte, wie Kartenhäuser. Der ganze Raum war voller Bilder, aber man konnte sie nicht direkt betrachten, es war ein Gefühl wie im Flipper. Im Kunstverein Wolfsburg haben wir dann gar keine Leinwände gezeigt. Wir haben uns erst während der Fahrt dahin überlegt, was wir machen. Wir gaben uns das naheliegende Thema „Autos und Sex" und malten vor Ort Bilder und Texte direkt auf die Wände. Innerhalb von fünf Stunden waren wir fertig und alle waren zufrieden. Außer den VW-Managern, die den Raum mieden. Für uns war das ein Test, ob man sich untereinander noch motivieren kann, sich anfeuern kann, sich übertreffen will. Eine Art selbstgebastelter Situationismus, man versetzt sich in eine aufregende Situation und versucht, diese Stimmung produktiv zu machen. Irgendwann, um 1982/83 rum, hat Maenz gesagt, er kann nur noch mit dreien von uns weiterarbeiten – mit Dahn, Dokoupil und mir. Zu der Zeit war der Kontakt zwischen uns schon nicht mehr eng, und es war auch klar, dass jeder den eigenen Weg geht. Ich fand die Auflösung der Gruppenform zu früh, aber die anderen fanden's nicht. Mich reizte die Reibung zwischen Gruppen-Ego und Selbst-Ego. [...]

Die *Spex* war ein autodidaktisches, politisches Projekt. Die Idee von Gerald Hündgen und mir war es, auf der Basis der Punk- und New-Wave-Bewegung und der eigenen Musikbegeisterung ein teilnehmendes Forum als Zeitschrift aufzubauen, ähnlich den Stadtmagazinen. Ursprung war die alte linke Idee der Gegenöffentlichkeit, selber etwas in die Öffentlichkeit tragen, was sonst nirgendwo zu lesen war. Diese Zeitschrift sollte uns gehören, denen, die das machen, die Idee des Selbstverlages also. Im September 1980 erschien die erste Ausgabe. Wir waren alle Autodidakt*innen.

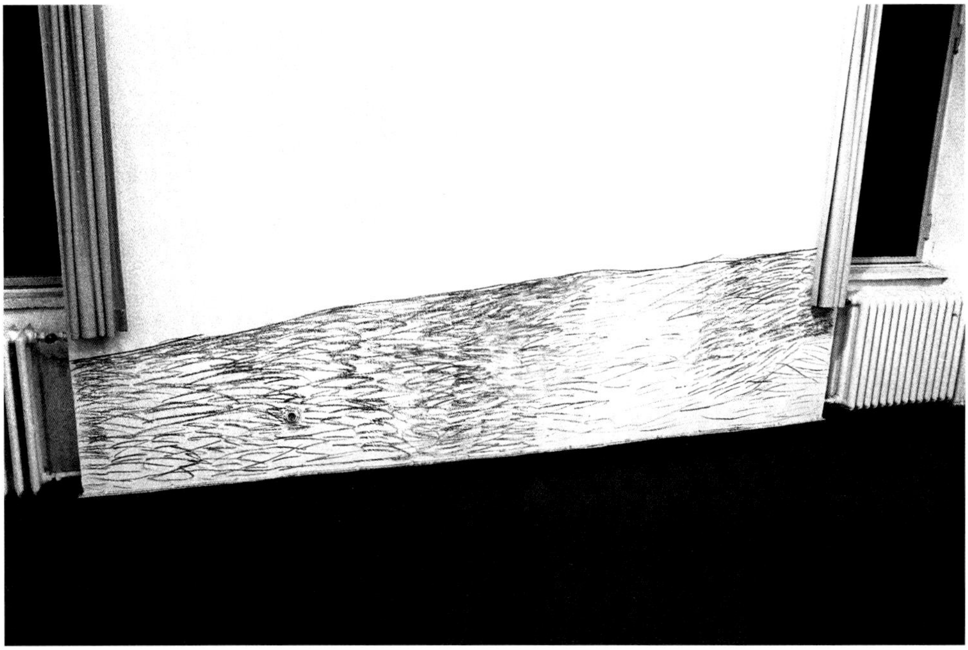

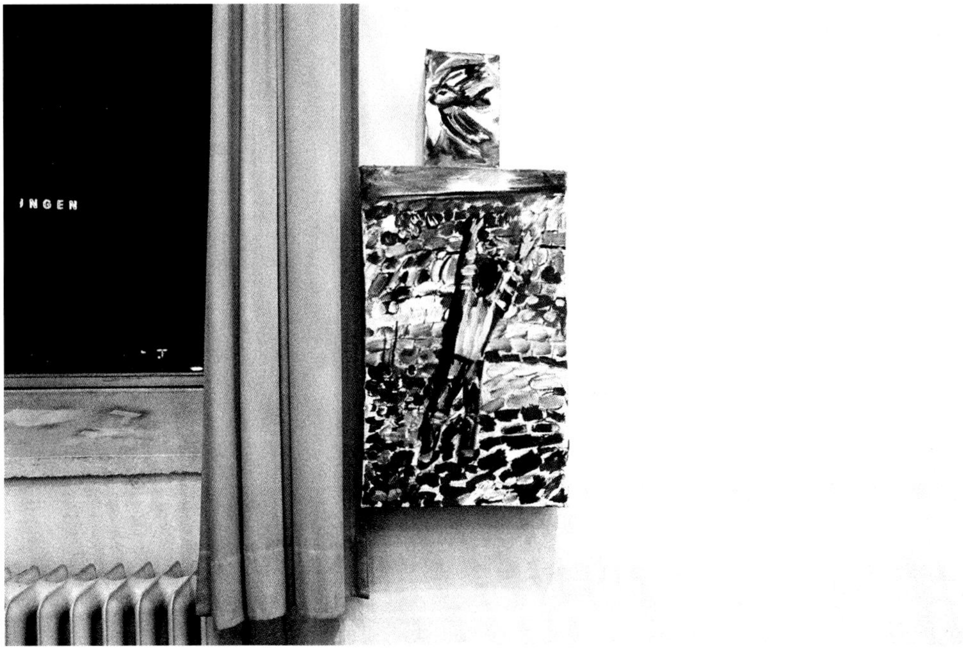

Auch wenn das Perlhuhn leise weint, BBK Hahnentorburg, Köln / Cologne, 1980, Fotos / photos: Lothar Schnepf

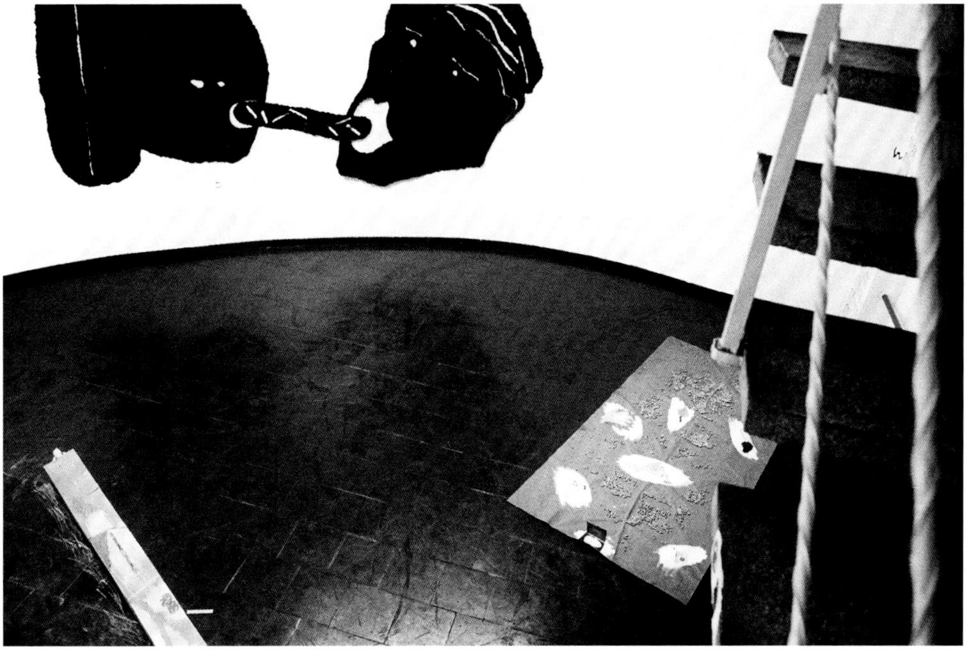

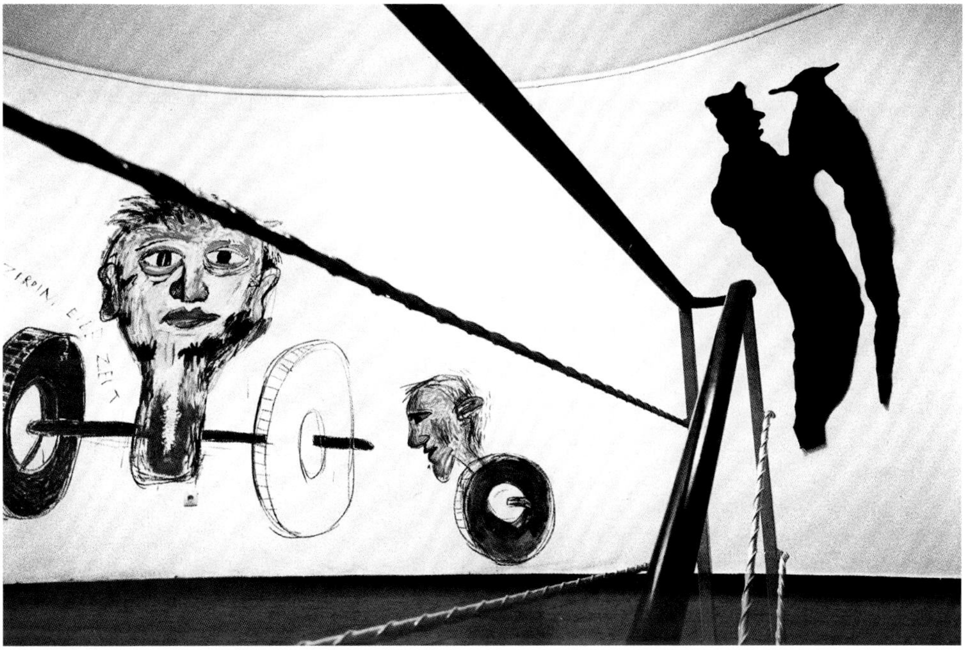
ZEIT

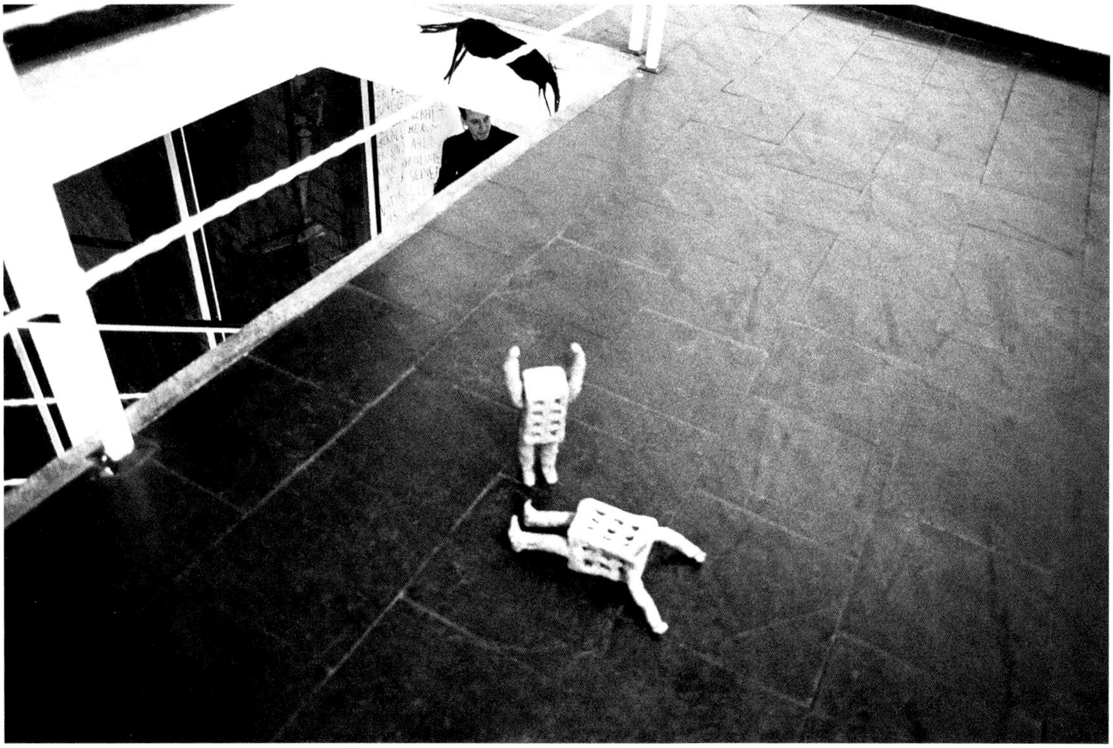

Auch wenn das Perlhuhn leise weint, BBK Hahnentorburg, Köln / Cologne, 1980,
Fotos / photos: Lothar Schnepf

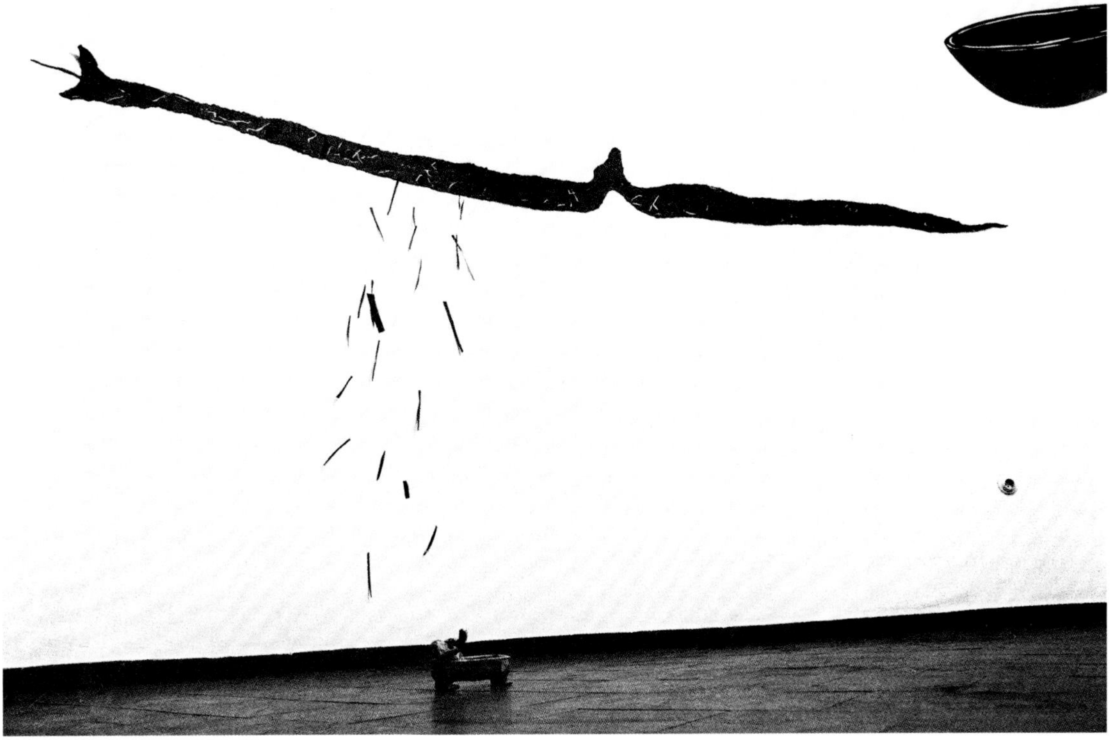

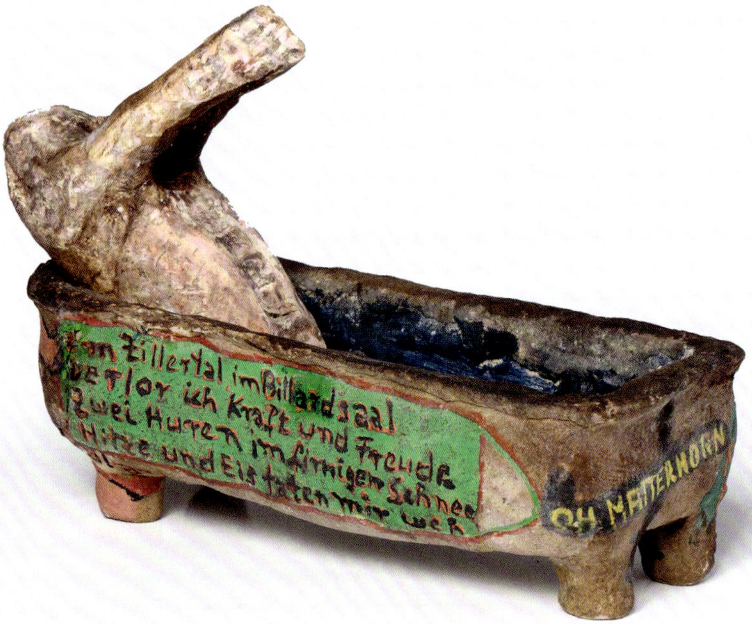

Peter Bömmels, *Betendes Brot in der Badewanne*, 1979, bemaltes Fimo / painted polymer clay, 13 × 22,5 × 8,5 cm

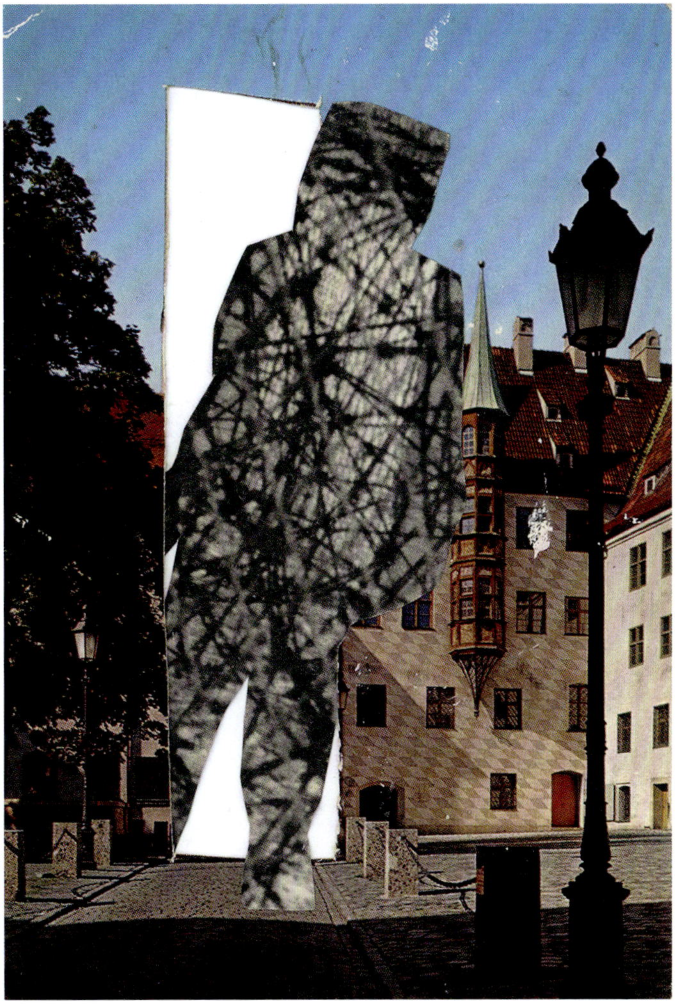

Peter Bommels, *Ohne Titel*, 1978, collagierte Ansichtskarte / collage postcard, 14,5 × 10 cm

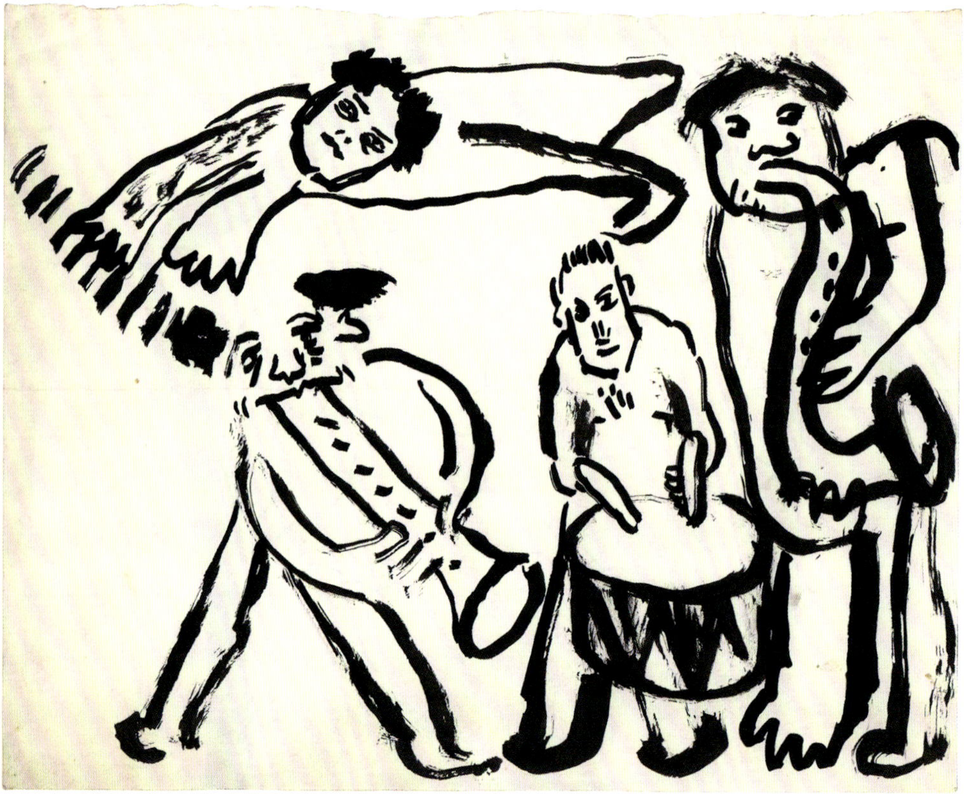

Jiří Georg Dokoupil, *Ohne Titel (The Wirtschaftswunder)*, 1982, Tusche auf Papier / India ink on paper, 23,4 × 29,5 cm

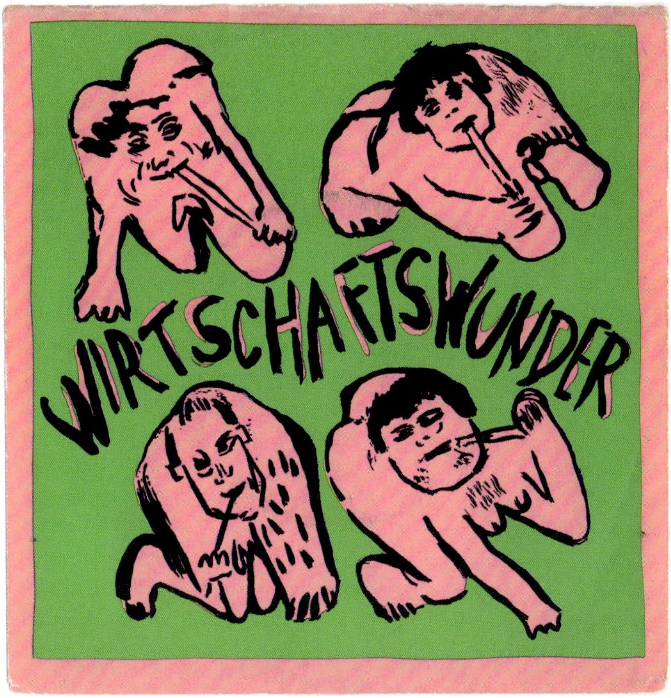

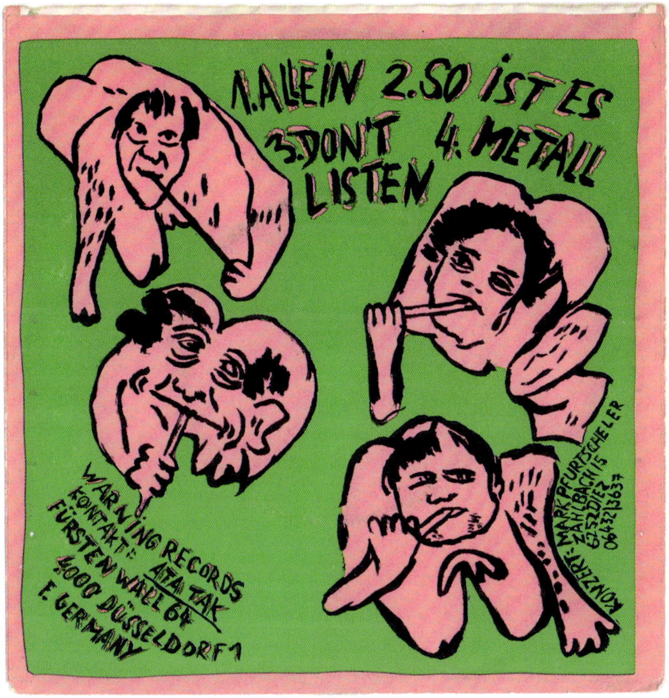

The Wirtschaftswunder, *Allein*, 1980, Single, Warning Records, Düsseldorf,
Design: Jiří Georg Dokoupil

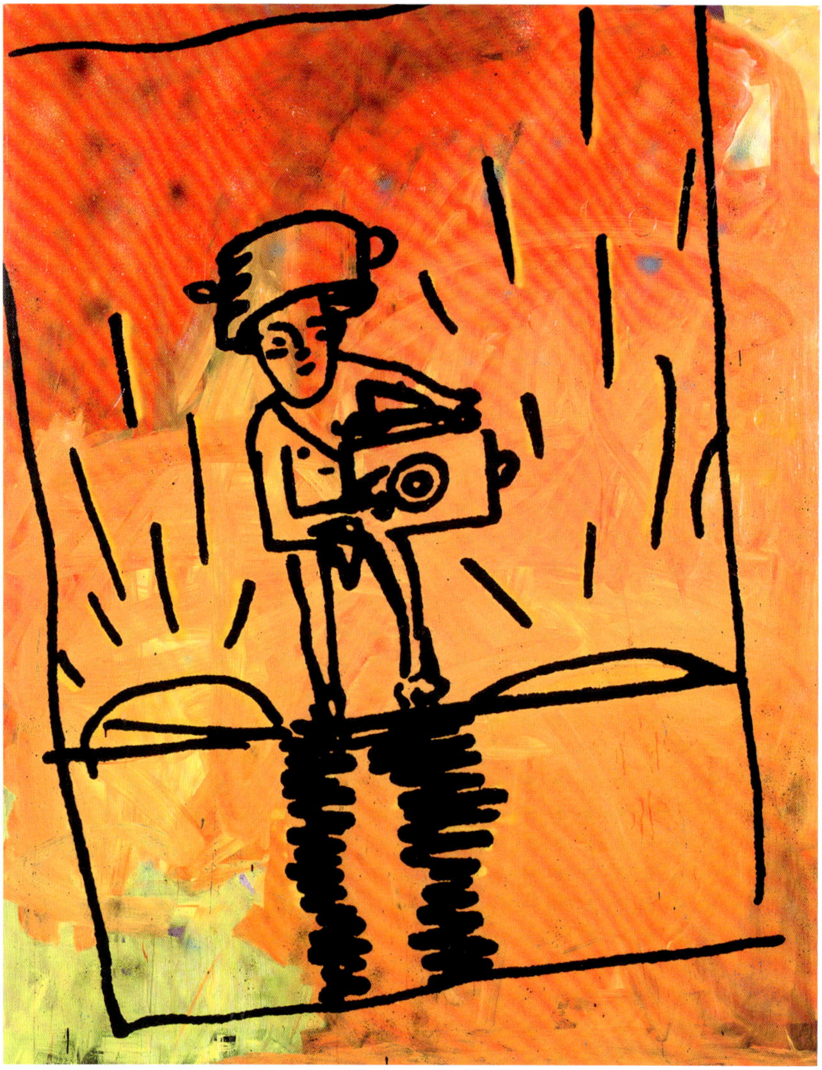

Walter Dahn, *Ohne Titel (Der Fotograf)*, 1986, Acryl, Siebdruck und Schellack auf Leinwand / acrylic, silkscreen, and shellac on canvas, 250 × 200 cm

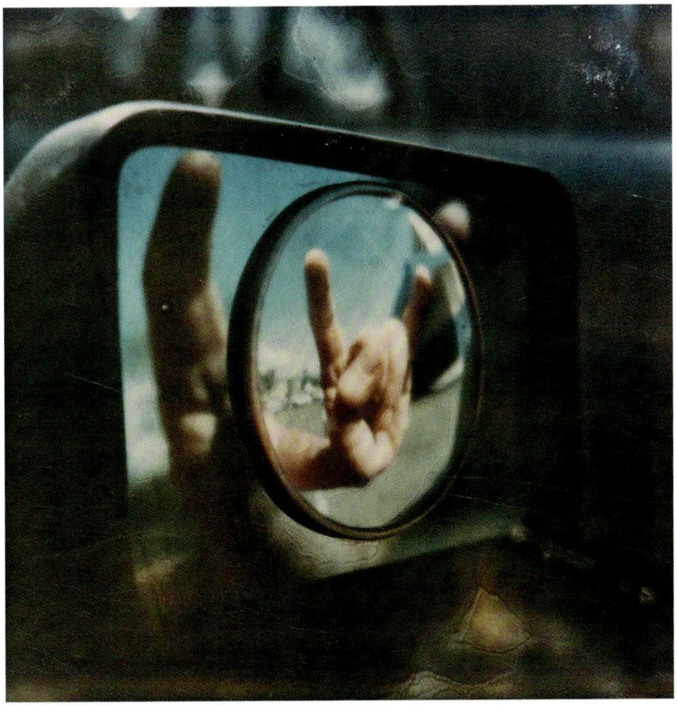

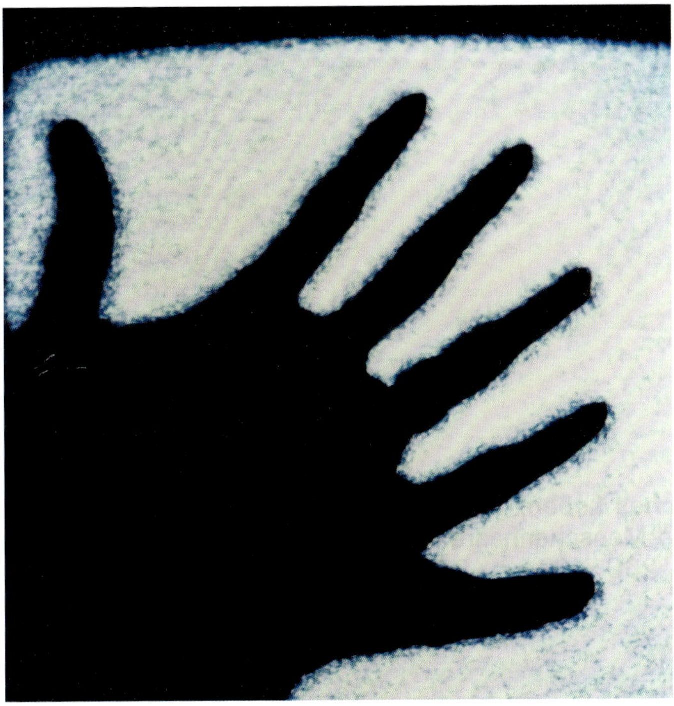

Walter Dahn, *Ein Riese füttert einen hungrigen Zwerg*, 1984/87, C-Print, 50 × 50 cm
Walter Dahn, *Mögliche Fernsicht*, 1986, C-Print, 50 × 50 cm

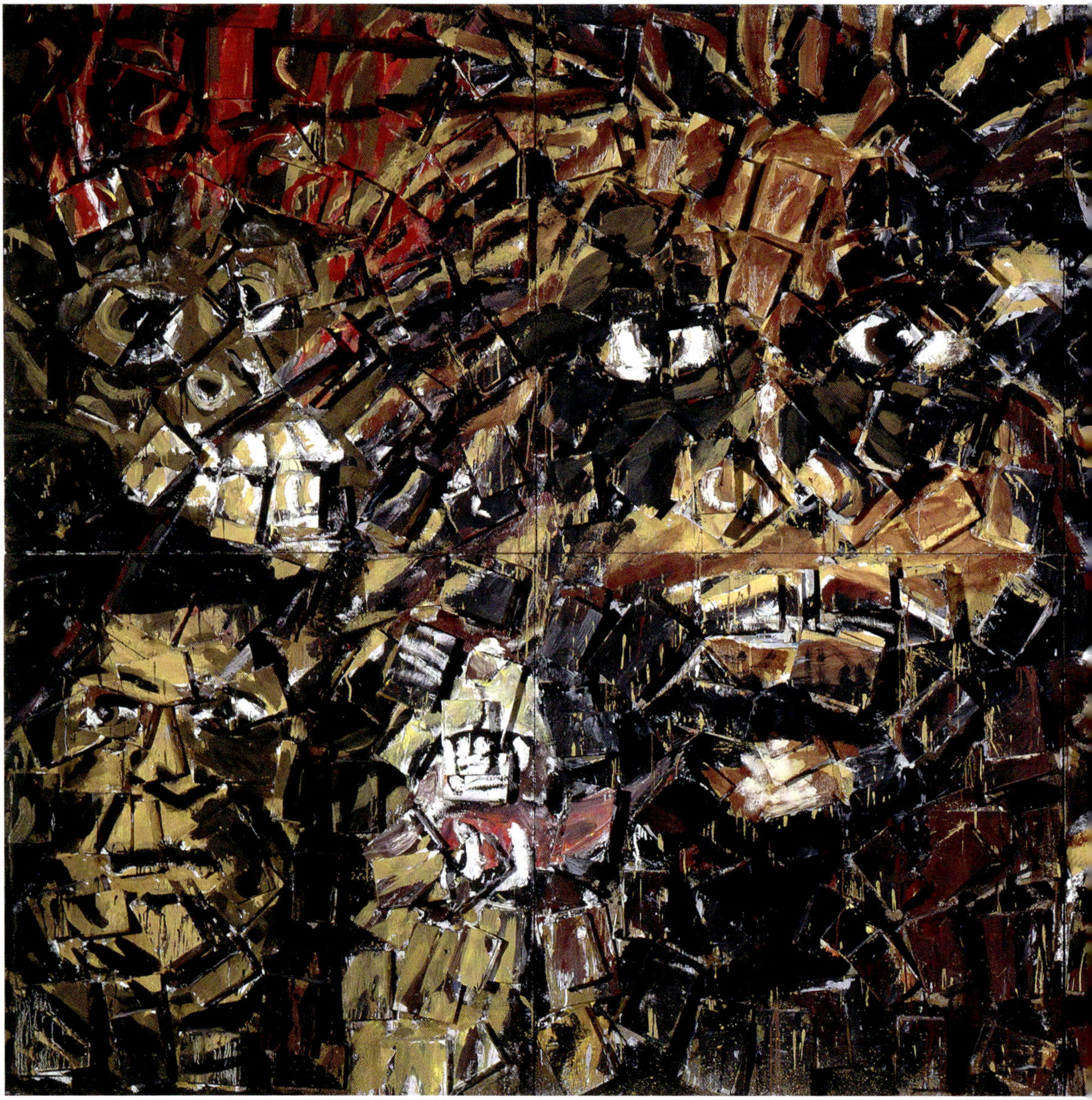

Jiří Georg Dokoupil, *Gott, zeig mir deine Eier*, 1982, Acryl, Öl und Bücher auf Rupfen u

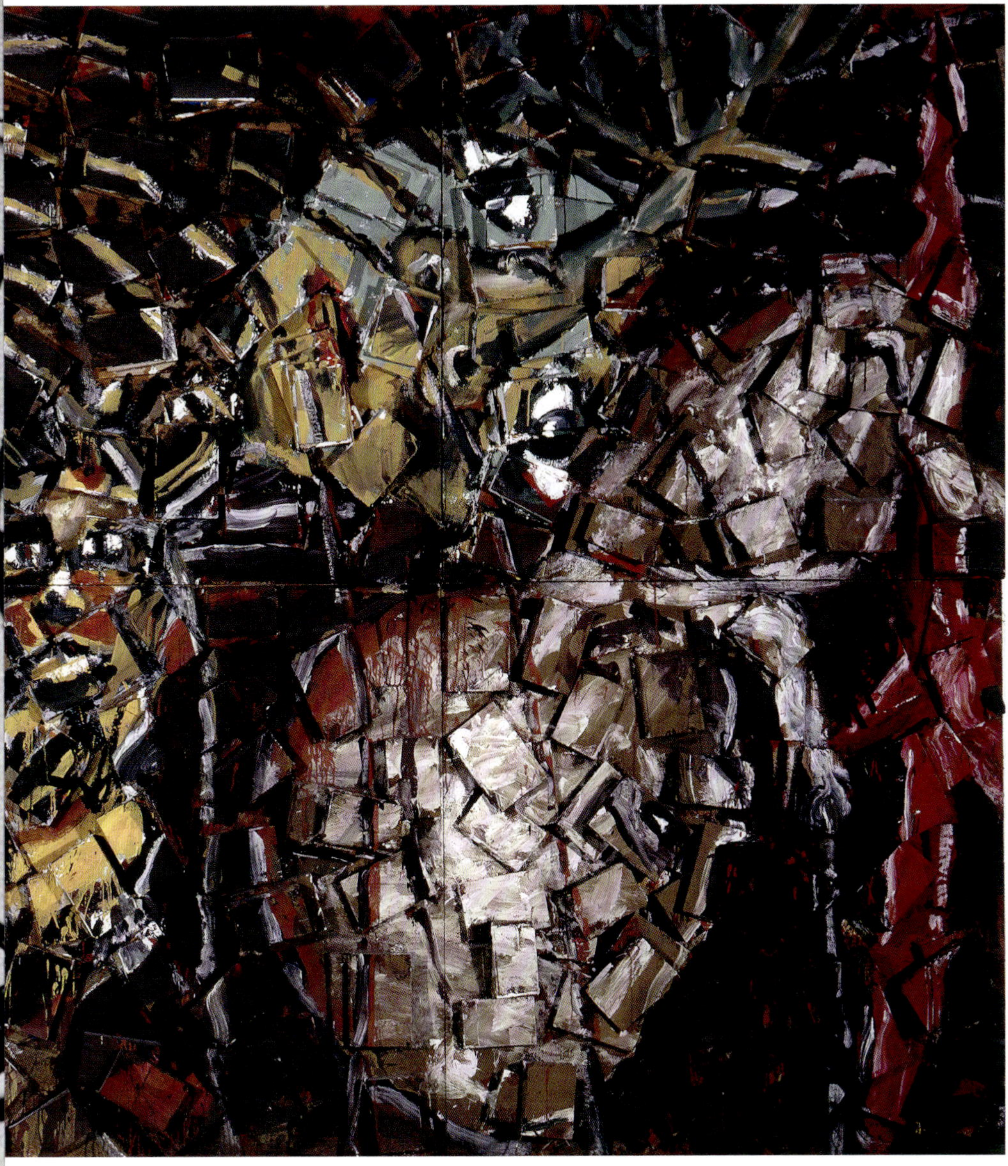

olzplatten / acrylic, oil, and books on jute and wooden boards, 300 × 600 cm

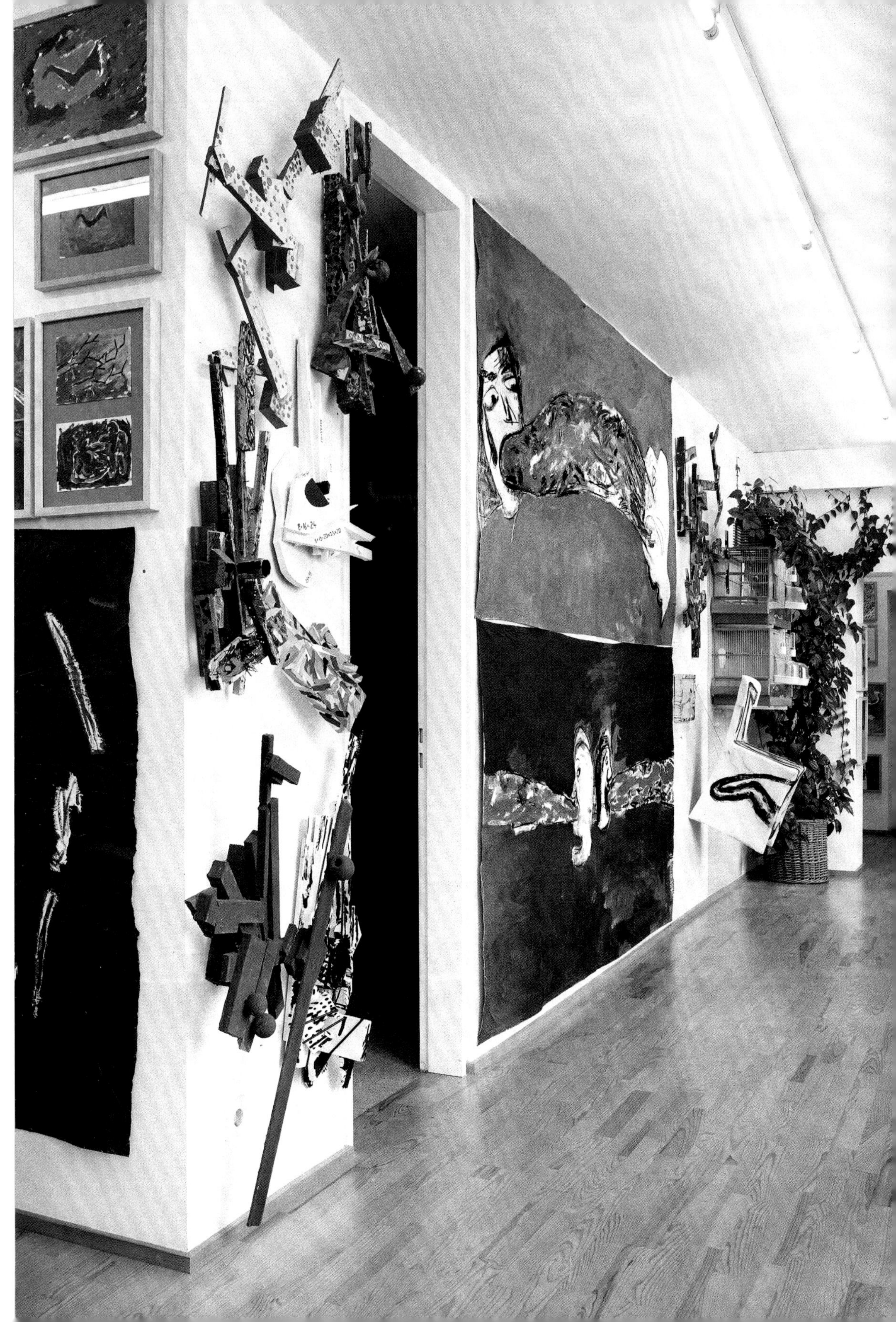

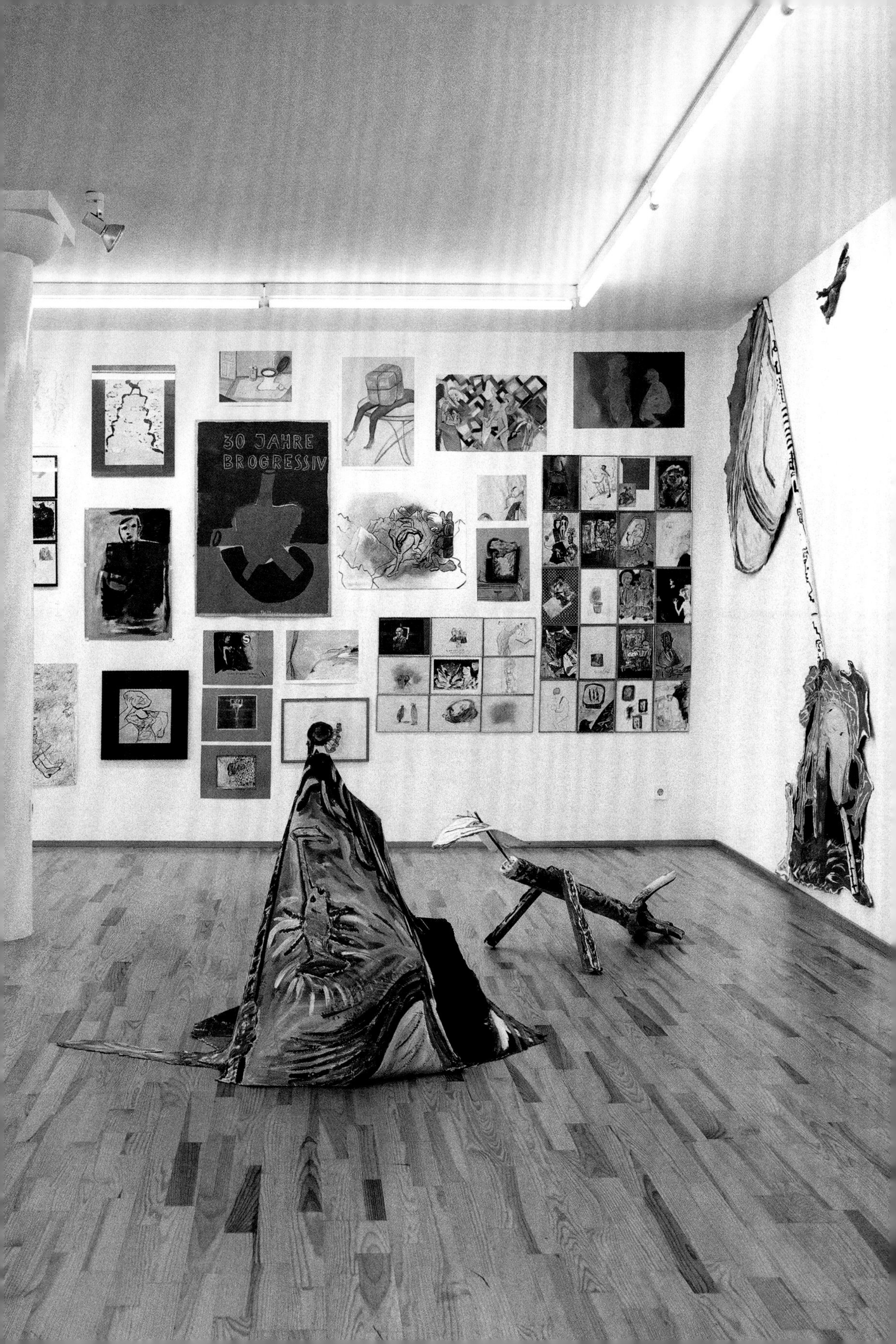
30 JAHRE
BROGRESSIV

Programm / Program
Flyer, Buch Handlung Welt, Hamburg, Februar / February 1978

Buch Handlung Welt zeigt Filme und Diaserien von ...
Flyer, Buch Handlung Welt, Hamburg, 1978

2. außerordentliche Veranstaltung in Bild und Ton: Aktion Pisskrücke. Geheimdienst am Nächsten
Flyer, Künstlerhaus Hamburg e. V., Hamburg, 1980, Design: Martin Kippenberger

Bettina Semmer, *Ich mach Frauenkunst*
Flyer, Buch Handlung Welt, Hamburg, 1982

Werner Büttner, Albert Oehlen, *Das Licht von der anderen Seite*
Flyer, Buch Handlung Welt, Hamburg, 1978

Markus Oehlen, *Wandmalerei*
Flyer, Buch Handlung Welt, Hamburg, 1981

Walter Dahn, Jiří Georg Dokoupil, *Entweder Kirk Douglas oder die Sonne im Nil*
Flyer, Buch Handlung Welt, Hamburg, 1980

Bettina Sefkow, *Von einem Blinden mit dem Munde gemalen*
Flyer, Buch Handlung Welt, Hamburg, 1978

(354–355) *Mülheimer Freiheit & Interessante Bilder aus Deutschland*, Galerie Paul Maenz, Köln / Cologne, 1980, mit Werken von / with works by Peter Bömmels, Werner Büttner, Walter Dahn u. a. / et al., Fotos / photos: Lothar Schnepf

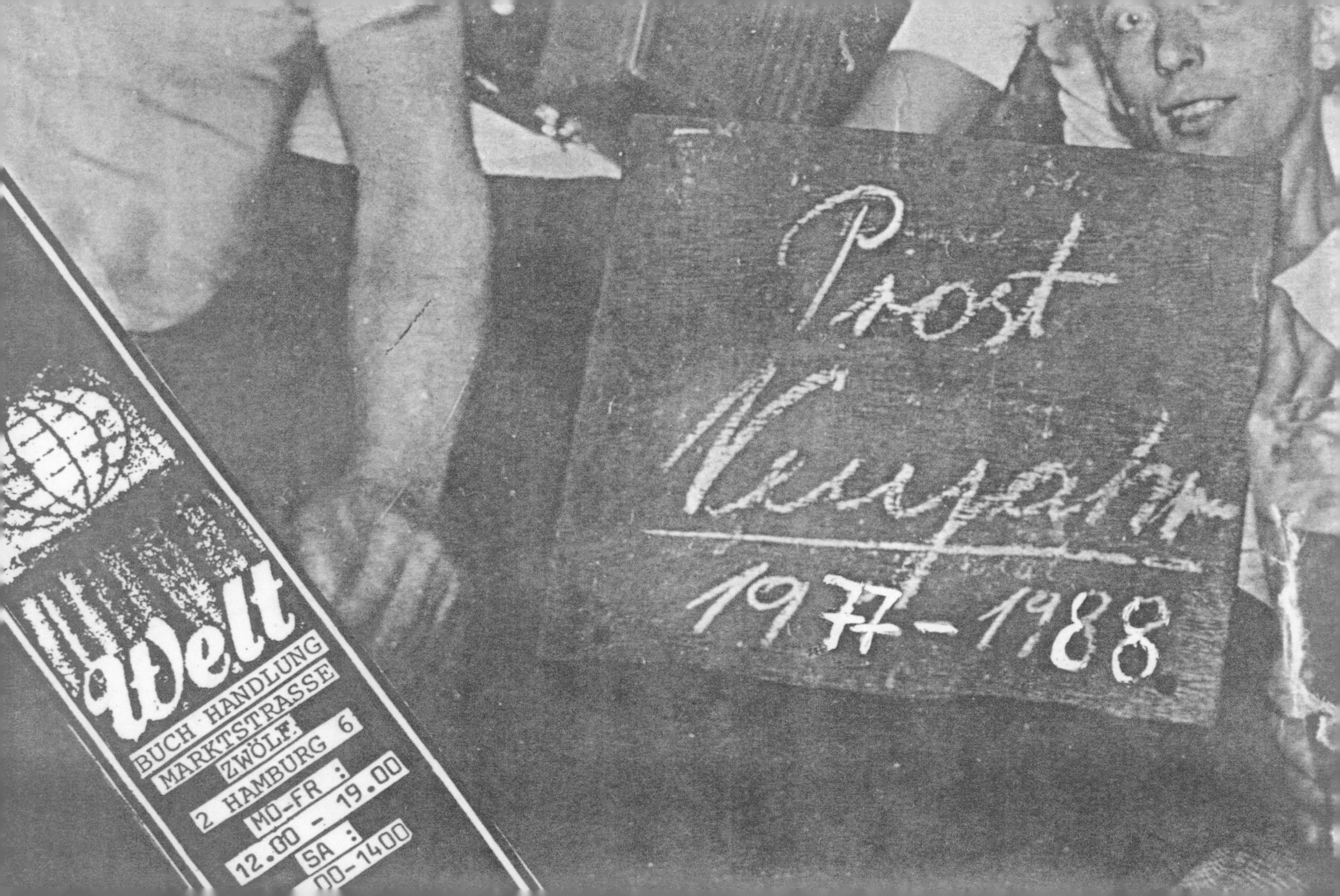
Prost
Neujahr
1977-1988
Welt
BUCH HANDLUNG
MARKTSTRASSE
ZWÖLF
2 HAMBURG 6
MO-FR :
12.00 - 19.00
SA :
00-1400

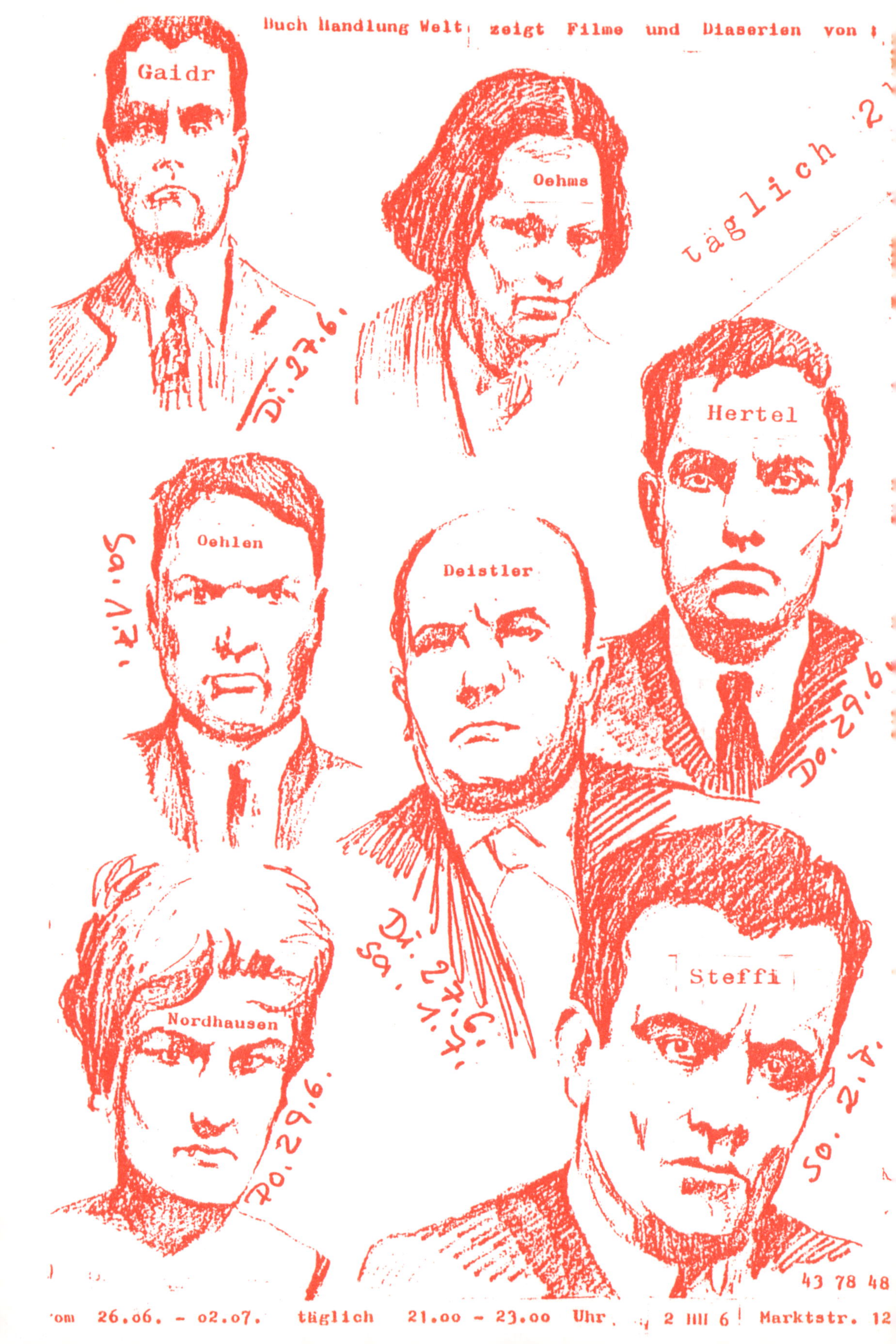

Buch Handlung Welt zeigt Filme und Diaserien von :
täglich 2
Gaidr
Di. 27.6.
Oehms
Hertel
Do. 29.6.
Oehlen
Sa. 1.7.
Deistler
Di. 27.6.
Sa. 1.7.
Nordhausen
Do. 29.6.
Steffi
So. 2.7.
43 78 48
vom 26.06. - 02.07. täglich 21.00 - 23.00 Uhr 2 HH 6 Marktstr. 12

Eröffnungsveranstaltung

am 9. April 1980 um 19.00 Uhr
im Künstlerhaus
Weidenallee 10b   2 Hamburg 6

Musik:
Sven Ake Johansson
Zwischenopfer

Unkostenbeitrag 10,— DM

Geöffnet Mi., Fr., Sa.   von 18.00 — 20.00 Uhr und nach Vereinbarung
Ausstellungsdauer bis zum 19. April   Tel.: 45 70 20

Wandbild in der Buch Handlung Welt Marktstr.12 Hamburg 6

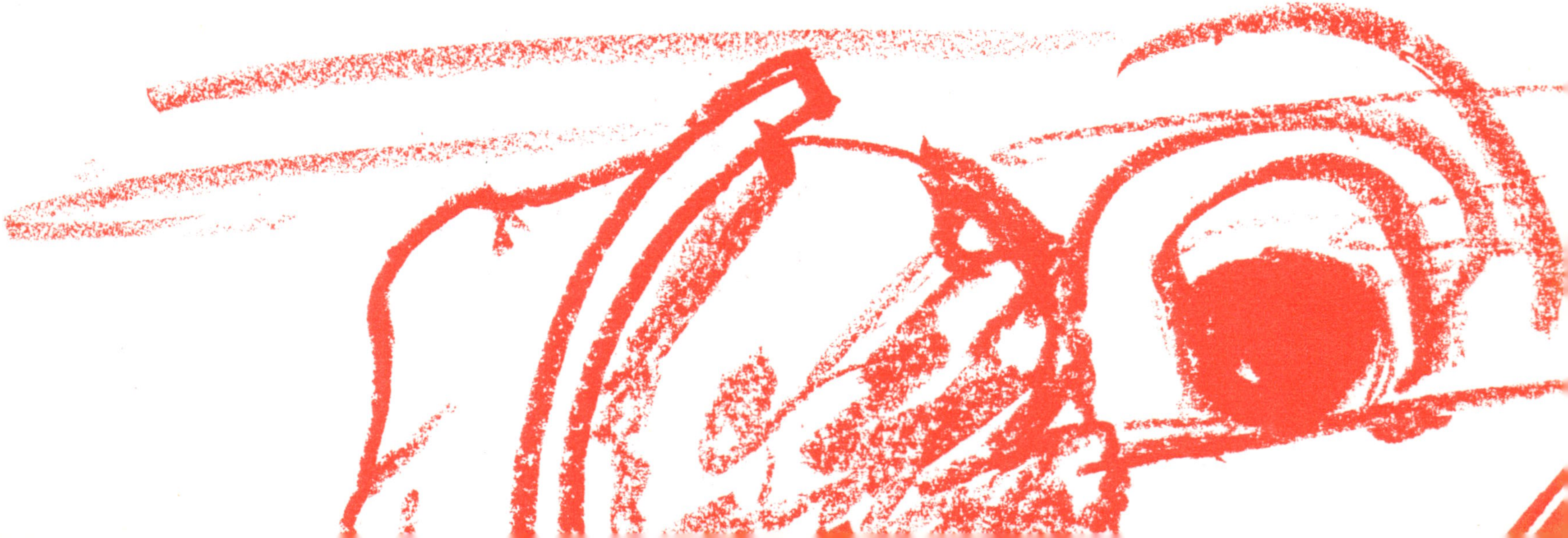

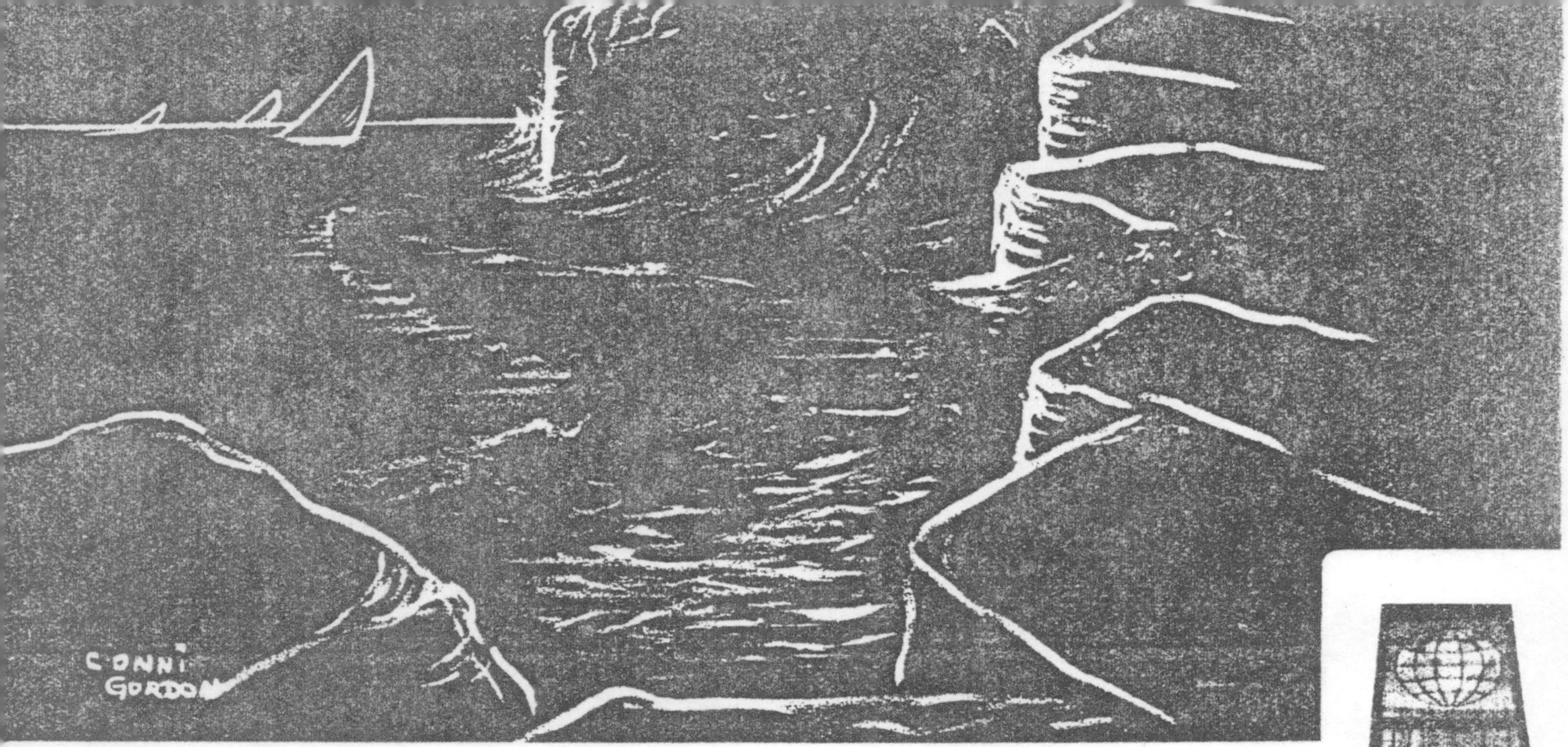

albert oehlen - werner büttner

das licht von der anderen seite

eröffnung: 5.2.1978 um 21 Uhr

BUCH HANDLUNG
MARKTSTRASSE ZWÖI
2 HAMBURG 6
43 78 48

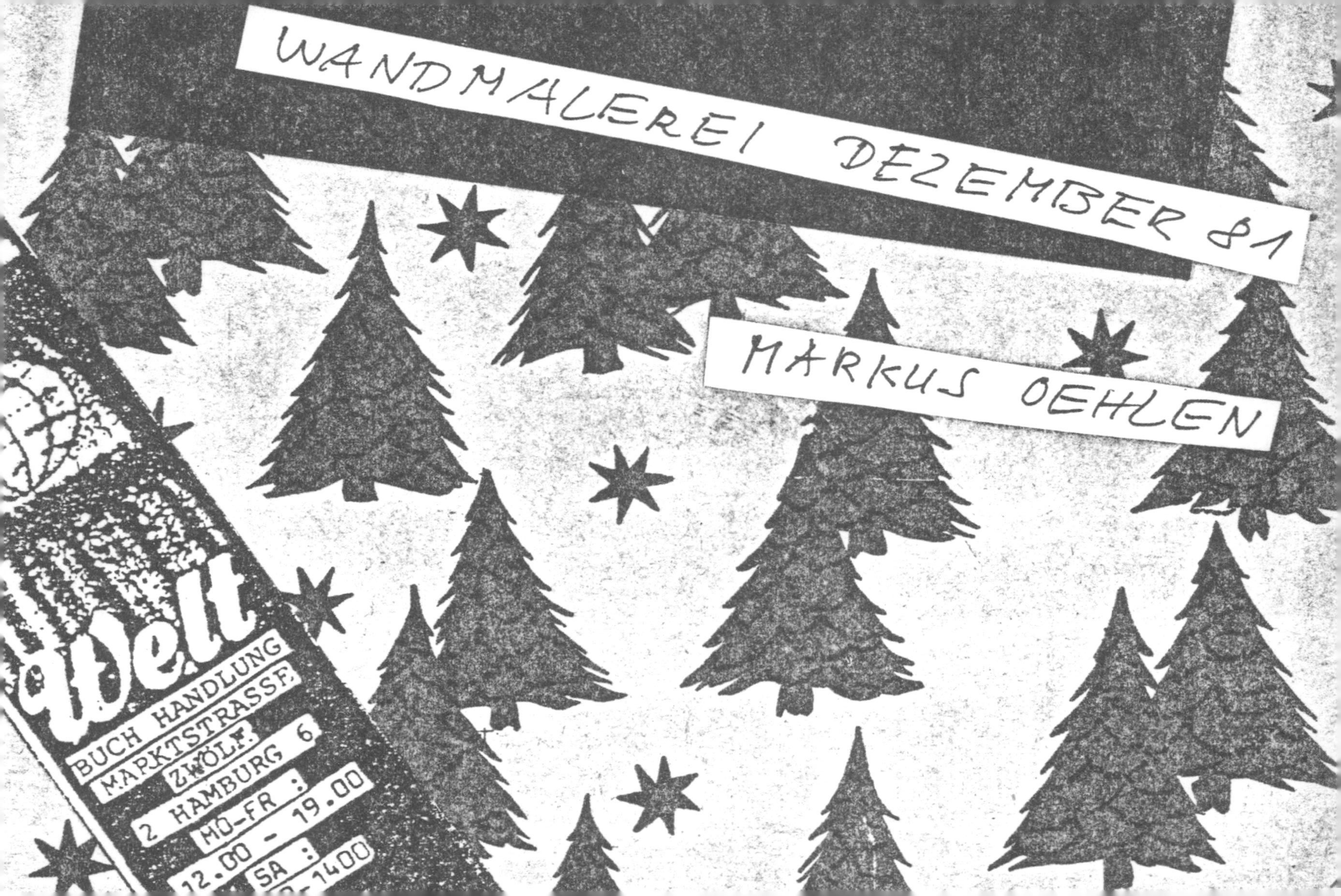
WANDMALEREI DEZEMBER 81
MARKUS OEHLEN
Welt
BUCH HANDLUNG
MAPKTSTRASSE
ZWÖLF
2 HAMBURG 6
MO-FR :
12.00 - 19.00
SA :

ENTWEDER KIRK DOUGLAS
ODER DIE SONNE IM NIL.

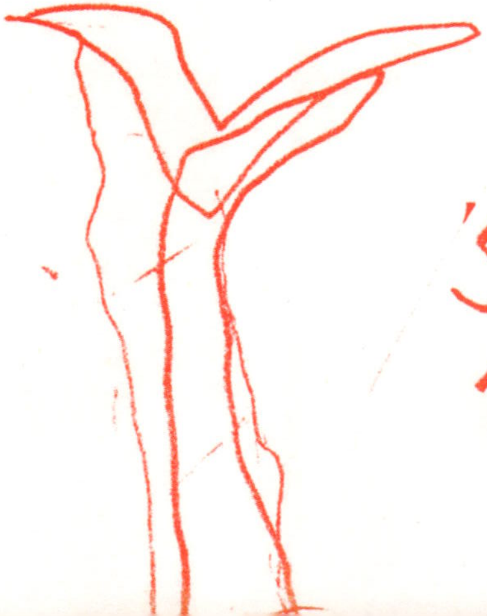

DIE WANDAQUARELLE
SIND VOM 10.4. BIS
10.5. ERÖFFNET.

WELT BUCH HANDLUNG: WAND/MALEREI

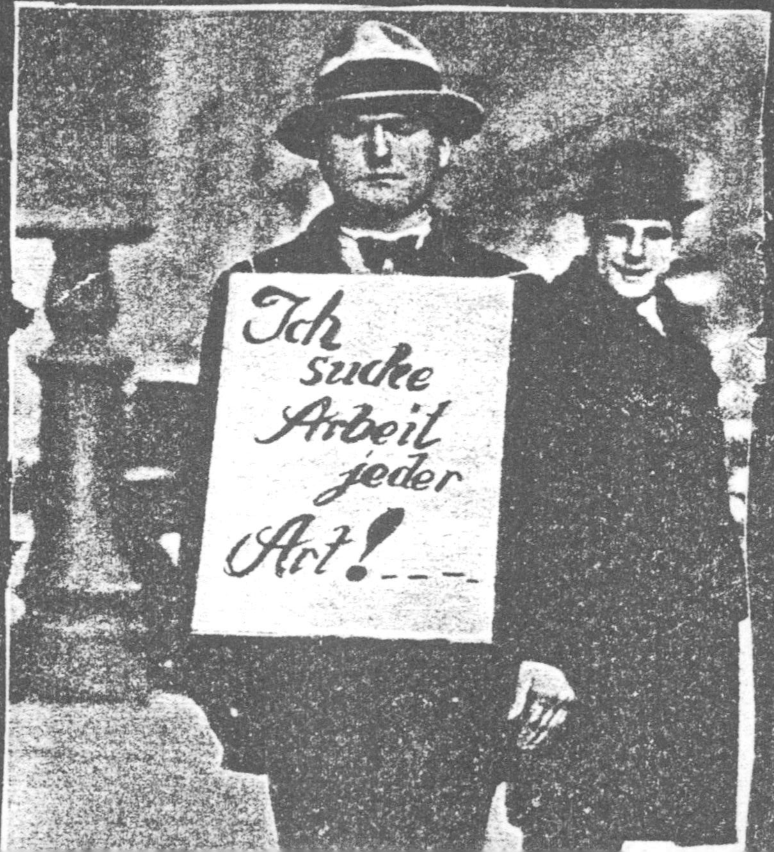

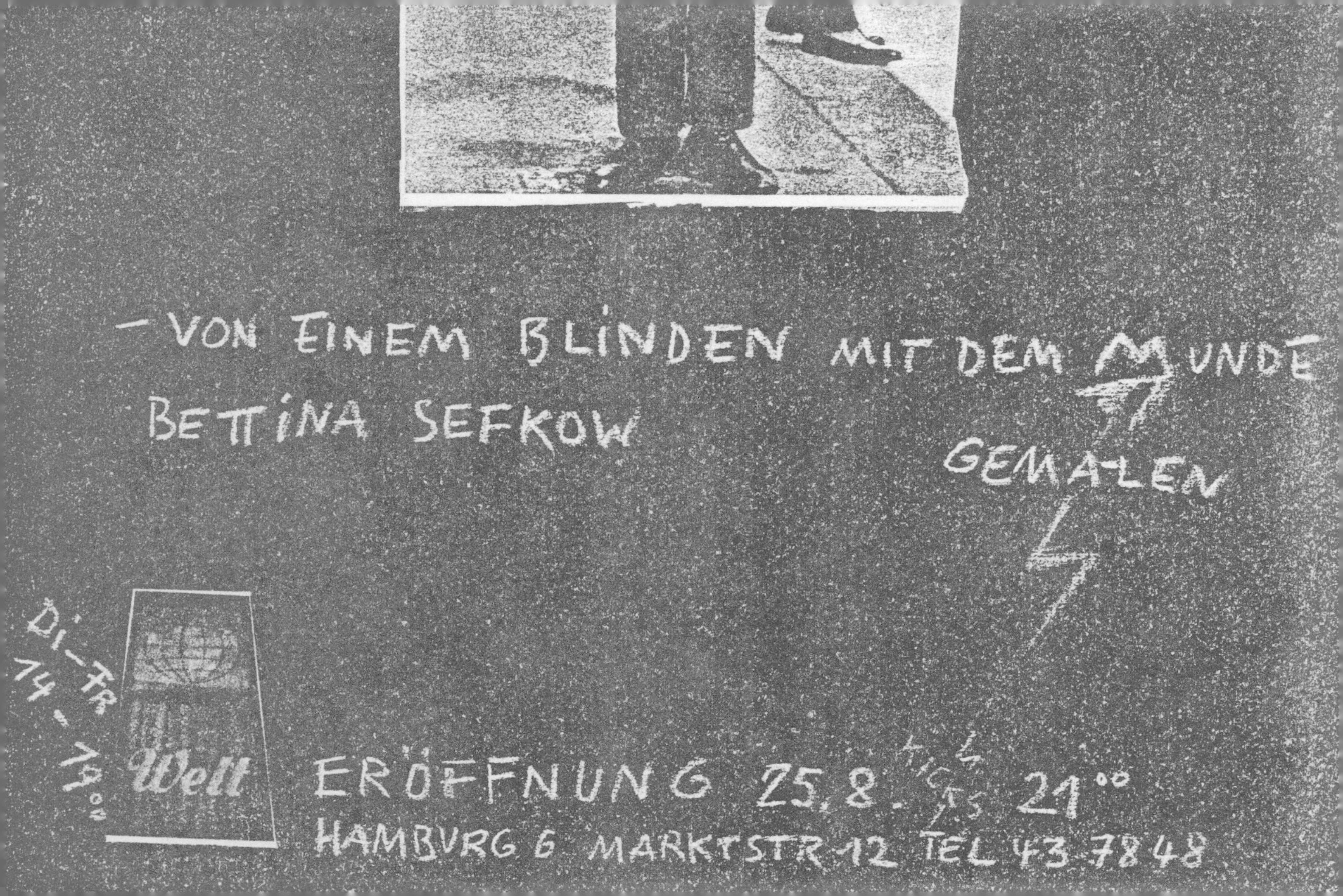
– VON EINEM BLINDEN MIT DEM MUNDE
BETTINA SEFKOW
GEMALEN
Di–Fr
14 - 19⁰⁰
Welt
ERÖFFNUNG 25.8. 21⁰⁰
HAMBURG 6 MARKTSTR 12 TEL 43 78 48

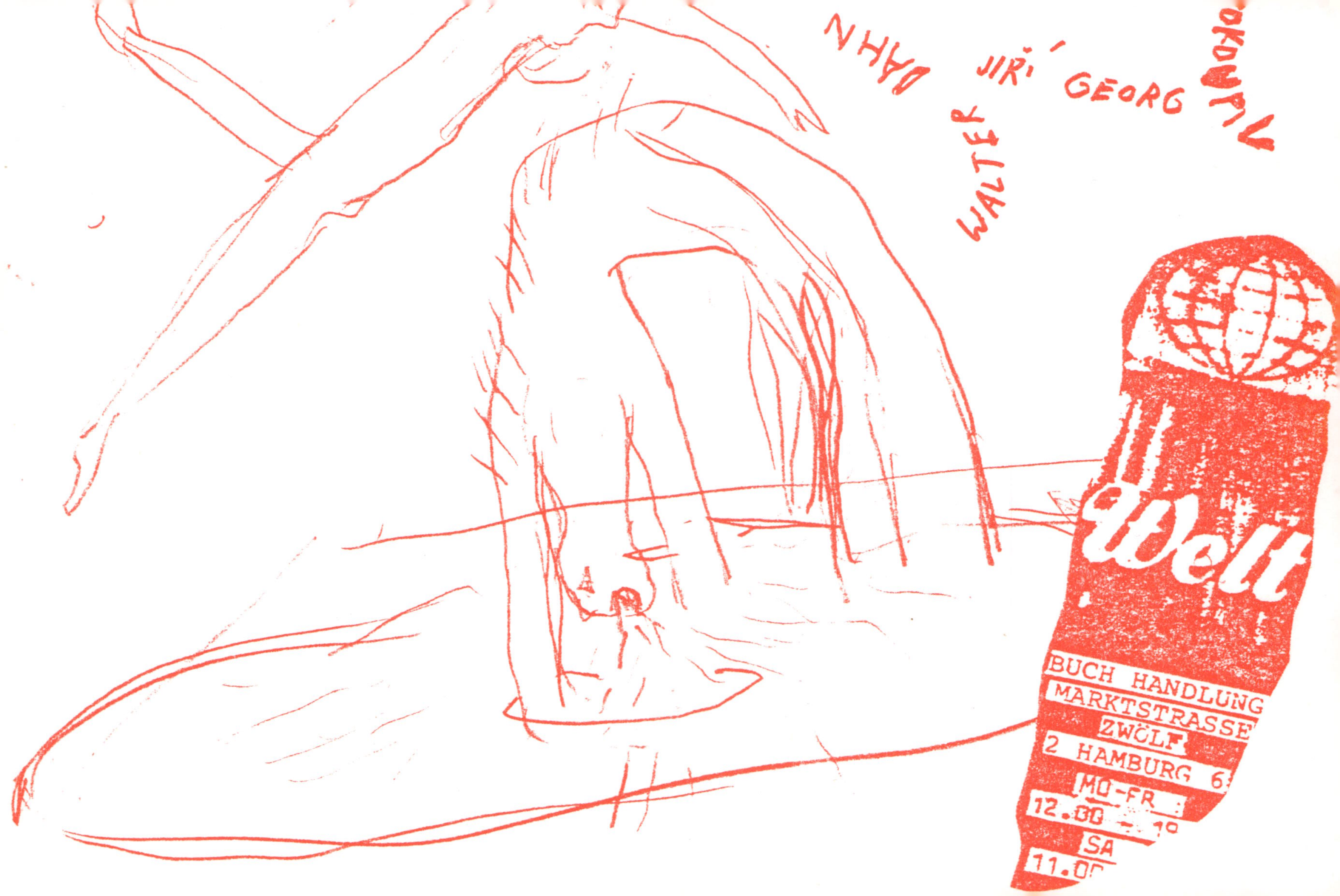
WALTER DAHN
JIRÍ GEORG
OKOUPIL
Welt
BUCH HANDLUNG
MARKTSTRASSE
ZWÖLF
2 HAMBURG 6
MO-FR
12.00 - 19
SA
11.0

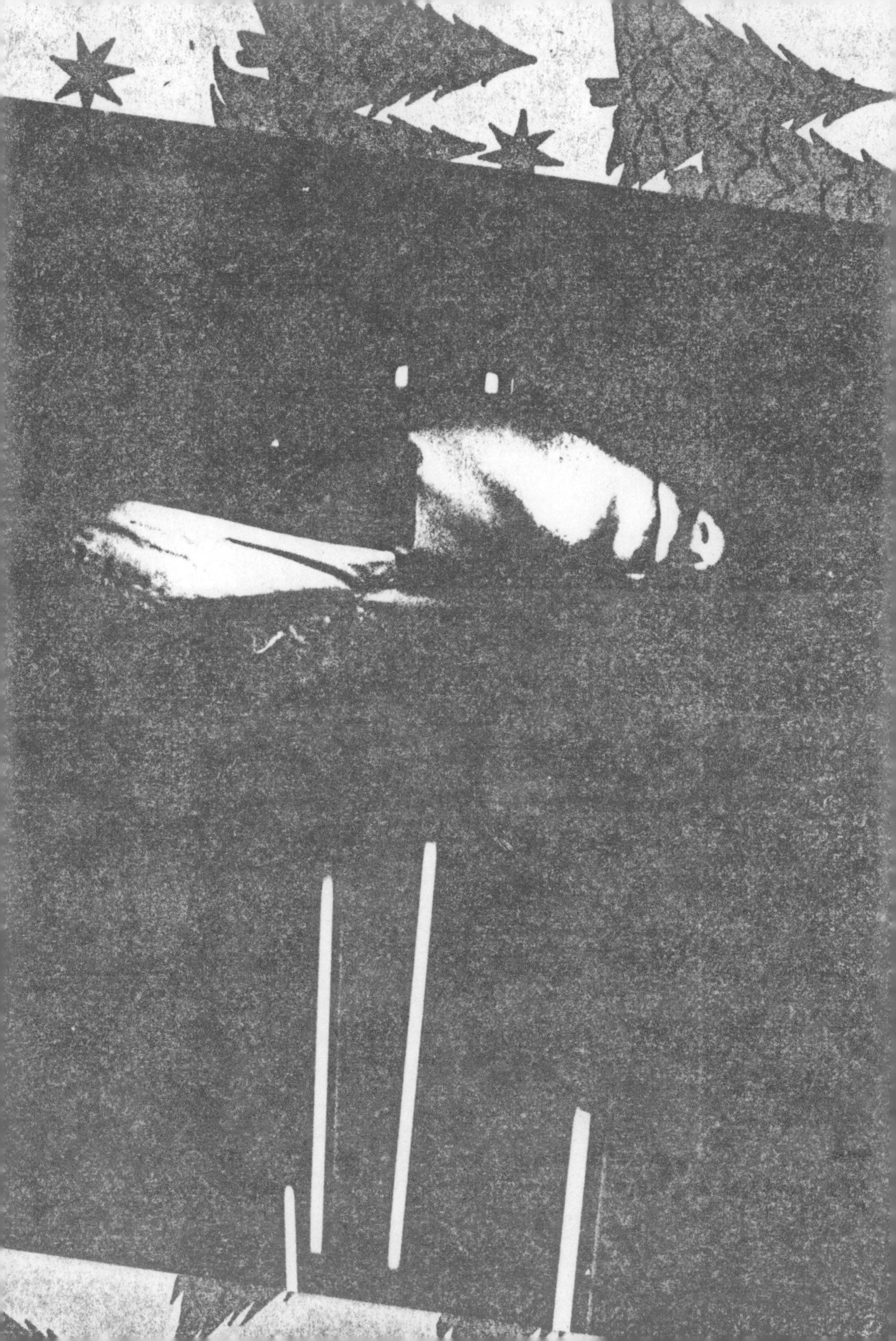

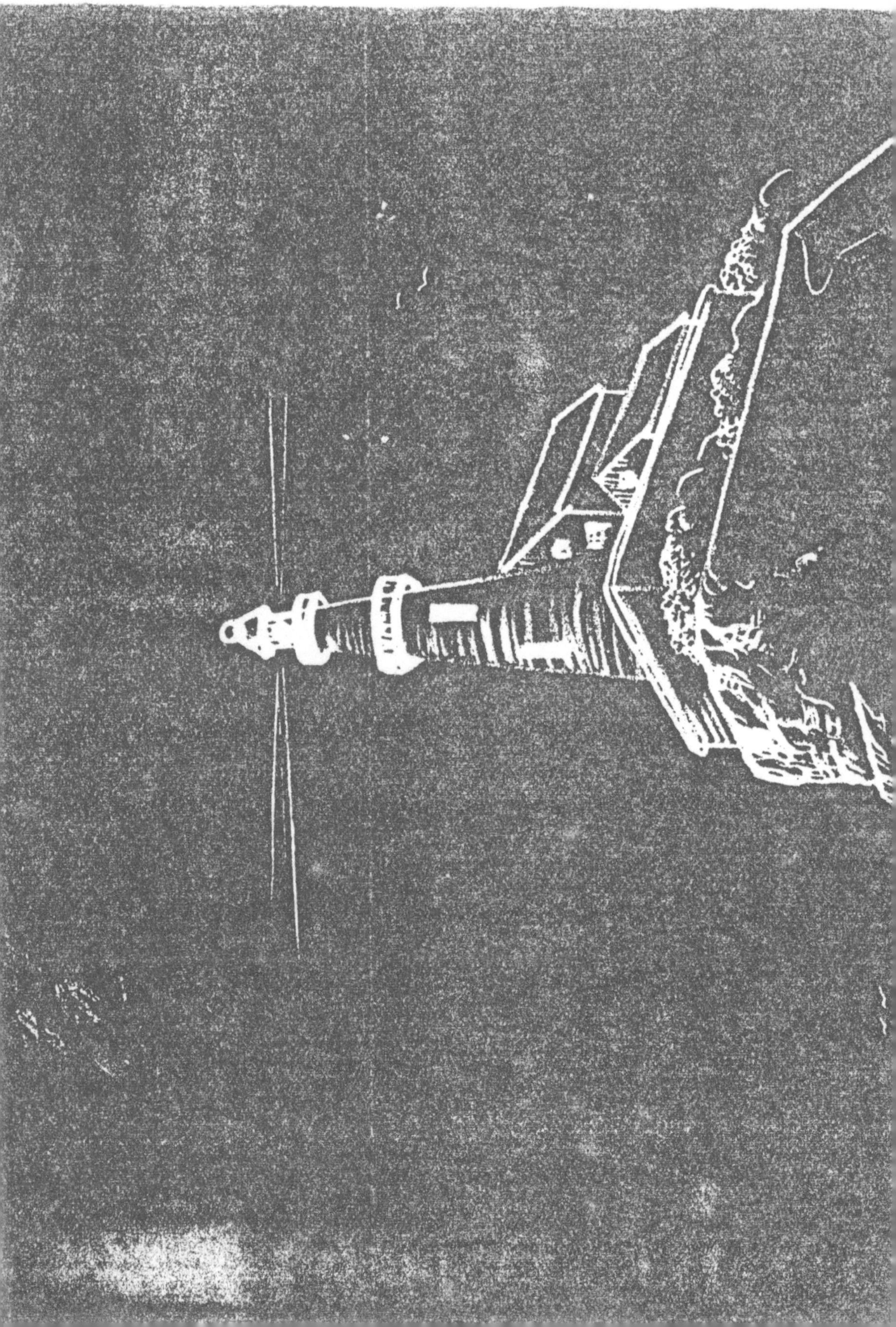

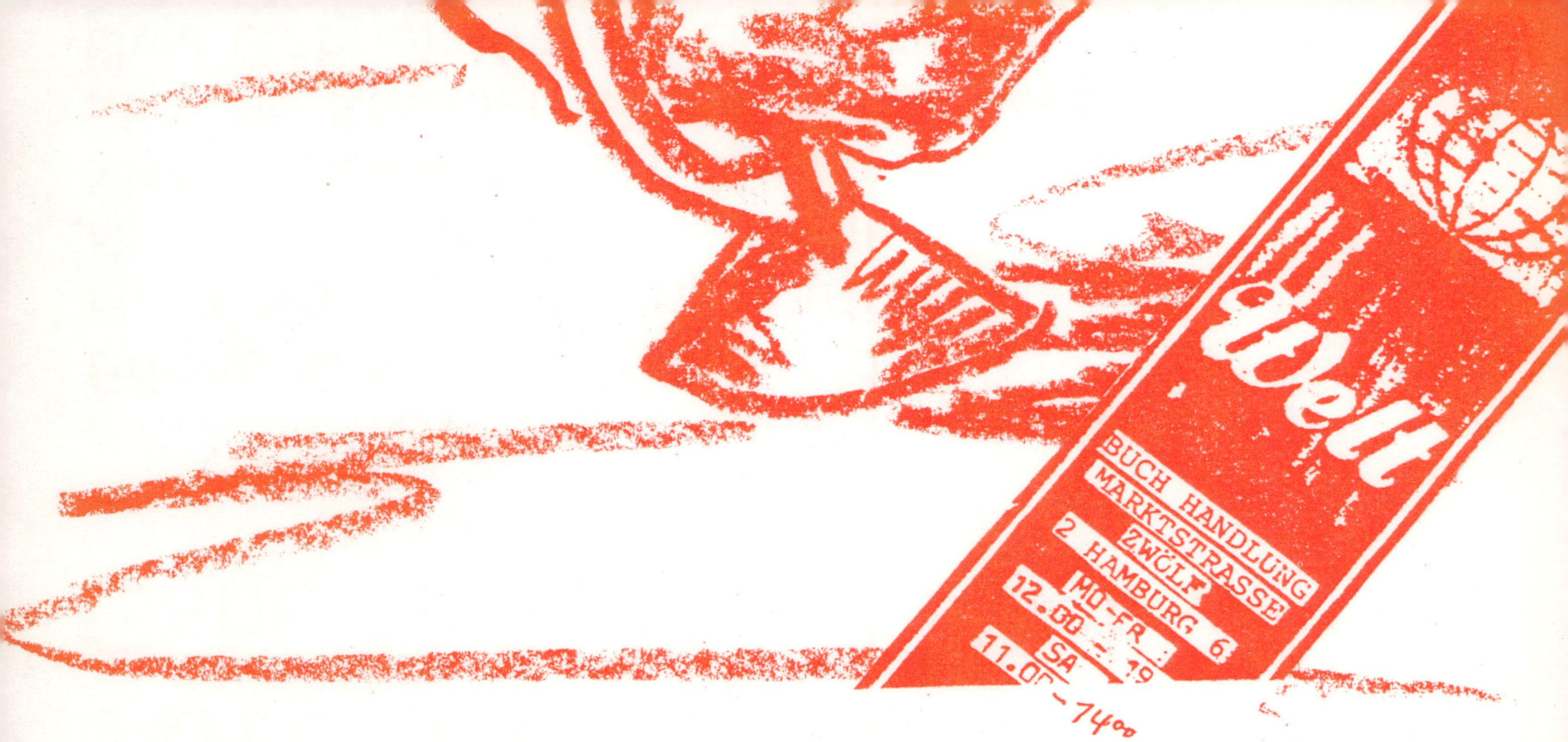

Bettina Semmer

Eröffnung Montag den 31.5.82 19 Uhr

2. außerordentliche Veranstaltung
in Bild und Ton

Aktion Pisskrücke

Geheimdienst am Nächsten

mit Albert Oehlen, Brigitta Rohrbach,
Erinna König, Georg Herold,
Hilka Nordhausen, Ina Barfuß,
Klaus Hübner, Marcus Oehlen,
Martin Kippenberger, Michael Deistler,
Michael Krebber, Thomas Wachweger,
Uwe Gabriel, Werner Büttner.

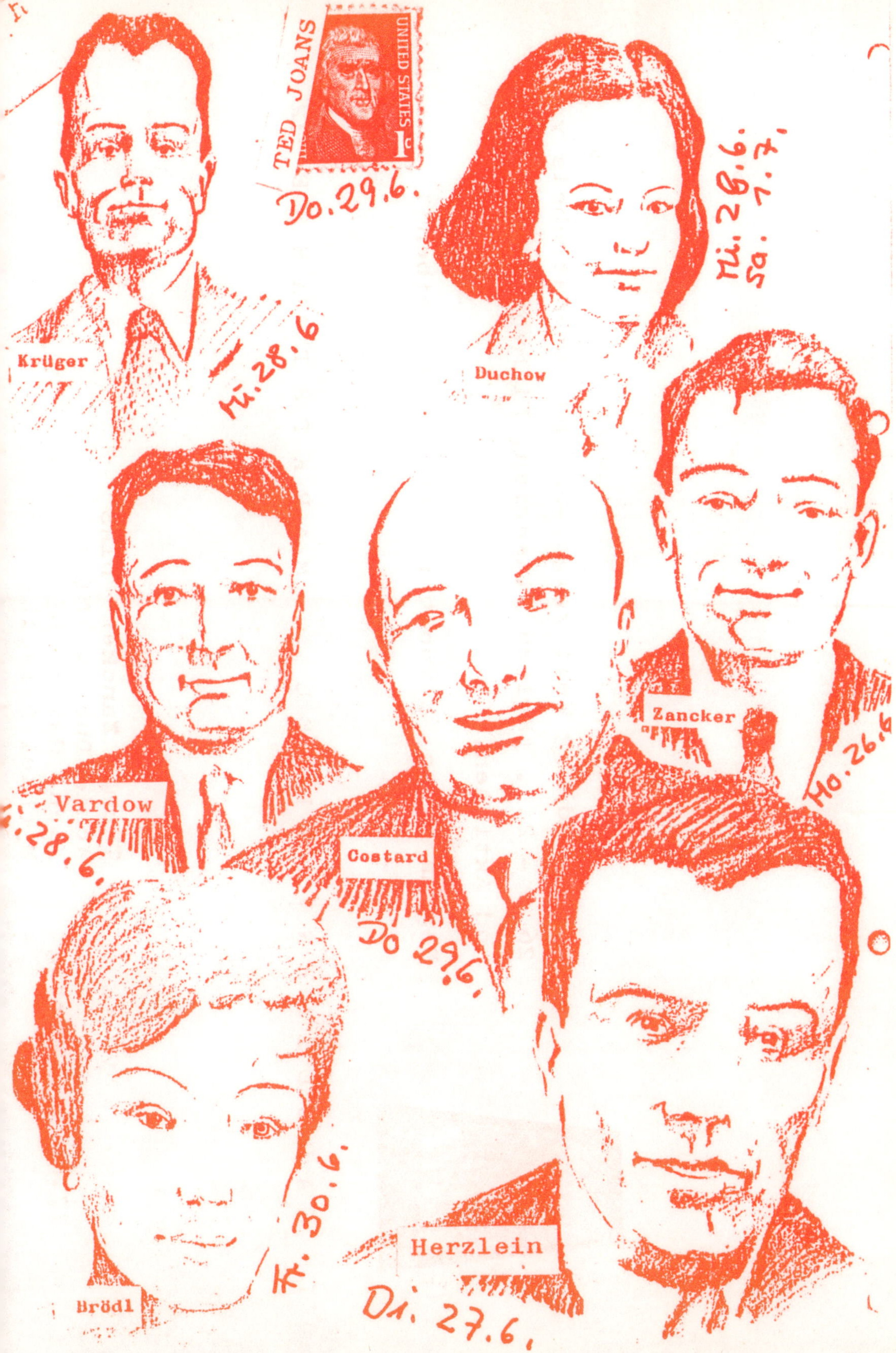
TED JOANS
UNITED STATES
Do.29.6.
Krüger
Mi.28.6
Duchow
Mi.28.6.
Sa.7.7.
Zancker
Mo.26.6
Vardow
.28.6.
Costard
Do 29.6.
Brödl
Fr.30.6.
Herzlein
Di.27.6.

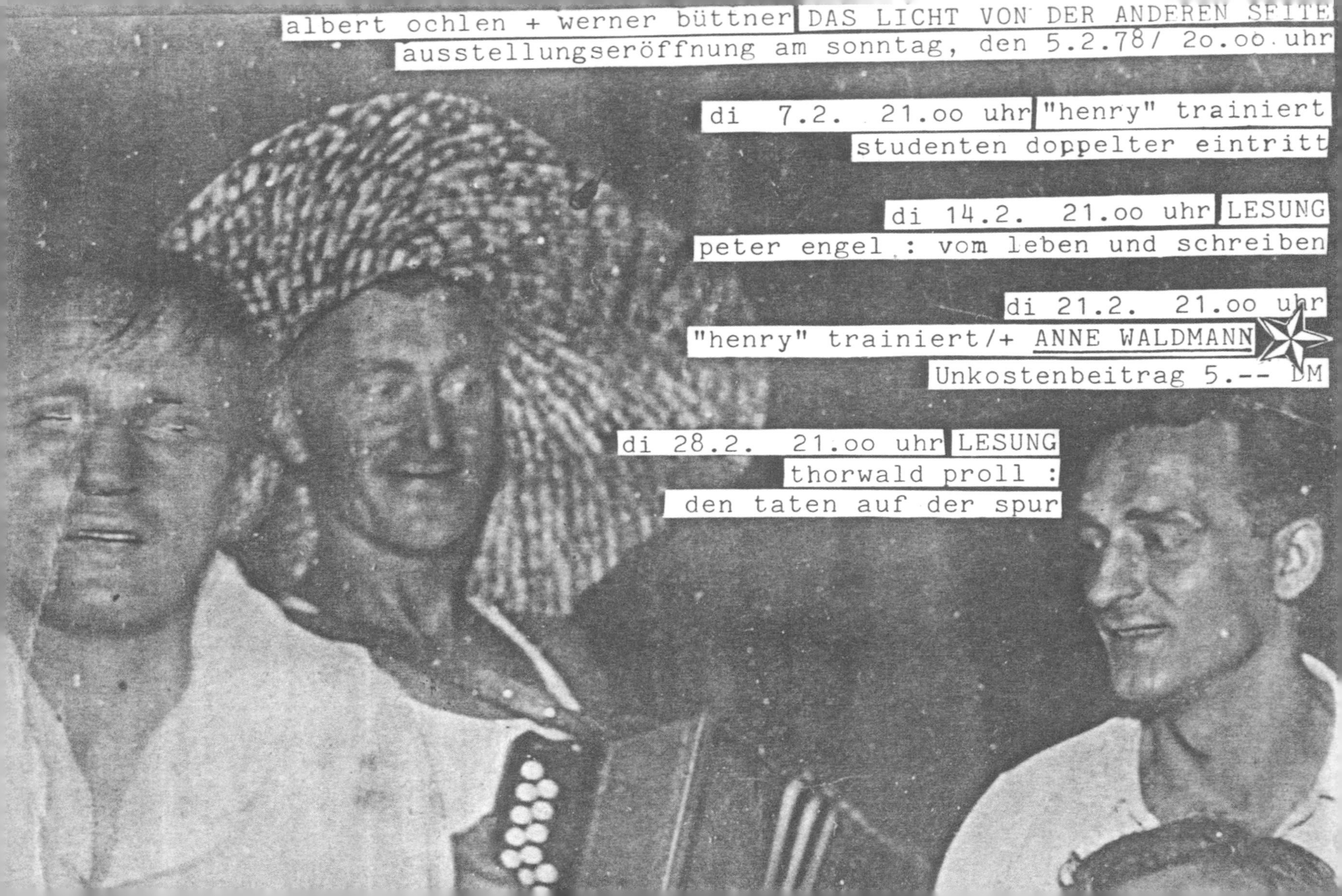
albert ochlen + werner büttner DAS LICHT VON DER ANDEREN SEITE
ausstellungseröffnung am sonntag, den 5.2.78/ 20.00 uhr
di 7.2. 21.00 uhr "henry" trainiert
studenten doppelter eintritt
di 14.2. 21.00 uhr LESUNG
peter engel : vom leben und schreiben
di 21.2. 21.00 uhr
"henry" trainiert/+ ANNE WALDMANN
Unkostenbeitrag 5.-- DM
di 28.2. 21.00 uhr LESUNG
thorwald proll :
den taten auf der spur

STADT AACHEN

NEUE GALERIE - SAMMLUNG LUDWIG

LES NOUVEAUX FAUVES
DIE NEUEN WILDEN

SAMMLUNG LUDWIG

19. Januar bis 21. März 1980

In *Les Nouveaux Fauves – Die Neuen Wilden*, exh. cat. Neue Galerie – Sammlung Ludwig, Aachen 1980, n.p.

Wolfgang Becker

Les Nouveaux Fauves / Die Neuen Wilden: Proposal for a Study

This is the catalogue of an exhibition that presumes to present North American, French, and German artists under a common title that looks like the name of a style—and is at the same time that of the new inventory, the documentation of a passion for collecting that has been preceded by several others. Collecting, along with its laws and limits, therefore determines the selection of the artists and works of this show, which was also the preliminary goal of a periodic commitment by the collector couple Ludwig.

Society's reception of works of art has, as a whole, a pragmatic side nowadays, one that depends on the laws of the free market and the advertising industry. It is most evident where collectors contribute to determining the reception of new art movements.

By relating the three geographically defined groups of artists to each other, we present a simultaneity of their reception of our collection, as if it represented the simultaneity of their discovery in the art public. However, the German artists Baselitz, Immendorff, Lüpertz, and Penck have been known in the Federal Republic, Switzerland, and the Netherlands for around ten years, the "old masters" Simon Hantaï, Claude Viallat, and Louis Cane have been discussed by French art criticism since 1967, and Neil Jenney, Miriam Schapiro, and Robert Zakanitch are also "seasoned" artists with eventful resumes.

The simultaneity that our exhibition insinuates is thus not necessarily that of a generation or a group of artists communicating with each other. It instead reflects the needs of the art public that are articulated with varying focuses by art criticism and the exhibition services. If most of the artists on display are currently in the focus of public attention, it is because they seem to give an account of certain needs that we are called upon to consult. Here are a few, roughly outlined: colorfulness—heat—expression—spontaneity—casualness—unrest—emotion—experience—history—orient—Gesamtkunstwerk—synthesis—communication—praxis.

We can therefore imagine that the artists who are now highlighted for a broad public by major exhibitions turn against those who have not fulfilled these needs, who have been colorless, cold, expressionless, calculating, obsessive, calm, emotionless, ahistorical, academic, analytical, uncommunicative, and out of touch with praxis. Perhaps the image of the adversary defined in this way can contribute to identifying our new heroes.

In the first half of the 1960s, the Berlin-based artists Lüpertz and Baselitz as well as their friend Ralph Winkler, aka A. R. Penck, who was born in Dresden, set themselves apart from contemporary North American art—Pop Art—that dominated the public European art scene. This breakaway led them back to their own schools—via northern European forms of Art Informel, such as CoBrA, to early German Expressionism. Against Pop Art's metropolitan, cynical denigration of pictorial contents and languages, they introduced a swaggering, dark pathos, attempting to create "anti-pictures" "without a style" (Baselitz) and gradually developing their strictly individualistic signatures. In his late works that are on view here, Baselitz retains his apparent indifference toward the motif by continuing to paint familiar objects upside down, but he steps up the expressivity of his application of paint into the casualness of a rough sketch to such an extent that the motifs remain visible merely as occasions for paintings.

Aus: *Les Nouveaux Fauves - Die Neuen Wilden*, Ausst.-Kat.
Neue Galerie – Sammlung Ludwig, Aachen 1980, o. S.

Wolfgang Becker

Les Nouveaux Fauves / Die Neuen Wilden: Vorschlag zu einer Untersuchung

Dieser Katalog ist der einer Ausstellung, die sich anmasst, nordamerikanische, französische und deutsche Künstler unter einem gemeinsamen Titel vorzustellen, der so aussieht wie eine Stilbezeichnung – und zugleich der des neuen Bestandes, Dokument einer Leidenschaft des Sammelns, dem mehrere andere vorausgegangen sind. Das Sammeln, seine Gesetze und seine Beschränkungen bestimmen also die Auswahl der Künstler und der Werke dieser Ausstellung, die zugleich das vorläufige Ziel eines periodischen Engagements des Sammlerehepaares Ludwig war.

Die Geschichte der Aufnahme von Kunstwerken durch die Gesellschaft hat insgesamt heute eine pragmatische, von Gesetzen der freien Markt- und Werbewirtschaft abhängige Seite. Sie tritt am deutlichsten dort hervor, wo Sammler die Rezeption neuer Kunstströmungen mit bestimmen.

Wenn wir hier drei geografisch bestimmte Künstlergruppen zueinander ordnen, so zeigen wir eine Gleichzeitigkeit ihrer Rezeption in unserer Sammlung, als wäre sie stellvertretend für die Gleichzeitigkeit ihrer Entdeckung in der Kunstöffentlichkeit.
Die deutschen Künstler Baselitz, Immendorff, Lüpertz und Penck sind aber in der Bundesrepublik, der Schweiz, den Niederlanden seit etwa 10 Jahren bekannt, der „Altmeister" Hantaï, Claude Viallat und Louis Cane werden in der französischen Kunstkritik seit 1967 diskutiert, und Neil Jenney, Miriam Schapiro und Robert Zakanitch sind ebenso „gestandene" Künstler mit bewegungsvollen Lebensläufen.

Die Gleichzeitigkeit, die unsere Ausstellung suggeriert, ist also nicht notwendigerweise die einer Generation, nicht die einer in sich kommunizierenden Künstlergruppe, sondern reflektiert Bedürfnisse der Kunstöffentlichkeit, die von der Kunstkritik und den Ausstellungsdiensten schwerpunktartig artikuliert werden. Wenn die meisten der Künstler unserer Ausstellung heute im Mittelpunkt öffentlicher Aufmerksamkeit stehen, dann scheinen sie bestimmten Bedürfnissen Rechenschaft zu geben, die wir zu befragen haben. Hier sind einige, roh umrissen:
Farbigkeit – Hitze – gestalteter Ausdruck – Spontaneität – Lockerheit – Unruhe – Emotion – Erlebnis – Geschichte – Orient – Gesamtkunstwerk – Synthese – Kommunikation – Praxis.

Wir können uns also vorstellen, dass die Künstler, die jetzt durch grosse Ausstellungen in das Licht der grossen Öffentlichkeit treten, sich gegen jene wenden, die diesen Bedürfnissen nicht entsprochen haben. Die also farblos, kalt, ausdruckslos, kalkulierend, besessen, ruhig, emotionslos, geschichtslos, akademisch, analytisch, kommunikationsarm und praxisfremd waren. Vielleicht trägt das so definierte Feindbild dazu bei, unsere neuen Helden zu bestimmen.

Die Berliner Lüpertz und Baselitz und der ihnen nahestehende Dresdener Ralph Winkler – A. R. Penck setzen sich in der ersten Hälfte der 60er Jahre gegen die zeitgenössische nordamerikanische Kunst – die pop art – ab, die die öffentliche europäische Kunstszene beherrschte. Diese Absetzung führte sie in ihre eigenen Schulen zurück – über nordeuropäische Ausprägungen des informel wie COBRA bis zum deutschen Frühexpressionismus. Gegen die großstädtisch zynische Abwertung der Bildinhalte und -sprachen der pop art führten sie ein kraftmeierisches, dunkles Pathos ein, versuchten, „Anti-Bilder" „ohne Stil" (Baselitz) herzustellen und entwickelten langsam ihre streng individualistischen Handschriften. Baselitz erhält sich in seinen späten Werken, die wir hier zeigen, dadurch, dass er weiterhin vertraute Gegenstände auf dem Kopf malt,

Lüpertz, on the other hand, has found a "style" that determines the demands he makes both on the social role of the artist and on the picture. Since 1963 he has been working with the concept of "dithyramb" and presenting his paintings "enthusiastically, buoyantly" as "songs of praise," "ceremonious poems." The turn to content of great sublimity ("Death," "Spring") and to a monumental pictorial language expressed with emotive formulae reveals the degree to which he has departed from everything we deemed "modern" in art in the 1960s: the embracing of mass media and their technologies, the socially minded activities of the artist, the analytical irony. The work of Anselm Kiefer leads us completely away from the present to the engagement with social themes that belong to a specifically German awareness—presented in a language that is rough and incomplete and seeks to elude quick consumption.

I came upon the title *Les Nouveaux Fauves - Die Neuen Wilden* while visiting *Paris - Berlin* at the Centre Pompidou in Paris, because I found that the show did not sufficiently answer the question as to what the Fauves and the German Expressionists in around 1910 had in common and what distinguished them from each other, and because I think it is worthwhile to examine whether the commonalities and differences can be seen again today—if we start from the assumption that recourses to Fauvism and Expressionism are discernible both here and there. For example: Does the "vertigo" ("le Vertige"), the tendency toward ecstatic idealization, toward metaphysics, the proximity of visual art, literature, and philosophy, which made German Expressionism so fascinating and frightening for the French, recur today in Baselitz, Penck, Lüpertz, and Kiefer? Or: Do we currently see in French art the same degree of painterly discipline, rationality of taste, striving for balance and harmony—and the same social noncommitment—that we saw in Matisse and his circle? And finally, what do the Americans contribute, who—with clear reference to Matisse—appear to be reappraising the global history of ornamentation with large fabrics in pretentious colors?

This exhibition is not the result of a study, it is meant to prompt one. That is why today we only raise questions and do not give answers.

There appears to be nothing that would allow a comparison between the German and French artists of this exhibition—except for the expressivity tending toward pathos that has evolved with both Cane and Viallat in the past years. Since the mid-1960s, the artists' group Supports/Surfaces, based on a thorough theoretical dealing with Matisse and the American artists Ad Reinhardt, Barnett Newman, Morris Louis, and Frank Stella, as well as on a politico-cultural discourse, has transformed pictures into objects, or rather merged picture support and picture surface. They were inspired by the older Hantaï. When these folded, sewn, tamponed, and loosely hanging cloths dyed with earthy substances became known, they appeared as variants of contemporary abstract painting that existed both in Europe and America. Only Viallat has expanded the idea of the object by retaining the pompoms and fringes on the found lengths of fabric or lending them the form of a garment. Viallat loves the associative proximity to ethnology and non-European ornamentation that we can find in the American works. Yet he refrains from direct citation, thus unmistakably keeping closest to the cut papers of Matisse.

Supports/Surfaces went through the political generational crisis of 1968 just like their German colleagues. Did the group follow the French tradition of always making aesthetic instruments out of politico-cultural demands? Does that distinguish them from the German artists of their generation?

The French Supports/Surfaces group presented the genre of slack, freely suspended fabric pictures for the first time (if we leave aside the silk cloths of the *Hoarfrost* series for which Robert Rauschenberg became known in 1974).

die scheinbare Gleichgültigkeit gegenüber dem Motiv, steigert aber den Ausdruck des Malauftrages so in die Lockerheit einer groben Skizze hinein, dass die Motive nur noch als Bildanlässe sichtbar sind.

Im Gegensatz zu ihm hat Lüpertz zum „Stil“ gefunden, der seinen Anspruch an die gesellschaftliche Rolle des Künstlers ebenso bestimmt wie den an das Bild. Seit 1963 arbeitet er mit dem Begriff „Dithyrambe“ und trägt seine Bilder „begeistert, schwungvoll“ als „Loblieder“, „feierliche Gedichte“ vor. Die Wendung zu Inhalten von grosser Erhabenheit („Der Tod“, „Der Frühling“) und zu einer monumentalen Bildsprache in Pathosformeln zeigt den Grad der Absetzung von allem, was wir in den 60er Jahren als „modern“ in der Kunst empfunden haben: die Öffnung zu den Massenmedien und ihren Techniken, die gesellschaftsnahe Aktivität des Künstlers, die analytische Ironie. Vollends führen uns die Arbeiten von Anselm Kiefer aus der Gegenwart in die Beschäftigung mit geschichtlichen Inhalten, die einem spezifisch deutschen Bewusstsein angehören – vorgetragen in einer Sprache, die roh und unfertig sein und sich damit der raschen Konsumption entziehen will.

Ich habe den Titel „Les Nouveaux Fauves – Die Neuen Wilden“ in der Ausstellung „Paris – Berlin“ im Pariser Centre Pompidou gefunden, weil ich dort die Frage ungenügend beantwortet fand, was den „Fauves“ und den deutschen Expressionisten um 1910 gemeinsam war und was sie trennte, und weil ich für diskussionswürdig halte zu untersuchen, ob Gemeinsamkeiten und Verschiedenheiten heute wieder auftreten – wenn wir davon ausgehen, dass hier wie dort Rückbezüge zum Fauvismus – Expressionismus sichtbar sind. Beispielsweise: Tritt der „Taumel“ („le Vertige“), die Neigung zur ekstatischen Überhöhung, zur Metaphysik, die Nähe von Bildkunst, Literatur und Philosophie, die die Franzosen an den deutschen Expressionisten faszinierte und abschreckte, heute bei Baselitz, Penck, Lüpertz und Kiefer wieder auf? oder: Beobachten wir in der französischen Kunst heute den gleichen Grad von malerischer Disziplin, Rationalität des Geschmacks, des Strebens nach Ausgleich und Harmonie – und der gesellschaftlichen Unverbindlichkeit, den wir bei Matisse und seinem Kreis gesehen haben? Und was schliesslich fügen jene Amerikaner hinzu, die – in deutlichem Bezug zu Matisse – mit grossen Tüchern in prunkenden Farben die Ornamentgeschichte dieser Welt aufzuarbeiten scheinen?

Diese Ausstellung ist nicht Ergebnis einer Untersuchung, sondern soll ihr Anlass sein. Darum stellen wir die Fragen nur, beantworten sie heute aber nicht.

Es gibt scheinbar nichts, das einen Vergleich zwischen den deutschen und den französischen Künstlern dieser Ausstellung gestattete – es sei denn jene zum Pathos neigende Expressivität, die sich bei Cane ebenso wie bei Viallat in den letzten Jahren entwickelt hat. Die Künstlergruppe „Supports/Surfaces“ (= Bildträger – Bildflächen) hat seit der Mitte der 60er Jahre auf der Basis gründlicher theoretischer Auseinandersetzungen mit Matisse und den Amerikanern Ad Reinhardt, Barnett Newman, Morris Louis und Frank Stella und auf der Basis eines kulturpolitischen Diskurses Bilder in Gegenstände verwandelt oder: Bildträger und Bildfläche eins werden lassen. Dabei hat ihr der ältere Hantaï als Anreger gedient.
Als diese mit erdnahen Stoffen eingefärbten, gefalteten, zusammengenähten, tamponierten, lose herabhängenden Tücher bekannt wurden, erschienen sie wie Varianten einer zeitgenössischen abstrakten Malerei, die ebenso in Europa wie in Amerika existierte. Nur Viallat hat den Objektgedanken fortentwickelt, indem er Troddeln und Fransen an vorgefundenen Stoffbahnen belässt oder ihnen Gewandformen gibt. So tritt langsam die Serialität des gleichförmigen Tamponierens als Kompositionsprinzip in den Hintergrund. Viallat liebt die Assoziationsnähe zur Völkerkunde und zur aussereuropäischen Ornamentik, die wir in den amerikanischen Werken wiederfinden. Doch er versagt sich das direkte Zitat und hält damit unverwechselbar am stärksten die Nähe zu den geschnittenen Papieren von Matisse.

A cloth on the wall is something different than a picture; it lacks a frame, a demarcation; it is not window but curtain. It is not static but moves; it appears to be part of a performance. The fabrics of Kim MacConnel and Robert Kushner were originally elements of performances. Kushner first became known for his humorous, satirical fashion shows in which he improvised fantastical costumes from a loose stock of textile fragments of various origin, either alone or with female collaborators. And it must be pointed out that MacConnel's "pagode" piece was the prop of the performance *Mr. Burt his Memory of Mr. White his Fantasy of Mr. Dunstable his Musick/Pagode,* offering protection to two musicians with toy pianos and organs. The music reproduced here is part of the piece.

One is familiar with this process of props becoming autonomous from the Happening and Fluxus movement around the year 1960, and in the case of Kushner, a specific New York tradition allowed the evocation of the window dressings and fashion shows of Oldenburg. This tradition also upholds the love of trivial, used, worn-out, millionfold reproduced image motifs typical of Pop Art, most purely maintained in the wallpaper and decorative fabric industry (it hardly needs mentioning that now, from this new perspective, works by American and European Pop artists based on wallpaper are being dug up; what is more important, though, is that artists such as MacConnel reference Cubist collages and paintings by Picasso and Braque, who as a matter of course made use of wallpaper and newspapers).

Just as Pop Art countered the ossified emotive formulae of Abstract Expressionism, we can venture to regard this new group brought together by galleries and critics in New York as a reaction to the pictorial asceticism and intellectualism of Minimal and Conceptual Art, because the reaction becomes discernible as a break in the oeuvre of some of the protagonists.

The high sensitivity determining all the competitive achievements in a compact art center such as the island of Manhattan even turns fathers into accomplices. In a very obvious manner, artists such as Lichtenstein and Stella have been demonstrating their interest in the seriality and expressive pictoriality of historical ornaments in these years.

In the United States, we can presume a much higher awareness of the history of American arts and crafts and Native American art than by us. The national self-understanding lends an importance unknown to us to the objects of that history. This ethnological inclination accompanies American art and is presently becoming more distinct. It is not virulently nationalistic, however, but has more to do with the global ambition of partaking in world art.

Anyone seeking possibilities to order the pictures produced in this world ultimately arrives at laws determined by ornamentation and discovers that these laws are derived from old artisanal techniques. Their anti-modernist, anti-technological affects lead them to a tangible romanticism that in our exhibition reveals itself most obviously where it merges with a feminist stance. Joyce Kozloff, Miriam Schapiro, and Valerie Jaudon, as proponents of an aggressive feminism, have jointly developed image forms in which everyday decorative objects are cited in a provocative, monomaniacal, boisterous, and ironically naive fashion.

What does this engaging with Middle and Far Eastern ornamentation that distinguishes MacConnel, Smyth, Schapiro, Jaudon, and Kozloff imply? The marketable names of styles are deceptive: "pattern painting" and "decoration art," based on the understandable wish to celebrate themselves as ornament, deny that we are again dealing with non-usable art that cites customs.

But here the proximity to the object of use, to wall decoration, curtains, wallpaper, tiled interiors, reveals the determined desire to depart from the academic practice of the panel painting, to disavow painting that analyzes itself, to open up color surfaces into three-dimensional space, to enliven the

Die Gruppe „Supports/Surfaces“ ist ebenso 1968 durch die politische Generationskrise geschritten wie ihre deutschen Kollegen. Folgte sie einer französischen Tradition, kulturpolitische Forderungen immer ästhetisch zu instrumentalisieren? Unterscheidet sie das von den deutschen Künstlern ihrer Generation?

Die französische „Supports/Surfaces“-Gruppe hat uns zum ersten Mal jene Gattung ungespannter, freihängender Bildtücher vorgeführt (nehmen wir die Seidentücher der „Hoarfrost“-Serie aus, die Robert Rauschenberg 1974 bekannt gemacht hat).

Ein Tuch an einer Wand ist etwas anderes als ein Bild; ihm fehlt der Rahmen, die Abgrenzung; es ist nicht Fenster, sondern Vorhang. Es steht nicht fest, sondern bewegt sich, es scheint Teil einer Aufführung zu sein. Die Tücher von Kim MacConnel und Robert Kushner sind nach ihrer Herkunft Versatzstücke zu performances. Kushner wurde zuerst durch seine witzigen, satirischen Modeschauen bekannt, in denen er allein oder mit Partnerinnen aus einem lockeren Reservoir von Tuchfetzen verschiedenster Herkunft phantastische Kostüme improvisierte. Und man muss wissen, dass das Stück „Pagode“ von MacConnel in unserer Ausstellung Requisit der performance „MR. BURT HIS MEMORY OF MR. WHITE HIS FANTASY OF MR. DUNSTABLE HIS MUSICK / PAGODE“ war und zwei Musikern mit zwei Spielzeugklavieren und -orgeln Schutz bot. Die jetzt reproduzierte Musik ist Teil des Stückes.

Dieser Vorgang, dass Requisiten sich verselbständigen, ist aus der happening- und fluxus-Bewegung um 1960 bekannt, und eine spezifische New Yorker Tradition erlaubte es, bei Kushner an die Schaufensterdekorationen und Modeschauen von Oldenburg zu erinnern. In dieser Tradition bleibt auch die der pop art eigene Liebe zu trivialen, abgenutzten, ausgeleierten, millionenfach reproduzierten Bildmotiven erhalten, die sich am reinsten in der Tapeten- und Dekorationsstoffe-Industrie erhalten hat (es versteht sich, dass jetzt, unter diesem neuen Blickwinkel, Werke von pop-Künstlern aus Amerika und Europa ausgegraben werden, die auf Tapeten basieren; wichtiger ist aber, dass Künstler wie MacConnel sich auf kubistische Collagen und Gemälde von Picasso und Braque beziehen, die selbstverständlich Tapeten wie Zeitungen benutzt haben).

Wendete sich die pop art gegen die erstarrenden Pathosformeln des abstrakten Expressionismus, so können wir uns erlauben, diese neue, in New York von Galerien und Kritikern zusammengefasste Gruppierung in einer Reaktion auf die bildnerische Askese und Kopflastigkeit der minimal und conceptual art zu sehen, weil die Reaktion im oeuvre einiger der Protagonisten als Bruch sichtbar wird.

Die hohe Sensibilität, die in einem kompakten Kunstzentrum wie der Insel Manhattan alle kompetitiven Leistungen bestimmt, macht sogar die Väter zu Komplizen. Überdeutlich tragen Künstler wie Lichtenstein und Stella in diesen Jahren ihr Interesse an der Serialität und expressiven Bildhaftigkeit historischer Ornamente vor.

Wir können in den Vereinigten Staaten ein ungleich höheres Bewusstsein als bei uns für die Geschichte des amerikanischen Kunsthandwerks und die der Kunst der Indianer voraussetzen. Das nationale Selbstverständnis gibt Gegenständen dieser Geschichte ein Gewicht, das wir nicht kennen. Diese ethnologische Neigung begleitet die amerikanische Kunst und tritt heute stark hervor. Sie ist aber nicht virulent nationalistisch, sondern schliesst eher den globalen Anspruch ein, an der Weltkunst teilzuhaben.

Wer nach Möglichkeiten sucht, die Bilder, die in dieser Welt hergestellt werden, zu ordnen, stösst am Ende auf Gesetze, die von der Ornamentik bestimmt werden, und entdeckt, dass die Gesetze der Ornamentik sich ableiten aus alten handwerklichen Techniken. Seine anti-modernistischen, anti-technologischen Affekte führen ihn zu einer handgreiflichen Romantik, die in unserer Ausstellung am deutlichsten dort durchschlägt, wo sie sich mit einer feministischen Haltung verbindet. Joyce Kozloff, Miriam Schapiro und Valerie Jaudon haben als Vertreterinnen eines aggressiven Feminismus –

compositional principle of the series through gestures or color modulations, and to present a compositional spontaneity—provided that a knowledge of global art history exists. The intermediate position of American art schools between Europe and East Asia allows us to understand the inimitable mixture of pictorial heritages—just as we can understand that German artists such as Baselitz deal with Russian artists of the past.

The sensual attack of these fabrics is powerful. Yet it cannot be overlooked that this uplifting manifestation of joie de vivre is saturated with irony, fluttering, blowing, indeed not fixed.

It needn't be mentioned that the works of Miriam Schapiro, Joyce Kozloff, Kim MacConnel, and Robert Kushner have nothing in common with those of Markus Lüpertz and Georg Baselitz, Anselm Kiefer and Jörg Immendorff—except for a distinct pathos, a longing for the expression of grandness, exuberance, and triumphal appearance. Under this common denominator, we have tried to relate the works of our exhibition to each other. The questions raised by these posited interrelations will keep us busy for a year.

In 1980, Wolfgang Becker, the founding director of the Neue Galerie – Sammlung Ludwig, later the Ludwig Forum für Internationale Kunst, presented works newly acquired by Peter and Irene Ludwig under the exhibition title *Les Nouveaux Fauves – Die Neuen Wilden.* The group show featured works of the American Pattern and Decoration movement, the French artist group Supports/Surfaces, and a few German painters, including Georg Baselitz, Jörg Immendorff, and A. R. Penck. With the chosen title, Becker established a connection between these various contemporary positions and the French Fauvists of classical modernism. Whereas the Fauvists revolted against the academic painting of the Salon d'Automne at the beginning of the twentieth century, Becker describes the turn toward large-format painting over the course of the 1970s, which he firmly considers to be an international phenomenon, as an impulse running contrary to established currents like Conceptual Art, increasingly perceived as overly intellectual. The term "Neue Wilde" coined as part of the exhibition was quickly adopted by the media and art critics as a label for a number of young figurative painters in Germany, without Becker having shown any of their work in the original exhibition. *Les Nouveaux Fauves – Die Neuen Wilden* marked the beginning of a series of exhibitions by Becker that, based on the collecting by Peter and Irene Ludwig, were devoted to the latest "anti-academic" currents in art, including the New York graffiti scene.

in Verabredung – Bildformen entwickelt, in denen provozierend monomanisch, übermütig, ironisch naiv Gebrauchsgegenstände mit schmückender Funktion zitiert werden.

Was bedeutet diese Auseinandersetzung mit der Ornamentik des Vorderen und Hinteren Orients, die MacConnel, Smyth, Schapiro, Jaudon und Kozloff auszeichnet? Die marktgängigen Stilbezeichnungen täuschen: „pattern painting" und „decoration art" wollen aus dem verständlichen Wunsch, sich selbst als Ornament anzupreisen, verleugnen, dass wir es noch einmal mit gebrauchsferner, gebräuchezitierender Kunst zu tun haben.

Die Nähe zum Gebrauchsgegenstand, zur Wanddekoration, zum Behang, zur Tapete, zum gekachelten Interieur zeigt aber hier den entschlossenen Wunsch, von der akademischen Praxis des Tafelbildes abzurücken, die Malerei, die sich selber analysiert, zu desavouieren, Farbflächen in den Raum zu öffnen, das kompositorische Prinzip der Reihung gestuell oder durch Farbmodulationen zu beleben und eine gestalterische Spontaneität – globale Kunstgeschichtsbildung vorausgesetzt – vorzutragen. Die Mittelstellung der amerikanischen Kunstschulen zwischen Europa und Ostasien macht die unnachahmliche Mischung bildnerischer Erbschaften verständlich – wie es ebenso verständlich erscheint, dass deutsche Künstler wie Baselitz z. B. sich mit russischen Künstlern der Vergangenheit beschäftigen.

Der sinnliche Ansturm dieser Tücher ist gewaltig. Dennoch ist nicht zu übersehen, dass diese erhebende Manifestation der Lebensfreude mit Ironie gesättigt ist, flatternd, verwehend, durchaus nicht festgemacht.

Es bedarf keiner Erwähnung, dass die Werke von Miriam Schapiro, Joyce Kozloff, Kim MacConnel und Robert Kushner mit denen von Markus Lüpertz und Georg Baselitz, Anselm Kiefer und Jörg Immendorff nichts gemein haben – es sei denn jenes ausdrückliche Pathos, jene Sehnsucht nach der Expression von Grösse, Exuberanz und triumphaler Erscheinung. Unter diesem gemeinsamen Nenner haben wir die Werke in unserer Ausstellung zueinanderzuordnen versucht. Die Fragen, die diese Zueinanderordnung aufwirft, werden uns ein Jahr lang beschäftigen.

Wolfgang Becker, Gründungsdirektor der Neuen Galerie – Sammlung Ludwig, des späteren Ludwig Forum für Internationale Kunst, präsentierte 1980 unter dem Ausstellungstitel *Les Nouveaux Fauves – Die Neuen Wilden* Neuankäufe von Peter und Irene Ludwig. In der Gruppenschau waren Werke der amerikanischen Pattern and Decoration-Bewegung, der französischen Künstlergruppe Supports/Surfaces sowie einiger deutscher Maler, darunter Georg Baselitz, Jörg Immendorff und A. R. Penck, zu sehen. Mit seiner kunsthistorisch anmutenden Bezeichnung stellte Becker eine Verbindung zwischen den unterschiedlichen zeitgenössischen Positionen und den französischen Fauves der klassischen Moderne her. Während die Fauves zu Beginn des 20. Jahrhunderts gegen die akademische Malerei des Salon d'Automne aufbegehrten, beschreibt Becker die Hinwendung zur großformatigen Malerei im Laufe der 1970er-Jahre, die er dezidiert als internationales Phänomen beobachtet, als einen gegenläufigen Impuls zu etablierten und zunehmend als intellektualisiert wahrgenommenen Strömungen wie der Konzeptkunst. Der im Zuge dieser Ausstellung geprägte Begriff der „Neuen Wilden" wurde binnen kürzester Zeit von Medien und Kunstkritik als Label für eine Reihe junger figurativer Maler*innen in Deutschland herangezogen, ohne dass Becker diese in der „Ur-Schau" gezeigt hätte. *Les Nouveaux Fauves – Die Neuen Wilden* markierte den Anfang einer Reihe von Ausstellungen Beckers, die sich ausgehend von der Sammeltätigkeit Peter und Irene Ludwigs neuesten „anti-akademischen" Kunstströmungen, zum Beispiel der New Yorker Graffitiszene, widmeten.

Thomas Bayrle
Only Five Minutes

The “new painters” have a “new attitude.”
They live in a market economy and they know it.
They often form groups.
They’re publicized, the same as in the music business.
They call themselves—New Image—Artbrakers—Mülheimer Freiheit—Wilde.
People photograph them.
Mapplethorpe photographs them.
Good art dealers discover them.
Museums instantly exhibit them.—It all goes very quickly.
They’ve only got five minutes.
They’ve known that since Warhol.
They paint quickly.
They paint whatever takes their fancy.
Often at the exhibition venue.
They’re free of conventions, or conventional.
They don’t care about style, or they paint style.
They work like washing machines.
They “cleanse the environment.”
They stuff paint in.
They slap paint on.
Silicone on oil—vinegar in Bakelite—coffee over cake.
They were born in a supermarket.
They come from Kaufhof.
They paint “horrendously.”
They “fit” the era.
They “bend with the wind.”
They promise nothing.—These painters are NEW.
They paint FALSELY with total honesty.

Underground there are seated figures made from ebony—bodybuilding trained—with woodcut faces and transistor radios—the neighbors move anxiously away ... “Thank God I’m cleverer ... but what if he, nevertheless ... ?”
Lurking, elastic energy everywhere ... it gives us a headache ... on the levels ... It’s denser ... less porous ... surrounded by machines ... little automata everywhere ... robots ... checkouts ... beep beep.—It makes a lot of people nervous.
What they’ve “learned” no longer applies.
Others now feel “really good.”
They wallow in a cacophony of shells and cassettes.
Bathe in the daily newspaper gruel ... in the scraps of headlines ... splashing in towns ... NOW—live—NOW ...

The “present” rolls up into a ball.
Attracts everything.
Hurls the past, tears the future—back to the moment.

Thomas Bayrle
Nur 5 Minuten Zeit

Die „Neuen Maler" haben eine „Neue Haltung".
Sie leben in der Marktwirtschaft und wissen das.
Sie bilden oft Gruppen.
Wie im Musikgeschäft, werden sie bekannt gemacht.
Sie nennen sich – New Image – Artbrakers – Mülheimer Freiheit – Wilde.
Man fotografiert sie.
Mapplethorpe fotografiert sie.
Gute Händler entdecken sie.
Museen stellen sie sofort aus. – Es geht alles sehr schnell.
Sie haben nur 5 Minuten Zeit.
Das wissen sie, seit Warhol.
Sie malen schnell.
Sie malen, was ihnen gefällt.
Oft am Ort der Ausstellung.
Sie sind frei von Konvention, oder konventionell.
Sie kümmern sich nicht um Stil, oder malen Stil.
Sie arbeiten wie Waschmaschinen.
Sie „reinigen die Umwelt".
Sie stopfen Farbe rein.
Sie placken Farbe drauf.
Silikon auf Öl – Essig in Bagalit – Kaffee über Kuchen.
Sie sind im Supermarkt geboren.
Sie kommen aus dem Kaufhof.
Sie malen „grauen-haft".
Sie „passen" in die Zeit.
Sie „hängen die Fahne in den Wind".
Sie versprechen nichts. – Diese Maler sind NEU.
Sie malen pottehrlichen FAKE.

In „B-Ebenen" sitzen Körper aus Ebenholz – bodybuilding-trainierte – mit Holzschnittgesichtern und Kofferradios – ängstlich rücken die Nachbarn ab ... „Gott sei Dank bin ich klüger ... aber wenn er trotzdem ...?"
Lauernde, federnde Kraft überall ... das macht uns Kopfweh ... in den Ebenen ... Es ist dichter ... lückenloser ... von Maschinen umstellt ... überall die kleinen Automaten ... Robots ... Kassen ... pip pip. – Viele werden da nervös.
Was sie „gelernt" haben, stimmt nicht mehr.
Andere fühlen sich jetzt „richtig wohl".
Sie suhlen sich im Gestammel aus Muscheln und Kassetten.
Baden im täglichen Zeitungsbrei ... in den Fetzen der Überschriften ... in den Städten planschen sie ... JETZT – leben – JETZT ...

„Gegenwart" ballt sich zusammen.
Zieht alles an.
Schleudert Vergangenheit, reißt Zukunft – zurück auf den Moment.

Fifty years after the communist version of “collective culture,” it’s solid enough for that, the world has solidified—in a thicket of machinery.
Form armies of—workers—tins—onions—chocolates—cars—Greens—liberals—rightwingers—leftwingers—no matter the context—masses of the similar—of the same—as never before.
“Individual, self-determining,” they float like lumps in broths and sauces ... in the arteries of huge conglomerates of wildly proliferating entanglements in the economy and manufacturing ... rattled by waves—fads—obsessions—desires.

That’s a good situation for art.
It has to change!
Wash clean, become quicker, become more fluid.
There are no criteria any more! (Achille Bonito Oliva)—what a chance—to define new ones—in motion—flowing—like the clouds.
The kind that come and go—in keeping with technological reality ... like oil greasing societies.
There’s been enough practice ... the concept of art extended to language—gums—bodies for years ... what was Beuys preaching for ... that’s reality after all ... and that’s the new space ... why shouldn’t it be used?
An existential art praxis means saying yes to the “automatic body,” more sweating—less “mindfuck!”—push the body into the middle, don’t just see it as a launch vehicle for “beautiful ideas.”

Doing—feeling—acting treads where “planning” is stuck to the ground.

In 1981, the artist Thomas Bayrle, at the time a professor at the Staatliche Hochschule für Bildende Künste – Städelschule, wrote an article on the Neue Wilde for the *Frankfurter Rundschau.* His text refrains from employing the usual means of art-historical analysis or criticism, instead circling in on the contemporary spirit of euphoria with a staccato-like language and delivery that in its abruptness reflects the improvised and at times pointedly flippant-to-confrontational tone of the young artists. Bayrle’s text was featured on a single page with an article by the art critic Peter Iden, a withering piece of criticism entitled “Hochgemute Nichtskönner” (Light-Hearted Incompetents). Iden’s text is typical of the skeptical reactions in the German feuilletons. He criticized the intentional anti-virtuosity of the artists, judging it to be an indulgent, insubstantial act of rebellion, and thus a gesture that could not justify the lack of quality in working with the motifs and the painterly execution. With its sympathetic openness and experimental language, Bayrle’s piece reads like an energy-charged objection to Iden’s vehement criticism.

50 Jahre nach der kommunistischen Version von „kollektiver Kultur“ ist es Dicht genug dazu, hat sich die Welt verdichtet – im Maschinengestrüpp.
Bilden Armeen von – Werktätigen – Dosen – Zwiebeln – Pralinen – Autos – Grünen – Liberalen – Rechten – Linken – egal, von was – Massen von Ähnlichem – Gleichem – wie nie zuvor.
„Individuell, sich selbst bestimmend“, schwimmen sie als Brocken in Brühen und Saucen ... in den Arterien von riesigen Konglomeraten wild wuchernder Wirtschafts- und Produktionsverknotungen dahin ... durchgerüttelt von Wellen – Moden – Süchten – Wünschen.

Das ist eine gute Situation für Kunst.
Sie muß anders werden!
Reinwachsen, schneller werden, liquider werden.
Es gibt keine Kriterien mehr! (Achille Bonito Oliva) – was für eine Chance – Neue zu bilden – in Bewegung – im Fluß – gleich den Wolken –.
Welche, die kommen und gehen – der technischen Realität entsprechend ... wie Öl Gesellschaften schmierend.
Es wurde lange genug geübt ... der Kunstbegriff auf Sprache – Gaumen – Körper seit Jahren ausgedehnt ... wozu hat Beuys gepredigt ... das ist doch Realität ... das ist doch neuer Raum ... wieso soll er nicht genutzt werden?
Kunst existentiell ausüben heißt, den „automatischen Körper“ bejahen, mehr schwitzen – weniger „Hirnfick!“ – den Body in die Mitte schieben, ihn nicht nur als Trägerrakete sehen für „schöne Ideen“.

Handeln – Fühlen – Agieren tritt dahin, wo „Planen“ am Boden klebt.

Der Künstler Thomas Bayrle, damals Professor an der Staatlichen Hochschule für Bildende Künste – Städelschule, schrieb 1981 in der *Frankfurter Rundschau* über die „Neuen Wilden“. Sein Text bedient sich nicht der Mittel kunsthistorischer Analyse oder Kritik, sondern umkreist die gegenwärtige Aufbruchstimmung mit einem Stakkato-artigen Sprachduktus, der in seiner Schnelligkeit dem improvisierten und dabei bisweilen betont flapsigen bis konfrontativen Ton der jungen Künstler*innen Rechnung trägt. Bayrles Beitrag wurde auf einer Seite mit der vernichtenden Kritik „Hochgemute Nichtskönner“ des Kunstkritikers Peter Iden abgedruckt. Idens Text kann als stellvertretend für die skeptischen Reaktionen des deutschen Feuilletons verstanden werden. Er kritisierte den anti-virtuosen Gestus der Künstler als kurzweiliges, substanzloses Rebellieren, das ihm zufolge den Mangel an Qualität im Umgang mit Motivik und formaler Umsetzung nicht zu rechtfertigen vermochte. In direkter Konfrontation mit Idens Kritik erscheint Bayrles Beitrag in seiner wohlwollenden Offenheit und experimentellen Sprache als energiegeladene Gegenrede.

In *Junge Kunst aus Westdeutschland '81*, exh. cat. Galerie Max Hetzler, Stuttgart 1981, n.p.

Gudrun Inboden

The Categories of Modernism—Perplexed

Although there is no lack of exhibitions, that is to say first-hand information, on the production of young artists from Western Europe and America who are starting to cause a stir, and although numerous well-meaning neologisms already designate what is new, a critical debate has yet to commence. The large number of swiftly coined terms best reveals the prevailing perplexity: "Wilde Malerei," "Neue Welle," "New Imaginism," "Nouvelle Peinture," "Post-" and "Transavantgarde" have rapidly become noncommittal buzzwords. They fail to hit home. Since this is not due to a lack of accuracy, the reason must lie elsewhere. Apparently the desire to name the phenomenon misses the phenomenon itself. The habit of grasping art as a continuous sequence of styles that can be historicized, and of gauging their respective significance according to their degree of innovation is expressed—a bit insecurely—by these tentative names. They assert the new—but with a twofold meaning: as something that has not been there before and as something that is there anew. The innovative aspect is retracted in the same breath and with the same word with which it was proffered. As if one sensed that it did not hold water as a criterion. And one dallies with a turn to conservatism. The old and the new become the same in an unrealistic way. The tension and the space between the two dissipate. Where, then, is the "Neue Malerei" [new painting] really to be situated?

The helplessness in the face of the unsuitability of tried and tested criteria for classifying and assessing the most recent productions is certainly not just a symptom of an art criticism that is no longer in charge, but foremost of its subject matter that is not commensurable with it anymore.

The keyword "innovation," in light of which criticism no longer feels comfortable and that it can't apply in a convincing manner, derives from the context of aesthetic modernism, where the aspect of the new has the function of confronting the aesthetic and historical consciousness of the times with topicality, or incorporating topicality in this consciousness. In this context, the new unmistakably contains what has not been there before. Conservatism is its opposite pole. From the perspective of modernism, innovation amounts to opposition, but not—and this is crucial—for the sake of innovation. Avant-garde art may have addressed art itself to a great extent, but to reproach it for this reason means that one has understood nothing about it. If one describes it as pure formalism, one disavows the 1920s in Russia, for one thing, and disregards that the high degree of (also formal) self-reflectivity corresponds with a high degree of historical awareness. The art of modernism grasping itself as obliged to the historical context can only engender meaning by gaining clarity with respect to its own means. For its self-understanding is neither defined nor ensured by society. The social raison d'être, which has been lost for good, demands opposition and thus self-reflectivity from modernist art, if it does not want to forfeit its historical position.

From this perspective, the new of the "new" art can first be defined negatively: it does not pretend to be innovative—the formal solutions are familiar; it does not give the impression of being directed against anything or anyone—elements of the mundane world appear neutrally adopted or anecdotally interpreted; self-reflection cannot be sensed—the narrative moment and the immediacy of the formal implementation leave no room for this, and there can be

Aus: *Junge Kunst aus Westdeutschland ’81*,
Ausst.-Kat. Galerie Max Hetzler, Stuttgart 1981, o. S.

Gudrun Inboden
Die Kategorien der Moderne – Ratlos

Obwohl es an Ausstellungen sprich Information aus erster Hand über die Produktion der gerade erst von sich reden machenden jungen Künstler in Westeuropa und den USA nicht fehlt und obwohl bereits eine Reihe wohlmeinender Begriffsneuschöpfungen das Neue benennt, steht eine kritische Verständigung darüber noch aus. Die Vielzahl der eilig erfundenen übergreifenden Vokabeln verrät am ehesten Ratlosigkeit: „Wilde Malerei“, „Neue Welle“, „New Imaginism“, „Nouvelle Peinture“, „Post-“ und „Trans-avantgarde“ sind rasch zu unverbindlichen Schlagworten geworden. Sie treffen nicht ins Schwarze. Da mangelnde Treffsicherheit nicht der Grund dafür sein kann, liegt die Ursache anderswo. Offenbar geht der Wunsch nach Benennbarkeit des Phänomens an diesem selber vorbei. Die Gewohnheit, Kunst als kontinuierliche Folge historisierbarer Stile zu begreifen und ihren jeweiligen Stellenwert an ihrem Innovationsgrad zu messen, spricht sich – ein wenig unsicher geworden – in den Nennversuchen aus. Sie beteuern das Neue – aber mit zweierlei Sinngebung: von noch nicht dagewesen und von erneut wieder dasein. Das Innovative wird im selben Atemzug und mit demselben Wort zurückgenommen, mit dem es vorgebracht wird. Als spürte man, daß es als Kriterium nicht stichhält. Und man liebäugelt mit einer Wendung ins Konservative. Das Alte und das Neue werden auf unrealistische Weise einander gleich. Zwischen beiden schwinden die Spannung und der Raum. Wo ist nun wirklich die „Neue Malerei“ anzusiedeln?

Die Hilflosigkeit angesichts der Unbrauchbarkeit bewährter Kriterien zur Einordnung und Einschätzung der jüngsten Produktion ist gewiß nicht ausschließlich symptomatisch für eine unzuständig gewordene Kritik, sondern zunächst für ihren ihr nicht länger kommensurablen Gegenstand. Das Stichwort Innovation, bei dem der Kritik nicht mehr recht wohl ist und das sie doch nicht überzeugend ersetzen kann, entstammt dem Kontext der ästhetischen Moderne.
In ihm hat der Gesichtspunkt des Neuen die Funktion, die Aktualität dem ästhetischen und geschichtlichen Bewußtsein der Zeit entgegenzuhalten bzw. sie ihm einzuverleiben. Hier beinhaltet das Neue unmißverständlich das noch nicht Gewesene. Das Konservative ist sein Gegenpol. Aus der Sicht der Moderne ist Innovation gleich Opposition, jedoch nicht – und das ist entscheidend – um der Innovation willen. Die Kunst der Avantgarde hat zwar in hohem Maße die Kunst selbst thematisch gemacht, doch daraus einen Vorwurf gegen sie ableiten heißt nichts an ihr verstehen. Wenn man ihr bloßen Formalismus bescheinigt, verleugnet man einmal die 20er Jahre in Rußland, und man übersieht, daß der hohe Grad an Selbstreflexion (auch formaler Art) einem hohen Grad an geschichtlichem Bewußtsein entspricht. Die dem historischen Kontext verpflichtet sich sehende Kunst der Moderne kann nur dadurch Sinn erzeugen, daß sie über die ihr eigenen Mittel Klarheit gewinnt. Denn ihr Selbstverständnis wird ihr von der Gesellschaft weder definiert noch garantiert. Die ein für allemal verlorene gesellschaftliche Existenzberechtigung fordert die Kunst der Moderne zur Opposition und damit zur Selbstreflexion heraus, will sie ihren geschichtlichen Standort nicht einbüßen.

Von hier aus läßt sich das Neue an der „Neuen“ Kunst zunächst negativ bestimmen: Es gibt sich nicht innovativ – die formalen Lösungen sind vertraut –; es macht nicht den Eindruck, gegen irgendetwas oder irgendwen gerichtet zu sein – Bestandteile der Alltagswelt erscheinen neutral übernommen oder anekdotisch interpretiert –; Selbstreflexion ist nicht herausspürbar – das

no talk of a critical distance to the social environment.

When mentioning artists of the older generation such as Palermo, Polke, or Richter as trailblazers in this context, one should not withhold the crucial differences. These artists have created an iconography from reality and in contradiction to it, which in the sense of modernism assumes an enlightening function—pictures that mirror false consciousness and can only do so via the consistent reflection upon the form.

Aesthetic and historical experience—the interdependent categories of cultural modernism—no longer coincide in the production of the younger generation—something that becomes evident in the mundane fact that traditional means (without being critiqued) bring forth what is temporally new. Historical thought feels as if it were reduced to absurdity. What it can discern is that the thematic preconditions decisive for modernism are no longer given: Against whom should the individual oppose, when no authority is tangible, not to speak of responsible, anymore; when polarity not only doesn't exist but is not tolerated from the outset; when, instead, a generalized pluralism merely feigns the infinite diversity of possibilities of existence? What can be said in positive terms is that art produced in the spirit of modernism is anachronistic today, tilting at windmills. The art of the younger generation quite evidently puts an end to a historical thought that envisions utopias, and in this respect it is contemporaneous. Its noncommittal, private character, its arbitrary dealing with (art-) historical citations, its lack of reflection, are less signs of naivety than indications of a spontaneous uninhibitedness toward all the so-called sociocultural values that have long lost their credibility. They have become so unappealing that the artists do not even relate to them negatively. They have abandoned the context—at first each on their own, quite privately; and with astounding and at times apocalyptic verve, they now still give rise to a certainly not unproductive perplexity.

The heated debates about the Neue Wilde coincided with the discussion, emerging at the dawn of the 1980s, about the end of the avant-garde and the advent of postmodernism. With her essay, the art historian and curator Gudrun Inboden characterizes the uncertainty felt when the logic of avant-garde progress is questioned, a challenge the Neue Wilde also appeared to be expressing. The "return" to figurative painting and its purported revival of ideas like the object-bound unity of a work or subjective expression seemed at times to be an attack on the developmental logic of recent art history and a theory of art that used the tradition of gestural painting as a negative foil to advocate a broadened concept of art. There was, furthermore, disagreement as to whether the "new" painting, understood as seeking to once again tap into the potentialities of an expressionist notion of art, was to be supported or rejected. Or if it was, instead of a revival of classical values, rather a postmodernist carnivalesque play with styles and motifs that was tantamount to a swansong for the utopias of modernism and the revolutionary aspirations pursued by avant-garde practice. Inboden's essay was published in the exhibition catalogue for the early group show *Junge Kunst aus Westdeutschland '81* (Young Art from West Germany '81) held at the Galerie Max Hetzler in Stuttgart. Max Hetzler, who shortly after moved his headquarters to Cologne, the hub of the art market at the time, would become an important gallerist in the figurative painting scene of the 1980s.

erzählerische Moment und die Unmittelbarkeit der formalen Umsetzung lassen dafür keinen Raum, von kritischer Distanz zur gesellschaftlichen Umwelt kann nicht die Rede sein –.

Wenn man in diesem Zusammenhang Künstler der älteren Generation wie Palermo, Polke, Richter als Wegbereiter zitiert, so sollte man dabei nicht die gravierenden Unterschiede unterschlagen. Diese Künstler haben aus der Realität und in Widerspruch zu ihr eine Ikonographie herausgebildet, die im Sinne der Moderne eine aufklärende Funktion übernimmt – Bilder, die ein falsches Bewußtsein spiegeln und dies nur tun können durch eine konsequent reflektierte Form hindurch.

Ästhetische und geschichtliche Erfahrung – die einander bedingenden Kategorien der kulturellen Moderne – fallen in der Produktion der jüngeren Generation nicht mehr zusammen – deutlich schon an der banalen Tatsache, daß traditionelle Mittel (ohne der Kritik unterworfen zu werden) das zeitlich Neue hervorbringen. Geschichtliches Denken fühlt sich ad absurdum geführt. Was es einsehen kann, ist, daß die für die Moderne ausschlaggebenden inhaltlichen Voraussetzungen nicht mehr gegeben sind: Gegen wen sollte der Einzelne noch opponieren wollen, wenn keine Instanz mehr greifbar geschweige verantwortlich ist, wenn Polarität nicht nur nicht existiert, sondern von vornherein nicht geduldet ist, wenn stattdessen ein verallgemeinernder Pluralismus die unendliche Vielfalt von Existenzmöglichkeiten nur vortäuscht?

Soviel jedenfalls läßt positiv sich sagen: Heute aus dem Geist der Moderne heraus entstehende Kunst ist anachronistisch, ein Kampf gegen Windmühlen. Diesen Schlußpunkt unter ein für Utopien tragfähiges Geschichtsdenken setzt die Kunst der jungen Generation überdeutlich, und darin ist sie ihrer Zeit gemäß. Ihr unverbindlicher privater Charakter, ihr beliebiger Umgang mit (kunst-)historischen Zitaten, ihre Reflexionslosigkeit verraten weniger Naivität als vielmehr eine spontane Ungeniertheit all den sogenannten gesellschaftlich-kulturellen Werten gegenüber, die ihrer Glaubwürdigkeit längst verlustig sind. So unattraktiv sind diese geworden, daß die Künstler sich nicht einmal negativ auf sie beziehen. Sie sind ausgestiegen aus dem Kontext – zunächst jeder für sich ganz privat, und mit erstaunlicher, manchmal apokalyptischer Verve verursachen sie im Moment noch – eine gewiß nicht unfruchtbare Ratlosigkeit.

Die hitzigen Debatten um die „Neuen Wilden" überschnitten sich mit der Anfang der 1980er-Jahre aufkommenden Diskussion um das Ende der Avantgarde und den Anbruch der Postmoderne. Die Kunsthistorikerin und Kuratorin Gudrun Inboden benennt mit ihrem Aufsatz die Verunsicherung angesichts der Infragestellung avantgardistischer Fortschrittslogik, der auch die „Neuen Wilden" Ausdruck zu verleihen schienen. Die „Rückkehr" zur figurativen Malerei und deren vermeintliche Erneuerung von Konzepten wie etwa der objekthaften Werkeinheit oder des subjektiven Ausdrucks wirkten bisweilen wie ein Angriff auf die Entwicklungslogik der jüngsten Kunstgeschichte und einer Kunsttheorie, die die Tradition der gestischen Malerei als Negativfolie für einen erweiterten Kunstbegriff heranzog. Dabei war man sich uneins darüber, ob die „neue" Malerei nun als Rückgriff auf einen expressionistischen Kunstbegriff zu befürworten oder abzulehnen sei. Oder hatte man es anstatt mit einer Wiederbelebung klassischer Werte nicht viel eher mit einem postmodernen, karnevalesken Spiel mit Stilen und Motiven zu tun, das einem Abgesang auf die Utopien der Moderne und den revolutionären Anspruch avantgardistischer Praxis gleichkam? Inbodens Aufsatz erschien in dem Ausstellungskatalog der frühen Gruppenschau *Junge Kunst aus Westdeutschland '81* in der Galerie Max Hetzler in Stuttgart. Max Hetzler, der seinen Sitz kurze Zeit später ins damalige Kunstmarktzentrum Köln verlagerte, sollte zu einer wichtigen Galeristenfigur im Umfeld der figurativen Malerei der 1980er-Jahre werden.

In *Artforum* 20, no. 1, September 1981, pp. 33–39

Wolfgang Max Faust

"Du hast keine Chance. Nutze sie!" With It and Against It: Tendencies in Recent German Art

"Expressionist revival," "violent painting," "return of the Fauves," "back to the esthetic of shock," or simply "artists are painting again!"—such are the reactions that have been aroused by the youngest, newest generation of German artists. Their work evokes everything from wild praise to outright enmity—in other words, strong emotional reactions, which show that these artists have struck a nerve, have hit on something. And this "something" has more than local significance, standing as it does in the context of the fundamental reorientation that Western art is currently undergoing.

After an art from and for the head—conceptual art, the esthetic reductions of Minimal art, and Italian *Arte Povera*—after the schoolroom-for-society of Joseph Beuys, after artistic experimentation with technological media, after body art, after performance art, we are now witnessing a rediscovery of simple, spontaneous drawing and painting. At first this may strike one as a nostalgic (or even reactionary) return to long-neglected traditions; on closer view one realizes that a shift is taking place, and that these artists have esthetic positions which are truly new, though consciously historicist.

That this should be occurring with particular vehemence in West Germany—exhibitions of the new painting in Cologne, Groningen [*sic*], Munich, Berlin, and Karlsruhe are witness—is due in part to the general sociocultural situation in this country (West Germany). After the Second World War, as a result of barbarian Nazi policy, Germany had almost no vanguard art, and turned to one international stream after another for nourishment. France, then the United States and the revival of past phases of the international pre-war avant-gardes became the fixed points around which West German art revolved. This was reinforced by general trends elsewhere that attempted through art to arrive at "universally" meaningful statements in which the importance of individual and regional character was reduced, whether it related to the history of art or to the history of a given nation. To put it bluntly, the art that rapidly established itself in West Germany after the war reflected the power structures of resurgent capitalism.

The economic predominance of the United States brought with it American art which, like any other American product, was seeking (and found) a world market. The '60s were the decade of the wide-open American image. But the more crisis-prone American society showed itself to be, the less stable its political and moral tenets in practice became, and the more European artists drew away from this new-found authority; by the time the '70s ended, specifically European artists were again at the forefront of avant-garde discussion. Fundamental reevaluations of the shape and purpose of contemporary art had taken place in Western Europe during the '70s, and they were based (again, but for the first time since the war) on what was clearly a specifically European approach. Surprisingly, only now, looking back, does this become apparent. Significant European artists are concentrating (once again, but with a radical difference) on self-knowledge, self-image, self-expression, and on the problem of their representation and the making of esthetic objects.

From the late '70s on, painters such as Francesco Clemente, Sandro Chia, Enzo Cucchi, Mimmo Paladino, and Nicola De Maria have examined the connection between personal statement and painting

Wolfgang Max Faust

„Du hast keine Chance. Nutze sie!" Dafür und dagegen: Tendenzen in der jüngsten deutschen Kunst

„Revival des Expressionismus", „heftige Malerei", „Rückkehr der Fauves", „zurück zur Schockästhetik" oder einfach „Künstler malen wieder!" – das sind einige der Reaktionen auf die jüngste, neueste Generation deutscher Kunstschaffender. Ihre Arbeiten lösen sowohl überbordendes Lob als auch unverhohlene Feindseligkeit aus – starke emotionale Reaktionen also, die zeigen, dass diese Künstler*innen einen Nerv getroffen haben, auf etwas gestoßen sind. Und dieses „Etwas" hat nicht nur lokale Bedeutung, denn es steht im Kontext einer gegenwärtig stattfindenden grundlegenden Neuorientierung der Kunst im Westen.

Nach einer Kunst, die aus dem Kopf und für den Kopf gemacht wurde – der Konzeptkunst und den ästhetischen Reduktionen des Minimalismus sowie der italienischen Arte povera –, nach Joseph Beuys' Klassenraum für die Gesellschaft, den künstlerischen Experimenten mit technischen Medien und Performancekunst, beobachten wir nun eine Wiederentdeckung der einfachen und spontanen Zeichnung und Malerei. Das mag einem zunächst wie eine nostalgische (oder gar reaktionäre) Rückkehr zu lange vernachlässigten Traditionen erscheinen. Doch bei genauerer Betrachtung bemerkt man, dass eine Verschiebung stattfindet und diese Künstler*innen ästhetische Positionen einnehmen, die wirklich neu, jedoch bewusst historistisch sind.

Dass dies mit besonderer Vehemenz in Westdeutschland stattfindet – bezeugt durch Ausstellungen in Köln, Groningen [sic], München, Berlin und Karlsruhe –, hat zum Teil mit der allgemeinen soziokulturellen Situation in diesem Land zu tun. Nach dem Zweiten Weltkrieg als Folge der barbarischen Nazipolitik gab es in Deutschland fast gar keine avantgardistische Kunst. Für Inspiration wandte man sich einer internationalen Strömung nach der anderen zu. Fixpunkte, um die sich die westdeutsche Kunst drehte, waren erst Frankreich, dann die USA und schließlich die Wiederbelebung vergangener Phasen der internationalen Vorkriegsavantgarden. Verstärkt wurde dies durch allgemeine Trends andernorts, die versuchten, mittels Kunst zu „universell" bedeutungsvollen Aussagen zu gelangen, wobei sie die Wichtigkeit des individuellen und regionalen Charakters ignorierten, sei es in Bezug auf die Kunstgeschichte oder die Geschichte der jeweiligen Nation. Um es ganz unverblümt auszudrücken, spiegelte die Kunst, die sich in Westdeutschland nach dem Krieg rasch etablierte, die Machtstrukturen des wiederauflebenden Kapitalismus wider.

Mit der wirtschaftlichen Vormacht der USA ging die amerikanische Kunst einher, die, wie jedes andere amerikanische Produkt, einen Weltmarkt suchte (und fand). Die 1960er-Jahre waren das Jahrzehnt des grenzenlosen amerikanischen Bildes. Doch je krisengefährdeter sich die amerikanische Gesellschaft erwies, desto weniger stabil wurden ihre politischen und moralischen Grundsätze in der Praxis und desto weiter entfernten sich die europäischen Künstler von dieser neugefundenen Autorität. Gegen Ende der 1970er-Jahre waren insbesondere die europäischen Künstler wieder an vorderster Front der Avantgarde-Diskussion. Grundlegende Neubewertungen der Gestalt und des Zwecks der zeitgenössischen Kunst fanden in den 1970er-Jahren in Westeuropa statt, und sie gründeten (erneut, aber das erste Mal seit dem Krieg) auf einer ganz klar spezifisch europäischen Herangehensweise. Überraschenderweise wird dies erst jetzt im Rückblick erkennbar. Bedeutende europäische Künstler konzentrieren sich (erneut, aber radikal anders) auf die Darstellbarkeit von Selbsterkenntnis, Selbstbild und

as art, between (art) history and subjective experience in coded paintings, and images-ciphers. To avoid misunderstanding at the outset, this inquiry cannot be (although it has been) equated with a search for personal identity through the medium of art. Quite the contrary: what stands to be debated is a frame of reference in which the orientation points are ego, society, and art. Questions of the unity of style and originality in painting and drawing viewed against the background of an "esthetics of dispersion" are the crucial terms of the discussion. In the wake of the impersonal esthetic that dominated the past two decades, artists' present concern with the relation between subjectivity and esthetic symbol-making can hardly be expected to lead back to the old search for a personal style. The idea of "style" itself has become suspect, much as it was to artists like Marcel Duchamp, Francis Picabia, and the late Pablo Picasso. Yet even their work, which originally dropped into modern art with the impact of a bombshell, now raises not much more than an ironic smile among the young generation. Sons will challenge their fathers, of course, but what is different about this particular confrontation is the choice of weapons—this time it is the embrace.

When discussing questions of style, we have accustomed ourselves to thinking in terms of regions and epochs. We consider style to be a general esthetic category that includes a characteristic relation of author to work. The artist finds self when he or she finds style; through style, the identity of a subject manifests itself and is rendered visible. And stylistic change is the ostensible embodiment of artistic development, negating what is and establishing what is to be.

The social and cultural experience of the '60s and '70s, which led from idealism and optimism to retrenchment and resignation, has affected the way in which the subsequent generation is seeing itself. "Du hast keine Chance. Nutze sie!" (You haven't got a chance. So use it!) is a popular slogan in the alternative scene in Germany. So is "Wir wollen Alles. Und zwar jetzt!" (We demand everything. And now!). This sort of anarchism, asking for an immediate change (a someplace else in the here and now) rejects the previous crusades for social change and the sacrificing of individuality for a cause. New German art reflects this attitude faithfully. It is an attitude toward society (with it and against it) that might be called "productively anarchic." It includes personal idiosyncrasy and the esthetic signs and gestures that render it visible to others, granting a new quality of tension to the relationship between style and the subjective view. "Style" (to the artists I am discussing) means adaptation, a conforming drive that superficially mirrors the forces at work in their society. If you want to be "somewhere else," their reasoning goes, you have no use for a static point of view. You have to change continually; to keep moving you have to be "here" and yet keep your lines of escape open. This subversive view of style retroactively affects the way people experience and define themselves. By no longer striving for individuated identity, the subjects experience themselves as multiplicities. They find themselves in discontinuity and in contradiction, by continually stepping across the line.

This stasis-in-motion, which in visual art is apparent in self-contradiction, mimicry, or refusal to conform to critical expectations, reflects the process of what contemporary European thinkers, particularly in France (Gilles Deleuze, Félix Guattari, and Jean-François Lyotard) call the "epistemological shifts" or "dislocations" in our century. In analyzing modern culture, these men have detected a move away from logocentrism and anthropocentrism that is counterbalanced by a move toward a type of experience which accords to wishes (*le désir*) a revolutionary meaning. Central to this view is the idea that experience moves in the here and now, that its goal is less revolution than "becoming revolutionary"; discovering, in other words, a state of society beyond capitalism, yet

Selbstausdruck sowie auf die Produktion ästhetischer Objekte.

Seit den späten 1970er-Jahren untersuchten Maler*innen wie Francesco Clemente, Sandro Chia, Enzo Cucchi, Mimmo Paladino oder Nicola De Maria die Verbindung zwischen persönlicher Aussage und Malerei als Kunst, zwischen (Kunst-)Geschichte und subjektiver Erfahrung in kodierten Gemälden und Bildchiffren. Um sogleich Missverständnisse zu vermeiden: Man kann diese Erkundung nicht mit der Suche nach persönlicher Identität durch das Medium der Kunst gleichsetzen (obwohl dies getan worden ist), ganz im Gegenteil. Was zur Debatte steht, ist ein Referenzrahmen, in dem das Ich, die Gesellschaft und die Kunst die Orientierungspunkte bilden. Fragen zur Einheit des Stils und der Originalität in Malerei und Zeichnung sind, vor dem Hintergrund einer „Ästhetik der Zerstreuung" betrachtet, die zentralen Begriffe in dieser Diskussion. Angesichts der unpersönlichen Ästhetik, die in den letzten beiden Jahrzehnten vorherrschte, kann man in der gegenwärtigen Auseinandersetzung der Künstler mit dem Verhältnis von Subjektivität und der Produktion ästhetischer Symbole kaum erwarten, dass sie sich zurück auf die alte Suche nach einem persönlichen Stil begeben. Denn die Vorstellung von „Stil" selbst ist suspekt geworden, wie sie es auch für Kunstschaffende wie Marcel Duchamp, Francis Picabia oder den späten Pablo Picasso war. Doch selbst die Arbeit dieser Künstler*innen, die einst wie eine Bombe in der modernen Kunst einschlug, ruft wenig mehr als ein ironisches Lächeln bei der jungen Generation hervor. Natürlich stellen Söhne ihre Väter infrage, doch was diese spezielle Konfrontation unterscheidet, ist die Wahl der Waffen – dieses Mal ist es eine Umarmung.

Bei Diskussionen über Fragen des Stils haben wir uns daran gewöhnt, in Regionen und Epochen zu denken. Wir betrachten Stil als eine allgemeine ästhetische Kategorie, die eine charakteristische Beziehung zwischen Autor und Werk bezeichnet. Der Künstler findet zu sich, wenn er einen Stil findet; durch den Stil manifestiert sich die Identität eines Subjekts und wird dadurch sichtbar. Und Veränderungen des Stils verkörpern angeblich eine künstlerische Entwicklung, sie negieren das Bestehende und etablieren das, was sein soll.

Die gesellschaftlichen und kulturellen Erfahrungen der 1960er- und 70er-Jahre, die von Idealismus und Optimismus zu Rückzug und Resignation führten, haben das Selbstbild der nachfolgenden Generation beeinflusst. „Du hast keine Chance. Nutze sie!" ist ein populärer Slogan der deutschen Alternativszene, wie auch „Wir wollen alles. Und zwar jetzt!". Diese Form von Anarchismus, die sofortige Veränderung verlangt (ein anderswo im Hier und Jetzt), lehnt die vorangegangenen Feldzüge für sozialen Wandel und die individuelle Aufopferung für eine Sache ab. Die neue deutsche Kunst ist eine getreue Widerspiegelung dieser Haltung zur Gesellschaft (mit ihr und gegen sie), die man vielleicht als „produktiv anarchisch" bezeichnen könnte. Sie umfasst persönliche Idiosynkrasien und die ästhetischen Zeichen und Gesten, die diese Haltung für andere sichtbar machen, wodurch ein qualitativ neues Spannungsverhältnis zwischen Stil und subjektiver Sicht entsteht. „Stil" ist (für die Künstler, um die es hier geht) Anpassung, ein konformistischer Trieb, der auf oberflächliche Weise die Kräfte, die in der Gesellschaft am Werk sind, widerspiegelt. Wenn du „woanders" sein willst, so ihre Argumentation, nützt dir ein statischer Blickwinkel gar nichts. Du musst dich ständig verändern; um in Bewegung zu bleiben, musst du „hier" sein, aber gleichzeitig deine Fluchtlinien offen halten. Diese subversive Betrachtung von Stil beeinflusst rückwirkend die Art und Weise, wie sich die Menschen erleben und definieren. Indem sie nicht mehr nach individualisierter Identität streben, erfahren sich die Subjekte als Vielheiten. Indem sie ständig die Linie überschreiten, finden sie sich in einem Zustand der Diskontinuität und des Widerspruchs.

Dieser Stillstand-in-Bewegung, der sich in der bildenden Kunst als Selbstwiderspruch, Nachahmung oder Weigerung, kritische Erwartungen zu erfüllen, zeigt,

within capitalism itself. This present-oriented "becoming revolutionary" is not directed at finding a new unity, or a new truth, but at rendering visible and tangible human wishes and desires, even if these desires should include "regressive," "bourgeois," or "non-revolutionary" elements. In art, this process is evidenced in the refusal to formulate intentions, and the turn, instead, to spontaneity and improvisation as effective vehicles for the articulation of ideas. For the sake of expressive intensity, every program, every preconceived notion must be avoided, whether it concerns style, subject, theme, or some aspect of ideology that is incidental to the actual process of making itself.

In wanting to be both "with it and against it" at the same time, young German artists are very much in tune with the theory of knowledge outlined above. They attempt to avoid two pitfalls that trapped most of their predecessors, namely, blind affirmation on the one hand, and an overly critical, reductive approach on the other. By trying to find traces of the good life in the bad, they would escape the suffocating apathy that is everywhere evident. Almost no means of escape is too shallow. Trusting to chance and mood, a young artist may invent an unheard-of image or dig into the grab bag of art history, producing a work in which the highly personal is on the same footing with the stylistic quote. This brand of late-modern eclecticism is a slap in the face of originality. It is meant to be. Dilettantism is a useful tool when it comes to making works of art that call our very notion of a work of art into question.

Behind this attitude one senses a need for rigorous self-examination, achieved through the making of images—not, however, in the hope of attaining final and viable results, but in the knowledge that every answer will turn up ten even tougher questions. This, I suppose, is the lesson of the modernist tradition, a tradition (to change the metaphor) that young artists are (at the moment) exploiting like a veritable gold mine—particularly the expressionist veins, and most particularly, the German mother lode. Besides the Expressionists, this includes the immediately preceding generation of artists; men such as Anselm Kiefer, Georg Baselitz, Sigmar Polke, Markus Lüpertz, Jörg Immendorff, A. R. Penck, Gerhard Richter, and Karl Horst Hödicke, who in the '70s took their stand against the social and cultural status quo. The work of these artists—some of whom are not much older than their students—forms the connecting link to the pre-war generation. "Students," however, is a misnomer—the younger artists, buoyed by a view of things that comes straight out of Pop, punk, and New Wave, consider themselves adepts of an esthetic that is the property of their generation and no other. Perhaps that is why the new tendencies have been primarily regional, with groups in Berlin, Düsseldorf, Hamburg, Munich, and Cologne, each of which seems to be attempting an artistic reorientation from a different perspective. The fact that these local groups are anything but provincial has to do with an important determinant of German post-war art—political circumstances make it necessary to keep a sharp eye on international developments. Seen in this light, recent German art has a significance that extends beyond Germany's borders. It represents one manifestation of a change in esthetic outlook that is going on throughout the Western world, the core of which is opposition to any and all forms of coercion, be they social, personal, or exerted by the weight of history.

The challenge represented by young painters' inquiry into the relationship between style, self, and image has found its most convincing formulation in Berlin, in what is known as "Heftige Malerei" ("violent painting"). Living in the permanent crisis of a divided, walled-in city has made thinking in alternatives second nature to Berlin's inhabitants. Besides, social engagement in art has always been stronger here than in other German cities. Since Dada, since George Grosz, Otto Dix, and John Heartfield, Berlin has been synonymous with an aggressive, satirical, realistic art devoted to probing

entspricht einem Prozess, den zeitgenössische europäische Theoretiker*innen, besonders in Frankreich (Gilles Deleuze, Félix Guattari und Jean-François Lyotard), als die „epistemologischen Verschiebungen“ oder „Dislokationen“ in unserem Jahrhundert bezeichnen. In ihren Analysen der modernen Kultur haben diese Leute eine Bewegung weg von Logozentrismus und Anthropozentrismus beobachtet, die ausgeglichen wird durch eine Bewegung hin zu einer Art Erfahrung, die dem Begehren *(le désir)* eine revolutionäre Bedeutung zuspricht. Die zentrale Idee dieser Sichtweise ist, dass Erfahrungen im Hier und Jetzt gemacht werden, dass das Ziel weniger die Revolution als das „Revolutionär-Werden“ ist – mit anderen Worten die Entdeckung eines gesellschaftlichen Zustandes jenseits des Kapitalismus, der sich aber innerhalb des Kapitalismus selbst befindet. Diesem gegenwartsorientierten „Revolutionär-Werden“ geht es nicht um die Entdeckung einer neuen Einheit oder Wahrheit, sondern darum, menschliche Wünsche und Begehren sichtbar und greifbar zu machen, auch wenn sie „regressive“, „bourgeoise“ oder „nichtrevolutionäre“ Elemente beinhalten. In der Kunst zeigt sich dieser Prozess in der Weigerung, Intentionen zu formulieren, und der Hinwendung zu Spontaneität und Improvisation als wirkungsvollen Vehikeln für die Artikulation von Ideen. Um der expressiven Intensität willen muss jegliches Programm, jegliche vorgefasste Idee vermieden werden, sei es hinsichtlich des Stils, des Sujets, des Themas oder der ideologischen Aspekte, die für den eigentlichen Produktionsprozess nebensächlich sind.

Indem sie zugleich „dafür und dagegen“ sein wollen, agieren die jungen deutschen Künstler ganz im Sinne der oben skizzierten Erkenntnistheorie. Sie versuchen, zwei Fallen zu vermeiden, in die die meisten ihrer Vorgänger geraten sind, blinde Affirmation oder eine überaus kritische, reduktive Herangehensweise. Nach Spuren des guten Lebens im schlechten zu suchen, könnte eine Möglichkeit sein, der allgegenwärtigen erstickenden Apathie zu entkommen. Fast kein Mittel der Flucht ist zu geistlos. Indem er auf Zufall und Stimmung setzt, könnte ein junger Künstler ein unerhörtes Bild erfinden oder in die Grabbelkiste der Kunstgeschichte greifen und eine Arbeit produzieren, in der das sehr Persönliche einem Stilzitat gleichberechtigt gegenübersteht. Diese Spielart eines spätmodernen Eklektizismus ist ein Schlag ins Gesicht der Originalität. Und das soll sie auch sein. Der Dilettantismus ist ein nützliches Werkzeug, wenn es darum geht, Kunstwerke zu schaffen, die die Vorstellung eines Kunstwerks selbst infrage stellen.

Hinter dieser Haltung spürt man das Bedürfnis nach einer rigorosen Selbsterkundung mittels der Produktion von Bildern – allerdings nicht in der Hoffnung, endgültige und gangbare Resultate zu erzielen, sondern in dem Wissen, dass jede Antwort zehn noch schwierigere Fragen nach sich ziehen wird. Ich denke, das ist die Lehre aus der Tradition der Moderne, einer Tradition (um die Metapher zu wechseln), die die jungen Kunstschaffenden (derzeit) wie eine veritable Goldmine ausbeuten – besonders deren expressionistische Adern und ganz besonders die deutsche Hauptader. Neben den Expressionist*innen ist es auch die unmittelbare Vorgängergeneration von Kunstschaffenden, sind es Leute wie Anselm Kiefer, Georg Baselitz, Sigmar Polke, Markus Lüpertz, Jörg Immendorff, A. R. Penck, Gerhard Richter und Karl Horst Hödicke, die in den 1970er-Jahren gegen den gesellschaftlichen und kulturellen Status quo opponierten. Die Arbeit dieser Künstler – von denen einige nicht viel älter sind als ihre Studierenden – bildete das Bindeglied zur Vorkriegsgeneration. Allerdings ist „Studierende“ eine unzutreffende Bezeichnung – inspiriert durch eine Betrachtungsweise, die direkt aus Pop, Punk und New Wave stammt, begreifen sich die jungen Künstler*innen als Adepten einer Ästhetik, die ausschließlich der eigenen Generation gehört. Vielleicht ist das der Grund, weshalb die neuen Tendenzen in erster Linie regional sind, mit Gruppen in Berlin, Düsseldorf, Hamburg, München und Köln, die sich jeweils um eine künstlerische Neuorientierung aus einer

behind the facade of middle-class pretention and prosperity. "Violent painting," represented by Rainer Fetting, Salomé, Bernd Zimmer, and Helmut Middendorf is no exception.

Their subjects are big-city subjects in manifestations specific to Berlin: the New Wave scene, minorities, and the latent violence produced by the concrete disasters of public housing. The attitude expressed in their paintings is quite different from that of their immediate predecessors. Whereas the "Ugly Realism" of a Wolfgang Petrick, a Peter Sorge, or Klaus Vogelgesang took a closed, if critical view of the political and artistic status quo, the "violent painters" react immediately and emotionally to it, not as reformers so much as directly concerned individuals. The feeling justifies the image, they claim, not without casting an occasional fascinated glance back at "the great tradition." It is easy enough to find parallels between their work and that of the German Expressionists, though in the former case historical proximity seems to breed at least some measure of critical distance. Nowadays artists who want to paint themselves into art history cannot afford to jettison experiment altogether, if only to justify the borrowings and affinities with solutions already found by others. If pure belligerence often seems to result, it has less to do with the subjects of the paintings than with their treatment. Garish color, provocatively loose paint handling, and aggressive themes all arise from these artists' obsession with developing a pictorial repertoire that adequately presents both spontaneous experience and historic knowledge. And the history that concerns the "Violents" is one of outsiders, loners, pariahs who had and have one thing in common, namely, the guts not to conform; to go their own way. Yet compared to their models, the better known of which, other than the Expressionists, are Paul Gauguin, Vincent van Gogh, and Edvard Munch, these young "Fauves" cannot be said to be lonely, for they belong to an alternative scene, to a subculture whose turf is as much New York as Berlin. Indeed, their use of tradition is only another aspect of this yearning to belong, a kind of autosuggestive proximity to those who expressed themselves out of deep, inescapable need, who suffered pain and ecstasy, found and destroyed themselves. Thus the visions of these young artists express vicarious experience. This makes their work fascinating and ambiguous.

In the paintings of Fetting, Salomé, Middendorf, and Zimmer one finds obvious echoes of Ernst Ludwig Kirchner, Emil Nolde, Erich Heckel, and Otto Mueller, all artists whose work has enjoyed a revival of interest in recent years. It is their subjects—the big city, its nightlife, the egocentric self-portrait, the landscape seen with a city-dweller's nervous eye—that reappear on the canvases of the "Violents." The question then is: what is new and therefore what is significant about the way the "Violents" relate self to subject, subject to style?

Fetting rings continual changes on this theme. He takes subjects that fascinate him through endless variations. Obsessive repetition seems to promise an escape, or at least relief from an obsessive vision. Using painterly means, he raises questions concerning the possibilities of a new painting. A successful canvas acts as a kind of security against those existing mundane forces that would deny the subjective view its meaning. In the act of painting an artist may define the terms of and defend his right to self-expression, yet—and this is borne out in Fetting's work—his claim to self-expression remains fragmentary and threatened. His gesture may have more yearning about it than reality.

An even more steadfast concentration on the self as a subject for art is found in the work of Salomé. In gestures and poses that are both self-appreciating and self-castigating he identifies ego with image and presents the result in his art. Salomé began as a performance artist and those earlier existential concerns continue to inform the canvases, on which he gives free play to his personality—and sensuality—made public.

unterschiedlichen Perspektive heraus zu bemühen scheinen. Die Tatsache, dass die örtlichen Gruppen alles andere als provinziell sind, hat mit einer wichtigen Determinante der deutschen Vorkriegskunst zu tun – die politischen Umstände machen es notwendig, die internationalen Entwicklungen genau im Auge zu behalten. So gesehen besitzt die jüngste deutsche Kunst eine Relevanz, die über die Grenzen Deutschlands hinausgeht. Sie ist die Manifestation einer Veränderung in der ästhetischen Einstellung, die im gesamten Westen stattfindet und der es im Wesentlichen um eine Opposition gegen sämtliche Formen von Zwang geht, seien diese nun gesellschaftlich, persönlich oder durch die Last der Geschichte verursacht.

Die Herausforderung, die die Befragung der jungen Maler*innen hinsichtlich des Verhältnisses zwischen Stil, Selbst und Bild darstellt, ist in Berlin durch die sogenannte „Heftige Malerei“ am überzeugendsten formuliert worden. Das Leben in der permanenten Krise einer geteilten, eingemauerten Stadt hat das Denken zur alternativen zweiten Natur der Bewohner*innen gemacht. Zudem ist das soziale Engagement der Kunst in Berlin schon immer ausgeprägter gewesen als in anderen deutschen Städten. Seit Dada, seit George Grosz, Otto Dix und John Heartfield ist Berlin gleichbedeutend mit einer aggressiven, satirischen, realistischen Kunst, der es darum geht, hinter die Fassade der bürgerlichen Überheblichkeit und Prosperität zu blicken. Die „Heftige Malerei“ von Rainer Fetting, Salomé, Bernd Zimmer und Helmut Middendorf bildet da keine Ausnahme.

Ihre großstädtischen Sujets sind spezifisch Berliner Erscheinungen: die New-Wave-Szene, Minderheiten und die latente Gewalt, die durch die Betonkatastrophen des öffentlichen Wohnungsbaus verursacht wird. Die in ihren Gemälden zum Ausdruck kommende Haltung unterscheidet sich erheblich von der ihrer unmittelbaren Vorgänger. Während der „hässliche Realismus“ eines Wolfgang Petricks, Peter Sorges oder Klaus Vogelgesangs einen geschlossenen, wenn auch kritischen Blick auf den politischen und künstlerischen Status quo warf, reagieren die „heftigen Maler“ unmittelbar und emotional darauf, weniger als Reformer denn als direkt betroffene Individuen. Das Gefühl rechtfertigt das Bild, sagen sie, ohne auf einen zuweilen faszinierten Blick zurück zur „großen Tradition“ zu verzichten. Leicht findet man Parallelen zwischen ihren Arbeiten und denen des deutschen Expressionismus, obwohl im Fall der Ersteren eine historische Nähe zumindest ein gewisses Maß an kritischer Distanz zu erzeugen scheint. Heutzutage können Künstler*innen, die sich in die Geschichte hineinmalen wollen, nicht gänzlich auf Experimente verzichten, auch wenn es nur darum geht, die Anleihen und Affinitäten mit Lösungen zu rechtfertigen, auf die schon andere gekommen sind. Wenn die reine Streitlust oft das Ergebnis zu sein scheint, hat das weniger mit den Sujets der Gemälde als mit deren Behandlung zu tun. Grelle Töne, eine provokant lockere Handhabung der Farbe und aggressive Themen entstehen alle aus der Besessenheit dieser Kunstschaffenden von der Entwicklung eines bildlichen Repertoires, das sowohl spontane Erfahrung als auch historisches Wissen adäquat darstellt. Und die Geschichte, um die es den „Heftigen“ geht, ist die der Außenseiter, Einzelgänger und Parias, die eines gemeinsam haben, nämlich den Mumm, sich nicht anzupassen, ihren eigenen Weg zu gehen. Doch verglichen mit ihren Vorbildern, zu denen neben den Expressionisten auch Paul Gauguin, Vincent van Gogh und Edvard Munch als die Bekannteren gehören, kann man von diesen „Wilden“ nicht behaupten, sie seien einsam, denn sie gehören zur alternativen Szene, zu einer Subkultur, deren Terrain New York genauso wie Berlin umfasst. Tatsächlich ist ihre Nutzbarmachung der Tradition nur ein weiterer Aspekt dieser Sehnsucht nach Zugehörigkeit, einer autosuggestiven Nähe zu denjenigen, die sich aus einem tiefen, unentrinnbaren Bedürfnis heraus ausdrückten, die Schmerz und Ekstase erlitten haben, die zu sich fanden und sich zerstörten. Die Visionen dieser jungen Künstler drücken also nachempfundene Erfahrungen aus. Das macht ihre

It is precisely this publicity-oriented style that makes Salomé's work important, for it represents an attempt to formulate a more general style that could express the esthetic of a specific minority and its need for self-realization.

Though their subjects differ, Middendorf and Zimmer are also concerned with subcultural rapprochement. While Middendorf depicts the hunting grounds of urban natives, Zimmer paints landscapes that look like the refuges of which they dream. Contradiction and tension make these exuberant visions interesting, though problems arise whenever the pictorial thinking behind them concentrates solely on a kind of neoexpressionist fulfillment of the subject at hand. It's the old ogre again, the one every artist has to face—that the relationship of theme to expression, content to form, must be thought out anew with every work if the result is not to give the impression of sheer helpless activity for activity's sake. If that balance is not found, the subjective and spontaneous painting that was supposed to be liberating will soon stagnate into a new, very colorful, academic style.

Painting today is invariably painting about the possibility of painting. This statement applies to all modern painting, of course, although in the present context it seems particularly worthwhile to think about its implications. What is new about the present context, is simply that what was once taken for granted in art is no longer. The past decade's issues project into this, and the debate still turns on the relation between subjective view and esthetic sign, between painting and experience. Thus the historic view intrudes into thinking in recent art, which must consider both the doubt that has been shed on the traditional conception of self as well as the media-derived insights of contemporary esthetic theory.

New German art illustrates this dichotomy. In what way, an artist might ask in a Cologne, Berlin, or Düsseldorf loft, does someone look for, find, understand, experience the self through painting? What relationship does a work build up between image and self? Where does style come into the equation? What meaning does painting qua painting communicate? How can a painting be an answer if no questions are asked, that is, if the work has no preconceived aim? The Berlin artists known as "violent" are trying to solve these problems by employing historically mediated, expressive means. A diametrically opposed approach would be to count on the decorative possibilities of painting, or to make art of a stylistic arbitrariness that would resist any attempt to pin it down.

Both of these approaches were apparent recently in two large exhibitions, "Rundschau Deutschland" (German Comprehensive, Munich), and "Bildwechsel" (Change of View, West Berlin). The plurality of attitudes, the confrontation and merging of the most varied points of view that were so much in evidence in these shows amounted to the clearest statement of the late-modern canon that I have yet seen. Irritatingly, there was not the slightest trace of a search for anything truly new, some "avant-gardistic" twist that might revitalize or even reinterpret the tradition; every embryonic innovation dissolved in the vortex of the present, amid the scattered arbitrary flotsam of the past. One of these bits of wreckage, so to speak, was the pleasingly painted surface, which, concealing self-examination under a veil of beautiful forms, colors, lines, and planes, seemed to be ashamed of the fact that art had ever had an existential dimension.

Stefan Szczesny, a painter working in Munich, takes his cue from Henri Matisse. Szczesny pushes those beautiful surfaces, that arose naturally from a deep-felt *joie de vivre,* with contemporary determination to a simplicity of form and color that borders provocatively on the banal. Similar approaches are found in the work of Düsseldorf artists—Horst Gläsker, Jürgen Meyer, Fernand Roda are three—who put the painterly question in terms of good, striking composition and message, surely mirroring the ambience of that city,

Arbeit so faszinierend und vieldeutig.

In den Gemälden von Fetting, Salomé, Middendorf und Zimmer findet man offensichtliche Anklänge an Ernst Ludwig Kirchner, Emil Nolde, Erich Heckel und Otto Mueller – Künstler, deren Arbeit in den letzten Jahren wieder ins Zentrum des Interesses gerückt ist. Es sind ihre Sujets – die Großstadt, das Nachtleben, das egozentrische Selbstporträt, die Landschaft aus der nervösen Sicht des Städters –, denen man auf den Leinwänden der „Heftigen“ wiederbegegnet. Die Frage lautet nun: Was ist neu und folglich bedeutsam an der Art und Weise, wie die „Heftigen“ das Selbst zum Sujet und das Sujet zum Stil in Beziehung setzen?

Fetting variiert dieses Thema ständig. Er widmet sich Sujets, die ihn faszinieren, in unendlichen Variationen. Zwanghafte Wiederholung scheint das Versprechen eines Auswegs oder zumindest die Entlastung von einer obsessiven Vision in sich zu bergen. Mit malerischen Mitteln fragt er nach den Möglichkeiten einer neuen Malerei. Ein gelungenes Bild fungiert als eine Art Sicherheit gegen jene alltäglichen Kräfte, die die subjektive Sicht ihrer Bedeutung berauben. Im Akt des Malens kann der Künstler die Bedingungen bestimmen und sein Recht auf Selbstausdruck verteidigen. Dennoch – und das ergibt sich aus Fettings Arbeit – bleibt der Anspruch auf Selbstausdruck fragmentarisch und bedroht. Seine Geste hat womöglich mehr mit Sehnsucht als mit Realität zu tun.

Eine noch stärkere Konzentration auf das Selbst als Gegenstand der Kunst findet man in der Arbeit von Salomé. In Gesten und Posen, die sowohl selbstwürdigend als auch selbstkasteiend sind, identifiziert er das Ich mit dem Bild und präsentiert das Resultat in seiner Kunst. Salomé begann als Performancekünstler und seine früheren existenziellen Anliegen beeinflussen nach wie vor seine Bilder, in denen er seiner Persönlichkeit – und seiner Sinnlichkeit – in der Öffentlichkeit freien Lauf lässt. Es ist genau dieser auf Öffentlichkeit orientierte Stil, der Salomés Arbeit relevant macht, denn was er zu formulieren versucht, ist ein allgemeinerer Stil, der der Ästhetik einer bestimmten Minderheit und deren Bedürfnis nach Selbstverwirklichung Ausdruck verleihen könnte.

Obgleich ihre Sujets andere sind, beschäftigen sich Middendorf und Zimmer ebenfalls mit subkultureller Verständigung. Während Middendorf die Jagdgründe der Urban Natives abbildet, malt Zimmer Landschaften, die wie die Refugien aussehen, von denen diese träumen. Widerspruch und Spannung machen diese überbordenden Visionen interessant, allerdings ergeben sich Probleme, wenn sich das zugrunde liegende bildliche Denken nur auf eine Art neo-expressionistische Erfüllung des jeweiligen Gegenstandes konzentriert. Es ist wieder das alte Ungeheuer, mit dem sich jeder Kunstschaffende auseinandersetzen muss: Mit jeder Arbeit muss das Verhältnis zwischen Thema und Ausdruck, Inhalt und Form, neu durchdacht werden, wenn das Ergebnis nicht den Eindruck einer schier hilflosen Aktivität um der Aktivität willen erwecken soll. Wird dieses Gleichgewicht nicht gefunden, wird die subjektive und spontane Malerei, die eigentlich befreien sollte, alsbald stagnieren und zu einem neuen farbenfrohen akademischen Stil werden.

Malerei heute ist zwangsläufig Malerei über die Möglichkeit der Malerei. Diese Aussage trifft natürlich auf jegliche moderne Malerei zu, aber im gegenwärtigen Kontext scheint es besonders lohnenswert zu sein, über die Folgen nachzudenken. Neu am heutigen Kontext ist, dass das, was einst als selbstverständlich in der Kunst galt, heute nicht mehr selbstverständlich ist. Die Themen des vergangenen Jahrzehnts ragen da hinein, und die Debatte dreht sich immer noch um das Verhältnis zwischen subjektiver Sicht und ästhetischem Zeichen, zwischen Malerei und Erfahrung. Folglich dringt in der neueren Kunst die historische Sicht in das Denken ein, das sowohl den Zweifel an der traditionellen Vorstellung vom Selbst als auch die medialen Erkenntnisse der zeitgenössischen ästhetischen Theorie berücksichtigen muss.

Die neue deutsche Kunst veranschaulicht diese Dichotomie. Wie, fragt sich ein/e Künstler*in in einem Kölner, Berliner

"Europe's office-desk." The opposite pole to this "pretty art" is a type of painting that derives its imagery mostly from trivial genres, inserting pieces of them whole and undigested into a painterly context. The Düsseldorf group "Normal" (Peter Angermann, Milan Kunc, Jan Knap) and the independents Andreas Schulze and Stephan Dillemuth exploit the themes and styles of German kitsch and trivial art, i.e. cliché landscapes. What they are attempting to do is to force acceptance of artistic or pseudo-artistic phenomena that are generally thought to be below notice. At the same time they announce their repudiation of the "tradition of the new"—the idea that artists must innovate or die. Despite their point of view, these artists are prone to a dogmatism that ironically reveals an innate weakness for the very things they would denounce, or establish as being all too normal.

By contrast, the paintings of the Hamburg artists Albert Oehlen and Werner Büttner, and those of Ina Barfuss and Thomas Wachweger of Berlin, revolve around the difficulty of making a frank statement that raises an important issue. The scenes they choose are again slices of German reality—what it means to be a German at the beginning of the '80s, or what the media and public opinion makers say it means. An aggressiveness of approach is evident in the work of these artists, often bringing them precariously close to caricature, with its obviousness of form and message. These artists do not consider the painted image the place to conduct a dialogue with self, or to reflect on the circumstances of mental and material existence, as was *de rigueur,* say, in Analytic Painting (you see what you see). Their return to figuration does not necessarily mean that they relocate pictorial conception in the context of conceptual meaning (you read what you see). Rather, the figurative elements in their work serve only as stimuli, suggesting a theme, instead of stating it outright, and thereby frustrating attempts to label the work and its meaning, either in terms of its subject or of the success with which it brings form and content into equilibrium.

The open-ended attribution of meanings, which takes up certain strands of conceptual art in order to transform them, is the starting point for six artists who have joined forces in Cologne under the name of the street their studio is located on, "Mülheimer Freiheit." In keeping with the "liberty" of their title, this group is loosely organized, has no platform to push, and no aim that would stratify or hamper their efforts. The character of new German art being described here is found at its most extreme in this group. Rather than a unified style, theirs is a convergence of opposites, and they accept mutual influence to the point of collaborating in changing teams on common works. The poles between which this new esthetic oscillates are the *art brut* of Peter Bömmels, who is self-taught, and the highly eclectic and syncretist images of Jiří Georg Dokoupil. What both these artists have in common with the other members of the group—Gerard Kever, Hans Peter Adamski, Walter Dahn, and Gerhard Naschberger—might be described as a willful dissociation of the factors of subjectiveness and style.

The "for you/me/us anything goes" of "Mülheimer Freiheit" sees the painted image as a site of transient fascination that represents not the unity of one ego but a multiple subjective view. The result is "freestyle art," a term whose athletic associations this group (like the boxer-artist Arthur Cravan) accepts. In the arena of images, an artist's visions and longings face a showdown with his or her knowledge of art history. A momentary irritation caused by some picture from a magazine or television ad, an art book or a dream battles with the need to make an image that is authentically of and about the self. The fight, of course, will probably end either in a complete indifference to style or in a conscious use of stylistic inconsistency, where Cubist quotes share the canvas with Nazi-like male figures, expressionist

oder Düsseldorfer Loft womöglich, sucht, findet, versteht und erlebt man das Selbst mittels der Malerei? Welche Beziehung stellt eine Arbeit zwischen Bild und Selbst her? An welcher Stelle spielt der Stil eine Rolle? Welche Bedeutung vermittelt Malerei qua Malerei? Wie kann ein Gemälde eine Antwort sein, wenn keine Fragen gestellt wurden, das heißt wenn das Werk kein vorgegebenes Ziel hat? Die sogenannten „heftigen“ Berliner Künstler*innen versuchen diese Probleme dadurch zu lösen, dass sie historisch vermittelte Ausdrucksformen nutzen. Ein diametral entgegengesetzter Ansatz bestünde darin, auf die dekorativen Möglichkeiten der Malerei zu setzen oder eine Kunst zu machen, deren stilistische Beliebigkeit jegliche Zuordnungsversuche verhindern würde.

Beide Herangehensweisen waren kürzlich in zwei großen Ausstellungen zu beobachten: *Rundschau Deutschland* (München) und *Bildwechsel* (Westberlin). Die Vielfalt der Haltungen, die Konfrontation und Verschmelzung verschiedenster Standpunkte, die in diesen Ausstellungen so offensichtlich wurden, markierten die bisher klarste Aussage zum spätmodernen Kanon, die mir bisher begegnet ist. Irritierend war, dass es nicht die leiseste Spur einer Suche nach etwas wirklich Neuem gab, nach einer „avantgardistischen“ Wendung, die die Tradition vielleicht wiederbeleben oder sogar neu interpretieren könnte; jede noch so kleine Innovation verflüchtigte sich im Wirbel der Gegenwart, im verstreuten Treibgut der Vergangenheit. Eines dieser Trümmerteile, wenn man so will, war die angenehm bemalte Oberfläche, die – die Selbstuntersuchung unter einem Schleier von schönen Formen, Farben, Linien und Flächen verbergend – sich der Tatsache zu schämen schien, dass Kunst jemals eine existenzielle Dimension besaß.

Stefan Szczesny, ein in München arbeitender Maler, nimmt sich Henri Matisse zum Vorbild. Er drängt diese wunderschönen Oberflächen, die aus einer tief empfundenen Lebensfreude auf natürliche Weise entstanden sind, mit einer zeitgenössischen Entschlossenheit zu einer Einfachheit von Form und Farbe, die auf provozierende Weise an das Banale grenzt. Ähnliche Ansätze findet man in den Arbeiten der Düsseldorfer Künstler*innen – etwa Horst Gläsker, Jürgen Meyer, Fernand Roda –, die die Frage der Malerei im Sinne der guten, beeindruckenden Komposition und Aussage stellen, was sicherlich das Ambiente dieser Stadt, die als „Europas Bürotisch“ gilt, widerspiegelt. Den entgegengesetzten Pol dieser „hübschen Kunst“ bildet eine Malerei, die ihre Bildwelten meist aus trivialen Genres bezieht und Teile davon unverdaut in einen malerischen Kontext einfügt. Die Düsseldorfer Gruppe Normal (Peter Angermann, Milan Kunc, Jan Knap) und die unabhängigen Künstler Andreas Schulze und Stephan Dillemuth verwenden Themen und Stile des deutschen Kitschs und der trivialen Kunst, wie etwa Klischeelandschaften. Sie versuchen eine Akzeptanz für künstlerische oder pseudokünstlerische Phänomene zu erzwingen, die generell als nicht beachtenswert gelten. Zugleich verkünden sie ihre Ablehnung der „Tradition des Neuen“ – der Vorstellung, dass Künstler*innen erneuern müssten, wenn sie nicht scheitern wollen. Trotz ihrer Sichtweise sind diese Künstler*innen anfällig für einen Dogmatismus, der ironischerweise eine innere Schwäche für genau die Dinge offenbart, die sie verurteilen oder als allzu normal beurteilen würden.

Im Unterschied dazu kreisen die Gemälde der Hamburger Künstler Albert Oehlen und Werner Büttner und die der Berliner Künstler*innen Ina Barfuss und Thomas Wachweger um die Schwierigkeit, eine offene und ehrliche Aussage zu einem wichtigen Thema zu machen. Ihre Szenen sind wieder Ausschnitte aus der deutschen Realität – was es bedeutet, zu Beginn der 1980er-Jahre ein Deutscher zu sein, oder was die Medien und die öffentlichen Meinungsmacher sagen, dass es bedeutet. Eine aggressive Herangehensweise ist in den Arbeiten dieser Künstler*innen evident und rückt sie aufgrund der Offensichtlichkeit von Form und Aussage häufig gefährlich nahe an die Karikatur. Sie fassen das gemalte Bild nicht als den geeigneten Ort für einen Dialog

streetwalkers with Altamira deer. The label "New Subjectivism" is not precise enough to cover the refusal that lies behind this approach—the refusal to play the role of the autonomous artist who has something to say that only he or she can say.

The obsessive image production of "Mülheimer Freiheit" is not meant to enlighten or teach, but to seduce. They demand an acceptance from the viewer that, like fabled motherly love, asks no questions and expects no thanks. Their paintings are blasts of sheer joy in contradiction, overflowing the single painting to flood entire series (like the one consisting of over fifty pictures by Walter Dahn, all of which tell the story of "A Painter with No Ideas"). Transformation becomes the focus of esthetics; the artist a quick-change artist; the work a way station for an individuality that explores itself through art by dissipating itself in it. This happens without anxiety, shame, or regret; the act of making announces that these makers, at least, are through with following the commands either of the art market or of those internalized coercions, those little programmatic voices that tell you what is visionary or what is not. This artistic stance can be compared to transpolitics—we (the people, the artists) exist in the here and now and someplace else simultaneously—we are both "with it and against it." Clearly this is a precarious stance. The social relevance so desired of art during the past two decades is replaced—not by its opposite, a radically personal idiolect—but by a visual language that stems from identification with a social group. Living in West German reality now—with its rabid consumerism, its unemployment, its fear of terrorism, its electronic monitoring of daily existence, its burgeoning alternative movements—these artists are attempting to find a place. They seek neither refuge from "real reality," nor a cure for its sick glamor, but simply a place to be, now—a point from which, living symbiotically with, or even parasitically on accepted structures of self-experience and behavioral norms of society, they can divert, redirect, even transform them. Its makers would communicate seeing the same thing in a different way, not suggest therapies, design utopias, or proclaim truths, whether of a social, intellectual, esthetic, or anthropological nature. The structure of this art is no longer metaphoric but metastatic: a realm of proliferating appearances that play with every conceivable reference offered by history as well as by evanescent individual viewpoints and obsessions. This is a dangerous, but curiously optimistic art, one that is both obvious and tricky, which shows what it wants without revealing what it knows.

mit dem Selbst oder ein Nachdenken über die Umstände der geistigen und materiellen Existenz auf, wie es etwa für die analytische Malerei unerlässlich war (du siehst, was du siehst). Ihre Rückkehr zur Figuration bedeutet nicht unbedingt, dass sie die bildliche Konzeption in den Kontext einer begrifflichen Bedeutung rücken (du liest, was du siehst). Vielmehr dienen die figurativen Elemente in ihrem jeweiligen Werk lediglich als Anregungen, die auf ein Thema anspielen statt es offen anzusprechen. Dadurch scheitern Versuche, das Werk und seine Bedeutung zu benennen, sei es im Sinne seines Gegenstandes oder des Erfolgs, mit dem es Form und Inhalt in ein Gleichgewicht bringt.

Die ergebnisoffene Zuweisung von Bedeutung, die bestimmte Stränge der Konzeptkunst aufgreift, um sie zu verändern, bildet den Ausgangspunkt für sechs Künstler, die sich in Köln unter dem Namen der Straße, in der sich ihr Atelier befindet, zusammengeschlossen haben: „Mülheimer Freiheit“. Entsprechend der „Freiheit“ in ihrem Namen ist diese Gruppe locker organisiert, sie hat keine Agenda, die propagiert wird, keine Zielsetzung, die ihre Arbeit unterteilen oder einschränken würde. Der Charakter der hier beschriebenen deutschen Kunst ist bei dieser Gruppe am stärksten ausgeprägt. Statt eines einheitlichen Stils geht es ihnen darum, Gegensätze zusammenzubringen. Sie akzeptieren den gegenseitigen Einfluss in einem solchen Ausmaß, dass sie in wechselnden Teams an Werken zusammenarbeiten. Die Pole, zwischen denen ihre neue Ästhetik schwankt, sind einerseits die Art brut von Peter Bömmels, einem Autodidakten, und andererseits die höchst eklektischen und synkretistischen Bilder von Jiří Georg Dokoupil. Was diese beiden Künstler mit den anderen Gruppenmitgliedern – Gerard Kever, Hans Peter Adamski, Walter Dahn und Gerhard Naschberger – gemeinsam haben, könnte man als die bewusste Trennung der Faktoren Subjektivität und Stil beschreiben.

Die „Für dich/mich/uns geht alles“-Haltung der Mülheimer Freiheit betrachtet das gemalte Bild als Ort der vergänglichen Faszination, der nicht die Einheit eines Ichs, sondern eine multiple subjektive Sicht darstellt. Das Ergebnis ist „Freestyle-Kunst“, ein Begriff, dessen sportliche Assoziationen die Gruppe (wie schon der Boxer-Künstler Arthur Cravan) akzeptiert. In der Arena der Bilder werden die Visionen und Sehnsüchte des/der Künstler*in in einem Showdown mit dessen/deren Kenntnissen der Kunstgeschichte konfrontiert. Eine kurze Irritation, die durch ein Bild in einer Zeitschrift oder Fernsehreklame, durch ein Kunstbuch oder einen Traum ausgelöst wird, kämpft mit dem Bedürfnis, ein Bild zu malen, das authentisch vom Ich stammt und handelt. Natürlich wird der Kampf entweder in einer vollkommenen Gleichgültigkeit gegenüber dem Stil oder in der bewussten Verwendung einer stilistischen Inkonsistenz enden, wo kubistische Zitate mit naziähnlichen Männerfiguren oder expressionistische Straßenprostituierte mit dem Altamira-Reh die Leinwand teilen. Das Label „neuer Subjektivismus“ ist nicht präzise genug, um die Weigerung, die hinter dieser Haltung steckt, zu beschreiben – die Weigerung, die Rolle des autonomen Kunstschaffenden zu spielen, der etwas zu sagen hat, das nur er oder sie sagen kann.

Die obsessive Bildproduktion der Künstler der Mülheimer Freiheit soll nicht aufklären oder belehren, sondern verführen. Sie verlangen vom Betrachtenden Akzeptanz, wie die berühmte Mutterliebe, die keine Fragen stellt und keinen Dank erwartet. Ihre Gemälde sind Ausbrüche schierer Freude am Widerspruch, die über das einzelne Bild hinausfließt und ganze Serien flutet (so die mehr als fünfzig Bilder von Walter Dahn, die alle die Geschichte eines „Malers ohne Idee“ erzählen). Transformation rückt in den Fokus der Ästhetik; der/die Künstler*in wird zum/zur Verwandlungskünstler*in; die Arbeit zu einer Zwischenstation für eine Individualität, die sich selbst mittels Kunst erforscht, indem sie sich in ihr auflöst. Das geschieht ohne Angst, Scham oder Bedauern; der Akt des Machens besagt, dass diese Macher zumindest mit der Befolgung der Befehle des Kunstmarkts oder den verinnerlichten Zwängen, den kleinen programmatischen

Wolfgang Max Faust

The art historian Wolfgang Max Faust is one of the voices instrumental in supporting and vindicating the so-called Neue Wilde. Essays like "Du hast keine Chance. Nutze sie!" (You Haven't Got a Chance. So Use It!), laid the foundations with regards to art history for the narrative of a long overdue "return" of figurative painting, which was understood as the genuinely European or specifically German countermovement to the established, allegedly American-dominated "camp" of Conceptual Art. Faust's support for "new German" painting found its most prominent expression in the study of 1982, *Hunger nach Bildern. Deutsche Malerei der Gegenwart* (Hunger for Pictures: Contemporary German Painting), which he co-authored with Gerd de Vries. Both authors were closely associated with the circle around the gallerist Paul Maenz. The development of the latter's gallery activities can also be read as an indication of the shift in attitude taking place in the art world; in 1980, Maenz began including in his program, until then dominated by Conceptual and Minimal Art, works by the Cologne artists of the Mülheimer Freiheit. The title "Hunger nach Bildern" quickly became a catchy slogan for characterizing the painting style of the Neue Wilde. At the same time, however, the study may also be understood as an attempt to undertake something more audacious—to revise the lineaments of the art canon and emphasize a specifically German painting tradition. As the authors saw it, this tradition had been marginalized since the 1960s and 1970s, and therefore was now all the more forcefully playing a major role in contemporary art. Faust and de Vries traced a line of development between the Neue Wilde and painters like Georg Baselitz and Markus Lüpertz, who, despite the differing contexts and the significant generation gap, were ultimately considered within the United States representatives of a "German Neo-Expressionism."

Stimmen, die dir sagen, was visionär ist und was nicht, gebrochen haben. Diese künstlerische Haltung ist mit Transpolitik vergleichbar – wir (die Menschen, die Kunstschaffenden) existieren im Hier und Jetzt und zugleich woanders – wir sind zugleich „dafür und dagegen“. Das ist ganz klar eine prekäre Haltung. Die gesellschaftliche Relevanz, die man sich in den vergangenen beiden Jahrzehnten von der Kunst wünschte, wird ersetzt – nicht durch deren Gegenteil, etwa einen radikal persönlichen Idiolekt, sondern durch eine visuelle Sprache, die aus der Identifikation mit einer sozialen Gruppe herrührt. In der heutigen westdeutschen Realität lebend – mit ihrem fanatischen Konsumverhalten, ihrer Arbeitslosigkeit, ihrer Angst vor Terrorismus, ihrer elektronischen Überwachung des Alltags –, suchen diese Künstler*innen einen Ort. Sie suchen weder Zuflucht vor der „realen Wirklichkeit“ noch ein Mittel gegen deren kranken Glamour, sondern schlicht einen Ort, an dem man jetzt sein kann – einen Punkt, von dem aus man die akzeptierten Strukturen der Selbsterfahrung und die Verhaltensnormen der Gesellschaft, mit denen man symbiotisch oder sogar parasitär lebt, in eine andere Richtung lenken und womöglich transformieren kann. Die Macher dieser Kunst würden die Wahrnehmung der gleichen Sache anders kommunizieren und nicht Therapien oder Designutopien vorschlagen oder Wahrheiten proklamieren, seien sie gesellschaftlicher, intellektueller, ästhetischer oder anthropologischer Art. Die Struktur dieser Kunst ist nicht mehr metaphorisch, sondern metastatisch: Sie ist ein Bereich wuchernder Erscheinungen, die mit allen denkbaren Verweisen spielen, die die Geschichte und die flüchtigen, individuellen Sichtweisen und Obsessionen zu bieten haben. Es handelt sich um eine gefährliche, aber merkwürdig optimistische Kunst, die zugleich offensichtlich und verzwickt ist, die zeigt, was sie will, ohne zu verraten, was sie weiß.

Bei dem Kunsthistoriker Wolfgang Max Faust handelt es sich um eine der maßgeblichen Stimmen zur Unterstützung und Legitimierung der sogenannten „Neuen Wilden“. Essays wie „Du hast keine Chance. Nutze sie!“ bildeten das kunsthistorische Fundament für das Narrativ einer längst überfälligen „Wiederkehr“ der figurativen Malerei, die als genuin europäische beziehungsweise deutsche Gegenbewegung zu dem etablierten, vermeintlich amerikanisch dominierten „Lager“ der Konzeptkunst verstanden wurde. Fausts Engagement für die „neue deutsche“ Malerei schlug sich am prominentesten in der 1982 erschienenen Untersuchung *Hunger nach Bildern. Deutsche Malerei der Gegenwart* nieder, die er zusammen mit Gerd de Vries verfasste. Beide Autoren stammten aus dem engen Umfeld des Galeristen Paul Maenz. Auch die Entwicklung von dessen Galerietätigkeit kann als Gesinnungswechsel in der Kunstwelt gelesen werden, insofern er ab 1980 unter anderem die Kölner Maler der Mülheimer Freiheit in sein vor allem durch Konzeptkunst und Minimal Art dominiertes Programm aufnahm. Der Titel „Hunger nach Bildern“ avancierte schnell zu einem griffigen Slogan für die Malerei der „Neuen Wilden“. Die Publikation kann allerdings als darüber weit hinausgehender Versuch einer Kanonrevision zugunsten einer deutschen Malereitradition verstanden werden. Diese wurde den Autoren zufolge seit den 1960er- und 1970er-Jahren marginalisiert, um nun umso deutlicher ins Zentrum des gegenwärtigen Geschehens zu treten. Faust und de Vries ziehen dabei eine Entwicklungslinie zwischen den „Neuen Wilden“ und Malern wie etwa Georg Baselitz oder Markus Lüpertz, die in den USA schließlich trotz unterschiedlicher Kontexte und über die maßgebliche Generationslücke hinweg als „German Neo-Expressionism“ rezipiert wurden.

In *12 Künstler aus Deutschland*, exh. cat. Kunsthalle Basel, Basel 1982, n.p.

Jean-Christophe Ammann
On the Exhibition

Exactly a year ago, on March 13 [1981], the exhibition *Rundschau Deutschland* opened its doors in Munich. It inspired a raft of similar shows in Germany, but above all it triggered critical controversy. The present exhibition was first mooted in November 1979 when I saw a more or less improvised show at the Hahnentor in Cologne by Klaus Hübner, Peter Bömmels, Hans Peter Adamski, Walter Dahn, and Jiří Georg Dokoupil, which made a deep impression on me (see *Kunstforum International,* no. 39, 1980, p. 183, and no. 48, 1981–82, pp. 41–47). It was accompanied by a publication called *Kirschblüte.** Of course people immediately connected it with the work being done by the younger generation of Italian artists (Paul Maenz was showing them in Cologne), as though this were a direct influence. But those people were missing something important—the fact something similar was happening in German bands, most notably in a band by the name of Deutsch Amerikanische Freundschaft (DAF). At the time Peter Bömmels was working at the magazine *Spex* (as he did until quite recently), which mainly focused on these new bands in the international scene. Jiří Georg Dokoupil's brother is in a band called Wirtschaftswunder. Both Markus (in particular) and Albert Oehlen played in bands; in Berlin, Salomé and Castelli founded the band Geile Tiere. The terms "Wild Painting," "New German Painting," and "New German Wave" (referring to music) need not be discussed here, because they are no more than catchalls for a development that is in fact immensely complex.[1]

An important aspect of this development is "playfulness,"[2] which is demonstrated here in a manner that should actually be of interest to a great many more people. At a time when logjams in the economy and in politics have proved to be completely insurmountable obstacles (with the corresponding, psychological public feedback), artists have created room for maneuver—"playgrounds"—that even art in the 1970s could not muster. And they make radical use of these playgrounds, exploring themes, motifs, and even painting itself, intuitively and without prejudice. "Logjams" (and maybe more) arise in art when the codices of meaning in these playgrounds and in potential pathways gain too much power, when—in this kind of status quo—a self-fulfilling dynamic arises of its own accord and, on principle, censors and imposes taboos on innovative strategies.

The room for maneuver that artists carved out for themselves in the late 1970s has seen them systematically working to do away with theses overpowering codices of meaning. There is nothing that cannot be introduced into art. Everything is simultaneously present and, first and foremost, is viewed impartially. This de-hierarchization naturally establishes a different terminology and language that are primarily about an individual's self-image, his or her own feelings and desires. This could be seen as a model of sorts, because it facilitates a process of transformation in art, a process that opens out its own room for maneuver in all directions and also represents a fundamentally new response to reality.

The extent to which ideas of this kind are in fact seen in new German music is evident from the following excerpts from an interview with musicians Robert Görl and Gabriel Delgado-López, both from DAF, which was published in *Wochenzeitung* (*WoZ,* November 20, 1981) and in *Musik-Express* (*ME,* February 2, 1982).

Aus: *12 Künstler aus Deutschland*, Ausst.-Kat. Kunsthalle Basel, Basel 1982, o. S.

Jean-Christophe Ammann
Zur Ausstellung

Vor einem Jahr, auf den Tag genau am 13. März [1981], wurde in München die Ausstellung „Rundschau Deutschland“ eröffnet. Sie bewirkte eine grössere Zahl von ähnlichen Ausstellungen in Deutschland und vor allem eine kontroverse Kritik. Die Ausstellung hier entstand im Ansatz bereits im November 1979, als ich im Hahnentor in Köln eine eher improvisierte Ausstellung von Klaus Hübner, Peter Bömmels, Hans Peter Adamski, Walter Dahn und Jiří Georg Dokoupil sah. Eine Ausstellung, die mich sehr betroffen machte (siehe Kunstforum International Nr. 39, 1980, S. 183, und Nr. 48, 1981/82, S. 41–47). Sie war begleitet von einer mit „Kirschblüte“ bezeichneten Publikation.* Natürlich wurde sogleich die Verbindung zu den jüngeren italienischen Künstlern hergestellt (die Paul Maenz in Köln zeigte), gleichsam als unmittelbarer Einflussbereich. Dabei übersah man etwas Wesentliches: dass nämlich zur selben Zeit eine ähnliche Entwicklung bei deutschen Bands festzustellen war, vorab bei einer Gruppe, die sich „Deutsch-Amerikanische Freundschaft“ (DAF) nennt. Peter Bömmels arbeitete zu dieser Zeit und noch bis vor kurzem an der Zeitschrift ‚Spex‘, die sich in erster Linie mit diesen neuen Musikgruppen auf internationaler Ebene beschäftigt. Der Bruder von Jiří Georg Dokoupil spielt in einer Gruppe, die „Wirtschaftswunder“ heisst. Vor allem Markus, aber auch Albert Oehlen, spielten in Gruppen, und Salomé begründete in Berlin mit Castelli die „Geilen Tiere“. „Wilde Malerei“, „Neue deutsche Malerei“, „Neue deutsche Welle“ (auf die Musik bezogen) sind Bezeichnungen, über die man im Weiteren gar nicht diskutieren muss, weil sie doch nur eine Entwicklung global benennen, die in sich höchst komplex ist.[1]

Ein wichtiges Moment in dieser Entwicklung ist das *Spielerische*[2], und das wird mit einer Modellhaftigkeit vorgetragen, die eigentlich sehr viel mehr Leute interessieren müsste. Die Künstler haben zu jenem Zeitpunkt, wo sich die Engpässe in Wirtschaft und Politik als ein schier unüberwindliches Hindernis herausstellten (mit entsprechendem Feedback psychologischer Natur in der Öffentlichkeit), Spielräume erarbeitet, die auch die Kunst in den siebziger Jahren nicht aufzuweisen hatte. Und diese Spielräume werden radikal genutzt, indem vorurteilslos und intuitiv mit Themen, Motiven und der Malerei selbst umgegangen wird. „Engpässe“ (und vielleicht nicht nur) in der Kunst entstehen dann, wenn die Bedeutungskodizes der Spielräume und der möglichen Wege übermächtig werden, wenn in einem solchen status quo eine Eigendynamik um ihrer selbst willen entsteht, die neue Strategien, auch aus Gründen des Prinzips, tabuisiert und zensuriert.

Die Spielräume, die sich die Künstler Ende der siebziger Jahre erarbeitet haben, bestehen darin, dass sie systematisch an der Auflösung dieser übermächtigen Bedeutungskodizes gearbeitet haben. Es gibt nichts, was nicht in die Kunst eingebracht werden kann. Alles ist gleichzeitig vorhanden und wird primär als wertfrei betrachtet. Diese Enthierarchisierung bewirkt natürlicherweise eine neue Benennung und somit auch Sprache, die primär mit dem eigenen Selbstverständnis zu tun haben, den eigenen Gefühlen und Wünschen. Insofern besteht hier eine Modellhaftigkeit, weil sie einen Umwandlungsprozess in der Kunst ermöglicht, der ihren Spielraum in alle Richtungen hin geöffnet hat und der auch ein grundsätzlich neues Verhalten der Wirklichkeit gegenüber darstellt.

Wie stark solche Überlegungen auch in der neuen deutschen Musik vorhanden sind, zeigen die folgenden Interview-Auszüge mit Robert Görl und Gabriel Delgado-López,

WoZ: Do you see yourselves as a band pursuing a politically motivated path?

Gabi: We're a political band that doesn't advocate any particular politics but that talks about reality and desires. We talk about everything, from love to politics. But we don't preach and we don't have any messages—we pass on information and try to fill information gaps. For example, there's an intellectual elite that denies the masses could have anything resembling intelligence and claims the masses are stupid, although barely any of those intellectuals ever bother to make direct contact with them. But the masses aren't stupid, they're just less well informed than some other people. So we want to convey information via records to a mass audience.

ME: On *Gold und Liebe* you sing, "Children are cruel, children need gold." What's that about?

Gabi: It's perfectly simple. We're very interested in one thing in particular: in innocence. Children are innocent. And we try to be largely innocent. So we play around with various things. Children, they're capable of torturing mice—but still remain absolutely innocent. In other words, utterly cruel yet wholly pure at the same time. And that leads to a way of looking at things that diverges from Western binary thinking, namely that everything is either good or evil. There is in fact a kind of innocence that elevates people above that. And suddenly you have the freedom to play around with everything.

ME: Don't you worry that this idea can't come across without someone analyzing the song?

Gabi: That's only one aspect of it. The other is that children and people in general all want gold. And gold is always held up as the ultimate in desirable. By gold I also mean somewhere to live, for instance. Gold is used here as a symbol of things that are just part of daily life, like a home. But there are people who don't have a home. And they need one. So when their homes are taken away from them, they set up squats—like in Berlin.

ME: Do you actually believe your records are necessary? Are you trying to bring about change?

Gabi: ...DAF wants to reclaim a lot of things for people. Love songs that have been stolen from the masses by all the Toms, Dicks, and Harrys who have turned them into a completely falsified, perverted form. We're taking the love songs back. And we're taking the gold back. We're even taking words like "young" and "strong" back. Regardless of how they were used before—be it badly or well. We're giving things back to people by first taking them back for ourselves, without bias.

WoZ: Are you aware of the responsibility you are shouldering when you say that every ideology is shit—pulling the rug out from under the feet of your audience, abandoning them to their dilemma, to their own helplessness?

Gabi: Ideologies are only ever crutches. If you throw away those crutches then of course you feel unsure and have to learn to walk without them.

...A lot of what we do, of what the younger generation in general does these days, isn't open to rational explanation, or perhaps only in the specific slang they use. It certainly can't be articulated by your smart elitists.

WoZ: So have you cast off the shackles of rationalism?

Gabi: To a certain extent. The thing is, people have been thinking and acting analytically for far too long—in every respect, from politics to love. And in music, too. Although this mindset has led to a very secure, well-planned way of living, any intuitive engagement with things has been completely lost.

WoZ: So, in your work, where is the engagement with this, shall we say, broadly indefinable thing?

Robert: Dreams and desires should be realized, made real. These things instigate change, in society too. Everything changes, it just takes time. Things won't change in a matter of months. That's why protest often descends into chaos, or can even turn

den beiden Musikern der DAF, erschienen in der *Wochenzeitung* (WoZ, 20.11.81) und im *Musik-Express* (ME, 2.2.82).

WoZ: Versteht Ihr Euch als eine Band mit politisch motivierter Stossrichtung?

Gabi: Wir sind eine politische Band, die keine bestimmte Politik vertritt, sondern Wirklichkeit und Wünsche beschreibt. Wir beschreiben alles, von Liebe bis Politik. Aber wir sind keine Prediger und bringen auch keine Botschaften – wir geben Informationen weiter und versuchen, das Informationsgefälle abzubauen. Da gibt es doch z. B. diese geistige Elite, die der Masse abspricht, so was Ähnliches wie Intelligenz zu haben, und behauptet, die Masse sei dumm, obwohl sich unter den Intellektuellen kaum jemand die Mühe nimmt, direkt mit ihr in Berührung zu treten. Die Masse ist jedoch nicht dumm, sie hat einfach weniger Informationen als gewisse andere Leute. Deshalb wollen wir Informationen per Schallplatte an ein Massenpublikum weitergeben.

ME: Auf GOLD UND LIEBE singt Ihr: „Kinder sind grausam, Kinder brauchen Gold". Was steckt dahinter?

Gabi: Das ist ganz einfach. An einer ganz bestimmten Sache sind wir sehr interessiert: nämlich an der Unschuld. Kinder sind unschuldig. Wir versuchen auch weitgehend unschuldig zu sein. Deswegen spielen wir mit verschiedenen Dingen. Kinder, die können eine Maus foltern – und dabei absolut unschuldig sein. Also absolut grausam und gleichzeitig total rein. Und daraus ergibt sich eine Form, Dinge zu betrachten, die sich von diesem westlichen Dualismus-Denken entfernt: Alles sei entweder gut oder böse. Es existiert einfach so eine Unschuld, die den Menschen darüber erhebt. Und darin hat man dann auf einmal die Freiheit, mit allem zu spielen.

ME: Fürchtet Ihr nicht, dass dieser Gedanke ohne Interpretation des Stücks gar nicht rüberkommt?

Gabi: Das ist jetzt nur ein Teilaspekt. Der andere Aspekt ist der, dass Kinder oder Menschen allgemein Gold wollen. Und Gold auch dauernd propagiert wird. Mit Gold meine ich zum Beispiel auch eine Wohnung. Gold symbolisiert hier Sachen, die inzwischen zum täglichen Leben gehören, wie eben eine Wohnung. Es gibt aber auch Leute, die haben gar keine Wohnung. Sie brauchen aber eine. Und wenn denen die Wohnung genommen wird, dann werden – wie in Berlin – Häuser besetzt.

ME: Glaubt Ihr denn eigentlich, dass Eure Platten notwendig sind? Wollt Ihr Veränderungen erreichen?

Gabi: ...DAF will vieles für die Leute wieder zurückholen. Liebeslieder, die den Massen geklaut wurden durch irgendwelche Heinies. Die das in einer ganz falschen, pervertierten Form gebracht haben. Wir holen uns die Liebeslieder wieder. Wir holen uns das Gold wieder. Wir holen uns sogar solche Vokabeln wieder wie „jung" und „stark". Ohne irgendeinen Respekt davor, ob das früher mal falsch oder gut benutzt wurde. Wir geben den Leuten Sachen wieder, indem wir sie erst einmal für uns ganz wertfrei zurückholen.

WoZ: Seid Ihr Euch einer Verantwortung bewusst, wenn Ihr sagt: Jede Ideologie ist Scheisse, und damit den Zuschauer/-hörer seiner Orientierungshilfen beraubt, ihn im Dilemma, in seiner Hilflosigkeit sitzen lasst?

Gabi: Ideologien sind doch eigentlich nur Krücken. Wirft man diese Krücken ab, dann ist man selbstverständlich unsicher und muss lernen, ohne sie zu gehen.

...Vieles, was wir machen, was die heutige Jugend generell macht, ist doch nicht mehr rational erklärbar, bestenfalls noch in der spezifischen Slangsprache der Jugendlichen selbst. Ganz sicher aber nicht mehr durch irgendwelche gescheite Eliteleute zu formulieren.

WoZ: Habt Ihr denn die Ketten der Rationalität abgelegt?

Gabi: Teilweise schon. Sieh, es ist zu lange analytisch gedacht und vorgegangen worden. In allen Belangen, von der Politik bis zur Liebesbeziehung. Und auch in der Musik. Diese Einstellung hat zwar zu einer sehr sicheren und gut geplanten Lebensform geführt, aber die intuitive Auseinandersetzung mit Sachen ist absolut untergegangen.

bloody. But then it's over again, and the people who have been beaten black and blue for their cause are the losers.

Gabi: Resistance and protest, making a negative statement—that's all good, but it's not enough. You have to go at it intuitively, physically, because our bodies have been so endlessly crippled and because it's specifically in the body that things happen intuitively, that animalistic things happen.

ME: Which direction do you want to steer people in?

Robert: First of all, we want to change the overall atmosphere of people's lives.

Gabi: Part of that is about rediscovering their bodies. Dance. Rhythm. That first has to be working for everything else to follow on. Powerful physical music. Secondly, the content should make people think. Because we talk about absolutely everything—from hate to love, from holding hands to S-M, from red to black, from white to gray. All in a new form. And using a new language.

In what follows here I will look more closely at individual artists, although each will be treated differently and it certainly won't be possible for me to do equal justice to them all.

The selection of works by Salomé is deliberately limited to the period from 1978 to 1980. In those three years Salomé produced works that have already achieved a certain status in art history. He introduced a personal world into his art and worked with it in a way that would never have been possible before. When sexuality broke into art in the late 1970s, it was ultimately nothing other than a new directness in the way people dealt with it. In his compositions—initially in his seasons paintings (1978)—it is expressed with an ironic undertone that puts his source materials into the right perspective. And kung fu is blatantly reconfigured as fisting (*Kung Fu,* 1980). A casual yet observant attitude to medialized reality is adjusted to Salomé's own leanings, but without losing distance. His use of eloquent pictorial elements should not be overlooked in terms of innovation. Although they may seem fundamentally traditional, in relation to this subject matter they undergo a stress test that shows them in a new light.

Rainer Fetting almost always paints several versions of a picture in order to hunt down the "inner picture," exploring the effect of different colors on its meaning. Since his paintings are precisely constructed, colors change and shift the psychic intensity that underpins them. His compositions embody the highest possible concentration of a momentary atmosphere: a whole array of experiences and insights culminates in one specific event. The painting *Große Dusche (Panorama)* [Large Shower (Panorama)] was the outcome of a year spent in New York, as was the painting *Mann mit Axt* [Man with Ax]. The intense nightlife of the twenty-four-hour city mingles with remembered visits to the sauna, with a brutal murder in the Anvil (an infamous bar). Memories, feelings, something glimpsed for a fraction of a second all extend into the permanence of a constantly recurring image, condense into a moment of erotic awareness, while indeterminacy and contradiction keep that atmospheric moment in enduring suspense.

In 1973, Luciano Castelli was already starting to create self-portraits in which he systematically and intuitively explored male-female interferences (see the exhibition *Transformer,* Kunstmuseum Luzern, 1974). When he relocated to Berlin some years ago, he and Salomé embarked on an intense collaboration, with Rainer Fetting joining them later. In Fetting's work, color, in its expansiveness, is basically primal; in Salomé's it expresses a physical state that arises from continuous movement; in Castelli's it is basically tied to the drawing hand. While his spontaneous gestures may convey a figurative, often crude event, their vehemence—be they object- or atmosphere-led—articulate and situate the contents of the composition just as powerfully. That comes across very clearly in the works on display here. The paint application and brushwork communicate

WoZ: Wie findet denn bei Euch die Auseinandersetzung mit diesem, sagen wir mal ganz allgemein, Unbestimmbaren statt?

Robert: Träume und Wünsche soll man verwirklichen, zur Realität machen. Solche Sachen führen Veränderungen herbei, auch im gesellschaftlichen Sinn. Alles ändert sich, es braucht nur seine Zeit. Innerhalb von ein paar Monaten kann sich nichts ändern. Deshalb ufert der Protest oft in ein Chaos aus, geht eventuell sogar blutig aus. Und danach ist's vorbei, und die, die sich für die Sache haben blutig schlagen lassen, sind dann die Verlierer.

Gabi: Verweigerung und Protestverhalten, ein negatives Statement setzen, das ist gut, aber es genügt nicht. Man muss intuitiv, körperlich an die Sache rangehen, weil der Körper halt unendlich verkrüppelt worden ist und gerade weil doch dort so intuitive, so tierische Sachen ablaufen.

ME: In welche Richtung möchtet Ihr die Menschen denn lenken?

Robert: Erst einmal wollen wir die allgemeine Atmosphäre ändern, in der Menschen leben.

Gabi: Dazu gehört erst einmal die Wiederentdeckung des Körpers. Tanz. Rhythmus. Das muss zuerst funktionieren, damit alles andere auch läuft. Starke körperliche Musik. Zweitens sollen die Leute von den Inhalten zum Nachdenken angeregt werden. Weil wir eben wirklich von Hass bis Liebe, von Händchenhalten bis Sado-Maso, von Rot bis Schwarz, von Weiss bis Grau alles beschreiben. Und das in einer neuen Form. Auch mit einer neuen Sprache.

Ich möchte im Folgenden auf die einzelnen Künstler etwas näher eingehen, wobei dies auf unterschiedliche Art geschehen wird, und sicherlich wird es mir nicht möglich sein, jedem gleichermassen gerecht zu werden.

Die Auswahl der Arbeiten von Salomé beschränkt sich bewusst auf die Jahre 1978–1980. Salomé hat in diesem Zeitraum Werke geschaffen, die bereits eine Art historischen Stellenwert in der Kunst einnehmen. Er hat eine persönliche Welt in sein Schaffen hineingetragen und verarbeitet, wie das vorher gar nicht möglich war. Der Einbruch der Sexualität in die Kunst gegen Ende der siebziger Jahre ist letztlich nichts anderes als die Unmittelbarkeit des Selbstverständnisses, mit ihr umzugehen. In seinen Arbeiten – vorab in den Jahreszeiten-Bildern (1978) – äussert sie sich mit jenem ironischen Unterton, der die verwendeten Vorlagen in die richtige Perspektive rückt. Und [der] Kung Fu[-kämpfer] wird schlicht und einfach umgedeutet, indem er als Faustficker in Aktion tritt („Kung Fu“, 1980). Der lässige und doch aufmerksame Umgang mit einer medialisierten Wirklichkeit wird mit den eigenen Vorzeichen in Einklang gebracht, ohne dass die Distanz verlorengeht. Der Einsatz der bildsprachlichen Mittel darf vom innovativen Standpunkt aus gesehen nicht verkannt werden. Sie erscheinen zwar primär traditionell; aber in Bezug auf ihren Gegenstand werden sie einer Belastungsprobe unterworfen, die sie in einem neuen Licht erscheinen lässt.

Rainer Fetting malt fast immer mehrere Versionen von einem Bild, um diesem „innern Bild“ auf die Spur zu kommen, um dessen Sinn bei verschiedenen Farbeinsätzen zu erfragen. Da die Bilder präzis aufgebaut sind, verändern und verlagern die Farben die psychische Intensität, die ihnen zugrunde liegt. Sie sind stets höchste Konzentration eines Stimmungsmomentes: Ein Umfeld von Erfahrungen und Erlebnissen mündet in ein spezifisches Ereignis. Das Bild „Grosse Dusche (Panorama)“ ist auf einen einjährigen New York-Aufenthalt zurückzuführen, ebenso das Bild „Mann mit Axt“. Die nächtliche Intensität der 24-Stunden-Stadt vermengt sich mit Sauna-Erinnerungen, einem brutalen Mord im „Anvil“ (ein berüchtigtes Lokal). Erinnerung, Empfundenes, in Sekundenbruchteil Gesehenes dehnen sich aus in die Dauer des immer wiederkehrenden Bildes, verdichten sich in einem Moment erotischer Erkenntnis, in welchem Unbestimmtheit und Gegensätzliches das Stimmungsmoment in der Schwebe halten.

Luciano Castelli hat schon ab 1973 begonnen, die Interferenzen von Maskulin-Feminin systematisch und intuitiv in

and contain instinct in a painterly form. In 1981, Werner Büttner published volume one of a book entitled *Schrecken der Demokratie* [Disasters of Democracy]. It is a collection of photocopied drawings with related statements. Under a drawing of worms in the ground and a birdlike creature gazing longingly upward are the words "Enthemmungsprozesse äussern sich im Anfang immer als gute Laune" [Processes of disinhibition always initially manifest as a good mood]. In another case, the words "Höchstleistung & Gegröle '81" [Peak Performance and Bawling '81] appear under an image of a house in a forbidding landscape with men's pants flying away in the sky. The connections between texts and images are both complex and polemic, indirectly revealing and ironic. And this is precisely the stance that also determines his painterly work. When a cylindrical piece of wood meets a squared block of timber on the high seas, this provides both the trigger and the title for a large-format painting (1981–82); it is both a concrete event and a metaphor that could be interpreted in more than enough ways (which I am deliberately not exploring, in order to leave the painting open). *Im Weinberg* [In the Vineyard] (1981) depicts an utterly desolate scene with vines, an open umbrella on the ground, and a wrinkled old crone wielding an ax. The colors are a clayish gray, the paint application is clayish gray, the mood is clayish gray. And suddenly we register some kind of an acrid smell.

In Albert Oehlen's work, too, there is a strong, content-related connection between motif, painting, and choice of colors. And it seems to me that precisely this content-related connection is a particular thematic interest of Oehlen's, although there is little overt indication of this. When he paints underwater images with eels gliding through human skulls, when he paints the interior of a museum of natural history, washing and changing rooms on the lower ground floor of the car manufacturing plant at Rosenberg, bifurcated branches with spider's webs, the seemingly deliberate, supercooled choice of motifs is the supercooled and equally precise answer as to what a pictorial motif can be and wants to be in relation to painting, and that is also the source of the colors, generally somber and lacking in light. Albert Oehlen himself commented on this, with Werner Büttner and Jörg Immendorff, in an interview for the magazine *Twen:*

"I think it's maybe not bad to talk about motifs for a moment. My criticism of the majority of new artists today is that they select some partial aspect of art history and decide to expand on that. First, as Büttner puts it, they seek out somewhere to stand and then they very slowly hunker down. But in the process these people forget that the thing they are tapping into sometimes had different meanings. That's to say, if you extract some aspect of Polke's working method and adapt it to use in your own work, you're completely ignoring what he meant by it and what drove him to seek out this or that material.

Immendorff: But that is stylistically legitimate, because—in his more developed phase—Polke's work has a lot to do stylistically with Picabia. And I think that's legitimate...

Oehlen: But what I wanted to say is that people tap into certain forms when there was content. As a yardstick I'd say that in the case of a good artist, who means something, the form arises from the content. It comes of its own accord, it's part of the package. And it's just right."

Volker Tannert's work is primarily thematic. It's basically all about restratification, relocation, and transformation. There are paintings with excavations, with incursions into the earth, with aggressive bloodletting, phlebotomy (burnout), with an arsonist and a burning house, with organ transplants, with entangled limbs in effect reversing above and below, left and right, with heads that simultaneously but with spatial differences grow out of overly long arm shapes. In Volker Tannert's work there is a very

Selbstdarstellungen zu erforschen (siehe Ausstellung *Transformer*, Kunstmuseum Luzern, 1974). Als er vor Jahren nach Berlin übersiedelte, begann eine intensive Zusammenarbeit mit Salomé und später mit Rainer Fetting. Während bei Fetting die Farbe als Ausdehnung etwas Primäres ist, bei Salomé eine aus der kontinuierlichen Bewegung erlebte Körperbefindlichkeit ausdrückt, gründet sie bei Castelli eher auf einem zeichnerischen Duktus. Die spontane Gestik umreisst zwar ein figürliches, oft krudes Geschehen, aber ihre Vehemenz – ob objekt- oder stimmungsgebunden – artikuliert und situiert ebenso stark die inhaltliche Dimension des Bildes. Das kommt in den Arbeiten hier auch deutlich zum Ausdruck. Die Farb- und Pinselspuren bezeichnen und beinhalten Instinktives in bildnerischer Form.

1981 hat Werner Büttner ein Buch herausgegeben unter dem Titel „Schrecken der Demokratie" (Bd. 1). Es handelt sich um fotokopierte Zeichnungen mit jeweils dazugehörendem Text. „Enthemmungsprozesse äussern sich im Anfang immer als gute Laune" steht unter der Zeichnung mit Regenwürmern im Boden und einem vogelähnlichen Wesen, das sehnsüchtig nach oben blickt. Oder: „Höchstleistung & Gegröle '81", und darüber steht ein Haus in düsterer Landschaft mit davonfliegenden Hosen. Die Beziehungen zwischen Text und Bild sind sowohl komplex als auch polemisch, indirekt entlarvend und ironisch. Und genau diese Haltung bestimmt auch sein malerisches Schaffen. Wenn ein Rundholz auf hoher See auf ein Kantholz trifft, so ist dies Anlass und Titel für ein grossformatiges Bild (1981/82), ist konkretes Ereignis und Metapher, für die es genügend Interpretationen gäbe (auf die ich bewusst nicht eingehe, um das Bild offen zu lassen). „Im Weinberg" (1981) ist ein völlig desolates Bild mit einer hackeschwingenden Hutzelfrau, Rebstöcken und einem aufgespannten Regenschirm am Boden. Die Farben sind graulehmig, das Bild ist graulehmig gemalt, die Stimmung ist graulehmig. Und plötzlich verspürt man noch eine Art beissenden Geruchs.

Auch bei Albert Oehlen gibt es eine starke inhaltliche Verbindung zwischen Motiv, Malerei und Farbwahl. Und ich meine, dass gerade diese inhaltliche Verbindung ein geradezu thematisches Anliegen von Oehlen ist, wobei vordergründig wenig darauf hinweist. Wenn er Unterwasserbilder malt mit Aalen, die durch menschliche Schädel gleiten, die Innenräume eines naturhistorischen Museums, die Wasch- und Umkleideräume unter der Motorenhalle am Rosenberg, Astgabeln mit Spinn-Netzen, so ist die scheinbar willkürliche und unterkühlte Motivauswahl die unterkühlte und ebenso präzise Antwort, was ein Bildmotiv sein kann und will in Bezug auf die Malerei, und entsprechend ergeben sich auch die Farben, eher lichtarm und düster. Albert Oehlen in einem Interview mit der Zeitschrift ‚Twen', zusammen mit Werner Büttner und Jörg Immendorff:

„Ich meine, es ist vielleicht gar nicht schlecht, mal auf die Motive zu kommen. Meine Kritik an dem Grossteil der jetzigen neuen Künstler ist die, dass sie sich einen Teilaspekt aus der Kunstgeschichte raussuchen und den ausbauen wollen. Erst sucht man sich, wie der Büttner sagt, ein Stehplätzchen, und dann geht man langsam in die Hocke. Dabei vergessen diese Leute aber, dass das, woran sie angeknüpft haben, mal 'ne wechselnde Bedeutung hatte. Also wenn man sich jetzt mal aus der Arbeitsweise von Polke einen Aspekt rausnimmt und den adaptiert, um da weiterzuarbeiten, ignoriert man völlig, was der gemeint hat und was für Motive der gehabt hat, überhaupt dieses oder jenes Material zu entdecken.

Immendorff: Stilistisch ist das ja legitim, denn Polke hat stilistisch sehr viel mit – in der entwickelteren Phase – Picabia zu tun. Und ich find das legitim...

Oehlen: Worauf ich aber hinauswollte, ist, dass die Leute formell dort anknüpfen, wo Inhalt war. Und zwar würde ich also als Massstab sagen, bei einem guten Künstler, der eine Bedeutung hat, ergibt sich das Formelle aus dem Inhalt. Es kommt von selber, es wird einfach mitgeliefert. Es stimmt dann einfach."

clear sense of how he reduces painting, of his determination to, so to speak, contain a metaphor in the form of a painterly diagram. His work specifically demonstrates the way that, with daunting inventiveness, he opens up a topic and renders it susceptible to new impulses.—An important feature of his work is that the figures are exposed to moments of both passive and active energy: experiencing-as-agent and experiencing-as-recipient, they appear to express a need for mutation, or rather, a relocation and expansion of their potential and capacity for feeling and perceiving.

What can be described as a theme in Tannert's art appears more closely tied into the pictorial idea in work of the Mülheimer Freiheit artists (with the exception of Peter Bömmels). For all their differences, there is still common ground: a similar lifestyle, constant contact with each other, shared interests, and definitely the determination to achieve a wide artistic appeal without engaging in compromise—as is also seen very clearly in new German music.

Peter Bömmels's art is also primarily thematic. His painting is introverted and takes the form of cryptic "stories" that are nonetheless gripping, because their progress and connections have an intrinsic coherence that appears decodable to the observant viewer. In fact, his pictures are easier to recount than to describe; they have the hidden depth of fairytales. Their subject matter revolves around the many-sided "I" of the artist, which—with all its nuances—is the same as everyone's "I." A 1982 painting in which dripping breasts are forming a stalagmite is entitled *Eine Hölle gleicht der andern* [One Hell Is Like the Next]; in *Gletscherbeben, blutig* [Glacier Shards, Bloody], realized in 1981, one figure is dissipating in the icy wind, while another, connected to it, stalks along with a spidery gait.

Gerhard Naschberger's works are so complex that flushing out their meaning is a real challenge. In my view, his aim is ultimately to present a banal motif in a state of ecstatic enlightenment. *Im Wald* [In the Forest] is the title of one work from 1981: flames are bursting out from a horse's head penetrated by branches. In the painting *Abends* [In the Evening] (1981), two blue hands plead with the sunset. But their plea is kept at a distance by a continuous sequence of pieces of card, overpainted and glued to the composition. Naschberger is striving here to bathe something unremarkable in the glow of the irrevocable. There is a connection here to Bömmels. At a coffee table in the Folkwang Museum, Bömmels talks of "faith, hope, and love" and Walter Dahn retaliates with "power, hate, and pathos." It's not about identifying with terms of that kind, but about being able to deal with them. Naschberger shows this very clearly by unexpectedly, inventively focusing on things that we—in a metaphorical sense—would rather ignore. And it seems to me that above all in his case there is a very pronounced urge to make the impossible true.

At the moment I find Gerard Kever the hardest to grasp. He spent a lengthy period engaged in "alternative civilian service" and was not able to forge ahead in his work to the same extent as the others; but the determination and force with which he takes hold of often very contradictory subjects is just astounding. In his approximately three-by-three-meter painting *Die Kaffeeschmuggler* [The Coffee Smugglers] (1982), in a *High Noon* atmosphere with a hazy desert wind, we see the blindfolded smugglers shortly before their execution. A fist with a huge red flag reaches into the scene from the lower edge of the picture. The whole thing has an air of "Venceremos"; it's also a manifesto for the deceived and a caricature of ideology. At around the same time he painted a large-format picture with a realistic-looking figure seen from behind, whose head—done in black brushstrokes and turned toward the viewer—looks like that of an animal. Clinging onto the figure's back with its claws there is an animal that, like the burden of history, dictates the figure's gait and nature. On the left side, like the writing on the wall, there is a rapid sketch

Volker Tannerts Schaffen ist thematisch ausgerichtet. Es hat grundsätzlich mit Umschichtungen, Verlagerungen und Umwandlungen zu tun. Es gibt Bilder mit Ausschachtungen, mit Einbrüchen in die Erde, mit aggressiven Blutanzapfungen, Aderlassen (Verausgabung), mit einem Brandstifter und einem brennenden Haus, mit Organtransplantationen, mit Verschränkungen von Gliedern im Sinne einer Umkehrung von oben und unten, von links und rechts, mit Köpfen, die gleichzeitig und räumlich verschiedenen, überlangen Armverläufen entwachsen. Bei Volker Tannert wird deutlich spürbar, wie er die Malerei reduziert, wie er die Metapher malerisch gleichsam in Form eines Diagramms zu bewältigen sucht. Gerade bei ihm zeigt sich, wie er ein Thema mit einem anspruchsvollen Erfindungsreichtum öffnet und es neuen Impulsen gegenüber durchlässig macht. – Wichtig ist in seinem Schaffen, dass die Figuren sowohl passiven als auch aktiven Energiemomenten ausgesetzt sind: Handelnd-erlebend und erlebend-empfangend scheinen sie ein Mutationsbedürfnis auszudrücken oder, besser: eine Verschiebung und Ausdehnung von Empfindungs- und Wahrnehmungsfähigkeiten und -möglichkeiten.

Was bei Tannert als Thema bezeichnet werden kann, erscheint bei den Künstlern der Mülheimer Freiheit stärker an die Bildidee gebunden (mit Ausnahme von Peter Bömmels). Bei allen Unterschieden gibt es Gemeinsames: eine ähnliche Lebensweise, einen ständigen Kontakt untereinander, übergreifende Interessen und sicher – was in der neuen deutschen Musik deutlich wird – das Bestreben, künstlerische Breitenwirkung zu erzielen, ohne Kompromisse einzugehen.

Bei Peter Bömmels steht ebenfalls eine thematische Ausrichtung im Vordergrund. Seine Malerei ist introvertiert und entfaltet sich in kryptischen „Geschichten“, die nichtsdestoweniger spannend sind, weil die Abläufe und Verbindungen eine innere Kohärenz aufweisen, die sich dem betrachtenden Auge als entschlüsselungsfähig darbietet. In der Tat lassen sich seine Bilder weniger beschreiben, wohl aber erzählen, haben das Untergründige von Märchen. Ihr Inhalt kreist um das vielfältige Ich des Künstlers, das in all seinen Schattierungen auch das Ich eines jeden ist. „Eine Hölle gleicht der andern“ heisst ein Bild von 1982, in dem tropfende Brüste Stalaktiten bilden; „Gletscherbeben, blutig“ ein Bild von 1981, in dem eine Figur sich im Eiswind auflöst und eine andere, mit ihr verbunden, spinnenartig einherstelzt.

Gerhard Naschbergers Arbeiten sind in einem Masse komplex, dass es eine echte Herausforderung ist, ihnen auf die Spur zu kommen. Ich glaube, es geht ihm letztlich darum, ein banales Motiv in einen Zustand ekstatischer Erleuchtung zu versetzen. „Im Wald“ nennt sich ein Werk von 1981: Aus einem von Ästen durchbohrten Pferdekopf brechen Flammen aus. Im Bild „Abends“ (1981) beschwören zwei blaue Hände einen Sonnenuntergang. Aber die Beschwörung wird durch die durchgehend aufgeklebten und übermalten Kartonelemente auf Distanz gehalten. Was Naschberger anstrebt, ist, dem Unscheinbaren die Glut des Unwiderruflichen zu verleihen. Hier gibt es eine Verbindung zu Bömmels. Am Kaffeetisch im Folkwang Museum in Essen spricht Bömmels von „Glaube, Liebe, Hoffnung“, und Walter Dahn kontert mit „Macht, Hass, Pathos“. Es geht nicht darum, sich mit solchen Begriffen zu identifizieren, sondern darum, mit diesen umgehen zu können. Naschberger zeigt es deutlich, indem er unerwartet, erfinderisch auf Dinge eingeht, die man – im übertragenen Sinn – gerne übersieht. Gerade bei ihm – so scheint mir – ist der Drang, das Unmögliche wahr zu machen, ausgeprägt vorhanden.

Gerard Kever ist für mich zur Zeit noch am schwierigsten fassbar. Er hat einen viele Monate umfassenden Zivildienst hinter sich und konnte sein Schaffen nicht in dem Masse vorantreiben wie die andern; aber die Entschiedenheit und Wucht, mit der er oft sehr Widersprüchliches in den Griff bekommt, ist erstaunlich. In dem rund dreimal drei Meter grossen Bild „Die Kaffeeschmuggler“ (1982) stehen in einer Stimmung von „High Noon“ und diesigem Wüstenwind die Schmuggler mit verbundenen Augen kurz vor der Exekution. Eine Faust stösst mit

of the face of Adolf Hitler above a campfire.—In Kever's art there is no interruption in the path from the drawing to the painting. Small-format black brush drawings with erotic motifs are redone—quite naturally and ironically—in a large format (*Kleine Allegorie* [Small Allegory], 1981), as are the drawings telling drugs stories with powerfully spatial imagery (*Ohne Titel* [Untitled], 1982).

The paintings of Hans Peter Adamski are positively subversive in their gentleness and notable for their use of highly diverse materials. Regardless of whether a work is executed in charcoal, torn card, watercolors, poster paint, oil, or dispersion paint, and regardless of the format, Adamski consistently turns his widely varied subject matter into full-fledged pictorial events. This in turn means that his works always—unnervingly—appear to be merely a matter of course. Carefully formed figures from the erotic imagery of the Far East mingle with black-painted "demons" of the kind that only Adamski can paint. The sex games are ironically transformed into an encounter between his own painting and a quote (*Die Schwere* [Gravity], 1981). In *Schule von Athen* [School of Athens] (1982), a hybrid animal-human creature sits in a landscape with two intertwined listeners; to the left another listener or viewer stands stock still. The composition is painted in black on wrapping paper and measures 214 by 450 centimeters. The atmosphere calls to mind murmuring, Ubu, an ominous stupor, but also a landscape darkening at twilight, when outlines become blurred. In this case the painting is primarily filled by the sense of something lurking; other compositions convey an almost summery lightness, although this only partially chimes with the content, as seen for instance in *Erbsenherz* [Pea Heart] (1980): a large heart (with pea plants) spouting blood dominates the picture plane; a yellow figure is lingering in the leaves, calmly gazing at a cross in its hand.

Walter Dahn and Jiří Georg Dokoupil often collaborate on paintings. Their ability to respond to each other's ideas and to tease out the common threads in their divergence is remarkable in the extreme and was on show very recently at Galerie 't Venster in Rotterdam.

For some time now, Dokoupil's aim has been to demarcate particular pictorial ideas. Although these ideas are as ever replete with diametrically opposed drivers and contents, they still undergo considerable development within their given zones. In the series *Studien zu einem neuen Menschenbild I–V* [Studies for a New Concept of the Human Being I–V] (1982), the human being endures an astonishing, disconcerting mutation, which is registered by the artist with a similar degree of astonishment and no doubt also not without irony. For whenever it's claimed yet again that humans have alienated themselves from nature and that it is necessary to return to nature, Dokoupil shows a person successfully completing a particular experiment, which goes like this: first the figure kneels on the ground, its head in the earth; a dried fir tree grows out of its backside up into the night sky; at the tip of the tree, like a radar, there is an eye. In the second work, a male figure has one arm raised, angled above his head. The whites of his eyes shine like Boris Karloff's in *The Mummy.* And his fingernails gleam just as strongly; but in the once bushy armpit a window of sorts opens up onto a landscape. The third work consists of layered, growth-like limbs with a large eye resting on them. The fourth work depicts a headless torso with one arm outstretched and an open hand; lying on the hand there is a head with its eyes turned toward heaven. In the last work, an arm on a headless torso seen from behind turns into another dried fir tree.—In *Fruchtwasser I und II* [Fruit Water I and II] (1981), Dokoupil painted a loving mother and a clean boy's head with short hair (both as large-format paintings), and in 1982 he decided to paint two abstract compositions, again in gigantic formats, one organic, the other using the basic forms: circle, triangle, and rectangle. Both of these works use excess and solemnity to undermine certain pictorial concepts.

einer riesigen roten Fahne über die untere Bildbegrenzung in die Landschaft. Das Ganze sieht nach „Venceremos“ aus und ist gleichzeitig Manifest der Hintergangenen und Karikatur von Ideologie. Im gleichen Zeitraum malt er ein grossformatiges Bild mit einer realistischen Rückenfigur, deren dem Betrachter zugewandter Kopf in schwarzen Pinselstrichen ein tierhaftes Aussehen besitzt. In den Rücken gekrallt befindet sich ein Tier, das, wie die Last der Geschichte, Gang und Natur der Figur bestimmt. Auf der linken Seite erscheint menetekelhaft, in wenigen Zügen umrissen, das Antlitz Adolf Hitlers über einem Lagerfeuer. – Der Weg von der Zeichnung zum Bild wirkt bei Kever bruchlos. Kleinformatige schwarze Pinselzeichnungen mit erotischen Motiven finden sich wie selbstverständlich und ironisiert im Grossformat („Kleine Allegorie“, 1981), ebenso die Zeichnungen mit Drogen-Geschichten in Bildern mit starker Räumlichkeit („Ohne Titel“, 1982).

Die Bilder von Hans Peter Adamski sind von einer geradezu subversiven Sanftheit und durch den Einsatz verschiedenster Materialien geprägt. Ob in Kohle, gerissenem Karton, Aquarell, Plakatfarbe, Öl oder Dispersion ausgeführt, und in welchem Format auch immer, gelingt es Adamski, seine verschiedensten Bildhinhalte in eigentliche Bildereignisse umzuwandeln. Das bedeutet im Besonderen, dass seine Werke immer eine geradezu irritierende Selbstverständlichkeit besitzen. Da bewegen sich sorgfältig gestaltete Figuren aus dem Bereich der fernöstlichen Erotik zusammen mit schwarzgemalten „Dämonen“, wie sie nur Adamski malt. Die Sexspiele werden ironisch ihrer selbst überführt, gleichsam als Begegnung von eigenem Bild und Zitat („Die Schwere“, 1981). In der „Schule von Athen“ (1982) sitzt ein tiermenschähnliches Wesen mit zwei ineinander verschränkten Zuhörern in einer Landschaft; links davon steht wie ein Sack ein weiterer Zuhörer oder Betrachter. Das Werk ist in Schwarz auf Packpapier gemalt und misst 214 × 450 cm. Die Stimmung erinnert an Gemurmel, an Ubu, an bedrohliche Stumpfheit, aber genausosehr an eine Landschaft beim Eindunkeln, wenn Umrisse nicht mehr erkennbar sind. Hier ist es das Lauernde, das im Vordergrund steht, bei anderen Arbeiten eine gleichsam sommerliche Beschwingtheit, die aber nur bedingt mit dem Inhalt übereinstimmt, wie dies z. B. in „Erbsenherz“ (1980) sichtbar ist: Ein grosses, Blut sprühendes Herz mit Erbsengewächs bestimmt die Bildfläche; in den Blättern ruht eine gelbe Figur, die gelassen ein Kreuz in der Hand betrachtet.

Walter Dahn und Jiří Georg Dokoupil malen des öftern auch gemeinsame Bilder. Ihre Fähigkeit, aufeinander einzugehen, das Gemeinsame im Unterschiedlichen herauszukristallisieren, ist in hohem Masse bemerkenswert und war erst kürzlich in der Galerie ’t Venster in Rotterdam zu sehen.

Dokoupils Bestreben läuft seit einiger Zeit auf eine Eingrenzung bestimmter Bildideen hinaus. Bildideen, die zwar weiterhin von geradezu gegensätzlicher Motorik und Inhaltsdimensionen erfüllt sind, jedoch innerhalb ihres Bereiches eine stärkere Ausbildung erfahren. In der Reihe „Studien zu einem neuen Menschenbild I–V“ (1982) erfährt die menschliche Figur mit Staunen und Betroffenheit eine Mutation, die vom Künstler mit ebensolchem Staunen und sicherlich nicht ohne Ironie wahrgenommen wird. Denn wenn es immer wieder heisst, dass sich der Mensch der Natur entfremdet habe, und dass es notwendig sei, sich der Natur zuzuwenden, lässt Dokoupil seinen Menschen dieses Experiment bestehen, und das sieht dann wie folgt aus: Zuerst kniet er am Boden, den Kopf in der Erde; aus seinem Hintern wächst eine vertrocknete Tanne in den nächtlichen Himmel; auf ihrer Spitze befindet sich, einem Radar ähnlich, ein Auge. Im zweiten Werk erhebt eine männliche Figur ihren Arm, der über den Kopf gewinkelt ist. Das Weiss der Augen blinkt wie jenes von Boris Karloff in „The Mummy“. Und ebenso stark leuchten die Fingernägel; in der einst buschigen Achselhöhle aber öffnet sich eine Art Fenster mit Landschaft. Die dritte Arbeit besteht aus geschichteten, wulstartigen Gliedern, auf denen ein grosses Auge ruht. Die vierte Arbeit zeigt

Walter Dahn is no less eclectic and, as a painter, no less accomplished than Jiří Georg Dokoupil. He has done a series of head shots, which clearly refer to the situation of the artist painting today. He knows all about painters' problems and their need for spontaneous artistic activity, yet there is also an unmistakable intellectual or reflective impulse in his work. It would simply be wrong to imagine this were a new kind of painting from the gut, so to speak. What once polarized into reflective painting on one side and spontaneous on the other, has long since been ditched! The natural intermingling of both has become a real-life creative given.

In *Modell für Kulturrevolution* [Model for Cultural Revolution] (1981–82), a head elongates upward. To its left are houses, to the right trees. Flanking the head there are hands: the left hand is setting fire to the houses with a torch, the right hand is holding a ladder. It recalls themes explored by Dokoupil, but also the notion of a picture painting itself (with contents that, ironically coming into their own, develop some sort of momentum). In another head shot, entitled *Psychologisches Modell* [Psychological Model] (1981), two legs push sideways into the face above the eyes, and above that, again, there are two arms and hands, in some kind of a dispute. The face seems uninvolved. It registers with some astonishment what is happening inside its head. This composition is painted in gray on a black ground that the outlines have been extracted from. *Landschaft* [Landscape] is the title of a painting done in 1982. A huge face fills the picture plane. The left half of the face is taken up by an oversize eye with a black pupil and trees inserted at the side. Here, too, as in the previous composition, the focus is on the natural adaptability of a sensory organ that—in this case—changes according to its altered surroundings. And that's just it: the disproportion of the eyes alludes to the distortions in our perception of reality, or rather, in the way that reality is presented to us.

It is perhaps worth pointing out that these artists have a distinct prehistory, that for instance Dahn and Oehlen have known each other for many years, that the artists have experimented and explored their experiences in very different mediums—for example, with Adamski choosing photography—and that their engagement with painting meets a vital need to carve out a realm of emotional freedom that allows them to approach specific problems in the most widely diverse ways.

einen kopflosen Torso mit ausgestrecktem Arm und geöffneter Hand, auf der ein Kopf mit zum Himmel gerichteten Augen liegt. In der letzten Arbeit mündet der Arm eines kopflosen Rückentorsos in eine wiederum vertrocknete Tanne. – Dokoupil malt 1981 in „Fruchtwasser I und II" eine liebende Mutter und einen sauberen, kurzgeschorenen Jünglingskopf (beides grossformatige Bilder), und 1982 entscheidet er sich, abstrakte Bilder zu malen, ebenfalls Riesenformate, das eine organisch, das andere mit den Grundformen Kreis, Dreieck und Viereck. Beides Werke, die bis zum Exzess und mit Seriosität Bildbegriffe unterwandern.

Walter Dahn ist nicht weniger eklektisch und malerisch nicht weniger souverän als Jiří Georg Dokoupil. Es gibt von ihm eine Serie von Kopfbildern, die deutlich auf die Situation des malenden Künstlers von heute hinweisen. Er weiss um die Probleme und um sein Bedürfnis einer spontanen malerischen Tätigkeit, und gleichzeitig ist der intellektuelle bzw. reflektierende Impetus unverkennbar. Es wäre schlicht verfehlt, zu glauben, es gehe hier um eine neue sogenannte Bauchmalerei. Was sich einst in einer reflektierten und einer spontanen Malerei polarisierte und somit Welten trennte, ist heute längst über Bord! Die natürliche Durchdringung beider Seiten ist erlebtes schöpferisches Selbstverständnis.

In „Modell für Kulturrevolution" (1981/82) erfährt ein Kopf eine Ausdehnung nach oben. Auf der einen Seite sind Häuser aneinandergereiht, auf der rechten Bäume. Seitlich vom Kopf befinden sich Hände: Die linke Hand zündet mit einer Fackel die Häuser an, die rechte Hand hält eine Leiter. Das erinnert an die erwähnte Thematik von Dokoupil, aber auch an den Umstand: Das Bild malt sich selbst (Inhalte, die in ihrer ironischen Verselbständigung eine Art von Eigendynamik entwickeln). In einem andern Kopfbild, mit dem Titel „Psychologisches Modell" (1981), stossen über den Augen seitlich zwei Beine in das Antlitz und darüber zwei, gleichsam disputierende Arme und Hände. Das Gesicht erscheint wie unbeteiligt. Es nimmt mit Erstaunen wahr, was in seinem Kopf geschieht. Es handelt sich um ein grau gemaltes Bild auf schwarzem Grund, aus dem die Umrisse herausgearbeitet wurden. „Landschaft" heisst ein Gemälde von 1982. Ein riesiges Gesicht nimmt die Bildfläche ein. Die linke Gesichtshälfte stellt ein überdimensioniertes Auge dar mit schwarzer Pupille und seitlich eingefügten Bäumen. Auch hier, wie im vorausgegangenen Bild, geht es um die natürliche Anpassungsfähigkeit eines Wahrnehmungsorgans, das sich der veränderten Umgebung gemäss wandelt. Aber eben: Die Disproportion der Augen verweist auf die Verzerrung, mit der wir Wirklichkeit wahrnehmen, oder besser: mit der Wirklichkeit an uns herangetragen wird.

Vielleicht ist der Hinweis nicht unwichtig, dass diese Künstler eine klare Vorgeschichte haben, dass sich zum Beispiel Dahn und Oehlen seit vielen Jahren kennen, dass die Künstler hier ihre Erfahrungen in verschiedensten Medien experimentell erforscht haben – Adamski z. B. in der Fotografie –, und dass ihre Hinwendung zur Malerei einem vitalen Bedürfnis entspricht, sich einen emotionellen Freiraum zu erarbeiten, der das Angehen spezifischer Probleme in höchstmöglicher Diversität erlaubt.

1

Albert Oehlen (with Jörg Immendorff and Werner Büttner) in a hitherto unpublished interview in the magazine *Twen:* "When Expressionism emerged, or other trends for that matter, people wrote pamphlets and belligerently promoted them. But that doesn't happen any more, and that's another reason for dropping this term, because there isn't anyone trying to write a manifesto for 'violent painting' or trying to disseminate it as part of some ideology or even trying to really explain it.... And we can drop the term 'Neue Wilde' in just the same way that the label 'New Music' is no longer used for punk. The situation in music is much clearer, because you can easily see there how things will go in painting. There are some people with something to say and others with nothing."

2

Alain Cotta's first-rate *La Société ludique. La vie envahie par le jeu* (Paris: Grasset, 1980) is important here. It explores completely new patterns of behavior, some creative, in a society that is increasingly being changed by technology, the media, and the like. And this raises another point: in France, it is always writers, philosophers, and intellectuals who first "discover" any signs of change, of latent needs, and—often with great ease—lay claim to them. Artists in France then find themselves in the frustrating situation of, so to speak, having to confirm these findings. Fortunately that is not the case in Germany and Switzerland. Things happen; interpretations and possible explanations only appear after the event.

*

Ammann is referring here to the exhibition *Auch wenn das Perlhuhn leise weint*, which in fact took place at BBK Hahnentorburg in Cologne in 1980. "Klaus Hübner" is a fictive artist-persona; this name was chosen in the late 1970s by Walter Dahn and Jiří Georg Dokoupil when they first started to collaborate. In 1979, they applied in the name of Klaus Hübner for a grant from the Deutsch-Französisches Jugendwerk. The artists' magazine *Kirschblüte* was published independently of the exhibition at BBK Hahnentorburg.—Eds.

In 1982, the exhibition organizer and art historian Jean-Christophe Ammann curated *12 Künstler aus Deutschland.* Held at the Kunsthalle Basel, it was one of the first museum exhibitions to identify the emerging figurative painting as a generation or group phenomenon, thus presenting a perspective going beyond the differences between the individual artistic positions. Ammann's introductory catalogue text is one of the very first attempts to consider the painting practice of the featured (exclusively male) artists. Instead of references to the history of painting, Ammann draws on a young German band active in the (post-)punk and new wave scene, Deutsch Amerikanische Freundschaft, to understand and explain the "attitude" of the artists.

1

Albert Oehlen (mit Jörg Immendorff und Werner Büttner) in einem bisher unveröffentlichten Interview mit der Zeitschrift ‚Twen': „Als der Expressionismus aufkam, oder auch andere Richtungen, da haben die Leute Pamphlete geschrieben und die auch kämpferisch vertreten. Und das gibt es heute nicht, und das ist ein Grund mehr, diesen Begriff fallen zu lassen, weil es keinen gibt, der versucht, ein Manifest der ‚Heftigen Malerei' zu schreiben oder das irgendwie ideologisch zu propagieren oder auch nur richtig zu erklären. [...] Und wir können von dem Begriff ‚Neue Wilde' ebenso ablassen, wie jetzt die ‚Neue Musik' nicht mehr auf den Begriff Punk angewiesen ist. Die Situation in der Musik ist viel deutlicher, da kannst du genau sehen, wie es in der Malerei auch weitergehen wird. Da gibt es Leute, die was zu sagen haben, und da gibt es welche, die nichts zu sagen haben."

2

Alain Cotta hat mit seinem Buch „La Société ludique. La vie envahie par le jeu" (Paris, Grassel 1980) ein Buch von erstrangiger Bedeutung geschrieben. Es geht auf völlig neue, auch schöpferische Verhaltensmuster ein in einer zunehmend u. a. durch Technologie und Medien veränderten Gesellschaft. Darüber wäre auch nachzudenken: In Frankreich sind es stets die Schriftsteller, Philosophen und Intellektuellen, die jegliche Anzeichen von Veränderungen, von latenten Bedürfnissen zuerst „entdecken" und sich, oft souverän, zu eigen machen. Die Künstler sehen sich dann in der frustrierenden Situation, gewissermassen die Bestätigung hierfür zu liefern. In Deutschland und der Schweiz ist das glücklicherweise nicht der Fall. Die Dinge ereignen sich zuerst, und erst im Nachhinein erfolgen Interpretationen und Erklärungsmodelle.

*

Ammann bezieht sich auf die Ausstellung *Auch wenn das Perlhuhn leise weint*, die erst 1980 in der BBK Hahnentorburg in Köln stattfand. Bei „Klaus Hübner" handelt es sich um eine fiktive Künstlerfigur, unter deren Namen Ende der 1970er-Jahre erste gemeinsame Arbeiten von Walter Dahn und Jiří Georg Dokoupil entstanden und in deren Namen sich diese 1979 um ein Stipendium beim Deutsch-Französischen Jugendwerk bewarben. Die Künstlerzeitung *Kirschblüte* ist unabhängig von der Ausstellung in der BBK Hahnentorburg entstanden. [Anmerkung der Herausgeber*innen].

Mit *12 Künstler aus Deutschland* kuratierte der Ausstellungsmacher und Kunsthistoriker Jean-Christophe Ammann 1982 in der Kunsthalle Basel eine der ersten musealen Ausstellungen, die die junge figurative Malerei über die Unterschiede der einzelnen künstlerischen Positionen hinweg als Generations- oder Gruppenphänomen etablierten. Ammanns einführender Katalogtext ist der Versuch einer ersten Annäherung an die malerische Praxis der (ausschließlich männlichen) Künstler. Anstelle von Rückverweisen auf die Geschichte der Malerei zieht Ammann mit Deutsch Amerikanische Freundschaft eine junge deutsche Band aus dem Umfeld der (Post-)Punk- und New-Wave-Szene heran, um sich die „Haltung" der Künstler zu erschließen.

Diedrich Diederichsen

Embarrassing: On the Embarrassment of the Not-Embarrassing in Art

It happened overnight, almost imperceptibly. When I first started to think for myself, there were friends of mine who would scrutinize even the most harmless pleasure—if it was in the slightest aesthetically mediated—to test whether the accompanying experience was progressive or escapist, that is to say, reactionary. Although I, like everyone else, struggled with this terror, I was impressed by their relentless search for truth, and I learned a life lesson: nothing can be simultaneously true and false.

Art criticism, particularly the kind that is not marred with theoretical baggage (often nurtured in subcultural media outlets), generally relies on naive but nonetheless useful criteria, such as groundbreaking, tedious, entertaining, imitative, new, sleep-inducing, incendiary, emotional, cool, conceptual but also, rather often, progressive and reactionary. Especially in magazines such as this one, writers are often in a position to go beyond these naive criteria. They discover progressive art in a reactionary shell, groundbreaking features in tedium, excitement in monotony, and these days they even know that these kind of simple reversals no longer do justice to the present state of affairs.

But lately and all at once a different way of thinking has crept in for readers, a thought process that revolves around the dichotomy "embarrassing/not embarrassing." The graph showing the frequency of the word "embarrassing" in readers' letters, like the graph modeling the increase in the global population produced for the Club of Rome, obeys the law of exponential growth.

What is it about "embarrassing" and how does it connect with the concomitant impoverishment of other terms? Who benefits from the question whether a work of art or its professional processing in the form of features and reviews is embarrassing, that is to say, above all whether it's embarrassing or not embarrassing?

In the past, the long lost past, when the political function alone of a work of art was of decisive importance, the point was—for the sake of every even halfway intelligent and thus recalcitrant, confrontation-happy mind—to lever out the arguments of the orthodox at their weakest point; that was the form/content rhetoric. Form was seen as a translation of content. The presumption was that when artists began on the production of a work they knew down to the last detail what its content was and that they then deployed a form solely to render that content as comprehensible and memorable as possible. And it was the task of the critic to ferret out that beginning on the evidence of the finished product and then, depending on the given situation, to applaud it or decry it; the form would at best only be mentioned as an arts-pages aperçu by authors unable to forget their education.

That's what we opposed, we who believed art production had a momentum of its own, and who, secondly, specifically sought the contents of art in its form (and often found them there in much greater abundance) rather than in the subject matter or intentions.

For a long time the images of pop heroes were determined by the contents of their songs. That applied to Yes and the Sex Pistols alike: seeing Queen as a piece of shit or Roger Dean as a visionary and J. R. R. Tolkien as a writer. Both are linguistically referenceable attitudes, and as such contents, but at the same time also the core of the images and thus of the mythmaking point of reference for those pop musicians. Punk and seventies rock, on a not even politically reflected level, were engaged in the age-old altercation between escapist and realistic art. A rather crass matter.

Diedrich Diederichsen
Peinlich: Über das Peinliche des Unpeinlichen in der Kunst

Es geschah über Nacht, fast unmerklich. Als ich anfing zu denken, gab es Kameraden, die noch den harmlosesten Genuß, sofern er nur im geringsten ein ästhetisch vermittelter war, daraufhin untersuchten, ob das von ihm begleitete Erlebnis ein fortschrittliches oder ein eskapistisches, mithin reaktionäres war. Obwohl ich, wie jeder andere, unter diesem Terror litt, beeindruckte mich ihre unnachgiebige Wahrheitssuche, und ich nahm mit auf den Lebensweg, daß nichts gleichzeitig wahr und falsch sein kann.

Die Kunstkritik, und gerade die von keiner theoretischen Vorbelastung getrübte, wie sie in den Subkultur-eigenen Organen mehrheitlich gepflegt wird, bemüht in der Regel naive, aber deswegen nicht minder nützliche Kriterien wie originell, langweilig, unterhaltsam, epigonal, neu, einschläfernd, aufrührerisch, emotional, kühl, konzeptuell, aber eben auch oft fortschrittlich und reaktionär. Oft sind die Schreiber, gerade in einem Magazin wie diesem, in der Lage, über die naiven Kriterien hinauszugelangen. Sie entdecken das Fortschrittliche im vermeintlich Reaktionären, das Originelle im Langweiligen, das Aufregende in der Monotonie und sie wissen inzwischen sogar, daß derlei einfache Umkehrungen dem Stand der Dinge auch nicht mehr gerecht werden.

Doch in der Leserschaft hat sich neuerdings und über Nacht ein anderes Denken eingeschlichen, ein Denken, das um die Dichotomie „peinlich/unpeinlich“ kreist. Die Kurve der Häufigkeit der Vokabel „peinlich“ in Leserbriefen gleicht der die Vermehrung der Weltbevölkerung vorausberechnenden Kurve der Untersuchungen des Club of Rome, sie folgt dem Gesetz des exponentiellen Wachstums.

Was hat es mit dem „peinlich“ auf sich und wie hängt es mit der gleichzeitigen Verarmung an anderen Begriffen zusammen? Wem nützt die Fragestellung, ob ein Kunstwerk bzw. seine berufsmäßige Verarbeitung in Form von Features und Rezensionen peinlich, und zwar in erster Linie peinlich oder unpeinlich sei.

In jenen Zeiten, versunkenen Zeiten, da einzig die politische Funktion eines Kunstwerkes von entscheidender Bedeutung war, ging es darum, für jeden halbwegs intelligenten und damit auch renitenten, konfrontationslüsternen Kopf die Argumentation der Orthodoxen an ihrem schwächsten Punkt auszuhebeln; das war die Form/Inhalt-Rhetorik. Form galt als Übersetzung eines Inhaltes. Es wurde angenommen, daß jeder Künstler, am Beginn der Produktion seines Werkes, restlos wußte, was sein Inhalt sei, und er anschließend lediglich eine Form benutzte, um diesen Inhalt optimal verständlich und eindrücklich zu machen. Aufgabe des Kritikers war es nun, diesen Beginn der Produktion anhand des fertigen Produktes aufzuspüren und dann je nach Lage der Dinge zu rühmen oder zu denunzieren, ein Wort zur Form gab es allenfalls als feuilletonistisches Bonmot bei den Autoren, die ihre Erziehung nicht vergessen konnten.

Dem entgegengesetzt standen wir, die wir der Kunstproduktion Eigendynamik zugestanden und zweitens die Inhaltlichkeiten der Kunst gerade in der Form suchen wollten (und sie dort auch viel reichhaltiger vorfanden) als im Sujet oder in der Absicht.

Die Images der Pop-Helden waren lange Zeit von ihren Inhalten bestimmt. Das galt für Yes wie für die Sex Pistols: die Queen für ein Stück Scheiße zu halten oder Roger Dean für einen Visionär und J. R. R. Tolkien für einen Schriftsteller. Beide Haltungen sind sprachlich referierbare, somit Inhalte, gleichzeitig aber der Kern der Images und damit der mythenbildende Bezugspunkt der erwähnten Popmusiker. Zwischen Punk und Siebziger-Rock spielte sich, auf einem nicht einmal politisch reflektierten Niveau,

The discovery of pop as the antipode of rock changed that situation. Now the talk was of image strategies on one hand and the innate momentum of the artistic process on the other (if not in these terms). The image and the myth of pop—hitherto the bad, aggravating, commercial phenomena on the surface of real music—suddenly became part of pop, deliberately introduced and intended for the critical gaze.

At the same time, young painters started to emerge who saw their work as a totality of strategic actions. The political, up until then—crudely, and to cap it all, unromantically too—relegated as "content" to a formulaic, mechanistic process, had just emancipated itself through the incorporation of bedeviled form and was suddenly at one with the work as a whole. Pop wasn't political any more, it was politics.

During the course of these developments, an anarchist direction and a Marxist/Leninist direction evolved. The anarchist direction relied on the inherent dynamism of the simple pop song with its relatively generous room for maneuver, which facilitated the caprices, ferocities, excesses, and paroxysmal cries of desire, the fundamental rebellion of humankind. Meanwhile, the Marxist/Leninists imagined a musically sealed freight car that could be called ABC, for instance, and would deliver hot cargo right into the center of media fascism. Both produced some outstanding results, such as Gun Club (anarchists) and ABC (Marxists). Both collapsed, because of their euphoric naivety. But for a while both widened the horizon.

Now a generation is emerging that didn't grow up with that old altercation, but which only knows the test of the in any case hard-to-understand new one. What they do have is the old form/content dialectics, revived as an awareness that it's not enough just to say something: you also need to look like something, have a way of talking, a way of bouncing about in videos. They call the sum total of these activities "style."

But this "style" is not, as it was once intended, a means to an end, no, it's self-sufficient. It's an open intercity dining car, but it doesn't travel to Moscow, it's an hourly service between Hamburg and Munich. Sometimes it's delayed.

This violation of the newly established codes, these delays and imponderables are what are summed up in the notion of "embarrassing." Once strategy had degenerated into a convention, it communicated a new certainty that a life in popland was possible, where—instead of beauty, the true beauty of a means of altercation—the cheap beauty of fully functioning coexistence was on offer, the positively repellent beauty of a pluralism that involves the wholesale renunciation of ever being right. If this is disrupted, "embarrassing" is on everyone's lips, like the much-vaunted commonality of democrats.

But the ugliest thing of all is the way that some players manage to attain a puny, grubby authority when they—with their only remaining transcendence—decide something is "so embarrassing" that "it's good again."

I'm not complaining about the smooth surface of superficiality. I'm also not complaining about the beauty of a well-functioning work of art—if it is a work of art at all, that is. There's no need to go back to an age when the aims people pursued were still written *expressis verbis* on every cover and thus provided wonderful sacrifices for all kinds of pluralist appropriation strategies, and Lord knows I don't want young people to start dragging opinions around with them again. Opinions are still the pits. Although it's rather striking that the people howling "embarrassing!" are not short of "opinions." They are positively dripping with opinions and all feel the need to bleat.

Pop music, in fact not just pop music but all the arts, the whole edifice, is an unbelievably ridiculous business; however, taking it seriously according to its own laws, allowing it its own rules and aesthetic codes that may not be contravened, means writing off the potential, the insane ideological and aesthetic efficacy of this medium.

die uralte Auseinandersetzung zwischen eskapistischer und realistischer Kunst ab. Eine ziemlich grobe Sache.

Die Entdeckung von Pop als Antipode von Rock änderte diese Lage. Alle Welt sprach nun von Image-Strategien einerseits und von der Eigendynamik des künstlerischen Prozesses andererseits (wenn auch nicht in diesen Worten). Image und Mythos von Pop, bis dahin lästige, kommerzielle, böse, der eigentlichen Musik äußerliche Phänomene, waren plötzlich Bestandteil des Pop-Kunstwerkes, bewußt eingesetzt und Bestandteil des zu Kritisierenden.

Zur selben Zeit traten junge Maler in Erscheinung, die ihre Arbeit als eine Gesamtheit strategischer Maßnahmen begriffen. Das Politische, bis dahin, grob und zu allem Überfluß auch noch unromantisch, als „Inhalt" in einen formelhaften mechanistischen Prozeß verbannt, hatte sich gerade durch die Einbeziehung der verteufelten Form emanzipiert und war plötzlich mit dem gesamten Werk identisch. Pop war nicht mehr politisch, sondern Politik.

Dabei waren eine anarchistische und eine marxistisch/leninistische Richtung entstanden. Die anarchistische setzte auf die der relativ viel Spielraum freilassenden, einfachen Form von Pop-Songs innewohnende Dynamik, die Unberechenbarkeiten, Wildheiten, Überschreitungen und paroxystische Schreie des Wunsches, also das fundamentale Aufbegehren des Humanum ermöglichte. Die marxistisch/leninistische dachte sich einen musikalischen verplompten Güterwagen, der z. B. ABC heißen konnte und heiße Fracht direkt in das Zentrum des Medienfaschismus befördern würde. Beide brachten einige hervorragende Resultate, die Anarchisten z. B. den Gun Club, die Marxisten etwa ABC. Beide sind gescheitert, und zwar aufgrund ihrer euphorischen Naivität. Aber beide öffneten für eine Weile den Horizont.

Nun kommt eine Generation, die nicht mit der alten Auseinandersetzung aufgewachsen ist, sondern nur noch den Test der ohnehin schwer verständlichen neuen mitbekommen hat. Geblieben ist ihnen das Aufleben der alten Form/Inhalt-Dialektik als die Erkenntnis, daß es nicht reicht, nur etwas zu sagen: man muß noch dazu irgendwie aussehen, irgendwie reden, irgendwie auf Videos herumhoppeln. Die Gesamtheit dieser Tätigkeiten nennen sie „Stil".

Dieser „Stil" ist aber nicht, wie er mal gedacht war, ein Mittel zum Zweck, nein, er ist sich selbst genug. Es ist ein offener IC-Speisewagen, der nicht nach Moskau fährt, sondern zwischen Hamburg und München im Einstundentakt hin- und herkurvt. Manchmal verspätet er sich.

Diese Verletzung der neugewonnenen Umgangsformen, die Verspätungen und Unwägbarkeiten sind es, die im Begriff der „Peinlichkeit" auf den Punkt gebracht worden sind. Nachdem das Strategische zur Umgangsform degenerierte, vermittelte es eine neue Sicherheit, ein Leben in Popland war möglich, das statt der Schönheit, der wahren Schönheit eines Mittels zur Auseinandersetzung, die billige Schönheit eines funktionierenden Miteinander, die geradezu widerwärtige Schönheit eines Pluralismus bei totalem Verzicht auf jedes Rechthaben offerierte. Wird diese gestört, wird die „Peinlichkeit" beschworen, so wie jene vielgerühmte Gemeinsamkeit der Demokraten.

Aber das Allermieseste ist die Art und Weise, in der sich einzelne Vertreter zu einer kleinen, dreckigen Souveränität durchringen, wenn sie – einzige Transzendenz, die sie noch haben – etwas „so peinlich" finden, „daß es schon wieder gut ist".

Ich beschwere mich nicht über das Glatte oder das Oberflächliche. Ich beschwere mich auch nicht über die Schönheit eines wohl funktionierenden Kunstwerkes – wenn es denn ein Kunstwerk überhaupt ist. Es ist nicht nötig, zurückzugehen, zu einer Zeit, als die Zwecke, die man verfolgte, noch expressis verbis auf jede Hülle geschrieben standen und somit wunderbare Opfer abgaben für alle Arten von pluralistischen Vereinnahmungsstrategien, und ich möchte um Gottes willen nicht, daß die jungen Leute wieder anfangen, Meinungen mit sich herumzuschleppen. Meinungen sind immer noch das Letzte. Wobei es gerade auffällt, daß es den „Peinlich!"-Schreiern eben an

Anyone trying to exclude the profound embarrassment, indeed the beauty of some uglinesses from the world of pop, is paving the way for what has long since been achieved in jazz: the transformation of a direct, downright intelligent medium into bourgeois edification-shit.

In an interview reprinted in the book *Ursprung und Vision* [Origin and Vision]—the title speaks volumes about this attempt to regenerate archetyping, metaphysical shit—art journalist Grasskamp says to painter Albert Oehlen, "But you have also worked with mirrors, in that sense you have in part triggered that association (a certain impression of space—ed.) yourself." Oehlen replies, "When I inserted the mirrors into the paintings, I was aware there was something utterly awful about it. If people take that as an avant-garde step, which they're saying in the papers now, because the viewer can enter into the picture, it's just pathetic. But that's exactly what drove me to do something so banal." Grasskamp: "To debase the painting?" Oehlen: "To debase myself."

Because these days there's nothing more embarrassing than not-embarrassing art. Anyone these days who thinks they can get away with blithely producing meaningful, edifying work without also making a fool of themselves, is a liar. You can spot the good ones by the fact that they recognize this and work with it. That applies to people like Martin Fry and to John Cale or Prince (although I don't like him, for other reasons).

I remember an interview in this magazine with Gerald Hündgen and Hermann L. Gremliza, editor of *Konkret*. Gerald said to Gremliza that when he read Johannes Groß's *Tagebuch* [Diary] he got the impression that all the bourgeoisie had left to defend was their table manners, to which Gremliza responded, "But does it have anything else to defend?" That's where pop music is today, and all those who argue in the name of the not-embarrassing have a part in its demise, at a point where it's only trying to defend codes. Aesthetic etiquette.

The texts written by the critic and author Diedrich Diederichsen around 1980 are testimony to a burgeoning pop scene in Germany that, spanning various genres and art forms, sought to redefine the parameters of cultural practice. Having met in the subcultural milieu, Diederichsen personally knew and was friends with some of the artists identified with the label of Neue Wilde painting. In this essay, he discusses their painting and works from pop music in equal measure, defying entrenched conventional distinctions between the various art forms or between high and popular culture. Adopting a combative, at times polemical tone, Diederichsen not only considers what criteria are appropriate for judging art but also broaches the sensitive issue of what kind of relationship art itself needs to have to the rules set by criticism. Diederichsen's arguments revolve around the increasing prominence of the category "embarrassing/not embarrassing." He considers the category to be the expression of a safe "aesthetic etiquette" and contends that by adhering to them art is in effect diluting its inherent subversive sting. Behind his demand to acknowledge that the "embarrassing" is necessarily part of artistic production is a program targeting the mystique of the authentic and countering the emotional pathos of direct expressive creation, a pathos that some circles claim to be a signature characteristic of the painting of the Neue Wilde. The essay was published in *Spex,* a magazine devoted to pop culture founded in 1980 that employed a new language of direct subjective involvement.

„Meinungen" nicht mangelt. Sie alle meinen sich ja oft geradezu einen Ast ab und fühlen sich alle berufen, ihre kleinen individuellen Mäuler aufzureißen.

Popmusik, aber nicht nur die, sondern eigentlich alle Künste, ja der ganze Überbau, ist eine unglaublich lächerliche Angelegenheit; sie nach ihren eigenen Gesetzen ernstzunehmen, ihr Regeln, ästhetische Umgangsformen zuzugestehen, die nicht verletzt werden dürfen, bedeutet aber, die Potenzen, die irrsinnige ideologische und ästhetische Effizienz dieses Mediums abzuschreiben. Wer die tiefgehende Peinlichkeit, ja die Schönheit mancher Miesheiten aus der Popwelt heraushalten will, bereitet das vor, was im Jazz längst gelungen ist: die Umwandlung eines direkten, unverblümt-intelligenten Mediums in bürgerliche Erbauungsscheiße.

In einem Interview, das in dem Buch „Ursprung und Vision" – der Titel sagt eine Menge über den Versuch, archetypelnde, metaphysische Scheiße zu regenerieren – abgedruckt ist, fragt der Kunstjournalist Grasskamp den Maler Albert Oehlen: „Sie haben aber auch mit Spiegeln gearbeitet, insofern haben Sie diese Assoziation (gemeint ist ein gewisser Raumeindruck – d. Verf.) ja auch selbst verursacht." Oehlen daraufhin: „Als ich die Spiegel in die Bilder einmontierte, war mir klar, daß das was ungeheuer Elendes hat. Wenn man das als avantgardistischen Schritt betrachtet, wie es jetzt in den Zeitungen steht, weil der Betrachter sich ins Bild versetzen kann, ist das zum Heulen. Aber gerade das hat mich daran auch wieder gereizt, etwas dermaßen Plattes zu machen." Grasskamp: „Als Erniedrigung des Bildes?" Oehlen: „Als Erniedrigung meiner selbst."

Denn heutzutage gibt es nichts Peinlicheres als unpeinliche Kunst. Wer glaubt, heute als freier Sinnstifter und Erbauungsproduzent davonkommen zu können, ohne sich zum Affen zu machen, lügt. Gute Leute erkennt man daran, daß sie dies erkennen und damit arbeiten. Das gilt für jemanden wie Martin Fry, ebenso wie für John Cale oder Prince (den ich aus anderen Gründen aber nicht mag).

Ich erinnere mich an ein Interview, das Gerald Hündgen in diesem Blatt mit „Konkret"-Herausgeber Hermann L. Gremliza führte. Gerald fragte dabei Gremliza, er habe beim Lesen von Johannes Groß' „Tagebuch" den Eindruck gewonnen, die Bourgeoisie habe nichts anderes mehr zu verteidigen als ihre Tischmanieren, worauf Gremliza gegenfragte: „Hat sie denn etwas anderes zu verteidigen?" An diesem Punkt ist heute die Popmusik angelangt und die heute, die im Namen des Unpeinlichen argumentieren, haben ihren Anteil am Niedergang, an dem Punkt, wo sie nur noch Umgangsformen verteidigen will. Ästhetische Höflichkeiten.

Die um 1980 entstandenen Texte des Kritikers und Autors Diedrich Diederichsen sind Zeugnisse einer damals in Deutschland aufkommenden Genre- und Künste-übergreifenden Pop-Szene, die die Parameter kultureller Praxis neu zu bestimmen suchte. Diederichsen war mit einzelnen Künstler*innen, die unter dem Malerei-Label der „Neuen Wilden" gefasst wurden, aus dem subkulturellen Milieu bekannt und freundschaftlich verbunden. In diesem Aufsatz zieht er deren Malerei sowie Werke der Popmusik gleichermaßen zur Diskussion heran, ungeachtet der Unterscheidungen zwischen den Künsten oder zwischen Hoch- und Popkultur. In kämpferischem, bisweilen polemischem Ton stellt Diederichsen nicht nur die Frage nach den angemessenen Kriterien zur Beurteilung von Kunst. Auch das Verhältnis, das die Kunst selbst zu dem Regelwerk der Kritik einnehmen sollte, ist Thema des Textes. Diederichsens Argumente kreisen dabei um das vermehrte Aufkommen der Kategorie des „Peinlichen/Unpeinlichen". Diese betrachtet der Autor als Ausdruck abgesicherter „ästhetischer Umgangsformen", mit deren Befolgung sich die Kunst ihren eigenen subversiven Stachel ziehe. Hinter der von ihm im Gegenzug geforderten Anerkennung der notwendigen „Peinlichkeit" kultureller Produktion steht ein anti-authentisches Programm, das sich gegen das Pathos ungebrochen expressiven Ausdrucks positioniert, das in Teilen für die Malerei der „Neuen Wilden" in Anspruch genommen wurde. Der Aufsatz erschien in dem 1980 gegründeten Popkulturmagazin *Spex*, das sich durch eine neue, involvierte Sprache zur Diskussion von Popkultur auszeichnete.

Anmerkungen der Herausgeber*innen

Die Herausgeberschaft hat sich im vorliegenden Katalog um geschlechtergerechte Sprache bemüht. Dies soll nicht über das reale Missverhältnis hinwegtäuschen, dass sich die öffentlichen Debatten, Sammlungstätigkeiten und institutionellen Ausstellungen in Bezug auf die deutsche beziehungsweise europäische figurative Malerei und die „Neuen Wilden" um 1980 vornehmlich, in weiten Teilen sogar ausschließlich, auf männliche Künstler beschränken.

In den hier abgedruckten Reprints von Originaltexten der Zeit wurde die Rechtschreibung der entsprechenden Originalfassungen beibehalten. Offensichtliche Rechtschreibfehler wurden stillschweigend korrigiert. Die im Zuge dieser Publikation neu entstandenen Übersetzungen dieser Texte folgen in ihrer Bearbeitung hingegen den redaktionellen Richtlinien der übrigen Texte.

Editors' Notes

The editors have made every effort to ensure that the language used in the catalogue is gender neutral. This by no means wishes to ignore the reality that in public debates, collection activities, and exhibitions staged by institutions with respect to German and European figurative painting and the Neue Wilde circa 1980 there is a disproportionate or sometimes even exclusive focus on male artists.

The orthography of the original versions was maintained for the reprinted source texts. Obvious errors were silently corrected. The new translations of these source texts undertaken as part of this publication follow the editorial guidelines set out for the other texts.

Die Herausgeberschaft hat sich bemüht, alle Bildrechteinhaber*innen ausfindig zu machen. Sollte dies an einer Stelle übersehen worden sein, bitten die Herausgeber*innen um Mitteilung. Berechtigte Ansprüche werden im Rahmen der üblichen Vereinbarungen abgegolten. Falls nicht anders angegeben, liegt das Copyright bei den Künstler*innen und Fotograf*innen oder ihren Rechtsnachfolger*innen.

The editors have made every reasonable effort to locate and identify all copyright holders. Should any of these have been overlooked, the editors invite the authors or owners to contact them. Entitled claims will be settled within the framework of the usual agreements. Unless otherwise stated, the copyright lies with the artists and photographers or their legal successors.

Umschlagvorderseite / Front cover: *Die Letzte Nacht im S.O.36*, Berlin, 1979, Foto / photo: Achim Schächtele
Umschlagrückseite / Back cover: Hilka Nordhausen, *Ach, Malewitsch*, Wandarbeit / mural, Buch Handlung Welt, Hamburg, 1978

4, 336–341: © VG Bild-Kunst, Bonn 2019 / Walter Dahn; Fotos / photos: Lothar Schnepf
16, 25–26, 31: Fotos / photos: Carl Brunn
40, 81, 91, 115, 172–176, 345: © VG Bild-Kunst, Bonn 2019
44, 61: © VG Bild-Kunst, Bonn 2019 / Estate of Martin Kippenberger, Galerie Gisela Capitain, Cologne
47: Sammlung Inka Büttner; © Estate of Martin Kippenberger, Galerie Gisela Capitain, Cologne
48, 86: © ZickZack Platten
49: © VG Bild-Kunst, Bonn 2019 / Markus Oehlen / Estate of Martin Kippenberger, Galerie Gisela Capitain, Cologne
62: Sammlung Luciano Castelli; © VG Bild-Kunst, Bonn 2019 / Rainer Fetting; Courtesy Luciano Castelli
71: © VG Bild-Kunst, Bonn 2019 / Rainer Fetting
74: © VG Bild-Kunst, Bonn 2019; Courtesy Richard Saltoun Gallery, London
101, 135, 139, 142, 146, 222, 359, 370: © Estate of Martin Kippenberger, Galerie Gisela Capitain, Cologne
105: Courtesy Tom Dokoupil
110, 118, 178–179: Ludwig Forum für Internationale Kunst Aachen, Schenkung Peter und Irene Ludwig / Gift of Peter and Irene Ludwig; © VG Bild-Kunst, Bonn 2019; Fotos / photos: Carl Brunn
126: Ludwig Forum für Internationale Kunst Aachen, Schenkung Peter und Irene Ludwig / Gift of Peter and Irene Ludwig; © Anselm Kiefer; Foto / photo: Anne Gold
129: Ludwig Forum für Internationale Kunst Aachen, Leihgabe der Peter und Irene Ludwig Stiftung / Loan of the Peter and Irene Ludwig Foundation; © Georg Baselitz, 2019; Foto / photo: Carl Brunn
133, 148: © Estate of Martin Kippenberger, Galerie Gisela Capitain, Cologne; Foto / photo: Carl Brunn; Courtesy Hubert Kiecol
134, 147: © VG Bild-Kunst, Bonn 2019; Courtesy Archiv Peter Bömmels
137, 144: © Estate of Martin Kippenberger, Galerie Gisela Capitain, Cologne / Uli Kukulies / Andreas Rohé; Courtesy Kay Montag
138, 143, 223: © Estate of Martin Kippenberger, Galerie Gisela Capitain, Cologne; Courtesy Archiv Baumjohann
140–141: © Uli Kukulies / Andreas Rohé; Courtesy Archiv Baumjohann
156–159, 166–169: Berlinische Galerie, Landesmuseum für Moderne Kunst, Fotografie und Architektur; © VG Bild-Kunst, Bonn 2019
160–162: Sammlung Luciano Castelli; © VG Bild-Kunst, Bonn 2019
163: © Karlheinz Lubojanski; Courtesy Luciano Castelli
164–165: © VG Bild-Kunst, Bonn 2019; Fotos / photos: Ellen Valter; Courtesy Archiv Ludwig Forum für Internationale Kunst Aachen
170–171: © Helmut Metzner; Courtesy Luciano Castelli
177: Courtesy Helmut Middendorf
180, 206–207, 276–279, 348–351: Ludwig Forum für Internationale Kunst Aachen, Leihgabe der Peter und Irene Ludwig

Stiftung / Loan of the Peter and Irene Ludwig Foundation; © VG Bild-Kunst, Bonn 2019; Fotos / photos: Carl Brunn
181: Ludwig Forum für Internationale Kunst Aachen, Leihgabe der Peter und Irene Ludwig Stiftung / Loan of the Peter and Irene Ludwig Foundation; © Rainer Fetting; Foto / photo: Carl Brunn
182: Sammlung Alexandra Castelli; © VG Bild-Kunst, Bonn 2019; Foto / photo: Carl Brunn
188–189: © Estate of Martin Kippenberger, Galerie Gisela Capitain, Cologne; Courtesy Claudia Skoda
190–193: © Estate of Martin Kippenberger, Galerie Gisela Capitain, Cologne; Fotos / photos: Rich Richter; Courtesy Claudia Skoda
194–196: © Helmut Metzner; Courtesy Claudia Skoda
197–199: © VG Bild-Kunst, Bonn 2019; Courtesy Claudia Skoda
200: Courtesy Claudia Skoda
208: © VG Bild-Kunst, Bonn 2019 / Rainer Fetting; Courtesy Helmut Middendorf
209: Berlinische Galerie, Landesmuseum für Moderne Kunst, Fotografie und Architektur; © VG Bild-Kunst, Bonn 2019; Courtesy Archiv Bernd Zimmer
210: Sammlung Brennecke, Berlin; © Nachlass Anne Jud (Lisa Wismer)
211: © Nachlass Anne Jud (Lisa Wismer); Courtesy Sammlung Brennecke, Berlin
212, 215–219: © Achim Schächtele; Courtesy Archiv Baumjohann
213: Courtesy Archiv Baumjohann
214 (oben / top): © Jutta Henglein; Courtesy Archiv Baumjohann
214 (unten / bottom): © Helmut Metzner; Courtesy Archiv Baumjohann
220–221: © Estate of Martin Kippenberger, Galerie Gisela Capitain, Cologne / Eric Mitchell / Christine Hahn; Courtesy Kay Montag
224, 226: © Achim Schächtele
225: Archiv Buchhandlung Walther König; © Estate of Martin Kippenberger, Galerie Gisela Capitain, Cologne; Foto / photo: Carl Brunn
227: Privatsammlung, Berlin; © Estate of Martin Kippenberger, Galerie Gisela Capitain, Cologne / Achim Schächtele; Foto / photo: Carl Brunn
228–230: Privatsammlung, Berlin; © Estate of Martin Kippenberger, Galerie Gisela Capitain, Cologne / Achim Schächtele
236–237: Sammlung B. Rohrbach; © Brigitta Rohrbach; Fotos / photos: Jutta Henglein
238–243, 268–271: © Carmen Knoebel
244, 318 (oben / top), 319: © VG Bild-Kunst, Bonn 2019; Fotos / photos: Carl Brunn
245–250: © VG Bild-Kunst, Bonn 2019 / Estate of Martin Kippenberger, Galerie Gisela Capitain, Cologne / Markus Oehlen / ARCHIV Hilka Nordhausen / Uwe Gabriel / Brigitta Rohrbach / Walter Dahn; Fotos / photos: Uwe Gabriel; Courtesy Archiv Gabriel
272, 353: Courtesy Archiv Peter Bömmels
273–274: © VG Bild-Kunst, Bonn 2019 / ZickZack Platten
275: © Markus Oehlen / Pure Freude
280–281: Sammlung Grässlin, St. Georgen; © VG Bild-Kunst, Bonn 2019; Fotos / photos: Wolfgang Günzel
282: Sammlung Carmen Knoebel, Düsseldorf; © Markus Oehlen; Foto / photo: Carl Brunn
283–285: Ludwig Forum für Internationale Kunst Aachen, Leihgabe der Peter und Irene Ludwig Stiftung / Loan of the Peter and Irene Ludwig Foundation; © Estate of Martin Kippenberger, Galerie Gisela Capitain, Cologne; Fotos / photos: Carl Brunn
286: Archiv Buchhandlung Walther König; © Estate of Martin Kippenberger, Galerie Gisela Capitain, Cologne
292, 297: © ARCHIV Hilka Nordhausen
293: © VG Bild-Kunst, Bonn 2019; Fotos / photos: Hans-Jürgen Masch; Courtesy ARCHIV Hilka Nordhausen
294: © VG Bild-Kunst, Bonn 2019; Foto / photo: ARCHIV Hilka Nordhausen
295: © Estate of Martin Kippenberger, Galerie Gisela Capitain, Cologne / VG Bild-Kunst, Bonn 2019; Foto / photo: Michael Kellner; Courtesy ARCHIV Hilka Nordhausen
296: © VG Bild-Kunst, Bonn 2019 / Walter Dahn; Fotos / photos: Michael Kellner; Courtesy ARCHIV Hilka Nordhausen
298 (oben / top): © Bettina Sefkow; Foto / photo: ARCHIV Hilka Nordhausen
298 (unten / bottom): © Markus Oehlen;

Foto / photo: ARCHIV Hilka Nordhausen
299: © VG Bild-Kunst, Bonn 2019; Foto / photo: Henning Scholz; Courtesy ARCHIV Hilka Nordhausen
300: © Michael Kellner; Courtesy ARCHIV Hilka Nordhausen
316, 322–323: verschollen / lost; © VG Bild-Kunst, Bonn 2019; Fotos / photos: Bettina Semmer
317: © VG Bild-Kunst, Bonn 2019 / Johanna Kandl; Foto / photo: Rainer Fichel
318 (unten / bottom): © Christa Näher
320: Im Besitz der Künstlerin / Property of the artist; © VG Bild-Kunst, Bonn 2019; Foto / photo: Rainer Fichel
321: Groninger Museum; © VG Bild-Kunst, Bonn 2019; Foto / photo: Johannes Kramer
324–325: Im Besitz der Künstlerin / Property of the artist; © VG Bild-Kunst, Bonn 2019; Foto / photo: Bettina Semmer
326, 328: ARCHIV Hilka Nordhausen; © ARCHIV Hilka Nordhausen; Fotos / photos: Carl Brunn
327: Im Besitz der Künstlerin / Property of the artist; © Bettina Sefkow; Foto / photo: Carl Brunn
342: Im Besitz des Künstlers / Property of the artist; © VG Bild-Kunst, Bonn 2019; Foto / photo: Carl Brunn
343: Im Besitz des Künstlers / Property of the artist; © VG Bild-Kunst, Bonn 2019
344: Archiv Peter Bömmels; © VG Bild-Kunst, Bonn 2019
346: Ludwig Forum für Internationale Kunst Aachen, Leihgabe der Peter und Irene Ludwig Stiftung / Loan of the Peter and Irene Ludwig Foundation; © Walter Dahn; Foto / photo: Carl Brunn
347: © Walter Dahn; Courtesy Sprüth Magers
352: Im Besitz von / Property of Peter Bömmels; © VG Bild-Kunst, Bonn 2019 / Walter Dahn; Foto / photo: Carl Brunn
354–355: © VG Bild-Kunst, Bonn 2019 / Walter Dahn; Fotos / photos: Lothar Schnepf
357–358, 360–369, 371–372: Courtesy ARCHIV Hilka Nordhausen

Hans Peter Adamski, Christian Baumjohann, Thomas Bayrle, Wolfgang Becker, Peter Bömmels, Klaus D. Brennecke, Inka Büttner, Werner Büttner, Luciano Castelli, Walter Dahn, Diedrich Diederichsen, Jiří Georg Dokoupil, Hannah Eckstein, Rainer Fetting, Lisa Franzen, Albert Gabriel, G. L. Gabriel-Thieler, Nadine Hahn, Heinz Hanisch, Christian Haring, Alfred Hilsberg, Gudrun Inboden, Lena Ipsen, Tanja Keppler, Hubert Kiecol, Carmen Knoebel, Walther König, Eckhard Kunz, Zuzana Künzl, Marina Lachmann, Marlen Lienkamp, Paul Maenz, Helmut Metzner, Helmut Middendorf, Nuria Molina, Kay Montag, Christa Näher, Marlies Niermann, Markus Oehlen, Karl Pfefferle, Johanna Piesniewski, Ingrid Raab, Brigitta Rohrbach, Salomé, Achim Schächtele, Günter Schalich, Hans-Jörg Schalich, Hanna Schmandin, Lothar Schnepf, Corinna Schröder, Wilhelm Schürmann, Bettina Sefkow, Bettina Semmer, Claudia Skoda, Dusan Totovic, Uwe Trierweiler, Lisa Wismer-Jud, Bernd Zimmer

Diese Publikation erscheint anlässlich des Forschungsprojekts und der begleitenden Ausstellung / This catalogue is published on the occasion of the research project and the accompanying exhibition

Die Erfindung der Neuen Wilden. Malerei und Subkultur um 1980 / The Invention of the Neue Wilde: Painting and Subculture around 1980.

Ludwig Forum für Internationale Kunst Aachen, 12. Oktober 2018 – 10. März 2019 / October 12, 2018 – March 10, 2019

Publikation / Publication

Herausgeber*innen / Editors
Benjamin Dodenhoff, Ramona Heinlein

Konzept & Redaktion / Concept & editing
Benjamin Dodenhoff, Ramona Heinlein

Lektorat deutsch / German copyediting
Michael Ammann

Lektorat englisch / English copyediting
Jonathan Fox

Übersetzung / Translation
DE-EN: Paul Bowman (S. / pp. 149–155, 183–187, 201–205, 329–335 und / and Kommentare zu den Reprints / comments on the reprints), Fiona Elliott (S. / pp. 382–385, 406–427), Karl Hoffmann (S. / pp. 16–109, 231–235, 287–291, 374–381, 386–389), Good & Cheap Translators (S. / pp. 8–15, 251–267, 301–315)
EN-DE: Karl Hoffmann (S. / pp. 390–405), Christina Bösel (S. / pp. 110–131)

Gestaltung / Design
Jan Kiesswetter

Gesamtherstellung / Production
Printmanagement Plitt GmbH, Oberhausen

Erschienen im / Published by
Verlag der Buchhandlung Walther König
Ehrenstr. 4, D-50672 Köln

Bibliografische Information der Deutschen Nationalbibliothek
Die Deutsche Nationalbibliothek verzeichnet diese Publikation in der Deutschen Nationalbibliografie; detaillierte bibliografische Daten sind über http://dnb.d-nb.de abrufbar.

Bibliographic information published by the Deutsche Nationalbibliothek
The Deutsche Nationalbibliothek lists this publication in the Deutsche Nationalbibliografie; detailed bibliographic data are available in the Internet at http://dnb.d-nb.de.

Printed in Germany

Vertrieb / Distribution:

Germany, Austria, Switzerland / Europe
Buchhandlung Walther König
Ehrenstr. 4
D-50672 Köln
Tel: +49 (0) 221 / 20 59 6 53
verlag@buchhandlung-walther-koenig.de

UK & Ireland
Cornerhouse Publications Ltd. – HOME
2 Tony Wilson Place
UK – Manchester M15 4FN
Tel: +44 (0) 161 212 3466
publications@cornerhouse.org

Outside Europe
D.A.P. / Distributed Art Publishers, Inc.
75 Broad Street, Suite 630
USA - New York, NY 10004
Tel: +1 (0) 212 627 1999
orders@dapinc.com

ISBN 978-3-96098-570-9

Ausstellung / Exhibition

Direktor / Director, Ludwig Forum für Internationale Kunst Aachen
Andreas Beitin

Kurator*innen / Curators
Benjamin Dodenhoff, Ramona Heinlein

Ausstellungsgrafik / Exhibition graphics
DDT2w, Dusan Totovic, Werner Wernicke

Presse / Press
Jutta Göricke, Julia Zeh, Presseamt der Stadt Aachen

Art Handling
Thomas Bortfeldt, Martin Durham, Heinz Hanisch, Kalle Hommelsheim, Jörn Kruse, Heike Tödt

Ausstellungsteam / Exhibition team
Sonja Benzner, Daniel Brandt, Joachim Gabriel, Carolin Günther, Jaroslaw Gussmann, Nadine Henn, Karl-Heinz Jeiter, Kulturbetrieb der Stadt Aachen, Wolfgang Meehsen, Julia Rief, Hagen Scheer, Christina Sodermanns, Michael Weihmann, Werner Wosch

Ludwig Forum für Internationale Kunst Aachen

Ein Museum der stadt aachen

Förderer / Sponsors

Peter und Irene Ludwig Stiftung

Ministerium für Kultur und Wissenschaft des Landes Nordrhein-Westfalen

Unterstützer / Supporters

FREUNDE DES LUDWIG FORUMS FÜR INTERNATIONALE KUNST E.V.

ASEAG

STAWAG

WDR 3